ASCENT
CENTER FOR TECHNICAL KNOWLEDGE

Autodesk® Civil 3D® 2021
Autodesk Certified Professional
Exam Topics Review

Certification Preparation Guide

Imperial Units - 1st Edition

AUTODESK.
Authorized Publisher

ASCENT - Center for Technical Knowledge®
Autodesk® Civil 3D® 2021
Autodesk Certified Professional Exam Topics Review
Imperial Units - 1st Edition

Prepared and produced by:

ASCENT Center for Technical Knowledge
630 Peter Jefferson Parkway, Suite 175
Charlottesville, VA 22911

866-527-2368
www.ASCENTed.com

Lead Contributor: Jeff Morris

ASCENT - Center for Technical Knowledge (a division of Rand Worldwide Inc.) is a leading developer of professional learning materials and knowledge products for engineering software applications. ASCENT specializes in designing targeted content that facilitates application-based learning with hands-on software experience. For over 25 years, ASCENT has helped users become more productive through tailored custom learning solutions.

We welcome any comments you may have regarding this guide, or any of our products. To contact us please email: feedback@ASCENTed.com.

AS-C3D2101-RFC1IM-SG

Contents

SECTION 1: Points, Parcels, and Surveying

SECTION 2: Surfaces and Grading

SECTION 4: Corridors and Sections

Preface

Autodesk® Civil 3D® 2021: Autodesk Certified Professional Exam Topics Review is a comprehensive review guide to assist in preparing for the Autodesk Certified Professional: Civil 3D for Infrastructure Design exam. This certification preparation guide enables experienced users to review learning content from ASCENT that is related to the exam objectives. It is divided into sections that align with the topics in the exam. The beginning of each section includes a list of the objectives that are covered in that section and the corresponding chapter where the review content is presented.

This guide is intended for experienced users of the Autodesk Civil 3D software. New users of the Autodesk Civil 3D 2021 software should refer to the following ASCENT learning guides:

- *Autodesk® Civil 3D® 2021: Fundamentals*
- *Autodesk® Civil 3D® 2021: Fundamentals for Land Developers (Grading)*
- *Autodesk® Civil 3D® 2021: Fundamentals for Surveyors*

Autodesk Certified Professional Exam Objectives

Exam Objective	Chapter(s)
1.1 Create points using the point creation methods	
1.1.a Describe the difference between Survey and Coordinate Geometry (COGO) points	Ch. 1
1.1.b Create COGO points	Ch. 1
1.1.c Specify point parameters	Ch. 1
1.1.d Assign point styles and point label styles	Ch. 1
1.2 Modify point appearance and properties	
1.2.a Rotate point markers	Ch. 1
1.2.b Manage point styles	Ch. 1
1.2.c Edit point properties	Ch. 1
1.2.d Add and edit point labels	Ch. 1

Exam Objective	Chapter(s)
1.3 Create and use Point Groups to control point display	
1.3.a Create and modify Point Groups	Ch. 1
1.3.b Change the point group display order	Ch. 1
1.4 Create a parcel	
1.4.a Explain automatic parcel creation	Ch. 2
1.4.b Create a parcel by layout	Ch. 2
1.4.c Create a parcel from drawing objects	Ch. 2
1.4.d Create parcels by subdividing an existing parcel	Ch. 2
1.4.e Associate a parcel with a site	Ch. 2
1.5 Create and modify parcel styles and annotations	
1.5.a Describe the difference between parcel, parcel area, and parcel segment labels	Ch. 2
1.5.b Add and replace parcel labels	Ch. 2
1.5.c Define parcel styles	Ch. 2
1.5.d Create a parcel table	Ch. 2
1.5.e Convert a label to a tag	Ch. 2
1.5.f Rename and renumber parcels	Ch. 2
1.5.g Delete a parcel	Ch. 2
1.6 Understand the Civil 3D surveying tools	
1.6.a Work with linework code sets	Ch. 3
1.6.b Utilize the points in the Survey Database	Ch. 3
1.6.c Understand the use the Traverse Editor	Ch. 3
1.6.d Recognize the purpose of working with the Survey Figure Prefix Database	Ch. 3
1.6.e Understand the purpose of performing a Mapcheck Analysis	Ch. 2
2.1 Identify key characteristics of surfaces	
2.1.a Identify the parameters and display settings of surface styles	Ch. 4
2.1.b Understand a surface's build, how it was constructed and how it uses the data for calculations	Ch. 4
2.1.c Identify the data categories of a surface definition	Ch. 4

Exam Objective	Chapter(s)
2.1.d Define surface boundary types	Ch. 4
2.1.e Access and review surfaces statistics	Ch. 4
2.1.f Understand how and when to display Triangular Irregular Network (TIN) lines	Ch. 4
2.2 Create and edit TIN surfaces and volume surfaces	
2.2.a Create and edit TIN surfaces	Ch. 4
2.2.b Create a volume surface	Ch. 4
2.2.c Edit the properties of a surface definition	Ch. 4
2.2.d Create a TIN volume surface to compare two surfaces	Ch. 4
2.3 Create surface labels	
2.3.a Create spot elevation and slope labels	Ch. 4
2.3.b Add labels to single or multiple contour lines	Ch. 4
2.4 Identify examples of surface analysis	
2.4.a Identify the properties of a surface analysis type	Ch. 4
2.4.b Set the analysis parameters for a surface style	Ch. 4
2.4.c Perform a surface analysis	Ch. 4
2.5 Create and modify feature lines	
2.5.a Create feature lines	Ch. 5
2.5.b Edit feature lines geometry	Ch. 5
2.5.c Edit feature line elevations	Ch. 5
2.5.d Understand how objects interact with each other when they are part of the same site	Ch. 5
2.6 Create and modify sites and grading models	
2.6.a Create and modify sites	Ch. 5
2.6.b Create grading groups	Ch. 5
2.6.c Use grading creation and editing tools	Ch. 5
2.6.d Work with grading criteria	Ch. 5

Exam Objective	Chapter(s)
3.1 Create and modify alignments	
3.1.a Create an alignment from objects	Ch. 6
3.1.b Create offset alignments	Ch. 6
3.1.c Edit alignment constraints	Ch. 6
3.1.d Add lines, curves, and spirals to an alignment	Ch. 6
3.1.e Reverse the alignment direction*	See p. 6-1
3.1.f Apply widenings for a specified length along an alignment*	See p. 6-1
3.2 Create a surface profile	
3.2.a Create a surface profile along an alignment	Ch. 7
3.3 Create and modify a profile	
3.3.a Use profile creation tools	Ch. 7
3.3.b Edit layout profiles	Ch. 7
3.3.c Describe the purposes, features, and functions of the profile grid view	Ch. 7
3.3.d Explain how and when to add a vertical curve	Ch. 7
3.3.e Use profile grips	Ch. 7
3.4 Create profile views	
3.4.a Describe the relationship between profiles, profile views, and profile view bands	Ch. 7
3.4.b Identify available object types to project to a profile view*	See p. 7-1
3.4.c Create a profile view	Ch. 7
3.4.d Split a profile view	Ch. 7
3.5 Create alignment and profile annotations	
3.5.a Describe the relationship between the label type and how it is placed on the alignment/profile	Ch. 6
3.5.b Distinguish between station offset and station offset fixed point labels	Ch. 6
3.5.c Explain how to renumber tag labels*	See p. 6-1
3.5.d Work with alignment/profile labels	Ch. 6 Ch. 7
3.5.e Use alignment tables	Ch. 6

Exam Objective	Chapter(s)
6.1 Create Note label styles	
6.1.a Use the text component editor	Ch. 10
6.1.b Change the dragged state of a label	Ch. 10
6.1.c Apply a label set to an object	Ch. 10
6.2 Create view frames and sheets	
6.2.a Create view frames	Ch. 11
6.2.b Insert match lines on the view frames	Ch. 11
6.2.c Create sheets from a view frame group	Ch. 11
6.3 Identify when to use a Data Shortcut or an External Reference	
6.3.a Differentiate between a data shortcut and external reference	Ch. 12
6.3.b Explain the concepts and procedures for managing data shortcuts	Ch. 12
6.4 Create a reference to a Data Shortcut	
6.4.a Create a reference to a Data Shortcut	Ch. 12

*Objectives marked with an asterisk are not covered in this guide. Refer to each section for more information.

Prerequisites

- Access to the 2021.0 version of the software, to ensure compatibility with this guide. Future software updates that are released by Autodesk may include changes that are not reflected in this guide. The practices and files included with this guide might not be compatible with prior versions (e.g., 2020).

Note on Software Setup

This guide assumes a standard installation of the software using the default preferences during installation. Lectures and practices use the standard software templates and default options for the Content Libraries.

Students and Educators Can Access Free Autodesk Software and Resources

Autodesk challenges you to get started with free educational licenses for professional software and creativity apps used by millions of architects, engineers, designers, and hobbyists today. Bring Autodesk software into your classroom, studio, or workshop to learn, teach, and explore real-world design challenges the way professionals do.

Get started today - register at the Autodesk Education Community and download one of the many Autodesk software applications available.

Visit www.autodesk.com/education/home/

Note: Free products are subject to the terms and conditions of the end-user license and services agreement that accompanies the software. The software is for personal use for education purposes and is not intended for classroom or lab use.

Lead Contributor: Jeff Morris

Specializing in the civil engineering industry, Jeff authors training guides and provides instruction, support, and implementation on all Autodesk infrastructure solutions.

Jeff brings to bear over 20 years of diverse work experience in the civil engineering industry. He has played multiple roles, including Sales, Trainer, Application Specialist, Implementation and Customization Consultant, CAD Coordinator, and CAD/BIM Manager, in civil engineering and architecture firms, and Autodesk reseller organizations. He has worked for government organizations and private firms, small companies and large multinational corporations and in multiple geographies across the globe. Through his extensive experience in Building and Infrastructure design, Jeff has acquired a thorough understanding of CAD Standards and Procedures and an in-depth knowledge of CAD and BIM.

Jeff studied Architecture and a diploma in Systems Analysis and Programming. He is an Autodesk Certified Instructor (ACI) and holds the Autodesk Certified Professional certification for Civil 3D and Revit.

Jeff Morris has been the Lead Contributor for *Autodesk Civil 3D: Autodesk Certified Professional Exam Topics Review* since 2020.

In This Guide

The following highlights the key features of this guide.

Feature	Description
Practice Files	The Practice Files page includes a link to the practice files and instructions on how to download and install them. The practice files are required to complete the practices in this guide.
Sections	This guide is divided into sections that align with the topics in the Autodesk Certified Professional exam. The beginning of each section includes a list of the exam objectives that are covered in that section and their corresponding chapters.
Chapters	A chapter consists of the following - Exam Objectives, Instructional Content, and Practices. • **Exam Objectives** lists the Autodesk certification exam objectives that are covered in the chapter. • **Instructional Content**, which begins right after Exam Objectives, refers to the descriptive and procedural information related to various topics. Each main topic introduces a product feature, discusses various aspects of that feature, and provides step-by-step procedures on how to use that feature. Where relevant, examples, figures, helpful hints, and notes are provided. • **Practice** for a topic follows the instructional content. Practices enable you to use the software to perform a hands-on review of a topic. It is required that you download the practice files (using the link found on the Practice Files page) prior to starting the first practice.

Practice Files

To download the practice files for this guide, use the following steps:

1. Type the URLs *exactly as shown below* into the address bar of your Internet browser, to access the Course File Download pages for each file.

   Note: If you are using the ebook, you do not have to type the URLs. Instead, you can access the page simply by clicking the URLs below.

   https://www.ascented.com/getfile/id/hesperia
   https://www.ascented.com/getfile/id/repens
   https://www.ascented.com/getfile/id/aricia

   address bar of a browser

2. On the Course File Download page, click the **DOWNLOAD NOW** button, as shown below, to download the .ZIP file that contains the practice files.

3. Once the download is complete, unzip the file and extract its contents.

   The practice files folder location for Ch. 1 and 3 is: *C:\Civil 3D for Surveyors*
   The practice files folder location for Ch. 5 and 8 is: *C:\Civil 3D for Land Dev*
   The practice files folder location for Ch. 2, 4, 6, 7, 8, 9, 10, 11, and 12 is: *C:\Civil 3D Projects*

This guide contains practices from three different ASCENT learning guides, which have been combined to support the review of the Autodesk Certified Professional Exam objectives. **For all practices, it is important to pay close attention to the folder paths provided**. It is required that you do not change the location of the practice files folders. Doing so may cause errors when completing the practices.

Stay Informed!

To receive information about upcoming events, promotional offers, and complimentary webcasts, visit:

www.ASCENTed.com/updates

Points, Parcels, and Surveying

Exam Objective	Chapter(s)
1.4 Create a parcel	
1.4.a Explain automatic parcel creation	Ch. 2
1.4.b Create a parcel by layout	Ch. 2
1.4.c Create a parcel from drawing objects	Ch. 2
1.4.d Create parcels by subdividing an existing parcel	Ch. 2
1.4.e Associate a parcel with a site	Ch. 2
1.5 Create and modify parcel styles and annotations	
1.5.a Describe the difference between parcel, parcel area, and parcel segment labels	Ch. 2
1.5.b Add and replace parcel labels	Ch. 2
1.5.c Define parcel styles	Ch. 2
1.5.d Create a parcel table	Ch. 2
1.5.e Convert a label to a tag	Ch. 2
1.5.f Rename and renumber parcels	Ch. 2
1.5.g Delete a parcel	Ch. 2
1.6 Understand the Civil 3D surveying tools	
1.6.a Work with linework code sets	Ch. 3
1.6.b Utilize the points in the Survey Database	Ch. 3
1.6.c Understand the use the Traverse Editor	Ch. 3
1.6.d Recognize the purpose of working with the Survey Figure Prefix Database	Ch. 3
1.6.e Understand the purpose of performing a Mapcheck Analysis	Ch. 2

Points

Exam Objectives Covered in This Chapter

1.1.a Describe the difference between Survey and Coordinate Geometry (COGO) points

1.1.b Create COGO points

1.1.c Specify point parameters

1.1.d Assign point styles and point label styles

1.2.a Rotate point markers

1.2.b Manage point styles

1.2.c Edit point properties

1.2.d Add and edit point labels

1.3.a Create and modify Point Groups

1.3.b Change the point group display order

1.1 Points Overview

Within Civil 3D, there are three different types of points:

COGO is an abbreviation for Coordinated Geometry.

1. **COGO Points** reside in the drawing file and cannot be referenced into other drawings. There is little protection (other than locking the points); any Civil 3D user can add, manipulate, lock, or unlock COGO points. Therefore, they are mostly used as design points or stakeout points.

2. **Survey Points** reside in a protected survey database. Only users with proper permissions to the survey database folders can manipulate these points. They are inserted (or removed) from the drawings, thus can easily be shared among multiple drawings. They are used by the survey staff to create existing conditions and surfaces.

AutoCAD points are not covered in this guide. Consult other ASCENT AutoCAD guides or the AutoCAD Help for more information.

3. **AutoCAD Points** are regular AutoCAD objects with special properties for point display (**PDMODE** variable) and sizing behavior (**PDSIZE** variable). Beyond their standard AutoCAD use, they are not used much in Civil 3D.

Survey points are often used at the beginning of a project, while COGO points (for stakeout) are used at the end of a project. Surveyors collect data about existing site conditions (elevations, utilities, ownership, etc.) for the project. Their world is coordinates, which are represented by points. Each point has a unique number (or name) and a label containing additional information (usually the elevation of the coordinate and a short coded description).

There are no national standards for point descriptions in the surveying industry. Each organization or survey crew needs to establish its own conventions. There are no standards for symbols either. Each firm can have its own set of symbols. The symbols used in a submission set can be specified by the firm contracting the services.

Autodesk Civil 3D COGO/survey points are a single object with two elements: a point style and a point label style. A COGO/survey point definition is shown in Figure 1–1.

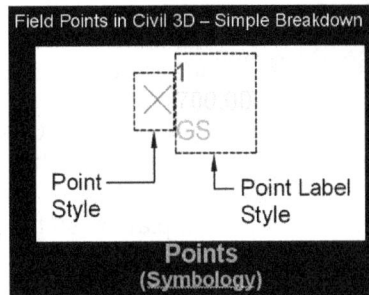

Figure 1–1

The following is important point information:

- A point style (no matter what it displays) is selectable with an AutoCAD **Node** object snap.

- Points can be displayed as an AutoCAD node, a custom marker, or a block.

A point label is not limited to the point's number, elevation, and description. A point label can contain lines, blocks, and other point properties. You can also set User-Defined point properties. For example, point labels might only display an elevation or description. This text can be manually overridden (as shown in Figure 1–2) or it can consist of intelligent variables that represent point characteristics (such as its convergence angle).

Figure 1–2

In U.S. state plane coordinate systems, the convergence angle is the difference between a geodetic azimuth and the projection of that azimuth onto a grid (grid azimuth) of a given point.

Point Marker Styles

A surveyor interacts with points daily. To easily use points in the Autodesk Civil 3D software, you need to have a basic understanding of their related styles.

The Autodesk Civil 3D software provides imperial and metric template files that contain several point styles: *Autodesk Civil 3D Imperial (NCS)* and *Autodesk Civil 3D Metric (NCS)*. These templates use the National CAD standards for their layers, and provide examples of styles that you can use in a project. To customize these styles, you need to modify and expand the list of point styles.

Customizing styles needs to be managed carefully. Consult with your CAD or BIM Manager as to the standards and procedures for such customization.

When installing the Autodesk Civil 3D software, the first thing you should do is to select one of these templates as your default template. Alternatively, your CAD or BIM Manager can develop styles to be used in your organization's drawing template file.

A point style defines a point's display, its 3D elevation, and its coordinate marker size. In the example shown in Figure 1–3, the point style is an X for a ground shot.

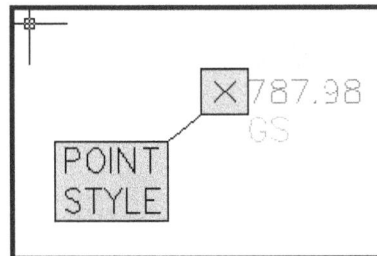

Figure 1–3

The Point Style dialog box has five tabs: *Information*, *Marker*, *3D Geometry*, *Display*, and *Summary*.

Information Tab

The *Information* tab names the style and sets the basic properties of the point style, as shown in Figure 1–4.

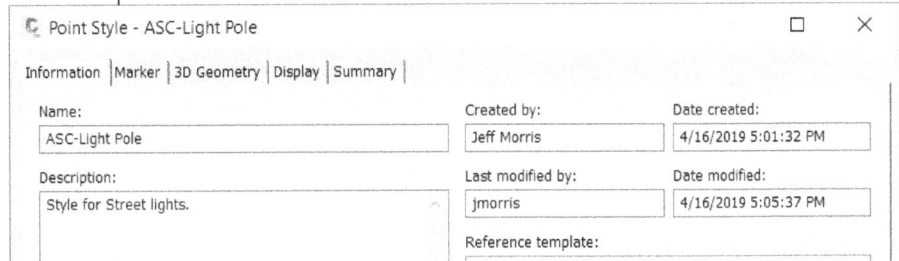

Figure 1–4

Marker Tab

The *Marker* tab supports three marker definition methods, as shown in Figure 1–5.

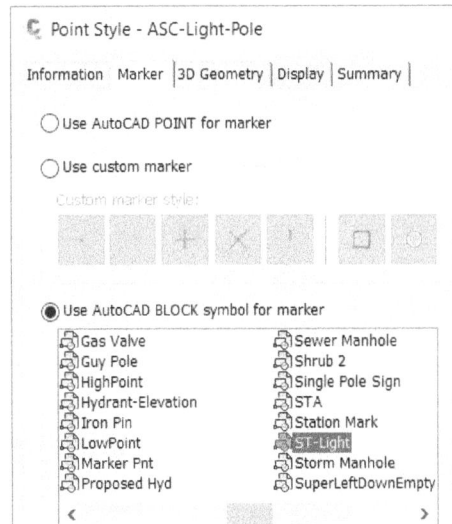

Figure 1–5

- **Use AutoCAD POINT [node] for marker:** All points in the drawing follow AutoCAD's **PDMODE** and **PDSIZE** system variables. You do not have independent control over points using this option. This option is seldom used.

- **Use custom marker:** This option creates markers similar to an AutoCAD point (node). However, the marker is controlled by the Autodesk Civil 3D software, and each point style can display a different combination of marker styles. When using this option, select the components of the style from the list of Custom marker style shapes. A custom marker can have shapes from the left and right sides. The first comes from one of the five icons on the style's left side, and you can optionally add none, one, or both shapes from the right.

- **Use AutoCAD BLOCK symbol for marker:** This option defines the marker using a block (symbol). The blocks listed represent definitions in the drawing. When the cursor is in this area and you right-click, you can browse to a location containing drawings that you want to include as point markers.

Options for scaling the marker are located in the marker panel's top right corner. The most common option is **Use drawing scale** (as shown in Figure 1–6), which takes the marker size (0.1000") and multiplies it by the current drawing's annotation scale, resulting in the final marker size. When the annotation scale changes, the Autodesk Civil 3D software automatically resizes the markers and their labels to be the appropriate size for the scale.

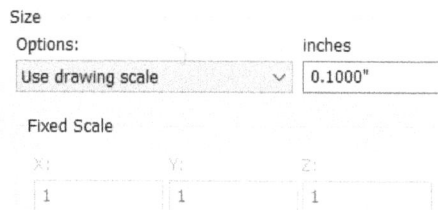

Size

Options:		inches
Use drawing scale	∨	0.1000"

Fixed Scale

X:	Y:	Z:
1	1	1

Figure 1–6

The other options are described as follows:

Use fixed scale	Specifies user-defined X, Y, and Z scale values.
Use size in absolute units	Specifies a user-defined size.
Use size relative to screen	Specifies a user-defined percentage of the screen.

3D Geometry Tab

The *3D Geometry* tab sets the point's elevation. The default option is **Use Point Elevation** (as shown in Figure 1–7), which displays the point at its actual elevation value.

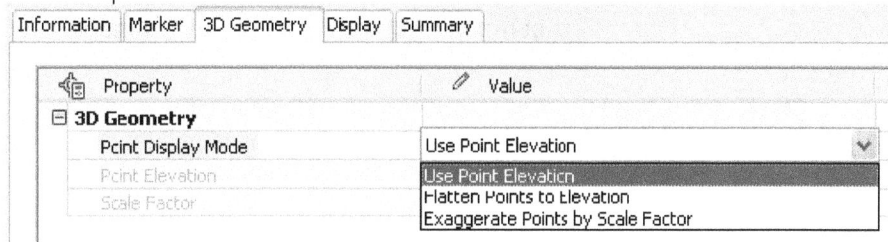

Figure 1–7

The other options are described as follows:

Flatten Points to Elevation	Specifies the elevation to which the point is projected (flattened). The Point Elevation cell highlights if this option is selected and is 0 elevation by default. When using an AutoCAD object snap to select a marker using this option, the resulting entity's elevation is the default elevation of 0. If selecting by point number or point object, the resulting entity is the point's actual elevation.
Exaggerate Points by Scale Factor	Exaggerates the point's elevation by a specified scale factor. When selecting this option, the Scale Factor cell highlights.

Display Tab

The *Display* tab assigns the marker and label layers, and sets their visibility and properties. Setting the property to **ByLayer** uses the layer's properties. Alternatively, you can override the layer properties by setting a specific color, linetype, or lineweight.

A style's View Direction value affects how the point and label components display in the plan, model, profile, and section views, as shown in Figure 1–8.

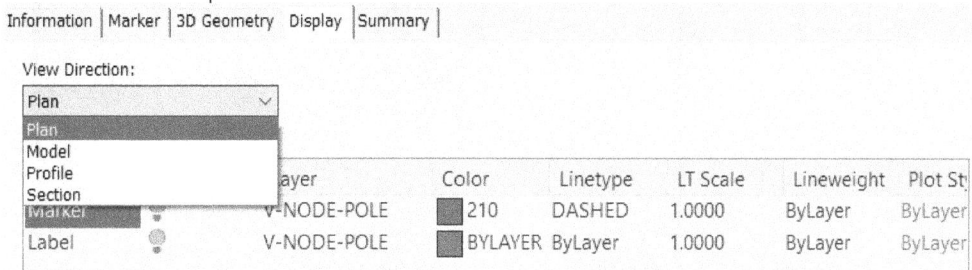

Figure 1–8

Summary Tab

The *Summary* tab is a report of all of the style's settings. Controlling a leader arrow from a label in the dragged state, points to the boundary of the marker (yes) or the center of the marker (no). It is also changed under **Marker>Leader**, and stops at marker. You can also edit style variables in this tab.

Point Label Styles

The Autodesk Civil 3D point label style annotates point properties beyond the typical point number, elevation and description. A typical point label style is shown in Figure 1–9.

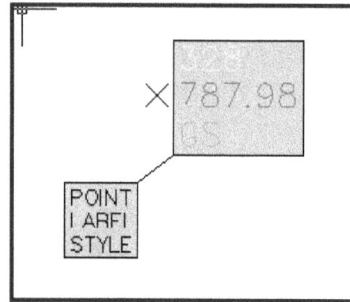

Figure 1–9

All Autodesk Civil 3D label style dialog boxes are the same. The basic behaviors for a label are in the settings in the Edit Label Style Defaults dialog box. The values in this dialog box define the label layer, text style, orientation, plan readability, size, dragged state behaviors, etc.

In the Toolspace>*Settings* tab, the drawing name and object collections control these values for the entire drawing (at the drawing name level) or for the selected collection (*Surface, Alignment, Point*, etc.) To open the Edit Label Style Defaults dialog box, select the drawing name or a heading, right-click, and select **Edit Label Style Defaults**, as shown in Figure 1–10.

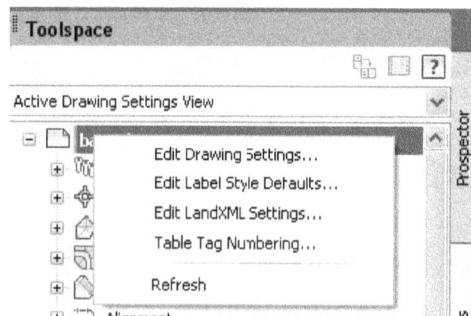

Figure 1–10

The Label Style Composer dialog box contains five tabs, each defining specific label behaviors: *Information*, *General*, *Layout*, *Dragged State*, and *Summary*.

Information Tab

The *Information* tab names the style and sets the basic properties of the label style, as shown in Figure 1–11.

Figure 1–11

General Tab

The *General* tab contains three properties, as shown in Figure 1–12:

- *Label:* The text style and layer.

- *Behavior*: The orientation.

- *Plan Readability*: The amount of view rotation permitted before the text is flipped to read from the bottom or right side of the sheet.

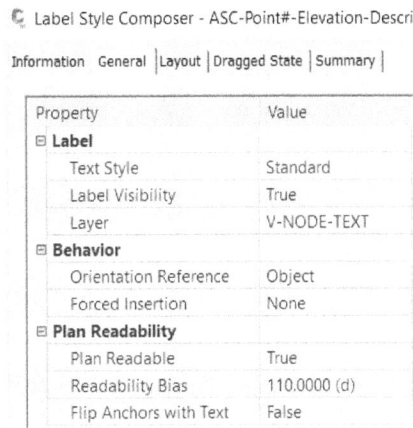

Figure 1–12

The *Label* property sets the *Text Style*, *Label Visibility*, and *Layer*. Select the *Value* cell next to the *Text Style* and *Layer* to open browsers and change their values. Selecting the *Label Visibility* cell displays a drop-down list containing the options **true** and **false**.

The *Behavior* property sets two variables that control the label's location. The *Orientation Reference* variable contains the three label orientation options.

Object	Rotates labels relative to the object's zero direction. The object's zero direction is based on its start to end vector. If the vector changes at the label's anchor point, the orientation updates automatically. This is the default setting.
View	Forces labels to realign relative to a screen-view orientation in both model and layout views. This method assumes that the zero angle is horizontal, regardless of the UCS or Dview twist. If the view changes, the label orientation updates as well. This is the recommended setting.
World Coordinate System	Labels read left to right using the WCS X-axis. Changing the view or current UCS does not affect label rotation. The label always references the world coordinate system.

Under the *Behavior* property, the **Forced Insertion** variable has three optional values that specify the label's position relative to an object. This setting only applies when the *Orientation Reference* is set to **Object**, and the objects are lines, arcs, or spline segments.

None	Maintains label position as composed relative to the object.
Top	Adjusts label position to be above an object.
Bottom	Adjusts label position to be below an object.

* **Note**: If you select **Top** or **Bottom**, the value of *Plan Readable* should set to **True**.

The *Plan Readability* property has three variables that affect how text flips when rotating a drawing view. Under the *Plan Readability* property, the *Plan Readable* variable has two options:

True	Enables text to rotate to maintain left to right readability from the bottom or right side of the drawing.
False	Does not permit text to flip. The resulting text might be upside down or read from right to left.

The *Readability Bias* variable is the amount of rotation required to flip a label to become left to right readable. The angle is measured counter-clockwise from the WCS 0 (zero) direction.

The *Flip Anchors with Text* variable has two options:

True	If the text flips, the text anchor point also flips.
False	The label flips, but maintains the original anchor point. The behavior is similar to mirroring the original text.

Layout Tab

The *Layout* tab defines the label contents, as shown in Figure 1–13. A label component is an object property that it labels. Point properties include northing, easting, raw description, etc. If User Defined properties are in use, they are also available. A label might have one component with several properties, or several components (each containing an object property) and regular text.

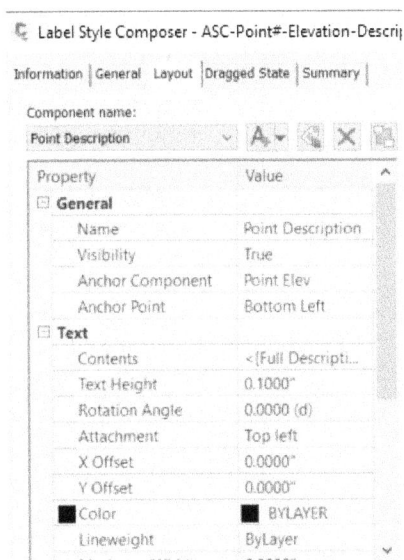

Figure 1–13

A point style label component can be text, lines, or blocks. Other object type label styles can include additional components, such as reference text, ticks, directional arrows, etc. To add a component, expand the drop-down list (shown in Figure 1–14) and select the component type.

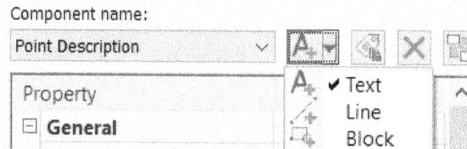

Figure 1–14

The remaining icons in the *Layout* tab are as follows:

	Copies the current component and its properties.
	Deletes the current component.
	Changes the display order of a label's components. For example, use this icon to change the draw order of the label's components (such as text above a mask).

Depending on the label component type, it might have any combination of three areas: **General**, **Text**, and **Border**.

- **General** defines how the label attaches to the object or other label components, its visibility, and its anchor point.

- If the label component is text, the **Text** property values affect how it displays its object property, as shown in Figure 1–15.

Figure 1–15

To set or modify a label's text value, select the cell next to *Contents* to display . Click to open the Text Component Editor dialog box.

The Text Component Editor dialog box (shown in Figure 1–16) defines the properties that the label annotates. When creating a label component, double-click on the text in the right pane to highlight it. In the left pane, select the property that you want to add, set the property's format values, and then click ⇨ to add the new property to the label component.

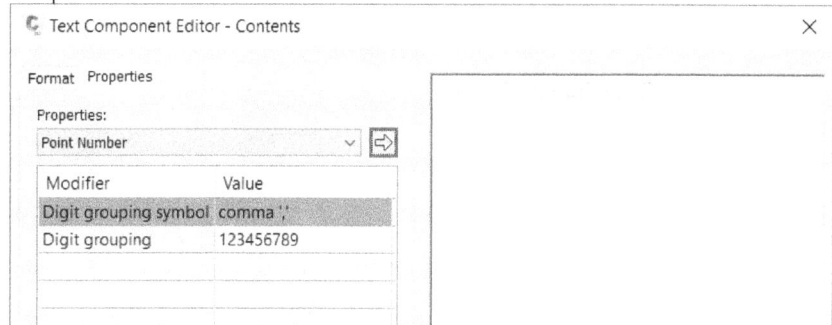

Figure 1–16

It is important to maintain the process order and to remember that the text on the right in brackets needs to be highlighted before you can revise its format values on the left, and then click ⇨ when you are ready to update it.

Dragged State Tab

The *Dragged State* tab has two properties: **Leader** and **Dragged State Components**. This tab defines how a label behaves when you are dragging a label from its original insertion point.

The *Leader* property defines whether a leader displays and what properties it displays. You can use the label's layer properties in the *General* tab (**ByLayer**) or override them by specifying a color, as shown in Figure 1–17.

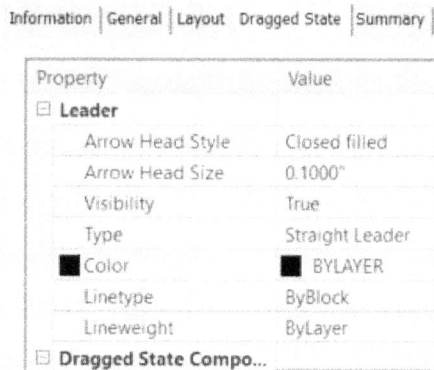

Figure 1–17

The **Dragged State Components** property defines the label component's display after it has been dragged from its original position. Select the cell next to *Display* to view the two display options, as shown in Figure 1–18.

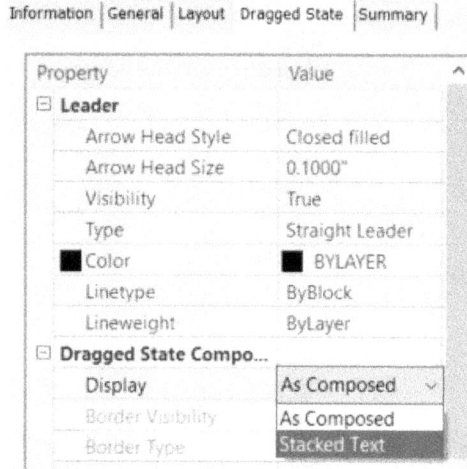

Figure 1–18

As Composed	The label maintains its original definition and orientation from the settings in the Layout panel. When you select **As Composed**, all of the other values become unavailable for editing.
Stacked Text	The label text becomes left justified and label components are stacked in the order listed in Layout's Component Name list. When you select **Stacked Text**, all of the blocks, lines, ticks, and direction arrows are removed. This is the recommended setting.

Summary Tab

The *Summary* tab lists the label component, general, and dragged state values for the label style. The label components are listed numerically in the order in which they were defined and report all of the current values.

1.2 Point Settings

When creating new COGO points, you must determine the next point number, as well as which elevations and descriptions to assign and how to assign them. To set the current point number, default elevations, descriptions, and other similar settings, use the Create Points toolbar's expanded area. Display this area by clicking ⯆ in the Create Points toolbar. The two areas, *Points Creation* (shown in Figure 1–19) and *Point Identity* (shown in Figure 1–20) contain the most commonly used values.

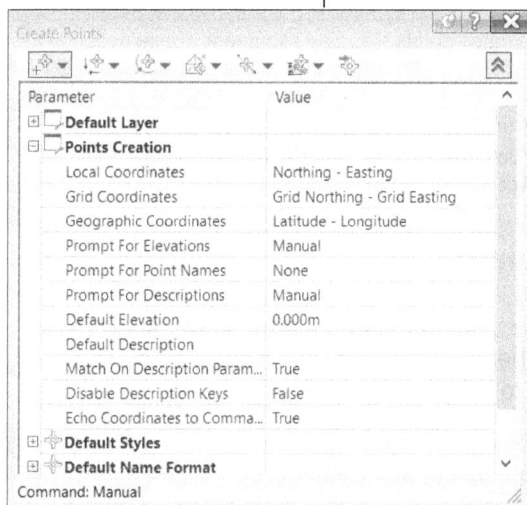

Figure 1–19

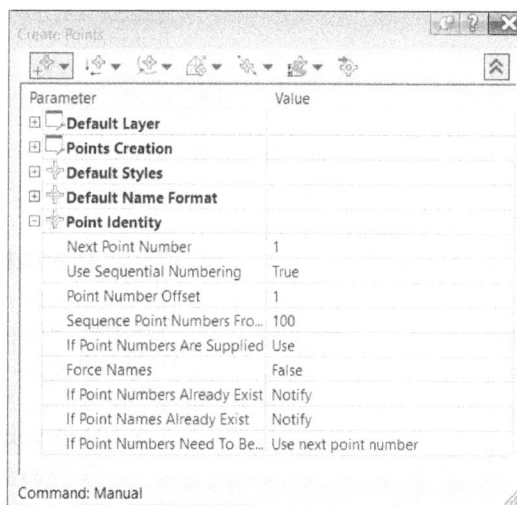

Figure 1–20

- Alternatively, you can select the Toolspace>*Settings* tab and expand the **Commands** collection, under the **Point** collection. Select **Create Points**, right-click, and select **Edit Command Settings**, as shown in Figure 1–21.

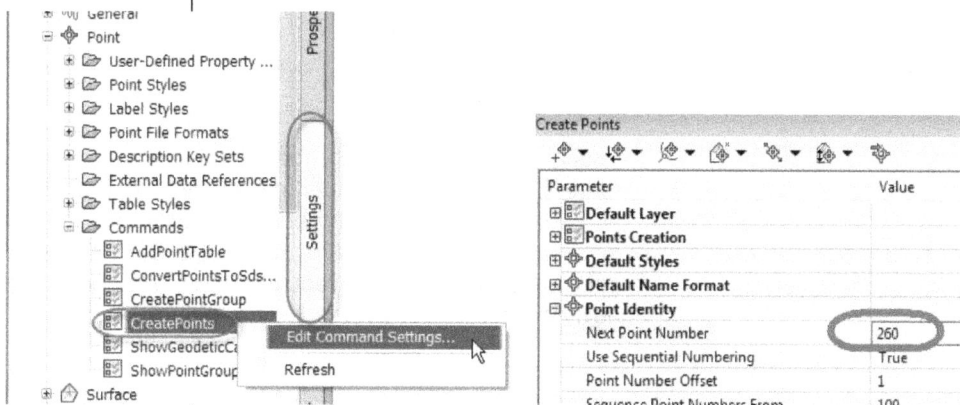

Figure 1–21

Points Creation Values

The *Points Creation* area affects prompting for elevations and descriptions. The two properties in this area are *Prompt For Elevations* and *Prompt For Descriptions*. These properties can be set as follows:

None	Does not prompt for an elevation or description.
Manual	Prompts for an elevation or description.
Automatic	Uses the **Default Elevation** or **Default Description** value when creating a point.
Automatic-Object	Creates points along an alignment whose description consists of the **Alignment name** and **Station**. This description is not dynamic and does not update if the alignment changes or the point is moved. You cannot set *Prompt For Elevations* to **Automatic-Object**.

Point Identity Values

The *Point Identity* area sets the default method of handling duplicate point numbers. If there are duplicate point numbers, there are four ways to resolve the duplication:

- Renumber the incoming point.
- Overwrite the existing point data.
- Merge the incoming point data with existing point data.
- Notify (and await further instructions).

If Notify is selected, then there are five options available:

These options are explained later in this chapter.

- Use next point number
- Add an offset
- Sequence from
- Overwrite
- Merge

This area's most critical property is *Next Point Number*. It is set to the first available number in the point list. If a file of imported point data uses point numbers 1-131 and 152-264, the current point number is 132 after importing the file. This value should be set manually to the next required point number before creating new points with the Create Points toolbar.

1.3 Creating COGO Points

Points can be created using the commands in the Create Points toolbar. These commands include:

- **Miscellaneous - Manual:** Creates a new point at specified coordinates.

- **Alignments - Station/Offset:** Creates a point at an alignment's specific station and offset. These points and their descriptions do not update if the alignment is modified or the point is moved. If you prefer a dynamic station and offset labels, consider using an Alignment label instead.

- **Alignments - Measure Alignment:** Creates point objects at a set interval, which is useful for construction staking. Again, these points do not update if the alignment changes.

- **Surface - Random Points:** Creates points whose elevation is from a specified surface. These points do update, but you must manually force the update. If you prefer a dynamic spot label, consider a Surface label instead.

Each icon in the Create Points toolbar has a drop-down list. If expanded, a command from the list can be selected to run, as shown in Figure 1–22.

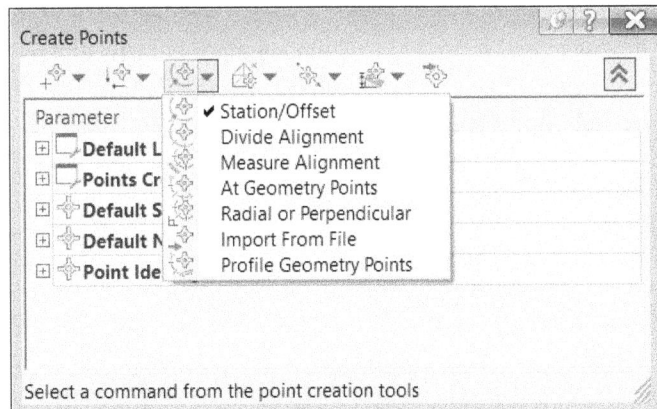

Figure 1–22

1.4 Description Key Sets

Description Keys categorize points by their field descriptions (raw description). If a point matches a Description Key entry, the point is assigned a point and label style, and a full description (a translation of the raw description). Description Key Sets can also scale and rotate points. The **Description Key Sets** collection is shown in Figure 1–23.

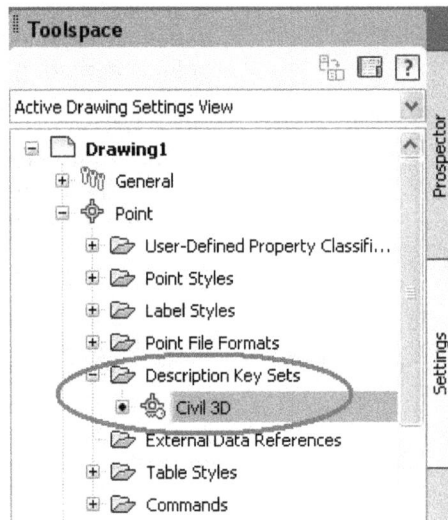

Figure 1–23

The Description Key's first five columns are the commonly used entries, as shown in Figure 1–24.

Code	Style	Point Label ...	Format	Layer	Scale Param...	Fixed Scale ...	Use drawin...	Apply to X-Y	Apply to Z	Ma
BRUSH*	☑ ASC-Tree Brush	☑ <default>	$2' $1 (TRUNK)	☑ V-NODE-TREE	☑ Parameter 2	☑ 25.000	☐ No	☑ Yes	☐ No	☐ P
CTREE*	☑ ASC-Tree C	☑ <default>	$2' $1 (TRUNK)	☑ V-NODE-TREE	☑ Parameter 2	☑ 25.000	☐ No	☑ Yes	☐ No	☐ P
DTREE*	☑ ASC-Tree D	☑ <default>	$2' $1 (TRUNK)	☑ V-NODE-TREE	☑ Parameter 2	☑ 25.000	☐ No	☑ Yes	☐ No	☐ P
SANMH*	☑ Sanitary Sewer Ma	☑ <default>	$*	☑ V-NODE-SSWR	☑ Parameter 1	☐ 1.000	☐ No	☐ No	☐ No	☐ P
STMMH*	☑ Storm Sewer Manh	☑ <default>	$*	☑ V-NODE-STRM	☑ Parameter 2	☑ 25.000	☐ No	☐ No	☐ No	☐ P

Figure 1–24

- To create a new Description Key row, select an existing code, right-click, and select **New**.

- To edit a Description Key code, double-click in the cell.

Code, Point, and Label Style

Description code is a significant part of data collection. Code assigned to a raw description triggers action by the Description Key Set. Each entry in the set represents all of the possible descriptions that a field crew would use while surveying a job. When a raw description matches a code entry, the Key Set assigns all of the row's values to the matching point (including point style and label style), translates the raw description, and possibly assigns a layer. Codes are case-sensitive and must match the field collector's entered raw description.

A code might contain wildcards to match raw descriptions that contain numbering or additional material beyond the point's description. For example, MH* would match MH1, MH2, etc. and UP* would match UP 2245 14.4Kv ACME. Common wild keys are described as follows:

# (pound)	Matches any single numeric digit. • Example: T# matches T1 through T9
@ (at)	Matches any alphabetic character. • Example: 1@ matches 1A through 1Z
. (period)	Matches any non-alphanumeric character. • Example: T. matches T- or T+
* (asterisk)	Matches any string of characters. • Example: T* matches TREE, TR-Aspen, Topo, or Trench
? (question mark)	Matches any single character. • Example: ?BC matches TBC or 3BC

Matching a Key Set entry for the code assigns a Point Style at the point's coordinates. If the *Point Style* is set to **Default**, the *Settings* tab's Point feature *Point Style* is used (set in the Edit Feature Settings dialog box), as shown in Figure 1–25.

Matching a Key Set entry also assigns a point label style to annotate important point values. This is usually a number, elevation, and description. If the *Point Label Style* is set to **Default**, the *Settings* tab's Point feature *Point Label Style* is used (set in the Edit Feature Settings dialog box), as shown in Figure 1–25.

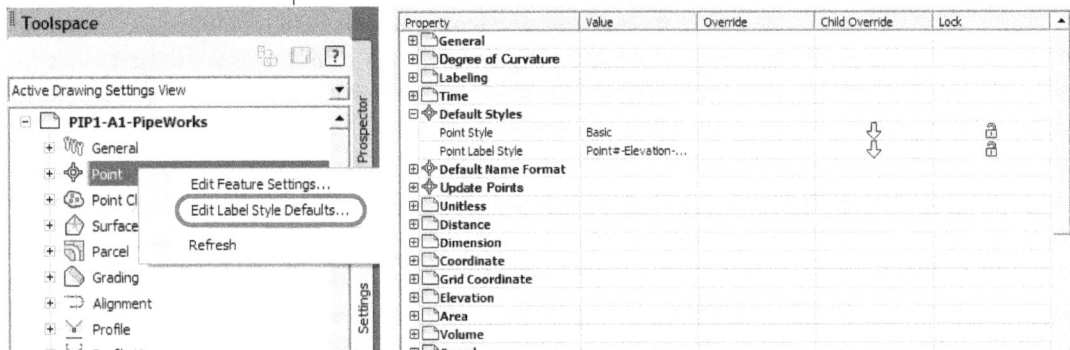

Figure 1–25

Format

The *Format* column translates the raw description (what the surveyor typed) into a full description (what you want it to read). When including spaces in a raw description, the Autodesk Civil 3D software assigns parameter numbers to each description element.

Parameters are represented by a $ sign, followed by a number. For example, the description *PINE 6* has two elements: PINE and 6, with PINE as parameter 0 ($0) and 6 as parameter 1 ($1).

When the *Format* column contains $*, it indicates that the software should use the raw description as the full description. The *Format* column can reorder the parameters and add characters to create a full description. For example, the raw description *PINE 6* can be translated to 6' PINE by entering **$1' $0**.

A complex raw description is as follows:

CTREE PINE 3.4

For the raw description to match the Description Key Set entry, the entry **CTREE** must have an asterisk (*) after CTREE (as shown in Figure 1–26). The raw description elements and their parameters are CTREE ($0), PINE ($1), and 3.4 ($2). The *Format* column entry of **$2' $1 (TRUNK)** creates a full description of **3.4' PINE (TRUNK)**

CTREE is used to differentiate between deciduous (DTREE) and coniferous (CTREE) trees. This way different point styles can be assigned.

(TRUNK) designates that the value corresponds to the trunk diameter, as opposed to the drip line of the tree.

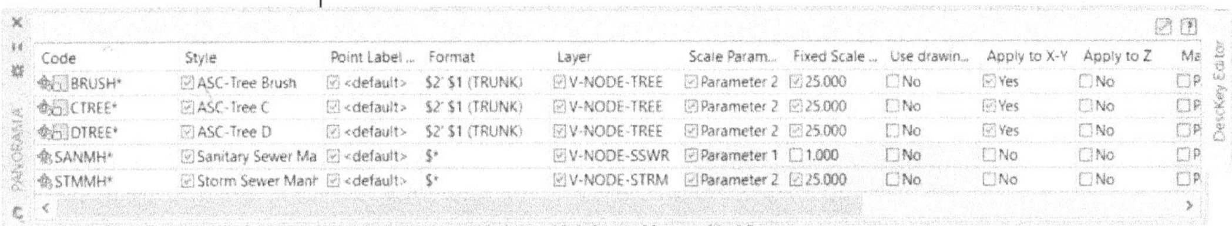

Code	Style	Point Label ...	Format	Layer	Scale Param...	Fixed Scale ...	Use drawin...	Apply to X-Y	Apply to Z	Ma
BRUSH*	☑ ASC-Tree Brush	☑ <default>	$2' $1 (TRUNK)	☑ V-NODE-TREE	☑ Parameter 2	☑ 25.000	☐ No	☑ Yes	☐ No	☐ P.
CTREE*	☑ ASC-Tree C	☑ <default>	$2' $1 (TRUNK)	☑ V-NODE-TREE	☑ Parameter 2	☑ 25.000	☐ No	☑ Yes	☐ No	☐ P.
DTREE*	☑ ASC-Tree D	☑ <default>	$2' $1 (TRUNK)	☑ V-NODE-TREE	☑ Parameter 2	☑ 25.000	☐ No	☑ Yes	☐ No	☐ P.
SANMH*	☑ Sanitary Sewer Ma	☑ <default>	$*		☑ V-NODE-SSWR	☑ Parameter 1	☐ 1.000	☐ No	☐ No	☐ No	☐ P.
STMMH*	☑ Storm Sewer Manh	☑ <default>	$*		☑ V-NODE-STRM	☑ Parameter 2	☑ 25.000	☐ No	☐ No	☐ No	☐ P.

Figure 1–26

If a point does not match any Description Key Set entry, it receives the default styles assigned by the **_All Points** group.

The *Layer* column assigns a layer to the matching point. If the Point Style already has a marker and label layer, this entry should be toggled off. The Description Key Set also contains the *Scale* and *Rotate Parameter* columns. In the example shown in Figure 1–26, the **3** for the trunk diameter can also be a tree symbol scaling factor when applied to the symbol's X-Y.

Practice 1a

Creating Autodesk Civil 3D Points

Practice Objective

- Create a point manually, and then zoom to it using transparent commands.

In this practice, a fire hydrant was located by GPS. You will add a point object to locate it manually.

Task 1 - Add a point object to the drawing.

1. Open **Points-A-Survey.dwg** from the *C:\Civil 3D for Surveyors\Working\Survey* folder.

2. If you are greeted with a splash screen about using Online Map Data, select **Remember my choice** and click **No**, as shown in Figure 1–27.

Geolocation - Online Map Data

Do you want to use Online Map Data?

Online Map Data enables you to use an online service to display maps in AutoCAD. Please sign into your Autodesk account to access online maps.

By accessing or using this service, you understand and agree that you will be subject to, have read and agree to be bound by the terms of use and privacy policies referenced therein: Online Map Data - Terms of Service.

☐ Remember my choice   Yes   No

Figure 1–27

3. In the *Home* tab>Create Ground Data panel, select **Points-Point Creation Tools** to display the Create Points toolbar.

4. Expand the toolbar by clicking ⥥, as shown in Figure 1–28.

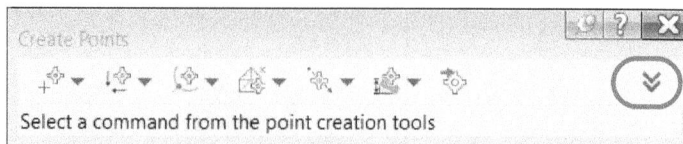

Create Points

Select a command from the point creation tools

Figure 1–28

5. In the *Point Identity* area in the dialog box, set the *Next Point Number* to **260** and collapse the toolbar by clicking ⥣.

6. Select the **Manual** option in the miscellaneous group in the toolbar, as shown in Figure 1–29.

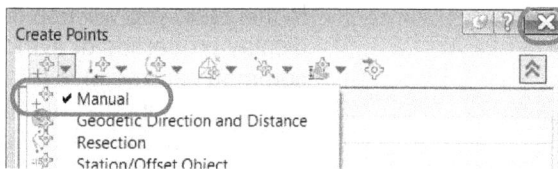

Figure 1–29

7. When prompted for a location, in the Command Line, type **6256069.30,2036634.25** and press <Enter> (or select the endpoint of the large red arrow).

8. When prompted for a description, type **HYD** and press <Enter>.

The period is a placeholder for the elevation field. Typing a zero is incorrect because 0 is a valid elevation.

9. When prompted for an elevation, press <Enter> to accept the default value of **<.>** (period), because the height is unknown.

10. Press <Enter> again to finish the command.

11. Close the Create Points toolbar by clicking the red **X** in the top right corner.

12. In the ribbon, in the *Transparent* tab, click (Zoom to Point) and type **260**.

13. In the Toolspace>*Prospector* tab, select the **_All Points** group, right-click, and select **Apply Description Keys**. The point updates to display the Hydrant symbol and its new description, as shown in Figure 1–30.

Before applying Description Keys

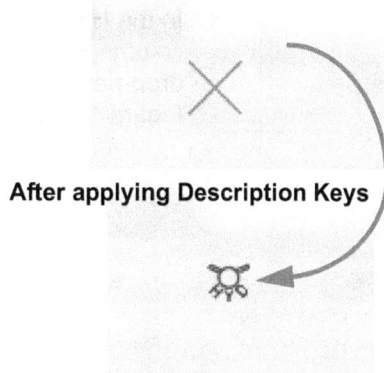

After applying Description Keys

Figure 1–30

14. Save the drawing.

Task 2 - Update the Description Key Set to use parameters.

In this task, you will use the Parameters feature to control the display properties of symbols in your drawings. The most common parameter is the **Scale** parameter. With this parameter, a surveyor will enter the size of a tree as part of the description and the description key file will insert a symbol scaled to the value provided by the surveyor. In this case, you want the pumpers on the hydrant to display correctly (i.e., running parallel to the road).

1. Continue working with the drawing from the previous task.

2. In the Toolspace>*Settings* tab, expand the **Point** collection and expand the **Description Key Sets** collection. Select **Ascent**, right-click, and select **Edit Keys**, as shown in Figure 1–31.

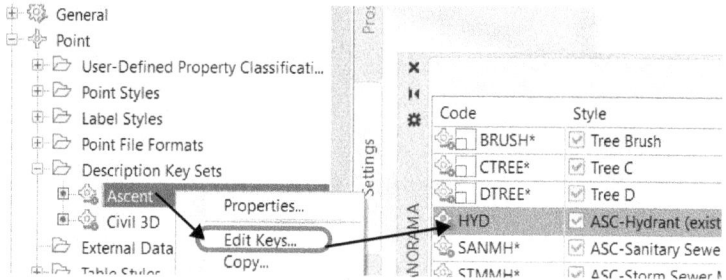

Figure 1–31

3. In the *HYD* row, *Code* column, type **HYD***. The asterisk symbolizes a wildcard, (i.e., any character after the letters HYD). In this example it is -5, parameter1, which you will enter in Step 6.

4. In the *HYD* row, select the checkbox in the *Marker Rotate* column, select the cell, and then select **Parameter1** in the drop-down list. The selected parameter is shown in Figure 1–32.

Code	Style	Point Label Styl	Apply to Z	Marker Rotate ...	Marker Fixed R...	Label Rotate Pa...	La
BRUSH*	Tree Brush	Point#-Eleva.	No	Parameter 2	0.0000 (d)	Parameter 2	
CTREE*	Tree C	Point#-Eleva	No	Parameter 2	0.0000 (d)	Parameter 2	
DTREE*	Tree D	Point#-Eleve	No	Parameter 2	0.0000 (d)	Parameter 2	
HYD*	ASC-Hydrant (existing)	ASC-Descrip	No	Parameter 1	0.0000 (d)	Parameter 2	
SANMH*	Sanitary Sewer Manhole	Point#-Elevat	No	Parameter 2	0.0000 (d)	Parameter 2	
STMMH*	Storm Sewer Manhole	Point#-Elevat	No	Parameter 2	0.0000 (d)	Parameter 2	

Figure 1–32

5. Click ☑ in the top right corner of the dialog box to close the Panorama view.

The -5 indicates the required rotation.

6. In Model Space, select the Hydrant point object, right-click, and select **Edit Points**. Change the *Raw Description* from *HYD* to **HYD -33** and press <Enter>.

7. Select the row, right-click, and select **Apply Description Keys**, as shown in Figure 1–33.

Point Num...	Easting	Northing	Point E...	N	Raw Descript...	Full Descript...	D...	Grid Easti...
⬦ 260	56069.3000'	36634.2500'			HYD 33	HYD 33	$*	56069.3000'	3

Renumber...
Datum...
Elevations from Surface...
Apply Description Keys

Figure 1–33

8. Click ☑ in the top right corner of the dialog box to close the Panorama view.

9. Note that the hydrant has been rotated to display the hydrant pumpers following the rotation of the road, as shown in Figure 1–34.

Figure 1–34

The label also displays the rotation angle text -5, which you do not want.

10. In the Toolspace>*Settings* tab, expand the **Point** collection and expand the **Description Key Sets** collection. Select **Ascent**, right-click, and select **Edit Keys**.

11. In the *HYD* row, change the *Format* from *$** to **HYDRANT**, as shown in Figure 1–35.

Code	Style	Point Label Style	Format
BRUSH*	☑ Tree Brush	☑ Point#-Elevation-Descri	$2' $1 (TRUNK)
CTREE*	☑ Tree C	☑ Point#-Elevation-Descri	$2' $1 (TRUNK)
DTREE*	☑ Tree D	☑ Point#-Elevation-Descri	$2' $1 (TRUNK)
HYD	☑ ASC-Hydrant (existing)	☑ ASC-Description Only	HYDRANT
SANMH*	☑ ASC-Sanitary Sewer Manl	☑ Point#-Elevation-Descri	$*

Figure 1–35

You still need to apply the changes.

12. Click ☑ in the top right corner of the dialog box to close the Panorama view.

13. In Model Space, select the Hydrant point object, right-click, and select **Apply Description Keys**. The changes are now applied, as shown in Figure 1–36.

Figure 1–36

14. Save the drawing.

1.5 Point Groups

Point groups organize points that share common descriptions and characteristics (such as existing storm, gas lines, building corners, etc.). Point groups also enable points to display different point or label styles. For example, a Landscape Architect needs to display different symbols for each tree species, while an Engineer only needs to display a generic tree symbol. The **Description Key Set** enables you to assign the tree species symbols for the Landscape Architect, and a point group enables generic tree symbols to override the symbols for the Engineer. Another function of a point group is to hide all of the points.

In the Autodesk Civil 3D software, point groups can be defined in the template along with a Description Key Set. When creating a new drawing from this template and importing points, they are assigned their symbols and can be sorted into point groups.

All points in a drawing belong to the **_All Points** point group. Consider this point group as the point database. It cannot be deleted and initially is not in a drawing until you add points. All new point groups include all drawing points or a subset of drawing points (copied points from the **_All Points** point group).

Defining Point Groups

To create a new point group, select the Toolspace>*Prospector* tab, right-click on the **Point Groups** collection and select **New**. Alternatively, in the *Home* tab, expand **Points** and select **Create Point Group**.

When you select **New** or **Create Point Group**, the Point Group Properties dialog box opens. It has nine tabs, most of them affecting the point group's definition.

- The *Point Groups*, *Raw Desc Matching*, *Include*, and *Query Builder* tabs add points to the point group. The *Exclude* tab removes points from a point group.

- The *Information* tab defines the point group's name. The *Point style* and *Point label style* should remain at their defaults, unless you want to use either style to override the assigned styles of the points in the point group. The points in the point group display their originally assigned styles until you toggle on the override.

A point group can be locked by toggling on the **Object locked** option to prevent any changes to the group. The Point Group Properties dialog box opens as shown in Figure 1–37.

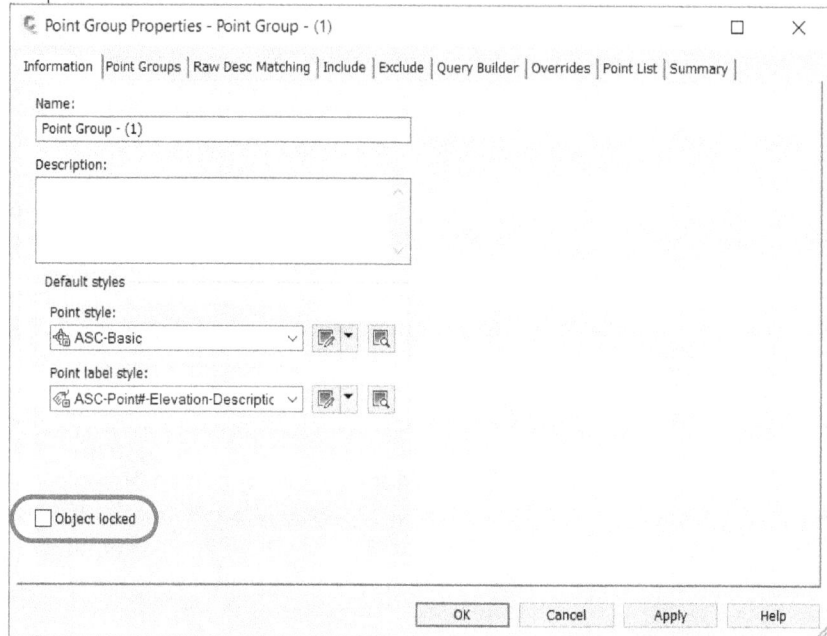

Figure 1–37

- The *Point Groups* tab lists the drawing's groups. A point group can be created from other point groups. When you select a point group name, the group and its points become members of the new point group. For example, the point group **Trees** is created from the point groups *Maple*, *Walnut*, *Oak*, etc.

- The *Raw Desc Matching* tab lists codes from the Description Key Code set. When you toggle on the code, any point matching the code becomes part of the point group.

- If you cannot select a point with the previous two methods, the *Include* tab enables you to include points by specifically entering in the selection criteria. The criteria include the point number (point number list or by selection), elevation, name, raw description, full description, and all points.

With numbers matching	Selects points by a point number range or list. When creating a list, sequential point numbers are hyphenated (1-20) and individual numbers are in a comma delimited list. A point list can include sequential and individual points (1-20, 14, 44, 50-60). Select **Selection Set in Drawing** to select the points in the drawing and list their point numbers at the top of the *Include* tab.
With elevations matching	Enables you to select points by entering a specific elevation or by specifying a minimum and maximum elevation. For example, valid entries include >100,<400, and >100. The first entry only includes points whose elevation is above 100, but less than 400. The second entry only includes points whose elevation is greater than 100. A point without an elevation cannot be selected using this method. An elevation range, defined by separating the start and end numbers with a hyphen, includes points whose elevation falls within the range (1-100). This can be combined with greater or less than symbols.
With names matching	Selects points based on matching their point names. Enter one or more point names separated by commas.
With raw/full descriptions matching	Selects points based on matching an entered raw or full description. Enter one or more descriptions separated by commas. You can use the same wildcards as the Description Key Set. Generally, this method uses the asterisk (*) as the wildcard after the description (e.g., PINE*, CTV*, CL*, etc.).
Include all points	Assigns all points in the drawing to the point group. When this option is toggled on, all other **Include** options are disabled.

- The *Exclude* tab has the same options as the *Include* tab, except for the **Include All Points** option.

- The *Query Builder* tab creates one or more expressions to select points. Each query is a row selecting points. As with all SQL queries, you combine expressions using the operators AND, OR, and NOT. You can also use parentheses to group expressions.

- The *Overrides* tab overrides the points in the point group's raw description, elevation, point style, and point label style. For example, you can override specific tree species symbols with a generic tree symbol, override a label style when displaying this group, or override the point and label style with none (to hide all points).

  The point group display order affects points and their overrides. To change how the point groups display, modify the point group display order.

- The *Point List* tab displays the point group's points. This tab enables you to review points that are currently in the point group. The *Summary* tab displays the point group's settings. You can print this tab as a report by cutting and pasting it into a document.

Updating Out of Date Point Groups

After defining point groups and adding points to a drawing, the group becomes out of date before assigning the points to the group. This enables you to verify that the points should become part of the group.

To review why a group is out of date, select the group, right-click, and select **Show Changes**. If the changes are correct, select **Update** to add the points to the group.

If you know that all of the groups displaying as out of date should be updated, right-click on the **Point Groups** collection and select **Update**. At this level, the command updates all of the point groups.

Overriding Point Group Properties

If a Description Key Set exists in the file, the points take on the symbol and label style assigned by the Description Key Set unless a point group override is toggled on. When working with points, you might want them to display different labels, have them not be visible, or display different symbols. Each required change is a function of a point group override.

A point group that contains all of the points and overrides their symbols and labels with none does not display any points. This is similar to freezing all of the layers involved with points.

A point group that changes the symbols that a group displays overrides the label styles assigned to the point in the point group. To display a different symbol, the point group overrides the assigned point styles.

To set the style and override the assigned styles, toggle on the point group in the *Overrides* tab and set the styles in the *Override* column of the point group, as shown in Figure 1–38.

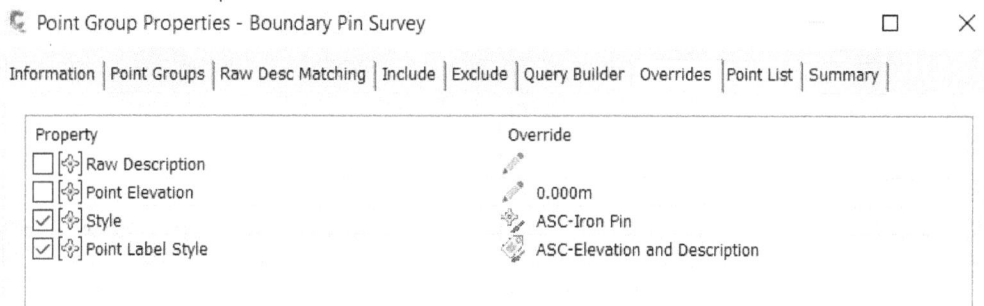

Figure 1–38

Point Groups Display Properties

When creating a point group, it is placed at the top of the point group list. The point group list is more than a list of point groups, it is also the Autodesk Civil 3D's point draw order. The Autodesk Civil 3D software draws the point groups starting from the bottom of the list to the top. If **_All Points** is the first drawn point group and the remaining point groups are subsets of all points, the individual point group does not display, but all of the points display.

To display point groups that are a subset of all points, you must create a point group whose purpose is to hide all points. This popular point group is commonly called **No Display**. With this group, any point group drawn after it displays its members without *seeing* the other points.

The Autodesk Civil 3D software draws point groups from the bottom to the top of the list. To manipulate the display order, right-click on the **Point Groups** collection in the Toolspace> *Prospector* tab and select **Properties**. The Point Groups dialog box opens, enabling you to modify the point group display order using the arrows on the right, as shown in Figure 1–39.

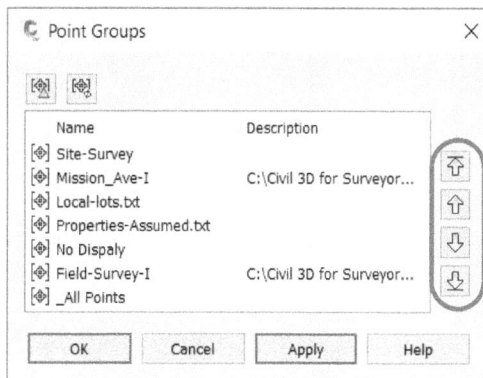

Figure 1–39

These arrows enable you to select the required point group and move it up or down in the list (or all of the way to the top or bottom of the list with one click, ⏫) in the hierarchy for display purposes. The Point Groups dialog box has two additional icons at the top. The first icon displays the difference between point groups and the second icon updates them all.

If you use Description Key Sets, a point displays the assigned point and label style when it is part of any point group. The only time the point displays another style is when you override the style (in the Point Group Properties dialog box, in the *Overrides* tab).

With the Description Key Set and display order shown in Figure 1–40, the points display their originally assigned point styles and point label styles.

Code	Style	Point Label ...	Format	Layer	Scale Param...	Fixed Scale ...	Use drawin...	Apply to X-Y	Apply to Z
☑ BRUSH*	☑ Tree Brush	☑ Point#-Elev	$2' $1 (TRUNK)	☑ V-NODE-TREE	☑ Parameter 2	☑ 25.000	☐ No	☑ Yes	☐ No
☑ CTREE*	☑ Tree C	☑ Point#-Elev	$2' $1 (TRUNK)	☑ V-NODE-TREE	☑ Parameter 2	☑ 25.000	☐ No	☑ Yes	☐ No
☑ DTREE*	☑ Tree D	☑ Point#-Elev	$2' $1 (TRUNK)	☑ V-NODE-TREE	☑ Parameter 2	☑ 25.000	☐ No	☑ Yes	☐ No
☑ HYD	☑ ASC-Hydrant (exist	☑ <default>	$*	☐	☑ Parameter 1	☐ 1.000	☐ No	☐ No	☐ No
☑ SANMH*	☑ Sanitary Sewer Ma	☑ Point#-Elev	$*	☑ V-NODE-SSWR	☑ Parameter 1	☐ 1.000	☐ No	☐ No	☐ No
☑ STMMH*	☑ Storm Sewer Manh	☑ Point#-Elev	$*	☑ V-NODE-STRM	☑ Parameter 2	☑ 25.000	☐ No	☐ No	☐ No

Figure 1–40

The **No Display** point group includes all of the points, but overrides the originally assigned point style and point label styles with **<none>**. When **No Display** is moved to the list's top, no points display. The Point Groups dialog box is shown in Figure 1–41.

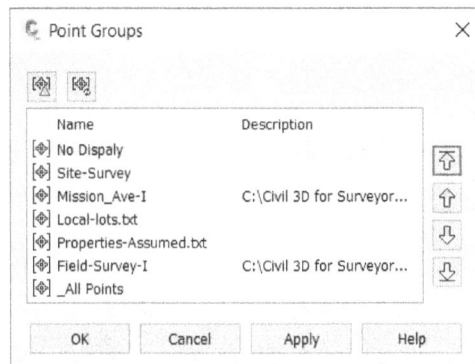

Figure 1–41

Survey Point Groups

Survey has the ability to create its own point groups. The points DO NOT need to reside in the drawing to produce survey point groups.

You can create these groups using one of the following three methods: There are three methods that create these groups:

1. **Survey Point Group by Import:** Import a survey file into a survey at the same time as the points are imported into a drawing. The Survey Toolspace automatically creates a point group that is the same name as the imported file.

2. **Manual selection:** Grouping the points in the drawing and selecting the points in the drawing to populate the survey point group. The issue with this method is that the points need to be grouped in the drawing, and that only those points display for the group being defined.

3. **Manual toggling:** Manually toggling what survey points are included in the survey point group. This method is the least desirable, because you have to toggle on each point in each group

Each method defines groups based on how you use the survey point database.

Practice 1b	# Creating Point Groups

Practice Objectives

- Create a point group.
- Rearrange the order of the point groups for display purposes.

In this practice, you will create point groups and change their properties and their display order.

Task 1 - Create point groups (Boundary Pin Survey).

1. Open **Points-C-Survey.dwg** from the *C:\Civil 3D for Surveyors\Working\Survey* folder.

2. In the Toolspace>*Prospector* tab, select **Point Groups**, right-click, and select **New**, as shown in Figure 1–42.

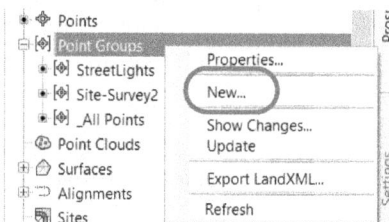

Figure 1–42

3. In the Point Group Properties dialog box, in the *Information* tab, set the following, as shown in Figure 1–43:

- *Name:* **Boundary Pin Survey**
- *Point style*: **ASC-Iron Pin**
- *Point label style*: **ASC-Elevation and Description**

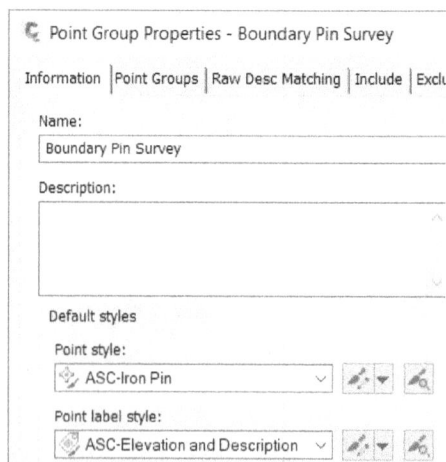

Figure 1–43

4. Select the *Include* tab. Select the **With raw description matching** option. Type ***IP.** (verify that a period follows IP) in the field to select all of the points that have the last three characters *IP.* (iron pin). You can confirm this in the *Point List* tab, as shown in Figure 1–44.

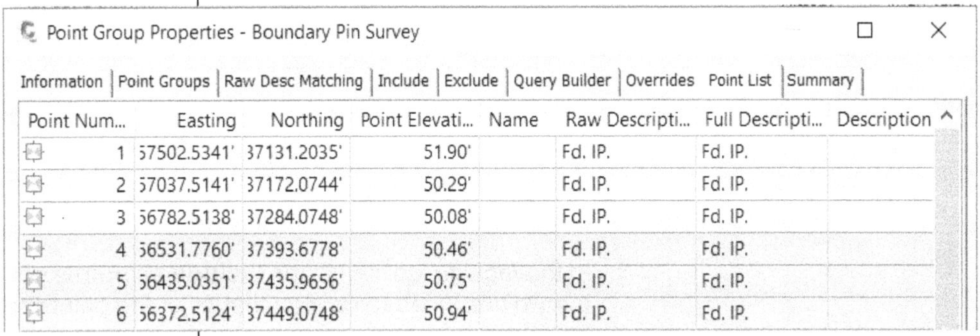

Point Num...	Easting	Northing	Point Elevati...	Name	Raw Descripti...	Full Descripti...	Description
1	57502.5341'	37131.2035'	51.90'		Fd. IP.	Fd. IP.	
2	57037.5141'	37172.0744'	50.29'		Fd. IP.	Fd. IP.	
3	56782.5138'	37284.0748'	50.08'		Fd. IP.	Fd. IP.	
4	56531.7760'	37393.6778'	50.46'		Fd. IP.	Fd. IP.	
5	56435.0351'	37435.9656'	50.75'		Fd. IP.	Fd. IP.	
6	56372.5124'	37449.0748'	50.94'		Fd. IP.	Fd. IP.	

Point Group Properties - Boundary Pin Survey

Information | Point Groups | Raw Desc Matching | Include | Exclude | Query Builder | Overrides | Point List | Summary

Figure 1–44

5. Click **OK** to close the dialog box and apply the changes.

Task 2 - Create point groups (No display).

Continue working with the drawing from the previous task. In this task, you will use the point group to control the points display. Not only will you be able to display the same point differently, but you will also be able to control the visibility of the points. This eliminates needing to use the Layer command to thaw and freeze layers.

1. Select **Point Groups**, right-click, and select **New** to create a new point group. In the *Information* tab, set the *Name* to **No display**.

2. Select **<none>** for both the *Point style* and the *Point label style*, as shown in Figure 1–45.

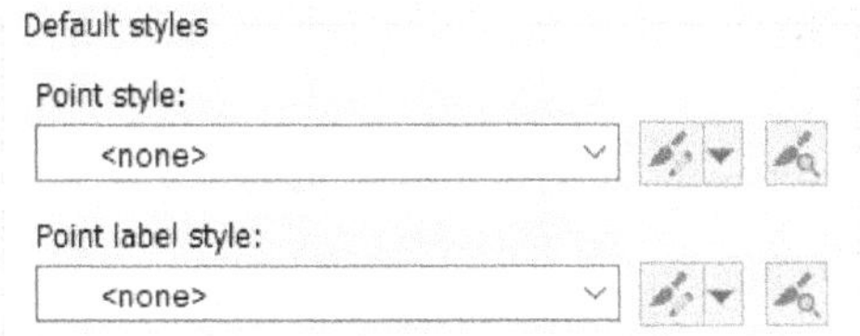

Default styles

Point style:
    <none>

Point label style:
    <none>

Figure 1–45

3. Select the *Overrides* tab and select **Style** and **Point Label Style**, as shown in Figure 1–46.

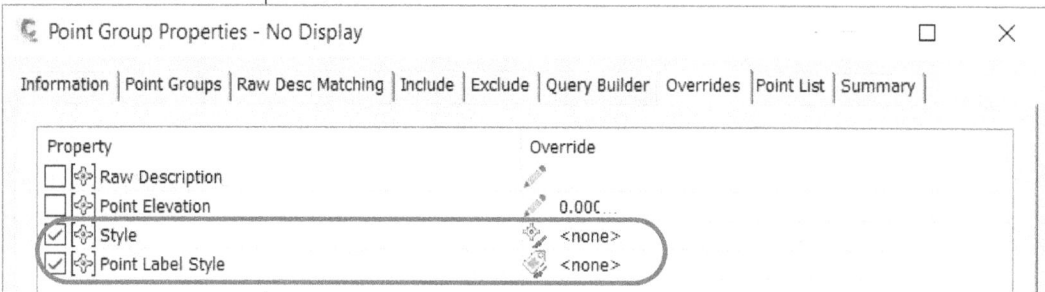

Figure 1–46

4. In the *Include* tab, select the **Include all points** option. Select the *Point List* tab to confirm that all of the points have been included.

5. Click **OK** to create the point group. Note that the points have disappeared because the newly created point group is at the top of the display order.

6. To control the hierarchy and the display of the point group style, select the Toolspace>*Prospector* tab, select **Point Groups**, right-click, and select **Properties**.

7. In the Point Groups dialog box, select the **No display** point group and move it to the top of the list by clicking ⬆. Select the **Boundary Pin Survey** point group and move it to the top of the list by clicking ⬆. Click **OK** to apply the changes. Only the points in the Boundary Pin point group are displayed. You might need to type **regen** in the Command Line (type **RE**, and press <Enter>).

8. In the Status Bar, ensure that the *Annotation Scale* is set to **1"=40'** (as shown in Figure 1–47) to change the point size in the drawing.

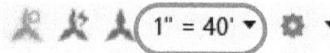

Figure 1–47

9. Save the drawing.

Task 3 - Modify the point group's properties.

With each Import Event in a survey database, a point group is generated automatically that contains the points that are imported. You will take the groundshots that were imported in the previous practice and change the properties of the point group.

1. In the Toolspace>*Prospector* tab, under **Point Groups**, select **Groundshots**, then right-click and select **Properties**, as shown in Figure 1–48.

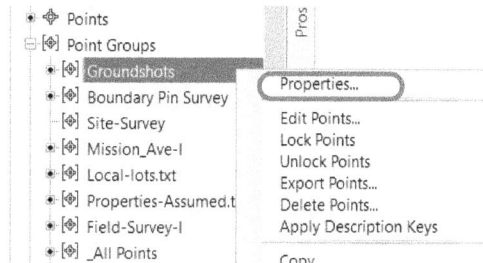

Figure 1–48

2. Note the description that was generated automatically by importing the points, as shown in Figure 1–49.

3. For the *Point style*, select **ASC-Bound**, and for the *Point label style*, select **ASC-Elevation Only**, as shown in Figure 1–49.

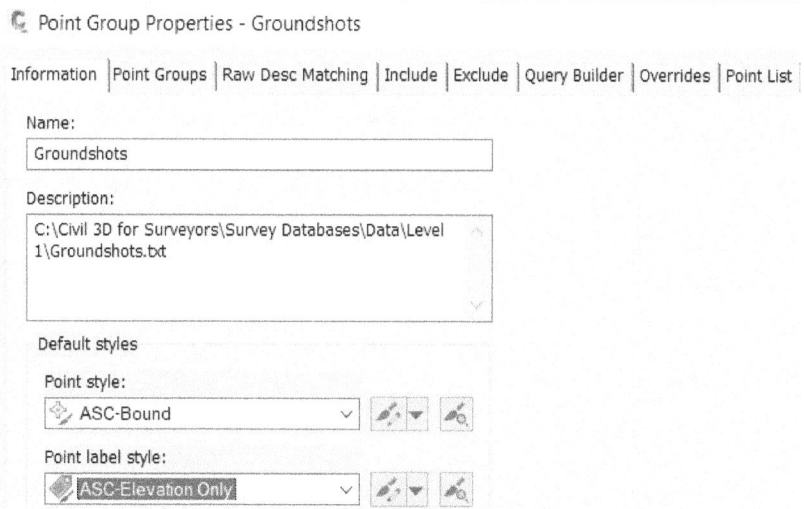

Figure 1–49

4. In the Point Groups dialog box, select the **Groundshots** point group and move it to the top of the list by clicking ⬆.

5. Select the **Boundary Pin Survey** point group and move it to the top of the list by clicking ⬆.

6. Click **OK** to apply the changes. You might need to type **regen** in the Command Line (type **RE**, and press <Enter>).

7. Experiment with moving point groups up and down the list to control the display of points. When done, select the **No display** point group and move it below the **Boundary Pin Survey** point group.

8. Save the drawing.

1.6 Reviewing and Editing Points

Reviewing and editing point data occurs throughout the Autodesk Civil 3D environment. It is as simple as selecting a point in the drawing, right-clicking, and selecting **Edit Points** You can also edit points using the right-click menu in the *Points* heading in the Toolspace>*Prospector* tab, as shown in Figure 1–50. Alternatively, you can select a point entry in the *Prospector's* preview area.

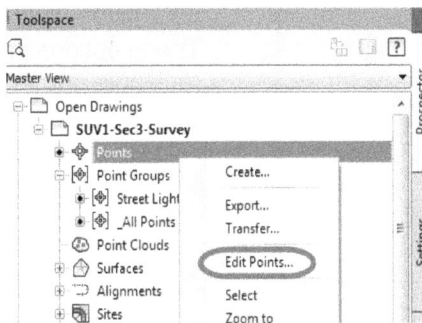

Figure 1–50

When selecting **Edit Points**, the Autodesk Civil 3D software displays the *Point Editor* tab inside the Panorama, as shown in Figure 1–51.

Point Num...	Easting	Northing	Point E...	N	Raw Descript...	Full Descript...	D...	Grid Easti...	Grid Nort...	Longitude	Latitude
22	56167.1890'	36620.5030'	202.68'		Fd. IP.	Fd. IP.		56167.1890'	36620.5030'	W117° 14' 57.49"	N33° 15' 05.61"
23	56167.3930'	36683.0530'	199.31'		Fd. IP.	Fd. IP.		56167.3930'	36683.0530'	W117° 14' 57.49"	N33° 15' 06.22"
250	55999.9650'	36668.5250'	204.75'		STMMH	STMMH	S*	55999.9650'	36668.5250'	W117° 14' 59.46"	N33° 15' 06.06"
251	56009.4790'	36658.7500'	204.95'		SANMH	SANMH	S*	56009.4790'	36658.7500'	W117° 14' 59.35"	N33° 15' 05.97"
252	55838.9710'	35674.7270'	230.67'		HYD 100	HYDRANT	HYD	55838.9710'	35674.7270'	W117° 15' 01.24"	N33° 14' 56.22"
260	56069.3000'	36634.2500'			HYD 33	HYDRANT	HYD	56069.3000'	36634.2500'	W117° 14' 58.64"	N33° 15' 05.73"
300	56396.1420'	37398.9810'	169.01'		BRUSH COTTOI	1.5' COTTONW	S2'	56396.1420'	37398.9810'	W117° 14' 54.88"	N33° 15' 13.33"
301	56357.1950'	37377.0080'	171.22'		BRUSH DOGW	2.4' DOGWOO	S2'	56357.1950'	37377.0080'	W117° 14' 55.33"	N33° 15' 13.11"
302	56340.8630'	37426.6040'	168.84'		BRUSH COTTOI	2.6' COTTONW	S2'	56340.8630'	37426.6040'	W117° 14' 55.53"	N33° 15' 13.60"
303	56560.9880'	37349.9030'	165.69'		BRUSH COTTOI	3.5' COTTONW	S2'	56560.9880'	37349.9030'	W117° 14' 52.93"	N33° 15' 12.86"
304	56469.5570'	37285.6370'	169.44'		BRUSH COTTOI	5.2' COTTONW	S2'	56469.5570'	37285.6370'	W117° 14' 54.00"	N33° 15' 12.21"
305	56439.4130'	37234.4250'	171.55'		BRUSH DOGW	1.2' DOGWOO	S2'	56439.4130'	37234.4250'	W117° 14' 54.35"	N33° 15' 11.70"
306	56376.1160'	37237.4380'	173.43'		BRUSH COTTOI	1.6' COTTONW	S2'	56376.1160'	37237.4380'	W117° 14' 55.09"	N33° 15' 11.73"
307	56718.5200'	37041.3900'	178.05'		BRUSH DOGW	3.7' DOGWOO	S2'	56718.5200'	37041.3900'	W117° 14' 51.04"	N33° 15' 09.82"

Figure 1–51

Repositioning Point Objects and Labels

When selecting a point, it displays multiple grips. The grips have different functions depending on their state (original vs. dragged).

Original State refers to a point label that has not been dragged from its original position. In this position, there are two grips available.

- Use the **rectangle** grip to:
  - Move the label
  - Rotate the label

  These options become available when you hover over the rectangle grip, as shown in Figure 1–52.

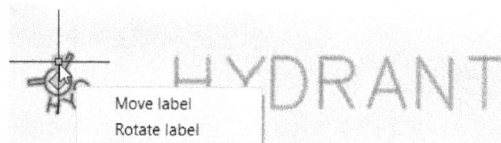

Figure 1–52

- Use the **diamond** grip to:
  - Move the point
  - Rotate both the label and marker
  - Rotate just the marker
  - Reset marker rotation (only available if the marker and/or the label have been rotated)
  - Reset all (only available if the marker and/or the label have been rotated)

  These options become available when you hover over the diamond grip, as shown in Figure 1–53.

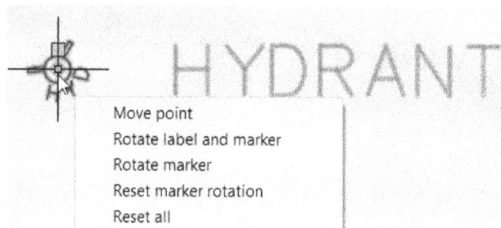

Figure 1–53

Dragged State refers to a point label that has been moved from its original position. In this position, the following grips are available.

- Use the **rectangle** label grip to:
    - Move the point
    - Rotate just the marker
    - Reset marker rotation
    - Reset all

    These options become available when you hover over the rectangle grip, as shown in Figure 1–54.

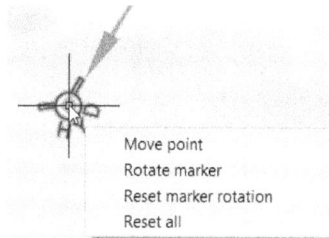

Figure 1–54

- Use the **diamond point object** grip to:
    - Move the label
    - Rotate the marker
    - Reset the label
    - Reset the label location
    - Reset all

    These options become available when you hover over the diamond grip, as shown in Figure 1–55.

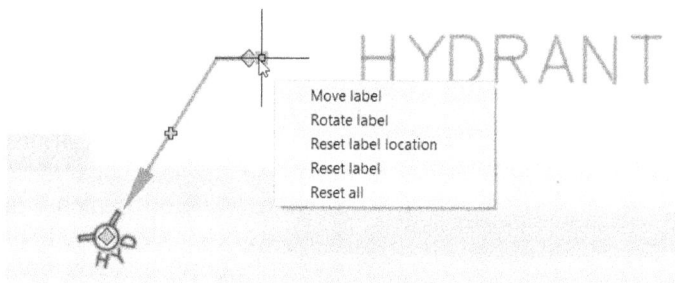

Figure 1–55

- Use the **+** (plus) grip to add vertices to the leader, as shown in Figure 1–56.

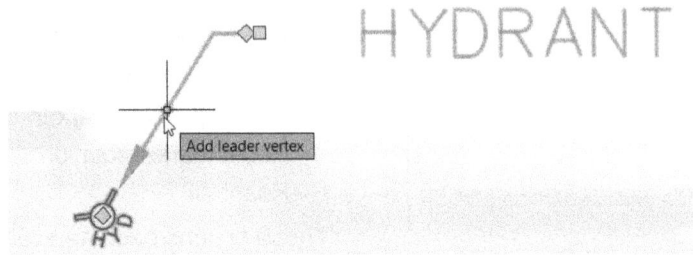

Figure 1–56

- Use the **-** (minus) grip to delete vertices from the leader, as shown in Figure 1–57.

Figure 1–57

Each label component can be modified and the change is only for that point.

Point objects can be set to automatically rotate to match the current view using style settings. If this is not preferred, they can have a rotation assigned directly through the AutoCAD Properties dialog box.

You can reset a label to its original position by selecting the point, right-clicking, and selecting **Reset Label**.

Each point label style has **Dragged State** parameters. These parameters affect the label's behavior when moving the label from its original label position. Depending on the **Dragged State** parameters, a label can change completely (Stacked text) or display as it was originally defined (As composed). Select the move point grip when you want to relocate the label.

An example of a dragged label is shown in Figure 1–58.

48
128.64
EOP

Figure 1–58

Practice 1c | Manipulating Points

Practice Objective

- Modify the label position for points to ensure that the plan is readable.

1. Open **Points-D-Survey.dwg** from the *C:\Civil 3D for Surveyors\Working\Survey* folder if you closed it previously.

2. In the Toolspace>*Prospector* tab, right-click on **Point Group** and select **Properties**.

3. Select the **No display** point group and click the <Down Arrow> or <Bottom> icon to move it to the bottom of the list, as shown in Figure 1–59.

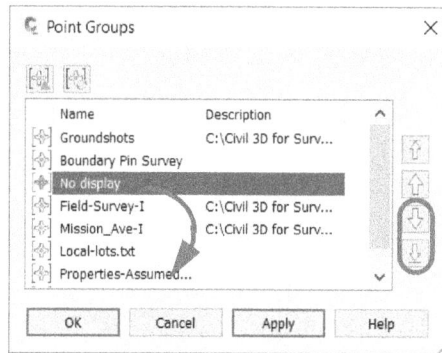

Figure 1–59

This positions the point at the center of the screen.

4. In the preview point list, scroll down until the point number **260** displays. Select it, right-click, and select **Zoom to**.

5. In the Status Bar, ensure that the *Annotation Scale* is set to **1"=40'** (as shown in Figure 1–60) to change the point size in the drawing.

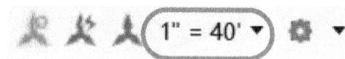

Figure 1–60

6. Select point **260** to display its grips. Select the Drag Label grip, as shown in Figure 1–61, to relocate the label.

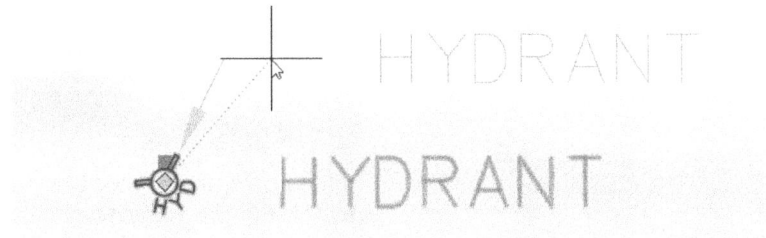

Figure 1–61

When selecting the cyan grip, it turns red.

7. With the label still displaying grips, hover on the Rectangle grip and select **Reset Label**.

8. With the label still displaying grips, hover over the Square label grip to display the options for moving, rotating, and additional sub item grips, as shown in Figure 1–62. Select **Rotate label** and rotate the label.

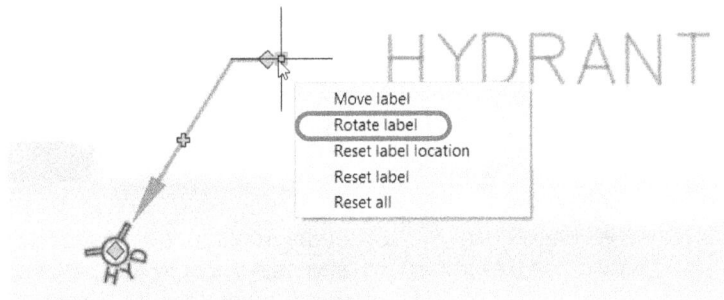

Move label
Rotate label
Reset label location
Reset label
Reset all

Figure 1–62

9. With the label still displaying grips, click the + (plus) grip to add a vertex to the leader, then select the - (minus) grip to delete the vertex.

10. Save the drawing.

Practice 1d | Point Locking and Editing

Practice Objective

- Prevent unwanted edits to points by locking them.

1. Open **Points-D-Survey.dwg** from the *C:\Civil 3D for Surveyors\Working\Survey* folder.

2. In the Toolspace>*Prospector* tab, select **Points** to display a point list in the *Prospector's* preview area.

3. Scroll through the list, select point number **10**, right-click, and select **Zoom to**.

4. In the drawing, select point **10** and note the move grip that displays at its marker, as shown in Figure 1–63.

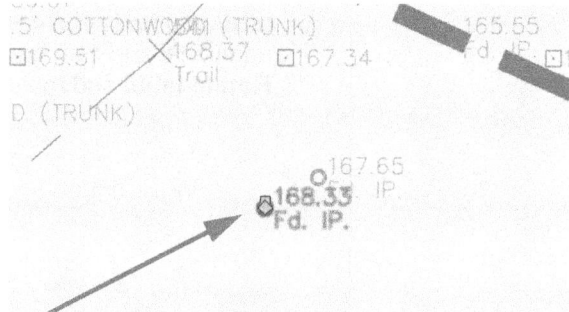

Figure 1–63

5. In the Toolspace>*Prospector* tab, select **Points**, right-click, and select **Lock**, as shown on the left in Figure 1–64. Note that the points in the *Prospector's* preview area now display the **Lock** icon, as shown on the right.

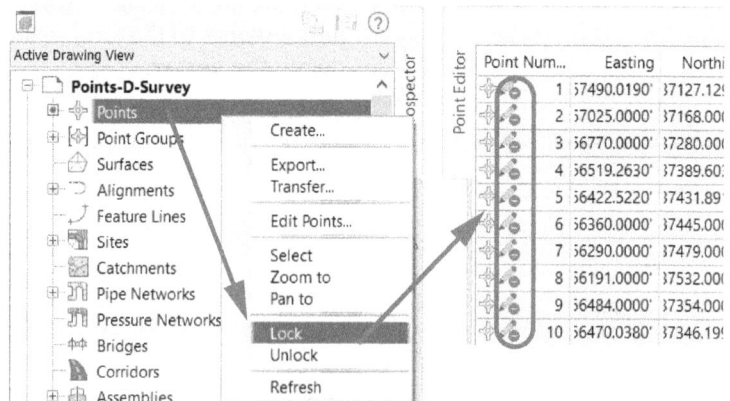

Figure 1–64

6. In the model, select point **10** and note that although the move grip is displayed, you cannot move the point, as shown in Figure 1–65.

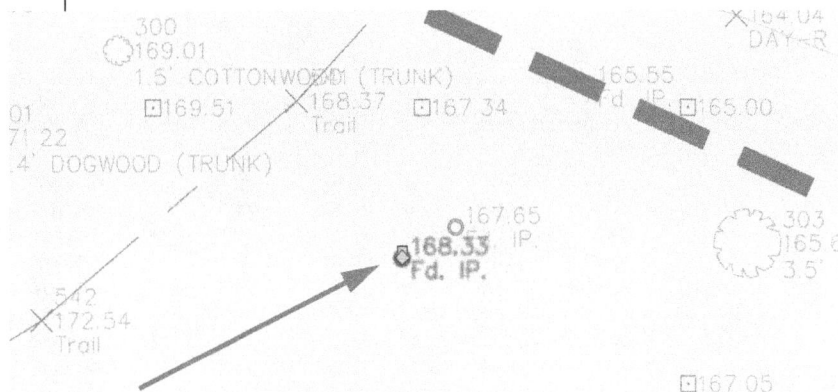

Figure 1–65

7. In the Toolspace>*Prospector* tab, select **Points**. Right-click and select **Edit Points**. The points display the **Lock** icon and the editor now has a gray background, as shown in Figure 1–66.

Point Num...	Easting	Northing	Point E...	N	Raw Descript...	Full Descript...	D...	Grid Easti...	Grid Nort...	Lonc ^
1	57490.0190'	37127.1290'	170.26'		Fd. IP.	Fd. IP.		57490.0190'	37127.1290'	W117° 14' 4
2	57025.0000'	37168.0000'	164.98'		Fd. IP.	Fd. IP.		57025.0000'	37168.0000'	W117° 14' 4
3	56770.0000'	37280.0000'	164.32'		Fd. IP.	Fd. IP.		56770.0000'	37280.0000'	W117° 14' 5
4	56519.2630'	37389.6030'	165.55'		Fd. IP.	Fd. IP.		56519.2630'	37389.6030'	W117° 14' 5
5	56422.5220'	37431.8910'	166.50'		Fd. IP.	Fd. IP.		56422.5220'	37431.8910'	W117° 14' 5
6	56360.0000'	37445.0000'	167.13'		Fd. IP.	Fd. IP.		56360.0000'	37445.0000'	W117° 14' 5
7	56290.0000'	37479.0000'	167.53'		Fd. IP.	Fd. IP.		56290.0000'	37479.0000'	W117° 14' 5
8	56191.0000'	37532.0000'	161.17'		Fd. IP.	Fd. IP.		56191.0000'	37532.0000'	W117° 14' 5
9	56484.0000'	37354.0000'	167.65'		Fd. IP.	Fd. IP.		56484.0000'	37354.0000'	W117° 14' 5
10	56470.0380'	37346.1990'	168.33'		Fd. IP.	Fd. IP.		56470.0380'	37346.1990'	W117° 14' 5
11	56139.0410'	37368.5910'	183.81'		Fd. IP.	Fd. IP.		56139.0410'	37368.5910'	W117° 14' 5
12	56076.0000'	37172.0000'	100.28'		Fd. IP.	Fd. IP.		56076.0000'	37172.0000'	W117° 14' 5

Figure 1–66

8. Select point **5** from the list of points. Scroll down the list, press <Shift> and select point **10**.

9. With points **5** to **10** highlighted right-click, and select **Unlock**. Note that the points no longer display the **Lock** icon and have a white background, as shown in Figure 1–67. These two things indicate that the points are available for editing.

Point Num...	Easting	Northing	Point E...	N	Raw Descript...	Full Descript...	D...	Grid Easti...	Grid Nort...	Lonc
1	57490.0190'	37127.1290'	170.26'		Fd. IP.	Fd. IP.		57490.0190'	37127.1290'	W117° 14' 4
2	57025.0000'	37168.0000'	164.98'		Fd. IP.	Fd. IP.		57025.0000'	37168.0000'	W117° 14' 4
3	56770.0000'	37280.0000'	164.32'		Fd. IP.	Fd. IP.		56770.0000'	37280.0000'	W117° 14' 5
4	56519.2630'	37389.6030'	165.55'		Fd. IP.	Fd. IP.		56519.2630'	37389.6030'	W117° 14' 5
5	56422.5220'	37431.8910'	166.50'		Fd. IP.	Fd. IP.		56422.5220'	37431.8910'	W117° 14' 5
6	56360.0000'	37445.0000'	167.13'		Fd. IP.	Fd. IP.		56360.0000'	37445.0000'	W117° 14' 5
7	56290.0000'	37479.0000'	167.53'		Fd. IP.	Fd. IP.		56290.0000'	37479.0000'	W117° 14' 5
8	56191.0000'	37532.0000'	161.17'		Fd. IP.	Fd. IP.		56191.0000'	37532.0000'	W117° 14' 5
9	56484.0000'	37354.0000'	167.65'		Fd. IP.	Fd. IP.		56484.0000'	37354.0000'	W117° 14' 5
10	56470.0380'	37346.1990'	168.33'		Fd. IP.	Fd. IP.		56470.0380'	37346.1990'	W117° 14' 5
11	56139.0410'	37368.5910'	183.81'		Fd. IP.	Fd. IP.		56139.0410'	37368.5910'	W117° 14' 5
12	56076.0000'	37172.0000'	198.39'		Fd. IP.	Fd. IP.		56076.0000'	37172.0000'	W117° 14' 5

Figure 1–67

10. In the Point Editor Panorama, double-click on point **10**. The cell switches to edit mode now that it has been unlocked.

11. Close the Panorama by clicking ☑ in the top right corner without making any changes.

12. In the drawing, select point **10**, right-click, and review the editing options in the right-click menu.

13. Press <Esc> to deselect the point.

14. Review the commands displayed in the ribbon. Because this is a contextual object, all of the entries are tools that are applicable to a point.

15. In the Toolspace>*Prospector* tab, select **Points**, right-click, and select **Unlock**.

16. Save the drawing.

Parcels

Exam Objectives Covered in This Chapter

1.4.a Explain automatic parcel creation

1.4.b Create a parcel by layout

1.4.c Create a parcel from drawing objects

1.4.d Create parcels by subdividing an existing parcel

1.4.e Associate a parcel with a site

1.5.a Describe the difference between parcel, parcel area, and parcel segment labels

1.5.b Add and replace parcel labels

1.5.c Define parcel styles

1.5.d Create a parcel table

1.5.e Convert a label to a tag

1.5.f Rename and renumber parcels

1.5.g Delete a parcel

1.6.e Understand the purpose of performing a Mapcheck Analysis

2.1 Introduction to Parcels

A Site under development (as shown in Figure 2–1), is the starting point for defining smaller parcels. The development's zoning agreement or covenants determine the size, setback, and other criteria for the new parcels. If a parcel is residential, there might be restrictions affecting minimum parcel areas, setbacks, and where to locate a house. If it is a commercial property, there might be restrictions or specific mandates for access, traffic control, parking spaces, etc. The **Parcel Layout** commands are used for subdividing larger parcels.

Figure 2–1

Sites, parcels, and alignments are closely related. Each can exist by itself and you do not need to have alignments associated with the parcels. However, you often start with a site boundary and then divide the site into smaller parcels by placing alignments within its boundary.

- Parcels are listed in the Toolspace, *Prospector* tab in the Sites branch, as shown in Figure 2–2.

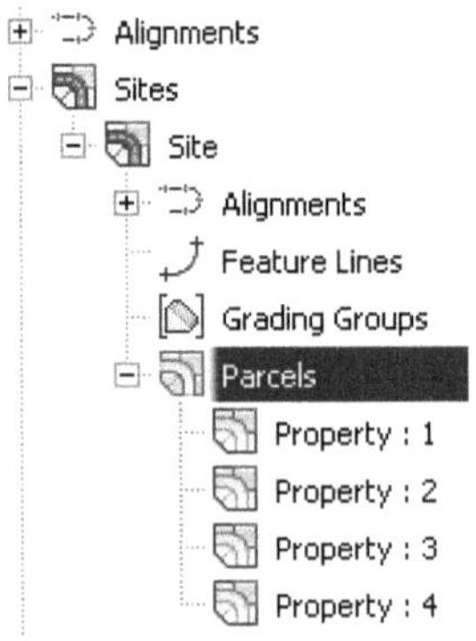

Figure 2–2

- When adding alignments to a site, the Parcels list is updated in the Toolspace, *Prospector* tab.

- As in all other Autodesk Civil 3D objects, Parcel object layers are controlled in the *Object Layers* tab of the Drawing Settings dialog box, as shown in Figure 2–3.

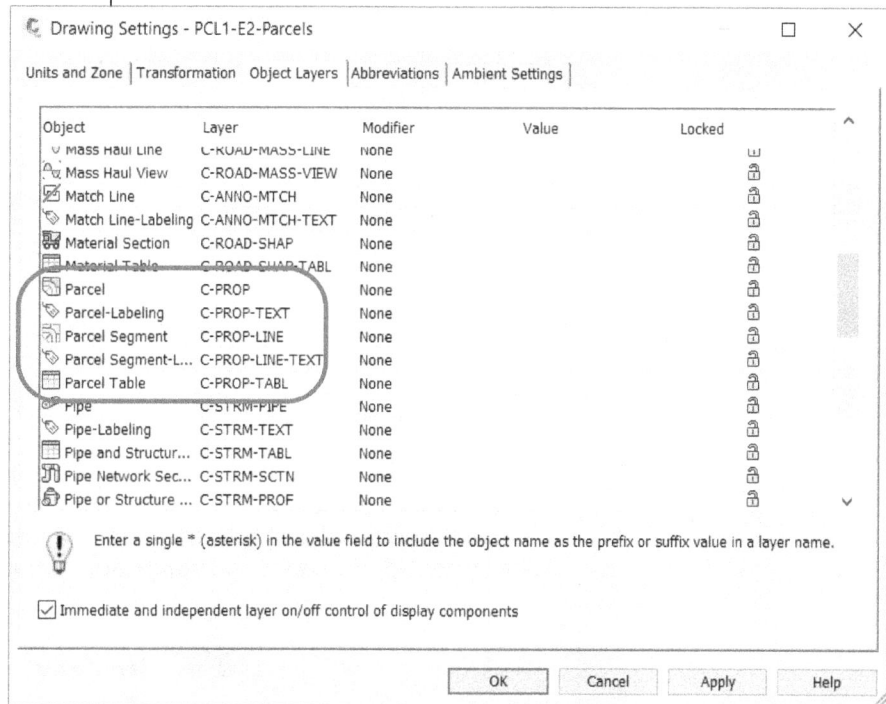

Figure 2–3

ROW Parcel

The right-of-way (ROW) parcel is related to the alignment and parcels. This special parcel represents land that is owned, maintained, and used for the community by a regulatory body (usually the local municipality or Department of Transportation). Typically, the ROW contains road, sidewalks, and utilities. The contents of the ROW depend on the covenants or agreements made before the site is developed. For example, in some cases, the sidewalks and utilities might be located within an easement outside the road ROW.

- The Autodesk Civil 3D software contains a **ROW** command, which creates a parcel using offsets from an alignment.

- A ROW parcel can represent the front yard definition of several potential parcels.

- While normal parcels automatically adjust to changes to an alignment, ROW parcels are static as shown in Figure 2–4. Therefore, you should only create ROW parcels after determining a final location for an alignment.

Figure 2–4

Parcel Style Display Order

Parcel segment display is controlled by parcel styles, and parcel lines can abut parcels with different styles. To open the Site Parcel Properties dialog box, select the *Parcels* collection (under *Sites*), right-click and select **Properties**, as shown in Figure 2–5.

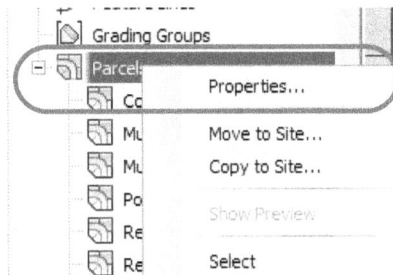

Figure 2–5

You can select which parcel style should take precedence in the *Parcel style display order* area of the Site Parcel Properties dialog box, as shown in Figure 2–6. Placing the style for the overall parent tract (the Site Parcel Style) at the top of the list causes the outside parcel lines to display differently than those inside.

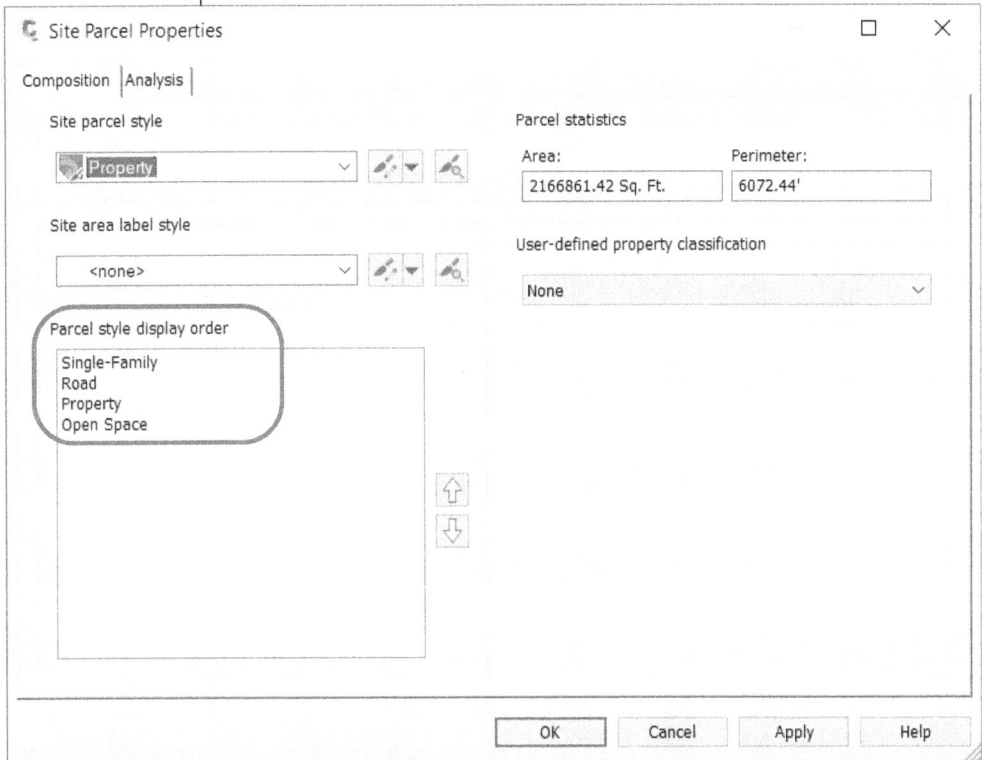

Figure 2–6

Parcel Properties

The properties of a parcel include its name, style, and an *Analysis* tab containing the parcel's area, perimeter, and point-of-beginning (POB). The Parcel Property's *Composition* tab displays the label style, area, and perimeter, as shown in Figure 2–7.

Figure 2–7

The *Analysis* tab contains a parcel boundary Inverse or Mapcheck analysis. In the upper right area of the tab, you can change the POB (Point of beginning) location and the analysis direction, as shown in Figure 2–8.

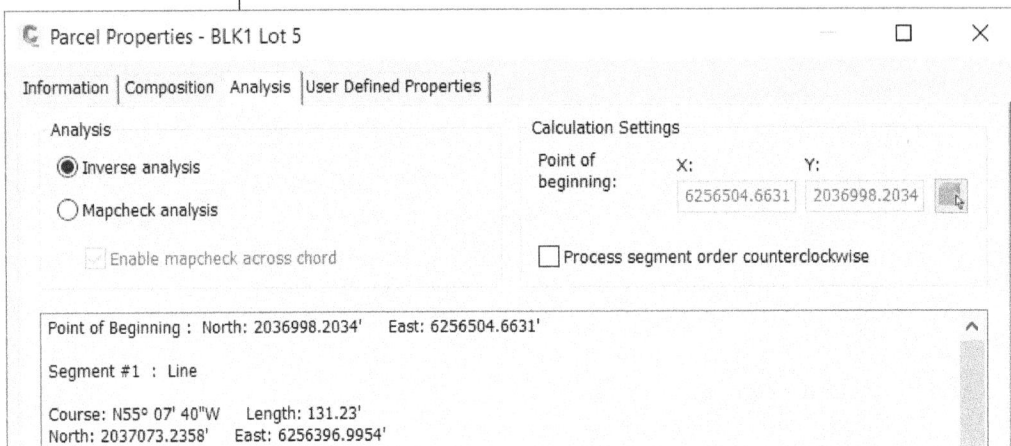

Figure 2–8

- The Mapcheck analysis precision is the same as the drawing distance precision.

- The Inverse report precision is set to the precision of the Autodesk Civil 3D software (10 to 12 decimal places).

- The default direction of a Mapcheck or Inverse analysis is clockwise. You can change the direction to counter-clockwise if required.

- A POB can be any vertex on the parcel's perimeter.

The *User Defined Properties* tab contains site-specific details, such as the *Parcel Number, Parcel Address, Parcel Tax ID*, and other properties you might want to define, as shown in Figure 2–9. Custom properties can be assigned to a drawing by using the *User Defined Property Classifications* area in the Toolspace, *Settings* tab, under the *Parcels* collection.

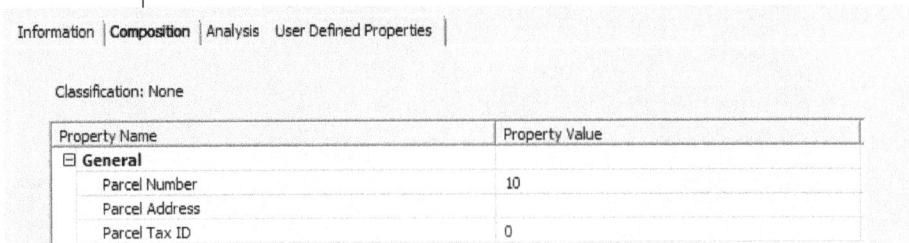

Figure 2–9

Parcel Labels and Styles

There are two types of parcel annotation: an area label for the parcel and the segments defining the parcel.

A parcel area label usually consists of a parcel's number or name, area, and perimeter, as shown in Figure 2–10. Most offices define their own parcel label styles. A parcel label style can include several additional parcel properties, address, PIN, Site name, etc.

In the Autodesk Civil 3D software, you select a parcel by selecting a parcel area label, not the parcel segments.

```
                        BLK1 LOT 2
                       10225.00 SQ FT
                         0.23 ACRES
```

Figure 2–10

Create Parcels from Objects

The Autodesk Civil 3D software can create parcels from AutoCAD objects, such as closed polylines and closed sequences of lines and arcs. Avoid gaps, multiple polyline vertices at the same location, and polylines that double-back over themselves, which might lead to errors in parcel layouts.

These objects can be selected in the current drawing or from an XREF. Note that Autodesk Civil 3D parcel lines in an XREF cannot be selected (only lines, arcs, and polylines can be selected). Additionally, Autodesk Civil 3D parcels created from AutoCAD objects do not maintain a relationship to the objects after creation.

Creating Right-of-Way Parcels

Once a site contains property that has been defined as a parcel and alignments have been generated, you are ready to start creating subdivision plans. One command that can speed up the process is **Parcels>Create ROW**. It automatically creates Right-of-Way parcels based on alignment setbacks.

ROW parcels do not automatically update when alignments change. Therefore, you might want to create ROWs after you are certain where you want the alignments to be for this alternative.

> **Hint: Multiple Alternatives in the Same Drawing**
>
> Sites enable you to organize alignments, parcels, and related data into separate containers, so that parcel lines from one site alternative do not clean up with parcel lines in others. However, sites do not offer layer or other kind of visibility control. Therefore, if you intend to have multiple parcel layout alternatives in the same drawing, you should consider placing parcel area labels and parcel segments on different layers.

Practice 2a

Create Parcels from Objects

Practice Objective

- Create parcels from objects in the drawing or external reference file.

Task 1 - Create a Site parcel from objects.

1. Open **PCL1-B1-Parcels.dwg** from the *C:\Civil 3D Projects\ Working\Parcels* folder.

2. In the *Home* tab>Create Design panel, expand **Parcel** and select **Create Parcels from Objects**, as shown in Figure 2–11.

Figure 2–11

3. In the model, select the polyline that represent the property boundary, as shown in Figure 2–12, and press <Enter>.

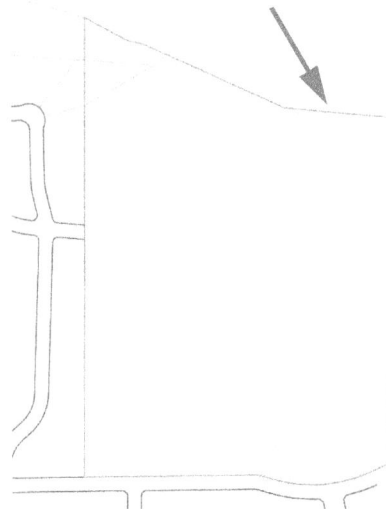

Figure 2–12

4. In the Create Parcels dialog box, set the following parameters, as shown in Figure 2–13, and then click **OK**.

- *Site:* **Site 1**
- *Parcel style:* **ASC-Property**
- *Area Label style:* **ASC-Name Area & Perimeter**
- Select **Automatically add segment labels**.
- *Parcel line segment label style:* **ASC-(Span) Bearing and Distance with Crows Feet**.
- Select **Erase existing entities**.

One parcel will be created with the parameters entered.

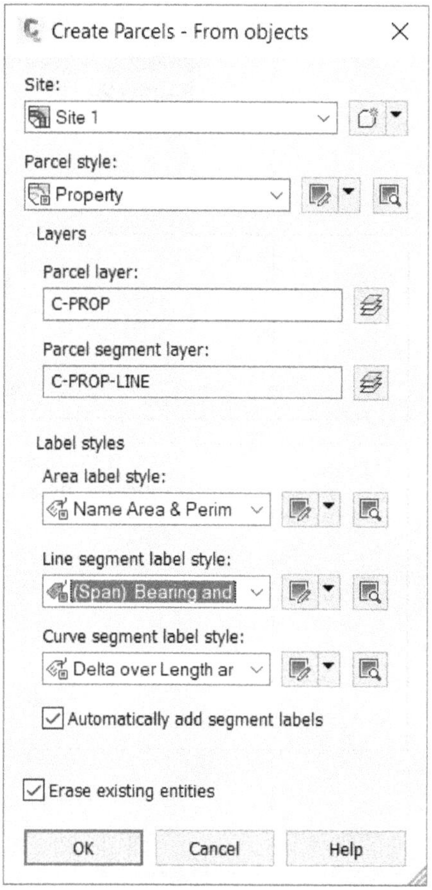

Figure 2–13

5. In the Toolspace, *Prospector* tab, expand the current drawing and select the **Sites>Site1>Parcels** node, as shown in Figure 2–14.

Note: If the + is not displayed next to Parcels, press <F5> to refresh the Toolspace, Prospector tab view.

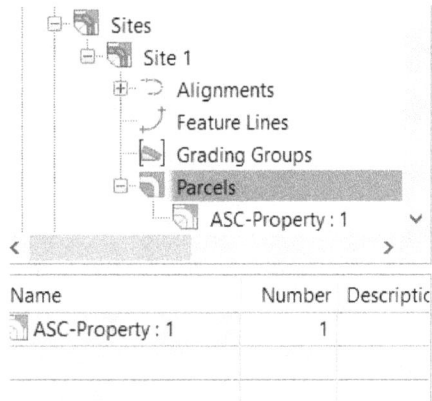

Sites
Site 1
Alignments
Feature Lines
Grading Groups
Parcels
ASC-Property : 1

Name	Number	Descriptio
ASC-Property : 1	1	

Figure 2–14

Task 2 - Create a new site and parcel from referenced objects.

You have received a drawing from the Land planning department that displays the street layout and different parcels. Using this plan, you will create parcels from XREF objects.

1. In the Toolspace, *Prospector* tab, right-click on the *Sites* collection and select **New**. Type **C3D Training** as the name and click **OK** to close the dialog box.

2. You now need to move the **ASC-Property:1** parcel from *Site 1* to the **C3D Training** site. Expand the *Site1* collection, expand the *Parcels* collection, right-click on the **ASC-Property:1** parcel and select **Move to Site**, as shown on the left in Figure 2–15.

3. In the Move to Site dialog box, select **C3D Training**, as shown on the right in Figure 2–15. Click **OK** to close the dialog box.

Figure 2–15

Note: To save time, the x-referenced drawing **Base-original Property**, has already been referenced. The zone and units for the project drawings were set. This enables you to geo reference the drawings using **Locate using Geographic data**, as shown in Figure 2–16.

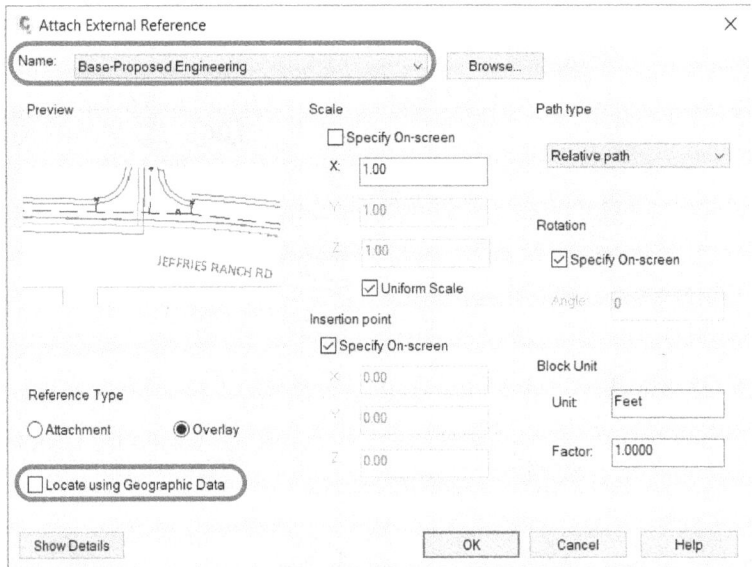

Figure 2–16

4. Thaw the layer **Base-originalProperty|C-PROP-LINE-N** and freeze the layer **Base-originalProperty|C-PROP-LINE-E**.

5. In the *Home* tab>Create Design panel, expand **Parcel** and select **Create Parcels from Objects**. Select XREF from the command options.

6. Use the AutoCAD Window selection or the Lasso Window selection method (click and drag the cursor towards the right side of the screen and then enclose the linework) to select all the linework. Press <Enter> to end the **XREF selection** command.

7. In the Create Parcels - From Objects dialog box, verify that the Site name is **C3D Training**. Clear the **Automatically add segment labels** option and keep the default values in the remaining fields, as shown on the right in Figure 2–17. Click **OK** to close the dialog box.

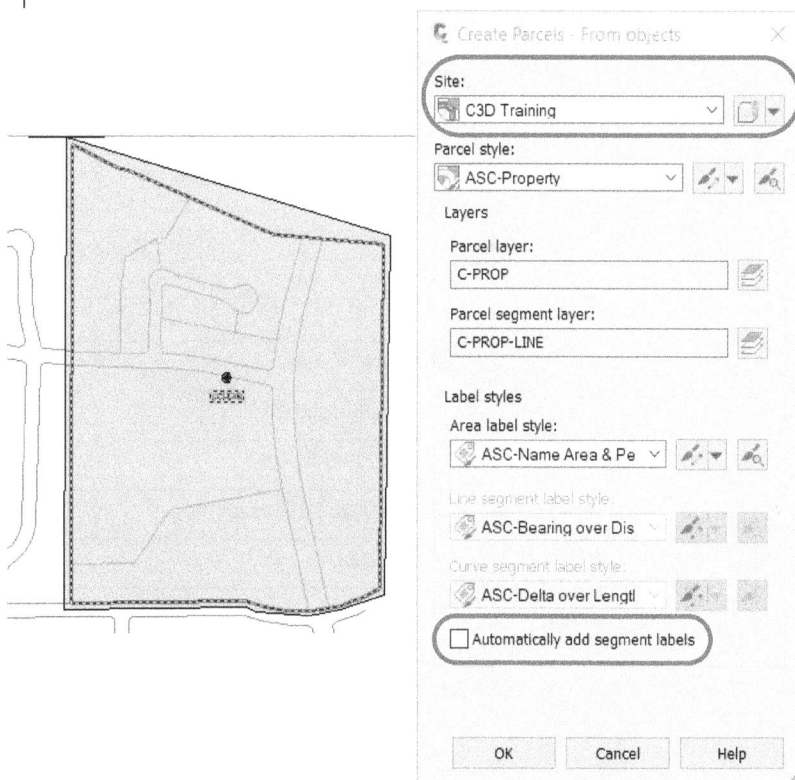

Figure 2–17

You may need to refresh the Toolspace by pressing <F5>.

8. The project site now has nine parcels. Select each parcel label and click (Parcel Properties) on the contextual *Parcels* tab>Modify panel.

The default parcel numbers may differ because they are randomly numbered.

9. In the Parcel Properties dialog box, in the *Information* tab, clear the **Use name template in parcel style** option, then rename the parcels according to the table in Figure 2–18.

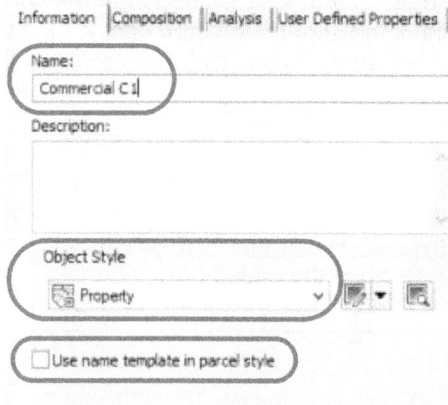

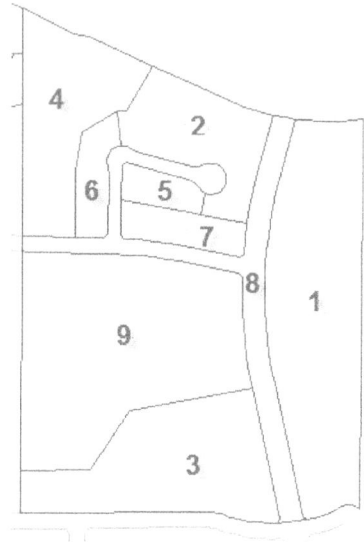

Figure 2–18

10. Using as a reference, set the parcel styles as follows:

Property Name	Style
1. **Commercial C1**	ASC-Property
2. **Multi Family MF**	ASC-Property
3. **Municipal Reserve MR**	ASC-Property
4. **Pond PUL**	ASC-Open Space
5. **Residential BLK2 R1**	ASC-Property
6. **Residential BLK1 R1**	ASC-Property
7. **Residential BLK3 R1**	ASC-Property
8. **Right Of Way**	ASC-Road
9. **School MSR**	ASC-Property

11. In the Toolspace, *Prospector* tab, expand *Sites*, expand the **C3D Training** site, right-click on *Parcels*, and select **Properties**, as shown in Figure 2–19.

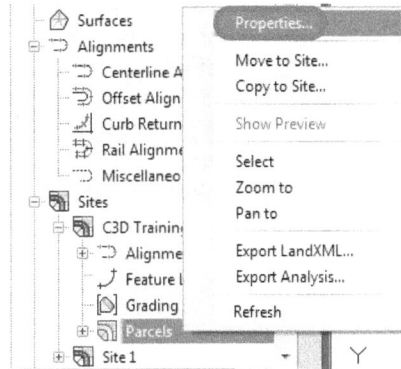

Figure 2–19

If the drawing does not look different after completing Step 13, you might need to adjust the draw order so that the XREF drawing is behind the existing drawing linework.

12. In the Site Parcel Properties dialog box, select **ASC-Property** in the *Parcel style display order* area, as shown in Figure 2–20. Click ⬆ to move it up in the list.

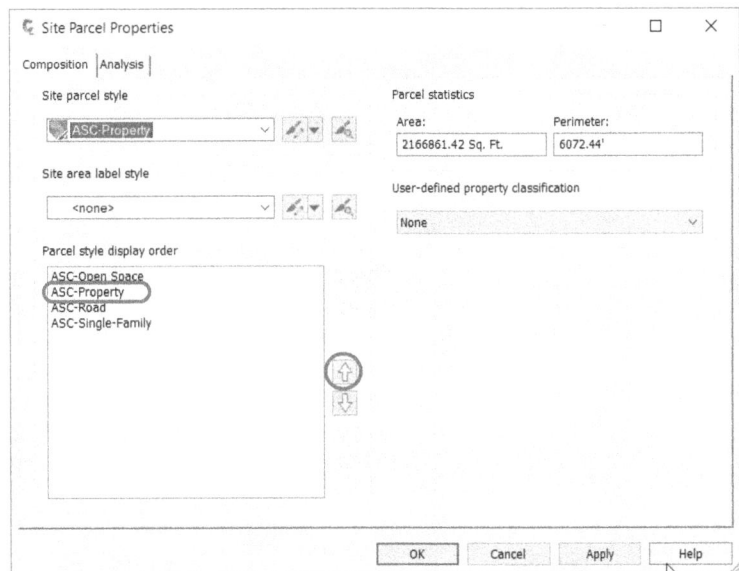

Figure 2–20

13. Click **OK**.

14. Save the drawing.

2.2 Creating and Editing Parcels

The **Create Parcel by Layout** tools can help you to quickly create a subdivision plan. Although these tools can make your job easier and are faster than manual drafting, they are only effective in creating the *last* side of new parcels. Therefore, you might need to create additional (or adjust) parcel lines manually to guide the Autodesk Civil 3D software to the best solution. For example, the area shown in Figure 2–21, requires you to create minimum 10,225 sq. ft. (0.23 acre) parcels.

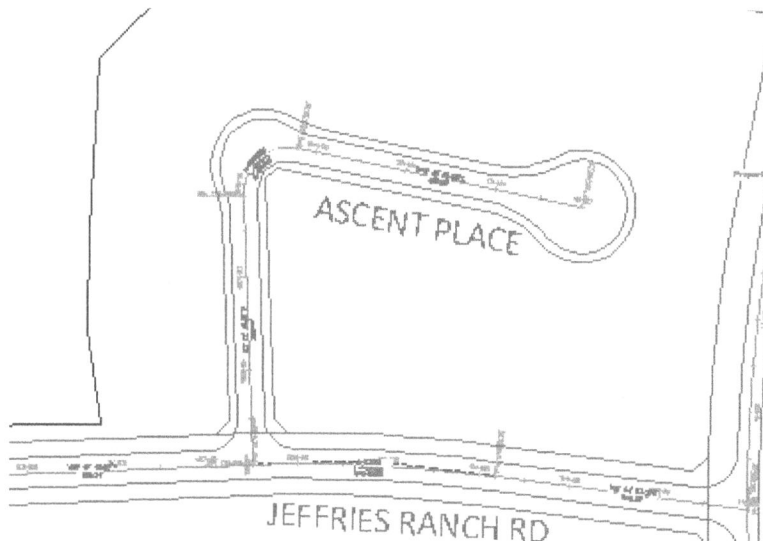

Figure 2–21

The back parcel lines (those along the west and south of the cul-de-sac area, and between Jeffries Ranch Rd and Ascent Place) were drawn manually and saved in a separate drawing file. Once inserted, they are used to guide the creation of the parcels next to Ascent Place. If you ask the Autodesk Civil 3D software to automatically subdivide this area, the result is a total of 15 residential lot parcels, as shown in Figure 2–22.

Figure 2–22

The various creation and editing techniques available in the Create Parcel by Layout toolbar include: Freehand tools, Slide Line tools, Swing Line tools, and **Free Form Create**.

Freehand

The ✏ (Line), ⌒ (Curve), and ⬜ (Draw Tangent - Tangent with No Curves) commands enable you to create lot lines without having to specify an area. In contrast, the following commands all create parcels based on a specified area.

Slide Line

The **Slide Line - Create** command enables you to subdivide a larger parcel by creating new parcel lines that hold a specific angle relative to the Right-of-Way, such as 90° or a specific bearing or azimuth. The **Slide Line - Edit** command enables you to modify a parcel to a specified area while holding the same angle from the ROW or a specific bearing or azimuth. The commands are shown in Figure 2–23.

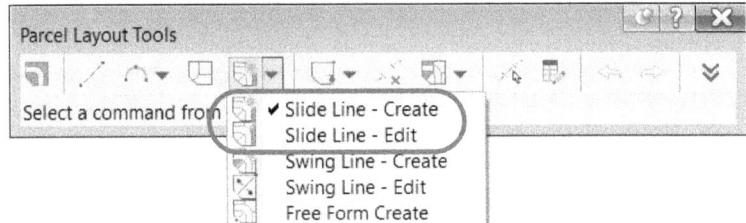

Figure 2–23

Swing Line

The **Swing Line - Create** command enables you to create a new parcel by creating a parcel segment that connects to a specified point, such as a property corner. The **Swing Line - Edit** command enables you to resize a parcel while specifying a lot corner. These commands are shown in Figure 2–24.

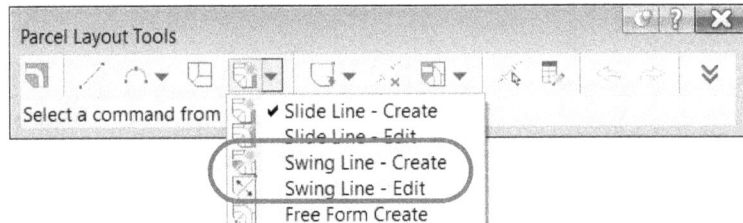

Figure 2–24

Free Form Create

The **Free Form Create** command enables you to create a new lot by specifying an area, attachment point and angle, or two attachment points.

Frontage

When using these tools, you are prompted to select a parcel interior point and trace its frontage geometry. This is a critical step. As you trace the frontage, the command creates a jig (heavy highlight) that recognizes the changing geometry of the frontage line work.

Practice 2b

Creating and Editing Parcels

Practice Objective

- Create and edit parcels to maximize the number of lots you can create with the required area and frontage.

You have three parcels zoned as single-family residential: Block1 (1.31ac), Block2 (0.94ac), and Block3 (1.47ac). Your client, the land developer, requires you to maximize the number of lots in these three parcels, while noting the minimum area and frontages as required by the Land Use bylaws.

1. Open **PCL1-C1-Parcels.dwg** from the *C:\Civil 3D Projects\ Working\Parcels* folder.

2. Select the preset view **Parcel-Create**.

3. In the *Home* tab>Create Design panel, expand **Parcel** and select **Parcel Creation Tools**. The Parcel Layout Tools toolbar displays.

4. Click ⮟ to expand the *Parcel Creation Tools* and enter the values shown in Figure 2–25. When finished, click ⮝ to collapse the expanded toolbar.

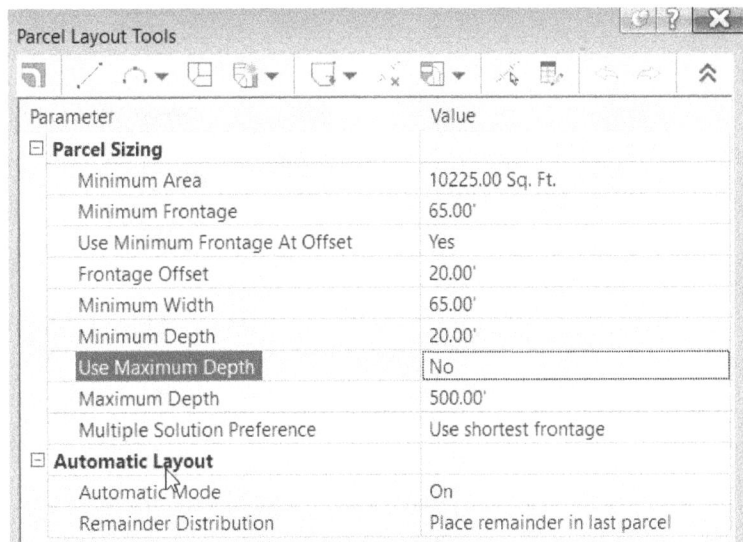

Parameter	Value
Parcel Sizing	
Minimum Area	10225.00 Sq. Ft.
Minimum Frontage	65.00'
Use Minimum Frontage At Offset	Yes
Frontage Offset	20.00'
Minimum Width	65.00'
Minimum Depth	20.00'
Use Maximum Depth	No
Maximum Depth	500.00'
Multiple Solution Preference	Use shortest frontage
Automatic Layout	
Automatic Mode	On
Remainder Distribution	Place remainder in last parcel

Figure 2–25

5. In the Parcel Layout Tools toolbar, expand ⬚ ▾ and select **Slide Line - Create**, as shown in Figure 2–26.

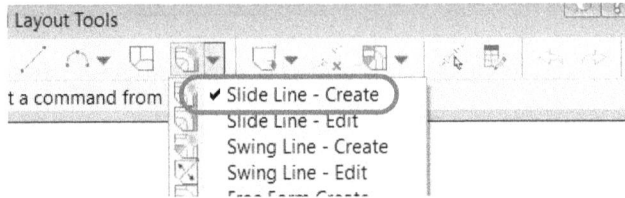

Figure 2–26

6. In the Create Parcels - Layout dialog box, set the following parameters, as shown in Figure 2–27:

- *Site:* **C3D Training**
- *Parcel style:* **ASC-Single-Family**
- *Area label style:* **ASC-Name Square Foot & Acres**

Figure 2–27

7. Click **OK** to accept the changes and close the dialog box.

8. When prompted to select the parcel to be subdivided, select the area label for parcel **RESIDENTIAL BLK1 R1**, as shown in Figure 2–28.

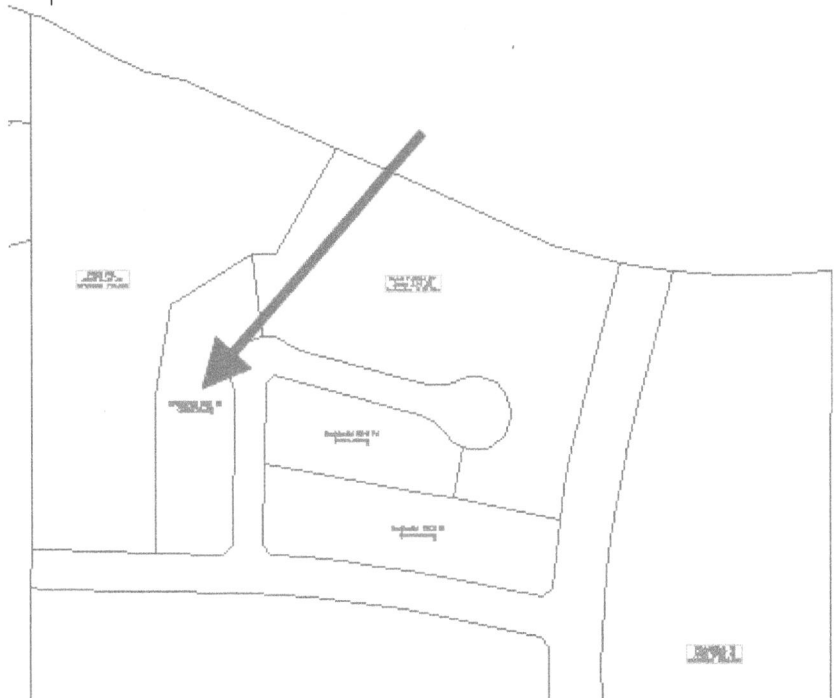

Figure 2–28

9. When you are prompted for the *starting point on frontage*, select the south end of the corner cut. Press <Ctrl>, right-click, and select **endpoint**.from the right-click menu. Then select the corner cut, **Pt 1**, shown in Figure 2–29.

10. When prompted for the *end point of the frontage*, set the end point of the property line to the north, **Pt 2**, as shown in Figure 2–29. Use the same process as the previous step to set the end point.

11. When prompted for the *angle of the property line* that will be used to define each lot, select a point east of the parcel near **Pt 3**, as shown in Figure 2–29. For the second point, press <Ctrl>, right-click, and select **Perpendicular**. Then select the line at Pt 4.

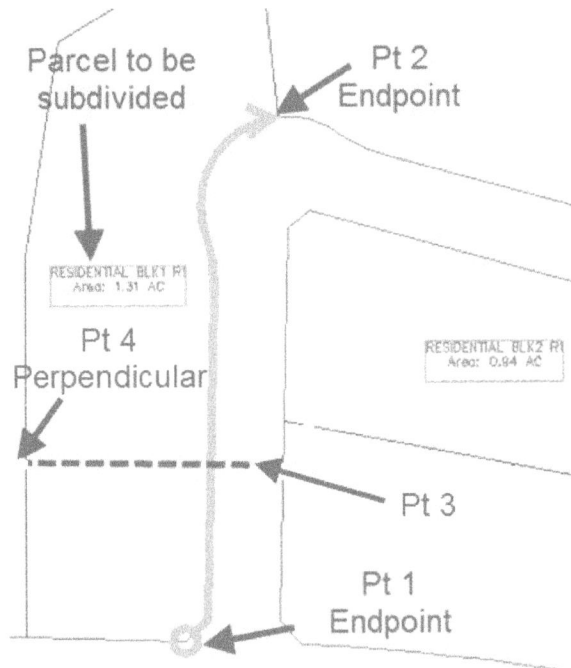

Figure 2–29

12. When prompted to *Accept results*, press <Enter>.

13. When prompted to select another parcel to subdivide, press <Esc> to end the command.

14. On the status bar, set the annotation scale to **1"=40'**.

15. Save the drawing.

2.3 Renumbering Parcels

Creating parcels using the methods that have already been taught results in inconsistent parcel numbering. Autodesk Civil 3D parcels can be renumbered individually using Parcel Properties, or in groups using **Modify>Parcel>Renumber/Rename**.

This command enables you to specify a starting parcel number and the increment you want to have between parcels. (It also enables you to rename your parcels based on a different name template.) When renumbering, the command prompts you to identify parcels in the order in which you want to have them numbered. The Renumber/Rename Parcels dialog box is shown in Figure 2–30.

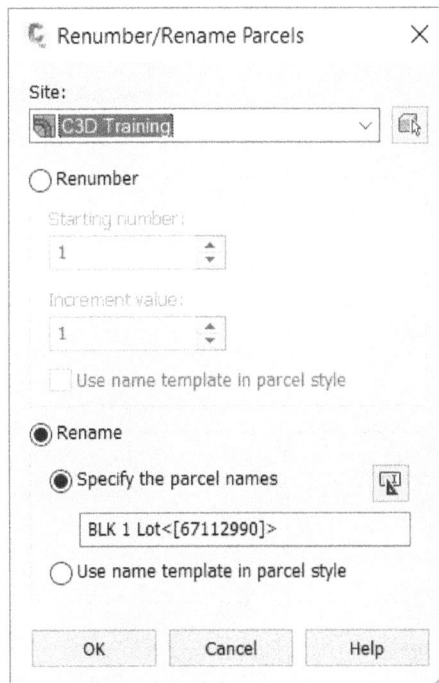

Figure 2–30

Hint: Renumber Odd and Even Parcels

If you need to have odd numbered lots on one side of the street, you can set the *Starting Number* to an odd number and the *Incremental Value* to **2**. Same procedure for even numbered lots on the opposite side.

Practice 2c

Rename/Renumber Parcels

Practice Objective

- Renumber the lots created so that they are in sequential order.

Task 1 - Rename and renumber parcels.

1. Open **PCL1-D1-Parcels.dwg** from the *C:\Civil 3D Projects\ Working\Parcels* folder.

2. Select the preset view **Parcel-Create**.

3. Before renaming the newly created parcels, you need to change the label style of the original parcel.
   - Select the parcel label **RESIDENTIAL BLK1 R1**.
   - Right-click, and select **Edit Area Selection Label Style**, as shown in Figure 2–31.
   - Select **ASC-Name Square Foot & Acres** as the style and click **OK** to apply the changes and close the dialog box.

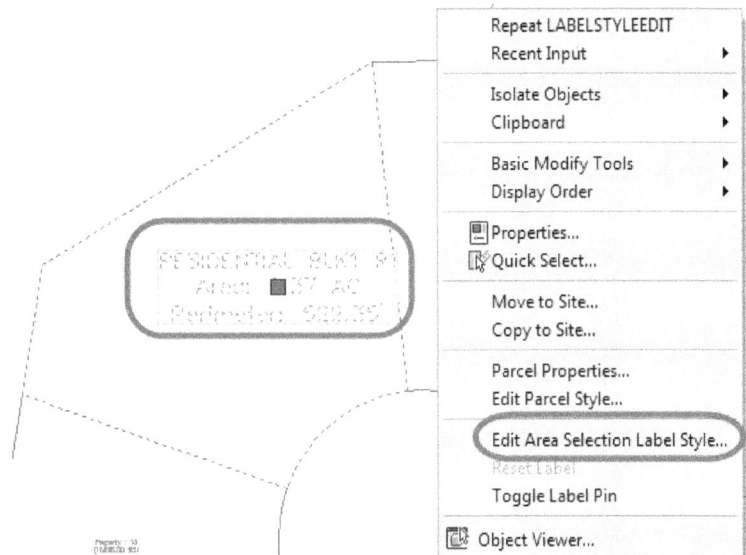

Figure 2–31

4. Rename and renumber the lots so that you have the same numbering system. In the *Modify* tab>Design panel, select **Parcel**. The *Parcel* contextual tab displays.

5. In the *Parcel* tab>Modify panel, click (Renumber/Rename), as shown in Figure 2–32.

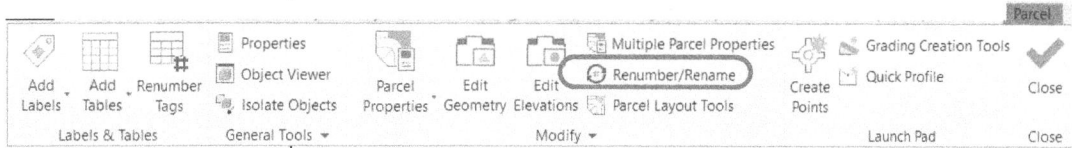

Figure 2–32

6. In the Renumber/Rename Parcel dialog box, set the following options, as shown in Figure 2–33:

   • Select **Rename**.
   • Select **Specify the parcel names**.

   • Click (Click to edit name template).

Figure 2–33

7. In the Name Template dialog box, set the following options, as shown in Figure 2–34:

   • Type **BLK1 Lot** followed by a space in the *Name* field.
   • Expand the Property Fields drop-down list.
   • Select **Next Counter** and click **Insert**.
   • Click **OK** to apply the changes and close the dialog box.

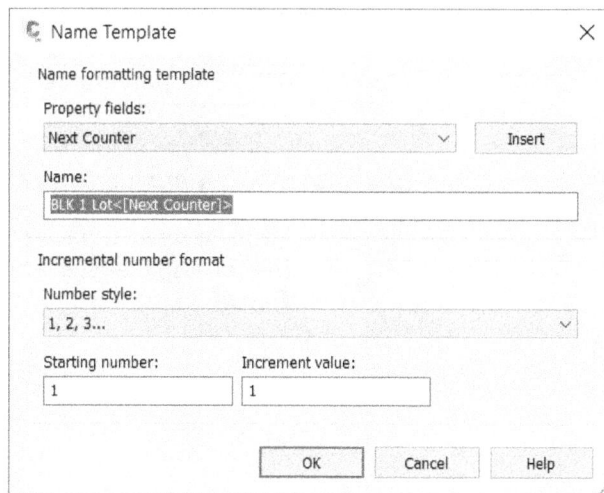

Figure 2–34

8. In the Renumber/Rename Parcel dialog box, click **OK** to accept the changes and close the dialog box.

9. When prompted for the points, select the two points shown in Figure 2–35. Press <Enter> to complete the selection and then press <Enter> again to exit the command.

Figure 2–35

10. Save the drawing.

Task 2 - Edit parcels using Swing Line - Edit.

In this task, you adjust the last three lots of the parcel suddivision so that they are more marketable.

1. You first need to adjust the Lot line between Parcel 3 and Parcel 4. In the *Home* tab>Create Design panel, select **Parcel**. In the expanded list, select **Parcel Creation Tools**.

2. Expand the Parcel Layout Tools toolbar and ensure the *Minimum Area* is set to **10225**, and the other settings as they were previously, in Figure 2–36. Click ⚑ to collapse the expanded toolbar.

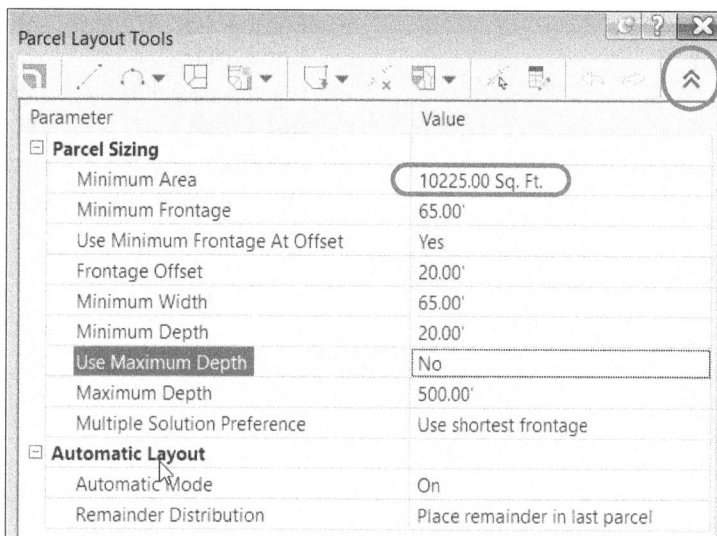

Figure 2–36

3. Select **Swing Line - Edit**, as shown in Figure 2–37.

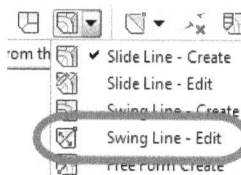

Figure 2–37

4. In the Create Parcel - Layout dialog box, set the following parameters:

   • *Site:* **C3D Training**
   • *Parcel Style:* **ASC-Single-Family**
   • *Area Label style:* **ASC-Name Square Foot & Acres**

5. You do not want to label segments, so do not enable this option. Click **OK** when done.

6. When prompted, complete the following, as shown in Figure 2–38:

    *   To select the parcel line to adjust, select the parcel line between Lot 3 and Lot 4.
    *   For the parcel to adjust, select **Lot 3**.
    *   For the *start frontage*, select the bottom right corner of **Lot 3, pt1**.
    *   For the *end of the frontage*, select the top right corner of **Lot 4, pt2**.
    *   For the *swing point*, select the end point of **pt3**.
    *   To accept the results, select **Yes**.

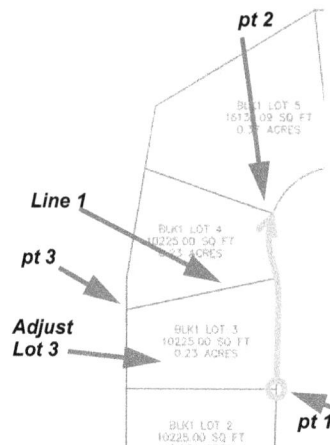

Figure 2–38

7. You have the required results for Lot 3. However, Lot 5 is larger than Lot 4. You want to create more evenly sized lots. Display the Parcel Layout Tools toolbar, if it is not open.

8. You could use the **Swing Line - Edit** command, however, you will use a more graphical approach.

9. Erase the parcel line between Lot 4 and Lot 5 using the (Delete Sub-entity) command in the *Parcel Layout Tools* toolbar. This causes both parcels to merge into one.

10. Add new parcel line by going to the **Add Fixed Line - Two Points** as shown in Figure 2–39.

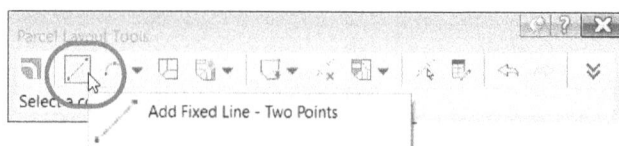

Figure 2–39

*Hint: Use the <Shift>+
right-click option to bring
up the AutoCAD Object
Snap overrides menu.*

11. In the Create Parcels - Layout dialog box, leave all the default options as they are. You will correct them after the parcels are created. Click **OK** to close the dialog box.

12. For the start point, select the endpoint of the western lot line.

13. For the end point, select (with the AutoCAD **Perpendicular** object snap) the arc of the Knuckle curve, as shown in Figure 2–40.

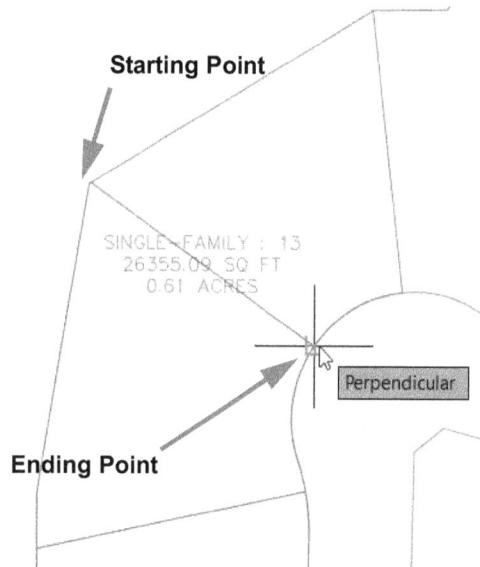

Starting Point

SINGLE-FAMILY : 13
26355.00 SQ FT
0.61 ACRES

Perpendicular

Ending Point

Figure 2–40

14. Press <Esc> to stop drawing fixed lines, then type **X** (or press <Enter>) to exit the Parcel Layout Tools.

15. Use the AutoCAD **March Properties** command. You can type **MA** to invoke it.

16. Select *BLK1 Lot 3 l*abel as the source object and select the two newly divided lots as the destination objects.Hit <Enter> to exit the command.

17. Renumber the two newly created lots as you did earlier in this practice.Remember to set the starting number to 4.

18. If time permits, repeat the steps above to subdivide the Parcels Block 2 and Block 3. If you do not complete the subdivisions for Parcels Block 2 and Block 3, you will need to open **PCL-E1-Parcels** in the next practice.

19. Save the drawing.

2.4 Parcel Reports

The Autodesk Civil 3D software contains several types of parcel reports. Parcel Inverse and Mapcheck data is available in the *Analysis* tab in the Parcel Properties dialog box, as shown in Figure 2–41. The report can be generated clockwise or counter-clockwise, and the point of beginning can be specified.

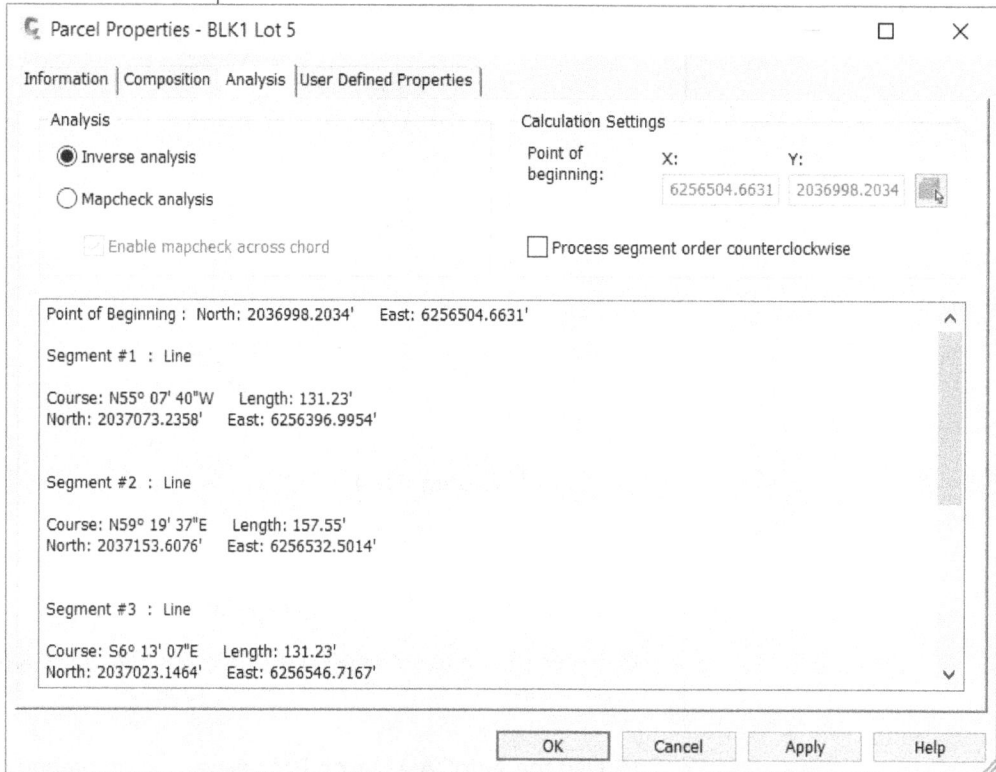

Figure 2–41

This dialog box does not enable output. If you want to generate a printable report, use the Autodesk Civil 3D Toolbox. It includes several stock Parcel-related reports (such as Surveyor Certificates, Inverse and Mapcheck reports, Metes and Bounds), as shown in Figure 2–42.

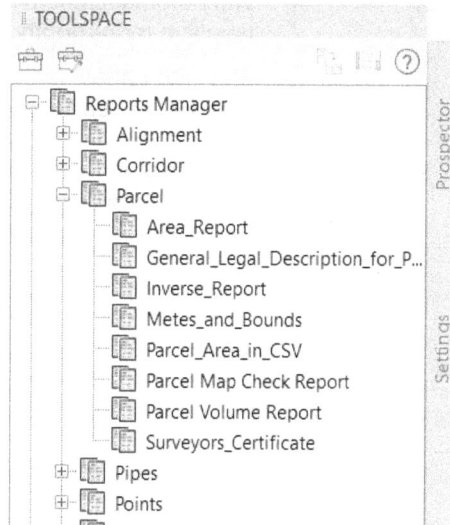

Figure 2–42

Once a report is run, it can be opened in a web browser, word processor, or spreadsheet application. Report settings (such as the Preparer's name) can be assigned by selecting **Report Settings** in the Toolspace.

2.5 Parcel Labels

Parcel area labels are a means of graphically selecting a parcel, such as when creating Right-of-Ways. In the Parcel creation and editing examples, the parcel segment labels were created for you automatically. This section explores the functionality of these labels in more depth.

The Add Labels dialog box (**Annotate>Add Labels>Parcel> Add Parcel Labels...**) can be used to assign the required label styles and place labels in the drawing. It can set the line, curve, and spiral styles and toggle between single and multiple segment labeling, and to access the Tag Numbering Table. The dialog box is shown in Figure 2–43.

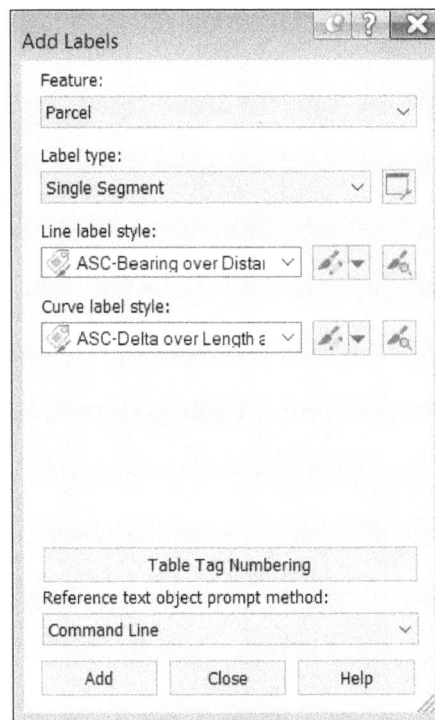

Figure 2–43

- Parcel labels, as with all Autodesk Civil 3D labels, are capable of rotating and resizing to match changes in the viewport scale and rotation.

- A segment label has two definitions: composed and dragged state. A dragged state can be quite different from the original label definition.

- The Autodesk Civil 3D software can label segments while sizing parcels.

- Labeling can be read clockwise or counter-clockwise around the parcel.

- Labels can be added through an external reference file using the same commands that label objects in their source drawing. This makes it easier to have multiple plans that need different label styles.

- The **Replace Multiple Labels** option is useful when you want to replace a number of parcel segment labels with another style. However, if you are labeling through an external reference file, labels created in the source drawing cannot be modified.

Parcel Area labels are controlled using Parcel Area Label Styles, which control the display of custom information (such as the parcel number, area, perimeter, address, etc.). For example, you can create more than one parcel area label if you need to show different parcel information on different sheets, as shown in Figure 2–44.

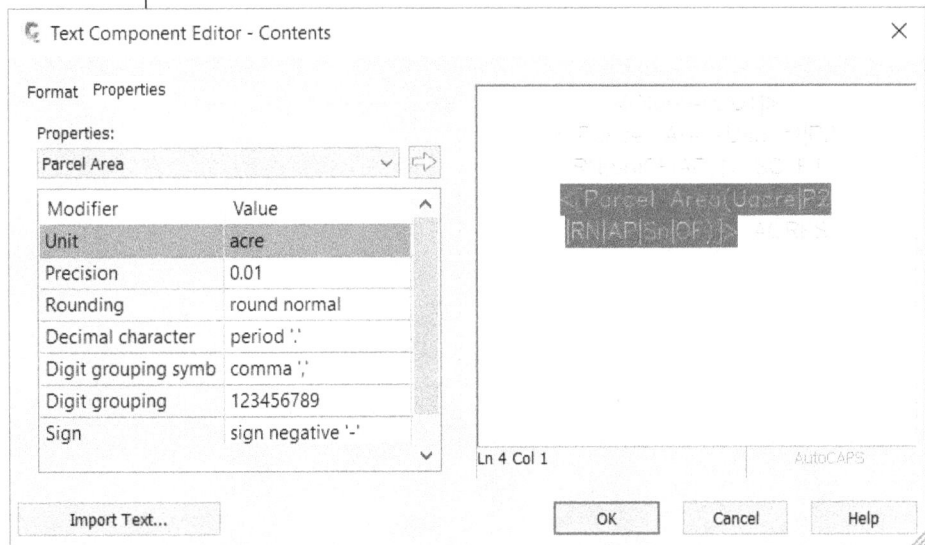

Figure 2–44

Parcel Segment labels annotate the line and curve segments of a parcel, as shown in Figure 2–45. You can label all of the segments of a parcel with one click or only label selected parcel segments.

Figure 2–45

All labels have two definitions: one for the original location, and another when it is moved from its original location. A dragged label can remain as originally defined or can be changed to stacked text. This is defined in the label style definition.

2.6 Parcel Tables

Parcel tables are an alternative to labeling individual parcel areas and segments. An example is shown in Figure 2–46.

Parcel Line and Curve Table			
Line #/Curve #	Length	Bearing/Delta	Radius
L2	6.42	N43° 08' 59.63"W	
L1	6.36	S46° 18' 04.79"W	
L3	1.08	S1° 18' 04.79"W	
L4	5.58	N52° 59' 46.62"E	
C1	11.38	19.75	33.00

Figure 2–46

When creating a table, the Autodesk Civil 3D software changes the parcel segment labels to an alpha-numeric combination, called a *tag*. A tag with an **L** stands for line and a **C** stands for curve. A segment's tag has a corresponding entry in the table.

- A table can only represent a selected set of label styles.

- The **Add Existing** option (shown in Figure 2–47) creates a table from existing objects. New objects are not added to the table. The **Add Existing and New** option creates a table with existing and new objects.

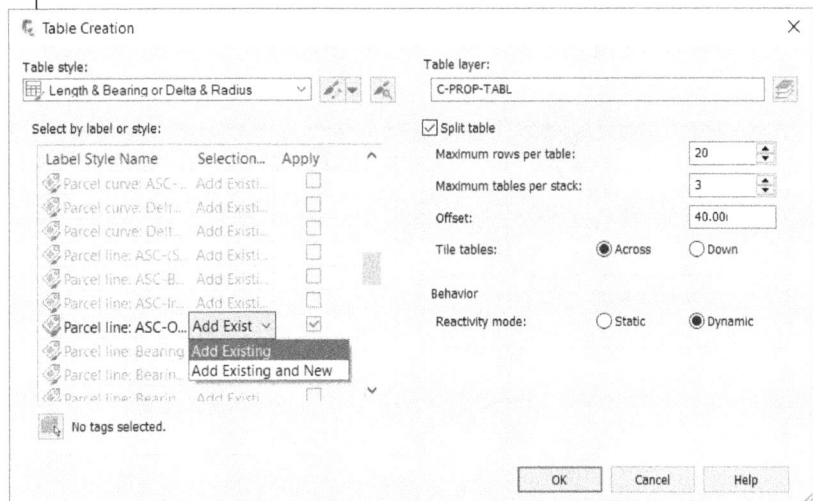

Figure 2–47

- A table can have a dynamic link between a segment's tag and table entry. If the segment changes, the table entry updates.

- The Autodesk Civil 3D software switches a label to a tag by changing the *Used In* mode from **Label and Tag Modes** to **Tag Mode**, as shown in Figure 2–48.

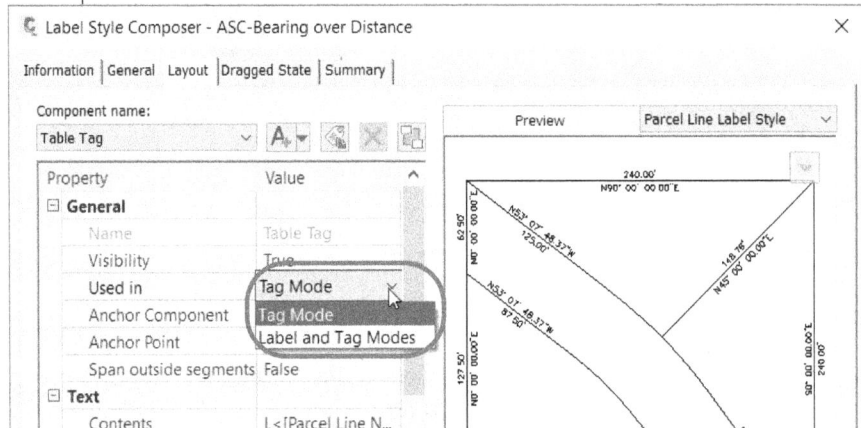

Figure 2–48

Practice 2d

Reporting On and Annotating the Parcel Layout

Practice Objectives

- Add labels, tags, and tables to the drawing to display useful parcel information.
- Create predefined reports to share useful parcel information in a textual format.

Task 1 - Add parcel labels.

1. Open **PCL1-E1-Parcels.dwg** from the *C:\Civil 3D Projects\ Working\Parcels* folder.

2. In the *Annotate* tab>Labels & Tables panel, click (Add Labels), as shown in Figure 2–49.

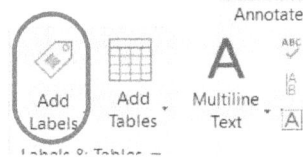

Figure 2–49

3. In the Add Labels dialog box, set the following parameters, as shown in Figure 2–50:
   - *Feature:* **Parcel**
   - *Label type:* **Multiple Segment**
   - *Line label style:* **ASC-Bearing over Distance**
   - *Curve label style:* **ASC-Delta over Length and Radius**
   - Once the parameters are set, click **Add**.

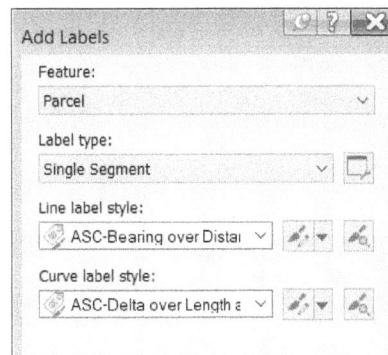

Figure 2–50

4. When prompted to select the Parcels that you want to annotate, select the single-family parcel labels in the BLK1 lot area.

5. When prompted for the label direction, select **Clockwise**.

6. Continue selecting single-family parcels and labeling them clockwise until all of the single-family parcels are labeled, including the parcels in BLK2 and BLK3.

7. Press <Enter> when finished labeling the parcels.

8. Select **X** in the Add Labels dialog box, or click **Close** to close the dialog box.

Parcels can also be labeled in an XREF file.

9. Save the drawing.

Task 2 - Create Line and Curve Segment Tables.

The labels are overlapping in a number of locations, making the drawing difficult to read. In this task, you try two methods to fix this. In the first method, you drag the label to a location in which there is no conflict. In the second method, you add a label tag and an associated table.

1. Select the preset view **Parcel-Tag1**. You may have to reset the Annotation scale back to what it was prior to changing the view.

2. Select the label **11.70'**, select the square grip, and drag to place the label in a location in which there is no conflict. Do the same for the label **21.48'**, as shown in Figure 2–51.

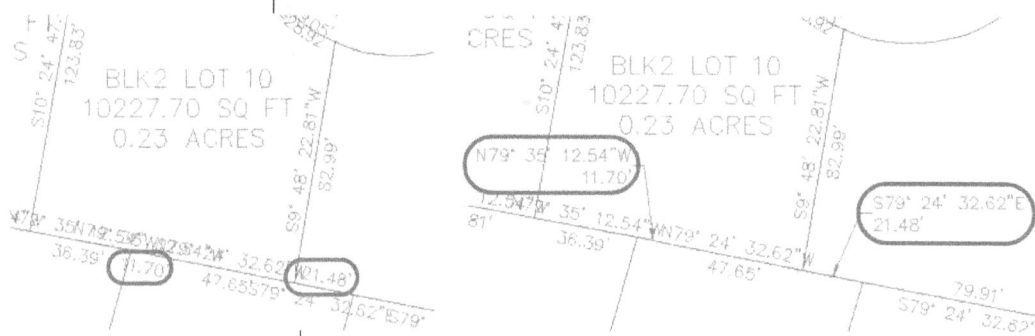

Figure 2–51

3. You will now add tags and a table. In the *Annotate* tab>
   Label & Tables panel, expand ⊞ (Add Tables) and select
   Parcel>Add segment, as shown in Figure 2–52.

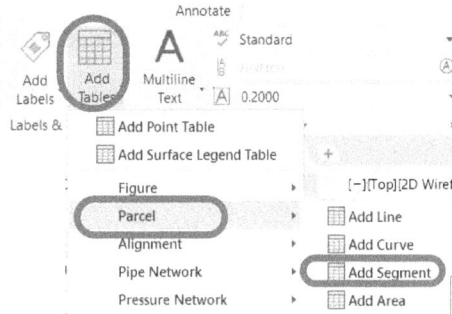

Figure 2–52

4. In the Table Creation dialog box, click ⊞ (Pick on screen)
   and select the labels shown in Figure 2–53. Press <Enter>
   when done.

Figure 2–53

5. When prompted to convert labels to tags or to not add labels, select **Convert all selected label styles to tag mode**.

6. Click **OK** to close the Table Creation dialog box.

7. When prompted for a location for the table, select a location in an open space, as shown in Figure 2–54.

Parcel Line and Curve Table			
Line #/Curve #	Length	Bearing/Delta	Radius
L2	6.42	N43° 08' 59.63"W	
L1	6.36	S46° 18' 04.79"W	
L3	1.08	S1° 18' 04.79"W	
L4	5.58	N52° 59' 46.62"E	
C1	11.38	19.75	33.00

Figure 2–54

8. Save the drawing.

Task 3 - Create a Parcel Area Table.

---

1. Continue working with the drawing from the previous task or open **PCL1-E2-Parcels.dwg**.

2. In the *Annotate* tab>Label & Tables panel, expand ⊞ (Add Tables) and select **Parcel>Add Area**.

3. In the Table Creation dialog box, in the *Select by label* or *style* area, select the style name **Name Square Foot & Acres**, as shown in Figure 2–55. All parcels with this style will be selected. Click **OK** to close the dialog box.

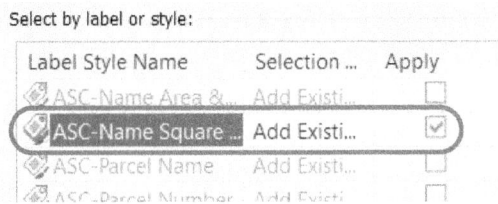

Select by label or style:

Label Style Name	Selection ...	Apply
ASC-Name Area & ...	Add Existi...	☐
ASC-Name Square ...	Add Existi...	☑
ASC-Parcel Name	Add Existi...	☐
ASC-Parcel Number	Add Existi...	☐

Figure 2–55

4. Select a location to insert the table into the drawing, as shown in Figure 2–56.

Parcel #	Area	Perimeter	Segment Lengths	Segment Bearings
				Parcel Area Table
3	12156.55	470.43	131.23 157.55 131.23 50.41	N55° 07' 40.10"W N59° 19' 36.65"E S6° 13' 06.61"E S59° 19' 36.65"W
5	11296.21	427.15	78.21 113.57 19.73 86.92 128.72	S79° 24' 32.62"E S6° 37' 06.81"W S52° 30' 45.23"W N79° 24' 32.62"W N16° 50' 42.05"E
9	10227.70	407.80	47.65 11.70 36.39 123.83 4.70 70.72 29.81 82.99	N79° 24' 32.62"W N79° 35' 12.54"W N79° 35' 12.54"W N10° 24' 47.46"E S75° 18' 31.56"E S56° 35' 41.15"E S52° 20' 32.14"E S9° 48' 22.81"W

Figure 2–56

5. Save the drawing.

Task 4 - Create a Parcel Report.

1. If the Toolspace, *Toolbox* tab is not displayed, go to the *Home* tab>Palettes panel, and click (Toolbox), as shown in Figure 2–57.

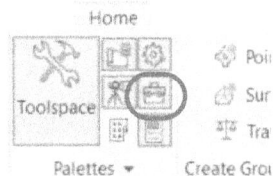

Figure 2–57

2. In the Toolspace, *Toolbox* tab, expand the *Reports Manager* and *Parcel* collections. Right-click on *Surveyor's Certificate* and select **Execute**.

3. In the Export to LandXML dialog box, click ⬚ (Pick from drawing), located at the bottom left of the dialog box.

4. When prompted to select a parcel, select one of the single-family lots that you created earlier and press <Enter>.

5. In the Export to XML Report dialog box, note that only the Lots you selected now display a checkmark. Click **OK** to close the dialog box.

6. In the Save As dialog box, stay in the default folder and type **ASC-Parcel-Report** for the report. Click **Save** to close the dialog box.

7. Review the report (as shown in Figure 2–58) and close the web browser.

Parcel BLK1 Lot 4

SURVEYOR'S CERTIFICATE

I, Preparer Registered Land Surveyor, do hereby certify that I have surveyed, divided, and mapped

more particularly described as:

Commencing at a point of Northing 2036905.451 and Easting 6256502.548 ;
thence bearing N 79-12-46.378 W a distance of 132.282 feet ;
thence bearing N 9-40-41.250 E a distance of 145.091 feet ;
thence bearing S 55-7-40.098 E a distance of 131.233 feet ;
thence along a curve to the LEFT, having a radius of 59.055 feet, a delta angle of 53° 19' 14.83",
and whose long chord bears S 8-12-42.487 W a distance of 52.996 feet ;
thence along a curve to the RIGHT, having a radius of 108.267 feet, a delta angle of 19° 44' 59.72",
and whose long chord bears S 8-34-25.067 E a distance of 37.135 feet ;
thence bearing S 1-18-4.794 W a distance of 3.580 feet to the point of beginning.

Said described parcel contains 14198.535 square feet (0.326 acres), more or less, subject to any and all
easements, reservations, restrictions and conveyances of record.

Figure 2–58

8. Save the drawing.

Surveying Tools

Exam Objectives Covered in This Chapter

1.6.a Work with linework code sets

1.6.b Utilize the points in the Survey Database

1.6.c Understand the use the Traverse Editor

1.6.d Recognize the purpose of working with the Survey Figure Prefix Database

Note: The objective *1.6.e Understand the purpose of performing a Mapcheck Analysis* is covered in *Chapter 2*.

3.1 Field Codes

During the survey pickup for each point, the surveyor assigns a field code that describes the point or line feature. This information is saved in the data collector and is output as an ASCII file. A line feature or connective code can be appended to a point description and indicates whether the feature line is a line segment or curve segment, and whether it is the beginning, continuation, or end of a segment.

Example

310,620918.3755,1907041.4409,53.0132, CL1 B

In this example, CL1 B is the field code in which:

- CL = An abbreviation that represents a center line.

- 1 = The center line number.

- B = The code in the linework code that is set to begin a figure.

Field codes are associated with both the Figure Prefix database and the description keys in the current drawing. If **CL** has been defined in the Figure Prefix Database (as shown in Figure 3–1), CL1 matches CL and is assigned the properties of the CL figure prefix, such as **Layer**, **Figure Style**, **Lotline** and **Breakline**.

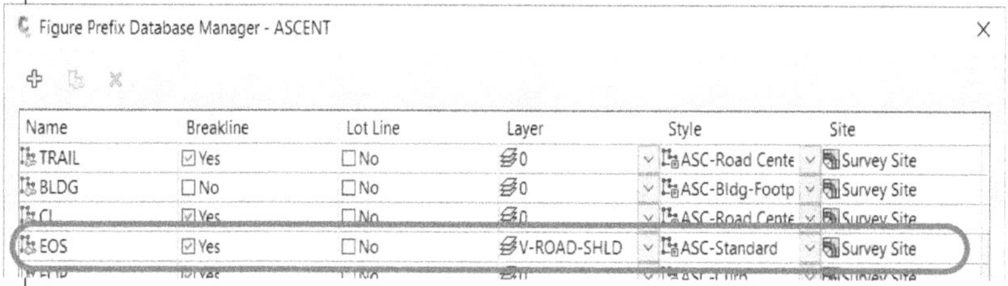

Note that when you import the survey data, you can omit the Begin code if the feature name matches a figure prefix that is defined in the current figure prefix database. If the feature name does not match a figure prefix, you must specify a Begin code.

Figure 3–1

If the survey point with the description CL1 B is placed in a drawing that has a description key of CL* (as shown in Figure 3–2), CL1 B matches the description key CL* and is assigned the point properties defined in the CL* description key, such as **Layer**, **Point Style**, and **Point Label Style**.

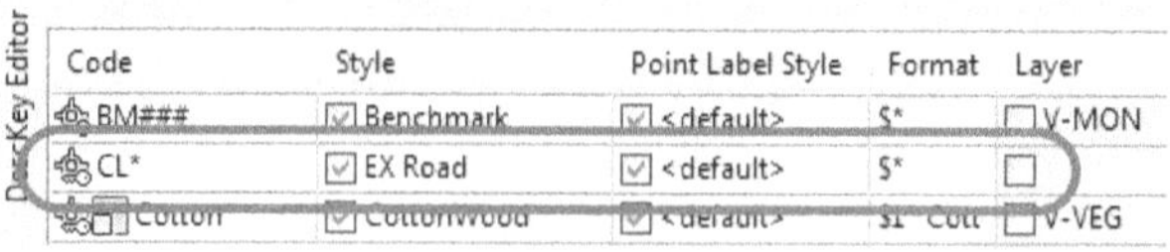

Figure 3–2

Linework Codes: Coding syntax

Some basic coding syntax rules are as follows:

CL1 B	It is recommended that you use <space> as the Field/Code delimiter property value (i.e., the <space> between the description CL1 and the B).
CL1 B/ Start of the centerline	A / <forward slash> is the recommended escape field code. It indicates that anything entered after the escape indicator is a comment.
CL1 B	Select **Yes** to specify that in CL1 B, CL1 matches the figure prefix of CL, and B is the Begin code. Select **No**, if you do not want the first instance of CL1 to automatically start a new figure named CL.

Linework Codes: Special Codes

CL1 B SW1 B B CL1 B SW1	**B** = Begin CL1 and SW1 are figure names. The letter B is the special code that is used to begin new figures named CL1 and SW1.
CL1 C SW1	**C** = Continue (Not used very much in practice) CL1 is a figure name. C continues the active figure named CL1. If the field code does not contain an explicit <Continue> code and the figure name in the field code matches an active figure, the figure is continued.
CL1 E SW1 B	**E** = End E is the End code. It continues an active figure with the name CL1 to this point and is then terminated (it is no longer an active). However, figure SW1 with the B code is starts at this point.
CL1 SW1 CLS	**CLS** = Close CLS is the Close code. A line segment is closed back to the starting vertex for the figure SW1. However, figure CL1 is still active and continues.
1,500,490,100.0 1,BC1 B H-4 V.1 H.5 H.75 V-.7 H2.25 V-.35	**H** = Horizontal offset H is the <Horizontal offset> code and -4 is the value for the first horizontal. **V** = Vertical Offset V is the <Vertical offset> code and .1 is the first vertical offset value, etc., for each of the remaining 3 offsets.
7,500,550,100.0 7,BC1 SO	**SO** = Stop offsets SO is the <Stop Offset> code. It terminates the offset for this figure.

Note that there are no spaces between RPN, CPN, or RECT, and the point number.

Linework Codes: Line Segment Codes

CL1 RPN CL1 RPN101	**RPN** = Recall point RPN is the Recall Point code. If a point is not supplied, it connects from the previous point to the current point and inserts a segment before the current point. If a point is supplied, as in the code CL1 RPN101, it connects from the current point to the indicated point.
CL1 B **CPN**101	**CPN** = Connect point A new figure CL1 is created at the current point, and a new figure with a single line segment is drawn to point 101 and called CL1.CPN101.
BLD1 RECT40	**RECT** = Rectangle A positive number indicates an offset to the right and a negative number indicates an offset to the left, which is relative to the direction of the line segment coming into the current point. If a number does not follow the Rectangle code, the code closes the figure by performing a perpendicular/ perpendicular line intersection between the previous segment coming into the current point and the first segment of the figure.
BLD1 RT X10.1 5 -12.2 -5 -12.2	**RT** = Right Turn Continues an active figure BLD1 to the current point, extends the current segment 10.1 units, and then draws perpendicular segments for each value
BLD1 X15.5	**X** = Extend BLD1 continues an active figure, X is the Extend code, and 15.5 is the value that the figure line segment is extended through the current point.

Linework Codes: Curve Segment Codes

CL1 BC	**BC** = Begin Curve BC indicates that the current point is the beginning of the curve segments.
CL1 EC	**EC** = End Curve EC indicates that the current point is the end of curve segments. You can have multiple figure points between the Begin and End curve segment codes.
CL1 CIR5.0	**CIR** = Circle CIR is the <Circle> code. It creates a new circular figure in which the current point is the radius point and 5.0 is the circle radius value.
CL1 OC	**OC** = Point On Curve OC is the Point On Curve code. The figure is continued and the point is evaluated as a point residing on a curve.

Practice 3a

Line Code

Practice Objective

- Correct errors in survey figures by editing the line code connotative file.

Task 1 - Review the survey data.

In this task, you review the errors that you will fix in the next task.

1. Open **LineCodes-C-Survey.dwg** from the *C:\Civil 3D for Surveyors\Working\Survey* folder.

2. If you are greeted with a splash screen about using Online Map Data, select **Remember my choice** and click **No**, as shown in Figure 3–3. (Since you have captured an online map in a previous chapter, you do not need to use Online Map Data.)

Figure 3–3

*If **Local-Metric** is not listed under Survey Databases, change your working folder to C:\Civil 3D for Surveyors\ Survey Databases\ Completed\Ascent Pointfiles.*

3. Continue working in the **Local-Metric** survey database. If required, right-click on the **Local-Metric** survey database to open it for editing.

4. Review the imported points file and note the errors that need to be fixed, as shown in Figure 3–4.
   - Close the building figure (A).
   - Correct the linecode in the imported points file (B).
   - Modify an offset line to display the back of the sidewalk (C).

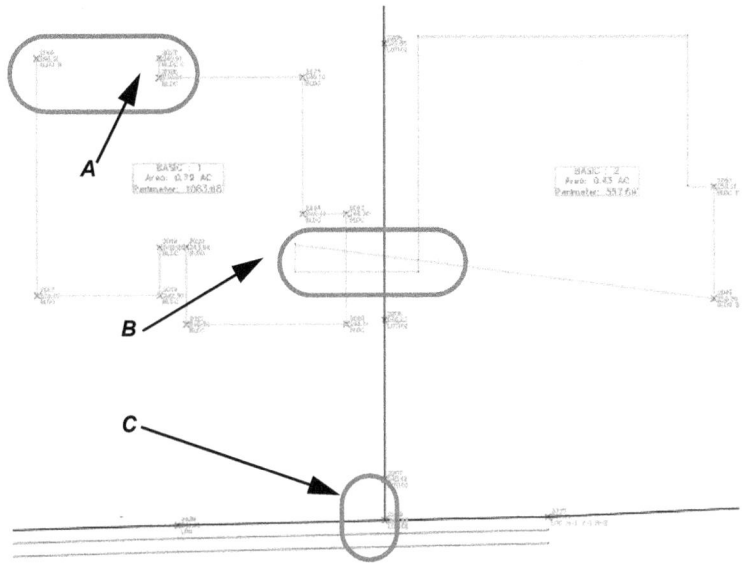

Figure 3–4

Labeling is covered in more detail later in this guide.

5. Select the figure shown in Figure 3–5. In the contextual ribbon, expand the **Add Label** menu and select **Single Segment**. Select the line segment shown in Figure 3–5 and note that the distance is 31.69 feet.

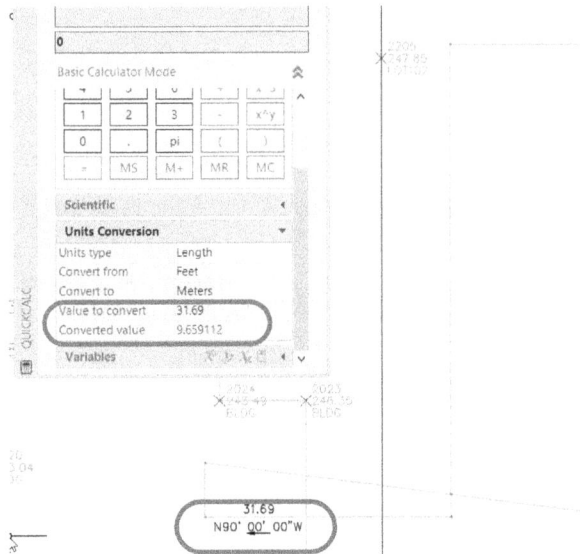

Figure 3–5

*<Ctrl>+<8> is a quick
way to launch the Quick
Calculator.*

6. Civil 3D's Quick Calculator tells us that 31.69' is the
   equivalent to 9.659m. As the metric survey database was
   inserted into the imperial drawing, it converted the units from
   meters to feet.

   • **Note:** Civil 3D will give no notification when it converts
     measurements between units.

Task 2 - Fix the line code survey file.

In this task, you will fix the error in the line code file.

1. Right-click on the **Local-Metric** survey database and select
   Properties, as shown in Figure 3–6.

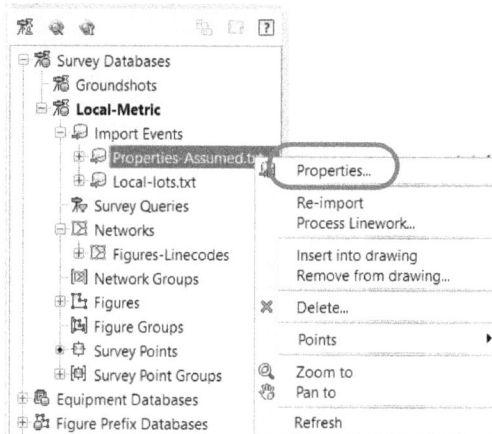

Figure 3–6

2. In the **Import Event Properties** window, by the *File* name,

   click ⊡ (Select) icon, as shown in Figure 3–7. The
   Properties-Assumed.txt imported text file opens in your
   default text editor.

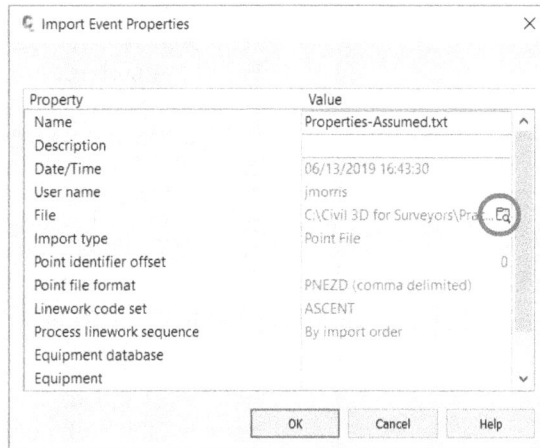

Figure 3–7

3. Prior to making any changes, save the file as **Properties-Assumed.ori** in the *C:\Civil 3D for Surveyors\Survey Databases\Data\Level 1* folder (as an archived *original* file). Save the file again as **Properties-Assumed.txt**. Click **Yes** to overwrite the file.

4. At point 2027, after **E** in the description, type **CLS** as shown in Figure 3–8. This fixes error "A" by closing building error 1 from point **16** to point **27**.

```
2026,5028.9361,9946.7723,73.4284,BLDG
2027,5030.3992,9946.7723,73.4284,BLDG E CLS
2028,5010.5005,9928.7677,72.4282,HOUSE
```

Figure 3–8

5. In the line for point **2050**, after the west edge of the building, -17.85 in a south direction, change *9.66* to **-9.66**, as shown in Figure 3–9. This will fix the building error "B".

```
2049,5012.1099,9990.2467,76.9132,BLDG B
2050,5020.5961,9990.2467,77.1798,BLDG RT x0 -2.05 11.41 -21.23 -17.85 -9.66 2.05 CLS
```

Figure 3–9

6. To create a back of sidewalk offset line, you will add a horizontal and vertical offset. The sidewalk only runs from the BC of the curb return. At point **2035** (shown in Figure 3–10), modify the code for the horizontal and vertical offset of the LOG to swap the side of the offset that represents the sidewalk. Delete the minus (-) from the H codes so that it is **LOG H1 V-1 H2**.

7. At point **2041** (shown in Figure 3–10), remove **SO** to continue the offset. SO is the code for "Stop Offset" and by removing this code, the offsets continue.

8. At point **2042** (also shown in Figure 3–10), remove the horizontal and vertical offsets. These offsets are redundant because the curb cut has been eliminated (in the above step).

```
2034,4996.4421,9998.1000,76.9104,LOG B LOT103        2034,4996.4421,9998.1000,76.9104,LOG B LOT103
2035,4995.5734,9977.0976,75.5193,LOG H-1 V-1 H-2     2035,4995.5734,9977.0976,75.5193,LOG H1 V-1 H2
2036,4994.9943,9948.1286,73.5023,LOG                 2036,4994.9943,9948.1286,73.5023,LOG
2037,4994.2704,9921.0427,71.5496,LOG                 2037,4994.2704,9921.0427,71.5496,LOG
2038,4994.5600,9909.1654,70.6753,LOG BC             2038,4994.5600,9909.1654,70.6753,LOG BC
2039,4996.7317,9903.0819,70.2459,LOG                 2039,4996.7317,9903.0819,70.2459,LOG
2040,5001.2199,9899.0263,70.0084,LOG                 2040,5001.2199,9899.0263,70.0084,LOG
2041,5008.4589,9898.1572,70.0576,LOG SO            2041,5008.4589,9898.1572,70.0576,LOG
2042,5016.5667,9899.7505,70.3261,LOG H-1 V-1 H-2    2042,5016.5667,9899.7505,70.3261,LOG
```

Figure 3–10

9. Save the text file and exit the text editor program.

10. Close the Import Event Properties dialog box by clicking **OK**.

11. In the *Survey* tab, in the current survey database collection, expand **Import Events**, right-click on **Properties-Assumed.txt**, and select **Re-import**, as shown in Figure 3–11.

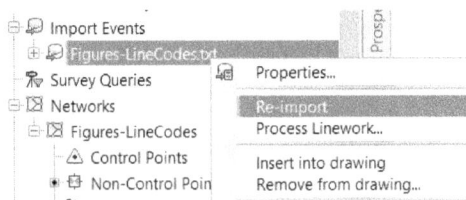

Figure 3–11

12. In the Re-import Points File dialog box, accept the defaults and click **OK**.

13. Now that the sidewalk has flipped, note that the parcel lines for the first lot intersect correctly, and a lot is created, as shown in Figure 3–12. However, also note that additional lots were inadvertently created for the sidewalk.

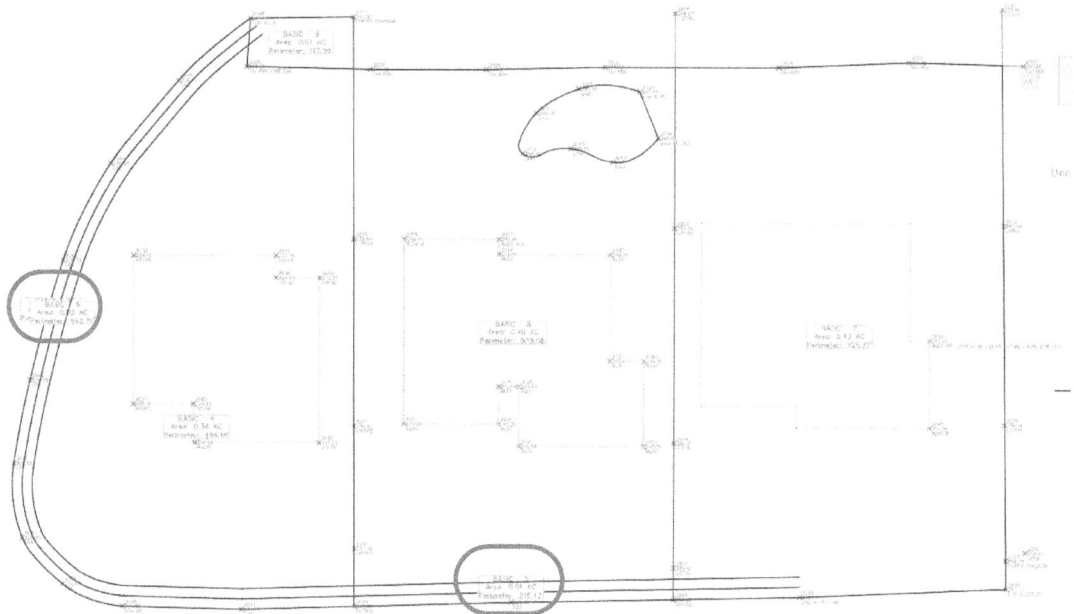

Figure 3–12

14. In the Transparent toolbar, click (Zoom to Point) and type **2001**. Zoom out to understand where this point is located in the drawing. Note that the point is a iron pipe found in the field. You will use this point to translate the survey database to a coordinate zone in the next practice.

15. Save the drawing.

3.2 Survey Figures

Survey figures consist of linework generated by coding and placed in a file that is imported into the Survey Database. A figure represents linear features (edge-of-pavement, toe-of-slopes, etc.)

Therefore, a figure has many functions, as follows:

- A figure displays linework in a drawing.

- All preset figures in a drawing can be defined as breaklines for a surface definition with one step.

- All preset figures in a drawing can be defined as parcel lines.

- A figure can be drawn as a pipe run. For example, a surveyor notices that only one pipe comes through a manhole. The surveyor then invokes a figure command to draw a survey figure that denotes the location of a pipe run. The Elevation Editor in the Autodesk Civil 3D software enables you to lower each survey figure at each manhole to the distance of what was measured in the field, and what was written on the manhole field notes as the flow elevation at the invert of the pipe run. The pipe functionality can make this line represent various types of locations within the circumference of the cross-sectional pipe and convert the survey figure into an existing pipe run.

- Any figure can be targets for *Width* or *Offset Targets* in a Corridor.

- Any figure can be targets for *Slope* or *Elevation Targets* in a Corridor (e.g., limits of construction for a road rehab project might be to the face of walk, which exists in the drawing as a Survey Figure, hence a target).

- It is recommended that you set up a Figure Prefix database and figure styles before importing any survey data to obtain the required entities in a drawing. As point and label styles and the Description Key Set need to exist before importing points, figure styles and entries in the Figure Prefix database need to exist before importing survey data.

Drawing Settings

The Drawing Settings dialog box (shown in Figure 3–13) sets a universal layer for figures. You can access these settings by selecting the drawing name in the Toolspace>*Settings* tab, right-clicking, and selecting **Edit Drawing Settings**. When selecting the *Object Layer* tab and scrolling to the bottom of the list, the default layer names are displayed.

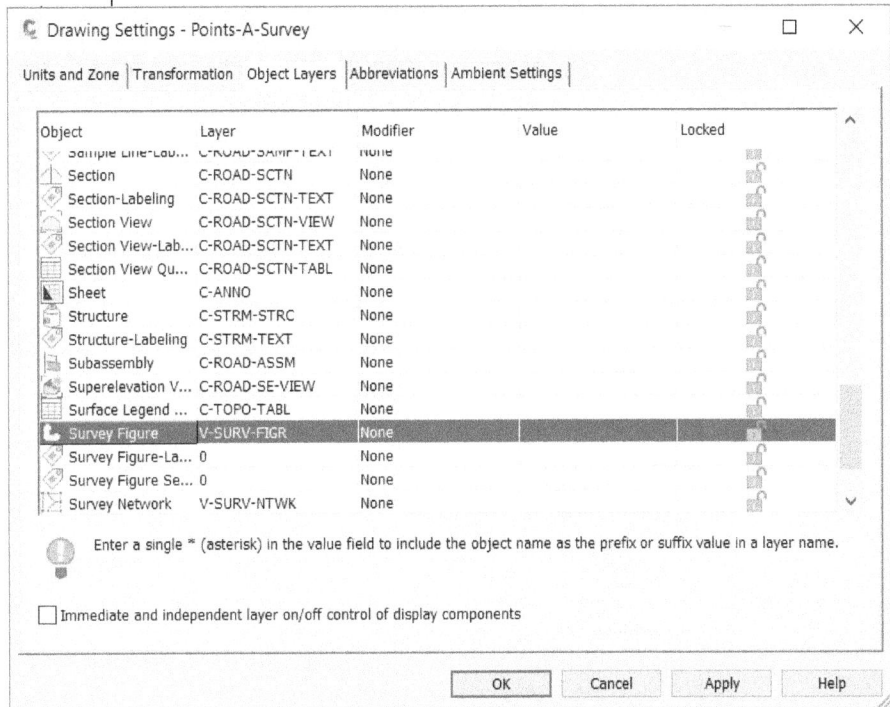

Figure 3–13

Your organization might have one or more default layers for each of the linework types. For example, edge-of-pavement, sidewalk, etc., each have their own layers in the drawing. To accomplish this, you need to define figure styles.

Figure Styles

Figure styles (found in the Toolspace>*Settings* tab) affect how the survey linework displays in a drawing. They should be part of your template file. These styles are not critical. However, to make figures work, you should define the layers they use in the drawing.

- Figure styles are tied to the Figure Prefix database.

- The Figure Prefix database assigns a figure style to a figure that is imported into a drawing.

- A figure style includes the layers for its linework and markers.

- A marker is a symbol placed on the figure's segment midpoints and end points. They call attention to the figure's geometry. Although a figure style includes marker definitions, they do not need to display.

Figures can be 3D and use the layers set in the *Display* tab in the Figure Style dialog box. The *Information* tab assigns a name to a style. The *Plan*, *Profile*, and *Section* tabs define how the marker displays in each of these views.The Figure Style dialog box is shown in Figure 3–14.

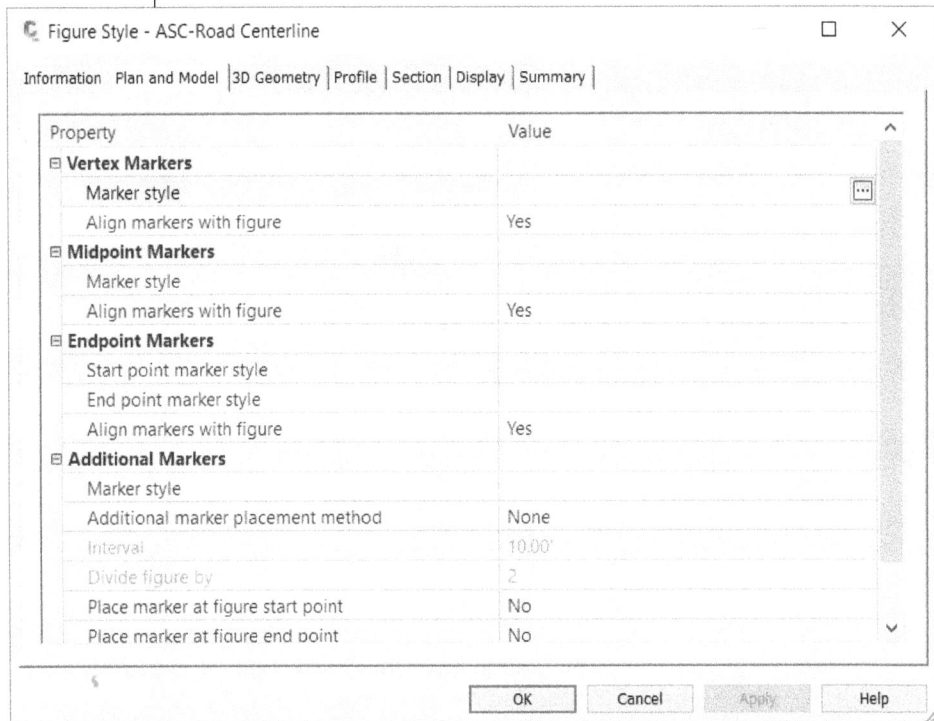

Property	Value	
⊟ **Vertex Markers**		
Marker style		[...]
Align markers with figure	Yes	
⊟ **Midpoint Markers**		
Marker style		
Align markers with figure	Yes	
⊟ **Endpoint Markers**		
Start point marker style		
End point marker style		
Align markers with figure	Yes	
⊟ **Additional Markers**		
Marker style		
Additional marker placement method	None	
Interval	10.00'	
Divide figure by	2	
Place marker at figure start point	No	
Place marker at figure end point	No	

Figure Style - ASC-Road Centerline

Tabs: Information | Plan and Model | 3D Geometry | Profile | Section | Display | Summary

Buttons: OK | Cancel | Apply | Help

Figure 3–14

The *3D Geometry* tab defines a figure's vertical behavior. By default, the elevation of the point defines the figure. The *Display* tab defines which figure's components display and which layers they use for plan, profile, and section views, as shown in Figure 3–15.

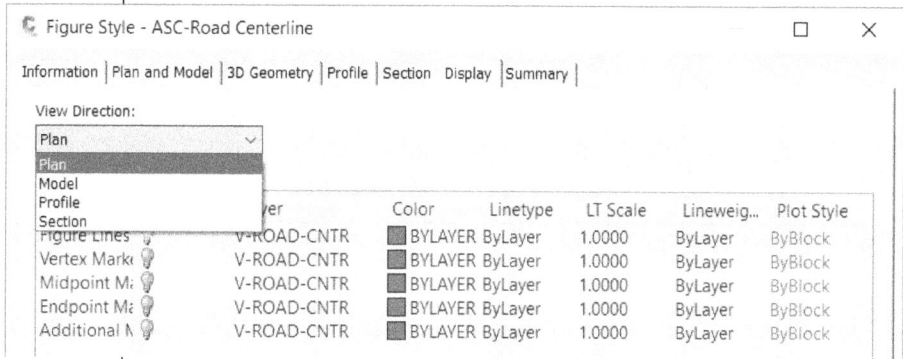

Figure 3–15

Figure Prefix Database

The Figure Prefix database, found in the Toolspace>*Survey* tab, does the following, as shown in Figure 3–16:

- Assigns the figure a style.

- Assigns the figure a layer. If you did not define any figure styles, you should at least assign a layer to correctly place the figure in the drawing.

- Defines whether the figure is a surface breakline. Toggling on the *Breakline* property enables you select all of the tagged survey figures and assign them to a surface without having to insert or select from a drawing.

- Defines whether the figure is a lot line (parcel segment). Toggling on the *Lot Line* property creates a parcel segment from the figure in the drawing and, if there is a closed polygon, assigns a parcel label and an entry in the designated site.

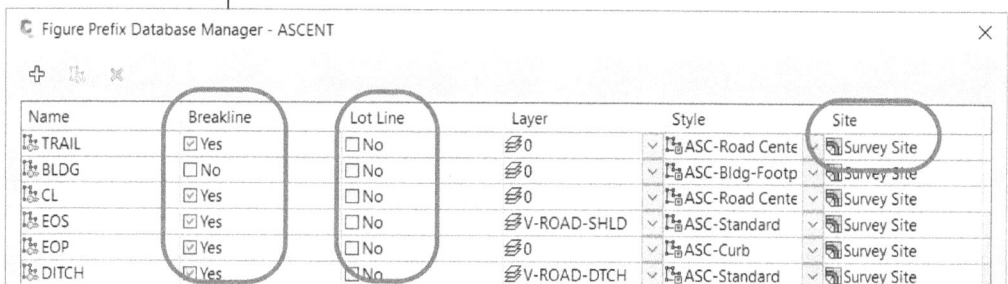

Figure 3–16

If the *Name* is **CL** (as shown in Figure 3–16), any figure starting with CL uses these settings. This is similar to using a Description Key Set, except that the entry in the Figure Prefix database does not need an asterisk (*). When inserting survey figures in the drawing, Survey checks the Figure Prefix database for style or layer values.

Practice 3b

Creating a Civil 3D Drawing Template

Practice Objectives

- Create a customized drawing template from an existing default template.
- Import Survey User Settings.
- Create a figure database for automatically stylizing linework on importing field book or ASCII files.

Task 1 - Create a drawing template.

1. In the ![C3D icon] (Application Menu), start a new drawing file using the **Autodesk Civil 3D (Imperial) NCS.dwt** template that is included with the software, as shown in Figure 3–17.

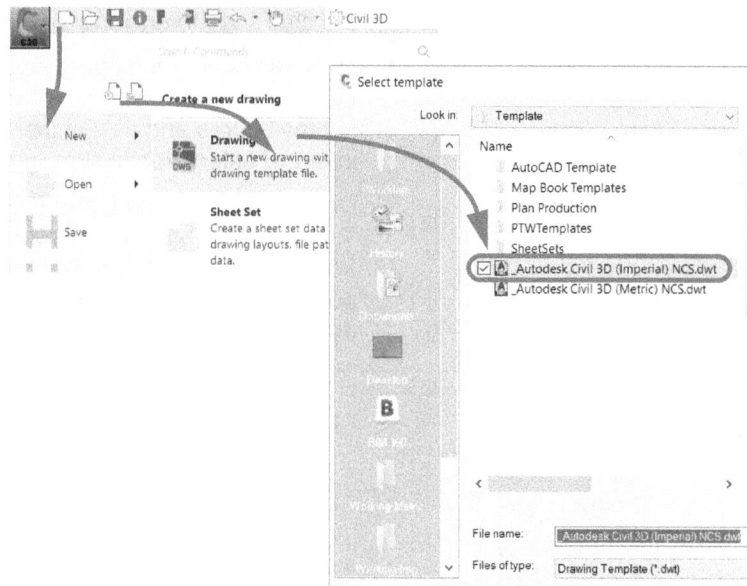

Figure 3–17

2. Click ![C3D icon] (Application Menu) and select **Save As>Drawing Template** as shown in Figure 3–18.

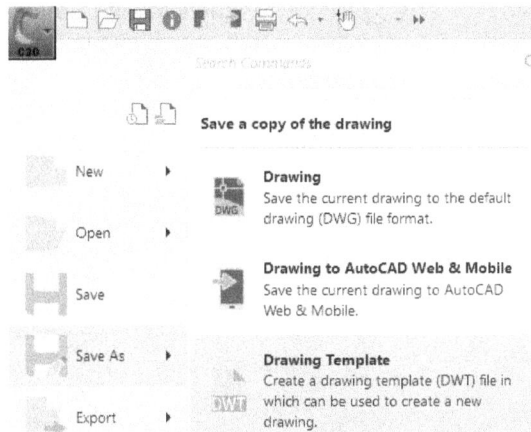

Figure 3–18

CA83-VIF designates the coordinate zone you use for this template.

3. Browse to the *C:\Civil 3D for Surveyors\Ascent-Config* folder and enter **XXX-C3D (CA83-VIF) NCS.dwt** as the template file name (substituting your initials for XXX) and then click **Save**.

4. In the *Template Options* dialog box, add an appropriate description for this newly created template, for example **Civil 3D Training template for Surveyors.**

5. Select the Toolspace>*Settings* tab, as shown in Figure 3–19.

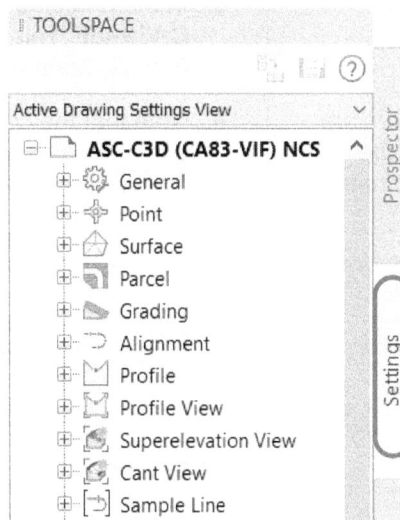

Figure 3–19

6. In the Toolspace>*Settings* tab, right-click on the drawing name (**XXX-C3D (CA83-VIF) NCS**, where XXX is your initials), and select **Edit Drawing Settings**.

7. In the Drawing Settings dialog box, select the *Units and Zone* tab, as shown in Figure 3–20.

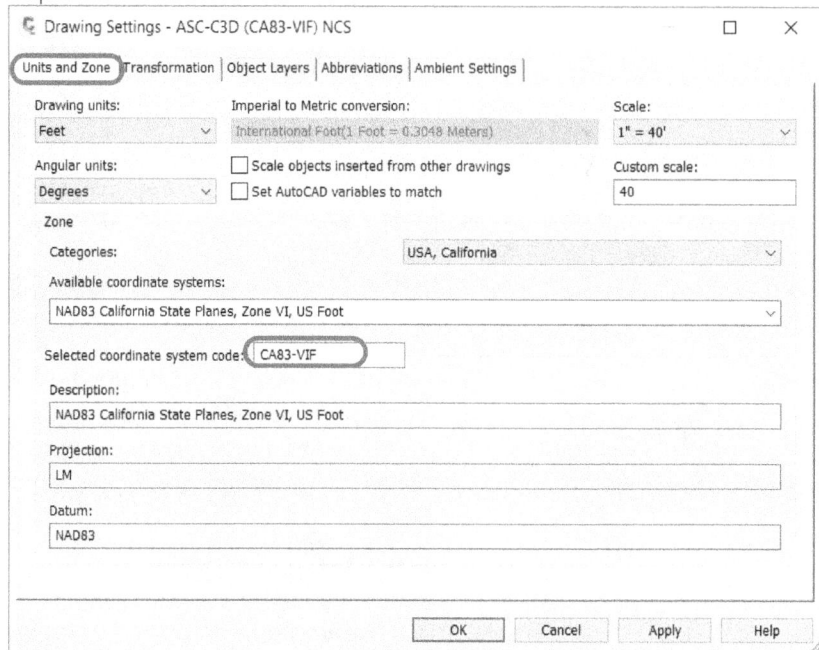

Figure 3–20

8. In the *Selected coordinate system code* field, enter **CA83-VIF**. This is the code for *NAD83 California State Planes, Zone VI, US Foot.*

These coordinates are in the vicinity of the CA83-VIF coordinate zone.

9. Note that the coordinates of the drawing are near **0,0**. In the command line, type **Zoom***,* and press <Enter>. Enter **C** (for Center), and then press <Enter> again.

10. For the coordinates, type **6256700, 2036200**. At the ensuing *magnification or height* prompt, type 5300 and press <Enter>.

11. Start the **Single Line text** command (type in **DTEXT** at the command line or select in the ribbon>*Annotate* tab>*Multiline Text* drop-down list), then select the center of the display as the insertion point.

12. Set the *text height* to **150** and the *rotation angle* to **33**.

13. Type the following, pressing <Enter> after each line (when done typing the last line, press <Enter> twice to finish):

DRAWING SET TO CA83-VIF COORDINATE SYSTEM.
GO TO DRAWING SETTINGS TO MODIFY IF NEED BE.
DELETE THIS MESSAGE.

14. Save the drawing template.

Task 2 - Import survey user settings.

Importing survey user settings will have no effect on a drawing template. You import the survey user settings now to establish the path to where the Figure Prefix Database resides.

1. In the Toolspace, select the Survey tab. Click ⚊ (Survey User Settings), as shown in Figure 3–21.

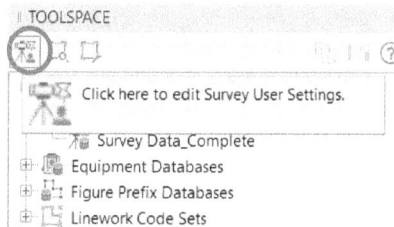

Figure 3–21

2. Click ⚊ (Import User Settings), as shown in Figure 3–22

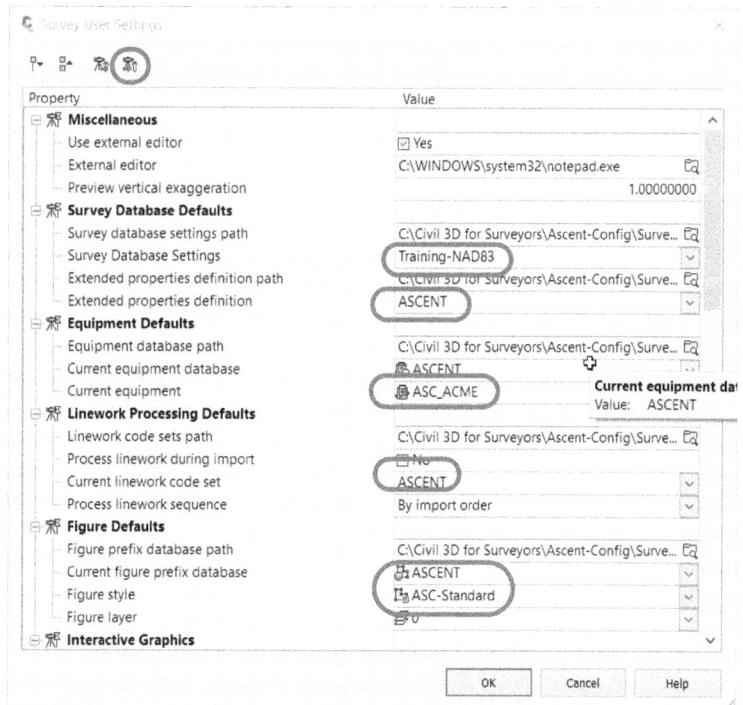

Figure 3–22

3. Browse to *C:\Civil 3D for Surveyors\Ascent-Config\Survey Settings* and select **ASCENT-Settings.usr_set**, then click **Open**.

4. Importing the user settings causes all branches to contract. You can expand each branch by clicking the **+** icon. A simple way of expanding all branches is to close the Survey User Settings window by clicking **OK** and reopening the file as you did in the first step of this practice.

5. Note how the paths have changed for the various entries.

6. Set the Survey User Settings drop-down lists as follows:

   - *Survey Database Setting*: **Training-NAD83**
   - *Extended properties definitions:* **Ascent**
   - *Current equipment database*: **Ascent**
   - *Current Equipment:* **ASC_ACME**
   - *Current linework code set*: **Ascent**
   - *Current figure prefix database*: **Ascent**
   - *Figure Style*: **ASC_Standard**

7. Click **OK** to exit the Survey User Settings.

8. Note that no changes were made in the template, so there is no need to save the drawing template. The changes were made to the *Survey User Settings.*

Task 3 - Create a Figure Prefix database.

---

1. Remain in the *Survey* tab of the Toolspace.

2. Right-click on **Figure Prefix Databases**, and select **New**. Set the *Name* to **XXX-Training** (substituting XXX with your initials).

3. Right-click on **XXX-Training** Figure Prefix database, and select **Make Current**.

4. Right-click on **XXX-Training** Figure Prefix database again, and select **Manage Figure Prefix Database**.

5. Click ✛ to create a new figure definition. The Autodesk Civil 3D software creates a default figure. Set the following, as shown in Figure 3–23:

- Change the *Name* to **Trail**.
- Set the *Breakline* to **Yes**.
- Verify that *Lot Line* is set to **No**.
- Set the *Layer* to **V-ROAD-CNTR**.
- Set the *Style* to **ASC-Road Centerline**.

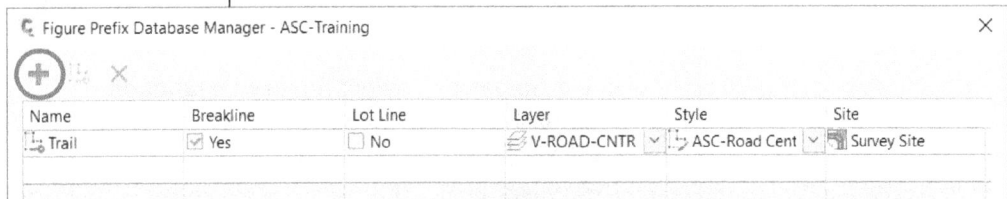

Name	Breakline	Lot Line	Layer	Style	Site
⌐ Trail	☑ Yes	☐ No	✍ V-ROAD-CNTR ⌄	⌐ ASC-Road Cent ⌄	▤ Survey Site

Figure 3–23

- Any figure starting with **Trail** is now selectable for a surface breakline and uses the **Road Centerline** style. Unlike the Description Key Set, an asterisk (*) is not required to match Trail1, Trail2, etc.
- The figure resides on the designated layer **V-ROAD-CNTR**.

6. Click ✛ to create a new figure definition and then set the following:

- Change the *Name* to **Building**.
- Verify that *Breakline* is set to **No**.
- Verify that *Lot Line* is set to **No**.
- Verify that *Layer* is set to **0**.
- Set the *Style* to **ASC-Buildings**.
- Click **OK** to exit the dialog box.

Since no layer was assigned, the figure resides on Layer **0**, however the style resides on layer **V-BLDG-OTLN**.

7. Close the drawing template. There is no need to save the drawing template, as the changes are recorded in the Figure Prefix Database, which resides in the path designated in the *Survey User Settings*.

3.3 The Survey Database

The Survey forking folder is the location for all of the Survey Databases and can be local or on the network. The preferred location is a network folder, in which you place the local Survey Databases. The Survey User Settings dialog box sets the defaults for all new Survey Databases. It is recommended to set them before starting Survey.

How To: Set the Working Folder for the Survey Database

1. In the *Survey* tab, select **Survey Databases**.
2. Right-click and select **Set working folder**, as shown in Figure 3–24.

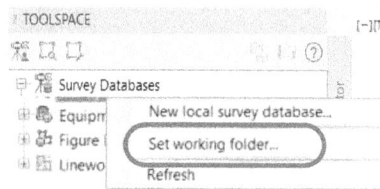

Figure 3–24

Survey Database

Survey Database folders cannot be deleted in the Autodesk Civil 3D Survey software. If you want to delete the working folder, it must be done through the Windows File Explorer.

A Survey Database is a subfolder in the working folder, as shown on the right in Figure 3–25. The Survey Working Folder contains the survey settings and the observation database. The database contains the survey's networks, figures, and survey points.

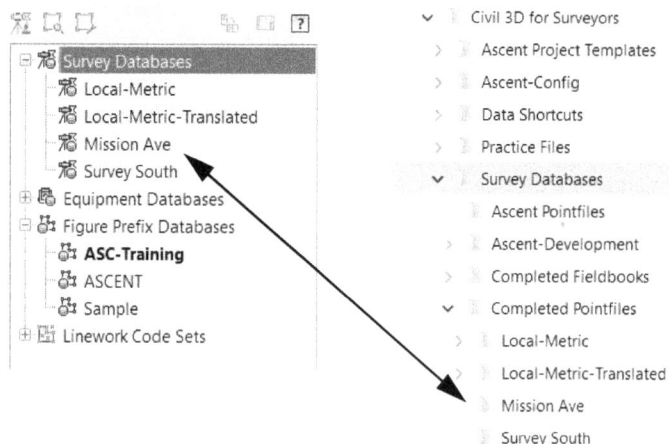

Figure 3–25

Each local Survey Database references files to perform some of its tasks.

- The Equipment database is an *.EDB file. The Equipment settings file contains values to estimate errors for the least squares adjustment process.

- The Figure Prefix database is an *. FDB file. The Figure Prefix database lists definitions for Survey figures (figure style and layers). The default location for these files is *C:\ProgramData\Autodesk\C3D 2021\enu\Survey.*

Survey has four nodes: **Import Events**, **Networks**, **Figures**, and **Survey Points**. **Import Events** is where files are imported into the survey's networks. The files can be a coordinate, field book, LandXML file, and points from a drawing. When importing a file, depending on its contents, the import results in figures and points. Information in the file also populates portions of survey's Network. When importing a coordinate or field book file containing only coordinates, the Figures and Survey Points nodes are used. When processing a file with observations, turned angles, zenith angles, slope distances, and setups, you use the network and its nodes.

Hint: Survey Database Migration to 2020 or 2021

The Survey Database format has changed as of the Autodesk Civil 3D 2020 software release. If you have existing Survey Databases that were created in an earlier format, they are marked and must be migrated, Right-click on the Survey Database and select **Migrate**. Select a new location for the updated Survey Database, as shown in Figure 3–26.

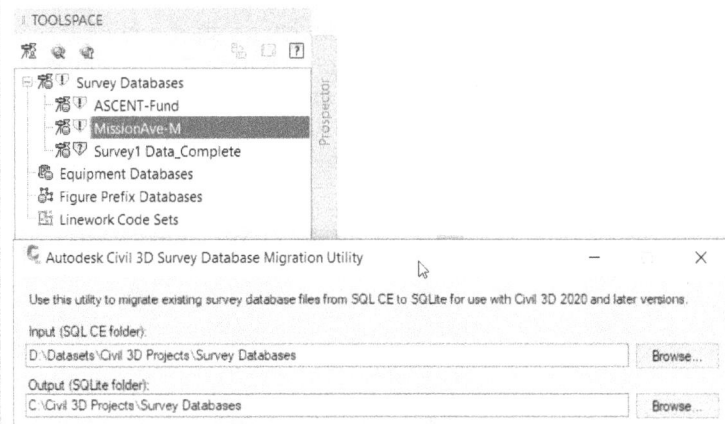

Figure 3–26

How To: Migrate a Survey Database

When the Survey Database has a yellow alert icon, it must be migrated.

1. Right-click on the Survey Database and select **Migrate**, as shown in Figure 3–27

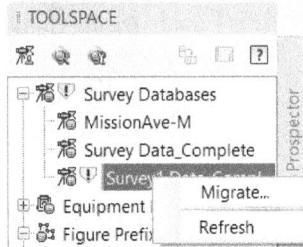

Figure 3–27

The Input and Output folders can be the same. However, it is recommended that you select a different folder to keep the original survey databases for archival purposes.

2. Click **Browse** to select the folder of the existing survey databases (Input), and the destination folder for where you want the migrated survey databases to reside (Output), as shown in Figure 3–28.

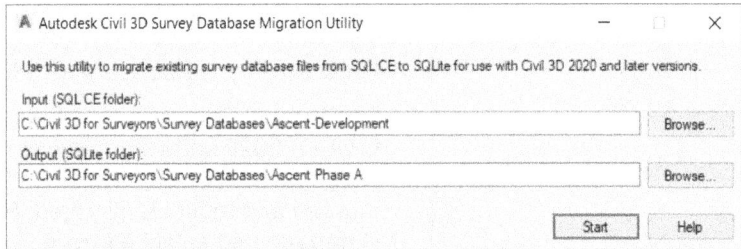

Figure 3–28

3. When the process is complete, a status window displays the results, as shown in Figure 3–29. Unsuccessful migrations are due to being too old (e.g., from AutoCAD Civil 3D 2012) or the databases have already been upgraded to the new version.

Figure 3–29

Survey Equipment Database

The Survey Equipment Database is used to define different Total Stations and their specific settings. However, these settings are not considered when importing data, because the actual equipment has already made the necessary adjustments when it generated the output files. The equipment database and its settings are only used when performing a traverse analysis in the Autodesk Civil 3D software, such as a least squares adjustment.

Within each Survey Equipment Database entry resides definitions specific to the values associated with a surveying instrument, such as the standard deviations associated with the measuring capabilities.

How To: Create an Equipment Database

1. In the *Home* tab>Palettes panel, click 🗠 (Survey Toolspace) to display the *Survey* tab, as shown in Figure 3–30.

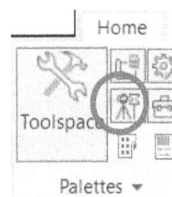

Figure 3–30

2. In the Toolspace, select the *Survey* tab.
3. Right-click on **Equipment Database** and select **New**, as shown in Figure 3–31. Enter an equipment database name, then click **OK** to accept and close the dialog box.

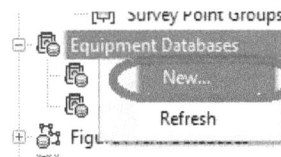

Figure 3–31

4. To open the Equipment Properties dialog box, select the equipment database, right-click, and select **Manage Equipment database**.
5. Review the settings. When done, click **OK** to close the dialog box.

6. By default, the Autodesk Civil 3D software saves the equipment database files in the *C:\ProgramData\Autodesk\ C3D 2021\enu\Survey* folder, as shown in Figure 3–32.

   • To change the path to a network drive, click 🛰 (Survey User Setting), scroll down to *Equipment Defaults*, and browse for a new path.

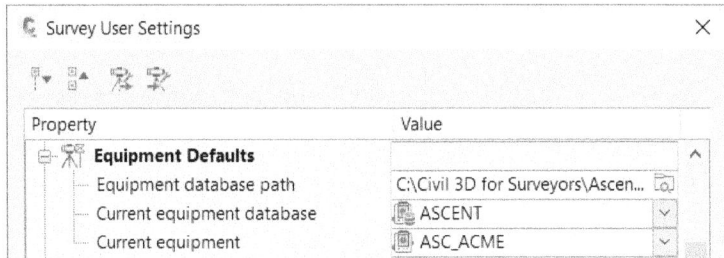

Figure 3–32

7. Review the settings. When done, click **OK** to close the dialog box.

How To: Create a Survey Database Using the Import Survey Data Command

1. In the *Home* tab>Create Ground Data panel, click 🔽 (Import Survey Data).
2. In the Import Survey Data dialog box, click **Create New Survey Database**. Enter a name and click **OK**.
3. In the Import Survey Data dialog box, select the new survey database and click **Edit Survey Database Settings**.
4. In the dialog box, under *Units*, for the *Coordinate Zone*, click ⋯ and select a coordinate system, as shown in Figure 3–33. Click **OK**.

Note that the survey can be done in any coordinate system, even if it does not match the project coordinate system. The Autodesk Civil 3D software converts the coordinates and units in the drawing.

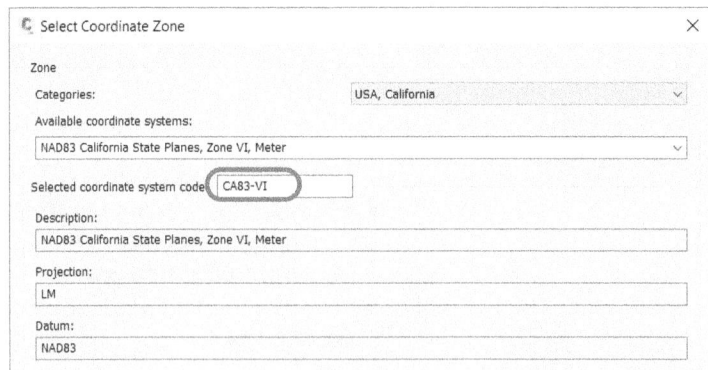

Figure 3–33

5. Set the *Direction*, *Temperature*, *Pressure*, and other settings, as shown in Figure 3–34. When done, click **OK** to close the dialog box.

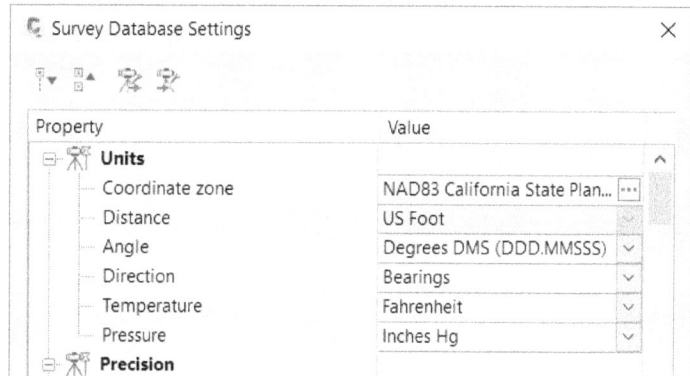

Figure 3–34

6. In the Import Survey Data dialog box, click **Next**.
7. Select the Data source type and browse for the file. Then click **Next**.
   - If the Data source type is set to **Point File**, specify the file format.
   - If the Data source type is set to **Points From Drawing**, click **Select points in current drawing**. Then, draw a selection window around the appropriate points and press <Enter>.
8. If a control network is required, click **Create New Network**. Then click **Next**.
   - If a control network in not required, just click **Next**.
9. Set the appropriate *Import Options* and click **Finish**.

How To: Create a Survey Database Without Importing Data at the Same Time

1. In the *Home* tab>Palettes panel, click 🔭 (Survey Toolspace) to display the *Survey* tab.
2. In the Toolspace, select the *Survey* tab.
3. Right-click on **Survey Databases** and select **New local survey database**.
4. Enter a name for the new database and click **OK**.

Open a Survey Database for Editing

Only one Survey Database can be opened at a time. When opened for editing, it prepares the survey for reading and writing. There are options to set the path or location for the Survey Database project files, as well as all of the settings.

- When you create a new Survey Database, a Windows folder is created with the same name.

- If you close a drawing with a survey open, the Survey Database closes automatically. You must start a new drawing or open en existing drawing, and then open the required Survey Database.

How To: Open a Survey Database

Double-clicking on the name of the survey database opens it as read-only.

1. Expand the **Survey Database** branch.
2. Select the survey database that you want to open, right-click and select **Open for edit** or **Open for read-only**, depending on your requirements, as shown in Figure 3–35.

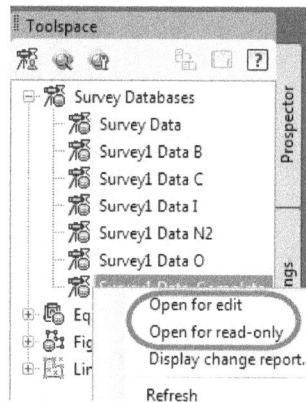

Figure 3–35

Practice 3c

Create a Survey Database

Practice Objectives

- Create three entries for the equipment database.
- Create two survey databases in preparation for importing survey data, one for metric data and one for imperial data.

Task 1 - Create an equipment database.

1. Start a new drawing. The Autodesk Civil 3D software will invoke your default drawing template. Since you will not be adding anything to the drawing, it does not matter which template you use.

2. If the Survey Toolspace is not displayed, in the *Home* tab> Palettes panel, click ⚓ (Survey Toolspace), as shown in Figure 3–36.

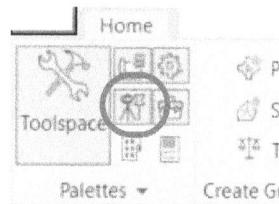

Figure 3–36

3. In the Toolspace, select the *Survey* tab.

4. To create an equipment database, right-click on **Equipment Database** and select **New**, as shown in Figure 3–37.
   - For the equipment database name, type **XXX-Equip** (substituting your initials for XXX), as shown in Figure 3–38.
   - Click **OK** to accept and close the dialog box.

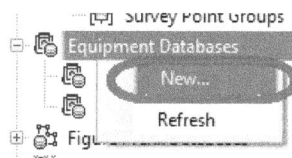

Figure 3–37

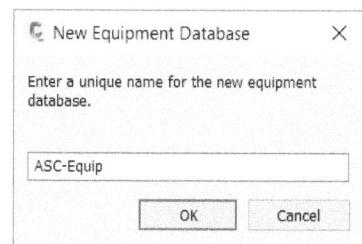

Figure 3–38

5. To open the Equipment Properties dialog box, select **XXX-Equip**, right-click, and select **Manage Equipment database**.

6. For the name, enter **XXX-ACME-M** (substituting your initials for XXX).

7. Ensure the unit for *Distance* is set to **Meter**, as shown in Figure 3–39.

8. Review the other settings.

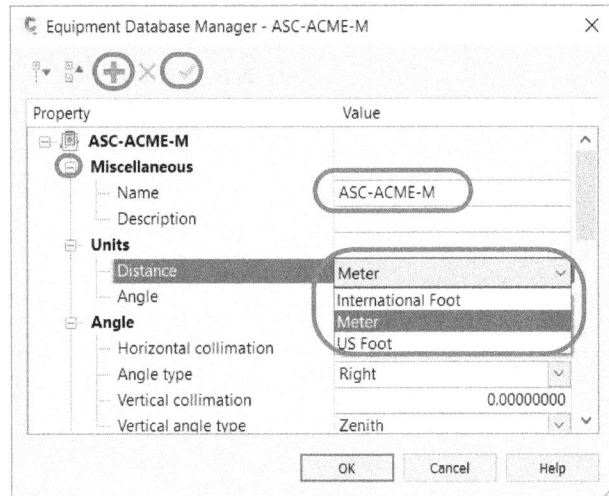

Figure 3–39

9. Click the ⊟ (minus sign) next to the **XXX-ACME-M** to collapse the branch.

10. Click the green plus (✢) to add a new set of equipment.

11. For the name, enter **XXX-ACME-USF** (substituting your initials for XXX).

12. Ensure the unit for *Distance* is set to **US Foot**.

13. Repeat Steps 10 to 12. For the name, enter **XXX-ACME-IF** (substituting your initials for XXX).

14. Ensure the unit for *Distance* is set to **International Foot**.

15. Collapse all three branches, then select **XXX-ACME-USF** and click the green checkmark (✓) to make it current.

16. When done, click **OK** to close the dialog box.

Task 2 - Create the Metric Survey Database.

1. In the *Survey* tab, right-click on **Survey Databases**, and select **Set working folder**, as shown in Figure 3–40.

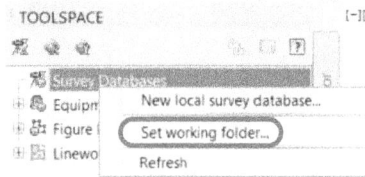

Figure 3–40

2. Browse to and select the *C:\Civil 3D for Surveyors\Survey Databases\Ascent-Development* folder. Click **Select Folder**.

3. In the Toolspace>*Survey* tab, right-click on **Survey Databases** and select **New local survey database**.

4. Set the *Name* to **Ascent Data-M** and click **OK**.

5. Right-click on the **Ascent Data-M** database and select **Edit Survey Database Settings**.

6. In the dialog box, under *Units*, for the *Coordinate Zone*, click ⋯ and select **NAD83 California State Planes, Zone VI, Meter**, as shown in Figure 3–41, and click **OK**.

Note that although some of the survey was done in CA83-VI and your drawings are in CA83-VIF, you can import the survey data to any coordinate system or units and the Autodesk Civil 3D software converts the coordinates and units in the drawing.

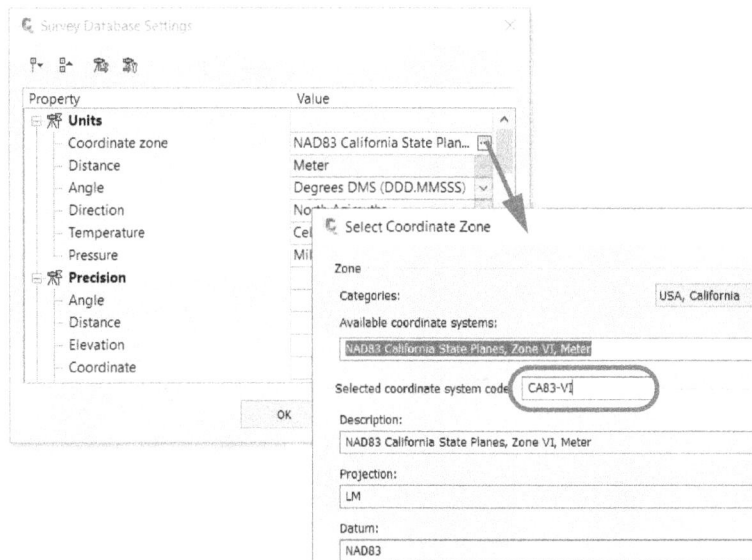

Figure 3–41

7. Set the following, as shown in Figure 3–42:
   - *Direction*: **North Azimuths**
   - *Temperature:* **Celsius**
   - *Pressure:* **Millimeters Hg**

Property	Value
⊟ 📷 **Units**	^
Coordinate zone	NAD83 California State Plan... ⋯
Distance	Meter
Angle	Degrees DMS (DDD.MMSSS) ∨
Direction	North Azimuths ∨
Temperature	Celsius ∨
Pressure	Millimeters Hg ∨

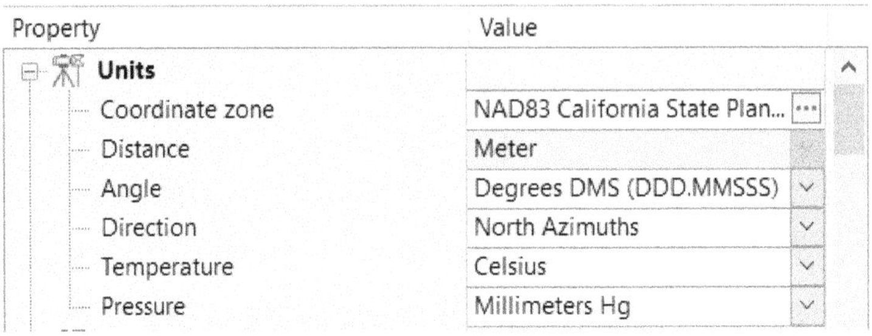

Figure 3–42

8. When done, click **OK** to close the dialog box.

Task 3 - Create the Imperial Survey Database.

---

1. In the Toolspace>*Survey* tab, right-click on **Survey Databases** and select **New local survey database**.

2. Set the *Name* to **Ascent Data-USF** and click **OK**.

3. Right-click on the **Ascent Data-USF** database and select **Edit Survey Database Settings**.

4. In the dialog box, under *Units*, for the *Coordinate zone*, click ⣿ and select **NAD83 California State Planes, Zone VI, US Foot**, as shown in Figure 3–43, and click **OK**.

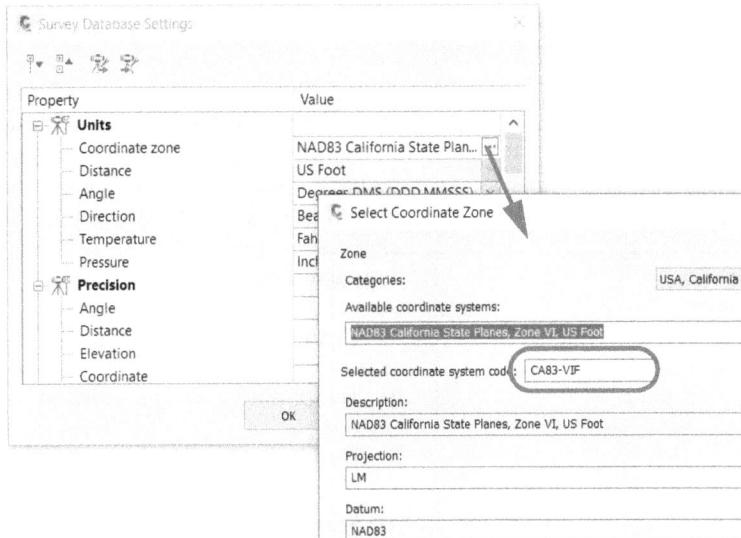

Figure 3–43

5. Verify that the following are set, as shown in Figure 3–44:
    - *Direction*: **Bearings**
    - *Temperature:* **Fahrenheit**
    - *Pressure:* **Inches Hg**

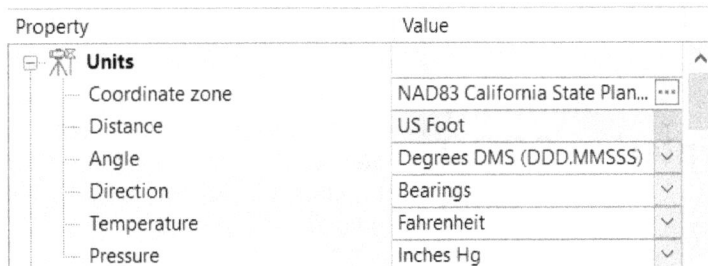

Figure 3–44

6. When done, click **OK** to close the dialog box.

7. Close the drawing. Note that no changes were made in the drawing, so there is no need to save it. The changes were made to the *Survey User Settings*.

3.4 Traverse Editor

Before the areas of a piece of land can be computed, it is required to have a closed traverse. The Traverse Editor (shown in Figure 3–45) assists in entering, editing, and outputting 2D traverse data. In addition, it can be used to enter a legal description of a property in table format making it easier to find and fix errors in data entry. Traverse data can be created in the following ways:

- From existing COGO data.

- By loading it from a polyline.

- By manually entering known data.

			Point Line Chord		Arc				Coordinate	
	Side	Occupied Point	Angle	Distance	Radial	Radius	Δ Angle	Length	North	East
1	Point	6257490.0191, ...							2037127.1292	6257490.
2	Line		S00° 26' 42.02"W	922.4138					2036204.7432	6257483.
3	Line		S00° 24' 20.08"W	508.3493					2035696.4067	6257479.
4	Line		S66° 03' 35.08"W	92.1845					2035658.9997	6257395.
5	Radial Arc				R90	627.1788	42°35'49"	466.28	2035637.9997	6256939.
6	Radial Arc				180	154.4828	-19°13'40"	51.84	2035646.1097	6256888.

Figure 3–45

Manually Entering COGO Data

Traverse data can be entered using a variety of formats and mathematical equations. The key when defining a traverse is to start by defining a point of beginning. Then, the sides of the traverse are defined. When entering data, keep the following guidelines in mind:

- The first Side type must be a point to represent the POB (point of beginning).

- The tab key is used to navigate between cells.

- Any data in red is considered invalid.

- Entered data is not affected if the traverse is adjusted, scaled, or rotated.

- Units of measure different from the project can be entered by typing **'** (feet) or **m** (meters). Once entered, the software converts the measurement to the project units.

Data Entry

Each vertex in a traverse can be manually entered or selected from the model. The following data types can be entered using the formats listed for each.

Side	The side field determines which fields become available for entering data. For example: If the Line option is selected, the Radius and Delta Angle fields become gray which indicates they cannot be modified. Five side types are available as follows: • Point • Line • Chord Arc • Radial Arc • Side Shot
Point	Creates only a COGO point in the drawing. The point of beginning or point of closure can be entered using (X,Y) to set the Latitude/Longitude values. When typing the values, use any of the following formats: • DDMMSS.ss • DD MM SS.ss • DD.MMSSss
Line	The direction of a line or curve from the last point can be set using the quadrant number and then the angle or by typing the bearing just as it is listed in the legal description. • Quadrant..Angle (1..45 = N 45 E) • N DD MM SS.ss E
Chord Arc	Chord arcs require an angle and distance to be entered at a minimum. You can also type the radius, delta angle, or length. Entered data displays in regular font. Calculated values (radius, delta angle, or length) are shown in italics. Multiple cells can be: • Angle/Direction • Distance • Radius • Delta Angle • Length

Radial Arc	Radial arcs require a radial direction and a radius to be entered at a minimum. You can also type the delta angle or length. Entered data displays in regular font. Calculated values (delta angle or length) are shown in italics. Multiple cells can be: • Radial Direction • Radius • Delta Angle • Length *If an arc is tangent to the last line, you can type L90 or R90 (left 90 degrees or right 90 degrees).
Unknown Value	Up to two values per traverse might be unknown. The Traverse Editor calculates the values based on other known values. Known values display in the Traverse Editor as regular text while calculated values display as italicized text. • Enter **U** in the cell.
Mathematical equations	A variety of mathematical equations can be entered to calculate a traverse parameter value. This enables you to calculate relative values based on known information. The following are valid operators: • + • - • / • * • ( )

Traverse Editor Options

- When entering new traverse data, you have the choice of producing lines, COGO points, or both in the drawing, as shown in Figure 3–46.

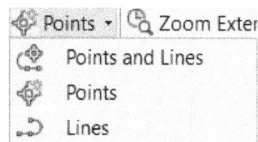

Figure 3–46

- You can control which zoom level the traverse information is displayed at in the drawing. Civil 3D can keep the extents of the whole traverse on the screen, zoom to the traverse element of the selected row of the Traverse Editor, or not change its zoom level, as shown in Figure 3–47.

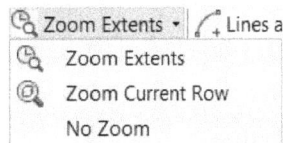

Figure 3–47

- You can choose to display only the traverse linear elements in the table or lines and arcs, as shown in Figure 3–48.

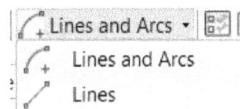

Figure 3–48

- Within the options ( ), you can choose how to handle conflicting points by overwriting the COGO point or creating a new one. You can also choose when to erase the traverse graphics that have been inserted into the drawing, as shown in Figure 3–49.

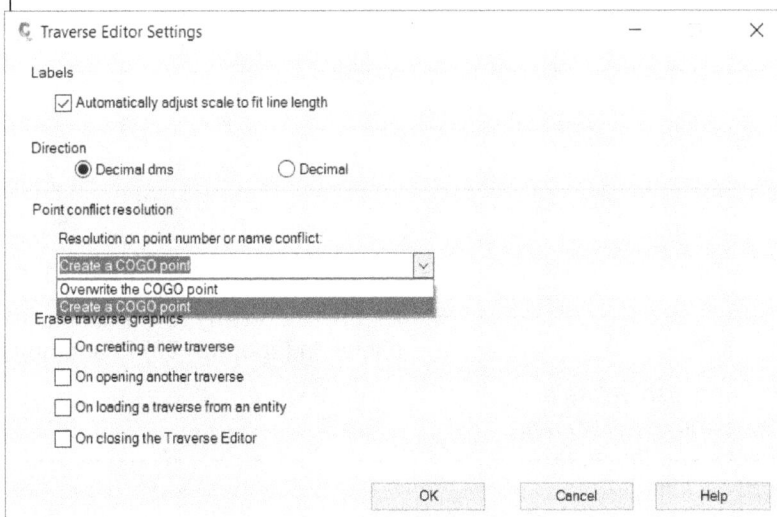

Figure 3–49

How To: Create a Traverse by Entering Data Manually

1. In the **Home** tab>Create Ground Data panel, expand **Traverse** and select (Traverse Editor).

Alternatively, you can click *(Select a point) and select an existing point in the model.*

2. To clear any existing data in the Traverse Editor, click (New).
3. In the first row, enter the **(X,Y)** value for the *Point of Beginning*.
4. In the Side type drop-down list, select the required option (as shown in Figure 3–50), and complete the required cells to the right of it.

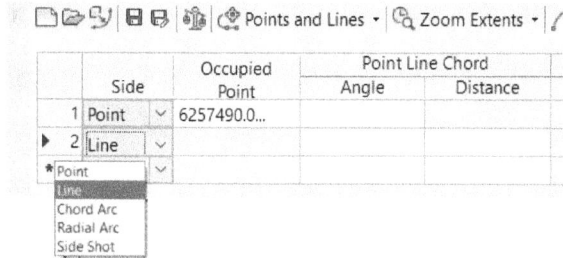

Figure 3–50

5. Repeat Step 4 until all segments of the traverse are entered.
6. To draw the traverse in the model, in the Traverse Editor palette, expand the Draw drop-down list and select which items you want in the model (Points and Lines, Points, or Lines), as shown in Figure 3–51. Review what is drawn in the model.

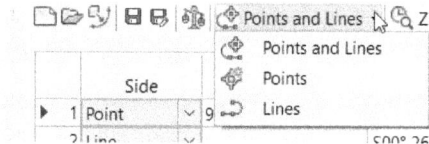

Figure 3–51

7. Right-click on any row and select **Insert Row After** (as shown in Figure 3–52) to add any missing segments.

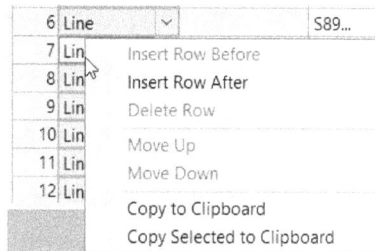

You can also delete a row or move a row up or down using the same right-click menu.

Figure 3–52

Practice 3d | Traverse Editor and Adjustment

Practice Objectives

- Add the property boundary to the model by typing in the legal description into the Coordinate Geometry Editor.
- Key entry traverse information in the Traverse Editor.
- Adjust the entered traverse in the Traverse Adjustment window.

In this practice, you will create a polyline from the previous legal description of a property boundary, as shown in Figure 3–53. This time, however, you will be using Traverse Editor tools, rather than drawing a polyline with transparent commands.

After realizing you missed a line of text in the legal description, you make edits to the boundary and import the polyline from the Traverse Editor into the drawing. You will then adjust the closure of the traverse with the Traverse Adjustment window.

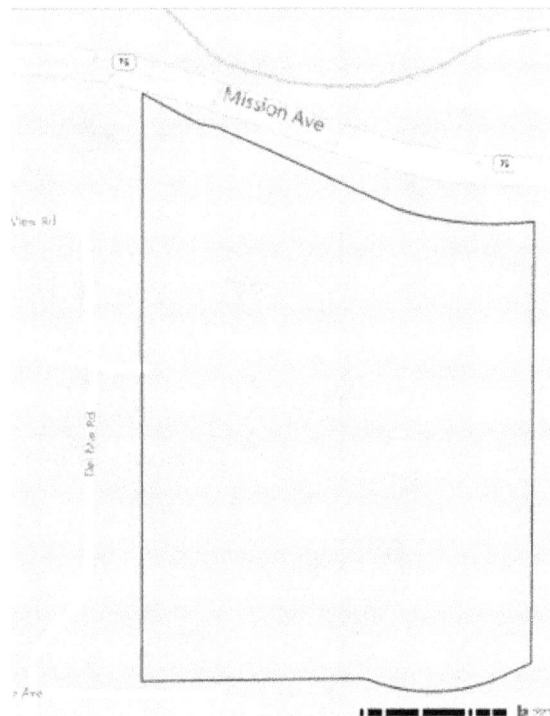

Figure 3–53

Task 1 - Manually enter a traverse boundary.

1. Open **Boundary-A2.dwg** from the *C:\Civil 3D for Surveyors\Working\Survey* folder.

2. In the *Home* tab>Create Ground Data panel, expand **Traverse** and select ⬦ (Traverse Editor).

3. To clear any existing data in the Traverse Editor, click ▢ (New).

4. For the first point, type **6257490.0191,2037127.1292**.

5. In the Side drop-down list, select **Line**, as shown in Figure 3–54.

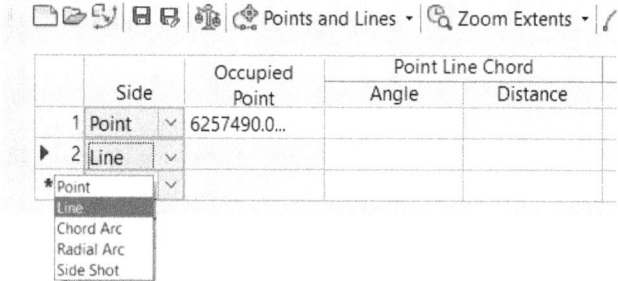

Figure 3–54

6. Set the following, taking care to use the spaces between the numbers and letters exactly as shown. Note that you can jump to the next cell by pressing <Tab>, and that <Up Arrow> and <Down Arrow> changes rows.
   - *Angle/Direction*: **S 00 26 42.2 W**
   - *Distance*: **922.4138**

7. Use the following table to set the remaining segments:

| Side Type | Point, Line, Chord | | | Arc | | |
	Angle/ Direction	Distance	Radial	Radius	Delta Angle
Line	S 00 24 20.8 W	508.3493			
Line	S 66 03 35.8 W	92.1845			
Radial Arc			L90	627.1788	42 35 49
Line	S 89 25 44.6 W	724.9442			
Line	N 00 11 9.9 E	1904.2647			
Line	S 61 50 15.3 E	135.9034			
Line	S 64 05 35.8 W	77.8201			
Line	S 78 09 29.2 E	63.8821			
Line	S 66 23 19.5 E	379.2248			
Line	S 66 17 17.4 E	278.5122			
Chord Arc	S 76 22 12 E	135.0030		1117.0	
Radial Arc			L90	1130.4720	-17

8. In the Traverse Editor palette, click 🖉 (Save Traverse to File As).

9. Browse to the *C:\Civil 3D for Surveyors\Working\ Survey\Data Files\Level 1* folder and type **BOUNDARY** for the traverse file. Click **Save**.

10. Close the Traverse Editor.

Task 2 - Make corrections to the traverse.

After you have run the report or drawn the traverse in the model, you might realize that you inadvertently missed a segment and put in the wrong angle or direction for another segment. In this task, you will add the missing segment and make any other corrections.

1. In the *Home* tab > Create Ground Data panel, click

   ⬥ (Traverse Editor).

2. In the Zoom drop-down list, select **Zoom Current Row** to zoom to the traverse element of the selected row of the Traverse Editor, as shown in Figure 3–55.

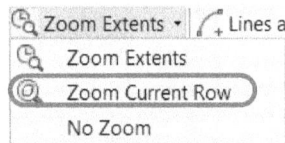

Figure 3–55

*If you did not save the file, select **NeedsCorrections.trv2** from the C:\Civil 3D for Surveyors\Survey Databases\Data\Level 1 folder.*

3. In the Traverse Editor, click 📂 (Load Traverse from File). Select the file you saved in the last task.

4. Note that the curve in line 5 is going in the wrong direction and that line 9 has a mistyped bearing. Correct it by doing the following:

   • In the *Radial* field of line 5, type R90 to change the direction of the curve from Left to Right, without changing the direction of the tangent.

   • In the *Angle/Direction* field of line 9, change the *Bearing* to **S 64 05 35.8 E** (change the **W** at the end to **E**).

5. Also note that the reverse curve is missing after line 5. To correct it, add a segment after line 5 by doing the following:

   • Right-click on line 6 and select **Insert Row Before**.

   • Change the *Side type* of the new line 6 to **Radial Arc**.

   • Set the *Radial* to **180**.

   • Set the *Radius* to **154.4828**.

   • Set the *Delta Angle* to **19 13 40**.

   • Note that the arc is going the wrong direction but has the correct length.

   • Copy the *length* value by highlighting it and pressing <Ctrl>+<C> on the keyboard.

   • In the *Delta Angle* field, type - (negative) in front of the angle value. Unfortunately, this causes the arc to lengthen.

   • Put the cursor in the Length field, press <Ctrl>+<V> to paste the correct length value.

   • Note the corrected linework in the model. If the negative disappears from the *Delta Angle* field, reinsert it.

6. Select row 14 and note that the arc is not tangent to the incoming line. To correct this, set the *Angle* to a negative value by putting a minus sign in front of the value (-06°55'45").

7. Note that even with these corrections, the traverse does not close properly. This means it needs to be adjusted. You could go directly to the Traverse Adjustment window by clicking the

   (Load Balance Tools) icon in the upper left corner. However, we will go the long way around in the next task.

8. In the Traverse Editor palette, click ![save icon] (Save Traverse As to File). Browse to *C:\Civil 3D for Surveyors\Survey Databases\ Data\Level 1* and save the file as **BOUNDARY-Corrected**.

9. Close the Traverse Editor palette by going to the side bar and clicking the **X** that appears, then save the drawing.

Task 3 - Adjust the traverse in the Traverse Adjustment window.

---

1. In the *Home* tab>Create Ground Data panel, click

   (Traverse Adjustment).

2. Click the **Select** button and browse to the folder and file name you saved in the previous task, or open *C:\Civil 3D for Surveyors\Survey Databases\Data\Level 1\ NeedsAdjustment.trv2*.

3. Click the **Settings** button and uncheck the Transit method so it does not show in the Traverse Adjustment window, as shown in Figure 3–56.

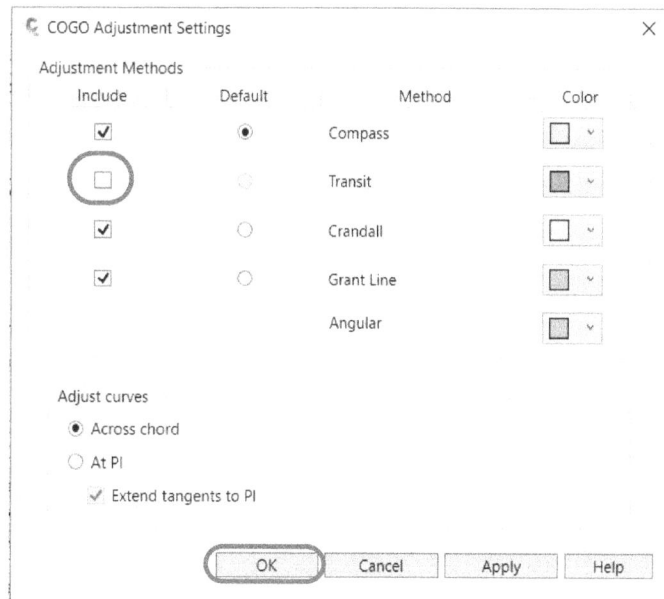

Figure 3–56

4. Click **OK** to return to the Traverse Adjustment window.

5. Ensure that **Compass** is selected in the Adjustment to apply drop-down list, as shown in Figure 3–57.

6. Click the **Generate Report** button and select **Current Adjustment to Apply**, as shown in Figure 3–57.

Adjustment to apply:	Compass		Generate Report	Apply Adjustment
Settings...			Current Adjustment to Apply	
			All Displayed Adjustment Methods	

Figure 3–57

7. Ensure the *Save as type* is set to **HTML**, browse to *C:\Civil 3D for Surveyors\Survey Databases\Data\Level 1*, and enter the *File Name* as **Boundary-Adjusted-Compass**.

8. Click the **Apply Adjustment** button, browse to *C:\Civil 3D for Surveyors\Survey Databases\Data\Level 1*, and enter the *File Name* as **Boundary-Adjusted-Compass**.

9. Click **OK** to close the Apply Adjustment alert box.

10. Click the **Done** button to close the Traverse Adjustment window.

11. Note that the curves have changed to straight segments. Adjusting traverses will do that.

12. Save and close the drawing.

Task 4 - Add a boundary to the Survey Database.

---

1. Open **Boundary-A3.dwg** from the *C:\Civil 3D for Surveyors\Working\Survey* folder.

2. If needed, in the *Survey* tab, right-click on **Survey Databases**, then select **Set working folder** and select the *C:\Civil 3D for Surveyors\Survey Databases\ Ascent-Development* folder.

3. Right-click on the **Ascent Data-USF** database and select **Open for Edit**.

4. Right-click on **Figures** and select **Create figure from object**, as shown in Figure 3–58.

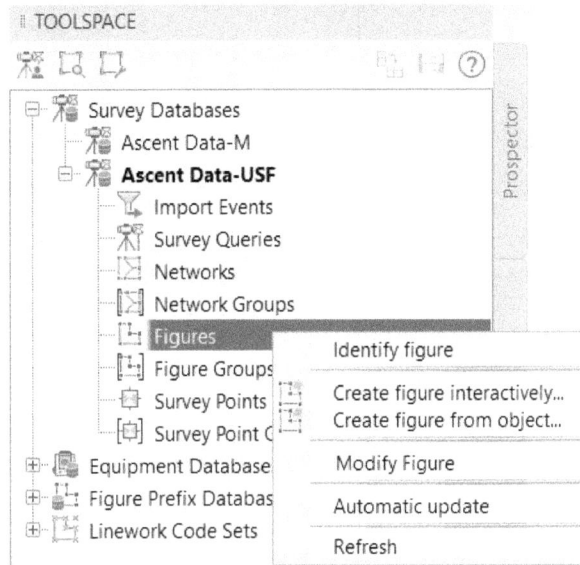

Figure 3–58

5. When prompted, select the red polyline representing the boundary traverse.

6. In the Create Figure From Object window, for the *Name*, type **Boundary**, and then select ASCENT for the *Current figure prefix database*. Do NOT associate survey points to vertices, as shown in Figure 3–59.

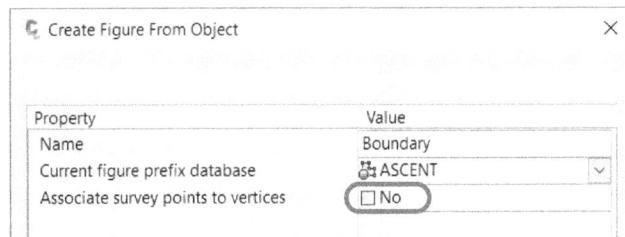

Property	Value
Name	Boundary
Current figure prefix database	ASCENT
Associate survey points to vertices	☐ No

Figure 3–59

7. Note that no changes were made in the drawing, so there is no need to save it. The changes were made to the *Survey Database*.

Surfaces and Grading

Exam Objective	Chapter(s)
2.4 Identify examples of surface analysis	
2.4.a Identify the properties of a surface analysis type	Ch. 4
2.4.b Set the analysis parameters for a surface style	Ch. 4
2.4.c Perform a surface analysis	Ch. 4
2.5 Create and modify feature lines	
2.5.a Create feature lines	Ch. 5
2.5.b Edit feature lines geometry	Ch. 5
2.5.c Edit feature line elevations	Ch. 5
2.5.d Understand how objects interact with each other when they are part of the same site	Ch. 5
2.6 Create and modify sites and grading models	
2.6.a Create and modify sites	Ch. 5
2.6.b Create grading groups	Ch. 5
2.6.c Use grading creation and editing tools	Ch. 5
2.6.d Work with grading criteria	Ch. 5

Surfaces

Exam Objectives Covered in This Chapter

2.1.a Identify the parameters and display settings of surface styles

2.1.b Understand a surface's build, how it was constructed and how it uses the data for calculations

2.1.c Identify the data categories of a surface definition

2.1.d Define surface boundary types

2.1.e Access and review surfaces statistics

2.1.f Understand how and when to display Triangular Irregular Network (TIN) lines

2.2.a Create and edit TIN surfaces

2.2.b Create a volume surface

2.2.c Edit the properties of a surface definition

2.2.d Create a TIN volume surface to compare two surfaces

2.3.a Create spot elevation and slope labels

2.3.b Add labels to single or multiple contour lines

2.4.a Identify the properties of a surface analysis type

2.4.b Set the analysis parameters for a surface style

2.4.c Perform a surface analysis

4.1 Styles in Depth

Styles are central to the Autodesk Civil 3D software. Their flexibility enables an Office or Company to create a unique *look* for their drawings. By changing the assigned style, you can change the composition of a profile view as shown in Figure 4–1.

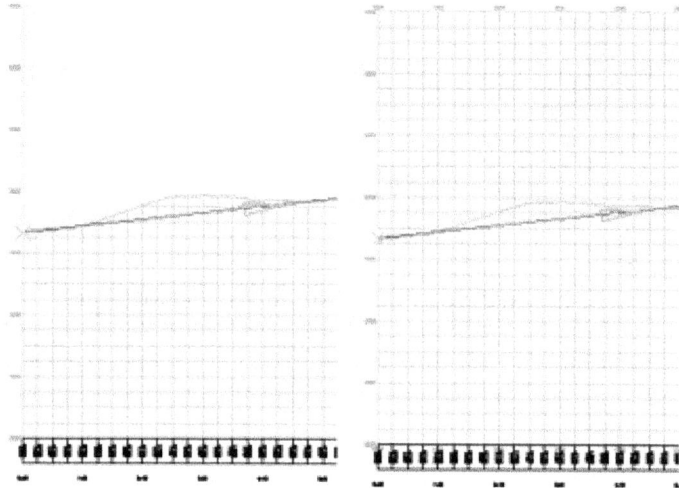

Figure 4–1

In the Toolspace, *Settings* tab, an object type branch identifies each style type and lists its styles below each heading. An example is shown in Figure 4–2.

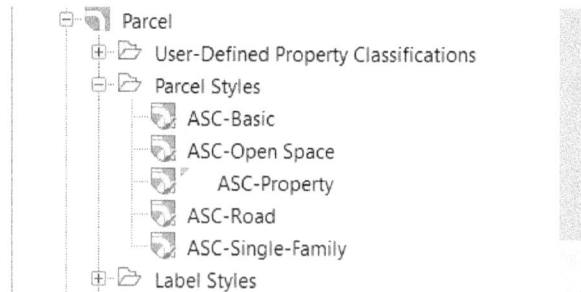

Figure 4–2

Object Styles

Object Styles stylize an object's data for display and print. To edit a style, in the Toolspace, *Settings* tab, right-click on the style and select **Edit**. Much of the work for the object styles is done in the *Display* tab. For certain objects, other tabs might need to be modified.

For example, in the Surface Style dialog box, the *Display* tab enables you to toggle on or off triangles, borders, contours, and other items, as well as define the layer, color, linetype, etc. that are assigned, as shown in Figure 4–3. The *Contours* tab sets the contour interval, smoothing, and other settings, as shown in Figure 4–4.

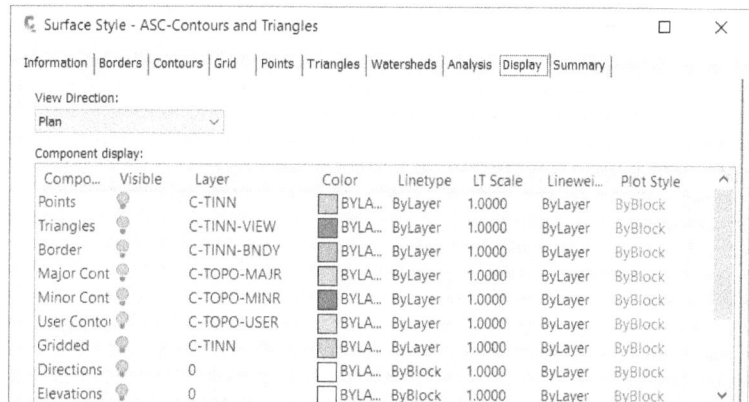

Figure 4–3

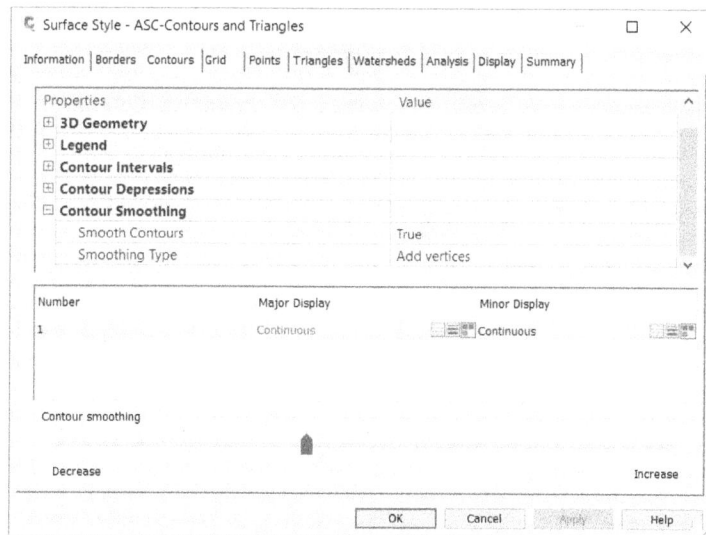

Figure 4–4

From the default Autodesk Civil 3D template, the respective Parcel Style dialog box for Open Space, Road, or Single Family, (as shown in Figure 4–5), define how each displays their segments and hatching by assigning different layers for the components. The other tabs are rarely used for the Parcel styles.

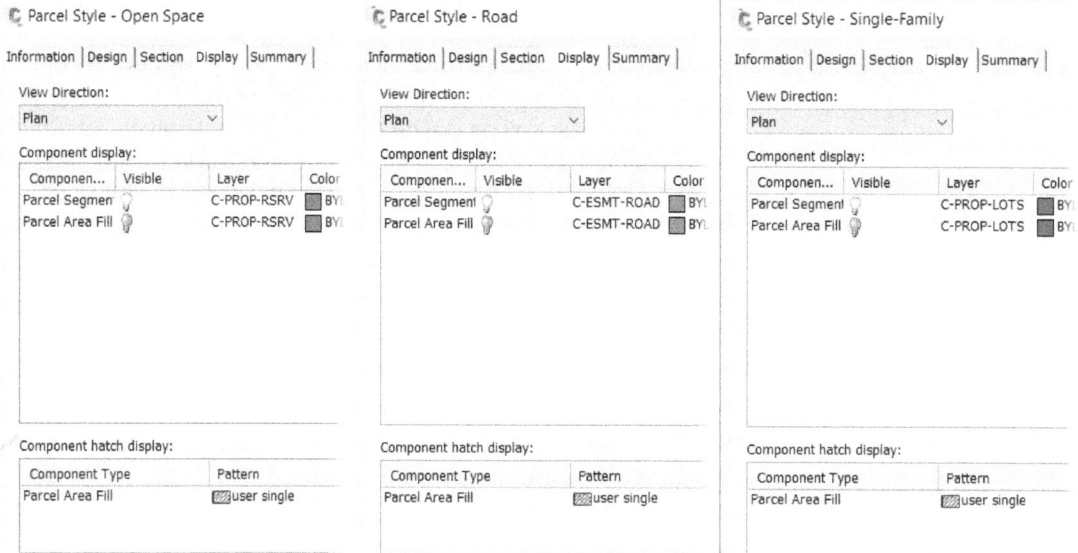

Figure 4–5

An object style represents a specific task, view, type, or stage in a process. For example, a surface style for developing a surface, reviewing surface properties, or documenting surface elevations as contours for a submission. For Parcels, styles represent a type such as open space, commercial, easement, single family, etc. One style can cause an object to look different in various views. For instance, you might want to display both the point and the label in the plan view but only the point marker in a model (3D view). As shown in Figure 4–6, there are four view directions to consider when creating an object style.

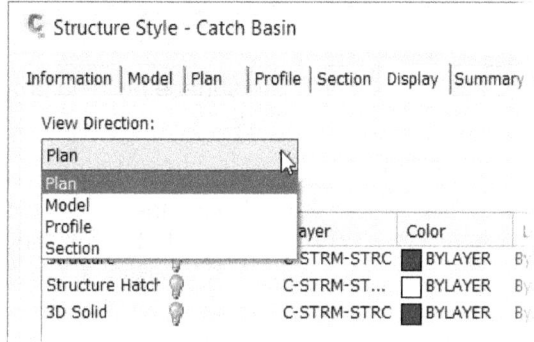

Figure 4–6

4.2 Surface Process

The surface building process can be divided into the following steps:

1. Assemble data.
2. Assign the data to a surface.
3. Evaluate the resulting surface.
4. Add breaklines, assign more data, modify the data, or edit the surface as required.

1. Assemble data

The first step in surface building is to acquire the initial surface data. This can be points, contours, 3D polylines, feature lines, AutoCAD® objects, ASCII coordinate files, and boundaries. Each data type provides specific information about a surface.

2. Assign data to a surface

Acquired data is assigned to a surface. Once assigned, the Autodesk Civil 3D software immediately processes this data and a surface object is created.

Surfaces are listed individually in the *Surfaces* collection in the Toolspace, *Prospector* tab. Each surface contains content information, as shown in Figure 4–7. The surface content includes *Masks, Watersheds,* and *Definition* elements. The *Definition* contains a list of all of the surface data that has been applied, including boundaries, breaklines, and points. The Toolspace, *Prospector* tab displays data for each type of surface data in the list view when one of these types is selected.

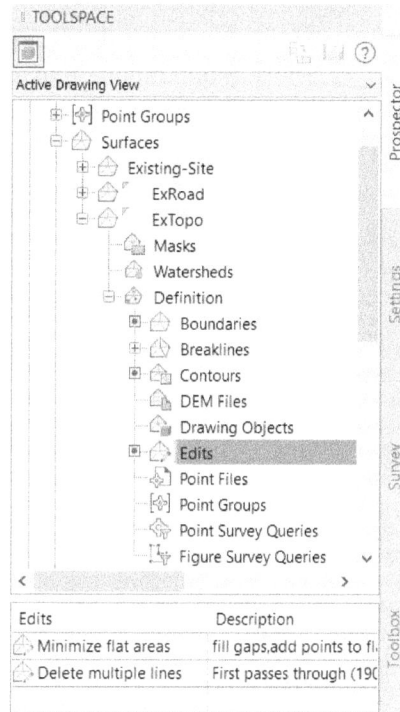

Figure 4–7

The Autodesk Civil 3D software processes the initial data into one of two types of surfaces. The first type, the **Triangulated Irregular Network** (TIN) surface, is the most common. With triangulated surfaces, surface points are connected to adjacent points by straight lines, resulting in a triangular mesh. Surfaces generated from contour lines have surface points created at their vertices, modified by weeding and supplementing factors. An example of this type of surface is shown in Figure 4–8.

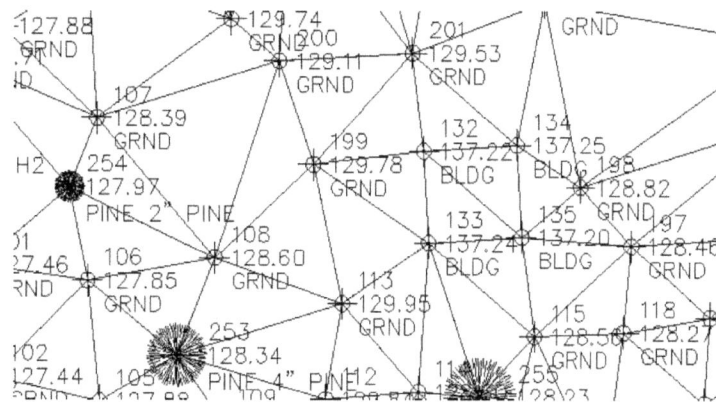

Figure 4–8

The second type of surface is a *Grid* surface. This surface interpolates and assigns an elevation from the surface data to each regular grid intersection. Most of the elevations at grid intersections are interpolated. **Digital Elevation Models** (DEMs) are a type of grid surface used in GIS applications. An example of this type of surface is shown in Figure 4–9.

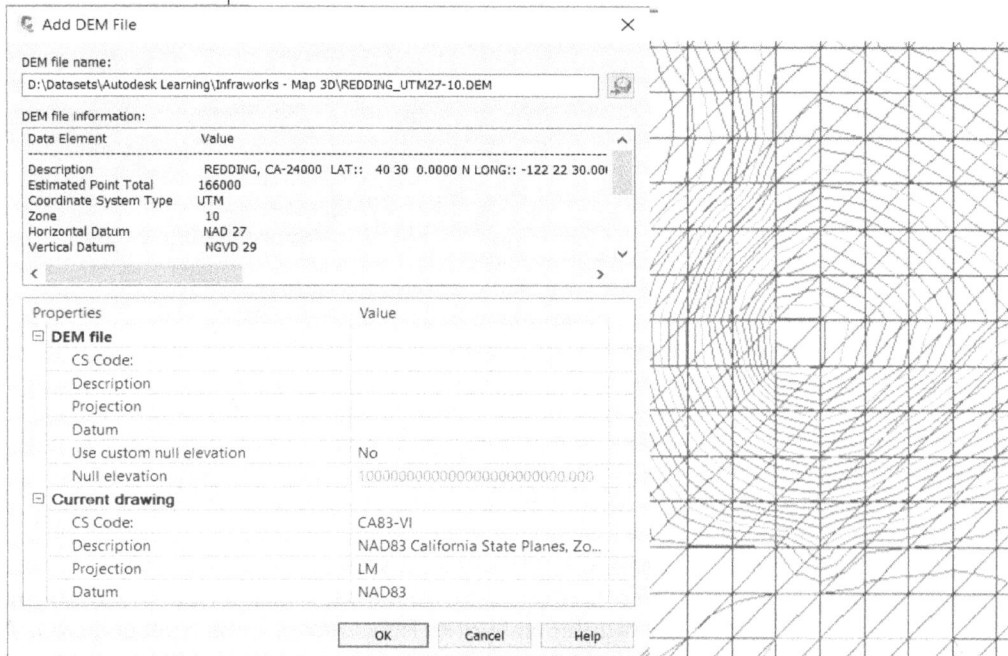

Figure 4–9

3. Evaluate the resulting surface

Surfaces, especially ones created from points, typically need some attention to represent them as accurately as possible. For any four adjacent surface points, there are two possible triangulations, as shown in Figure 4–10.

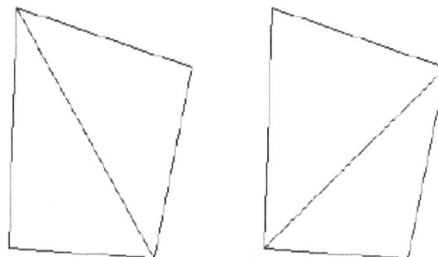

Figure 4–10

The differences can be difficult to envision when viewing the triangles from the TOP view, but these two configurations provide entirely different geometries. For example, note the surface shown in Figure 4–11.

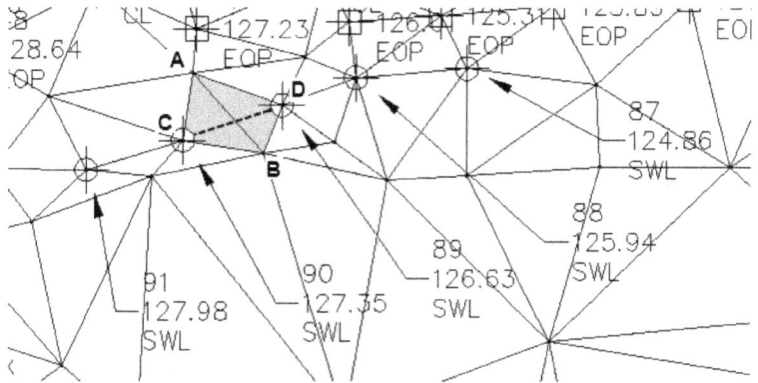

Figure 4–11

The triangulated points A, B, C, and D have a TIN line running from A to B. This configuration ignores the fact that C and D are both part of a continuous swale (SWL), indicated by the dashed line. In a 3D view, this configuration would resemble the example shown on the left in Figure 4–12. The correct triangulation has the triangle line *following* the linear feature rather than *crossing* it, as shown on the right.

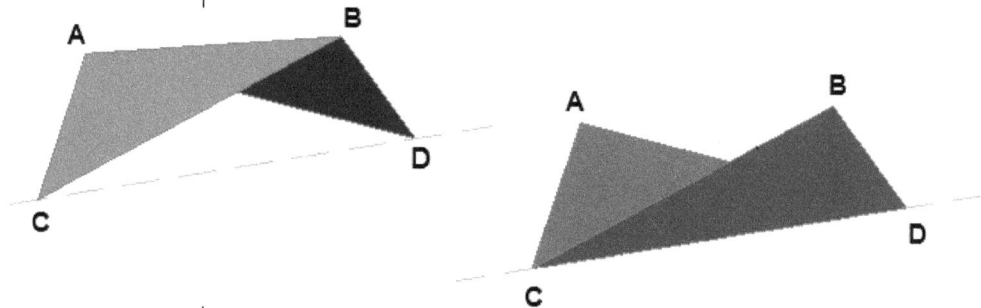

Figure 4–12

When creating surfaces, representing linear features correctly is extremely important. Examples of linear features include road center lines, edges-of-pavement, road shoulders, swales, berms, tops and bottoms of banks, and headwalls. Adding breaklines that follow linear features ensures that a terrain model is triangulated correctly along the features, rather than across them.

Other types of issues to watch out for include bad elevations (blown shots), elevations at 0 where there should be no chance of such elevation values, and points that were surveyed above or below the ground (e.g., the tops of fire hydrants). Unwanted triangles along the edges of the surface might connect points that should not be connected, which could also present problems.

In addition to the casual inspection of the triangles, surfaces can be evaluated by creating contour lines, reviewing the surface in 3D, and using the **Quick Profile** command.

4. Add breaklines, assign more data, modify the data, or edit the surface as required

After you have evaluated the surface, you can add the necessary breaklines or edit the surface directly to make adjustments. If the triangulation errors are isolated, editing the surface directly might be faster than creating and applying breaklines. For example, the triangulation issue in the previous *swale* example could be addressed by *swapping* the edge that crossed the swale center line. To do so, right-click on Edits under a Surface's definition in the Toolspace, *Prospector* tab and select **Swap Edge**, as shown in Figure 4–13.

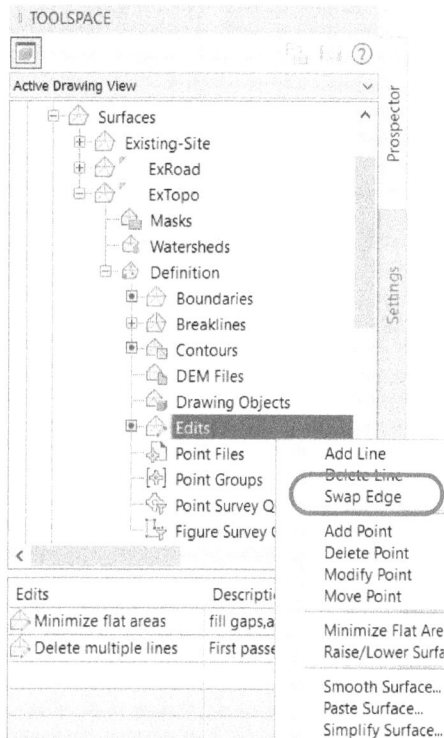

Figure 4–13

Other options enable you to add, move, modify, or remove points from the surface (but not change or erase the point object on which they were based), as well as add or remove triangle lines directly.

Minimize Flat Areas is a group of algorithms that can be used to minimize the number of flat areas created by contour data. **Raise/Lower Surface** enables you to raise and lower the entire surface by a set amount, and a **Smooth Surface** enables you to smooth surfaces using the **Natural Neighbor** or **Kriging** method. (Contour smoothing is handled through surface styles. These techniques smooth the actual surface geometry.)

4.3 Other Surface Data

DEM Files

Digital Elevation Models (DEMs) are grid-based terrain models primarily used by GIS applications to represent large areas. Since they are large-scale and grid-based, they are generally only used in the Autodesk Civil 3D software for preliminary design and other approximate tasks.

Drawing Objects

AutoCAD points, text, blocks, and other objects can be used as surface data. Individual Autodesk Civil 3D point objects can also be selected using the **Drawing Objects** option. Selected objects need to have a valid elevation value.

- All data added as drawing objects is considered point data.

- You can add 3D lines and polyfaces using this method, but each end point is treated as if it were a point object. Linework is not treated as contours or breaklines. The Add Points From Drawing Objects dialog box is shown in Figure 4–14.

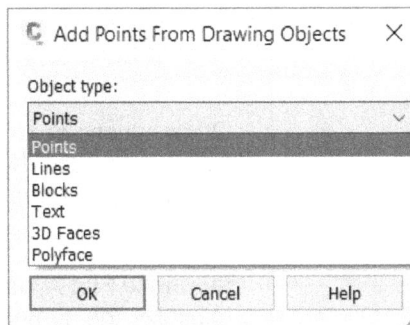

Figure 4–14

Point Files

Points in an ASCII point file can be used as surface data.

- You can use any import/export file format.

- This is an excellent way to create a large surface from a massive number of points, as it bypasses creating point objects, thereby reducing drawing overhead.

Point Groups

Using previously defined point groups in a surface definition enables you to isolate only the points on the ground to ensure that the tops of walls and invert elevations do not distort the surface, by not including these in the point group definition.

Point Survey Queries

Select points in a survey database can be used as surface data by creating a survey query. The point data is used, but point objects are not created.

- Dynamic references to the points provide a more seamless update if changes to the database or query are made.

- This is an excellent way to create a large surface from a massive number of points, as it bypasses creating point objects, thereby reducing drawing overhead.

- You can query the survey points required for creating a surface (similar to the point groups).

- Points from a survey query display under point groups in the surface definition.

Figure Survey Queries

Select figures in a survey database can be used as surface data. The figures are used as breaklines, but 3D polylines are not created in the drawing.

- Dynamic references to the figures provide a more seamless update if changes to the database or query are made.

- This is an excellent way to create a large surface from a massive number of figures, as it bypasses creating 3D polylines and turning them into breaklines, thereby reducing drawing overhead.

- Figures from a survey query display under breaklines in the surface definition.

Practice 4a	# Creating an Existing Ground Surface

Practice Objectives

- Add contour data and point data to a surface that already exists in the drawing.
- Creating a Surface style

In this practice, you will define the surface with surface data. You will use this model to create existing ground contours and for reference during the design. You will begin the model with the provided contours and the previously created **Existing Ground** point group.

Task 1 - Create a surface and set properties.

Ensure that you open the indicated file rather than continuing to work from the last exercise. Otherwise you will be missing information in your surfaces.

1. Open **SUF1-A1-Surface.dwg** from the *C:\Civil 3D Projects\Working\Surface* folder.

2. In the Toolspace, *Prospector* tab, select **Surfaces**, right-click, and select **Create Surface**.

3. For the *Type*, select **TIN surface**. For the *Name*, type **ExTopo** and for the *Style*, select **ASC-Contours 2' and 10' (Background)**, as shown in Figure 4–15.

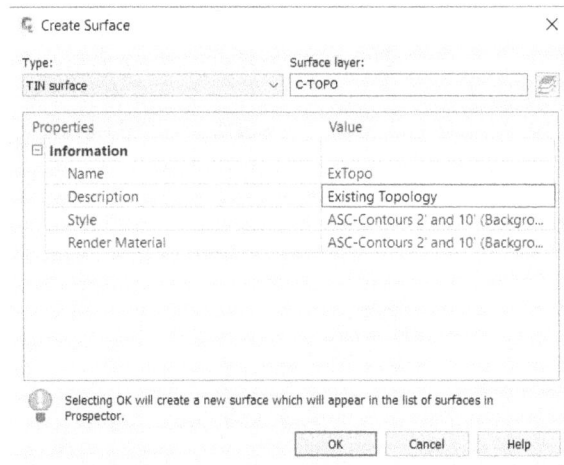

Figure 4–15

4. Click **OK** to accept the changes and close the dialog box.

5. Save the drawing.

Task 2 - Define a surface with contour data.

1. In the *Insert* tab>Block panel, click ⬚ (Insert Block) and select **Blocks from Library**, as shown in Figure 4–16.

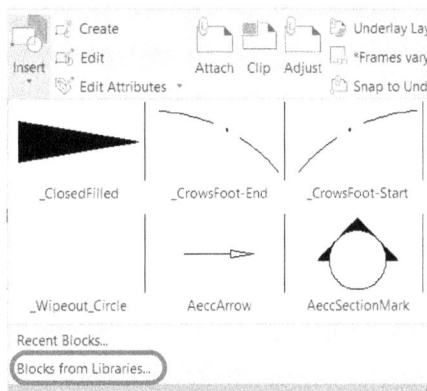

Figure 4–16

2. From the *C:\Civil 3D Projects\References\DWG\Existing* folder, insert **Site-Contours.dwg**, as shown in Figure 4–17.

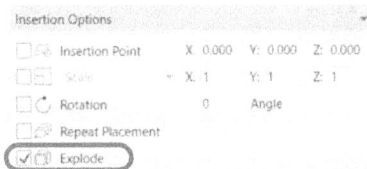

Figure 4–17

- Ensure that **Explode** is selected.

3. Confirm, in the *Insert - Geographic Data* dialog box, that you want to prompt for insertion point, as shown in Figure 4–18.

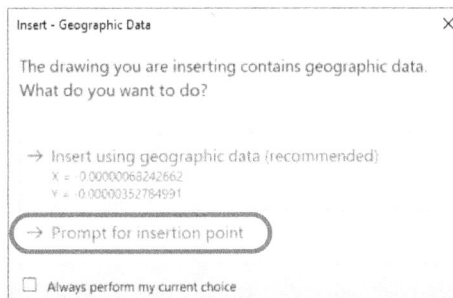

Figure 4–18

*If this setting is not changed, the **C-TOPO** layer will lock and the Autodesk Civil 3D software will not create the surface.*

4. In the *Home* tab>Layers panel, click [icon] (Isolate). Do the following before selecting the layers:

    • Type **S** for **Settings**.
    • Select **Off** and then select **Off** again to ensure that **layiso** does not lock the layer by changing the settings to toggle off isolated layers.

5. Select one major and one minor contour from the **Site-Contours.dwg** to isolate the layers **A-TOPO-MAJR** and **A-TOPO-MINR**.

6. Expand the *Surfaces* collection in the Toolspace, *Prospector* tab.

7. Expand the *ExTopo* surfaces collection and the *Definition* collection.

8. Select the **Contours** data element, right-click, and select **Add...**, as shown in Figure 4–19.

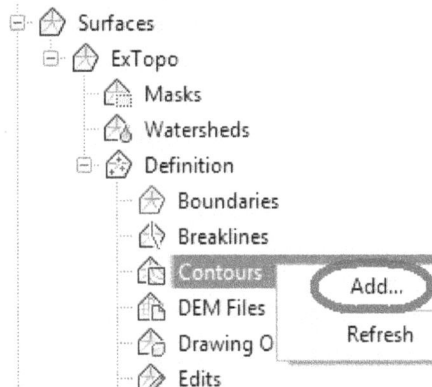

Figure 4–19

9. In the Add Contour Data dialog box, accept the defaults, as shown in Figure 4–20, and click **OK**.

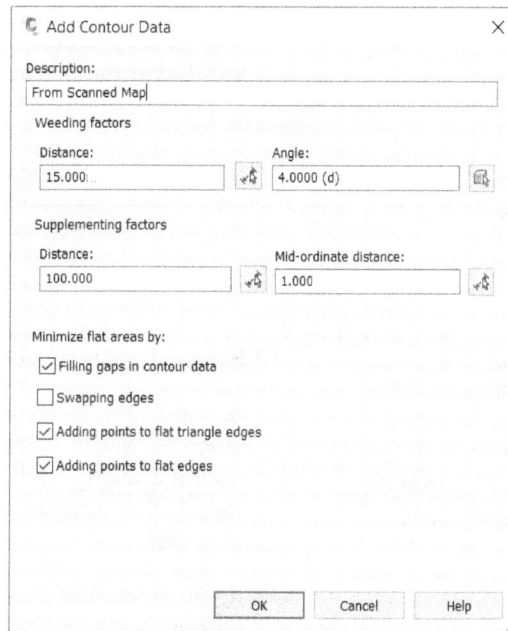

Figure 4–20

10. When prompted to select contours, use the AutoCAD window or crossing selection method to select all of the AutoCAD contour objects on the screen, as shown in Figure 4–21. Press <Enter> to end the command.

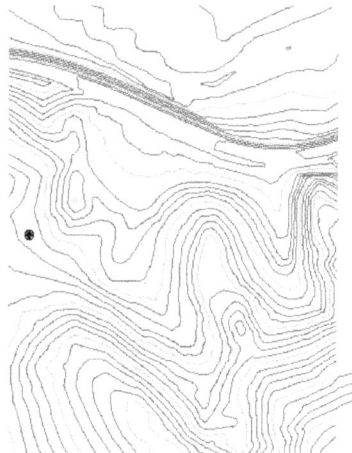

Figure 4–21

11. The Autodesk Civil 3D software has created a surface. However, only the original two isolated contour layers display, the surface is not displayed. You need to restore the previous layer state. To do so, click ⬛ (Unisolate) in the *Home* tab>Layer panel as shown in Figure 4–22.

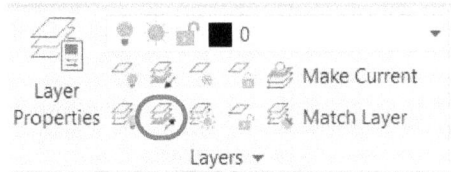

Figure 4–22

After freezing the original contours, if the contours for the new surface are not displayed, verify that the C-TOPO layer is not frozen.

12. Freeze the layers **A-TOPO-MAJR** and **A-TOPO-MINR** by clicking ⬛ (Layer Freeze) and selecting the contours you selected when adding contours to the surface. This will clean up the drawing while ensuring that you do not accidentally modify the surface by changing any of the original contour polylines.

13. If you select the green surface boundary or any contour line, the *Tin Surface: ExTopo* contextual tab displays, as shown in Figure 4–23.

Figure 4–23

14. Save the drawing.

Task 3 - Define surface with point data.

In examining the **ExTopo** surface more closely, note that although the internal site contours correctly reflect the surveyed point elevations, the original contours are out of date or have missing information in the area of the existing road, **Mission Avenue** (the road running east to west at the top of the site). However, you have a detailed survey of the road. Using this data, you will generate a surface.

1. Continue working with the drawing from the previous task or open **SUF1-A2-Surface.dwg**.

*If the points still display in the model, you might have to right-click on Point Groups and select **Update**.*

2. Although the point group that you use in this practice has been created, you should change the display order of the point groups to display them clearly. To do so, in the Toolspace, *Prospector* tab, right-click on *Point Groups* and select **Properties**. Move the **_No Display** point group to the top and then move the **ExRoad** point group above it.

3. In the Toolspace, *Prospector* tab, select the **Surfaces** collection, right-click, and select **Create Surface**.

4. In the Create Surface dialog box, select **TIN surface** for the surface type, type **ExRoad** for the surface name, and select **ASC-Contours 2' and 10' (Background)** for the style.

5. Click **OK** to accept the changes and close the dialog box.

6. Expand the *Surfaces* collection in the Toolspace, *Prospector* tab and expand the *ExRoad* collection.

7. Expand the *Definition* collection, select *Point Groups*, right-click, and select **Add…**.

8. In the Point Groups dialog box, select the **ExRoad** point group, as shown in Figure 4–24. Click **OK** to accept the changes and close the dialog box.

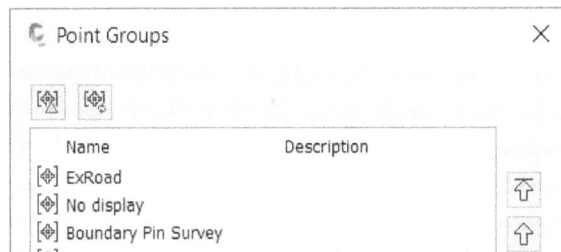

Figure 4–24

9. Save the drawing.

Task 4 - Create a surface contour style.

---

1. Continue working with the drawing from the previous task or open **SUF1-A3-Surface.dwg**.

2. Since there is very little grade change along the road, the frequency of the contours is small, making the surface difficult to see. Expand the *Surfaces* collection, right-click **ExRoad** and select **Surface Properties**.

3. In the Surface Properties dialog box, in the *Information* tab, expand ![icon] to the right of the *Surface style* field and select **Copy Current Selection**, as shown in Figure 4–25.

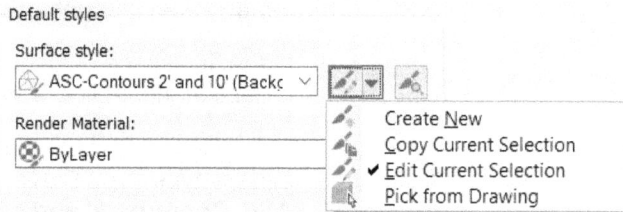

Default styles

Surface style:

ASC-Contours 2' and 10' (Backc

- Create New
- Copy Current Selection
- ✔ Edit Current Selection
- Pick from Drawing

Render Material:

ByLayer

Figure 4–25

4. In the *Information* tab, type **ASC-Contours 0.5' and 2.5' (Background)** for the style name, as shown in Figure 4–26.

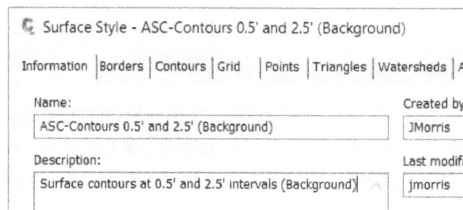

Surface Style - ASC-Contours 0.5' and 2.5' (Background)

Information | Borders | Contours | Grid | Points | Triangles | Watersheds | A

Name: Created by

ASC-Contours 0.5' and 2.5' (Background)   JMorris

Description: Last modifi

Surface contours at 0.5' and 2.5' intervals (Background)   jmorris

Figure 4–26

5. In the *Contours* tab, expand the *Contour Intervals* collection and type **0.5'** for the *Minor Interval* and **2.5'** for the *Major Interval*, as shown in Figure 4–27.

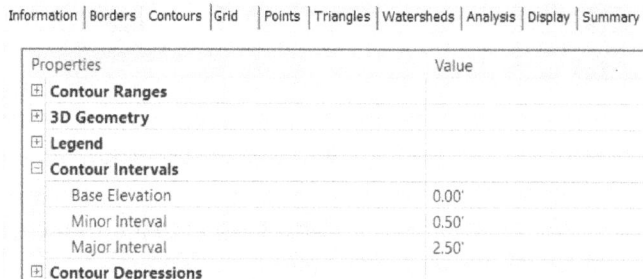

Information | Borders | Contours | Grid | Points | Triangles | Watersheds | Analysis | Display | Summary

Properties	Value
⊞ **Contour Ranges**	
⊞ **3D Geometry**	
⊞ **Legend**	
⊟ **Contour Intervals**	
Base Elevation	0.00'
Minor Interval	0.50'
Major Interval	2.50'
⊞ **Contour Depressions**	

Figure 4–27

6. Click **OK** to accept and close the Edit Style dialog box, and click **OK** to close the Surface Properties dialog box.

7. Zoom into the existing road at the north end of the site and note the detail contours identifying the crown of the road.

8. Save the drawing.

4.4 Breaklines and Boundaries

A surface can include data from boundaries, breaklines, contours, Digital Elevation Model files (DEMs), drawing objects (AutoCAD points, individual Autodesk Civil 3D points, lines, 3D faces, etc.), and point files. The *Boundaries* collection displays above the *Breaklines* collection under the surface's *Definition* (in the Toolspace, *Prospector* tab), as shown in Figure 4–28. However, you should generally add boundaries after adding breaklines to a surface. If you use the Data Clip boundary type, any data that you add to the surface (point file, DEM file, or breakline) is only added to the area within the boundary. In that case, breaklines can be added to the surface after a Data Clip boundary type. Surface edit operations are not affected by the Data Clip boundary.

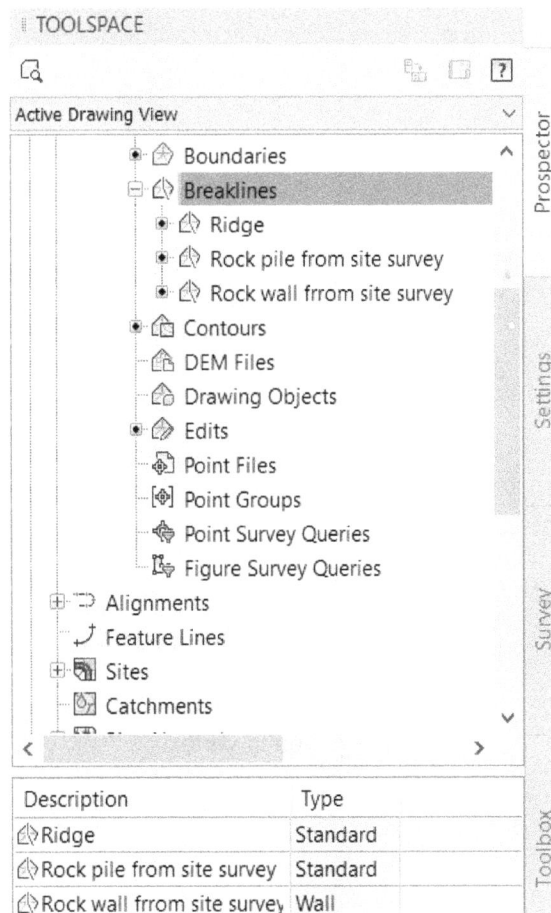

Figure 4–28

Breaklines

Breaklines affect surface triangulation and are important in point-based surfaces. Think of breaklines being a fold in a surface, much like a fold in a piece of paper. They ensure that terrain models are triangulated correctly along linear features, as shown in Figure 4–29.

Surface before breaklines have been applied along the center line of a road.

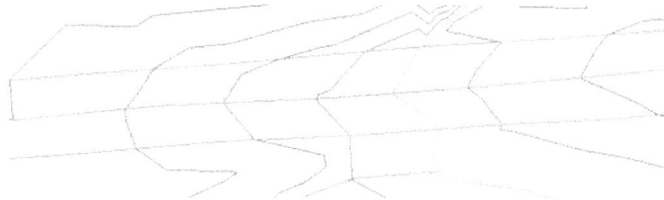

Surface after breaklines have been applied along the center line of a road.

Figure 4–29

- When adding a breakline to a surface, the Autodesk Civil 3D software creates an entry under the *Breakline>Definition* collections, based on a description that you supply.

- When you define multiple breaklines at the same time, the Autodesk Civil 3D software creates a single entry under the *Breaklines* collection. However, they are listed separately in the Toolspace, *Prospector* tab's List View.

- Breaklines can be defined as one of four types: **Standard, Proximity, Wall**, and **Non-Destructive**.

Standard Breaklines

A standard breakline is one that has valid elevations assigned at each vertex.

- Standard breaklines can be defined from 3D lines, 3D polylines, survey figures, or grading feature lines.

- The number of points generated along a breakline can be reduced by specifying a *Weeding* factor or increased by specifying a *Supplementing* factor, similar to weeding and supplementing factors for contour data.

- Curves in standard breaklines are approximated through the use of a mid-ordinate distance, similar to the way curved boundaries are resolved.

- When drawing 3D lines, polylines, or feature lines, you can use Autodesk Civil 3D's transparent commands. For example, using the **Point Object ('PO)** transparent command to select a point as a vertex of a 3D polyline prompts the Autodesk Civil 3D software to assign the point's elevation to the vertex of the polyline.

- Standard breaklines can also be defined from ASCII breakline data files (.FLT file extension).

Proximity Breaklines

Proximity breaklines do not need to have elevations at their vertices. A polyline at elevation 0 could be used as a proximity breakline. When a proximity breakline is defined, the Autodesk Civil 3D software automatically assigns vertex elevations from the nearest TIN data point, such as a nearby point object or contour line vertex.

- The Autodesk Civil 3D software can define proximity breaklines from 2D polylines or grading feature lines.

- The Autodesk Civil 3D software does not support curves in proximity breaklines. Arc segments are treated as if they were straight line segments.

- One of the default options in the surface *Build* area enables the conversion of all proximity (2D) breaklines into standard (3D) breaklines. After conversion, the breakline is listed as a standard breakline and has the same elevations as the point objects that are at each vertex.

Wall Breaklines

- A wall breakline can be used to represent both the top and bottom of a wall, curb, or other sheer face.

- Wall breaklines are defined by 3D lines, 3D polylines, or feature lines. When defining them from linework, the object itself is meant to define either the top or bottom of the wall.

- The other end of the wall (top or bottom) is defined interactively by entering the absolute elevations or height differences from the defining line.

- If a Wall breakline starts as a 2D polyline or feature line, it can contain curve segments.

- The number of points generated along a breakline can be reduced by specifying a *Weeding* factor or increased by specifying a *Supplementing* factor.

Survey Figures as Breaklines

Figures created by surveyors can be used as breaklines if a connection exists between the drawing and the survey database.

How To: Add Survey Figures as Breaklines

1. Open the survey database for editing.
2. In the Toolspace, *Survey* tab, expand the *Survey Data* collection and select **Figures**. The list of figures in the grid view displays at the bottom of the Toolspace.

3. Select the figures, right-click, and select **Create breaklines...**, as shown in Figure 4–30.

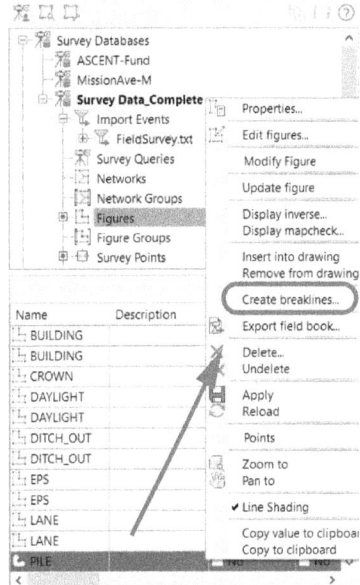

Figure 4–30

4. In the Create Breaklines dialog box, select the surface on which to place the breaklines, and then in the *Breakline* column, select **Yes** on to create the breaklines, as shown in Figure 4–31. Click **OK** to close the dialog box.

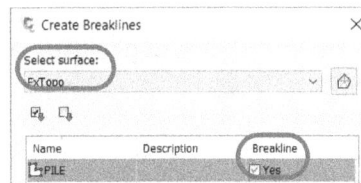

Figure 4–31

Boundaries

Boundaries provide interior or exterior limits to the surface triangulation. Boundaries are typically created from 2D closed polylines. There are four types of boundaries: **Outer**, **Hide**, **Show**, and **Data Clip**. An outer boundary should be one of the last items added to a surface, because adding data outside an existing boundary extends the surface past the boundary.

- An **Outer** boundary hides or excludes data outside its edge.

- A **Hide** boundary hides an interior portion of a surface to delineate features (such as water bodies and building footprints).

- A **Show** boundary displays a portion of a surface within a Hide boundary (e.g., to display an island in a pond).

- A **Data Clip** boundary acts as a filter on all data, including points, DEMs, and breaklines added to the surface after the creation of the Data Clip boundary. If a data clip boundary is used, any data added after it, that falls outside the data clip boundary, is ignored.

A boundary can contain arc segments. To better represent surface elevations around an arc, the Autodesk Civil 3D software uses a mid-ordinate value to calculate where the triangles interact with the boundary. The mid-ordinate value is the distance between the midpoint of the cord and the arc. The smaller the mid-ordinate value, the closer the surface data is to the original arc. An example is shown in Figure 4–32.

Figure 4–32

A boundary can limit a surface to the data within it. When you want to extend the triangulation exactly to a boundary line, select the **Non-destructive breakline** option in the Create Boundary dialog box. A non-destructive breakline fractures triangles at their intersection with the boundary. The resulting triangles preserve the original elevations of the surface at the boundary intersection as close as possible.

Non-destructive breaklines are rarely used in practice.

The example in Figure 4–33 shows the following:

1. The surface with a polyline is used as an outer boundary.
2. The boundary is applied without the **Non-destructive breakline** option. This is typically used when the boundary polyline is approximate and not meant to represent a hard edge. Triangles that lie under the boundary will be removed from the surface, resulting in a jagged edge.
3. The boundary is applied with the **Non-destructive breakline** option. Non-destructive breaklines are often used to create a specific termination limit for the surface (such as at a parcel boundary). Triangles that lie under the boundary will be trimmed back to the boundary, resulting in a smooth edge.

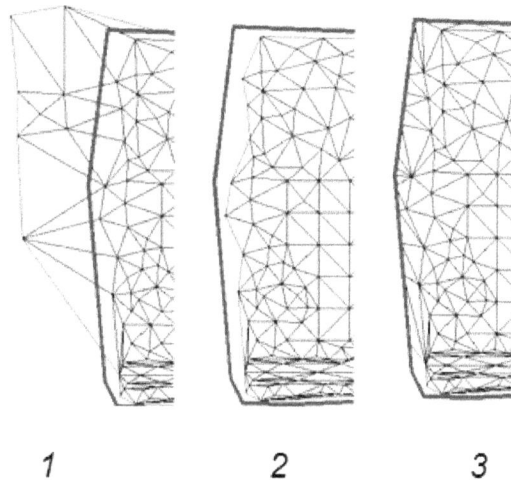

1   2   3

Figure 4–33

Practice 4b

Add Additional Data to an Existing Ground Surface

Practice Objective

- Improve the accuracy of a surface by adding various breaklines, such as standard breaklines, wall breaklines, and breaklines from survey figures.

Task 1 - Add surface breaklines.

TIN lines are generally created using the shortest distance between points. To further define a surface, you might need to supplement it with breaklines of ridges, ditches, walls, etc., that accurately define the surface. These breaklines prevent the software from triangulating directly between points that are bisected by a breakline. The breakline becomes part of the triangulation between the two adjacent points.

1. Open **SUF1-B1-Surface.dwg** from the *C:\Civil 3D Projects\Working\Surface* folder.

The contextual tab displays.

2. Select any part of the **ExTopo** surface in Model Space.

3. In the contextual *Surface* tab>Modify panel, select **Surface Properties** as shown in Figure 4–34. The Surface Properties dialog box opens.

Figure 4–34

4. In the *Information* tab, expand the Surface style drop-down list and select **ASC-Contours and Triangles**, as shown in Figure 4–35. Click **OK** to close the dialog box.

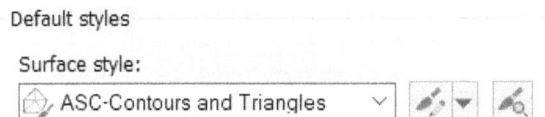

Figure 4–35

Now that the triangulations display, you will examine how adding a feature line impacts the surface.

5. In the *View* tab>Views panel, expand the drop-down list and select **Surf-Breakline**. This zooms into the breakline that is located north of the existing road as shown in Figure 4–36.

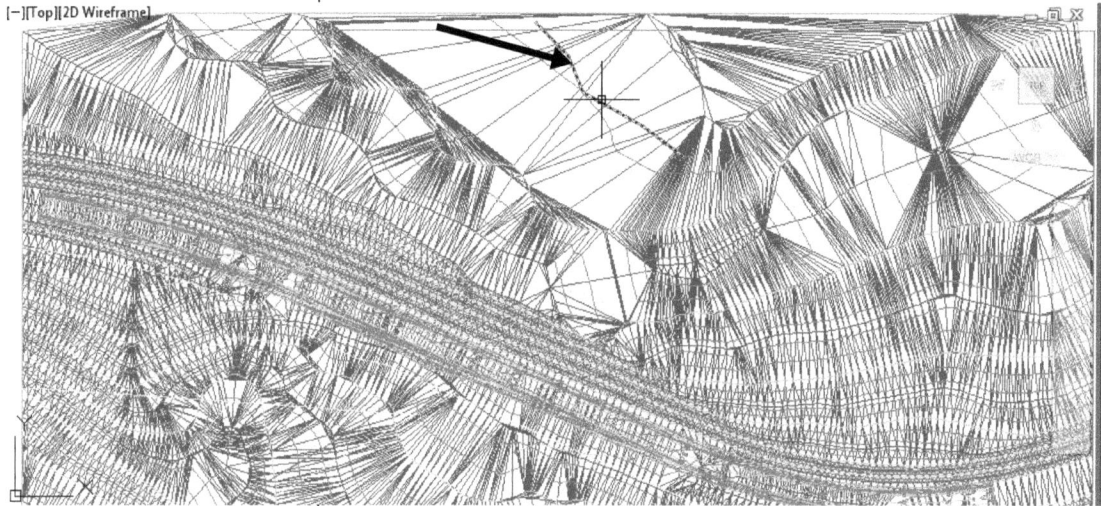

Figure 4–36

The triangulation crosses the breakline.

6. Expand the *Current Drawing* collection in the Toolspace, *Prospector* tab and then expand the *Surfaces>ExTopo> Definition* collections. Select **Breaklines**, right-click, and select **Add**, as shown in Figure 4–37.

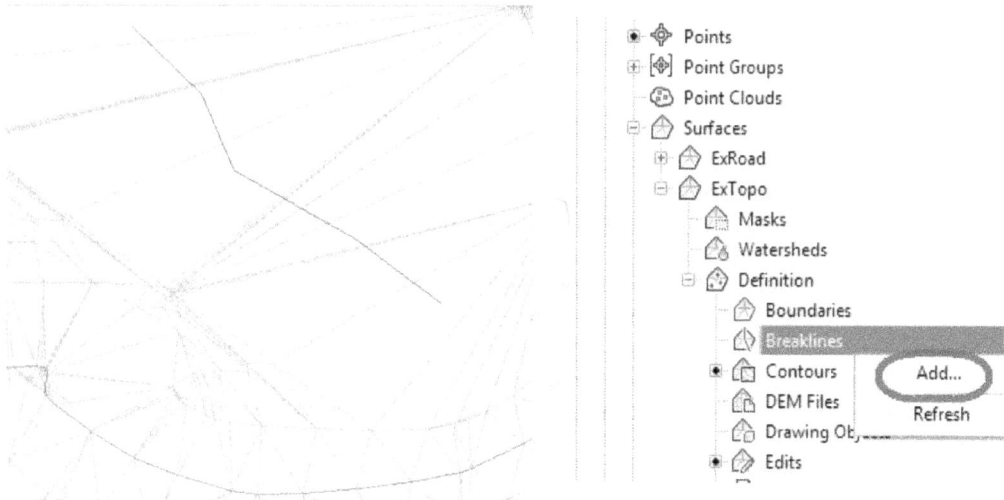

Figure 4–37

7. Type **Ridge** in the *Description* field, as shown in Figure 4–38. Accept all of the defaults and click **OK** to close the dialog box.

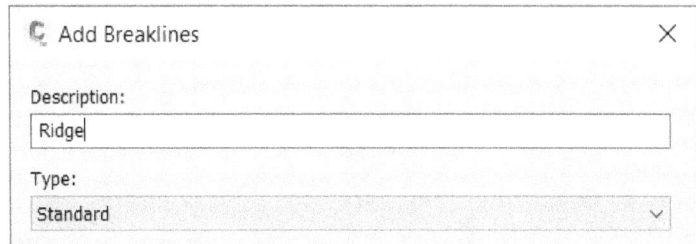

Figure 4–38

8. When prompted to select objects, select the red 3D polyline and press <Enter> to complete the command.

9. The surface should rebuild automatically. Note that the triangulation now takes the breakline into consideration, as shown in Figure 4–39.

*If the **ExTopo** surface is marked as out-of-date*

*, select the **ExTopo** surface, right-click, and select **Rebuild Automatic**.*

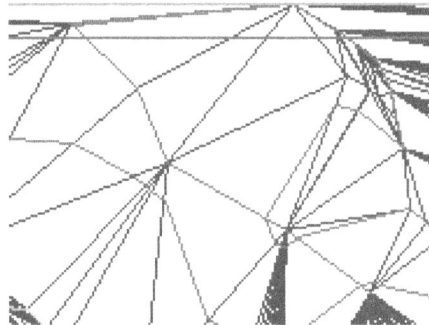

Figure 4–39

10. Save the drawing.

Task 2 - Set up the survey database.

In this practice, you will need to incorporate survey data into the surface. To do so, you must first establish a connection to the survey database. If you have not completed the practices in the Survey section, you will need to open the survey database **Survey Data_Complete** to open the connection.

In the Toolspace,

Survey tab, click 🏕 *in the Home tab>Palettes panel to toggle it on.*

1. If not already done, in the Toolspace, *Survey* tab, right-click on Survey Databases and select **Set working folder**, as shown in Figure 4–40.

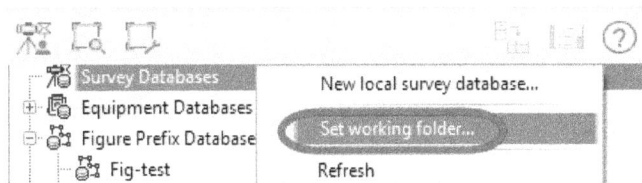

Figure 4–40

2. If need be, select the *Survey Databases* folder in the *C:\Civil 3D Projects\Survey Databases* folder, and click on the *Select Folder* button.

3. Select the survey database **Survey Data_Complete**, right-click, and select **Open for edit**, as shown in Figure 4–41. Do not double-click, this would open the survey database read-only.

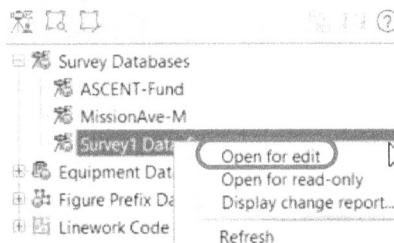

Figure 4–41

4. In the Toolspace, *Survey* tab, expand the *Survey Data_Complete* collection and select **Figures**. The list of figures in the grid view displays at the bottom of the Toolspace.

5. Select the figure **Pile**, right-click, and select **Create breaklines...**, as shown in Figure 4–42.

Figure 4–42

6. In the Create Breaklines dialog box, select **ExTopo** for the surface, and select the **Yes** option in the *Breakline* column to create breaklines, as shown in Figure 4–43. Click **OK** to close the dialog box.

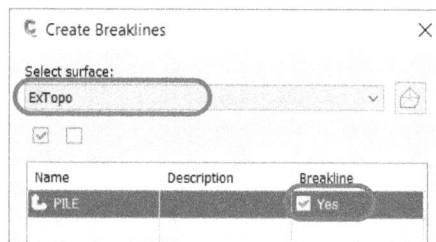

Figure 4–43

7. The Autodesk Civil 3D software will zoom in to the location of the breakline, and open the Add Breaklines dialog box. Type **Rock pile from site survey** in the *Description* field, and ensure that **Standard** is selected in the Type drop-down list, as shown in Figure 4–44. Click **OK** to close the dialog box.

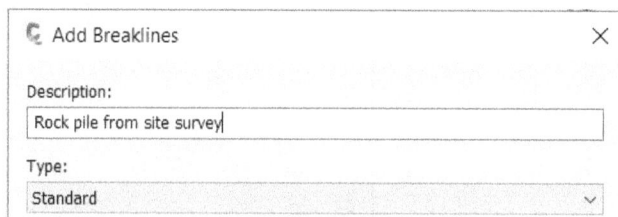

Figure 4–44

8. The Event Viewer vista in the Panorama opens. You have received a number of errors with crossing breaklines. You can zoom to the error by selecting **Zoom to** in the far right column. The reason for this error is that when building surfaces from contour-type objects, each of these objects becomes a breakline. By default, Civil 3D does not allow crossing breaklines. For now you need to clear these errors from the event log file.

9. Click **Action** in the Panorama and select **Clear All Events**, as shown in Figure 4–45.

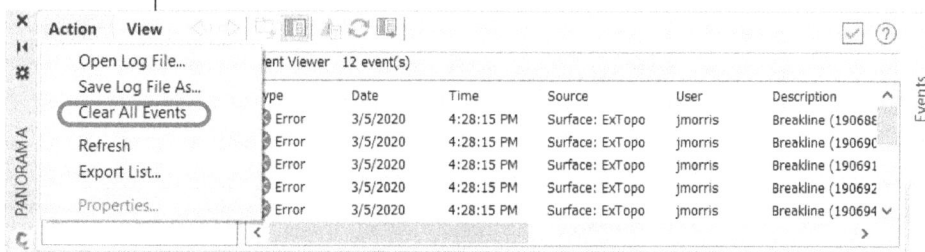

Figure 4–45

10. Close the Panorama by clicking ☑ (checkmark) in the dialog box.

11. In Model Space, select the **ExTopo** surface. The *Tin Surface: ExTopo* contextual tab displays. In the Modify panel, select **Surface Properties** as shown in Figure 4–46.

Figure 4–46

In practice, you should use this option with caution. Unless you use contours to build a surface, this option can produce unexpected results.

12. The Surface Properties - ExTopo dialog box opens. In the *Definition* tab, expand the *Build* collection and set the value of *Allow crossing breaklines* to **Yes**. Set the value for the *Elevation to use* field to **Use last breakline elevation at intersection**, as shown in Figure 4–47. When you have finished, click **OK**.

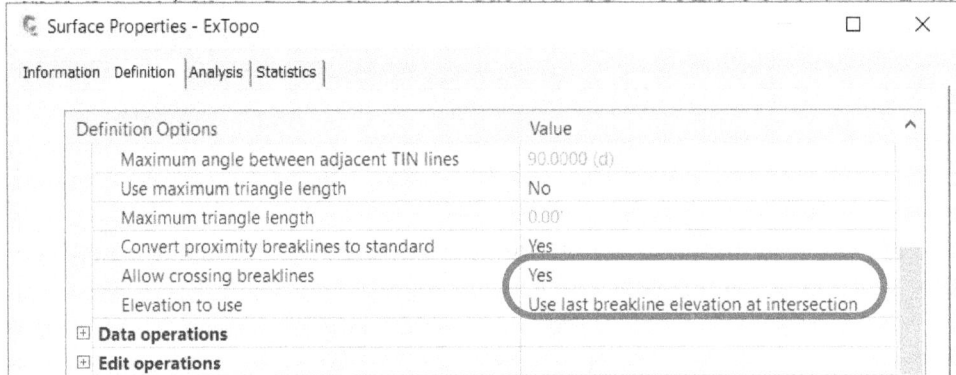

Figure 4–47

13. When prompted to *Rebuild the surface* or *Mark as out of Date*, select **Rebuild the surface**. When you review the surface contours, note that the surface has used the figure as a breakline.

14. Save the drawing.

Task 3 - Add a wall breakline.

In the task, you will add a wall breakline to the surface from figures that were created when the field books were imported.

1. Open the survey database **Survey Data_Complete**, if it is not already open.

2. In the Toolspace, *Survey* tab, expand the *Survey Data* collection and select **Figures**. Note the list of figures in the grid view at the bottom of the Toolspace.

3. Select the **Wall** figure, right-click, and select **Create breaklines**.

4. In the Create Breaklines dialog box, select the **ExTopo** surface and select the **Yes** option in the *Breakline* column to create breaklines. Click **OK** to close the dialog box.

5. The Autodesk Civil 3D software zooms in to the location of the breakline, and opens the Add Breaklines dialog box. Type **Rock Wall from site survey** in the *Description* field, and ensure that **Wall** is selected in the Type drop-down list, as shown in Figure 4–48. Click **OK** to close the dialog box.

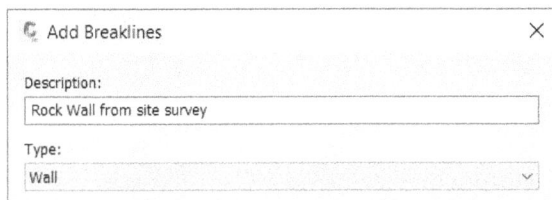

Figure 4–48

6. At the prompt to pick the offset side, select a point to the south of the wall break line, as shown in Figure 4–49.

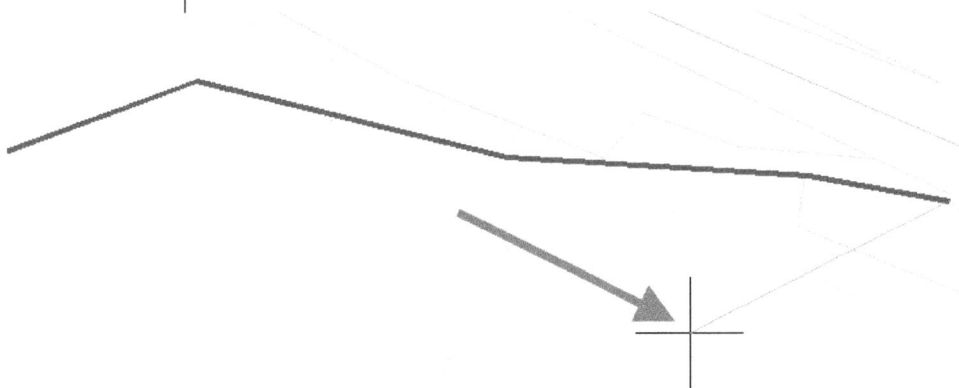

Figure 4–49

7. When prompted to select the option for the wall height, select the default **All** option because the wall has a constant height.

The wall has a constant height of 1.5 feet from the base.

8. When prompted for the elevation difference or elevation, type **1.5** and press <Enter>.

9. Save the drawing.

4.5 Surface Editing

There are three ways of adjusting surfaces graphically: using lines, points, and area edit tools (such as **Minimize Flat Areas** and **Smooth Surface**). All of these tools are available by right-clicking on the *Edits* heading in a surface's *Definition* area (Toolspace, *Prospector* tab), as shown in Figure 4–50. These editing tools are also available through the contextual tab of the surface.

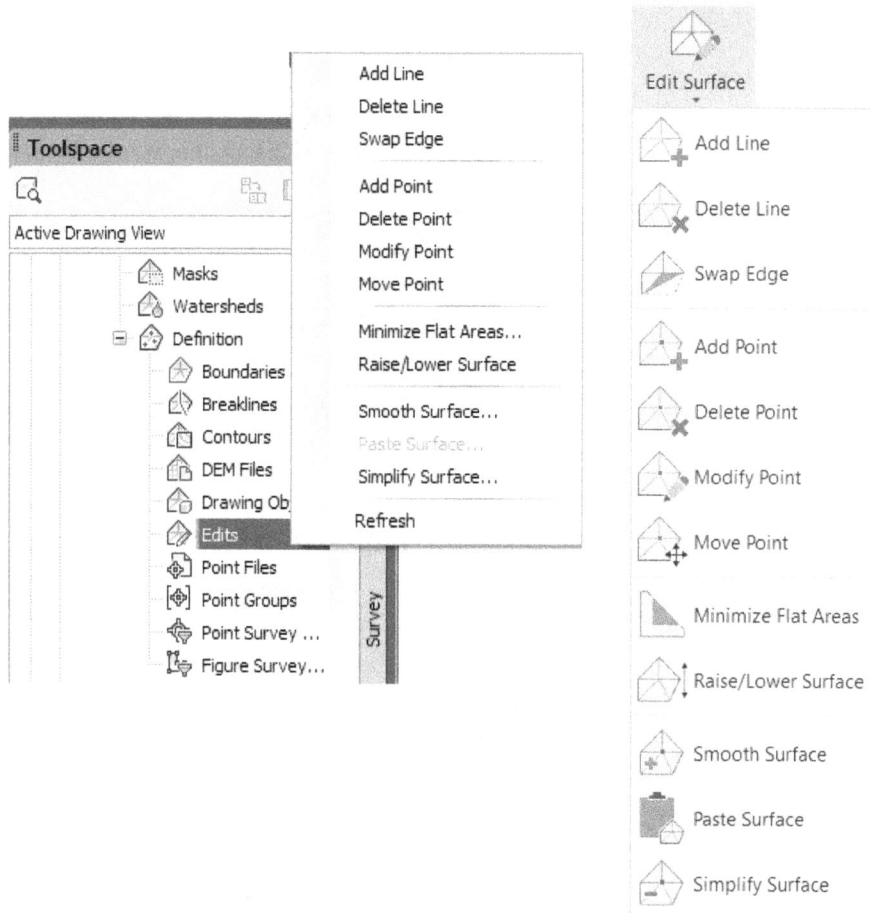

Figure 4–50

- The Autodesk Civil 3D software considers each graphical surface edit to be additional data that can be removed later.

- Most surface edits apply immediately. If the drawing item modifier icon displays (as shown in Figure 4–51), then an edit has rendered the surface out of date. When this happens, a surface should be rebuilt by right-clicking on the surface name in the Toolspace, *Prospector* tab and selecting **Rebuild**.

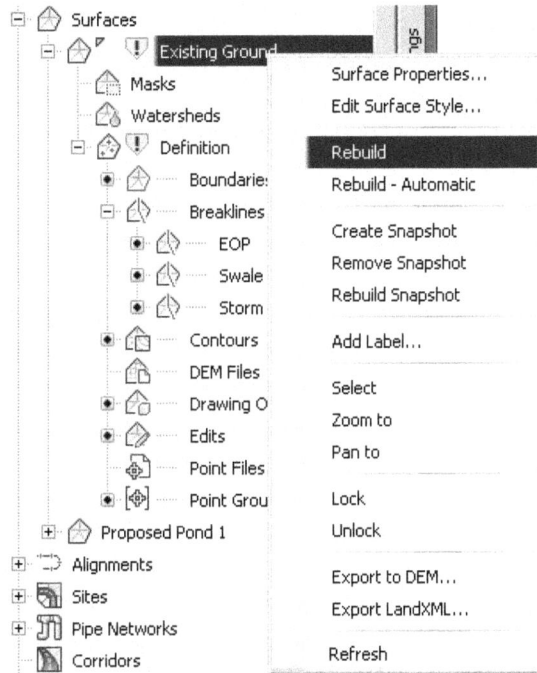

Figure 4–51

- To have a surface automatically rebuild as required, right-click on the surface name in the Toolspace, *Prospector* tab and select **Rebuild-Automatic**. However, toggling this option on increases the use of computer resources and graphics capabilities.

- To delete an edit from a surface permanently, remove it from the *Edits* list in Toolspace, *Prospector's* preview area or from the *Operations Type* list in the *Definition* tab in the Surface Properties dialog box.

Line Edits

The line editing commands include **Add Line**, **Delete Line**, and **Swap Edge**. The **Add Line** and **Delete Line** commands add or remove triangle lines. The **Delete Line** command is often only applied around the outside edge of a surface to remove unwanted edge triangulation. Deleting lines in the interior of a surface causes both of the triangles next to the removed line to be deleted, leaving a hole in the surface that needs to be repaired by adding another line.

If you are considering deleting a line only to replace it with the opposite diagonal, such as the central line shown in Figure 4–52, using the **Swap Edge** command instead might be more efficient.

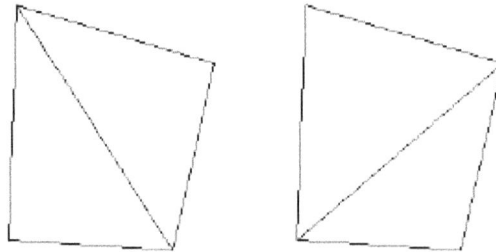

Figure 4–52

Adding an interior line that crosses many existing triangles swaps them where possible to adhere to the geometry represented by the added line. This method can be a good way of swapping multiple edges at the same time.

Point Edits

The Point editing commands can **Add**, **Delete**, **Modify**, or **Move** surface points. They do not affect point objects in the drawing, but rather the surface points created from them. Surface points can be adjusted or deleted as required.

When an Autodesk Civil 3D point object is adjusted (e.g., moved), the surface containing that point data might not be identified as being out of date nor update automatically. In this situation, you should rebuild the surface.

Simplify Surface

As the collection methods of surface data continue to evolve, yielding significantly larger data sets, the drawing file size increases in proportion to the surface data contained in the drawing. The Autodesk Civil 3D software has a limit of 2.5 million vertices for a surface. Once it exceeds this limit, the software prompts you to store surface data to an external file with an .mms extension. The resulting external surface files can be quite large. To avoid this, you can simplify your surface using the Simplify Surface wizard. Extra points can be removed from a surface without compromising its accuracy. Points that you might want to remove include points that are in an external point file or database, or redundant points in areas of high data concentration where the value of this extra information is minimal. There are two simplification methods available.

- **Edge Contraction:** This method simplifies the surface by using existing triangle edges. It contracts triangle edges to single points by removing one point. The location of the point to which an edge is contracted is selected so that the change to the surface is minimal.

- **Point Removal:** This method simplifies the surface by removing existing surface points. More points are removed from denser areas of the surface.

When you simplify a surface, you specify which regions of the surface the operation should address. The region options include using the existing surface border, or specifying a window or polygon. The **Pick in Drawing** icon enables you to select the region from the drawing. If a closed line exists in the drawing that you want to use as the region boundary, you can select the **Select objects** option and then use the **Pick in Drawing** icon to select the boundary. Curves in the boundary are approximated by line segments. The line segment generation is governed by a *Mid Ordinate Distance* value that you determine.

Once you have selected the region, the dialog box displays the *Total Points Selected In Region* value. You can refine the surface reduction options by setting a percentage of points to remove, the maximum change in elevation, or the maximum edge contraction error.

Smooth Contours

Although not a true surface edit, Autodesk Civil 3D surface contours can be smoothed to reduce their jagged appearance using the Surface Object Style settings. There are two approaches to this: the *Add Vertices* method and the *Spline Curve* method. The *Add Vertices* method enables you to select a relative smoothness from the slider bar at the bottom of the Surface Style dialog box, as shown in Figure 4–53.

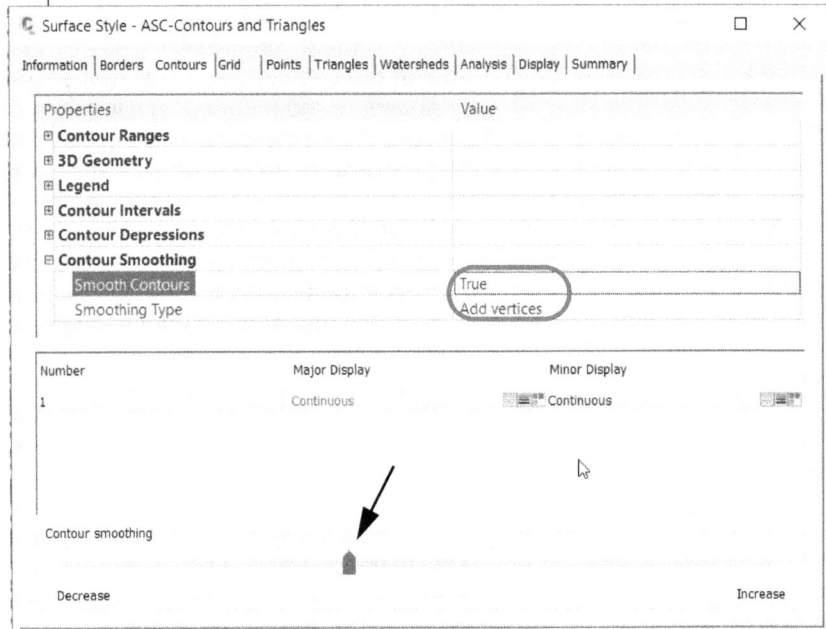

Figure 4–53

The *Spline Curve* method generates very smooth contours, but the contours are more liberally interpolated and might overlap where surface points are close together. This approach is best applied to surfaces with relatively few data points or in areas of low relief, as shown in Figure 4–54.

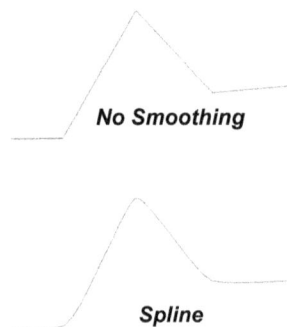

No Smoothing

Spline

Figure 4–54

Smooth Surface

The Smooth Surface edit introduces new, interpolated elevations between surface data. It is used to create a more realistic-looking terrain model, though not necessarily a more accurate one. Generally, surface smoothing works best with point-based surface data.

The Autodesk Civil 3D software has two smoothing methods: *Natural Neighbor* and *Kriging*.

- *Natural Neighbor* interpolates a grid of additional data points that produce a smoother overall terrain model.

- *Kriging* reads surface trends to add additional data in sparse areas.

Surface smoothing is applied by right-clicking on the *Edits* collection under a surface's *Definition* and selecting **Smooth Surface**. The Smooth Surface dialog box and example of surface smoothing are shown in Figure 4–55.

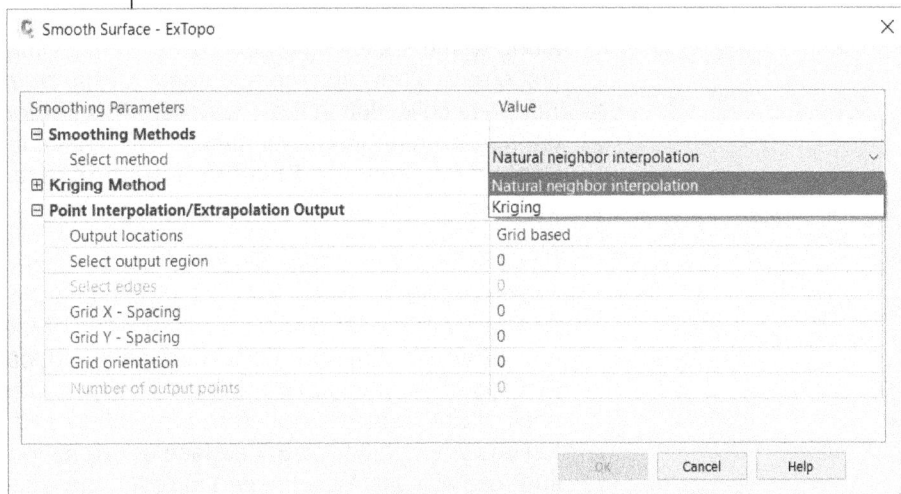

Figure 4–55

Copy Surface

The Autodesk Civil 3D software does not have a copy surface command, but surface objects can be copied using the AutoCAD **Copy** command (**Modify>Copy**). When copying surface objects, select the same base and then a second point to ensure that the surface is not moved during the copy. Another option is not to specify a base point, but simply give it a Displacement distance of 0,0,0, which means there is no displacement.

After a copy, a duplicate surface is created and displays in the Toolspace, *Prospector* tab. The copy has the same name as the original followed with a number in parenthesis, such as (1). These copied surfaces can be renamed as required. Surface copies are independent of each other and can be edited independently.

Surface Paste

The **Surface Paste** command enables the Autodesk Civil 3D software to combine multiple surfaces into a single surface. You might want to paste into a copy of a surface if you want to keep the original unmodified. For example, a finished condition surface is needed that includes a proposed surface (*Proposed*) along with the existing ground (EG). In this situation, you would first create a new surface and name it **Finished Ground**. In the *Surfaces* collection in the Toolspace, *Prospector* tab, right-click on the Finished Ground surface's *Edit* collection and select **Paste** to merge in the **Existing ground (EG)** and **Proposed** surfaces.

Once the command has executed, the surface's **EG** and **Proposed** surfaces are left unchanged, and the **Finished Ground** surface represents a combination of the two. If you did not create the **Finished Ground** surface, but pasted the **Proposed** surface into the **EG** surface, you would not have the original **EG** surface for reference in profiles and other places (unless you copied the EG surface as explained above). If surfaces are pasted in the wrong order, the order can be rearranged using the *Definition* tab in the Surface Properties dialog box.

Surfaces remain dynamically linked after pasting. Therefore, if the **Proposed** surface changes, the **Finished Ground** surface updates to display the change, when the **Finished Ground** surface is set to Rebuild Automatically.

Raise/Lower Surface

The **Raise/Lower Surface** command adds or subtracts a specified elevation value. This adjustment is applied to the entire surface. It is useful for modeling soil removal and changing a surface's datum elevation.

Adjusting Surfaces Through Surface Properties

In addition to the graphical edit methods, you can adjust surfaces by changing their surface properties. Surface property adjustments include setting a *Maximum triangle length* or *Exclude elevations* greater or less than certain values. You can also enable or disable the effects of certain surface data (such as breaklines and boundaries) by disabling them in the dialog box.

If dependent objects, such as polylines (used for contour definitions), breaklines, or any AutoCAD objects (used to define the surface), are deleted from the drawing, the **Copy deleted dependent objects** option will copy the definition of those objects into the surface object.

Without this option, the surface will lose the definition those objects had provided.

To locate these options (as shown in Figure 4–56), right-click on a surface in the Toolspace, *Prospector* tab and select **Surface Properties**.

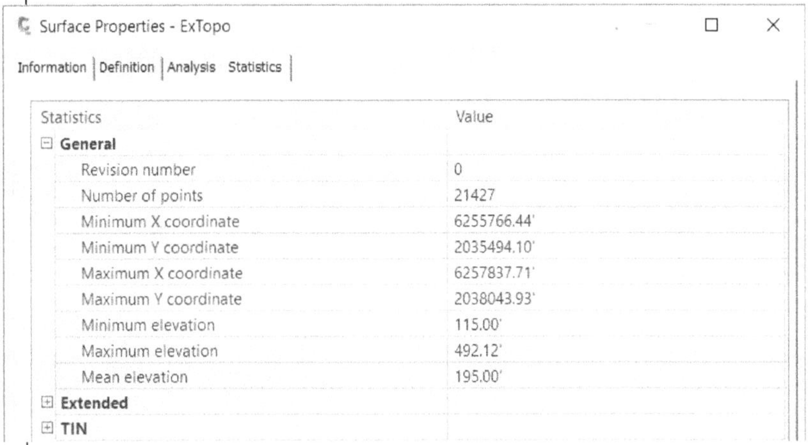

Statistics	Value
General	
Revision number	0
Number of points	21427
Minimum X coordinate	6255766.44'
Minimum Y coordinate	2035494.10'
Maximum X coordinate	6257837.71'
Maximum Y coordinate	2038043.93'
Minimum elevation	115.00'
Maximum elevation	492.12'
Mean elevation	195.00'
Extended	
TIN	

Surface Properties - ExTopo — Information | Definition | Analysis | Statistics

Figure 4–56

Copy Deleted Dependent Objects

If dependent objects, such as polylines (used for contour definitions), breaklines, or any AutoCAD objects (used to define the surface), are deleted from the drawing, this will copy the definition of those objects into the surface object. The surface will remain unaffected.

However, if such dependent objects are removed from the drawing without this option enabled, the surface will update to reflect the removal of these objects it was dependent on.

4.6 Surface Analysis Tools

Viewing a Surface in 3D

AutoCAD's default view, the overhead or plan view, is not the only way to view a surface. The AutoCAD **3D Orbit** command and the Autodesk Civil 3D **Object Viewer** tilt the coordinate space to display a 3D surface model. How the surface displays is dependent on the assigned style. You can view a surface in 3D using the Object Viewer or directly in the drawing window using the **3D Orbit** command. Both have similar navigation controls, but the Object Viewer enables you to review only your surface in 3D without changing your current view.

Both methods can display a wireframe (3D Wireframe and 3D Hidden), conceptual, or realistic view. By default, a Conceptual display is a cartoon-like rendering without edge lines, while a Realistic display has material styles with edge lines. Both viewing methods use the AutoCAD ViewCube, which uses labels and a compass to indicate the direction from which you are viewing a model.

The Object Viewer method is shown in Figure 4–57.

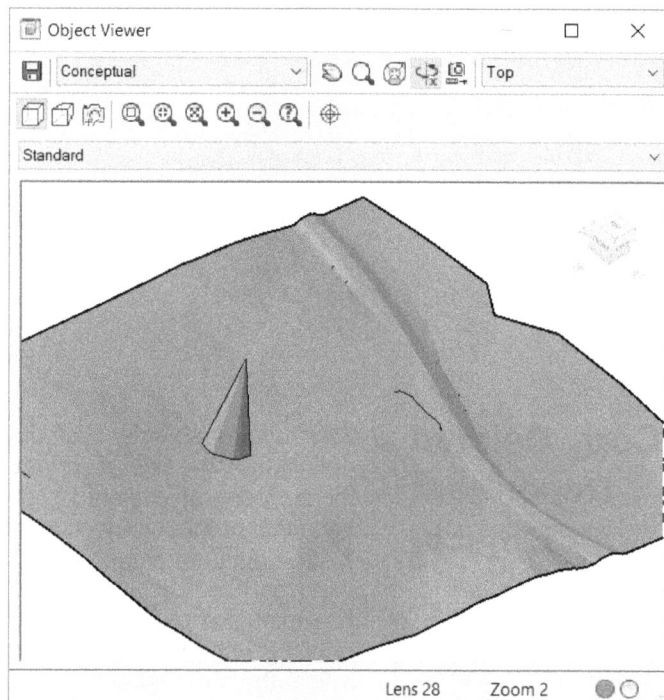

Figure 4–57

Quick Profile

Understanding the affect of breaklines and other data on a surface is critical to generating an accurate surface. The **Analyze>Ground Data>Quick Profile** command enables you to produce an instant surface profile with minimal effort. It is also accessible through the **Home>Profile** drop-down menu.

A *Quick Profile* is a temporary object, which disappears from the drawing when you save or exit. If you need a more permanent graphic, you should create an alignment and profile.

Quick Profiles can be created along lines, arcs, polylines, lot lines, feature lines, or survey figures, or by selecting points. In addition to the command being located in the *Analyze* tab, you can select one of the previously mentioned objects, right-click, and select **Quick Profile**. Two examples of the Quick Profile are shown in Figure 4–58.

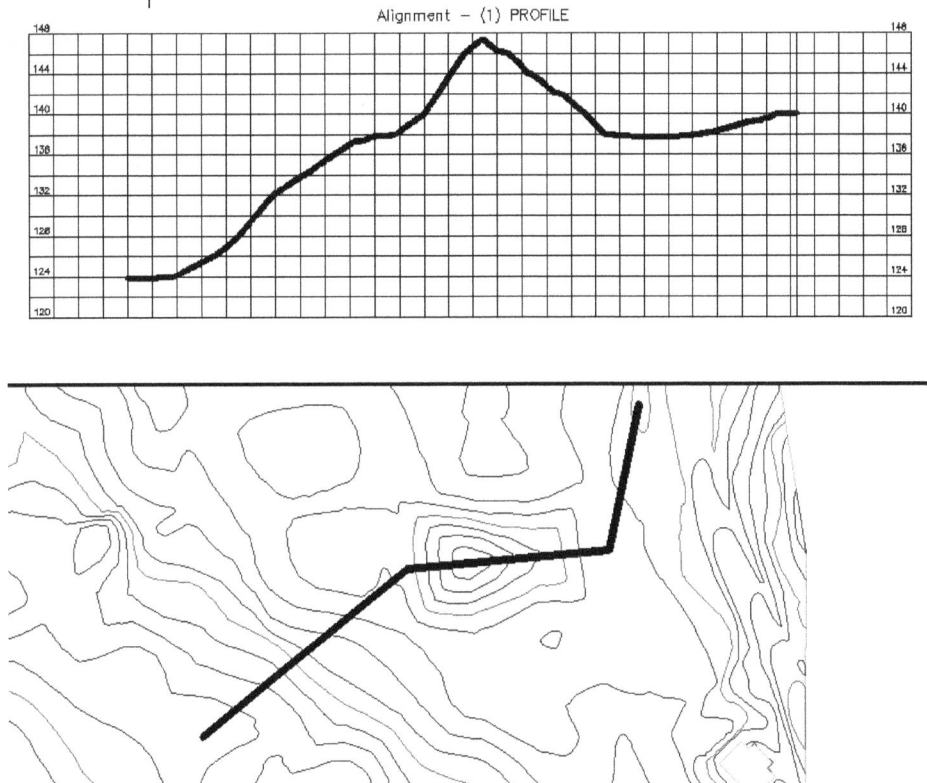

Figure 4–58

Practice 4c

Surface Edits

Practice Objective

- Edit a surface using definition options in the surface properties and commands found in the Toolspace.

In this practice, you will refine a previously created surface. The **ExTopo** surface has some triangulations that are not valid. You will eliminate these TIN lines using three methods: you will set options for the surface properties, delete TIN lines (triangle edges), and add a boundary to the surface. Each of these methods has advantages and disadvantages and should be used appropriately.

Task 1 - Copy deleted dependent objects.

1. Open **SUF1-C1-Surface.dwg** from the *C:\Civil 3D Projects\Working\Surface* folder.

*Ensure that the **ExTopo** surface is using the **Contours and Triangles** surface style.*

2. In Model Space, select the **ExTopo** surface. The *Tin Surface ExTopo* contextual tab will display. In the *Modify* panel, select **Surface Properties**, as shown in Figure 4–59.

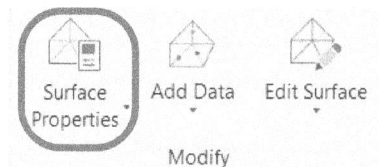

Figure 4–59

3. The Surface Properties dialog box opens. Select the *Definition* tab and expand the **Build** options in the *Definition Options* area.

4. Set the *Copy deleted dependent objects* value to **Yes**, as shown in Figure 4–60. Click **OK** to close the dialog box and accept the changes.

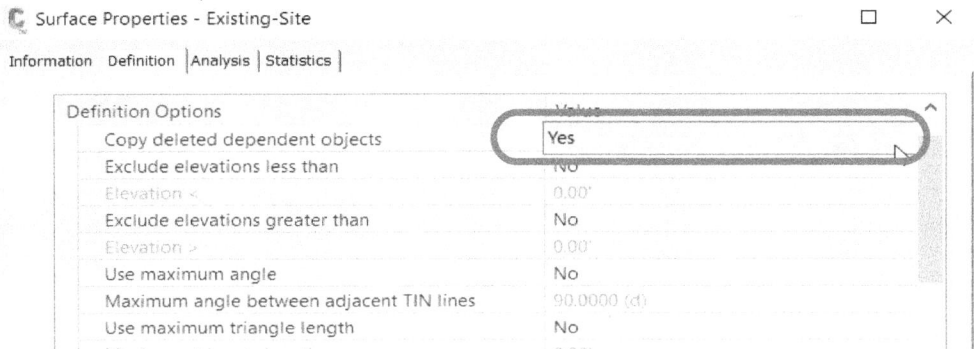

Figure 4–60

5. When prompted to *Rebuild the surface* or *Mark the surface as out-of-date*, select **Rebuild the surface**.

6. Save the drawing.

Task 2 - Delete lines.

Some triangles, along the eastern edge of the surface, need to be removed.

If you are not still in the drawing view from the previous task, select the View tab>Views panel, and select the preset view Surface-Edit.

1. Figure 4–61 shows the lines that you will be deleting.

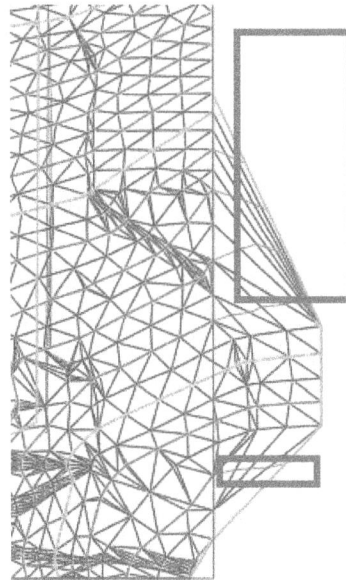

Figure 4–61

2. In Model Space, select the **ExTopo** surface. The *Tin Surface ExTopo* contextual tab will display. In the *Modify* panel, expand the ⬨ (Edit Surface) drop-down list, and select **Delete Line**, as shown in Figure 4–62.

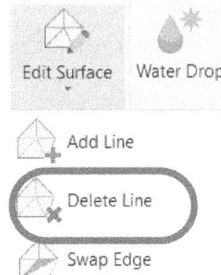

Figure 4–62

3. Select each of the required TIN lines in Model Space, as shown in Figure 4–63. When you have finished, press <Enter> to end the selection and press <Enter> to end the command.

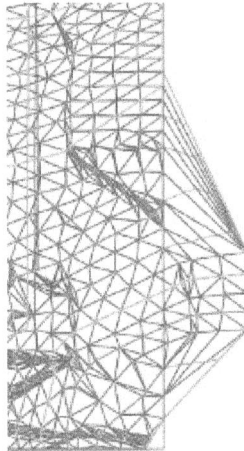

Before trimming   *After trimming*

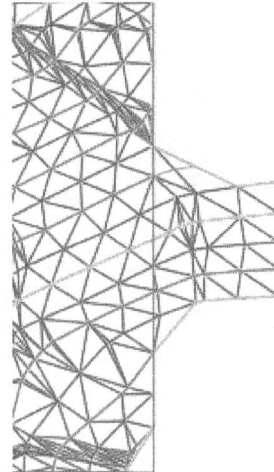

Figure 4–63

4. Save the drawing.

Task 3 - Add a boundary.

The **Delete Line** command can be effective, but might not efficiently clean up the edges of large surfaces. A surface boundary is useful if you have a well-defined boundary.

1. If necessary, select the *View* tab>Views panel and select the preset view **Surface-Edit**.

2. In Model Space, select the **ExTopo** surface. The *Tin Surface ExTopo* contextual tab will display. In the *Modify* panel, click

   (Add Data), expand the drop-down list and select **Boundaries**, as shown in Figure 4–64.

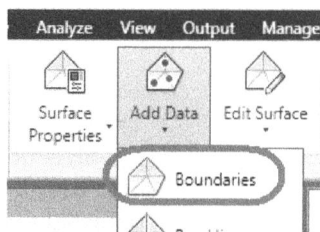

Figure 4–64

3. The Add Boundaries dialog box opens, as shown in Figure 4–65. Type **Limits** in the *Name* field, and select **Outer** in the Type drop-down list. Select the **Non-destructive breakline** option, because you do want to trim to this polyline shape. Otherwise, the dialog box options will erase all of the triangle lines that cross or are beyond the boundary. Click **OK** to accept the changes and close the dialog box.

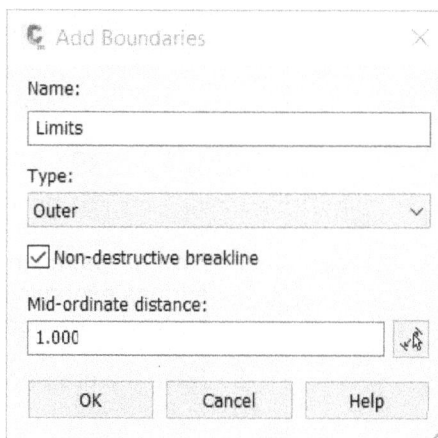

Figure 4–65

You might have to regen the screen to display the boundary.

4. When prompted to select an object, select the red polyline that represents the boundary, as shown in Figure 4–66.

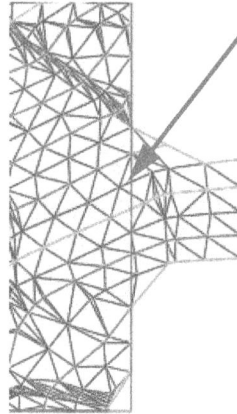

Figure 4–66

5. Examine how this boundary affected the surface. The boundary only trimmed the surface to the picked rectangle, but it did not extend the surface to the rectangle. This boundary is a dynamic part of the **ExTopo** surface.

6. Select the boundary line and move the grips. Note in the Prospector that the **ExTopo** surface is marked as being *Out of Date.* If necessary, right-click on the **ExTopo** surface and set it to *Rebuild - Automatic*, as shown in Figure 4–67.

Figure 4–67

7. Now as you change the polyline defining the boundary, the surface expands or contracts to match the change in the boundary. Restore the polyline to its original position.

8. Save the drawing.

Task 4 - Set the elevation range.

In reviewing the drawing, you need to address an error in the site. The original topographical contour file contains an invalid piece of data that has transferred to the surface.

1. Continue working with the drawing from the previous task or open **SUF1-C2-Surface.dwg**.

2. Select the preset view **Surf Elev Edit**.

3. In Model Space, as shown on the left in Figure 4–68, select the **ExTopo** surface, right-click, and select **Object Viewer**.

4. In the Object Viewer, click and drag the view, as shown on the right in Figure 4–68, to rotate the 3D view to identify the issue.

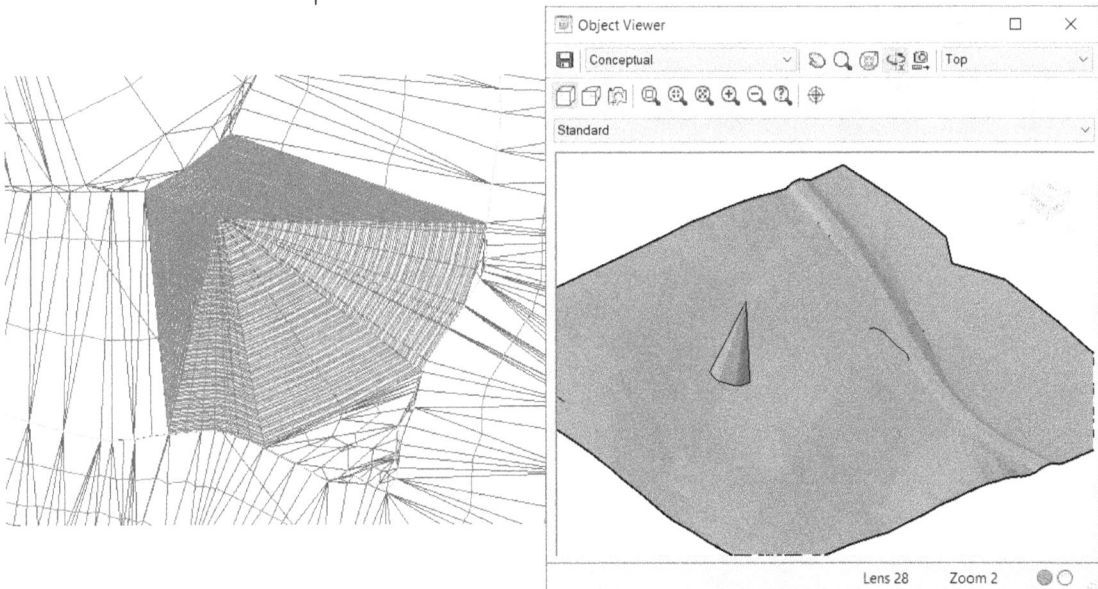

Figure 4–68

5. Close the Object Viewer by selecting **X** in the top right corner of the dialog box.

6. In Model Space, select the **ExTopo** surface. The *Tin Surface ExTopo* contextual tab will display. In the Modify panel, select **Surface Properties**. The Surface Properties dialog box opens.

7. Select the *Statistics* tab and expand the value list in the *General* area.

8. When you review the site conditions, note that the site ranges from an elevation of roughly 100' to 330'. However, the statistics indicate that the surface ranges from an elevation of 115' to 492.12', as shown in Figure 4–69.

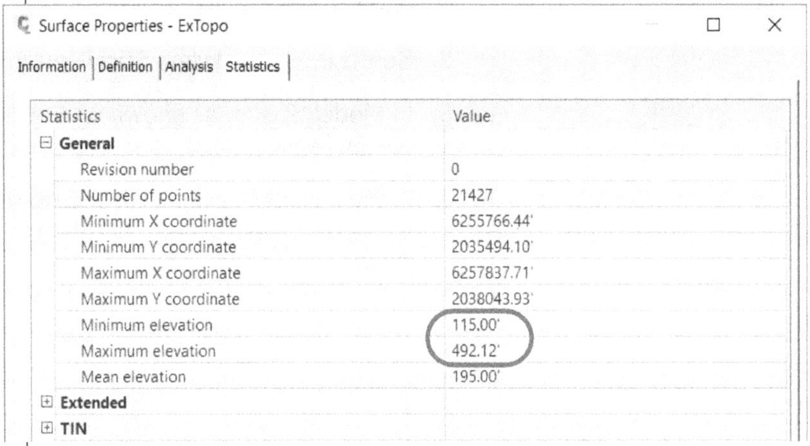

Figure 4–69

9. To correct the surface, select the *Definition* tab. Expand *Build* properties and set the *Exclude elevation less than* value to **Yes**. Set the *Elevation* < value to **100'**, the *Exclude elevation greater than* value to **Yes**, and the *Elevation* > value to **330'**, as shown in Figure 4–70.

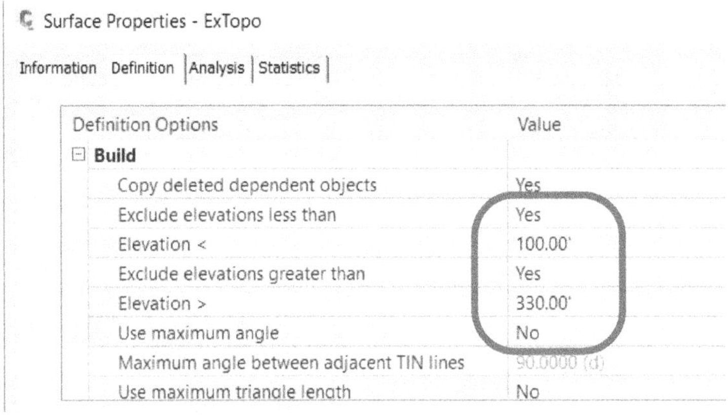

Figure 4–70

10. Click **OK** to accept the changes and close the dialog box.

All points that are above an elevation of 330' are removed and the error is fixed.

11. When prompted to *Rebuild the surface* or *Mark the surface as out-of-date*, select **Rebuild the Surface**.

12. Save the drawing.

Task 5 - Review edits in the Toolspace, *Prospector* tab and in the Surface Properties dialog box.

The history of all of the changes made to a surface is saved in the drawing. You can apply and remove these changes selectively to the surface.

1. If required, select the preset view **Surface-Edit**.

2. In the Toolspace, *Prospector* tab, expand the *Surfaces* collection and select the **ExTopo** surface. Right-click and select **Surface Properties**. In the Surface Properties dialog box, clear the **Add boundary** *Operation Type* (as shown in Figure 4–71), and click **Apply**.

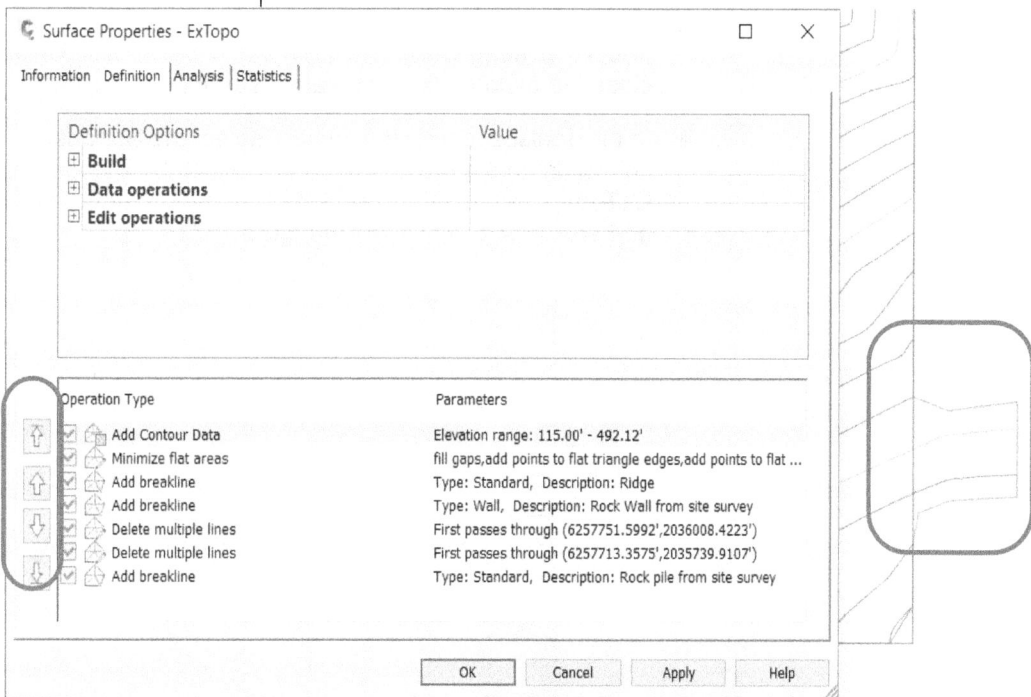

Figure 4–71

3. When prompted, select **Rebuild the Surface** in the Warning dialog box that opens. The boundary is ignored.

The boundary is once again used in the surface definition.

4. Re-select the **Add boundary** *Operation Type* and click **Apply**. When prompted, select **Rebuild the Surface** in the Warning dialog box that opens.

5. Save the drawing.

Task 6 - Create a composite surface.

In the preceding tasks, you created a surface from available contour data. However, the data around the existing road, **Mission Avenue** (the road running east to west at the top of the site), was inaccurate, so you surveyed the road and created a surface. You need to create a composite surface that represents the site condition combined with the road.

1. Select the preset view **Survey Main**.

2. In the Toolspace, *Prospector* tab, right-click on the *Surfaces* collection and select **Create Surface**.

3. Select **TIN surface** for the surface *Type*. Type **Existing-Site** for the surface name and **Composite surface of ExTopo and ExRoad** for the *Description*. Select **ASC-Contours 2' and 10' (Background)** for the surface *Style*. Click **OK** to close the dialog box and create a surface.

4. In the Toolspace, *Prospector* tab, select the *Surfaces* collection. In the preview list area, select the **ExRoad** and **ExTopo** surfaces. Right-click on the *Style* column heading and select **Edit**, as shown in Figure 4–72.

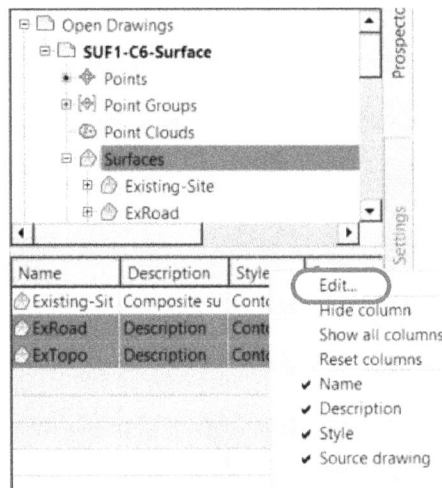

Figure 4–72

5. Set the surface style to **_No Display** and click **OK** to accept the changes and close the dialog box.

6. In the Toolspace, *Prospector* tab, expand the *Surfaces> Existing-Site>Definition* collections for that surface and select **Edits**. Right-click and select **Paste Surface...**, as shown in Figure 4–73.

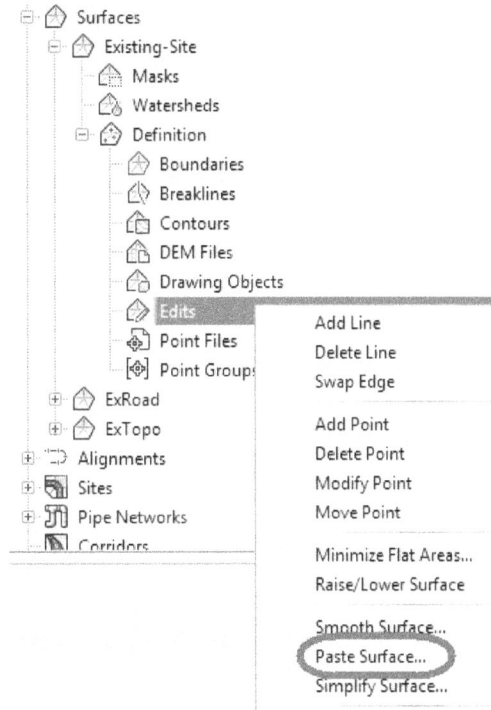

Figure 4–73

To select both surfaces, hold <Ctrl> when selecting the second surface.

7. In the Select Surface to Paste dialog box, select the **Ex Topo** and **Ex Road** surfaces, as shown in Figure 4–74. Once selected, click **OK** to close the dialog box.

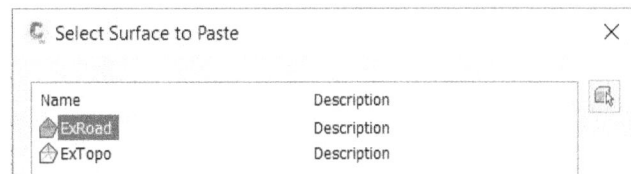

Figure 4–74

Note that the **ExRoad** surface was pasted first, followed by the **ExTopo** surface. In the area of overlap along the road, the **ExTopo** surface data will take precedence. This is not the required result.

8. In Model Space, select the **Existing-Site** surface from the surfaces listed in the *Surfaces* collection in the Toolspace, *Prospector* tab. The contextual tab for the surface object will display. Select **Surface Properties** in the ribbon panel. The Surface Properties - Existing Site dialog box opens. In the *Definition* tab, note the order of the paste operations, as shown in Figure 4–75.

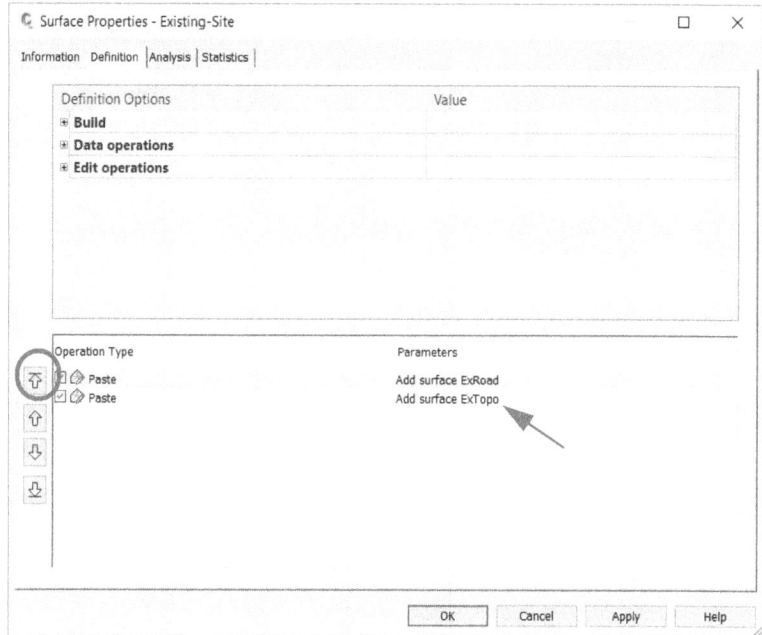

Figure 4–75

9. Select the **Paste** operation with the value **Add surface ExTopo** and move it to the top of the list by clicking ⬆.

10. Click **Apply**. When prompted to *Rebuild the surface* or *Mark the surface as out-of-date*, select **Rebuild the Surface**.

11. Click **OK** to exit the dialog box.

    As a consequence of the Autodesk Civil 3D software's dynamic abilities, any changes to either the **ExTopo** or **ExRoad** surface will be reflected in the **Existing-Site** surface.

12. Save the drawing.

4.7 Surface Labels

Surface labels can be used to label contour elevations, slope values, spot elevations, and watershed delineations. Label values update when the surface changes.

To create surface labels, in the *Annotate* tab>Labels & Tables panel, expand Add Labels and select **Surface** to access the surface label flyout menu, as shown in Figure 4–76.

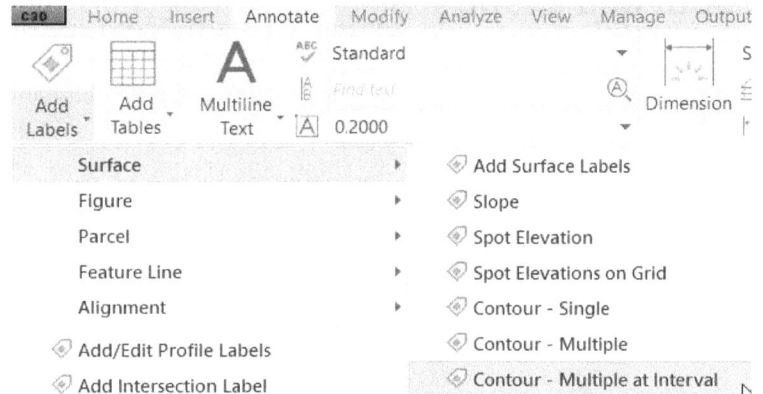

Figure 4–76

You can also click (Add Labels) to open the Add Labels dialog box, as shown in Figure 4–77. This dialog box enables you to select the feature and label type while being able to control the label style on the fly.

Figure 4–77

Contour Labels

Contour labels can be created individually, as multiples along a linear path, or as multiples along a linear path with repeated labels at a set interval. Multiple contours are aligned along an object called a *Contour Label Line*, which can be repositioned as needed, and in turn updates the position of its labels. These label lines have a selectable property that can make them visible only when an attached label is selected. If they are left visible, they should be placed on a non-plotting layer.

Spot and Slope Labels

Spot elevation and slope labels can be created as needed to annotate a surface. These are dynamic surface labels and not point objects, although they might look similar to points. Slopes can be measured at a single point or interpolated between two points.

4.8 Surface Volume Calculations

You can generate volume calculations in the Autodesk Civil 3D software in many ways. Surface-to-surface calculations are often used to compare an existing ground surface to a proposed surface to determine cut and fill quantities. In the Autodesk Civil 3D software, quantities can be adjusted by an expansion (cut) or a compaction (fill) factor. Surfaces representing different soil strata can be compared to each other to determine the volume between the soil layers. There are multiple ways of comparing surfaces to each other in the Autodesk Civil 3D software.

Volumes Dashboard

In the *Analyze* tab>Volumes and Materials panel, click

 (Volumes Dashboard).

The Volumes Dashboard creates a volume surface based on a graphical subtraction of one surface from the other, as shown in Figure 4–78.

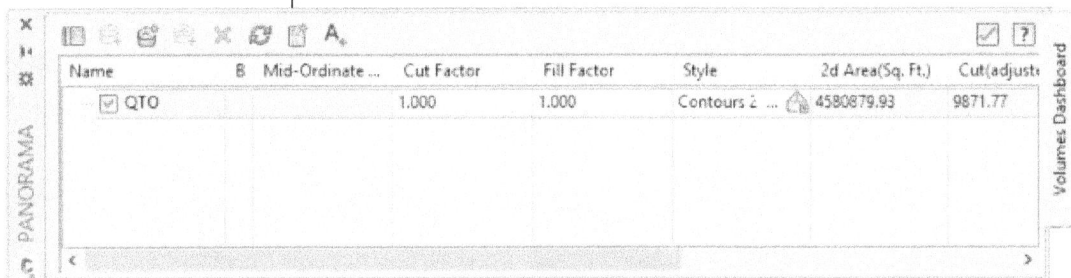

Name	B	Mid-Ordinate ...	Cut Factor	Fill Factor	Style	2d Area(Sq. Ft.)	Cut(adjuste
☑ QTO			1.000	1.000	Contours 2 ...	4580879.93	9871.77

Figure 4–78

The *Net Graph* column color displays in red if the surface difference results in a net cut, and green if it is a net fill. You can have multiple volume entries listed if you are comparing multiple surfaces. If any surfaces change, return to this vista and click

 (Recompute Volumes) to update the calculations. Alternatively, you can add another volume entry. Select the same two surfaces and compare before and after volume calculations.

Bounded Volumes

The area to calculate cut and fill can be limited by clicking

 (Add Bounded Volume). This limits the calculations to the area defined by a polyline, polygon, or parcel.

Volume Reports

The dashboard's cut/fill summary contents can be placed directly into the drawing by clicking A_+ (Insert Cut/Fill Summary) inside the Volumes Dashboard. In addition, you can create a volume report from the dashboard contents to include in specifications or other project documents by clicking 📝 (Generate Volume Report) inside the Volumes Dashboard.

Grid Volume or TIN Volume Surface

This method enables you to assign the surfaces you want to compare as object properties of a volume surface. The volume between the surfaces is calculated and included in the volume surface object properties. The TIN surface calculation is the same one conducted in the Volumes Dashboard. The Grid surface calculation is based on a grid of points interpolated from both surfaces, rather than all of the surface points of both. Grid surfaces tend to be less accurate, but faster to calculate and easier to prove by manual methods.

A grid of spot elevation labels that list the elevation differences between two surfaces can be generated from either a Grid Volume surface or TIN Volume surface. Once the volume surface is established, create the labels. In the *Annotate* tab>Labels & Tables panel, expand **Add Labels**, expand **Surface**, and select **Spot Elevations on Grid**, as shown in Figure 4–79.

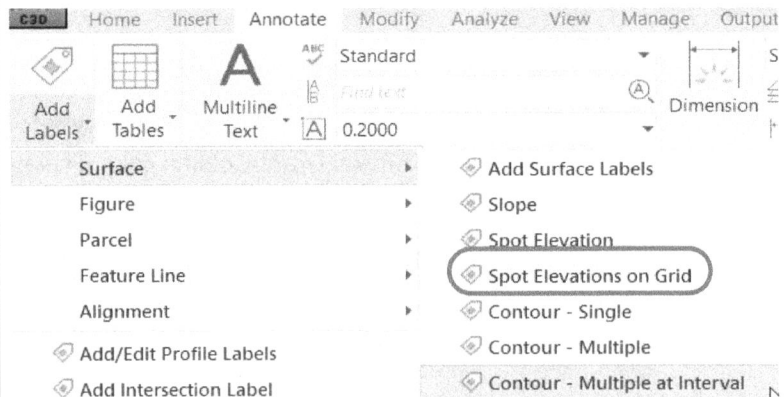

Figure 4–79

4.9 Surface Analysis Display

The Autodesk Civil 3D software can calculate and display many different surface analyses, including:

- **Contours:** This analysis can display contours differently based on their elevation ranges.

- **Directions:** This analysis can render surface triangles differently depending on which direction they face.

- **Elevations:** This analysis can render surface triangles differently depending on their elevation ranges.

- **Slopes:** This analysis can render surface triangles differently depending on their slope ranges.

- **Slope Arrows:** This analysis creates a dynamic slope arrow that points downslope for each triangle, colorized by slope range.

- **User-Defined Contours:** This analysis can display user-defined contours differently based on their elevation ranges.

- **Watersheds:** This analysis can calculate watershed areas, and render them according to area type. The AutoCAD Civil 3D watershed analysis usually results in a very large number of individual watersheds. Although a **Catchment Areas** command is available to assist in drawing the catchment areas, it is still up to the engineers to draw their own conclusions on how these should be merged together into catchment areas.

The above analyses are calculated on demand for each surface and their results are stored under the surface's Surface Properties.

In addition, the following separate utilities might be helpful when analyzing surfaces:

- **Check for Contour Problems:** Used to locate problems with the contour data, including crossing or overlapping contours. To access this command, in the *Surface* tab>expanded

  Analyze panel, select [icon] **Check for Contour Problems**, as shown in Figure 4–80.

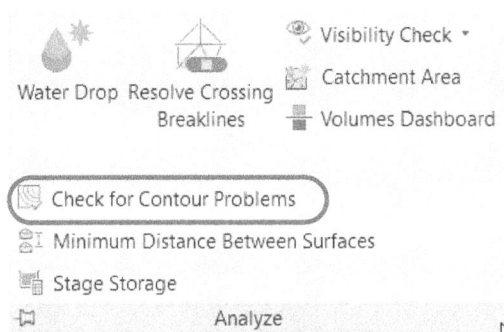

Figure 4–80

- **Resolve Crossing Breaklines:** Identifies and fixes any breaklines that create an invalid condition when two elevations exist at the intersection point of two breaklines. The breaklines can be found in the drawing, in a survey figure, or in the survey database. To access this command, in the *Surface* tab>Analyze panel, click [icon] (Resolve Crossing Breaklines).

- **Water Drop:** Draws a 2D or 3D polyline indicating the expected flow path of water across the surface from a given starting point. To access this command, in the *Surface* tab> Analyze panel, click [icon] (Water Drop).

- **Catchment Area:** Draws a 2D or 3D polyline indicating the catchment boundary and catchment point marker for a surface drainage area. To access this command, in the *Surface* tab>Analyze panel, click [icon] (Catchment Area). You should use this command in conjunction with the **Water Drop** command to determine an accurate placement of catchment regions and points.

- **Visibility Check>Zone of Visual Influence:** Analyzes the line of sight for 360 degrees around a single point. To access this command, in the *Surface* tab>Analyze panel, click

  (Visibility Check>Zone of Visual influence). This command is good for analyzing if towers, buildings, and other objects can be seen within a certain radius.

- **Minimum Distance Between Surfaces:** Identifies the (X,Y) location where two overlapping surfaces are the closest elevation. To access this command, in the *Surface* tab>

  Analyze panel, click (Minimum Distance Between Surfaces). If there is more than one location with the shortest distance between the two surfaces (because it is flat), then the location might be represented by a series of points, a line, or a closed polyline.

- **Stage Storage:** Calculates volumes of a basin from a surface, using either a surface or polylines to define the basin. To access this command, in the *Surface* tab>Analyze

  panel, click (Stage Storage). Either the *Average End Area* or the *Conic Approximation* method, or both are used to calculate volumes for the stage storage table.

Analysis Settings

You apply a surface analysis using the *Analysis* tab in the Surface Properties dialog box. In this tab, you can select the number of ranges and a legend table to be used. All of the remaining analysis settings are located in the *Surface Object* style, including whether to display in 2D or 3D, the color scheme, elevations, range groupings, etc. If you want to change the number of ranges or the range values, use the settings in this tab at any time.

Analysis Data Display

Overall visibility, layer, linetype, and related controls for analysis elements are managed using the *Display* tab in the Object Style dialog box, as shown in Figure 4–81. The component entries for *Slopes, Slope Arrows, Watersheds*, etc., are displayed. These can be set to display different settings and combinations of elements in 2D and 3D.

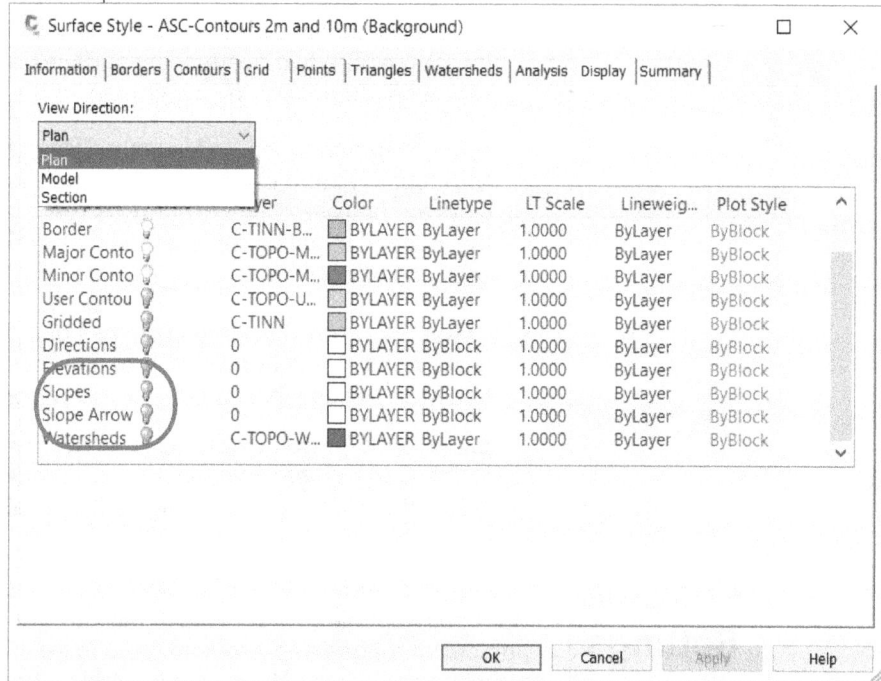

Figure 4–81

Practice 4d

Surface Labeling and Analysis

Practice Objective

* Communicate information about the surface by labeling and analyzing it.

Task 1 - Add surface labels.

1. Open **SUF1-D1-Surface.dwg** from the *C:\Civil 3D Projects\Working\Surface* folder.

2. Select the preset view **Surface Label**.

3. Select the **Existing-Site** surface in Model Space. In the contextual *Surface* tab>Labels & Tables panel, expand Add Labels and select the **Contour - Multiple**, as shown in Figure 4–82.

Figure 4–82

4. When prompted to select the first point, specify any point. When prompted for the next point, select a second and third point that creates a line intersecting all of the contours that you want to label, as shown in Figure 4–83. Press <Enter> when done.

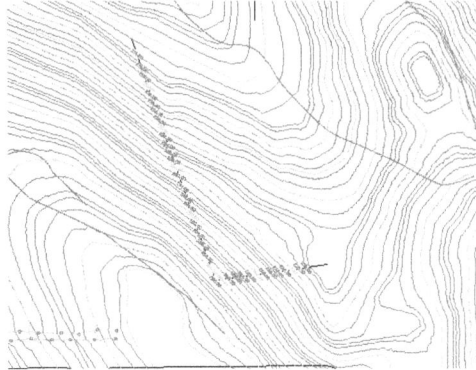

Figure 4–83

5. Move and reorient the contour label line. The labels update.

6. The *Display Contour Label Line* property can be set to only be visible when contour labels are selected. To change the visibility property, select the line in Model Space and select **Properties** in the contextual *Label* tab>General Tools panel. In the Properties dialog box, set the *Display Contour Label Line* property and the *Display Minor Contour Labels* property to **False,** as shown in Figure 4–84.

Figure 4–84

7. Close the Properties dialog box and press <Esc> to cancel your selection.

8. To have all of the future contour label lines behave this way in this drawing, select the *Settings* tab in the Toolspace. Select **Surface**, right-click, and select **Edit Feature Settings...,**as shown in Figure 4–85.

Once the grips disappear, the line is no longer displayed. Select a contour label to have the contour label line temporarily display for editing.

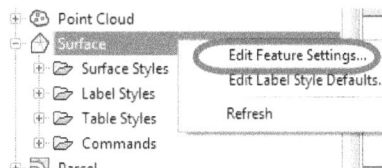

Figure 4–85

9. In the Edit Feature Settings dialog box, expand *Contour Labeling Defaults* and set the *Display Contour Label Line* property to **False** and change *Surface Contour Label Style Minor* to **<none>**, as shown in Figure 4–86. Click **OK** to accept the changes and close the dialog box.

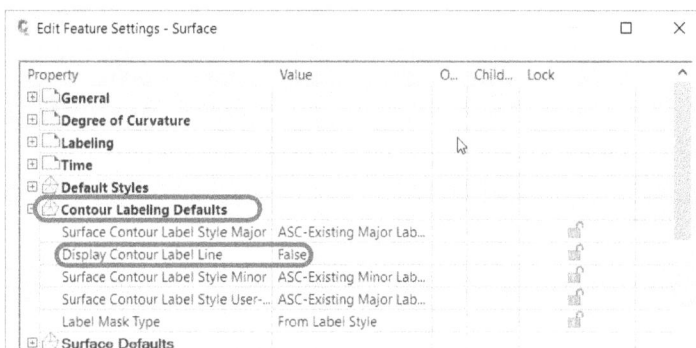

Figure 4–86

10. Select the **Existing-Site** surface again in Model Space. In the contextual *Surface* tab>Labels & Tables panel, expand Add Labels and select **Contour - Multiple**.

11. Select two points that will draw a line across some contours and press <Enter> when done. The contour label line and minor contour labels do not display.

12. Select the **Existing-Site** surface in Model Space. In the contextual *Surface* tab>Labels & Tables panel, expand Add Labels and select **Slope**.

13. To accept the prompt for the default One-point label, press <Enter>, and select a point in Model Space within the surface boundary. The Autodesk Civil 3D software will place the slope value at that point. When you finish placing the labels, press <Enter> to exit the command.

14. (Optional) Using the processes, experiment with labeling the surface with spot elevations and two point slopes. Note that you will be able to copy a label and place it at a different location. As the labels are dynamic, the values will change to reflect the surface information at the location of the label.

Task 2 - Perform a slope analysis.

1. Select the preset view **Survey Main**.

2. Select the **Existing-Site** surface in Model Space. In the contextual *Surface* tab>Modify panel, select **Surface Properties**.

3. In the *Information* tab in the Surface Properties dialog box, select **ASC-Slope Banding (2D)** as the surface style.

The Autodesk Civil 3D software calculates a range of values to fit within the specified number of ranges.

4. In the *Analysis* tab, select **Slopes** for the *Analysis type* and select **4** for the number of ranges to use. Click ⬇ (Run Analysis).

5. Change the range values for Range 4 of the Minimum Slope to 30.0% (leaving the Maximum Slope as is), Range 3 from 20% to 30%, Range 2 from 15% to 20% and Range 1 from 10% to 15%, as shown in Figure 4–87.

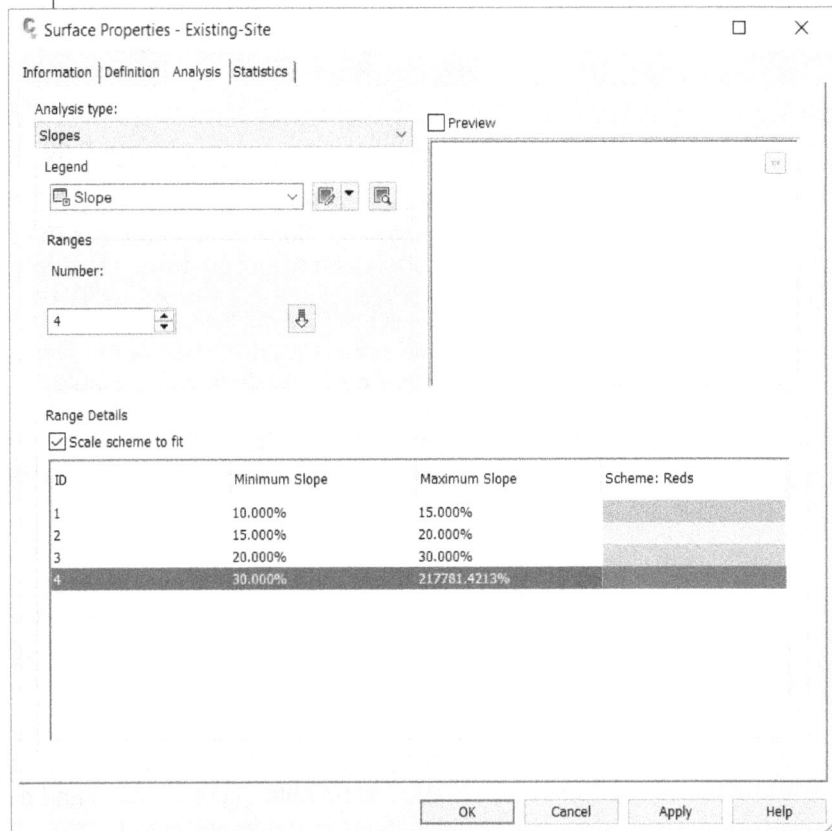

Figure 4–87

6. Change the range of colors for the slope range from light green to yellow to orange to red as shown in Figure 4–87. To change the color, click on it to open the Select Color dialog box, as shown in Figure 4–88, and select the required color. Click **OK** to close the dialog box.

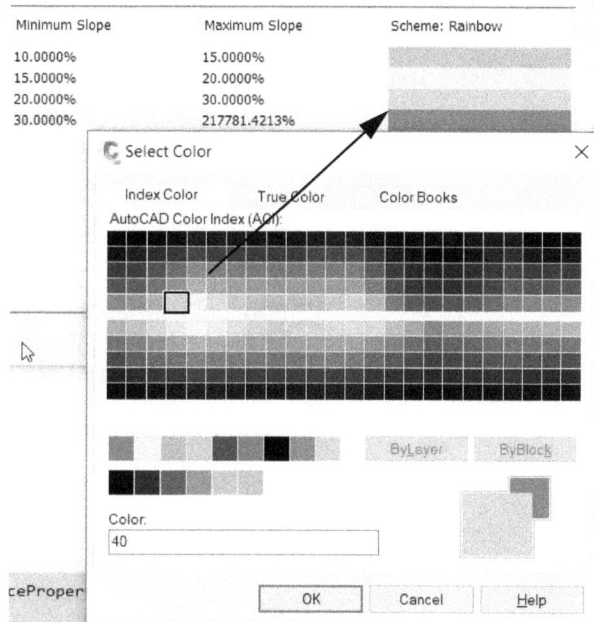

Figure 4–88

7. Click **OK** to close the dialog box and apply the changes. Press <Esc> to exit the surface selection.

8. Review the area that you want to develop. The slope ranges will be an issue.

9. You need to create a slope values table. Select the **Existing-Site** surface in Model Space. In the contextual *Surface* tab>Labels & Tables panel, select **Add Legend**.

10. Select **Slopes** from the command options, and then select **Dynamic** for a dynamic table.

11. When prompted for the top corner of the table (top left), select a location in an open area to the right of the surface, as shown in Figure 4–89. Press <Esc> to exit the selection.

Because this table is dynamic, any changes made to the surface or to the ranges in the analysis will update the table automatically.

Slopes Table				
Number	Minimum Slope	Maximum Slope	Area	Color
1	10.00%	15.00%	1116953.11	
2	15.00%	20.00%	585352.95	
3	20.00%	30.00%	155916.74	
4	30.00%	217781.42%	185938.85	

Figure 4–89

12. (Optional) Open the Surface Properties dialog box (Steps 3 to 7) and change the number of slope ranges or the values. The Model Space Legend table will be updated.

13. Save the drawing.

Chapter 5

Feature Lines

Exam Objectives Covered in This Chapter

2.5.a Create feature lines

2.5.b Edit feature lines geometry

2.5.c Edit feature line elevations

2.5.d Understand how objects interact with each other when they are part of the same site

2.6.a Create and modify sites

2.6.b Create grading groups

2.6.c Use grading creation and editing tools

2.6.d Work with grading criteria

5.1 Draw Feature Lines

When creating feature lines, ✎ (Create Feature Line) creates both straight and curved segments. Elevations are assigned at each vertex by typing an elevation value or by assigning an elevation from a surface that exists in the drawing.

How To: Draw a Feature Line

1. In the *Home* tab>Create Design panel, click ✎ (Create Feature Line).
2. In the Create Feature Line dialog box, set the site, enter a name for the feature line, and select a style for the feature line, as shown in Figure 5–1. Click **OK**.

Note that the conversion options are unavailable since the feature line is being drawn rather than created from an existing object.

Figure 5–1

3. In the Command Line you are prompted to *Specify start point:*. Pick a point in the drawing or type a coordinate value where the feature line starts.
4. In the Command Line you are prompted to *Specify elevation*. You can either type an elevation value or type **S** and press <Enter> to obtain a surface elevation at that point.

5. In the Command Line you are prompted to *Specify the next point*. Pick a point in the drawing or type a coordinate value to define the next end point.

6. Type the capital letter(s) from the following options to set the elevation:

Option	Description
Grade	A grade percentage is applied between the previous point and the next point.
SLope	A rise:run slope is applied between the previous point and the next point.
Elevation	The typed elevation is given to the next point.
Difference	An elevation is calculated for the next point by adding an amount to the previous point's elevation value.
SUrface	Obtain the elevation from a selected surface at the next point in the drawing.
Transition	Skips setting the elevation of the next point and subsequent points by pressing <Enter> until an elevation is assigned to the last point. The elevations for all intermediate vertices is calculated from a grade based on the distance between the first and last point and the change in elevation.

7. In the Command Line you are prompted to *Specify the next point*. Type **A** and press <Enter> to draw an arc.

8. Type the capitol letter from the following options to create the arc according to the required design parameters.

Option	Description
Arc end point	Pick an arc end point to complete the arc. The arc is automatically tangential to the previous segment.
Radius	Enter a radius and then pick the end point of the arc or type **L** to enter the arc length. The arc is automatically tangential to the previous segment.
Secondpnt	Pick a point to specify the second point through which the arc must pass. Then specify the arc endpoint by picking another point or typing **L** to set the arc length. This enables the arc to not be tangential to the previous segment.
Line	Returns to drawing straight line segments.
Undo	Undoes the last segment of the feature line.

Using feature line arcs avoids creating tessellated arcs. This is preferred when working with grading footprints because it creates many small grading faces joined by radial corners. If you use 3D polylines as surface breaklines for grading, tessellation occurs and slows down your drawing. You can use the **Fit Curve** command to convert tessellated arcs to true arcs.

Practice 5a

Draw a Feature Line and Create a Temporary Surface

Practice Objective

- Create a feature line and temporary surface which will be used to assign elevations to the vertices of another feature line.

For the Land Development drawings in this course, much of the preliminary work has already been done for the site development.

The completed corridors for Jeffries Ranch Road and Ascent Place, the Ascent Place knuckle and cul-de-sac target alignments, the Mission Avenue alignment, and the Existing-Site surface have been referenced through Data Shortcuts.

In this practice, you will create a temporary site, draw a feature line, create a temporary surface, and create a feature line and set elevations by grading.

Task 1 - Create a temporary site.

1. Open **PKLOT-A-Grading.dwg** from the *C:\Civil 3D for Land Dev\Working\Parking Lot* folder.

2. Hover over the Data Shortcuts and look at the tooltip that appears, as shown in Figure 5–2. Ensure that your **Data Shortcuts Working Folder** is set to *C:\Civil 3D for Land Dev\Data Shortcuts\Fundamentals* and the **Data Shortcuts Project Folder** to *Ascent-Development*. If not, right-click on Data Shortcuts to set the **Working Folder** and **Data Shortcuts Project Folder**.

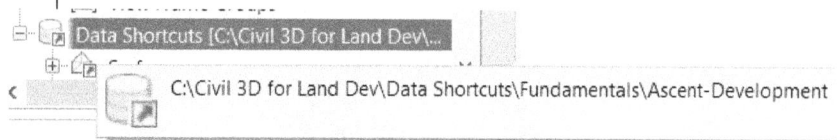

Data Shortcuts [C:\Civil 3D for Land Dev\...

C:\Civil 3D for Land Dev\Data Shortcuts\Fundamentals\Ascent-Development

Figure 5–2

3. In the *View* tab>Views panel, select **Parking Lot** as the view to zoom into the parking lot area, as shown in Figure 5–3.

Figure 5–3

4. In the *Prospector* tab, right-click on Sites and select **New**, as shown in Figure 5–4.

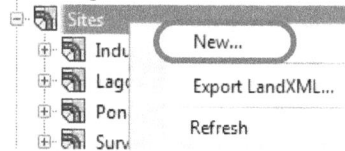

Figure 5–4

5. In the *Information* tab, for the *Name* type **Temp**, and click **OK**.

Task 2 - Draw a feature line.

1. In the *Home* tab>Create Design panel, click ⬜ (Create Feature Line).

2. In the Create Feature Lines dialog box, complete the following, as shown in Figure 5–5:
   - For the *Site*, select **Temp**.
   - For the feature line *Name,* type **CenterLine**.
   - For the *Style,* select **ASC-Basic Feature Line**.
   - Click **OK**.

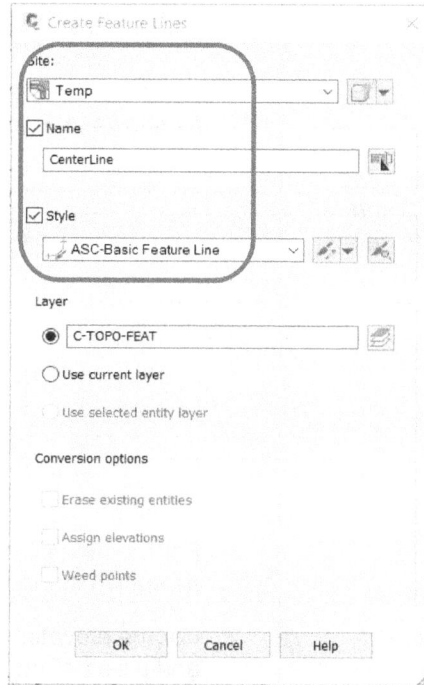

Figure 5–5

3. At the Command Prompt you will be prompted to pick a point.
   Using the **Endpoint** Osnap, click point one on the parking lot
   center line, as shown in Figure 5–6.

Figure 5–6

4. Type **S** and press <Enter> to have it find the elevation of a surface at that point.

5. When prompted for the surface, select **Road1** and click **OK**, as shown in Figure 5–7.

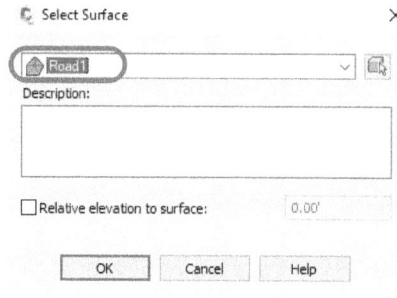

*If this dialog box does not open, type **S** and press <Enter> to select the surface.*

Figure 5–7

6. For the next point, use the **Endpoint** Osnap to pick point 2, as shown in Figure 5–6.

7. For the elevation, the default will be to set the grade. Type **-2** and press <Enter> to set the grade at 2% going down.

*If grade is not the default, type **G** and press <Enter> before setting the negative 2% grade.*

8. For the next point, use the **Endpoint** Osnap to pick point 3, as shown in Figure 5–6.

9. For the elevation, the default will be to set the grade. Type **-2** and press <Enter> to set the grade at 2% going down.

10. For the next point, use the **Endpoint** Osnap to pick point 4, as shown in Figure 5–6.

11. For the elevation, the default will be to set the grade. Type **4** and press <Enter> to set the grade at 4% going up.

12. Press <Enter> to end the command.

13. Save the drawing.

Task 3 - Create a temporary surface.

1. In the *Home* tab>Create Design panel, click (Grading Creation Tools).

2. In the Grading Creations Tools toolbar, click (Set Group).

---

3. In the Site dialog box, for the *Site name* select **Temp**, as shown in Figure 5–8. Click **OK**.

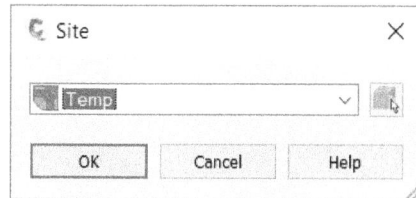

Figure 5–8

4. In the Create Grading Group dialog box, do the following, as shown in Figure 5–9:

   • For the *Name*, type **Temp Parking Lot**.
   • Select the **Automatic surface creation** option.
   • Select the **Volume Base Surface** option and ensure *Existing Site* is listed.
   • Click **OK**.

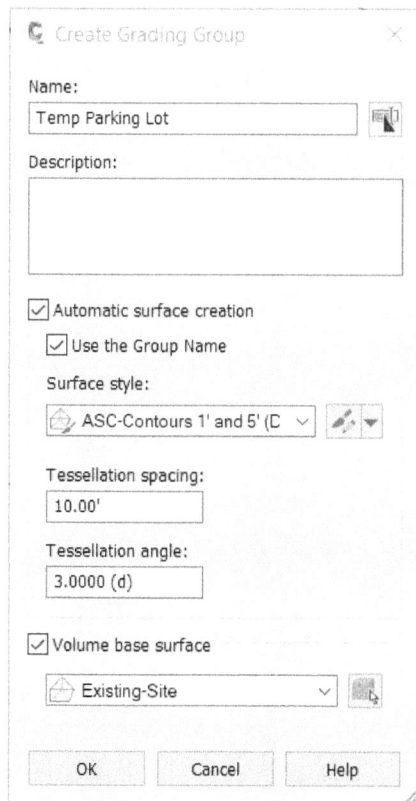

Figure 5–9

5. In the Create Surface dialog box, click **OK to** the defaults.

6. In the Grading Creation Tools toolbar, select **Grade to Distance** for the criteria, as shown in Figure 5–10.

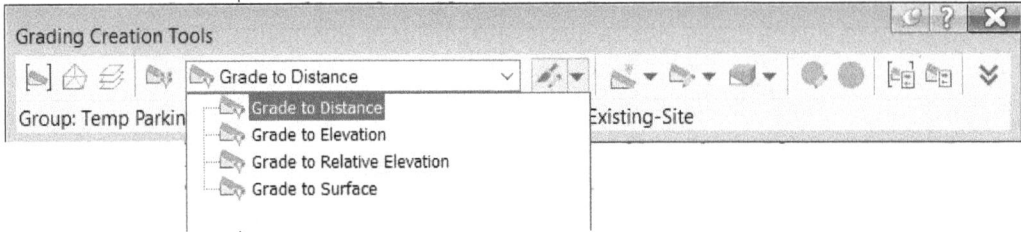

Figure 5–10

7. In the Grading Creation Tools toolbar, click (Create Grading.

8. In the drawing, select the CenterLine feature line that you created in the last task, as shown in Figure 5–11.

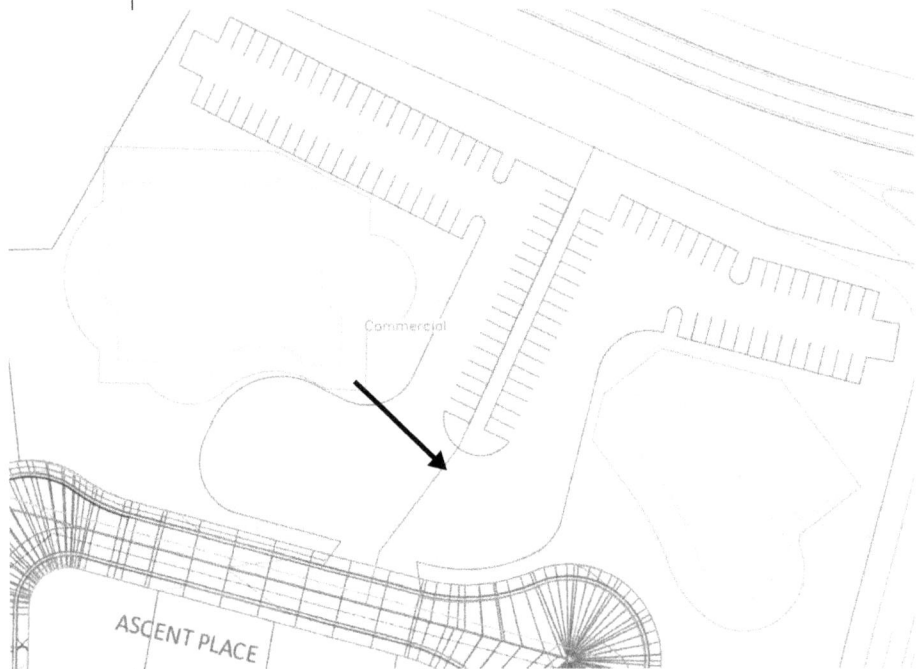

Figure 5–11

Note: If selecting the feature line is difficult, you might need to set the drawing order of the grading surface to the back.

9. When prompted for a side to which to grade, pick a point in the drawing to the right of the feature line. Press <Enter> to accept the default to grade the entire length of the feature line.

- For the *Distance*, type **235** and press <Enter>.
- For the *Format*, type **G** and press <Enter> for grade.
- For the *Grade* type **2** for a positive 2% slope.

10. Repeat Steps 2 to 9 to grade to the left side **265'** at a **2%** grade.

11. Press <Esc> to end the command.

12. Close the Grading Creation Tools toolbar.

13. Save the drawing.

Task 4 - Create a feature line and set elevations by grading.

1. In the *Home* tab>Create Design panel, expand the Feature Line drop-down list and click [icon] (Create Feature Line from Objects).

2. Type **X** and press <Enter> to select linework from the external reference file. Select the magenta line that represents the parking lot perimeter, as highlighted in blue in Figure 5–12. Press <Enter> to continue.

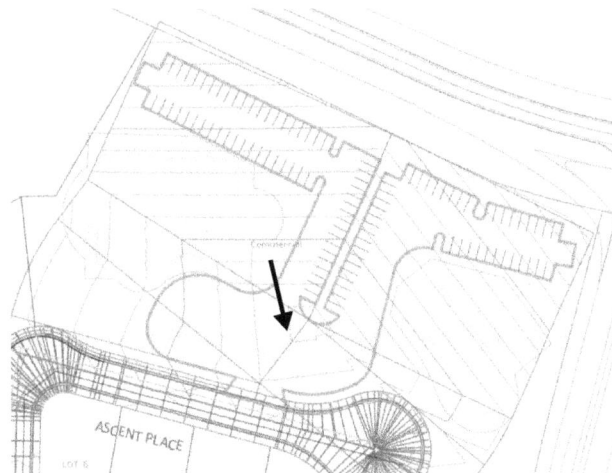

Figure 5–12

3. In the Create Feature Lines dialog box, complete the following, as shown in Figure 5–13:

- Leave the *Site* set to **Temp**.
- For the *Name*, type **Parking-Gutter**.
- Set the *Style* to **Parking Lot**.
- Verify that **Assign elevations** is selected.
- Click **OK**.

Figure 5–13

4. In the Assign Elevations dialog box, select **From gradings**, as shown in Figure 5–14. Click **OK**.

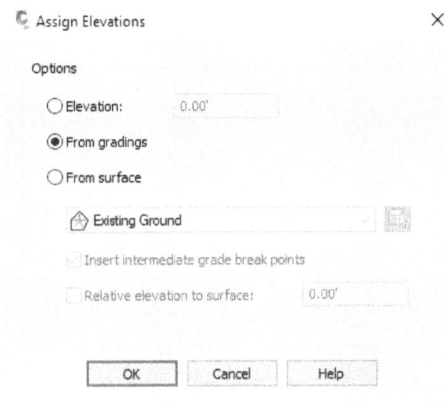

Figure 5–14

5. Save the drawing.

5.2 Copy or Move Feature Lines from One Site to Another

Feature lines must reside in a site to be created and used. If you use feature lines for grading, it is important that they reside in the same site as their grading group. Sometimes feature lines are created in the wrong site or need to be reused in other sites. In these cases you can move or copy a feature line from one site to another. You are able to copy or move the contents of an entire site (alignments, grading groups, parcels, and feature lines) to another site.

How To: Move or Copy Feature Lines

1. Select the object(s) to move or copy.
2. Right-click and select **Move to Site** or **Copy to Site**, as shown in Figure 5–15.

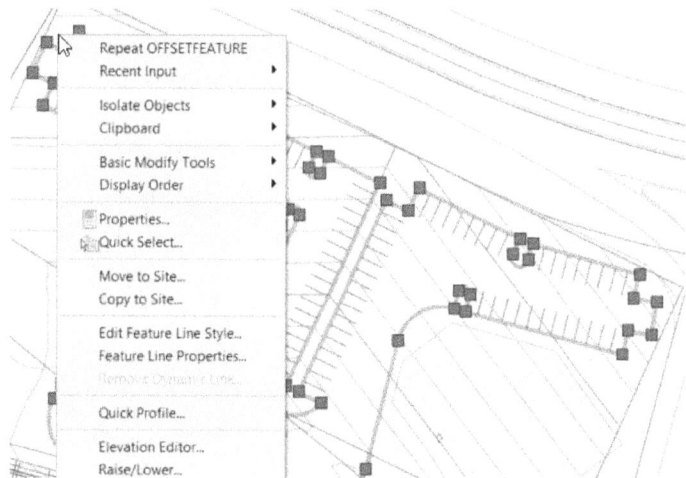

Figure 5–15

3. Another option is to select **Move to Site** or **Copy to Site** by expanding the *Feature Line* contextual tab>Modify panel, as shown in Figure 5–16.

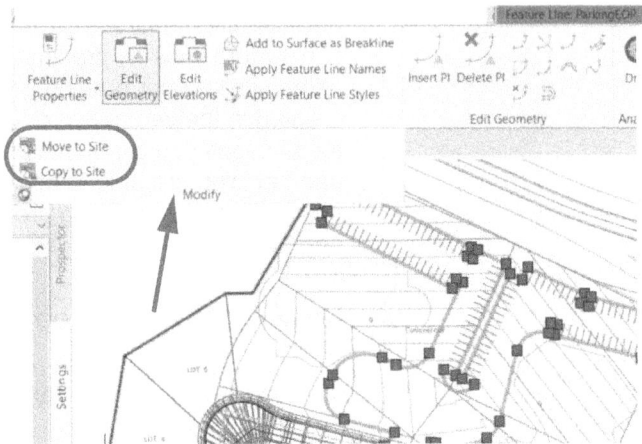

Figure 5–16

4. In the dialog box, select an option for the *Destination site*, as shown in Figure 5–17.

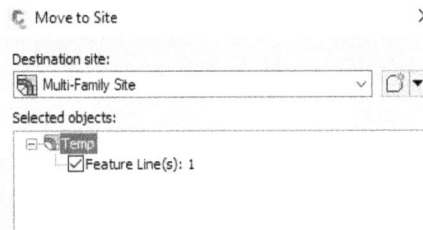

Figure 5–17

5.3 Feature Line Review

There are times when you cannot create a simple grading object. For example, the design criteria required for the pond cross-section shown in Figure 5–18 is too complex for just a grading group.

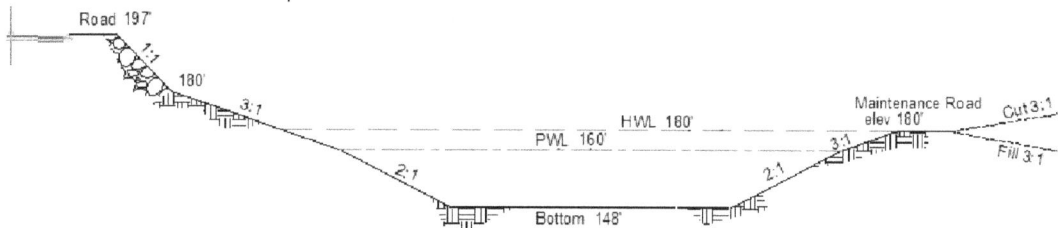

Figure 5–18

Each side of the pond requires different grading criteria:

- At the **South end** of the pond site is a road which has an elevation of 197'. The road is elevated at an average of 20' above the adjacent parcels. As a result, you use a 1:1 slope from the road so that you can create a pond base elevation of 180'.

- At the **North end** of the pond site, a maintenance access road is designed that is elevated 3' above the Permanent Water Level (PWL).

To grade the pond as shown in the cross-section, you must establish a base feature line that uses a common grading criteria. This involves the following:

- Creating a base feature line to the South (1:1 to elev 180').

- Creating a base feature line to the North (3:1 to elev 164').

- Joining the trimmed east and west feature lines to the north and south control feature lines.

- Grading the pond based on this new combined feature line.

Feature Line Contextual Tab

The *Feature Line* contextual tab (shown in Figure 5–19) contains commands that enable you to edit and modify feature lines. These include tools to edit feature line elevations and feature line geometry, such as **Break**, **Trim**, **Join**, and **Fillet** (which creates a true, 3D curve).

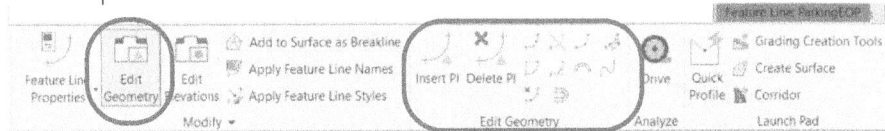

Figure 5–19

The **Create Feature Line** and **Create Feature Lines from Objects** commands are accessed in the *Home* tab>Create Design panel, expanded Feature Line drop-down list, as shown in Figure 5–20.

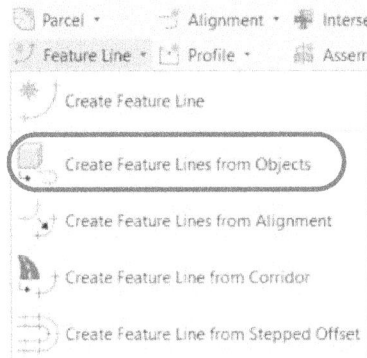

Figure 5–20

These commands can be used to draw feature lines from scratch and to establish an elevation at each vertex. You can also use existing objects to create feature lines and set the elevations of their vertices from surfaces and grading objects.

Practice 5b	# Feature Lines I

Practice Objective

- Create and edit feature lines using various tools.

For the Land Development drawings in this course, much of the preliminary work has already been done for the site development.

The completed corridors for Jeffries Ranch Road and Ascent Place, the Ascent Place knuckle and cul-de-sac target alignments, the Mission Avenue alignment, and the Existing-Site surface have been referenced through Data Shortcuts.

In this practice, you will define the perimeter of the pond using two methods of defining a feature line. You will create a feature line from a surface and then create a feature based on design elevations.

Task 1 - Create a feature line from a surface.

Mission Avenue is the northern boundary of the site and an existing subdivision bounds the western side. To establish a design control line for the north and west perimeters of the site, you will create a feature line that extracts elevations from the existing surface.

1. Open **POND-A-Grading.dwg** from the *C:\Civil 3D for Land Dev\Working\Pond* folder.

2. Hover over the Data Shortcuts and look at the tooltip that appears, as shown in Figure 5–21. Ensure that your **Data Shortcuts Working Folder** is set to *C:\Civil 3D for Land Dev\Data Shortcuts\Fundamentals* and the **Data Shortcuts Project Folder** to *Ascent-Development*. If not, right-click on Data Shortcuts to set the **Working Folder** and **Data Shortcuts Project Folder**.

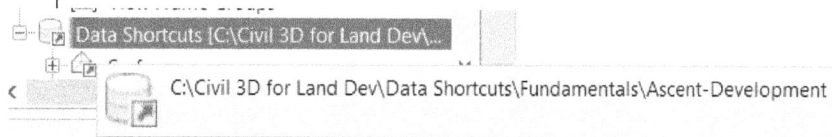

Data Shortcuts [C:\Civil 3D for Land Dev\...

C:\Civil 3D for Land Dev\Data Shortcuts\Fundamentals\Ascent-Development

Figure 5–21

You might need to type **Regen** *in the Command Line to display this polyline.*

3. In the *View* tab>Views panel, select the preset view **Storm Pond**. A red polyline displays along the north and west property lines, as shown in Figure 5–22.

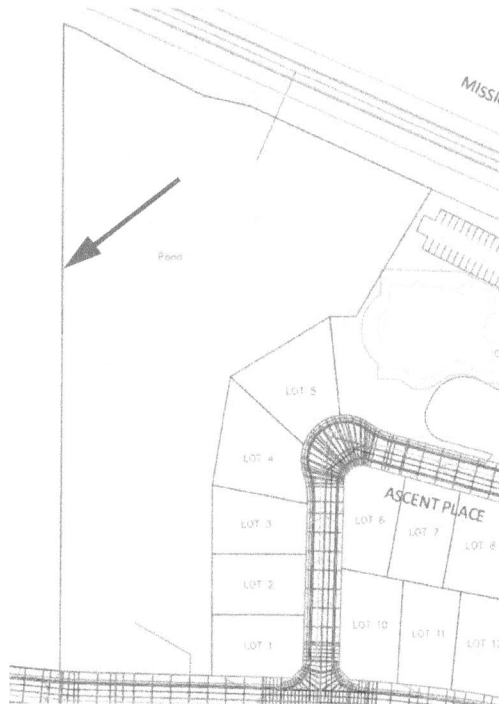

Figure 5–22

4. In the *Home* tab>Create Design panel, expand the Feature Line drop-down list and click (Create Feature Lines from Objects).

5. When prompted to *Select the object:*, select the red polyline shown in Figure 5–22. Press <Enter> when done.

6. In the Create Feature Lines dialog box, complete the following, as shown in Figure 5–23:

- For the *Site,* select **Pond Site**
- For the *Name,* type **North-West-Boundary**
- In the *Conversion options* area select the **Erase existing entities**, **Assign elevations**, and **Weed Points** options.
- Accept all of the other defaults and click **OK** when done.

Figure 5–23

7. In the Assign Elevations dialog box, complete the following, as shown in Figure 5–24.

   - Select the **From surface** option.
   - In the drop-down list, select **Existing-Site.**
   - Select the **Insert intermediate grade break points** option.
   - Click **OK** to accept the changes and close the dialog box.

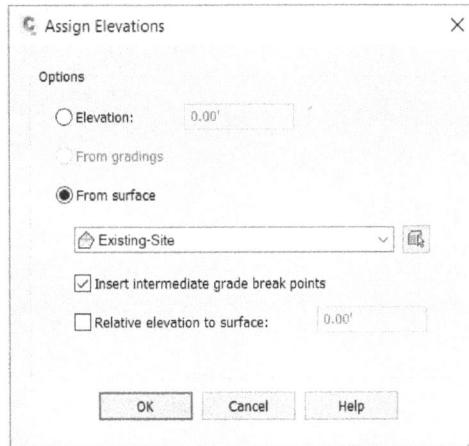

Figure 5–24

8. In the Weed Vertices dialog box, accept the defaults and click **OK**, as shown in Figure 5–25.

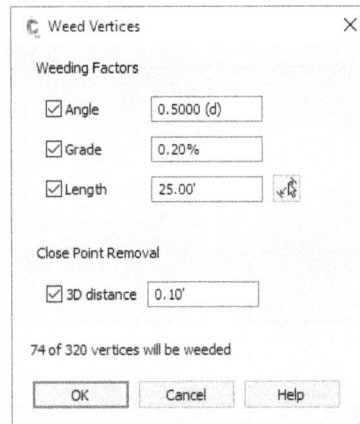

Figure 5–25

9. A feature line has been created for the north and west property lines of the site, with elevations matching the existing ground surface. Save the drawing.

Task 2 - Create a feature based on design elevations.

In this task you will create a feature line of the east perimeter of the pond. The grades at the east perimeter of the pond are governed by the rear grades of the lots or parcels.

1. Based on the street grades and types of lots that are required (Walkout Basements), elevations for the east property line have been roughly calculated. The last point (pt7) ties into the existing ground elevation that is controlled by Mission Avenue, as shown in Figure 5–26.

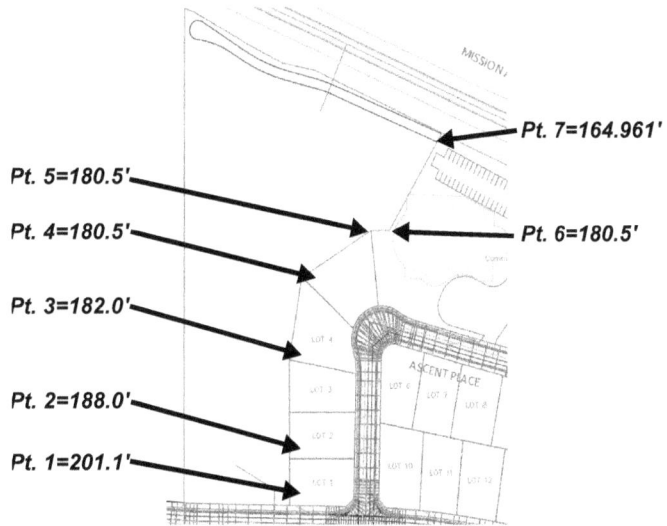

Figure 5–26

2. In the *Home* tab>Create Design panel, expand the Feature Line drop-down list and click ↲ (Create Feature Line).

3. In the Create Feature Lines dialog box, complete the following:
   - Select **Pond Site** for the site and select the option to name it.
   - For the *Name* type **East-Boundary**.
   - Accept all of the other defaults.
   - Click **OK**.

4. When prompted for the feature line points, using the **Endpoint** Osnap, select **Pt1**, as shown in Figure 5–26.

5. When prompted to *Specify elevation or [surface] <0.000>:* type **201.1** and press <Enter>.

6. When prompted for the next point, using the **Endpoint** Osnap, select **Pt2**, as shown in Figure 5–26.

7. You are prompted to *Specify grade or [SLope/Elevation/ Difference/SUrface/Transition] <0.00>:*. If the option is not set to accept elevations, type **E** and press <Enter> to set the default as the elevation.

8. Once the option has been set to accept elevations, you are prompted to *Specify elevation or [Grade/SLope/Difference/ SUrface/ Transition] <61.300>*. Type **188.0** and press <Enter>.

9. Continue selecting endpoints and entering elevations for all of the points as shown in Figure 5–26. When finished entering the elevation for the last point, pt7 (**164.961**), press <Enter> to exit the command.

10. Save the drawing.

5.4 Edit Elevations

The Grading Elevation Editor vista (as shown in Figure 5–27) enables you to add, modify, or vary the elevations of a feature line. The feature line data is organized into rows, where one row lists the data for an individual vertex.

Station	Elevation	Length	Grade Ahead	Grade Back
0+00.00	60.000'	729.550'	0.00%	0.00%
7+29.55	60.000'	82.272'	0.00%	0.00%
8+11.82	60.000'	0.643'	0.00%	0.00%
8+12.47	60.000'	63.341'	0.00%	0.00%
8+75.81	60.000'	91.491'	0.00%	0.00%
9+67.30	60.000'	2.995'	0.00%	0.00%
9+70.29	60.000'	103.000'	0.00%	0.00%

Figure 5–27

Other elevation editing tools are available on the *Feature Line* contextual tab>Edit Elevations panel. To access this panel, in the *Modify* tab>Design panel, click ↵ (Feature Line). The *Feature Line* contextual tab displays, click 🗂 (Edit Elevations). The Edit Elevations panel displays, as shown in Figure 5–28.

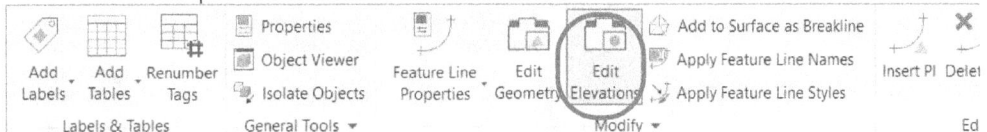

Figure 5–28

Each icon's function is as follows:

Icon	Command	Description
	Elevation Editor	Opens the Elevation Editor vista where you edit the vertex elevations of feature lines, survey figures, and parcel lines.
	Insert Elevation Point	Adds an elevation control to the feature line. Elevation points provide an elevation control without creating a new vertex. These points are Z-controls without X- or Y-components.
	Delete Elevation Point	Vertical grade breaks are anywhere other than horizontal vertices.

	Quick Elevation Edit	Displays elevation values at vertices and elevation points along a feature line or parcel line. Selecting one of these points enables you to edit it in the Command Line.
	Edit Elevations	Edits elevations at vertices along a feature line, parcel line, or 3D polyline as you step through each vertex in the Command Line.
	Set Grade/Slope Between Points	Sets the grade or slope between two points on a feature line, parcel line, or 3D polyline. The elevations between the two selected points are interpolated to maintain the grade/slope/elevation/elevation difference entered.
	Insert High/Low Elevation Point	Inserts a high or low break point where two grades intersect on a feature line, survey figure, parcel line, or 3D polyline.
	Raise/Lower by Reference	Raises or lowers a feature line, survey figure, parcel line, or 3D polyline a specified grade or slope from a selected COGO point or surface elevation.
	Set Elevation by Reference	Sets a single vertex elevation on a feature line, survey figure, parcel line, or 3D polyline a specified grade or slope from a selected COGO point or surface elevation.
	Adjacent Elevations by Reference	Sets elevations of one feature line, survey figure, parcel line, or 3D polyline based on a grade/slope/elevation/elevation difference from points on another feature running alongside the first feature.
	Grade Extension by Reference	Extends the grade of one feature line, survey figure, parcel line, or 3D Polyline across a gap to set the elevations of another feature and maintain the same slope.
	Elevations from Surface	Takes the elevations of all vertices from the surface if no vertices are selected. If a vertex is selected, it takes the surface elevation for just that vertex.
	Raise/Lower	Raises or lowers all of the feature line vertices by the elevation entered.

- You can edit the elevations of a feature line or parcel line before or after it becomes part of a grading group.

How To: Insert Elevation Points

1. In the *Feature Line* contextual tab>Modify panel, click

    (Edit Elevations).

2. In the Elevation Editor or in the *Feature Line* contextual tab>

    Edit Elevations panel, click (Insert Elevation Point).

3. Either pick a point along the feature line or enter a station
    where you want the new elevation point to be located.

4. At the Command line, type the station and press <Enter>.
    Then type the elevation and press <Enter>.

5. In the Grading Elevation Editor vista, the new station should
    be displayed, as shown in Figure 5–29.

Station	Elevation	Length	Grade Ahead	Grade Back
0+00.00	201.100'	13.000'	100.778%	100.778%
0+13.00	188.000'	67.863'	0.00%	0.00%
0+80.86	188.000	168.805	-3.55%	3.55%
2+49.67	182.000'	147.637'	-1.02%	1.02%

Figure 5–29

5.5 Edit Geometry

The Edit Geometry panel (shown in Figure 5–30) enables you to modify feature lines, survey figures, parcel lines, polylines, and 3D polylines. When working with feature lines, you must use these commands to make edits to feature line geometry, rather than the **Polyline Edit** command. To open the Edit Geometry panel, in the *Feature Line* contextual tab>Modify panel, click (Edit Geometry).

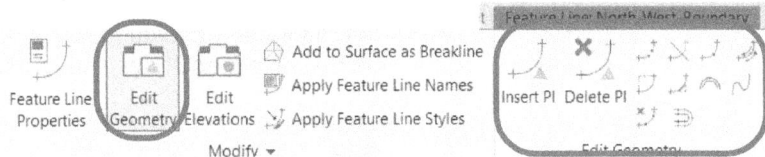

Figure 5–30

The tool functions are as follows:

Icon	Command	Description
	Insert PI	Adds a new vertex to a feature line, survey figure, parcel line, polyline, or 3D polyline giving you additional horizontal and vertical control.
	Delete PI	Removes a selected vertex from a feature line, survey figure, parcel line, polyline, or 3D polyline.
	Break	Creates a gap or break in a feature line, survey figure, or parcel line. The location selected when picking the object is the first point of the break unless otherwise specified.
	Trim	Removes part of a feature line, survey figure, or parcel line at the specified boundary edge.
	Join	Combines two feature lines, survey figures, parcel lines, polylines, or 3D polylines that fall within the tolerance distance set in the command settings.
	Reverse	Changes the direction of the stationing along a feature line, survey figure, parcel line, polyline, or 3D polyline.
	Edit Curve	Changes the radius of a feature line arc, parcel line arc, or survey figure arc.

	Fillet	Creates a curve between two segments of selected feature line(s), survey figures, parcel lines, or 3D polylines.
	Fit Curve	Places a curve between selected vertices of a feature line, survey figure, parcel line, or 3D polyline while removing vertices between the selected vertices. Useful for converting tessellated lines to true arcs.
	Smooth	Adds multiple arcs to feature lines or survey figures to assist in smoothing tessellated lines.
	Weed	Removes unnecessary vertices along feature lines, polylines, or 3D polylines based on defined angle, grade, length, and 3D distance values.
	Stepped Offset	Creates copies of a selected feature line, survey figure, polyline, or 3D polyline a specified horizontal and vertical distance away from the original object.

Break Feature Lines

Feature lines can be broken into two or more segments in order to have more control over surface elevations. It is common for existing ground surface contours or corridor feature lines to be used in a finish ground grading plan. However, the entire feature line might not be required. It is in these instances that it becomes necessary to use the feature line (Break) or (Trim) commands. The **Break** command allows you to break the feature line at selected points, as shown in Figure 5–31.

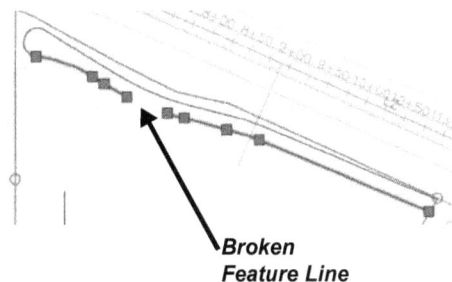

Broken
Feature Line

Figure 5–31

How To: Break a Feature Line

1. In Model Space, select the feature line that needs to be split into two feature lines.
2. In the *Feature Line* contextual tab>Modify panel, click

   ⬜ (Edit Geometry) to display the Edit Geometry panel.

3. In the Edit Geometry panel, click ⬚ (Break), as shown in Figure 5–32.

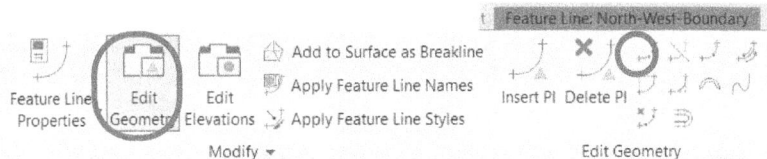

Figure 5–32

4. When prompted to select an object to break, select the feature line at the location where you want to place the first break point.
5. When prompted to select the second break point, click on the line at the second point.
   - If you need to provide a different first point, type **F** and press <Enter>. Click on the feature line to re-select the first break point, and then click on the feature line at the second break point location.

Trim Feature Lines

Feature lines can be trimmed at specified cutting edges. This allows you to ensure that feature lines do not go beyond a specific boundary. The specified boundary becomes the cutting edge, and then the feature line is removed up to the cutting edge, as shown in Figure 5–33.

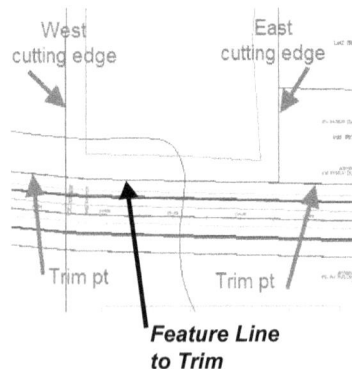

Figure 5–33

How To: Trim a Feature Line

1. In Model Space, select the feature line requiring trimming.
2. In the *Feature Line* contextual tab>Modify panel, click

    ⬚ (Edit Geometry) to display the Edit Geometry panel.

3. In the Edit Geometry panel, click ⤢ (Trim), as shown in Figure 5–34.

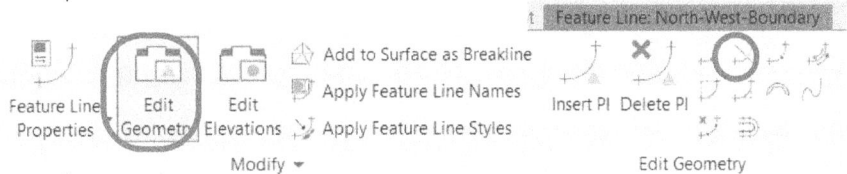

Figure 5–34

4. When prompted to select the cutting edge, select an object to trim to and press <Enter>.
5. When prompted to select the object to trim, select the feature line to trim on the side you wish to remove from the drawing.

Join Feature Lines

When two feature lines touch each other, end to end, at the same elevation, you can join them into one feature line, as shown in Figure 5–35. This is especially useful when you have used various commands to create the base feature lines, such as *Create Feature Line From Objects* or *Create Feature Line From Corridors*.

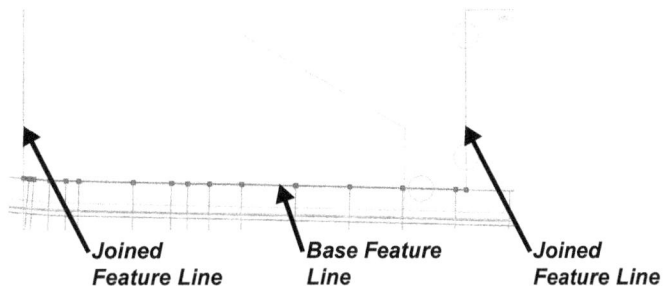

Joined Feature Line   *Base Feature Line*   *Joined Feature Line*

Figure 5–35

How To: Join Feature Lines Together

1. In the *Feature Line* contextual tab>Modify panel, click
   ⬚ (Edit Geometry) to display the Edit Geometry panel.

2. In the Edit Geometry panel, click ⌐ (Join), as shown in Figure 5–36.

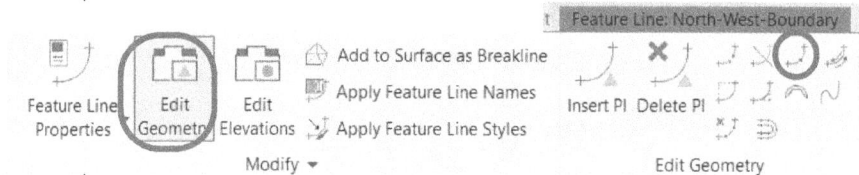

Figure 5–36

3. When prompted, select all the feature lines in the drawing that you want to join.
4. Press <Enter> to end the command
5. Press <Esc> to exit the feature line selection.

> **Hint: Fixing Feature Lines Which Fail to Join**
>
> If the ⌐ (Join) command does not join the selected feature lines, some grip editing might be required where lines do not intersect perfectly.
>
> Alternatively, you can change the command settings to set a tolerance factor. Changing the tolerance factor allows feature lines with a gap between them to join together as long as the gap is within the selected tolerance.

Practice 5c

Feature Lines II

Practice Objectives

- Edit feature line elevations by adding additional elevation points at locations other than the vertices.
- Create feature lines from corridors to speed up the creation process and ensure design coordination.

In this practice, you will modify feature line elevations, create a feature line from a corridor and edit feature line geometry.

Task 1 - Modify feature line elevations.

In the Grading Elevation Editor vista, you can make changes to the feature line design. Due to the grade difference between Jeffries Ranch Rd and the adjacent lot grade, the start of the feature line must be adjusted to display a 1:1 slope.

1. Open **POND-B-Grading.dwg** from the *C:\Civil 3D for Land Dev\Working\Pond* folder.

2. In Model Space, select the East-Boundary feature line you created in the last practice. In the *Feature Line* contextual tab>Modify panel, click ⬚ (Edit Elevations) to display the Edit Elevations panel, and then click ⬚ (Insert Elevation Point).

3. When prompted for a point, type **13** and press <Enter> at the Command Line (this is the station along the feature line).

4. When prompted for the *Elevation*, type **188.0'** and press <Enter>.

5. In the *Feature Line* contextual tab>Edit Elevations panel, click ⬚ (Elevation Editor) to open the vista. The new station should display with a circle icon indicating that it is an elevation point rather than a vertex, as shown in Figure 5–37.

Station	Elevation	Length	Grade Ahead	Grade Back
0+00.00	201.100'	13.000'	-100.77%	100.77%
0+13.00	188.000'	67.863'	0.00%	0.00%
0+80.86	188.000'	168.005'	3.55%	3.55%
2+49.67	182.000'	147.637'	-1.02%	1.02%

Figure 5–37

6. Save the drawing.

Task 2 - Create a feature line from corridor.

The grades at the south end of the pond are controlled by Jeffries Ranch Rd. In this task you will extract a feature from the corridor to establish the elevation of the south property line.

1. In the *View* tab>Views panel, select the preset view **Storm Pond**.

2. In the *Home* tab>Layers panel, ensure that the **C-ROAD-CORR** layer is toggled on. Regen the drawing, by typing **RE**in the Command Line.

3. In Model Space, select the Jeffries Ranch Rd corridor object, right-click, and select **Display Order>Bring to Front**.

4. In the *Home* tab>Create Design panel, expand the Feature Line drop-down list and click 　 (Create Feature Line from Corridor), as shown in Figure 5–38.

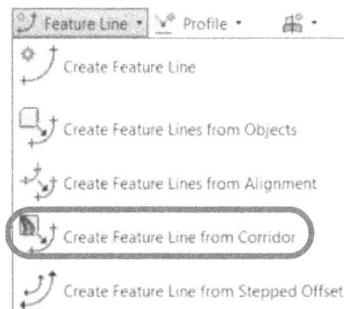

Figure 5–38

If it is difficult to select the corridor feature line, you can toggle on the selection cycling.

5. When prompted to select the corridor, click on Jeffries Ranch Rd.

6. When prompted to select the feature line, select the **north edge** (green or magenta) line, as shown in Figure 5–39. Press <Enter> to indicate that you are finished selecting feature lines.

7. In the Extract Corridor Feature Line dialog box, complete the following, as shown in Figure 5–39:

   • In the *Site* column, select **Pond Site**.

   • Click **Settings**.

   • Clear the **Dynamic link to the corridor** option.

   • Accept the remaining defaults.

   • Click **OK** to close the Settings dialog box.

   • Click **Extract**.

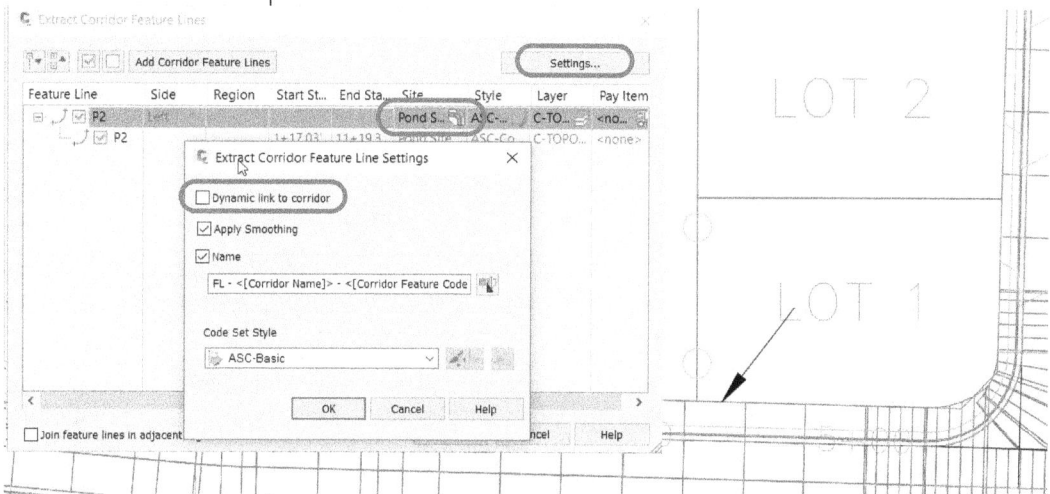

Figure 5–39

A message displays at the Command Line indicating that a feature line from <P2> has been created.

8. Save the drawing.

Task 3 - Edit feature line geometry.

1. In Model Space, select the newly created feature line, as shown in Figure 5–40. In the *Feature Line* contextual tab> Modify panel, click (Edit Geometry). In the Edit Geometry panel, click (Trim).

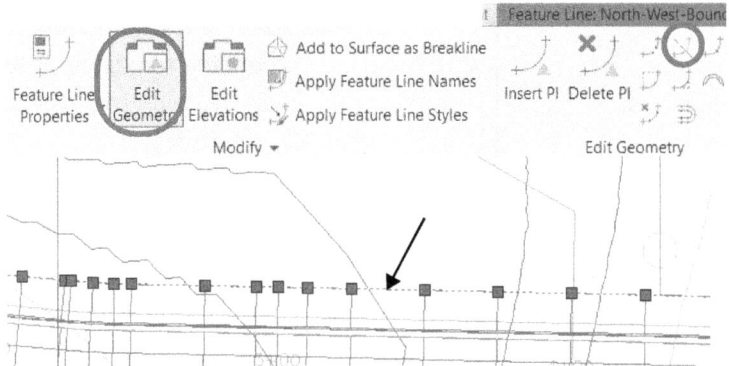

Figure 5–40

2. When prompted to select the cutting edge, select the east and west property lines of the pond and press <Enter> when done.

3. When prompted to select the object to trim, select the feature line at a point outside the pond property lines, west of the west cutting edge and east of the east cutting edge, as shown in Figure 5–41. Press <Enter> when done and press <Esc> to exit the feature object selection.

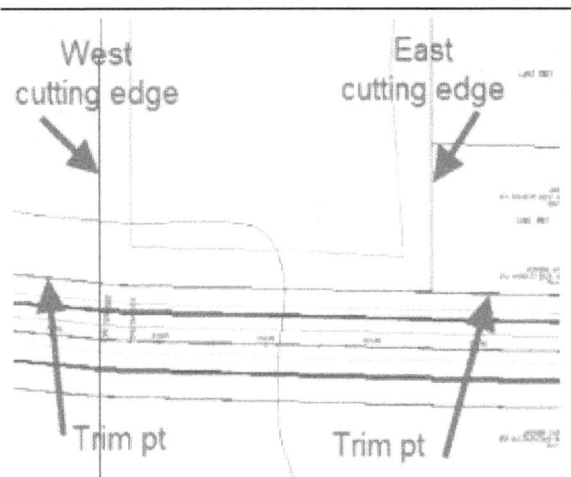

Figure 5–41

A feature line based on the corridor road design has now been created.

4. To join the three feature lines, select the feature line at the west side of the pond.

5. In the *Feature Line* contextual tab>Modify panel, click

     (Edit Geometry) to display the Edit Geometry panel,

    and then click (Join), as shown in Figure 5–42.

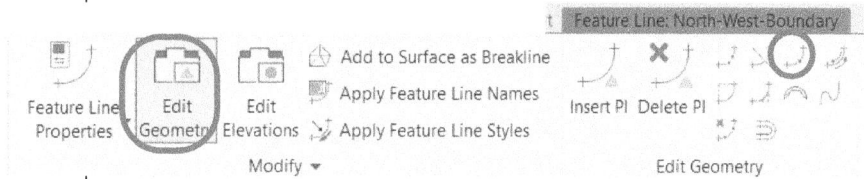

Figure 5–42

If the feature line fails to join any lines in this process, some grip editing might be required where lines do not intersect completely.

6. When prompted, select the feature line to the south and select the feature line to the east. Press <Enter> to end the command and press <Esc> to exit the feature line selection.

7. Save the drawing.

Practice 5d	# Pond Grading - Feature Line (Create Base Line)

Practice Objective

- Create and modify feature lines using grading objects and feature line editing tools.

In this practice, you will establish control feature lines at the north and south ends, as shown in Figure 5–43, and then create the pond outside rim feature line.

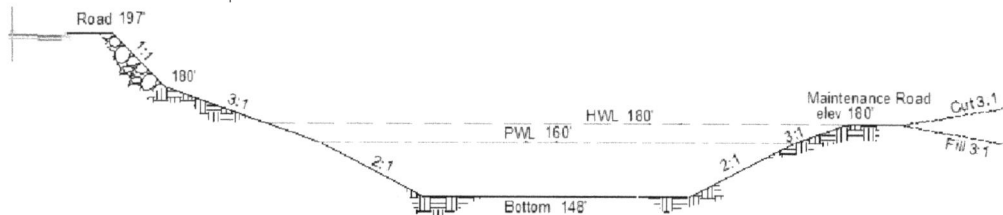

Figure 5–43

Task 1 - Establish control feature lines (south end).

1. Open **POND-C-Grading.dwg** from the *C:\Civil 3D for Land Dev\Working\Pond* folder.

2. In the *View* tab>Views panel, select the preset view **Storm Pond**.

3. In the *Home* tab>Create Design panel, expand the Grading drop-down list and click (Grading Creation Tools).

4. In the Grading Creation Tools toolbar, click (Set the Grading Group). Select **Pond Site** for the site and click **OK**, as shown in Figure 5–44.

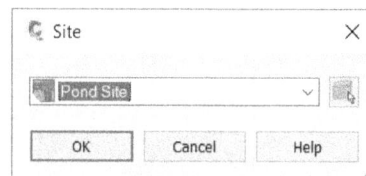

Figure 5–44

You will create a temporary grading object that creates pre-design information.

5. In the Create Grading Group dialog box, for the *Name* enter **Temp**, as shown in Figure 5–45. Clear the **Automatic surface creation** option and click **OK**.

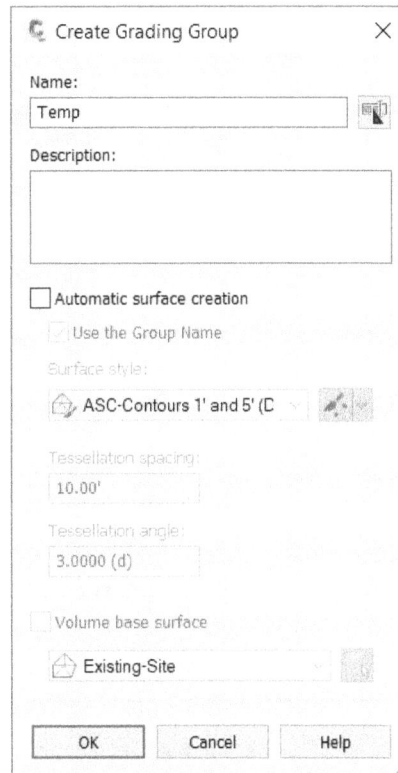

Figure 5–45

Establish a feature line with a **1:1** slope to an elevation of **180' using the following steps**.

6. In the Grading Creation Tools toolbar, set the *Criteria* as

   Grade to Elevation and click ![icon] (Create Grading), as shown in Figure 5–46.

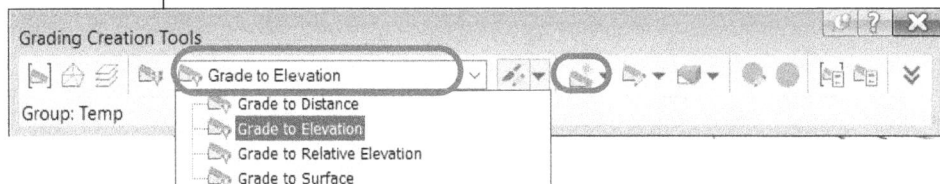

Figure 5–46

7. When prompted to select a feature, select the green pond boundary feature line that defines the perimeter pond site, as shown in Figure 5–47. If prompted to weed the feature line, select **Continue grading without feature line weeding**.

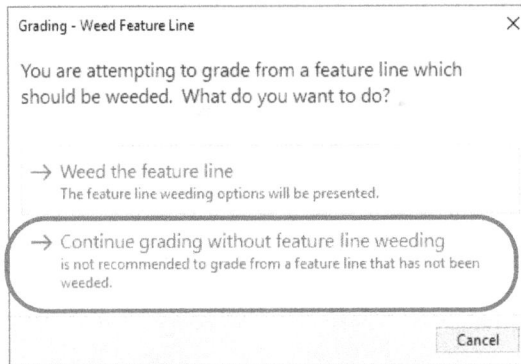

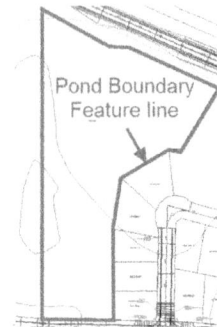

Grading - Weed Feature Line ✕

You are attempting to grade from a feature line which should be weeded. What do you want to do?

→ Weed the feature line
The feature line weeding options will be presented.

→ Continue grading without feature line weeding
is not recommended to grade from a feature line that has not been weeded.

Cancel

Pond Boundary
Feature line

Figure 5–47

8. When prompted for the side to grade, select a point inside of the pond.

9. Select **No** when prompted to *Apply to the entire length*.

10. When prompted for the start point, select the center of the green circle located on the west feature line and press <Enter> to accept <20+09.87'> for the station.

11. When prompted for the end point or length, select the center of the green circle located on the south feature line and press <Enter> to accept <23+77.50'> for the station.

12. When prompted for the elevation, type **180** and press <Enter>.

13. When prompted for the cut format, select **Slope**. Type **1** and press <Enter> to indicate a cut slope of 1:1.

14. When prompted for the fill format, select **Slope**. Type **1** and press <Enter> to indicate a fill slope of 1:1.

15. This defines the 1:1 slope from the road, as shown in Figure 5–48.

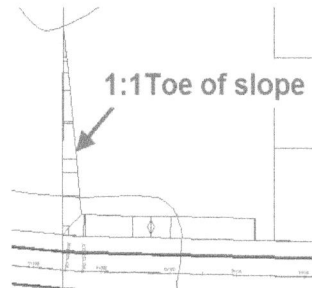

1:1 Toe of slope

Figure 5–48

Next you will determine where the 3:1 slope from the parcels to the east intersects the 1:1 slope of the pond.

*At any time, if you accidentally closed the **Grading** command, you just need to click*

(Create Grading).

16. When prompted to select a feature line, select the pond boundary feature line, which is the green line that defines the outer perimeter of the pond site.

17. When prompted for the grading side, select a point inside the pond.

18. When prompted for the start point, select the center of the southern-most cyan circle located on the east feature line and press <Enter> to accept <0+14.89'> for the station.

19. When prompted for the endpoint or length, select the center of the northern-most cyan circle located on the east feature line and press <Enter> to accept <0+69.25'> for the station, as shown in Figure 5–49.

Station:0

Figure 5–49

20. When prompted for the elevation, type **165** and press <Enter>.

21. When prompted for the cut format, select **Slope**. Type **3** and press <Enter> for a cut slope of 3:1.

22. When prompted for the fill format, select **Slope**. Type **3** and press <Enter> for a fill slope of 3:1.

This establishes the toe of slope where the 1:1 slope intersects the 3:1 slope.

23. Press <Esc> to end the feature line selection and select the **X** in the Grading Creation Tools toolbar to close the toolbar.

To use the toe of slope for further grading, the feature line that represents the toe of slope must be extracted from the grading object.

24. In Model Space, select the toe of slope feature line, right-click, and select **Move to Site...**, as shown in Figure 5–50.

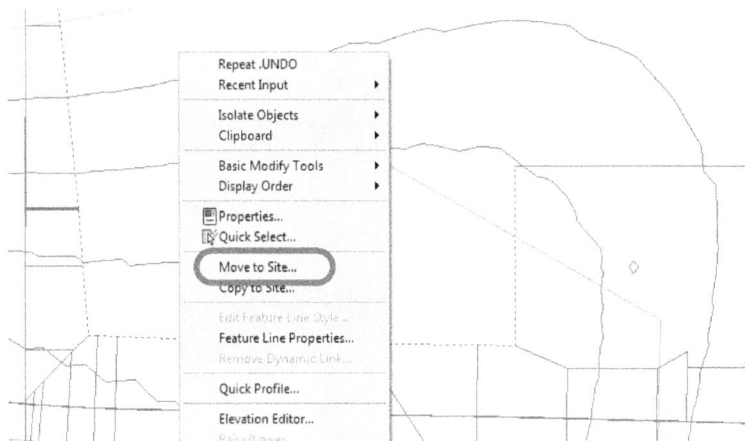

Figure 5–50

25. In the Move to Site dialog box, click **OK** to accept the default site, as shown in Figure 5–51.

It does not matter which site you place it in. By moving the feature line to a different site, the grading object is deleted, leaving just the toe of slope.

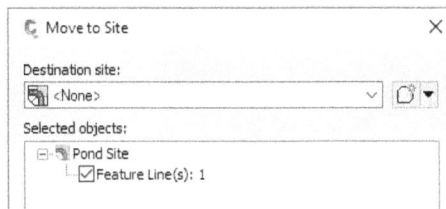

Figure 5–51

26. Select the feature line again and move it back to the **Pond Site**, as shown in Figure 5–52.

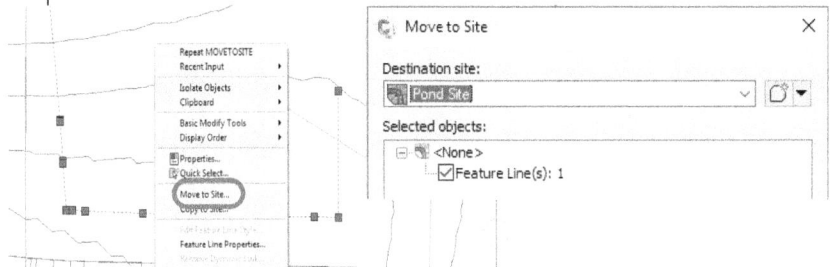

Figure 5–52

27. In Model Space, select the feature line. In the *Feature Line* contextual tab>Modify panel, click (Feature Line Properties).

28. In the Feature Line Properties dialog box, select the **Name** option and type **Toe of slope** in the *Name* field, as shown in Figure 5–53. Click **OK**.

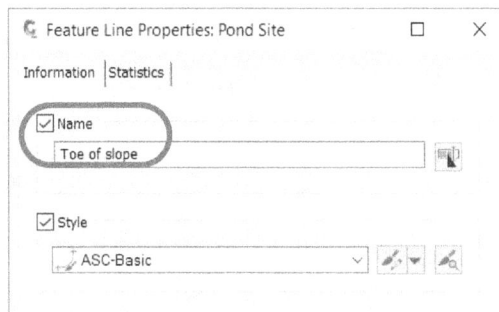

Figure 5–53

29. In Model Space, select the toe of slope feature line. In the *Feature Line* contextual tab>Modify panel, click (Edit Elevations). In the Edit Elevations panel, click (Elevation Editor).

In the Grading Elevation Editor vista, the elevation shown for station 2+84.74' is 172.50', as shown in Figure 5–54. The correct elevation is 180'.

1+66.15		180.000'	2.549'	-0.00%	0.00%
1+68.70		180.000'	0.004'	0.00%	0.00%
1+68.71		180.000'	5.575'	0.00%	0.00%
1+74.28		180.000'	25.002'	0.00%	0.00%
1+99.28		180.000'	17.561'	-0.00%	0.00%
2+16.84		180.000'	7.439'	0.00%	-0.00%
2+24.28		180.000'	10.040'	-0.00%	0.00%
2+34.32		180.000'	14.960'	0.00%	0.00%
2+49.28		180.000'	25.001'	0.00%	-0.00%
2+74.28		180.000'	10.454'	-71.74%	71.74%
2+84.74	180		48.266'	-15.54%	-15.54%
3+33.01		165.000'			

Figure 5–54

30. Select the elevation field for station 2+84.74, type **180**, and press <Enter>.

31. Click ✔ to close the Elevation Editor vista.

32. To join the toe of slope feature line to the east pond boundary, select the toe of slope feature line and select the east feature line to display all of the grips.

33. Select the last grip on the toe of slope feature line and drag it to the intermediate point on the east feature line, as shown in Figure 5–55.

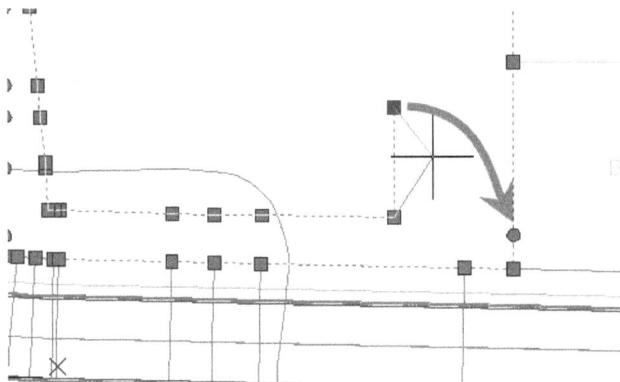

Figure 5–55

34. You have now defined the south pond feature line.

35. Save the drawing.

Task 2 - Establish control feature lines (north end).

In this task you will define the north pond feature line by determining the location of the Pond maintenance access road, based on a 3:1 grade from the existing boundary.

1. In the *View* tab>Views panel, select the preset view **Storm Pond**.

2. In the *Home* tab>Create Design panel, expand the Grading drop-down list and click (Grading Creation Tools).

3. In the Grading Creation Tools dialog box, set the *Grading Group* name to **Temp** (if not already set) and ensure that the grading criteria is set to **Grade to Elevation**.

4. Click (Create Grading) as shown in Figure 5–56, and select the Pond boundary feature line, which is the green line that represents the perimeter of the pond site.

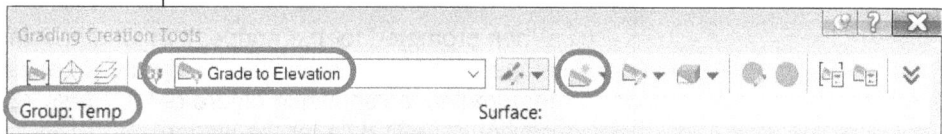

Figure 5–56

5. When prompted to weed the feature line, select **Continue grading without feature line weeding**.

6. When prompted for the side to grade, select a point inside the pond. Select **No** when prompted to *Apply to the entire length*.

7. When prompted for the start point, select the center of the magenta circle located on the northeast corner of the feature line, as shown in Figure 5–57. Press <Enter> to accept <7+88.94'> for the station.

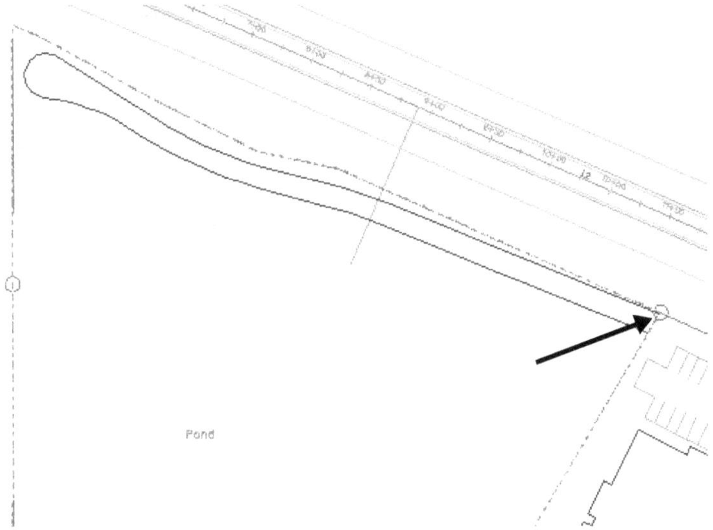

Figure 5–57

8. When prompted for the endpoint or length, select the center of the magenta circle located on the northern part of the west feature line, as shown in Figure 5–58. Press <Enter> to accept <15+31.82'> for the station.

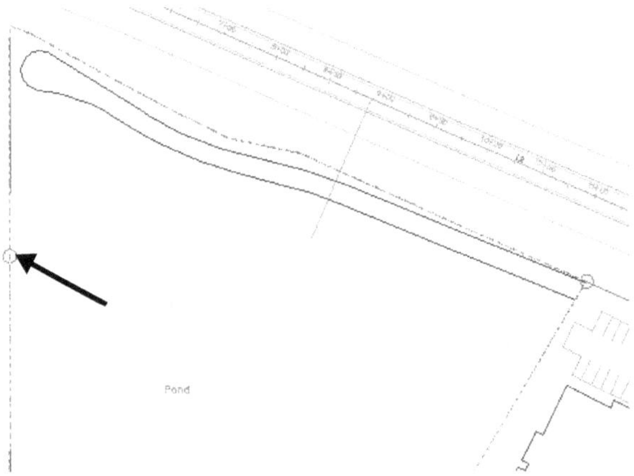

Figure 5–58

9. When prompted for the elevation, type **165.0** and press <Enter>.

10. When prompted for the cut format, select **Slope**. Type **3** and press <Enter> for a cut slope of 3:1.

11. When prompted for the fill format, select **Slope**. Type **3** and press <Enter> for a fill slope of 3:1.

12. Press <Esc> to exit the feature line selection. Select the **X** in the Grading Creation Tools toolbar to close the toolbar.

This grading object defines a 3:1 slope from the existing boundary and establishes the approximate location of the maintenance road. To save time, the access road has already been designed, as shown in Figure 5–59.

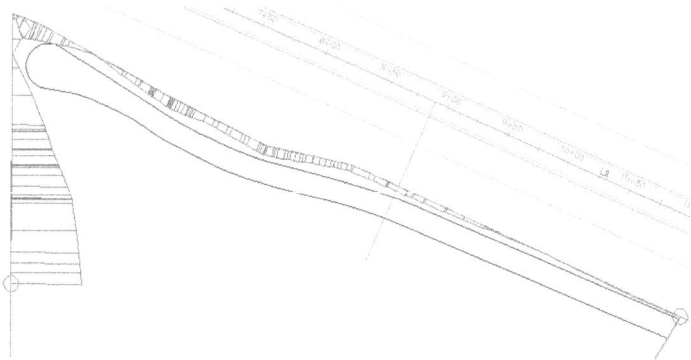

Figure 5–59

Based on the 3:1 cut and fill slope to an elevation of 164.4', you now have a feature line representing the access road. This access road has a maximum side slope of 3:1 to existing ground on the north side of the road. On the south side of the road, you continue to grade based on the design criteria for the pond.

13. You can erase the grading 3:1 maximum slope because it is no longer needed. In Model Space, select the grading object.

    In the *Grading* contextual tab>Modify panel, click (Delete Grading).

14. Save the drawing.

Task 3 - Create the pond's outside rim feature line.

---

1. Continue working with the drawing from the previous task.

2. In the *View* tab>Views panel, select the preset view **Storm Pond**.

This list displays the names of the feature lines, style, layer, and 2D length.

The Autodesk Civil 3D software highlights the appropriate feature line.

3. In the *Prospector* tab, expand the *Sites>Pond Site* collection. Select **Feature lines** and note the grid view that is usually at the bottom of the pane.

4. Select **Toe of slope** from the list, right-click and select **Select**, as shown in Figure 5–60.

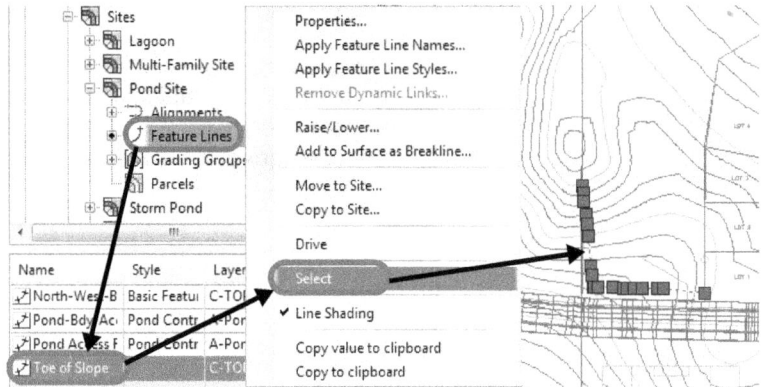

Figure 5–60

5. In the *Feature Line* contextual tab>Modify panel, click

    (Feature Line Properties).

6. In the Feature Line Properties dialog box, complete the following, as shown in Figure 5–61:
   - Change the *Name* to **Pond-Bdy-Control**.
   - Set the *Style* to **Pond Control Feature Line**.
   - Click **OK**.

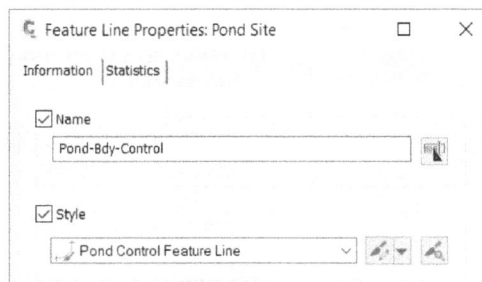

Figure 5–61

7. Press <Esc> to release the feature line.

8. Zoom in on the south end of the pond.

9. Select the feature line named **North-West-Boundary** that surrounds the pond.

10. In the *Feature Line* contextual tab>Modify panel, click
    ⬛ (Edit Geometry) if it is not already displayed. In the Edit
    Geometry panel, click ⤶ᵗ (Break), as shown in Figure 5–62.

Figure 5–62

11. Select the **North-West-Boundary** feature line again. Type **F**
    at the Command Line so that you can select the first and
    second point of the break. Pick a point south of the cyan
    circle to the south of the control feature line for the first point.
    Then pick the endpoint of the control line using Osnaps, as
    shown in Figure 5–63.

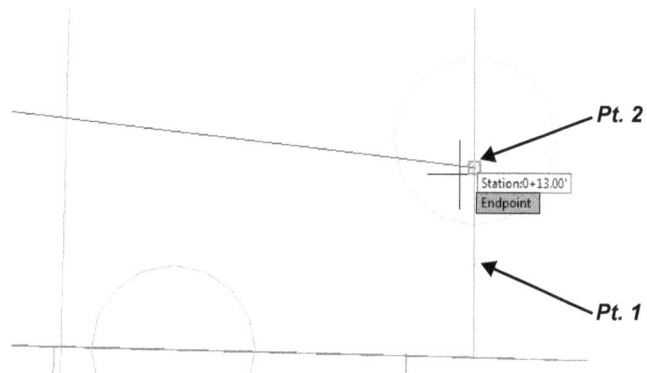

Figure 5–63

12. Select the **North-West-Boundary** feature line. In the *Feature
    Line* contextual tab>Modify panel, click ⬛ (Edit Geometry) if
    it is not already visible. In the Edit Geometry panel, click
    ⤶ᵗ (Break).

13. Select the **North-West-Boundary** feature line again. Type **F**
    at the Command Line so that you can select the first and
    second point of the break.

14. Pick a point inside the green circle to the south of the control feature line for the first point. Then pick the endpoint of the control line using Osnaps, as shown in Figure 5–64.

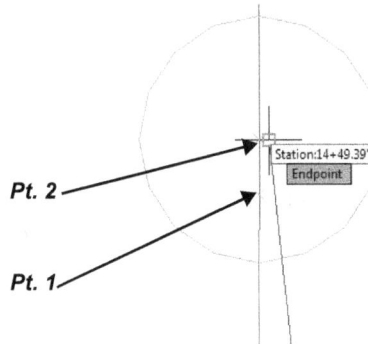

Figure 5–64

15. In the *View* tab>Views panel, select the **Storm Pond** view. Zoom into the north-east corner of the pond.

16. Select the **North-West-Boundary** feature line. In the *Feature Line* contextual tab>Modify panel, click ⬛ (Edit Geometry) if it is not already displayed. In the Edit Geometry panel, click ⬛ (Break).

17. Select the **North-West-Boundary** feature line again just north of the south line of the maintenance road (this is also the first point), as shown in Figure 5–65. Pick the endpoint of the south line of the maintenance road using Osnaps for the second point.

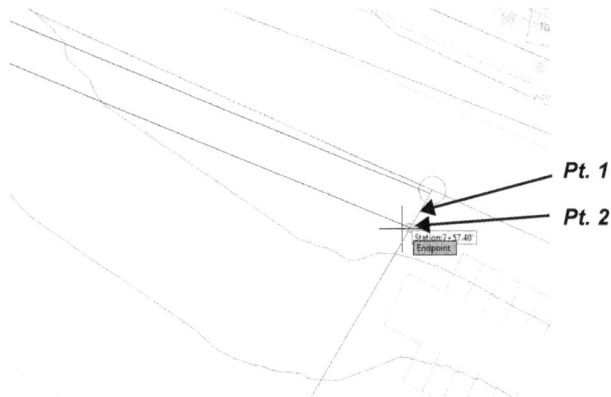

Figure 5–65

18. In the *View* tab>Views panel, select the **Storm Pond** view. Zoom into the north-west corner of the pond.

19. Select the **North-West-Boundary** feature line. In the *Feature Line* contextual tab>Modify panel, click (Edit Geometry) if it is not already displayed. In the Edit Geometry panel, click (Break).

20. Select the **North-West-Boundary** feature line again near the north-western corner of the pond (this is also the first point), as shown in Figure 5–66. Then pick the endpoint near station 5+98.05' (using Osnap) for the second point.

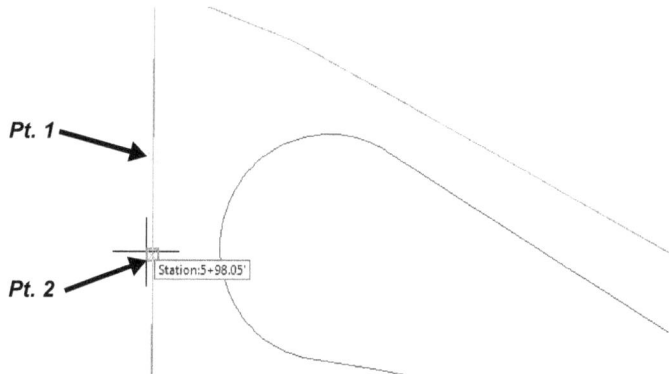

Pt. 1

Pt. 2

Station:5+98.05'

Figure 5–66

21. Select the west feature line. In the *Feature Line* contextual tab>Modify panel, click (Edit Elevations). In the Edit Elevations panel, click (Elevation Editor).

22. In the Elevation Editor vista, note that an elevation point is located at station 0+20.17 with an elevation of 170', as shown in Figure 5–67. You turn this into a regular vertex.

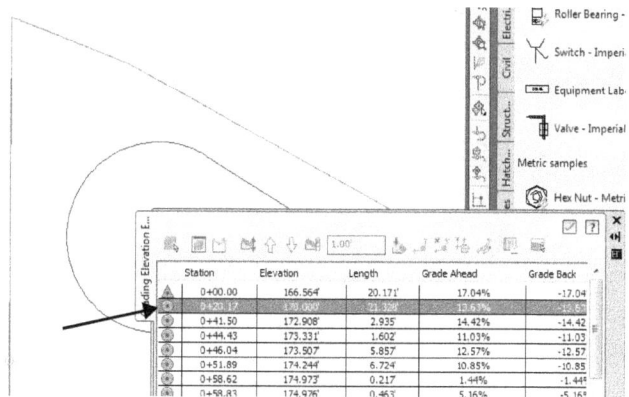

Station	Elevation	Length	Grade Ahead	Grade Back
0+00.00	166.564'	20.171'	17.04%	-17.04
0+20.17	170.000'	21.328'	13.63%	-15.65
0+41.50	172.908'	2.935'	14.42%	-14.42
0+44.43	173.331'	1.602'	11.03%	-11.03
0+46.04	173.507'	5.857'	12.57%	-12.57
0+51.89	174.244'	6.724'	10.85%	-10.85
0+58.62	174.973'	0.217'	1.44%	-1.44
0+58.83	174.976'	0.463'	5.16%	-5.16

Figure 5–67

23. Select the feature line again. In the *Feature Line* contextual tab>Modify panel, click 📁 (Edit Geometry). In the Edit Geometry panel, click ⟋⟍ (Insert PI).

24. At the Command Line, for *Distance* type **D** and press <Enter>. For the *Distance* value type **20.17** and press <Enter>. For the *Elevation* type **170** and press <Enter>. Press <Esc> to end the command.

25. Click ✔ to close the Elevation Editor vista.

26. Select the feature line. Using grips, move the first vertex to the endpoint of the southern boundary line of the maintenance road using Osnaps, as shown in Figure 5–68.

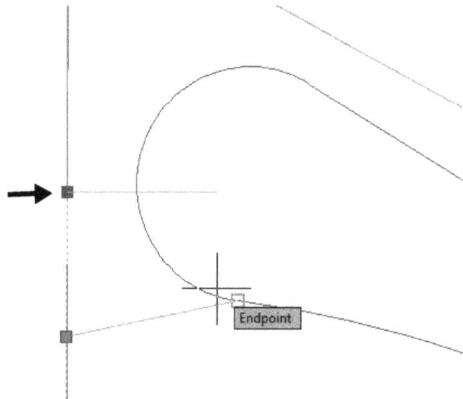

Figure 5–68

27. In the *View* tab>Views panel, select **Storm Pond** to restore the view.

28. To join all of the feature lines, select the feature line **Pond-Bdy-Control**. In the *Feature Line* contextual tab>Modify panel, click 📁 (Edit Geometry). In the Edit Geometry panel, click ⟋ (Join), as shown in Figure 5–69.

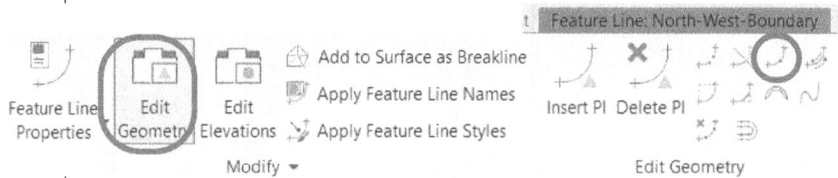

Figure 5–69

29. When prompted to select the connecting feature lines, select the feature line **Pond-Bdy-East** (2), **Pond-Bdy-North** (3), and **Pond-Bdy-West** (4), as shown in Figure 5–70. If you receive an error that they cannot be joined, you might need to grip edit the feature lines to snap them end to end.

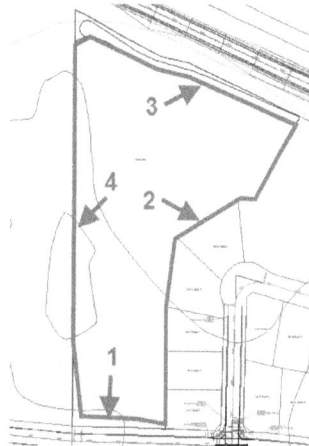

Figure 5–70

30. Press <Esc> to exit the feature line selection.

31. Select the feature line that runs along the Jeffries Ranch Road corridor to the south.

32. In the *Feature Line* contextual tab>Modify tab, click (Feature Line Properties).

33. In the Feature Line Properties, for the *Name* type **Pond-Bdy-South**. Click **OK**.

34. Select the feature line that runs along the north of the pond.

35. In the *Feature Line* contextual tab>Modify panel, click (Feature Line Properties).

36. In the Feature Line Properties, for the *Name* type **Pond-Bdy-North**. Click **OK**.

37. Save the drawing.

5.6 Pond Staging Volumes

An important part of designing ponds or basins is ensuring that the pond can hold the volume of water anticipated. This is often done using stage-storage calculations. Stage-storage defines the relationship between the depth of water and storage volume in the storage basin or pond.

Within the Autodesk Civil 3D software, you can calculate incremental and cumulative volumes using two different calculations, as shown in Figure 5–71 and described below. Whichever method is chosen, the Stage Storage command is used to complete the stage storage volume analysis.

- Average End Area: Calculates the volume between two cross sections.

- Conic Approximation: Calculates the volume between two sectional areas.

$$V = \left(\frac{A_1 + A_2}{2}\right)L \qquad V = \left(\frac{h}{3}\right)(A_1 + A_2 + \sqrt{A_1 A_2})$$

Average End Area Method Equation   **Conic Approximation Method Equation**

Figure 5–71

How To: Calculate the Stage Storage Volumes of a Pond or Basin.

1. Ensure that the contours are visible for the surface to analyze. This is done in the surface properties by selecting an appropriate surface style.
2. In the *Analyze* tab>expand the Design panel, and click

   ⬚ (Stage Storage).
3. In the Stage Storage dialog box, do the following, as shown in Figure 5–72.
   - Enter a *Report Title*.
   - Enter a *Project Name*.
   - Enter a *Basin Description*.
   - For the *Volume Calculation Method*, select either **Average End Area, Conic Approximation** or **Both**.
   - For the *Basin Definition Options*, select either **Define Basin from Entity** or **Use Manual Contour Data Entry**. Then, click **Define Basin**.

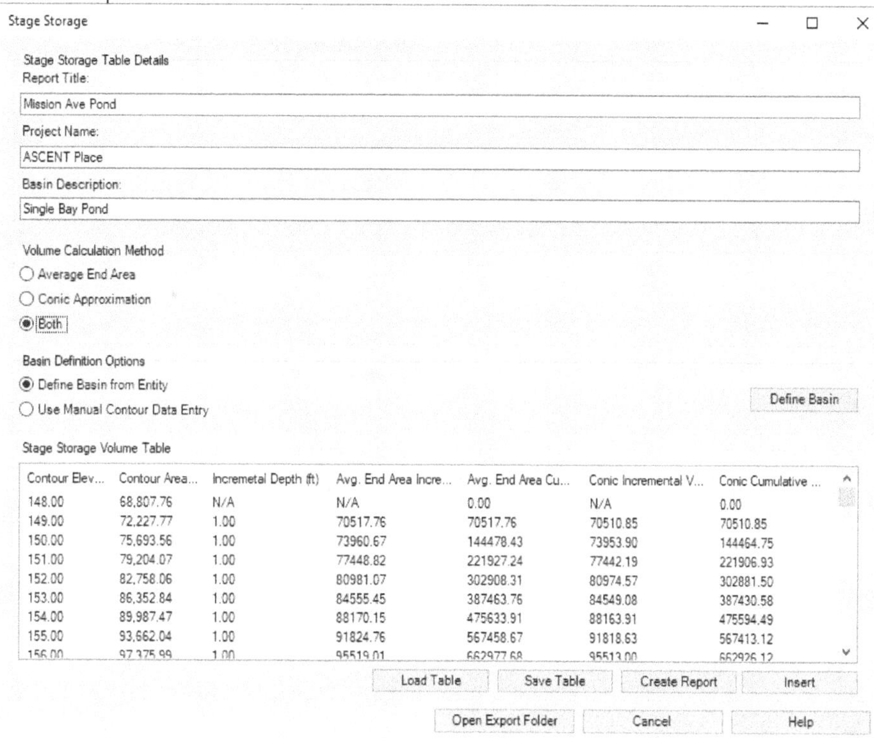

Figure 5–72

- If the **Use Manual Contour Data Entry** option is selected, a dialog box displays that enables you to manually enter the contour elevation and area, as shown in Figure 5–73.

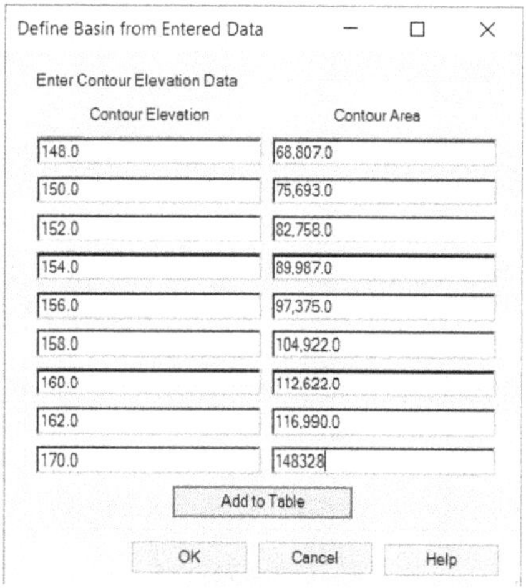

Figure 5–73

4. In the Define Basin from Entities dialog box, enter a *Basin Name*, and select one of the following options, as shown in Figure 5–74.

- **Define from Surface Contours:** Enables you to select a surface.
- **Define Basin from Polylines:** Enables you to select polylines representing surface contours.

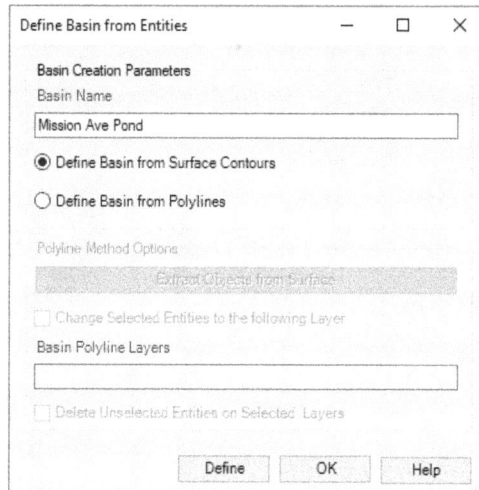

Figure 5–74

5. Then, click one of the following options to show the results:

- **Create Report:** Prompts you to save a *.txt file.
- **Insert:** Prompts you to select a point in the model to place the top left corner of the volume table.

SECTION 3

Alignments and Profiles

Exam Objective	Chapter(s)
3.4 Create profile views	
3.4.a Describe the relationship between profiles, profile views, and profile view bands	Ch. 7
3.4.b Identify available object types to project to a profile view*	*See p. 7-1
3.4.c Create a profile view	Ch. 7
3.4.d Split a profile view	Ch. 7
3.5 Create alignment and profile annotations	
3.5.a Describe the relationship between the label type and how it is placed on the alignment/profile	Ch. 6
3.5.b Distinguish between station offset and station offset fixed point labels	Ch. 6
3.5.c Explain how to renumber tag labels*	*See p. 6-1
3.5.d Work with alignment/profile labels	Ch. 6 Ch. 7
3.5.e Use alignment tables	Ch. 6

Alignments

Exam Objectives Covered in This Chapter

3.1.a Create an alignment from objects

3.1.b Create offset alignments

3.1.c Edit alignment constraints

3.1.d Add lines, curves, and spirals to an alignment

3.5.a Describe the relationship between the label type and how it is placed on the alignment/profile

3.5.b Distinguish between station offset and station offset fixed point labels

3.5.d Work with alignment/profile labels

3.5.e Use alignment tables

Note: The objectives *3.1.e Reverse the alignment direction, 3.1.f Apply widenings for a specified length along an alignment*, and *3.5.c Explain how to renumber tag labels* are not covered in this guide. Refer to the Civil 3D Help documentation to review this content.

6.1 Introduction to Alignments

An Autodesk Civil 3D alignment is an AEC object that resembles an AutoCAD® polyline. Alignments have rule-based constraints that make them very powerful design tools. Alignments can contain tangents (line segments), circular curves, and spirals.

The appearance and annotation of alignments are controlled by object and label styles. These styles are flexible, have an extensive list of label properties, and control layer assignments for objects and their labels.

Autodesk Civil 3D alignments can be created in the following ways:

- If previously defined, alignments can be imported from Autodesk LandXML®, from an Autodesk® Land Desktop project, or from InfraWorks conceptual roads.

- A polyline can be converted directly to an alignment. Converted polylines follow the direction of the original polyline object.

- An alignment can be created interactively using the Alignment Layout toolbar.

- Individual AutoCAD lines and arcs can be converted to alignments using the Layout toolbar as well.

When creating new alignments, remember that you can use transparent commands to draw line segments by **Angle and Distance**, **Bearing and Distance**, **Azimuth and Distance**, and **Deflection Distance**. These commands are available in the Transparent ribbon tab, as shown in Figure 6–1. They are extremely helpful when you need to stay within a specific right-of-way and you have the legal description of that right-of-way.

Figure 6–1

These Transparent Commands are also available in a toolbar, as shown in Figure 6–2.

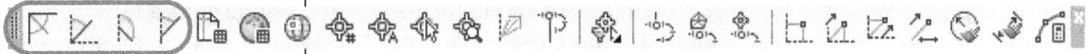

Figure 6–2

They are also available through the right-click menu when AutoCAD or Civil 3D is searching for a point, as shown in Figure 6–3.

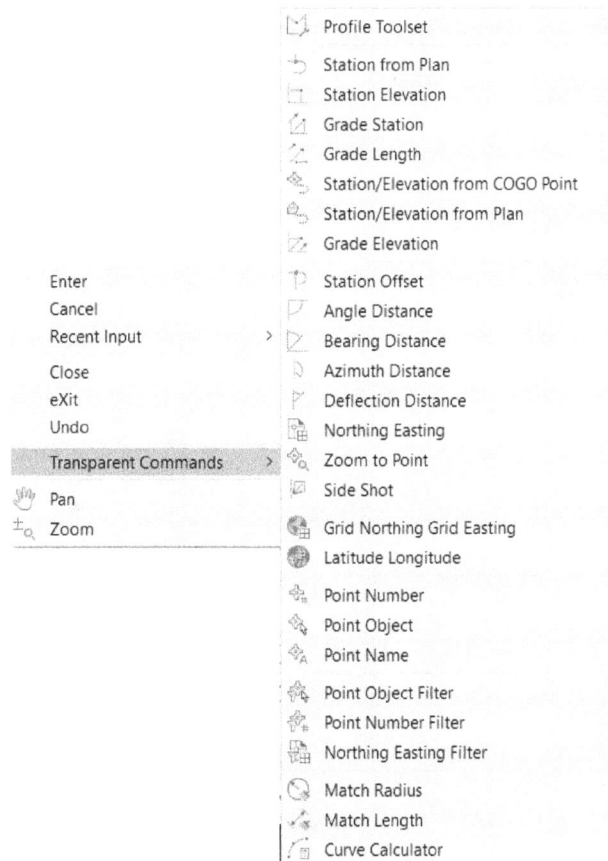

	Profile Toolset
	Station from Plan
	Station Elevation
	Grade Station
	Grade Length
	Station/Elevation from COGO Point
	Station/Elevation from Plan
	Grade Elevation
Enter	Station Offset
Cancel	Angle Distance
Recent Input >	Bearing Distance
Close	Azimuth Distance
eXit	Deflection Distance
Undo	Northing Easting
Transparent Commands >	Zoom to Point
Pan	Side Shot
Zoom	Grid Northing Grid Easting
	Latitude Longitude
	Point Number
	Point Object
	Point Name
	Point Object Filter
	Point Number Filter
	Northing Easting Filter
	Match Radius
	Match Length
	Curve Calculator

Figure 6–3

Criteria-Based Design

Default or custom standards can be used in the Autodesk Civil 3D software to evaluate alignment and profile designs. The Design Criteria Editor enables you to view, edit, or create criteria files (such as AASHTO tables). When you create a new alignment, the Create Alignment dialog box opens, as shown in Figure 6–4. You can tell the software what type of alignment you are creating to make intersection design easier later. The dialog box includes a *Design Criteria* tab that enables you to type the starting design speed, use criteria-based design, use a design criteria file, or use a design check set.

Figure 6–4

When an entity does not meet the criteria in the file it displays with a warning marker. Hover over the marker and note which criteria the entity violates, as shown in Figure 6–5.

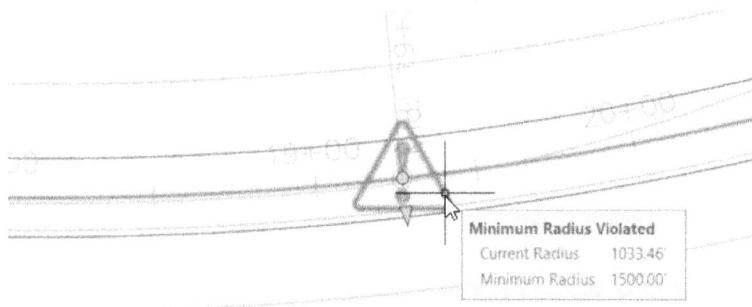

Minimum Radius Violated	
Current Radius	1033.46'
Minimum Radius	1500.00'

Figure 6–5

A warning marker also displays in the sub-entity and grid view editors when a violation occurs. This marker disappears when the value meets the required criteria.

Alignment Types

There are 5 different types of alignments that can be used in a design.

1. A **Centerline alignment** is the most commonly used type of alignment. You can use it when you know the location and design parameters of the centerline of the road, trail, or other linear feature being designed.

2. An **Offset alignment** is used to create transitions in a corridor design. You can use it when you want to target a transition line, such as a curb return, bus turnout lane, or other deviation from the original widths.

3. A **Curb Return alignment** is used when you want to base the design of the road from the curb location or when you need to connect the edges of two intersecting roadways.

4. A **Rail alignment** is the newest type of alignment. You can use it when you need to calculate curves along chords rather than arcs. It also enables you to set the track width and calculate cants.

5. A **Miscellaneous alignment** is available when the type of alignment you are creating does not fall into any of the other categories.

Alignment Segment Types

Each alignment tangent, circular curve, and spiral falls into one of three categories.

1. A **fixed segment** is one that is defined by specific criteria that only have a limited ability to be dynamically updated. Fixed curves hold their initial constraints (such as length and radius) and do not remain tangent at either end if a neighboring line segment is adjusted. You should avoid fixed curves in alignments that you might want to dynamically update (such as proposed alignments).

   Alignments imported from the Autodesk LandXML software contain all fixed segments. Alignment segments created from individual lines and arcs are also created as fixed segments. These fixed curves can be deleted and replaced with other types as required.

2. A **floating element** is one that depends entirely on the object before it in the alignment. If a preceding object is moved, stretched, or adjusted, a floating element (and everything following it) translates accordingly while holding all of the initial constraints (length, radius, pass-through-points, etc.).

   For example, the alignment shown in Figure 6–6 begins with a fixed line followed by a series of floating curves and a floating line that together define a cul-de-sac. Changing the end point of the fixed line causes all of the floating elements to translate while maintaining the original length of the floating line, and the original length, radius, and direction of the following curves. Floating elements only stay tangent at one end to neighboring segments if they are adjusted.

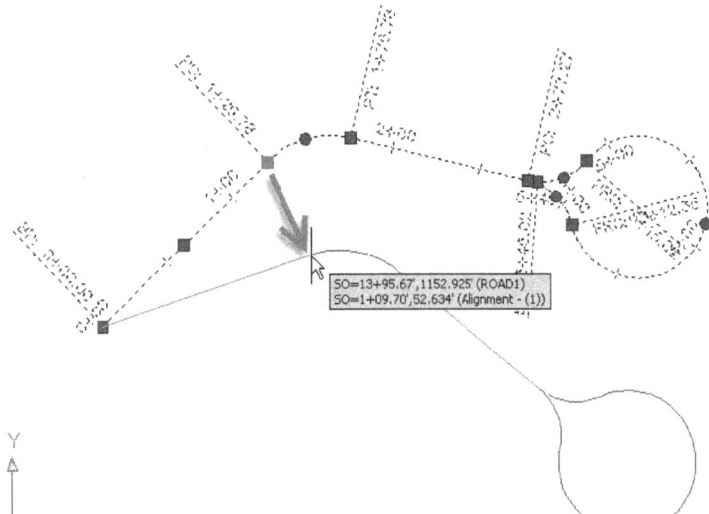

SO=13+95.67',1152.925' (ROAD1)
SO=1+09.70',52.634' (Alignment - (1))

Figure 6–6

3. A **free segment** is one that is adjusted if the geometry of either neighboring segment is changed. Free segments always adjust to remain tangent to adjacent segments at both ends. For example, the free line shown in Figure 6–7 was drawn connected to two fixed arcs. If either of the arcs were assigned a different property (such as a new radius), the line would be completely redrawn to remain tangent to both.

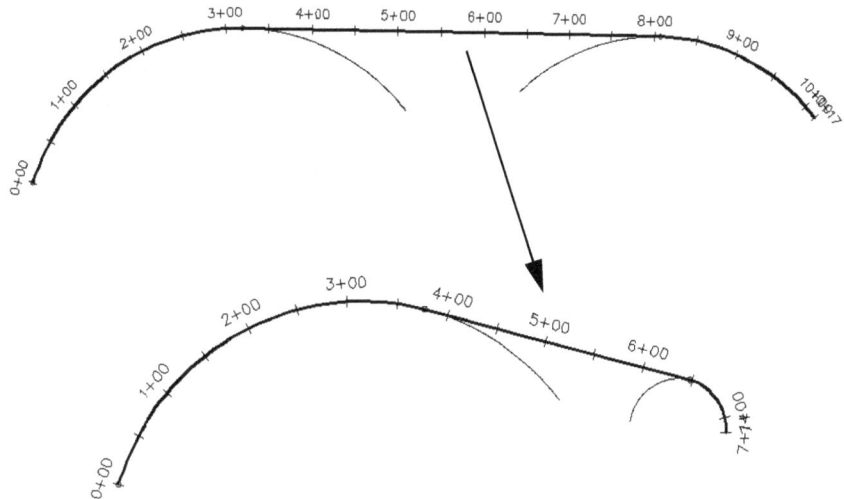

Figure 6–7

- Alignments created by layout and polyline are made of fixed lines and free curves and spirals. These tend to be the most flexible types of alignments.

- Because of their flexibility and ability to remain tangent through changes, free and floating elements are more useful in alignments that are subject to change, such as those for proposed roadway center lines.

Practice 6a

Creating Alignments from Objects

Practice Objective

- Create alignments from objects in the drawing or in an external reference file attached to the drawing.

In this practice, you will create horizontal alignments using two methods. First, you will create an alignment from an existing polyline that defines a road center line alignment. Second, you will create an alignment from a XREF file that defines a proposed center line alignment.

Task 1 - Create Alignment from a Polyline.

1. Open **ALN1-A1-Alignment.dwg** from the *C:\Civil 3D Projects\Working\Alignments* folder.

   In the drawing, the red polyline running east-west represents the existing center line alignment of Mission Avenue, as shown in Figure 6–8.

Figure 6–8

2. Set the **Working Folder** to *C:\Civil 3D Projects\Data Shortcuts\Fundamentals* and the **Data Shortcuts Project Folder** to *Ascent-Development*. Also, associate this drawing with the Ascent-Development project.

3. Reference the Existing-Site surface from the Ascent-Development project, leaving the name the same (as Existing-Site).

4. Change the style of the surface to **_No Display**.

5. In the *Home* tab>Create Design panel, expand Alignment, and select (Create Alignment from Objects), as shown in Figure 6–9. Select the west end of the polyline representing **Mission Ave polyline** (as shown in Figure 6–8) and press <Enter>.

Selecting the west end of the polyline identifies the start direction of the alignment.

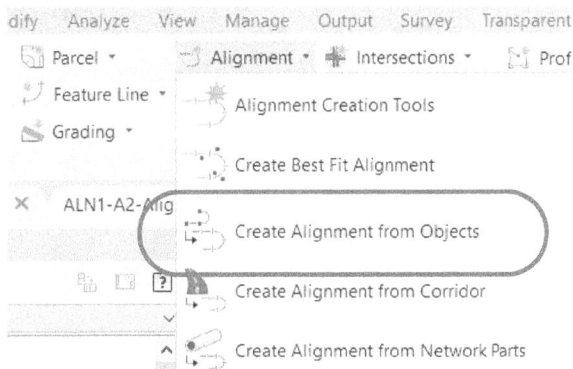

Figure 6–9

*If you want to reverse the direction of the alignment, you need to select **Reverse**.*

6. Verify that the alignment direction arrow is pointing East and press <Enter> to accept the alignment direction. If the direction arrow is pointing West, then press **R** to reverse the alignment direction.

Note: *By having an alignment in a site, any parcels in that same site will be divided by the alignment that bisects the parcel.*

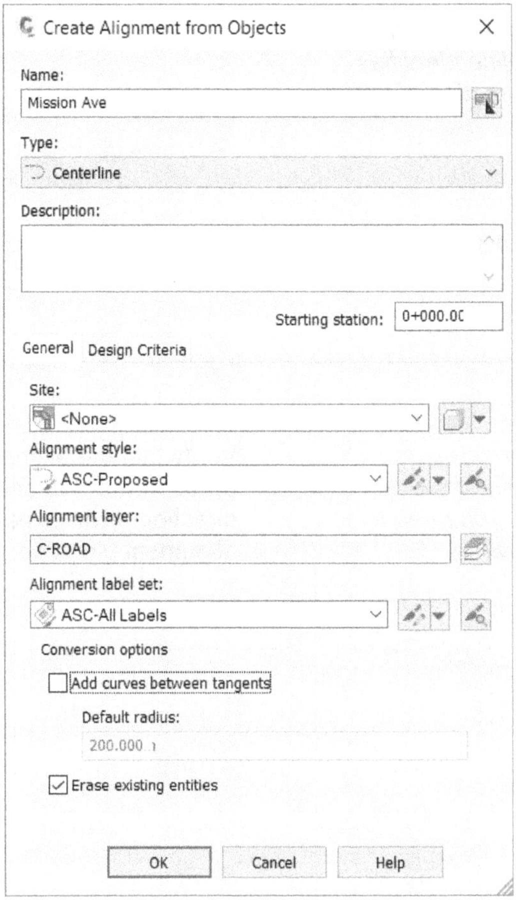

7. In the Create Alignment from Objects dialog box, assign the values shown in Figure 6–10 to define the properties of this alignment:
   - *Alignment name:* **Mission Ave**
   - *Type:* Leave as **Centerline**
   - *Description:* Type a description if required
   - *Starting station:* **0** (Even though this is an existing roadway and the starting station should be an existing value, you will leave it set to Zero for simplicity's sake).
   - *Site* (*General* tab): **None**
   - *Alignment Label Set:* **ASC-All Labels**
   - Clear the **Add curves between tangents** option.
   - Accept the remaining default values, but **do not** click **OK**, for you need to check the design criteria in the next step.

Figure 6–10

*The Autodesk Civil 3D software will reference the design criteria file **Autodesk Civil 3D Imperial (2011) Roadway Design Standards.xml**.*

An Autodesk Civil 3D alignment is created, complete with labeling.

8. Select the *Design Criteria* tab shown in Figure 6–11. Ensure that the following are set, then click **OK**:

   - Design speed is set to **60 mi/h**.
   - Both the **Use criteria-based design** and **Use design criteria file** options should be selected.

General   Design Criteria

Starting design speed:

60 mi/h

☑ Use criteria-based design

☑ Use design criteria file

C:\ProgramData\Autodesk\C3D 2021\enu\Data\Corridoi ⋯

Default criteria:

Property	Value
Minimum Radius Table	AASHTO 2011 US Customary...
Transition Length Table	2 Lane
Attainment Method	AASHTO 2011 Crowned Roa...

☑ Use design check set

Basic

Figure 6–11

9. Select the preset view **Aln-Warning**. Hover the cursor over the exclamation mark at approximately the station 19+26 on the alignment and note which design check was violated, as shown in Figure 6–12. In this case, the radius is 1033.46', but the minimum radius for a 60 mi/h road based on the AASHTO table must be greater than 1500'.

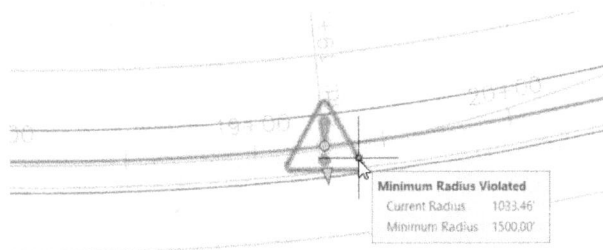

Minimum Radius Violated
Current Radius   1033.46'
Minimum Radius   1500.00'

Figure 6–12

10. Save the drawing.

Task 2 - Create an Alignment by Object (XREF).

1. Select the preset view **Aln-xref**.

2. In the *Home* tab>Create Design panel, expand **Alignment**, and select ⤳ (Create Alignment from Objects). When prompted to select an object, type **Xref** or **X** and press <Enter>. You will then be prompted to select a XREF object.

3. Select the west end of the polyline representing **Jeffries Ranch Rd** center line (the dashed gray line), as shown in Figure 6–13, and press <Enter>.

Selecting the west end of the XREF line identifies the start direction of the alignment.

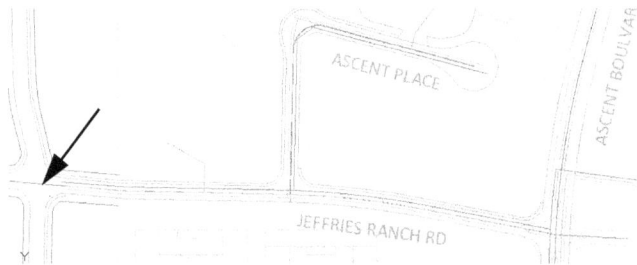

Figure 6–13

4. Verify that the alignment direction arrow is pointing East and press <Enter> to accept the alignment direction.

5. In the Create Alignment from Objects dialog box, type **Jeffries Ranch Rd** for the alignment name and accept all of the default values. Again you leave the starting station at Zero, although it is an existing roadway.

For this alignment, you will not be using design criteria.

6. In the *Design Criteria* tab, ensure that the **Use criteria-based design** option is cleared, as shown in Figure 6–14.

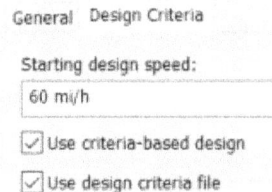

Figure 6–14

7. Click **OK** to close the dialog box and create the alignment.

8. Save the drawing.

6.2 Alignments Layout Tools

Alignments are created and edited using the Alignment Layout toolbar, which can be opened from the *Home* tab>Create Design panel. Expand Alignment and select ⤴ (Alignment Creation Tools), as shown at the top of Figure 6–15. The Alignment Layout Tools toolbar displays, as shown at the bottom of Figure 6–15.

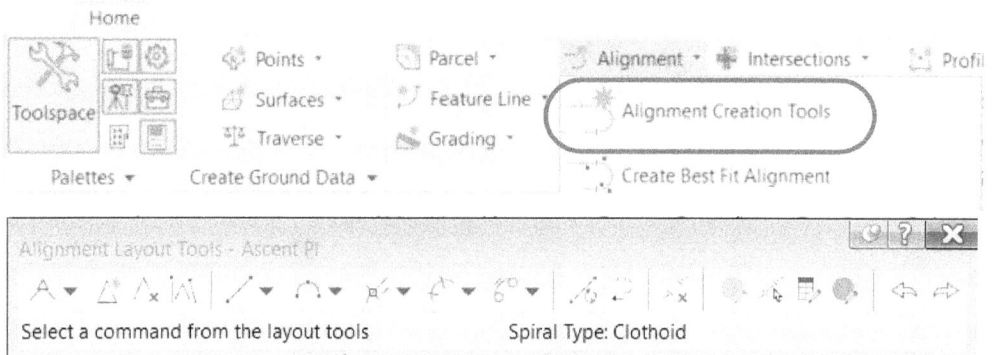

Figure 6–15

To create or add to an alignment interactively by locating new Points of Intersection (PIs), select one of the first two options in the Draw Tangents drop-down list, as shown in Figure 6–16.

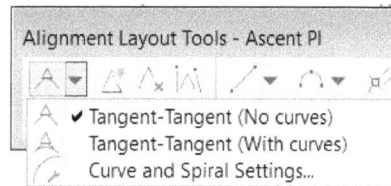

Figure 6–16

These two methods (with or without curves) are similar to drawing an AutoCAD polyline. If the **With Curves** option is selected, default curve information can be assigned in the Curve and Spiral Settings dialog box, as shown in Figure 6–17.

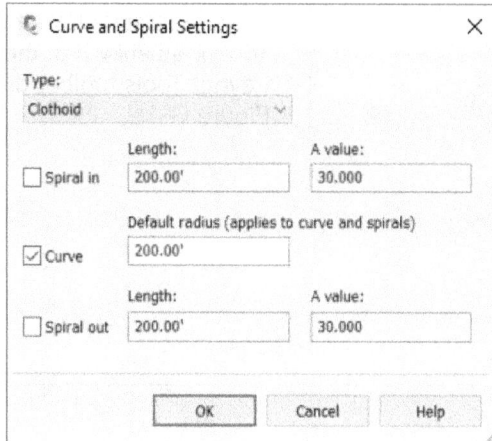

Figure 6–17

The Layout toolbar also includes tools that enable you to:

	Create new Points of Intersection (PIs).
	Delete PIs (and associated curves).
	Break apart PIs.
	Convert AutoCAD lines and arcs to alignment segments.
	Delete a line, circular curve, or spiral segment.
	Edit best-fit data for all entities.
	Select an individual segment for editing in the Sub-Entity Editor.
	Review and adjust alignment properties (length, radius, etc.) in the Alignment Entities Vista.
	Undo a recent alignment edit.
	Redo a recent alignment edit.

Most of the other tools in the Layout toolbar are intended for creating segments with various constraints.

Alignment Editing

In addition to the Edit tools available in the Alignment Layout toolbar, alignments can be edited using the AutoCAD **Modify** commands, such as **Move** and **Stretch**. Alignment entities can also be grip-edited into new positions. You can delete an alignment using the AutoCAD **Erase** command, or by right-clicking on the name of the alignment in the Toolspace, *Prospector* tab and selecting **Delete**. To open the Alignment Layout toolbar, expand Alignments and select **Edit Alignment Geometry**.

Practice 6b | Creating and Modifying Alignments

Practice Objective

- Create an alignment from scratch using the Alignment Layout tools.

In this practice, you will create a free form alignment, based on some design parameters. You will create an alignment for Ascent Place based on existing design data, as shown in Figure 6–18. According to this data, the street right-of-way extends north at a bearing of N1d18'04.79"E and then east at a bearing of S75d18'31.56"E. The north center line leg is 353.17' to the point of intersection and the east leg is -381.93' from the point of intersection. In addition, the center line of Ascent Place intersects Jeffries Ranch road at sta 5+79.13'.

Figure 6–18

Task 1 - Create an Alignment by Layout.

1. Open **ALN1-B1-Alignment.dwg** from the *C:\Civil 3D Projects\Working\Alignments* folder.

2. Select the preset view **Aln-Create**.

3. Toggle on *Selection* cycling by pressing <Ctrl>+<W>. The alignment object and XREF center line occupy the same location in space (as shown in Figure 6–19), and the selection cycling enables you to select the alignment.

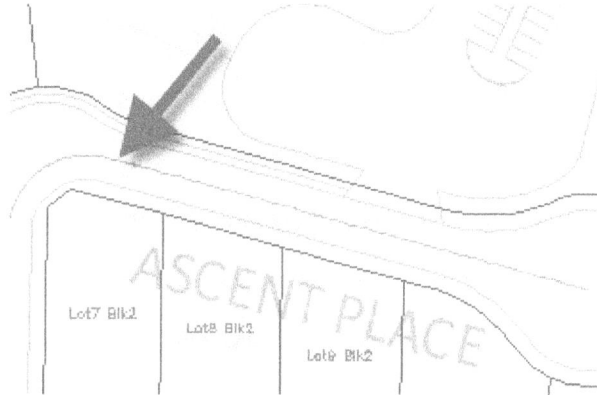

Figure 6–19

4. In the *Home* tab>Create Design panel, expand Alignment, and select (Alignment Creation Tools).

5. In the Create Alignment Layout dialog box, type **Ascent Pl** for the alignment name and accept all of the default values.

For this alignment, you will not be using design criteria.

6. In the *Design Criteria* tab, ensure that the **Use criteria-based design** option is not selected. Click **OK** to close the dialog box and create the alignment.

7. Expand the Tangent tool icon and select (Curve and Spiral Settings), as shown in Figure 6–20.

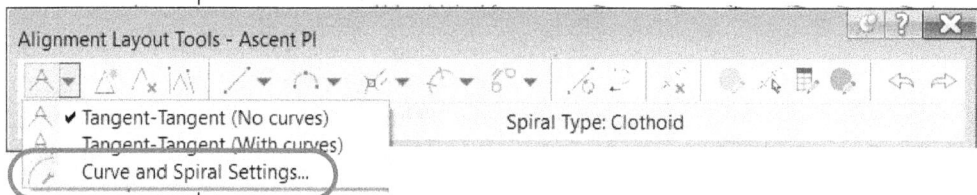

Figure 6–20

8. For the curve settings, ensure that the **curve** option is selected. Set the curve radius to **30.00'**, and click **OK** to close the Curve and Spiral Settings dialog box.

You want to start the alignment at a reference station to Jeffries Ranch Rd.

9. Expand the Tangent tool icon and select the

   ⒶⒶ (Tangent-Tangent (With curves)) to start creating the horizontal alignment.

10. When prompted for the start of the alignment, click

    ⍔ (Station Offset) on the *Transparent Commands* tab (or

    🔨 on the Transparent Tools toolbar).

11. When prompted for an alignment, select **Jeffries Ranch Rd**. In the Selection Cycling dialog box, click **Alignment**.

12. When prompted for a station, type **579.13'** and press <Enter>.

13. When prompted for the offset, type **0** and press <Enter>. Press <Esc> to exit the transparent command.

The Autodesk Civil 3D software has now established the starting location of the alignment by converting the station/offset to a X,Y value.

14. You will specify the next point using the transparent command to enter a bearing and a distance. Click (Bearing Distance) on the *Transparent Commands* tab and enter the following:

    • Type **1** and press <Enter> for the NE quadrant.
    • Type **1.180479** and then press <Enter> for the bearing.
    • Type a distance of **353.17'** and press <Enter>.
    • Press <Esc> to exit the transparent command.

15. You will specify the next point using the transparent command to enter a turned angle and a distance. Click

    ⍁ (Angle Distance) on the *Transparent Commands* tab and do the following:

    • Type **C** and press <Enter>, since you will be entering a counter-clockwise include angle.
    • Type the include angle of **76.6101** and press <Enter>.
    • Type **381.93** and press <Enter> for the distance.

16. Press <Esc> to exit the transparent command and press <Enter> to complete the horizontal alignment.

17. Close the **Alignment** layout tool by clicking **X** in the top right of the dialog box.

18. Save the drawing.

Task 2 - Edit Alignments.

1. Set **Aln-Curv Radius** as the active view.

2. Select the alignment **Ascent PI**. In the contextual Alignment tab>Modify panel, click (Geometry Editor).

3. In the alignment Tool Layout toolbar, click (Pick Sub-entity), as shown in Figure 6–21.

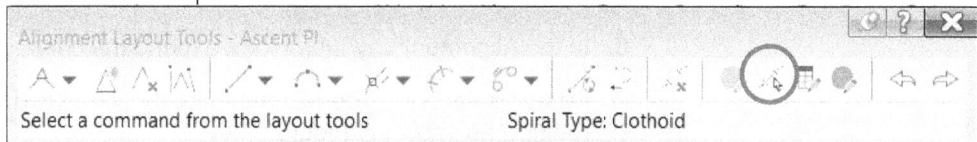

Alignment Layout Tools - Ascent PI

Select a command from the layout tools   Spiral Type: Clothoid

Figure 6–21

4. When prompted to select the sub-entity, select the curve. Change the radius to **50'** and press <Enter>, as shown in Figure 6–22.

Note that the radius dynamically changes in the graphics view.

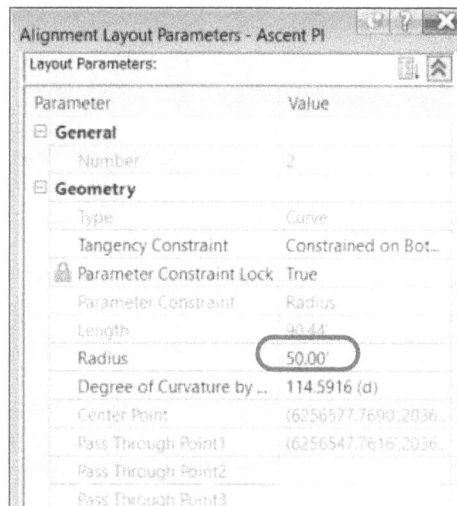

Alignment Layout Parameters - Ascent PI

Parameter	Value
General	
Number	2
Geometry	
Type	Curve
Tangency Constraint	Constrained on Bot...
Parameter Constraint Lock	True
Parameter Constraint	Radius
Length	90.44
Radius	50.00'
Degree of Curvature by ...	114.5916 (d)
Center Point	(6256577.7690;2036...
Pass Through Point1	(6256547.7616;2036...
Pass Through Point2	
Pass Through Point3	

Figure 6–22

5. Select (Delete Sub-entity) in the Alignment Layout toolbar, as shown in Figure 6–23. Select the curve and press <Enter> to exit the command.

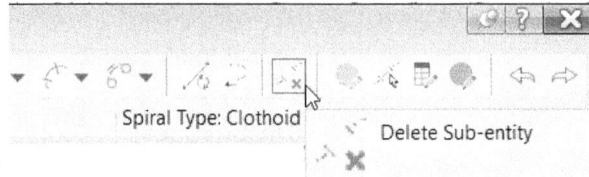

Spiral Type: Clothoid   Delete Sub-entity

Figure 6–23

6. In the Alignment Layout toolbar, expand the curve drop-down list and select (Free Curve Fillet (between two entities, radius)) as shown in Figure 6–24.

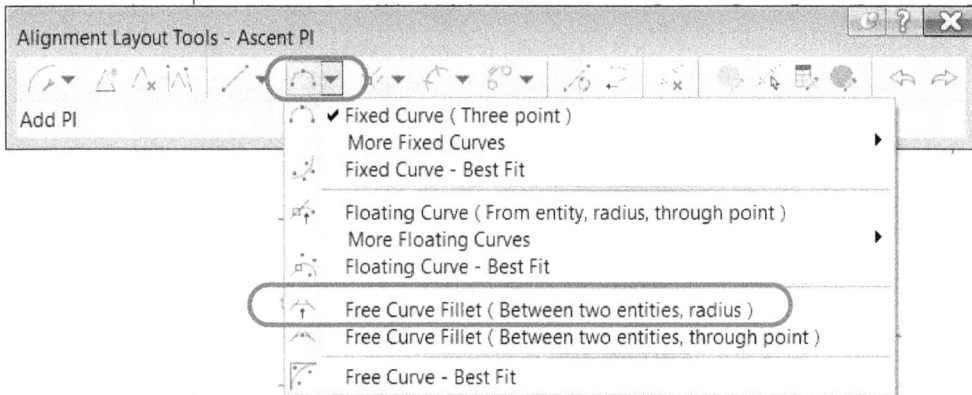

Alignment Layout Tools - Ascent PI

Add PI

✔ Fixed Curve (Three point)
More Fixed Curves
Fixed Curve - Best Fit

Floating Curve (From entity, radius, through point)
More Floating Curves
Floating Curve - Best Fit

Free Curve Fillet (Between two entities, radius)
Free Curve Fillet (Between two entities, through point)

Free Curve - Best Fit

Figure 6–24

7. Select the two tangents and press <Enter> to accept that the angle is **less than 180 deg**. For the radius, type **50'**, press <Enter>, and press <Enter> again to complete the command. The results are shown in Figure 6–25.

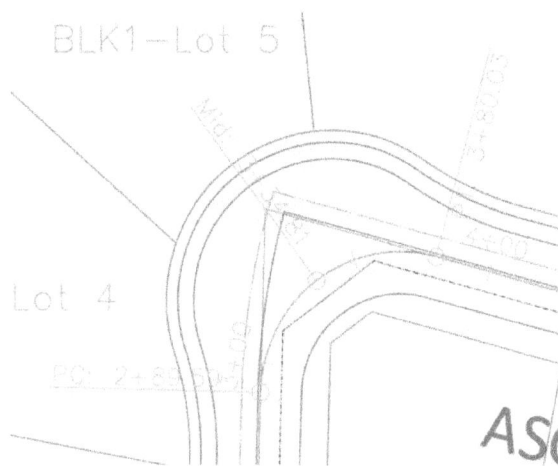

Figure 6–25

8. Close the Alignment Layout toolbar and save the drawing.

9. Save the drawing.

6.3 Labels and Tables

Alignment labels fall into two general categories: those controlled as a group using the **Edit Alignment Labels** command (referred to here as *Alignment Point Labels*), and those managed individually (referred to here as *Independent Alignment Labels*). Alignment labels of both types can be selected, repositioned, and erased separate from the alignment object itself.

Alignment Point Labels

Alignment point labels are organized into five categories, each of which is controlled by specific label styles:

- Major and Minor Stations

- (Horizontal) Geometry Points, such as Points of Curvature (PCs)

- Station Equations

- Design Speeds

- Profile Geometry Points, such as Points of Vertical Curvature (PVCs)

- Superelevation Critical Points

The Autodesk Civil 3D software enables you to organize various alignment point labels into **Alignment Label Sets**, as shown in Figure 6–26, to simplify adding a group of them at the same time.

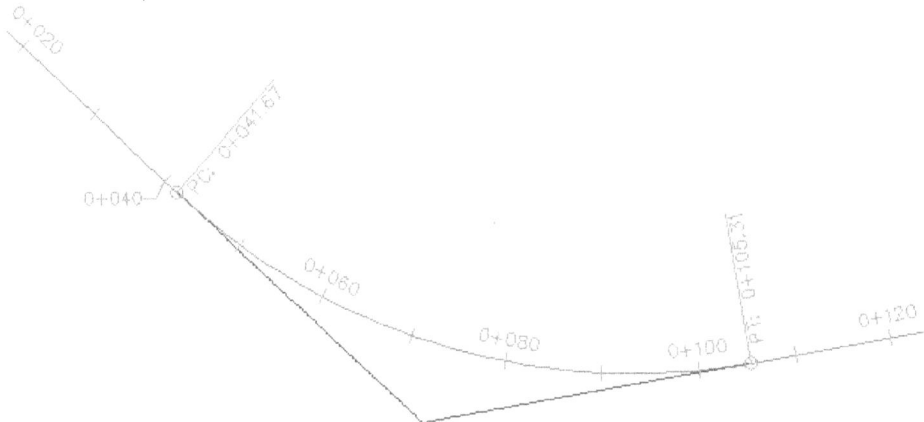

Figure 6–26

Alignment point labels are organized into *label groups*, so that when one is selected, all similar labels on the alignment are also selected, as shown in Figure 6–27. This enables you to change their properties (e.g., using the AutoCAD Properties dialog box), or erase them all at once.

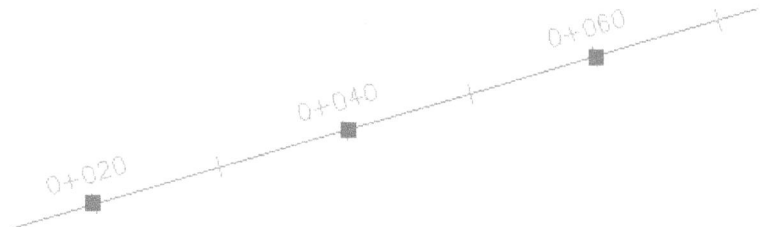

Figure 6–27

If you only want to select one of these labels (e.g., to erase one of them), hold <Ctrl> when selecting.

If you select an alignment and a large number of grips highlight, you have probably selected an alignment station label group, as shown in Figure 6–28. If you want to select the alignment itself (rather than the labels), press <Esc>, zoom in, and try again.

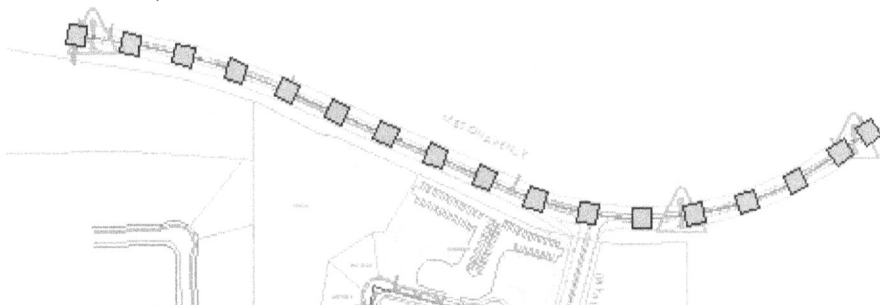

Figure 6–28

Alignment point labels can be added when the alignment is defined and can later be managed by right-clicking on an alignment and selecting **Edit Alignment Labels**. You can also edit existing labels by clicking on an alignment label element and selecting Edit Label Group from the contextual ribbon, as shown in Figure 6–29.

Figure 6–29

Independent Alignment Labels

Independent Alignment Labels can be used to add labels to alignment segments, and station and offset labels. They can be added using the Add Labels dialog box, which can be opened from the *Annotate* tab>Add Labels panel. Expand Alignment and select **Add Alignment Labels…**, as shown in Figure 6–30.

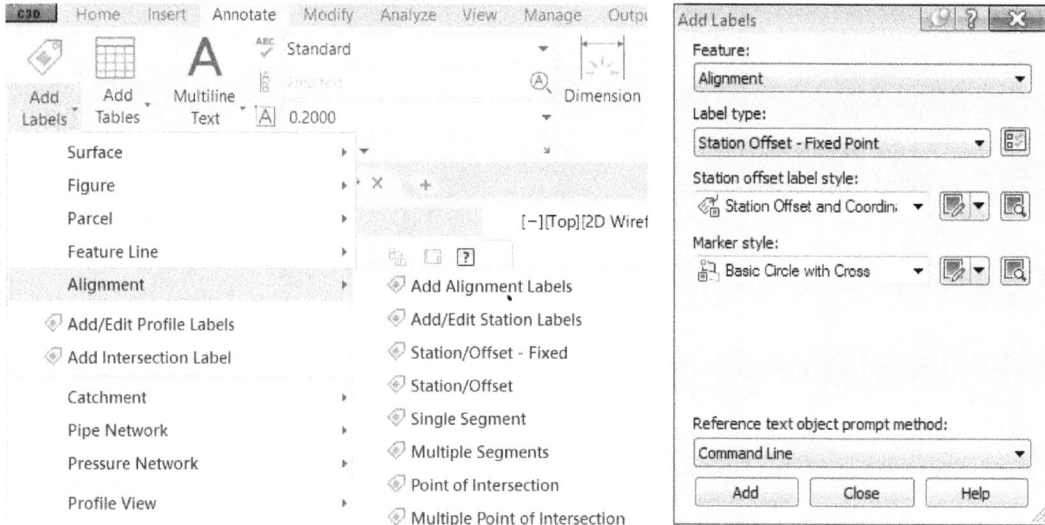

Figure 6–30

These labels include:

- **Station and offset label type:** (Shown in Figure 6–31), which moves with the alignment if it changes to maintain the same station and offset.

- **Station and offset – fixed point label type:** Does not move if the alignment changes, and its station and offset values update to reflect the alignment edit.

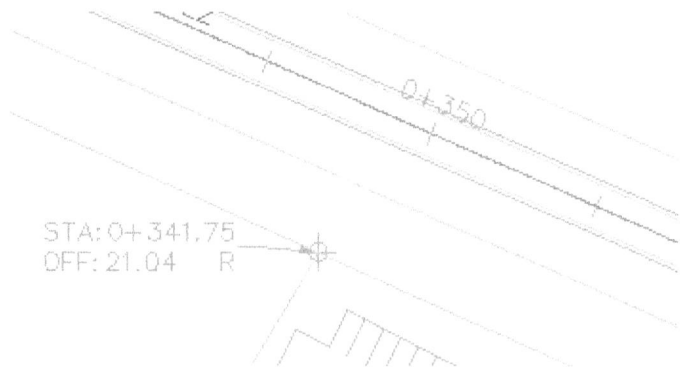

Figure 6–31

- **Single segment label type:** Adds a single line, curve, or spiral label to one alignment segment.

- **Multiple segment label type:** Adds a single line, curve, or spiral label to each alignment segment at the same time, as shown in Figure 6–32.

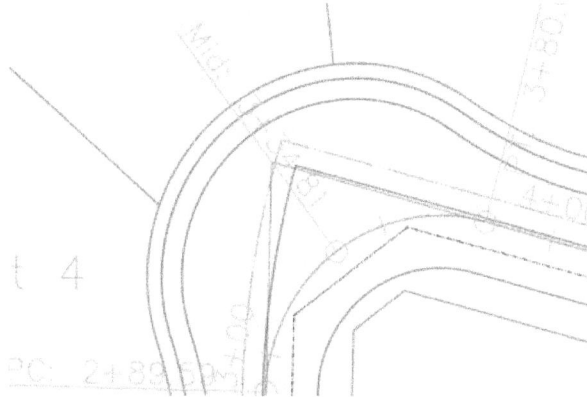

Figure 6–32

- **Point of intersection label type:** Adds a curve (or spiral-curve-spiral group) label at the tangent intersection, and labels the intersection of two tangents (sometimes called an *angle point*).

- **Multiple point of intersection label type:** Adds a curve (or spiral-curve-spiral group) to all of the intersections in the alignment.

Alignment Table Styles

If required, alignment segments can be given *tag* labels (such as **C1** shown in Figure 6–33) and the segment data can be tabulated. This is very similar to the procedures covered in the Parcels chapter for adding tags and tables.

Mission Ave				
Number	Radius	Length	Line/Chord Direction	A Value
L1		98.15	S81° 52' 26.21"E	
C1	2132.54	558.44	S74° 22' 19.17"E	
L2		743.16	S66° 52' 12.12"E	
C2	1033.46	1054.09	N83° 54' 37.46"E	
L3		110.26	N54° 41' 27.03"E	

Figure 6–33

Practice 6c | Alignment Properties and Labels

Practice Objective

- Communicate design information by adding alignment labels and tables.

Task 1 - Edit alignment properties.

1. Open **ALN1-C1-Alignment.dwg** from the *C:\Civil 3D Projects\Working\Alignments* folder.

2. Set **Aln-Warning** as the active view.

   When you created this alignment, you typed 100km/h as the speed. Note that, based on the design criteria, the radius is below the minimum. The warning displays in both the Model Space and in the Panorama view, as shown in Figure 6–34.

   - If the yellow triangular warning symbol is too small, zoom out and regenerate the drawing (**Regen** command). The symbol resizes itself proportionally to the screen size.

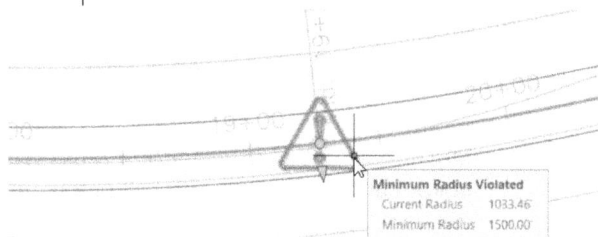

Minimum Radius Violated
Current Radius   1033.46
Minimum Radius   1500.00

No.	Type	Tangency Constraint	Parameter Constrain...	Parameter Co...	Length	Radius	Minimum Radius
1	Line	Not Constrained (Fixed)	🔒	Two points	98.15'		
2	Curve	Constrained on Both Sides (Free)	🔒	Radius	558.44'	2132.54'	1500.00'
3	Line	Not Constrained (Fixed)	🔒	Two points	743.16'		
4	Curve	**Constrained on Both Sides (Free)**	🔒	Radius	1054.09'	⚠ 1033.46'	1500.00'
5	Line	Not Constrained (Fixed)	🔒	Two points	110.26'		

Figure 6–34

You need to fix the properties of this alignment to reflect the correct speed.

3. Select the alignment **Mission Ave**. In the contextual *Alignment* tab>Modify panel, select ⬚ (Alignment Properties).

4. In the *Design Criteria* tab, change the *Design Speed* to **50 mi/h** and clear **Use design check set**, as shown in Figure 6–35, and click **OK** to exit.

- Now that you have the correct design speed, the radius is within the minimum requirements.

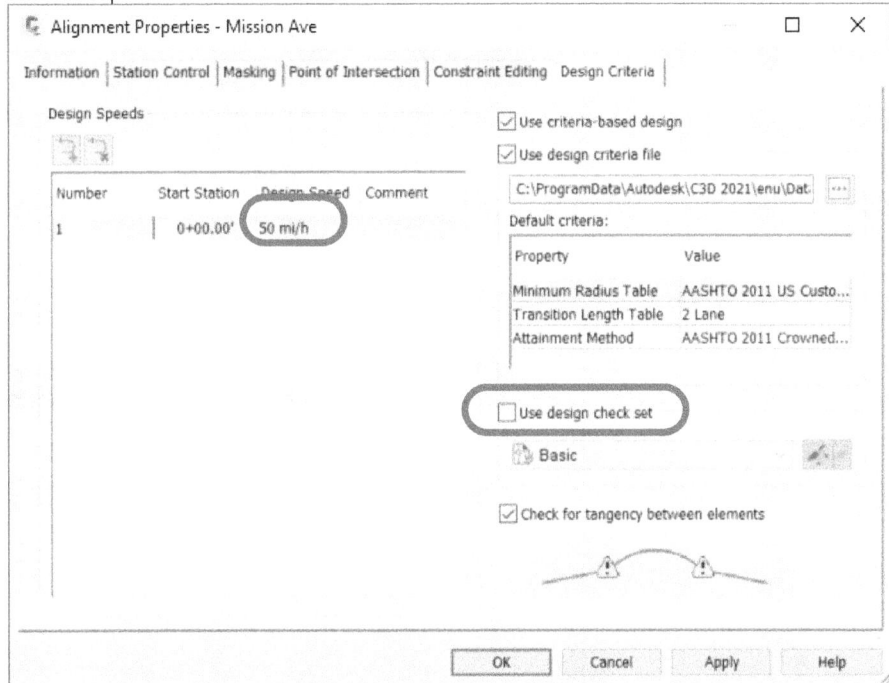

Figure 6–35

5. Press <Esc> to clear the selection and save the drawing.

Task 2 - Add and change alignment labels.

---

1. Currently, the station label intervals for Mission Ave. are every **100'**. Change it to show station labels at every **50'**. Select the alignment **Mission Ave**, right-click, and select **Edit Alignment Labels**.

2. In the Alignment Labels dialog box, change the *Increment* for the Major labels to **100'** and the Minor labels to **50'**, as shown in Figure 6–36. Click **OK** to close the dialog box and apply the changes.

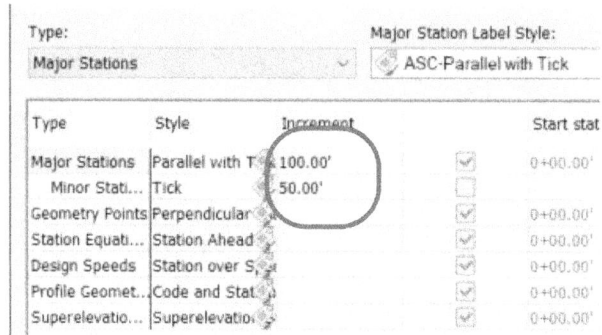

Type: Major Station Label Style:

Major Stations   ∨   ASC-Parallel with Tick

Type	Style	Increment		Start stat
Major Stations	Parallel with T	100.00'	✓	0+00.00'
Minor Stati...	Tick	50.00'	☐	
Geometry Points	Perpendicular		✓	0+00.00'
Station Equati...	Station Ahead		✓	0+00.00'
Design Speeds	Station over S...		✓	0+00.00'
Profile Geomet...	Code and Stat...		✓	0+00.00'
Superelevatio...	Superelevatio...		✓	0+00.00'

Figure 6–36

3. With the alignment Mission Ave still selected, expand Add Labels and select **Multiple Segment** in the Labels & Tables panel, as shown in Figure 6–37.

Figure 6–37

4. When prompted to select the alignment, select the **Mission Ave** alignment again (as shown in Figure 6–38), and press <Enter> to complete and exit the command.

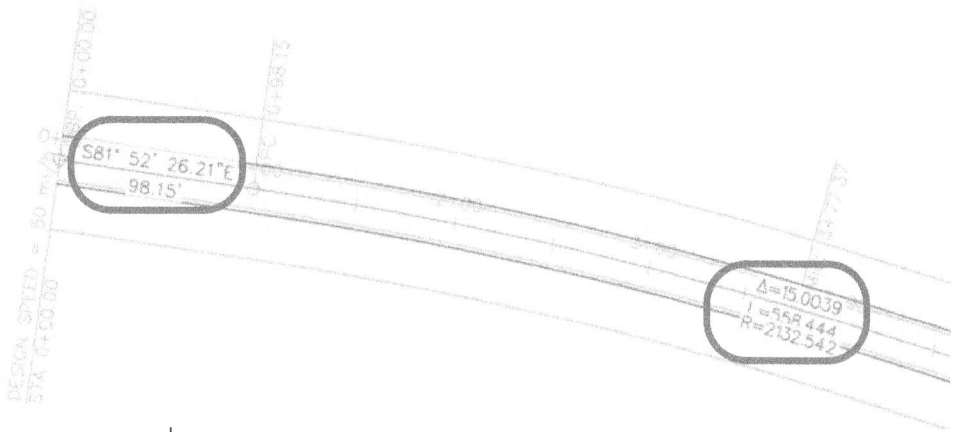

Figure 6–38

5. Select **Aln-Label** as the active view.

6. To create a Table listing the segments, select the alignment again, expand Add Tables and select **Add Segments** in the Labels & Tables panel, as shown in Figure 6–39.

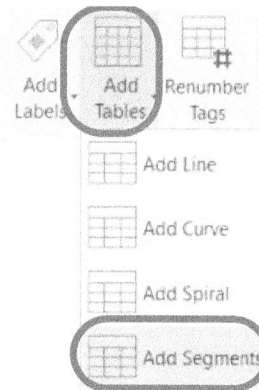

Figure 6–39

7. In the Alignment table creation dialog box, set the options as shown in Figure 6–40 and click **OK** when done.

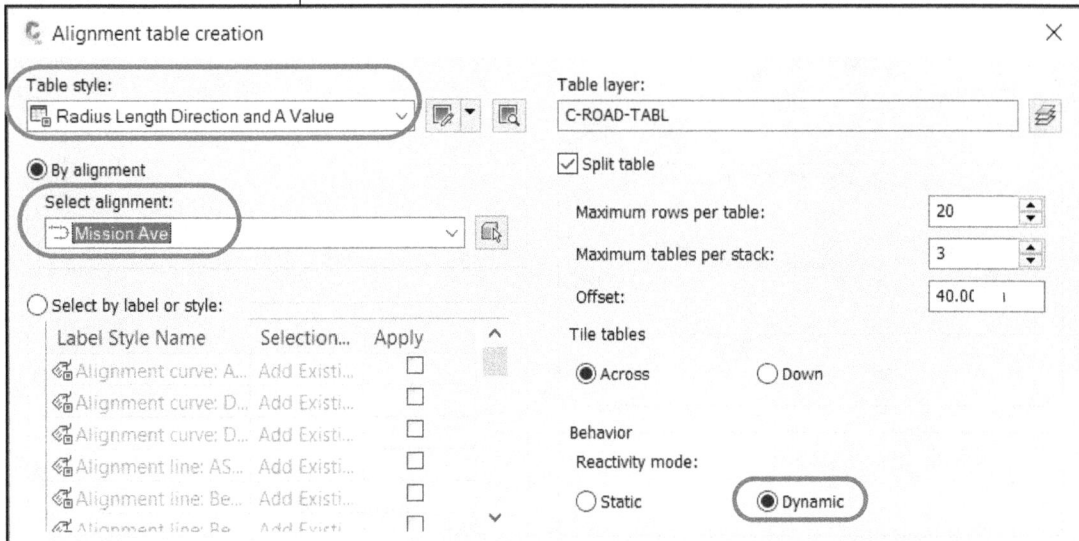

Figure 6–40

8. The Autodesk Civil 3D software will convert the labels to tags. Select a point in Model Space to set the location of the table, as shown in Figure 6–41.

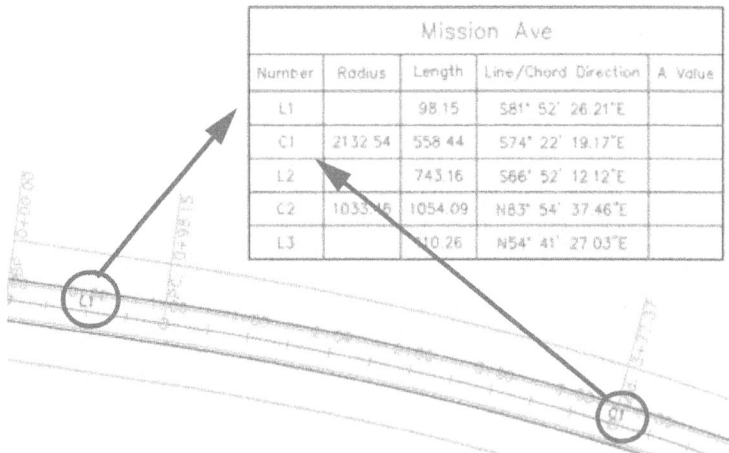

Figure 6–41

9. Select **Aln-Sta Label** as the active view.

10. Select the **Jeffries Ranch Rd** alignment and in the contextual tab, expand Add Labels and select **Station/Offset - Fixed Point** in the Labels & Tables panel, as shown in Figure 6–42.

Figure 6–42

11. Select the end point where the Ascent PI alignment intersects with Jeffries Ranch Rd, as shown in Figure 6–43. Because of all of the Autodesk Civil 3D labels around the intersection, it might be advisable to use either the Apparent or the Endpoint osnap.

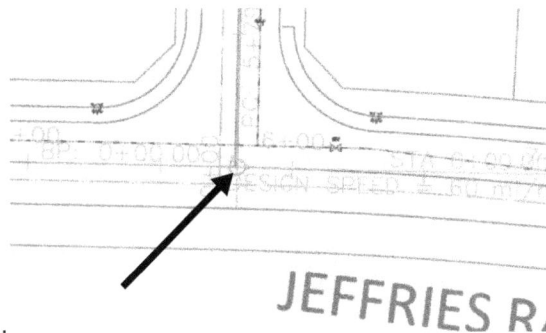

Figure 6–43

12. Press <Enter> to end the command and press <Esc> to clear the selection.

13. Select the label and using the Move grip, move the label to a location to avoid clutter, as shown in Figure 6–44.

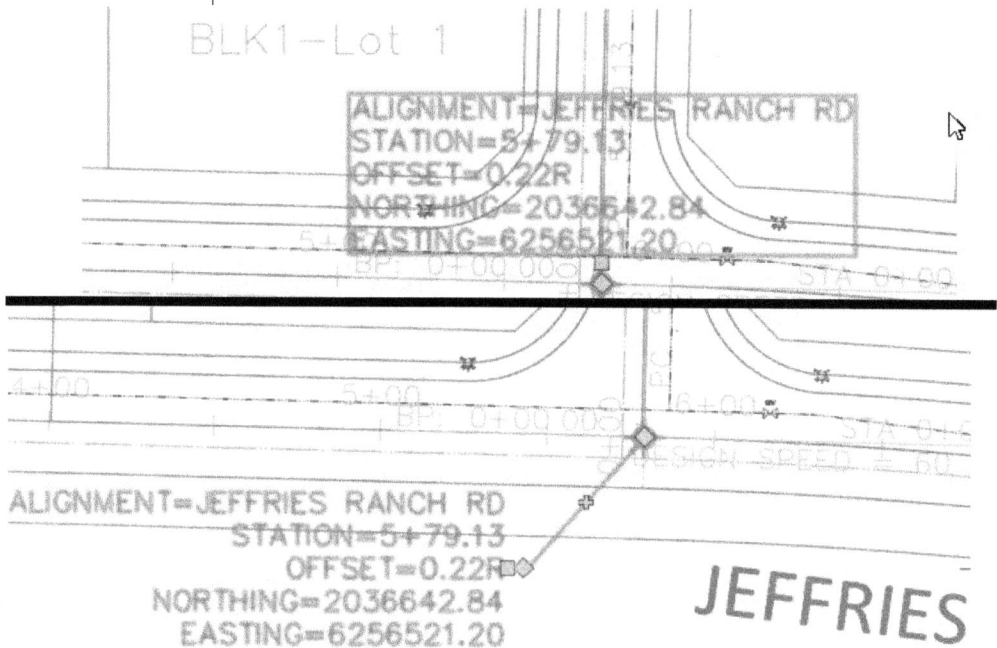

Figure 6–44

14. Save the drawing.

Chapter 7

Profiles

Exam Objectives Covered in This Chapter

3.2.a Create a surface profile along an alignment

3.3.a Use profile creation tools

3.3.b Edit layout profiles

3.3.c Describe the purposes, features, and functions of the profile grid view

3.3.d Explain how and when to add a vertical curve

3.3.e Use profile grips

3.4.a Describe the relationship between profiles, profile views, and profile view bands

3.4.c Create a profile view

3.4.d Split a profile view

3.5.d Work with alignment/profile labels

Note: The objective *3.4.b Identify available object types to project to a profile view* is not covered in this guide. Refer to the Civil 3D Help documentation to review this content.

7.1 Create Profiles from Surface

Most profile views display at least one profile based on a surface, such as from an existing ground terrain model. To create a profile from a surface, use the following steps:

1. In the *Home* tab>Create Design panel, click ⌂ (Profile> Create Surface Profile).
2. In the Create Profile from Surface dialog box (shown in Figure 7–1), select the required alignment and surface(s).
3. Enter the required station range.
4. Click **Add>>** to sample each surface based on these settings.

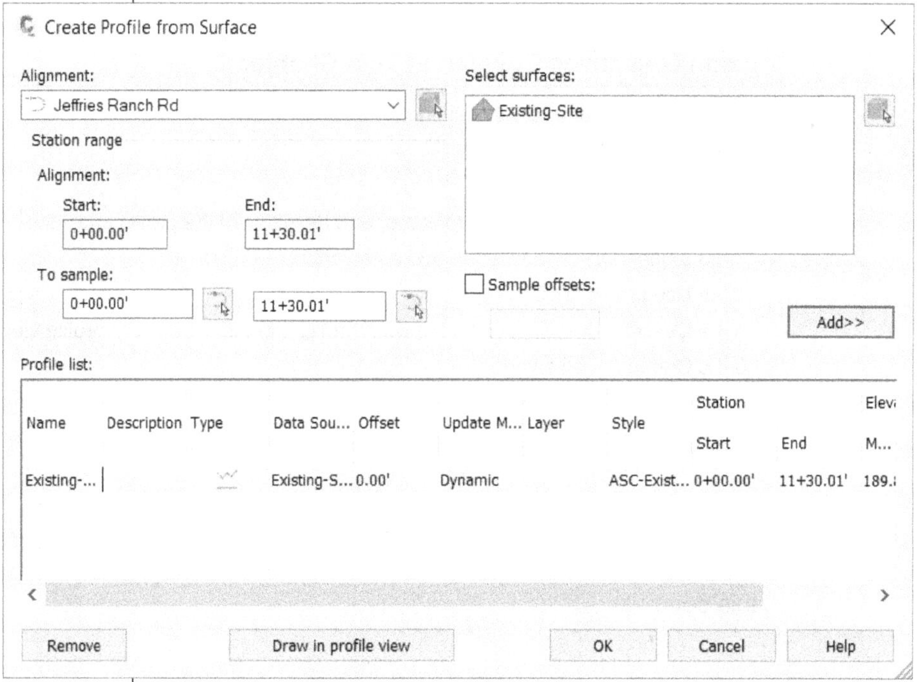

Figure 7–1

This creates a profile along the alignment itself with a zero offset. If you want to sample at an offset from the alignment, select the **Sample Offsets** option. Enter a positive (+) value to sample the right side and a negative (-) value to sample the left side of the alignment, and then click **Add>>**. You can sample multiple offsets by entering values one at a time and clicking **Add>>** after each or putting a comma between offset values to add them all at the same time.

There are two ways to exit this dialog box (other than clicking **Cancel**):

- If you do not have a profile view of this alignment in the drawing, click **Draw in profile view**. This opens the Create Profile View dialog box.

- If you already have a profile view of this alignment, click **OK** and any new profiles are added to the existing view. If you clicked **OK** accidentally without having a view in which to display the profile, go to the *Home* tab> Profile and Section

  Views panel, and click (Profile View>Create Profile View).

7.2 Create Profile View Wizard

You can create a profile view at any time using ⌐ (Profile View>Create Profile View). All of the settings selected in the wizard can be reassigned later using Profile View Properties (except for the alignment on which they are based).

*Clicking **Draw in profile view** in the Create Profile from Surface dialog box opens the same wizard.*

The *General* page in the Create Profile View wizard enables you to select the alignment that you want to work with and to assign the profile view a name, description, view style, and layer. The **Show offset profiles by vertically stacking profile views** option (shown in Figure 7–2) enables you to display offset profiles in a different view from the center line profile without overlapping.

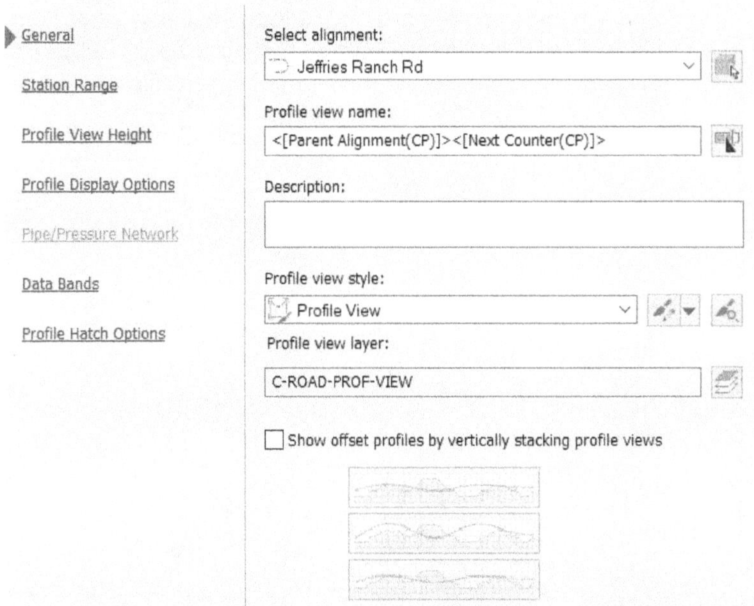

General ▶

Station Range

Profile View Height

Profile Display Options

Pipe/Pressure Network

Data Bands

Profile Hatch Options

Select alignment:

| Jeffries Ranch Rd | ∨ | |

Profile view name:

| <[Parent Alignment(CP)]><[Next Counter(CP)]> | |

Description:

| |

Profile view style:

| Profile View | ∨ | |

Profile view layer:

| C-ROAD-PROF-VIEW | |

☐ Show offset profiles by vertically stacking profile views

Figure 7–2

The *Station Range* page (shown in Figure 7–3) enables you to select the station range with which you want to work. The **Automatic** option includes the entire alignment's length.

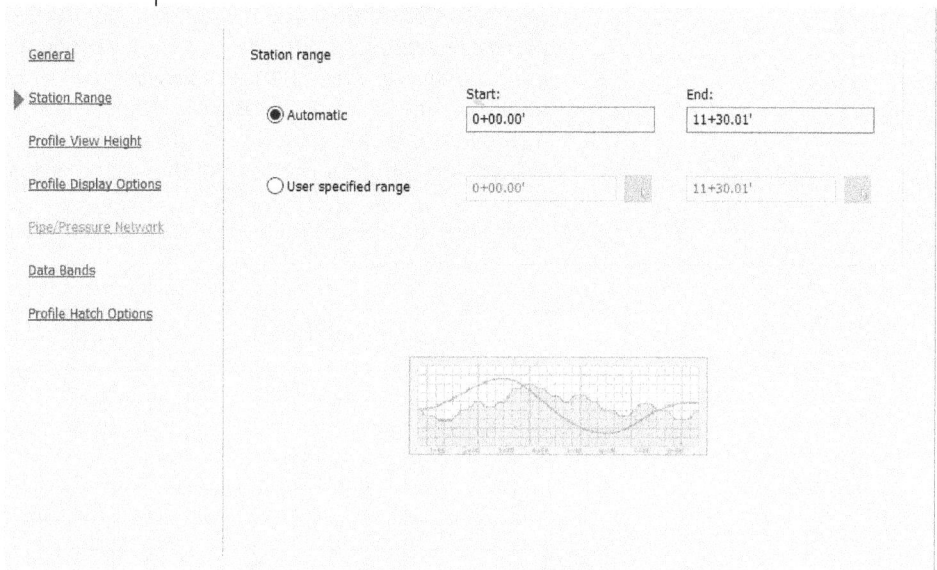

Figure 7–3

The *Profile View Height* page (shown in Figure 7–4) enables you to select the required height of the profile grid.

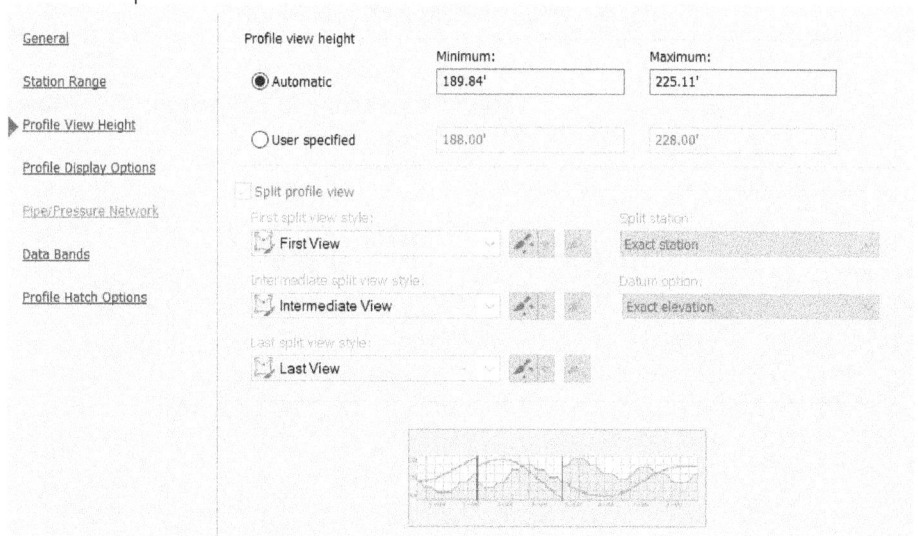

Figure 7–4

- The **Automatic** option creates a profile view that is sized to avoid having to be split.

- The **User Specified** option enables you to assign specific minimum and maximum heights to the profile view. If a profile in one of these views has an elevation below or above the specified values, the profile view is split to accommodate it. If a profile needs to be split you can assign different styles to control the different portions of the split profile.

Figure 7–5 shows a profile view that has been split.

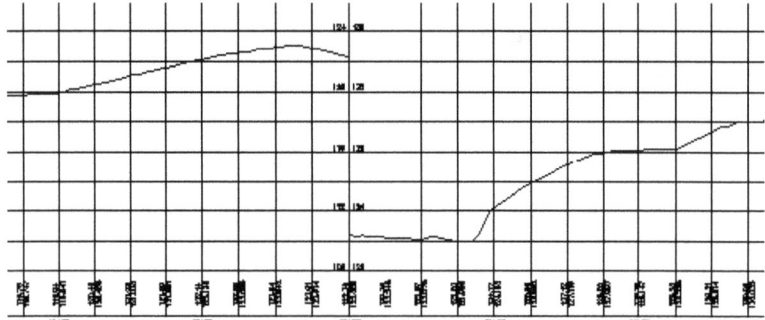

Figure 7–5

The *Stacked Profile* page (shown in Figure 7–6) enables you to set the number of stacked views, the gap between those views, and the styles for each one.

- This page is only available if you selected the **Show offset profiles by vertically stacking profile views** on the General page.

General

Station Range

Profile View Height

▶ Stacked Profile

Profile Display Options

Pipe/Pressure Network

Data Bands

Profile Hatch Options

Number of stacked views:

3

Gap between views:

0.00m

Top view style:

Top Stacked View

Middle view style:

Middle Stacked View

Bottom view style:

Bottom Stacked View

Specify profile and pipe network display options for each of the vertically stacked profiles in the following two pages.

Figure 7–6

The *Profile Display Options* page (shown in Figure 7–7) enables you to apply specific controls to profiles that display in the views.

Some of the most important options include:

- **Draw:** Disabling this option prevents the profile from being displayed in the view.

- **Style:** Sets the profile style to display in the profile.

- **Labels:** Sets the profile label set to display in the profile.

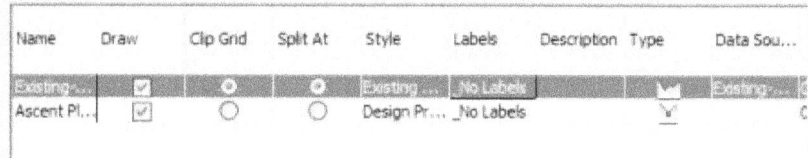

Figure 7–7

The *Data Bands* page (shown in Figure 7–8) enables you to select the bands that you want to include. Bands are additional profile information that can be included along the top or bottom of a profile. Bands are applied in this dialog box by selecting a Band Set.

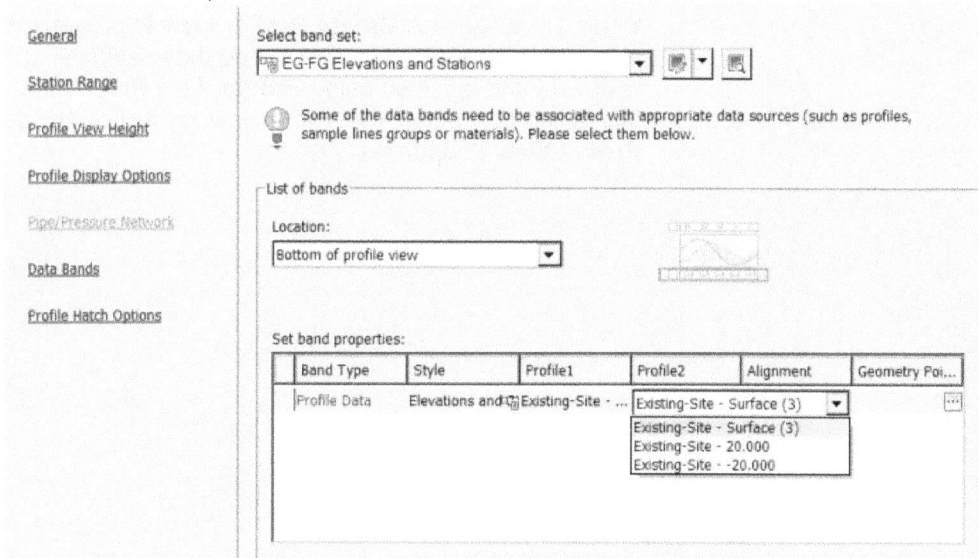

Figure 7–8

You can only create the **Profile Hatch** *when there are at least two profiles in the profile view.*

The **Profile Hatch** option is shown in Figure 7–9. You can hatch the profile according to the *Cut Area*, *Fill Area*, *Multiple boundaries*, or *From criteria* that you import. If you select one of these options, the software enables you to specify the upper and lower boundaries for the hatch area.

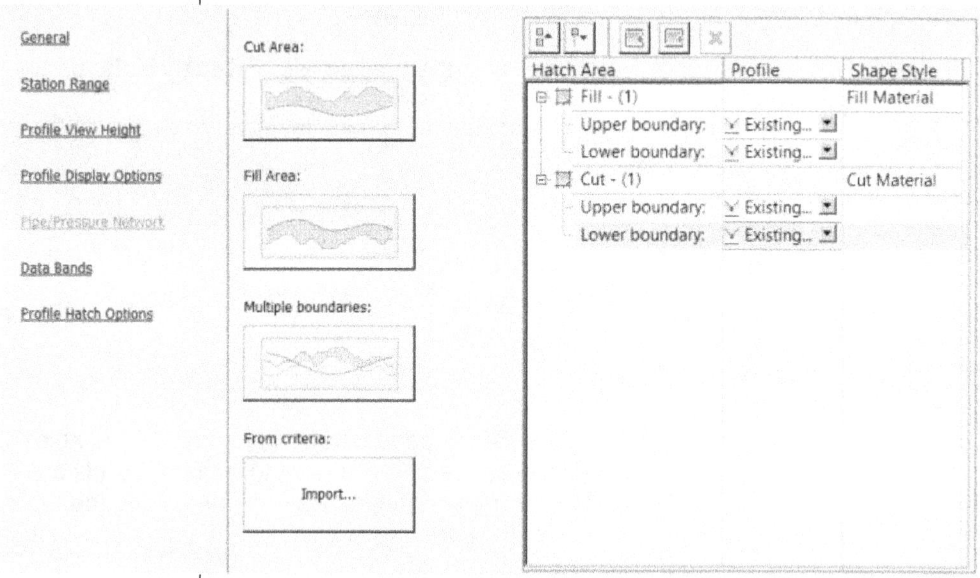

Figure 7–9

When satisfied, click **Create Profile View** to create the profile view. After the profile view is created these settings can be reviewed and adjusted using **Profile View Properties**. To open this dialog box, select the profile view, right-click and select **Profile View Properties**.

Practice 7a | Working with Profiles Part I

Practice Objective

*   Create profile views and the profile line of the existing ground.

In the following practices, you will create profile views and a profile vertical design. In a production collaboration environment, you can use data references to share data between team members, i.e., surfaces and horizontal alignments.

Based on specific design workflow, the horizontal alignment and design profiles often reside in the same drawing. This is the workflow that you will use. However, you can assume that the horizontal alignments are fixed and that you only need to reference them into the profile drawing. In that case, you can practice using data shortcuts or Vault shortcuts.

The *Existing-Site* surface is part of the Data-Shortcut Project *Ascent-Development* and has been referenced into this drawing. Its style has been set to *Border Only*.

Task 1 - Create surface profiles.

---

1. Open **PRF1-A1-Profile.dwg** from the *C:\Civil 3D Projects\ Working\Profiles* folder.

2. Hover the cursor over the Data Shortcuts and review the tooltip which displays, shown in Figure 7–10. Ensure that your Data Shortcuts are set so the **Working Folder** is set to *C:\Civil 3D Projects\Data Shortcuts\Fundamentals* and the **Data Shortcuts Project Folder** to *Ascent-Development*. If required, right-click on Data Shortcuts to set the **Working Folder** and **Data Shortcuts Project Folder**.

⊟·🗗 Data Shortcuts [C:\Civil 3D Projects\Data Shortc... ⌄

<   🗗   C:\Civil 3D Projects\Data Shortcuts\Fundamentals\Ascent-Development

Figure 7–10

3. In the *Home* tab>Create Design panel, click (Profile> Create Surface Profile), as shown in Figure 7–11.

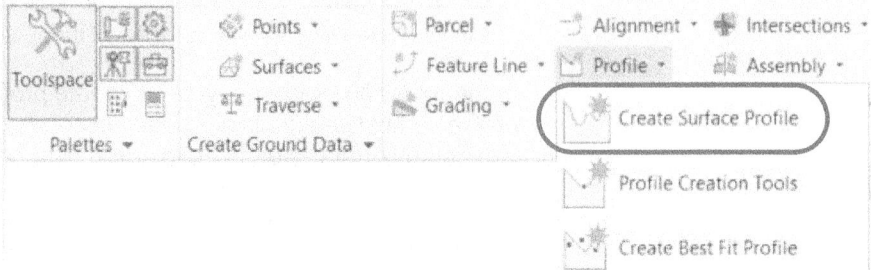

Figure 7–11

4. In the Create Profile from Surface dialog box:
   - Select the **Jeffries Ranch Rd** alignment.
   - Highlight the **Existing-Site** surface and click **Add>>**.
   - Click **Draw in profile view**, as shown in Figure 7–12.

This samples an existing ground profile along the center line, the entire length of Jeffries Ranch Rd.

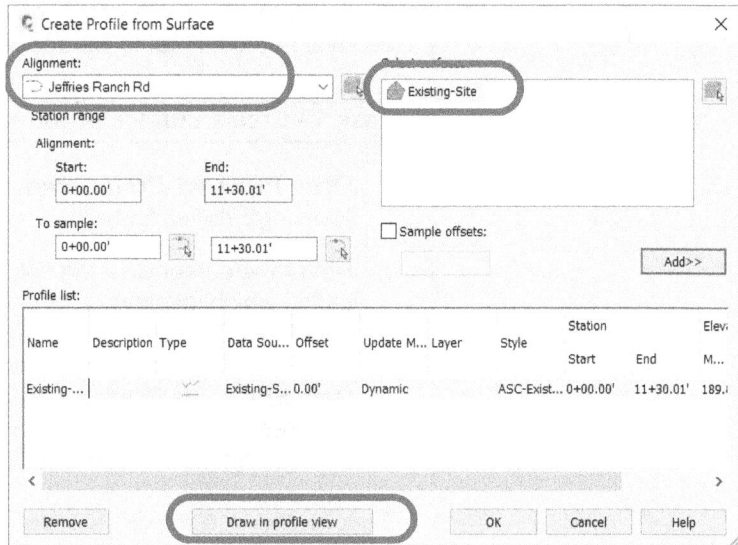

Figure 7–12

*If you clicked **OK** instead, expand Profile View and select **Create Profile View** in the Home tab>Profile & Section Views panel.*

5. In the Create Profile View wizard, set the following options, as shown in Figure 7–13:
   - In the *General* page, confirm **Jeffries Ranch Rd** as the alignment.
   - Set the *Profile view style* to **Profile View**.
   - Click **Next>**.

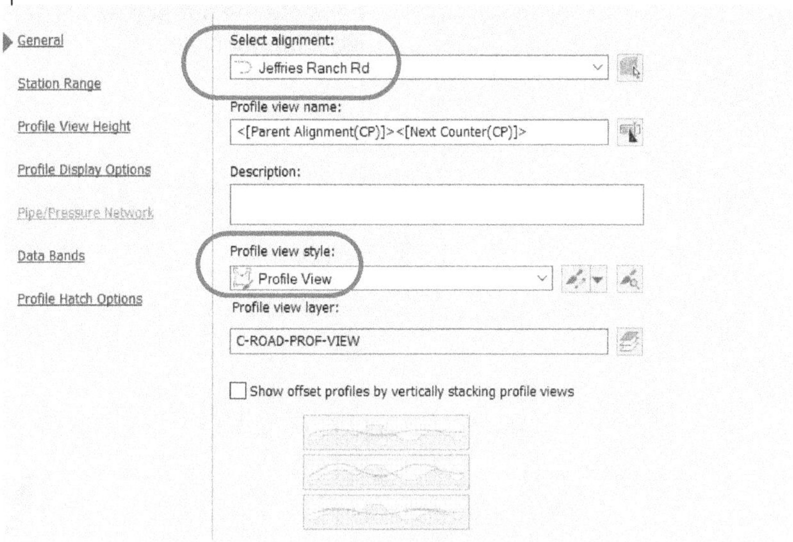

Figure 7–13

6. Accept the defaults in the *Station Range* page and click **Next>**.

7. Accept the defaults in the *Profile View Height* page and click **Next>**.

8. Accept the defaults in the *Profile Display Options* page and click **Next>**.

Note: *You will set which profiles to use for profiles 1 and 2 in the data bands after a finish ground profile has been created.*

9. In the *Data Bands* page, accept **EG-FG Elevations and Stations** for the band set, and click **Next>**.

10. In the *Profile Hatch Options* page, accept the default of no hatching and click **Create Profile View**.

11. If the event viewer displays, close it by clicking the checkmark in the top right corner. When prompted for a location for the profile, click a point to the right of the plan view to define the lower left corner of the Profile View, as shown in Figure 7–14.

   - **Note:** The surface profile displays although the surface contours are not displayed in the plan view. This is because the surface exists in the drawing but is set to a **No Display** style.

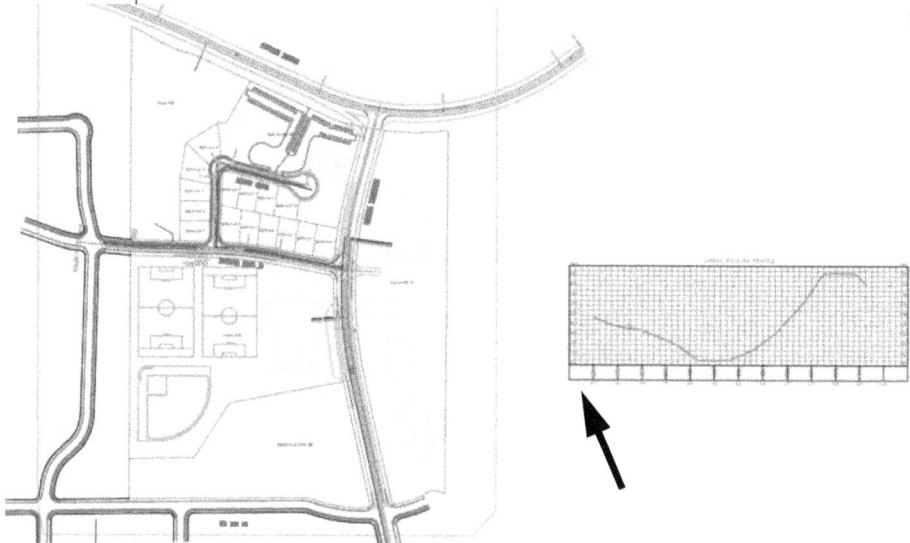

Figure 7–14

12. Repeat Steps 3 to 11 for the alignment **Ascent Pl**.

13. Save the drawing.

Task 2 - Adjust the Profile View.

You might sometimes be required to modify some of the selections that you made in the Create Profile View Wizard, specifically, the datum elevation or grid height. In this task, you will adjust the profile view.

1. Select the **Ascent PI** profile view, right-click, and select **Profile View Properties**, as shown in Figure 7–15.

*You can also select the Toolspace, Prospector tab and expand Alignments> Centerline Alignments> Ascent PI>Profile Views. Right-click on Ascent PI and select **Properties**.*

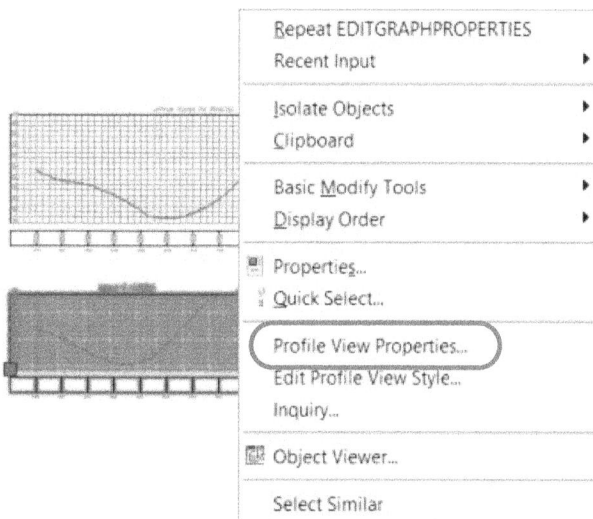

Figure 7–15

2. In the *Elevations* tab, select the **User specified height** option. Type a *Minimum* of **165** and a *Maximum* of **210**, as shown in Figure 7–16. Click **OK**.

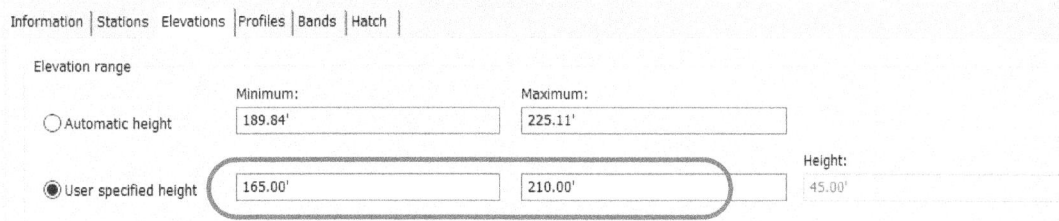

Figure 7–16

3. Save the drawing.

7.3 Finished Ground Profiles

Finished ground profiles (also referred to as proposed profiles or proposed vertical alignments) are often created interactively using the Profile Layout Tools toolbar, as shown in Figure 7–17. This is similar to how alignments are created by layout. The toolbar can be opened by going to the *Home* tab>Create Design panel and expanding Profile and selecting **Profile Creation Tools**.

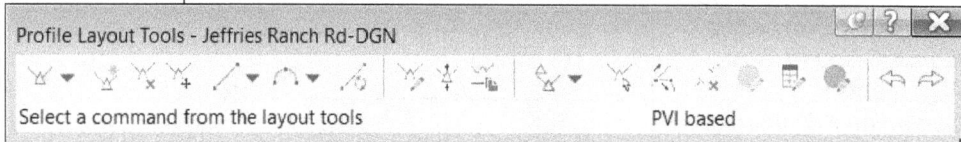

Figure 7–17

- Using these tools, you can add tangents and vertical curves.

- Vertical curves transition a vehicle from one tangent grade to another and occur in two situations: Crest (top of a hill) and Sag (valley).

- There are multiple types of vertical curves to transition between changing the tangent grades of a crest or sag: **Circular**, **Parabolic**, **Asymmetric Parabolic**, and **Best Fit**. Roadways almost always use parabolic (equal length) curves. Asymmetric parabolic curves are usually only used if layout constraints do not permit an equal-length curve. True circular curves are used in some parts of the world for low-speed rail design. Generally, they should *never* be used for roadways (which could lead to vehicle vaulting or bottoming out). Best fit curves follow the most likely path through a series of points.

- In the Toolspace, *Settings* tab, in the Profile heading, the Edit Features Settings set the default curve type, styles, and command settings.

Most vertical designs have regulations affecting the minimum and maximum values for tangent slopes, distances along tangents between vertical curves, and safety design parameters for passing sight and stopping sight distances. Refer to local design manuals for more information on these design constraints.

The points connecting tangents in a finished ground profile are referred to as a *Point of Vertical Intersection* (PVI).

7.4 Create and Edit Profiles

Similar to the Alignments Layout toolbar, the Profile Layout Tools toolbar contains an overall vista (Profile Grid View) and Profile Layout Parameters (segment data viewer). These vistas enable you to review and edit the vertical design. The settings used when creating a finished ground profile can be selected in the Draw Tangents flyout in the toolbar, as shown in Figure 7–18. This toolbar is used to edit any kind of profile, including profiles created from surfaces.

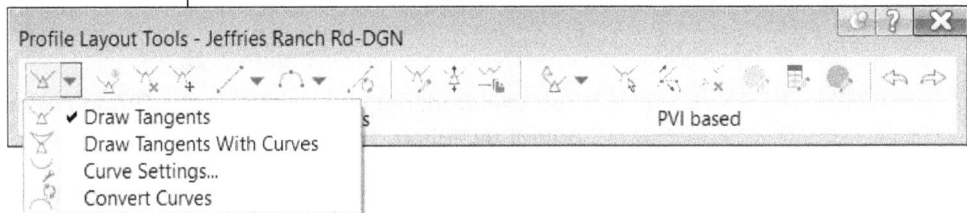

Figure 7–18

Other toolbar commands, enable you to **Add**, **Delete**, or **Move** individual tangents, PVIs, or vertical curve segments.

*   When editing a profile in the layout parameters or grid view, editable parameters display in black.

*   You can graphically edit a design profile using grips. As soon as you select the profile, a contextual tab (shown in Figure 7–19) displays in the ribbon that is specific to that profile.

Figure 7–19

- When graphically editing a vertical alignment, the tangents, PVIs, and vertical curves display grips that represent specific editing functions, as shown in Figure 7–20.

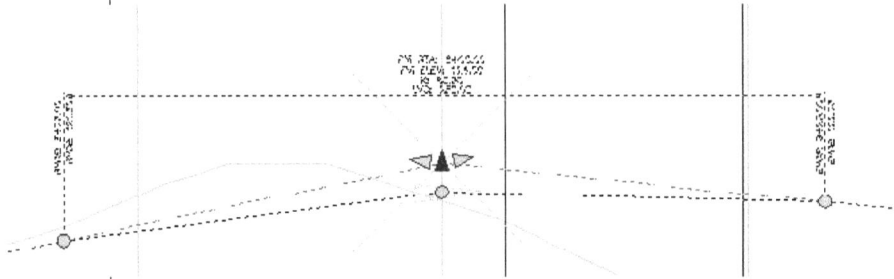

Figure 7–20

- The center triangular grip moves the PVI to a new station and/or elevation.

- The triangles left and right of the center extend the selected tangent, hold its grade, and modify the grade of the opposite tangent to relocate the PVI.

- The middle or end circular grips lengthen or shorten the vertical curve without affecting the location of the PVI.

- When you move the cursor to the original location of the grip, the cursor snaps to that location.

Transparent Commands

The Autodesk Civil 3D software has several transparent commands that can be extremely helpful when creating or editing a finished ground profile. They are listed below, in the order in which they display in the *Transparent* tab and in the toolbar on the right hand side of the drawing window, as shown in Figure 7–21.

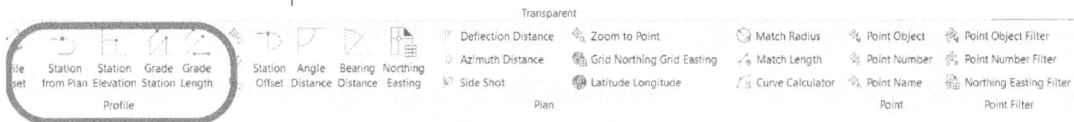

Transparent tab

Toolbar

Figure 7–21

The Transparent commands are also available through the right-click menu when AutoCAD or Civil 3D is searching for a point, as shown in Figure 7–22.

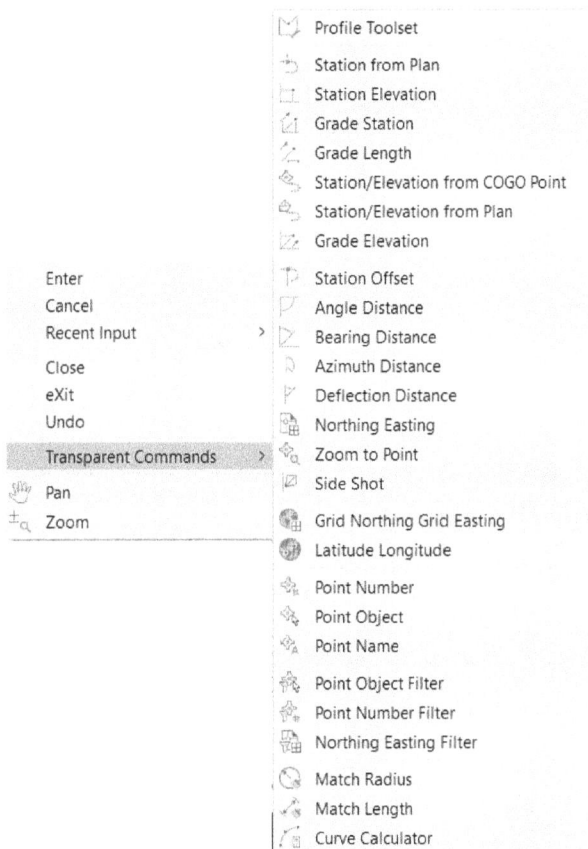

Figure 7–22

- **(Profile Station from Plan):** When creating or adjusting a PVI, this command enables you to pick a point in plan view next to the base alignment. The Autodesk Civil 3D software then calculates the station value automatically and prompts you for the elevation to use at that station.

- **(Profile Station and (surface) Elevation from Plan):** This command is similar, except that it enables you to determine an elevation from a surface.

- **(Profile Station and Elevation from COGO Point):** This command enables you to determine station and elevation values for a PVI based on the location of a point object.

- ⌐┐ **(Profile Station Elevation):** By default, when adding a PVI you are prompted for a drawing's X,Y location. If you would rather enter a station value and elevation, use this command.

- ⌐┐ **(Profile Grade Station):** This command enables you to locate a PVI based on a grade and an ending station value.

- ⌐┐ **(Profile Grade Elevation):** This command enables you to locate a PVI based on a grade and an ending elevation value.

- ⌐┐ **(Profile Grade Length):** This command enables you to locate a PVI based on a grade and tangent length.

Assigning Profile Band Elevations

Profile band elevations are assigned using Profile View Properties, in the *Bands* tab. When you create a profile view, you should review the band settings and verify that each profile band is assigned the correct profile in the *Profile1* and *Profile2* fields, as shown in Figure 7–23. The Autodesk Civil 3D software does not make any assumptions about which profile to use in either field.

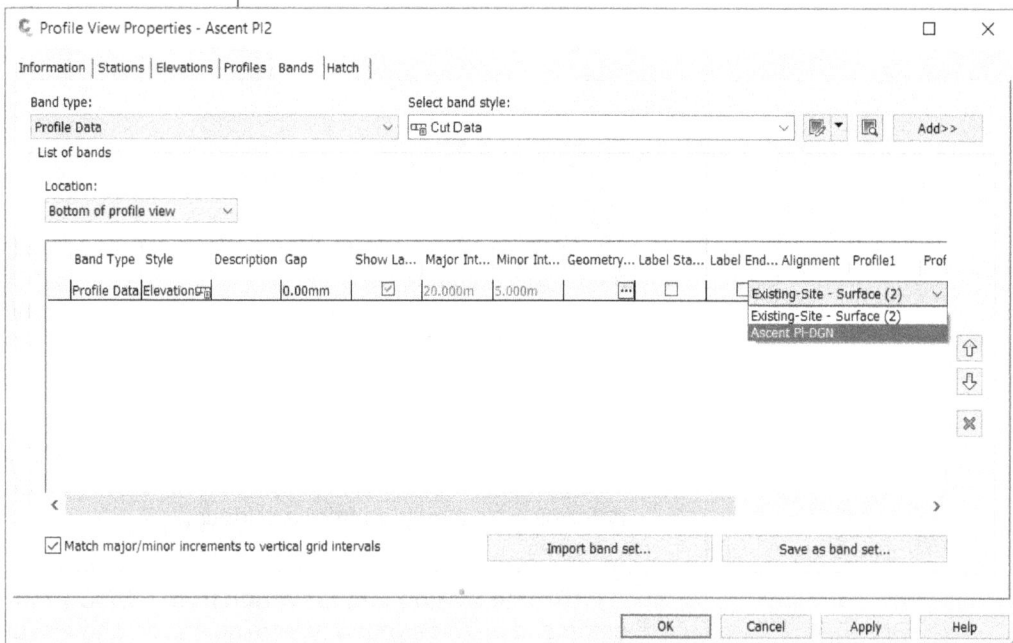

Figure 7–23

Using the styles supplied with the Autodesk Civil 3D templates, the existing ground surface would be assigned the *Profile1* field, and the finished ground profile would be assigned the *Profile2* field. This can be swapped depending on your organization's standards.

Profile Segment Types

Profile segments created by layout (tangent lines, parabolas, and circular curves) can be created as fixed, floating, or free.

Profile Labels

Profiles have dynamic labels that are organized into two categories:

- **Profile labels:** Include labels for Major and Minor Stations, Horizontal Geometry Points, Profile Grade Breaks, Lines, and Crest and Sag curves. These can be selected when the profile is created and managed later by right-clicking on a profile and selecting **Edit Labels**.

- **Profile View labels:** Include a Station & Elevation label type and a Depth label type. These are created by going to the *Annotate* tab>Labels & Tables panel, expanding Add Labels, expanding Profile View, and selecting **Add Profile View Labels**, as shown in Figure 7–24. They can be removed using the AutoCAD **Erase** command.

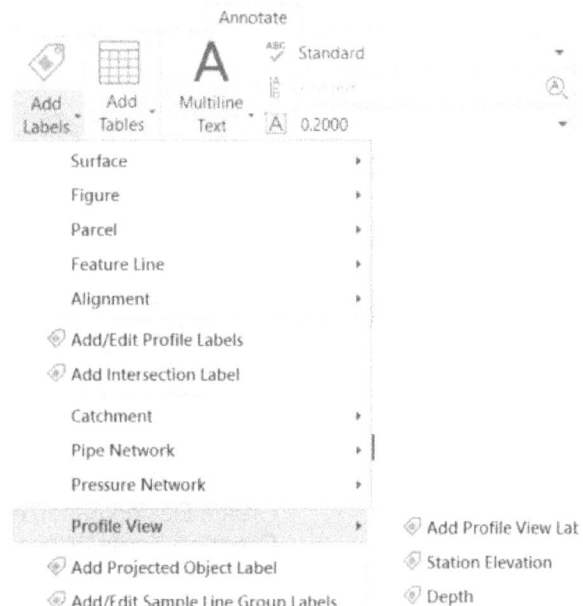

Figure 7–24

Practice 7b | Working with Profiles Part II

Practice Objective

- Create finished ground profiles using specific design parameters.

Before starting any type of design, you need to obtain all of the constraints. The tie in elevation for Jeffries Ranch Rd at the east end is 200.02', for this is an existing road to be lengthened. You also know that based on survey data that the tie in elevations at the west end at station 0+06.17' is 207.78', with an existing grade of approximately 3.80%. The cul-de-sac will be based on the grade of Jeffries Ranch Rd and an adjacent grade at Ascent Blvd. The low point overflow drainage in the knuckle will be addressed by an overland gutter to the pond. Figure 7–25 roughly shows the type of street drainage that you want to establish.

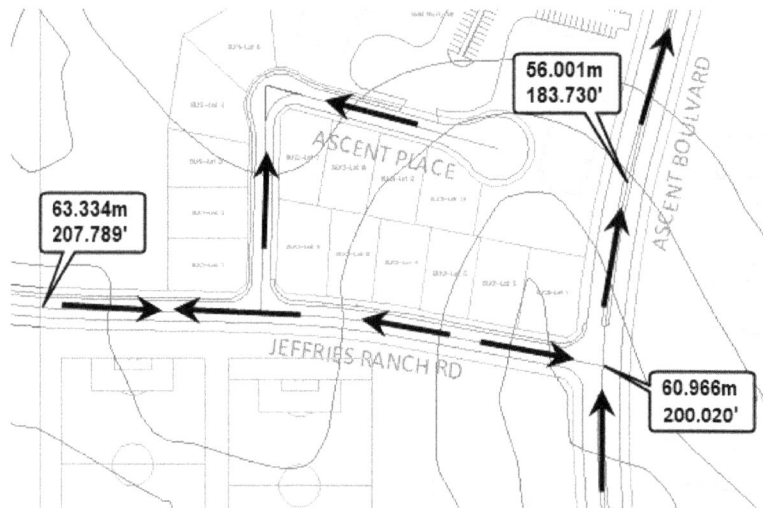

Figure 7–25

Task 1 - Create the Finished Ground Profile.

1. Open **PRF1-B1-Profile.dwg** from the *C:\Civil 3D Projects\ Working\Profiles* folder.

*Alternatively, select the **Jeffries Ranch Rd** profile view, and in the contextual tab>Launch Pad panel, select **Profile Creation Tools**.*

2. Zoom to the Jeffries Ranch Rd profile view. In the *Home* tab> Create Design panel, expand **Profile** and select **Profile Creation Tools**. When prompted to select a profile view, select the **Jeffries Ranch Rd** profile view.

3. In the Create Profile dialog box that opens, for the *Name,* click
    🖳 (Edit name template) to the right.

4. In the Name Template dialog box, set the following, as shown
    in Figure 7–26:
    *   In the *Property fields* field, select **Alignment Name** and
        then click **Insert**.
    *   In the *Name* field, after **<[Alignment Name]>**, type -**DGN**.
    *   Click **OK** to close the dialog box.

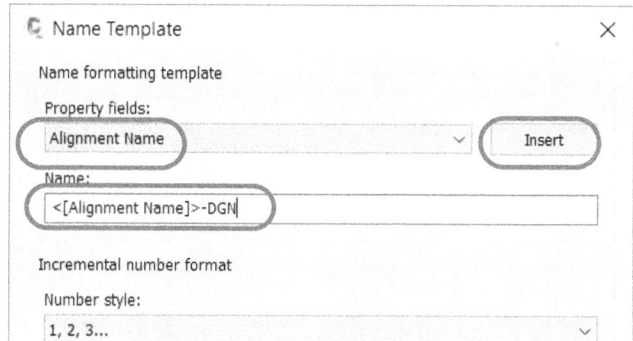

Figure 7–26

5. Set the *Profile style* to **ASC-Design Profile** and the *Profile
    label set* to **ASC-Complete Label Set** as shown in
    Figure 7–27. Click **OK**.

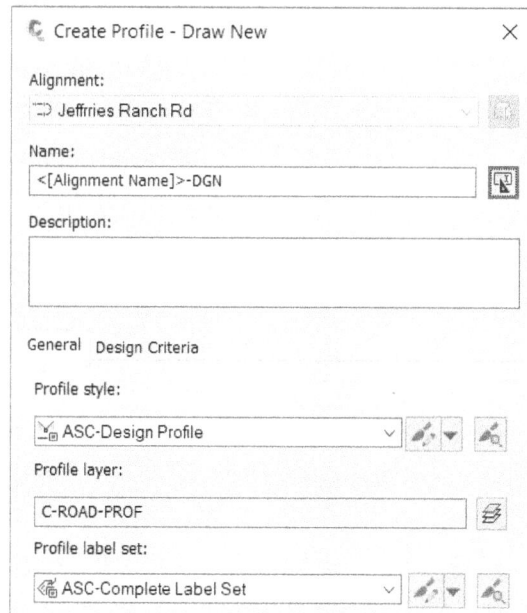

Figure 7–27

6. Expand the drop-down list in the Profile Layout Tools toolbar and select **Draw Tangents**, as shown in Figure 7–28. The Autodesk Civil 3D software prompts you for a start point, which indicates the location of the road's first PVI.

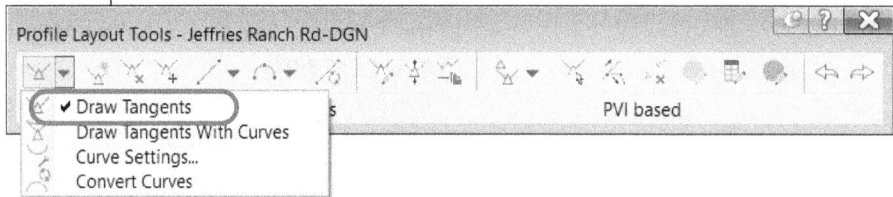

Figure 7–28

7. In the *Transparent* tab (or the toolbar or right-click menu), click ⌐. (Profile Station Elevation), and then proceed as follows:

   • Select any part of the Jeffries Ranch Rd profile view.
   • Type a starting station of **6.17'** and press <Enter>.
   • Type a starting elevation of **207.78'**, and press <Enter>.
   • Press <Esc> to exit this transparent command.

*You want to set the next point based on a grade to a given station, so you will use the **Profile Grade Station** transparent command.*

8. Click ⌐. (Profile Grade Station) in the *Transparent Commands* tab to enter a grade followed by a station, as follows:

   • For the grade, type **-3.79** and press <Enter> (to indicate -3.79%).
   • For the station, type **328.08'** and press <Enter>.
   • Press <Esc> to end the transparent command.
   • Press <Esc> again to end the layout command.

   The profile is shown in Figure 7–29. Close the Profile Layout Tools, as shown on the top right of Figure 7–29.

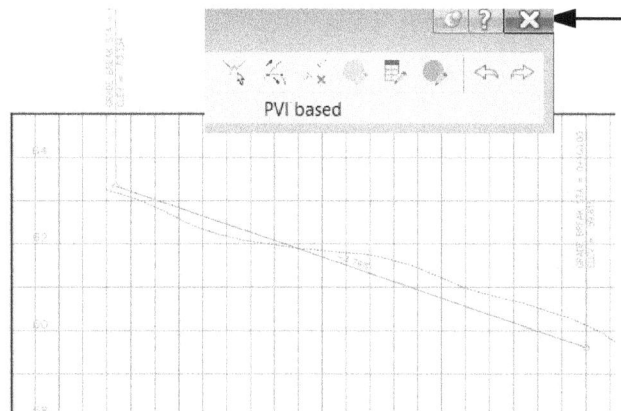

Figure 7–29

9. At any time, you can continue to edit a profile by selecting it, right-clicking, and selecting **Edit Profile Geometry**. In the Jeffries Ranch Rd profile view, select the **Jeffries Ranch Rd-DGN** grade line drawn in Step 8. In the contextual

   tab>Modify Profile panel, click ✎ (Geometry Editor) to edit it.

10. To continue adding PVIs, return to the Profile Layout Tools

    toolbar and expand ⬚▾ and select **Draw Tangents**. When prompted for the start point, snap to the end point of the last segment that you drew (i.e., **sta=328.08', elev=195.58'**).

11. In the *Transparent* tab, click ⤢ (Profile Grade Length), and then proceed as follows:
    - Select the **Jeffries Ranch Rd** profile view.
    - For the grade, type **0.8** and press <Enter>.
    - For the length, type **482.283'** and press <Enter>.
    - Press <Esc> to exit the transparent command.

12. To tie back to the final design point, click ⬚ (Profile Station Elevation) in the *Transparent* tab, and then proceed as follows:
    - Type an end alignment station of **1130.01'**and press <Enter>.
    - Type a tie in elevation of **200.02'** and press <Enter>.
    - Press <Esc> to exit the transparent command.
    - Press <Enter> to exit the **Draw Tangent** command.

13. In the Profile Layout Tools toolbar, click **X** to close it.

Task 2 - Adjust the FG Profile.

1. Select the **Jefferies Ranch Rd-DGN** profile that you drew in the previous task and note the grips that display.

2. In the contextual tab>Modify Profile panel, click
   ✎ (Geometry Editor).

The PVIs do not have any vertical curves. You will add them to the design using the **Free Vertical Curve (Parabola)** option, as shown in Figure 7–30. You could have also done this at the initial stage of the design using the **Draw Tangent with Curves** tool rather than the **Draw Tangent** tool.

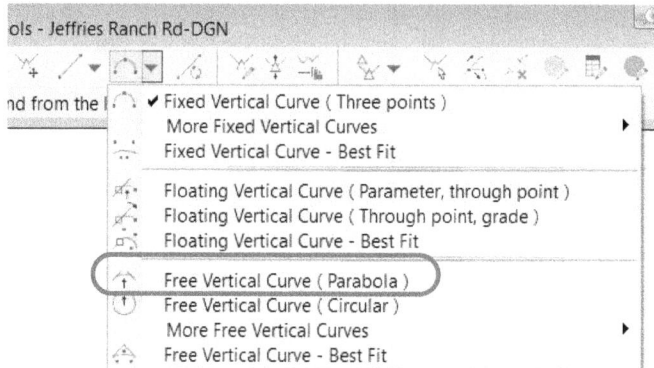

Figure 7–30

3. In the Curve pull-down, select ⬆️▼ (Free Vertical Curve (Parabola)), and when prompted to select the first entity, select the incoming grade (1) and then select the outgoing grade (2), as shown in Figure 7–31. Type **100'** for the length of vertical curve.

4. Do the same for the second vertical curve. Select entities (3) and (4) (as shown in Figure 7–31) and type **100'** for the length of the vertical curve. Press <Enter> to exit the command.

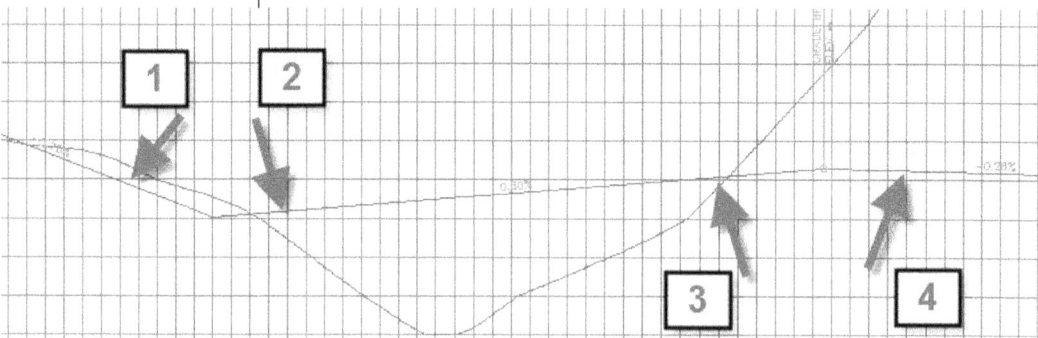

Figure 7–31

5. In the Profile Layout Tools toolbar, click 🔲 (Profile Grid View).

The Profile Entities vista should display in the Panorama.

6. The *Grade In* elevation at the station **11+30.01'** is **0.18%**. This is less than minimum, so you need to change it to **-0.8%** while maintaining both PVI stations. However, the elevation at station **8+10.37'** will be revised. Select the *Grade In* elevation and change *0.18* to **-0.8**, as shown in Figure 7–32.

No.	PVI Station	PVI Elevation	Grade In	Grade Out
1	0+06.17'	207.780'		-3.79%
2	3+28.08'	195.579'	-3.79%	0.80%
3	8+10.37'	199.438'	0.80%	0.18%
4	11+30.01'	200.020'	0.18%	

Figure 7–32

7. You will change the *Grade In* elevation at station **8+10.37'** to also be **0.80%**. Select the *Grade In* elevation and change it to **0.8**, as shown in Figure 7–33. This affects the elevation at station **3+28.08'**.

No.	PVI Station	PVI Elevation	Grade In	Grade Out
1	0+06.17'	207.780'		-3.79%
2	3+28.08'	195.579'	-3.79%	1.45%
3	8+10.37'	202.577'	1.45%	-0.80%
4	11+30.01'	200.020'	-0.80%	

Figure 7–33

At this point, the as built grade from station 0+06.17' is no longer 3.79%. However, from a simple calculation you know that if you move the PVI from station 3+28.08', elevation 198.72' to station **2+60.04'**, elevation **198.16'**, you will be able to preserve the 3.79% grade and the 0.8% minimum grade. There are two methods to accomplish this:

- Edit the station and elevation in the grid view, as shown in Figure 7–34.

No.	PVI Station	PVI Elevation	Grade In	Grade Out
1	0+06.17'	207.780'		-2.81%
2	3+28.08'	198.719'	-2.81%	0.80%
3	8+10.37'	202.577'	0.80%	-0.80%
4	11+30.01'	200.020'	-0.80%	

Figure 7–34

- Alternatively, in Model Space, move the PVI to a station and elevation. For training proposes, perform the more complex process of the two.

The following steps correct the grade.

8. In Model Space, select the **Jeffries Ranch Rd-DGN** grade line to display its grips.

9. At the **3+28.08'** PVI station, select the center PVI grip. For the new location, click 🔛 (Profile Station and Elevation).

   - When prompted for the profile view, select one of the grid lines of the Jeffries Ranch Rd profile view.
   - Type a station value of **260.04'** and press <Enter>.
   - Type an elevation value of **198.16'** and press <Enter>.

10. The grid view should have the values shown in Figure 7–35. Click the **X** in the Profile Layout Tools toolbar to close both the grid view and toolbar.

No.	PVI Station	PVI Elevation	Grade In	Grade Out
1	0+06.17'	207.780'		-3.79%
2	2+60.04'	198.160'	-3.79%	0.80%
3	8+10.37'	202.577'	0.80%	-0.80%
4	11+30.01'	200.020'	-0.80%	

Figure 7–35

Task 3 - Update profile bands.

The profile views display existing ground elevations in both the existing and proposed slots of the profile bands, as shown in Figure 7–36. In this task, you will change the right label to a finished ground profile label.

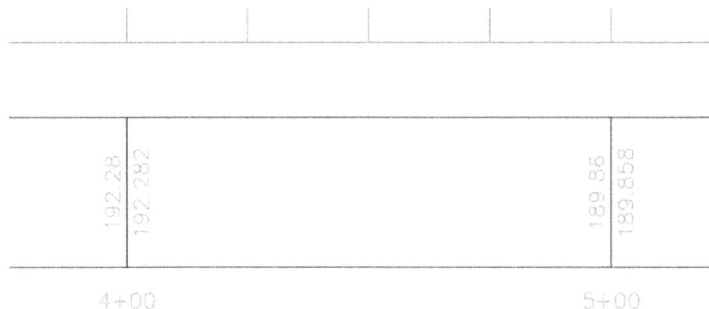

Figure 7–36

1. To update, select the Jeffries Ranch Rd profile view, right-click, and select **Profile View Properties**. In the *Bands* tab, assign Profile2 to reference Jeffries Ranch Rd-DGN, as shown in Figure 7–37. Click **OK**.

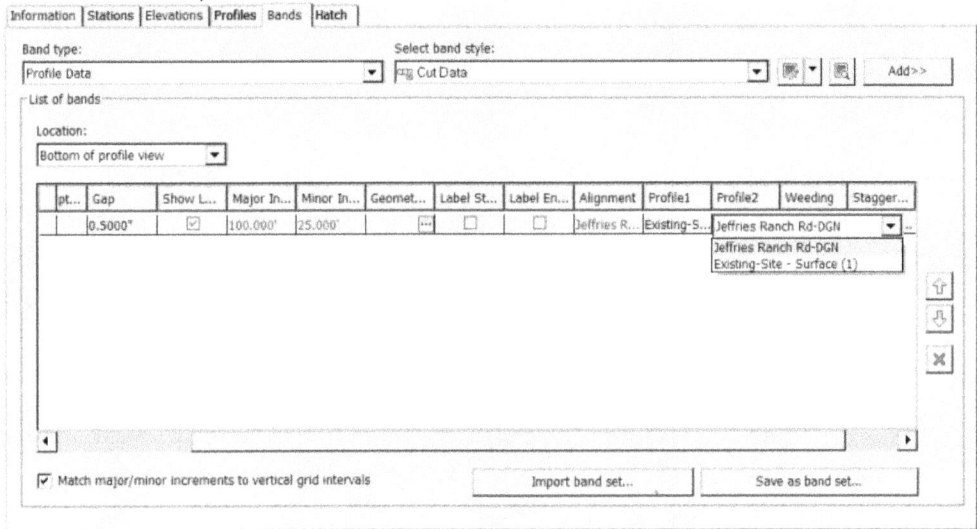

Figure 7–37

The profile band displays existing ground elevations on the left and design elevations on the right, as shown in Figure 7–38.

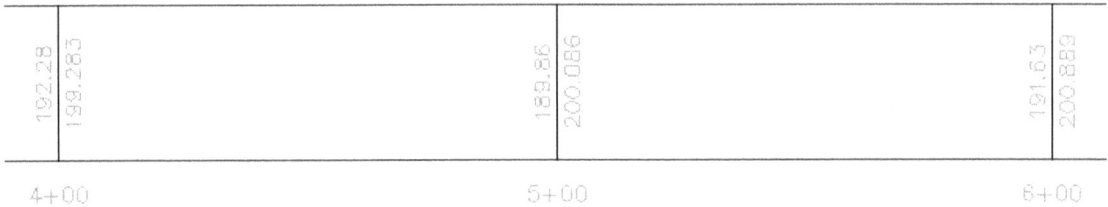

Figure 7–38

2. Save the drawing.

SECTION 4

Corridors and Sections

Chapter 8

Corridors and Sections

Exam Objectives Covered in This Chapter

4.1.a Create and assign basic assemblies and subassemblies

4.1.b Create a corridor

4.1.c Add multiple baselines to a corridor

4.1.d Add and edit targets (horizontal and vertical)

4.1.e Understand the concept of clearing corridor bowties

4.1.f Rebuild corridors

4.2.a Create objects from a corridor

4.3.a Create sample lines

4.3.b Create section sheets

4.3.c Edit sample line group properties

4.3.d Create section views

4.3.e Compute Materials

8.1 Assembly Overview

Assemblies

An *assembly* defines the attachment point of a roadway cross-section to the horizontal and vertical alignments. This attachment point occurs at the midpoint of the assembly marker (or assembly baseline), as shown in Figure 8–1. The 3D progression of the attachment point along the corridor is also sometimes referred to as the *profile grade line*.

Figure 8–1

Assemblies can be placed anywhere in a drawing (centerline of roads, curb returns, sidewalks, off ramps, railways, etc). Assembly styles only affect the display of the marker itself (i.e., color, layer, etc.).

Assembly Types

The type of road or railway that an assembly represents is important, especially if it is used in a corridor that requires superelevation axis of rotation or cant. When a superelevation or cant is calculated for an alignment, it is also important to select an assembly type that matches design needs. There are six types of assemblies:

- **Undivided Crowned Road:** Enables you to specify the axis about which the corridor is superelevated.

- **Undivided Planar Road:** Enables you to specify the axis about which the corridor is superelevated and the default highside location for planar roads.

- **Divided Crowned Road:** Enables you to specify the axis about which the corridor is superelevated and whether the median maintains its shape or becomes distorted as the corridor superelevates.

- **Divided Planar Road:** Enables you to specify the axis about which the corridor is superelevated and whether the median maintains its shape or becomes distorted as the corridor superelevates.

Railways are not covered in this course.

- **Railway:** Enables you to specify the cant about which the corridor is going to bank.

- **Other:** Used for all other types of corridors that are not listed above.

Subassemblies

Assemblies are assigned *subassemblies*, which represent individual components of the proposed cross-section (such as lane or curb subassemblies). Subassemblies attach to the left or right side of an assembly's attachment point. When building an assembly, you build from the middle out to the left or right edges.

- The library of stock subassemblies supplied with the Autodesk Civil 3D® software uses a wide array of dynamic parameters (e.g., dimensions of lane width and slope). These stock subassemblies routinely expand and evolve as Civil 3D matures from release to release.

- When parameter values change, the corridor model gets updated. Custom dynamic subassemblies can be created using the .net programming language, using the Subassembly Composer, which is an additional program that is included with Autodesk Civil 3D.

- You can create static subassemblies (without dynamic parameters) from polylines.

- Each point (vertex) of a subassembly can be assigned a name or *point code* for reference later. A point is a potential location for offset and elevation annotation. It is also a connection point for an adjacent subassembly. When such a point is stretched onto the next assembly, it generates a line (known as a *feature line*). For example, points are commonly assigned at edge-of-travelways, back-of-curbs, gutters, etc. Marker styles define the properties for points and their labels.

- Corridors generate *feature lines* at every location that is assigned a point code. These linear 3D objects can be used as input for surfaces and grading solutions.

- Lines in subassemblies are referred to as *links*. A link can be automatically given a slope or grade label in the cross-sections as required. When such a link is stretched onto the next assembly, it generates a plane, which can be used to create Civil 3D surfaces. Link styles define the properties of a link and its labels.

- A subassembly *shape* is an area enclosed by links. When such a shape is stretched onto the next assembly, it generates a solid, which can be assigned material types and can be used to calculate quantities. Shape styles define the display properties of a shape.

- Marker styles, feature line styles, and link and shape styles are all assigned based on a Code Set Style. The Code Set Style assigns the styles to be applied based on the codes assigned to these objects. Code Sets and each of these styles are all configured under the *Multipurpose Styles* collection in the Toolspace, *Settings* tab.

The example in Figure 8–2 shows an assembly containing lane, curb, and daylight subassemblies. This assembly has been assigned to display an offset and elevation marker (point) label at the edge of the lane, a pavement slope (link) label, and shape labels displaying the area of the sub-base.

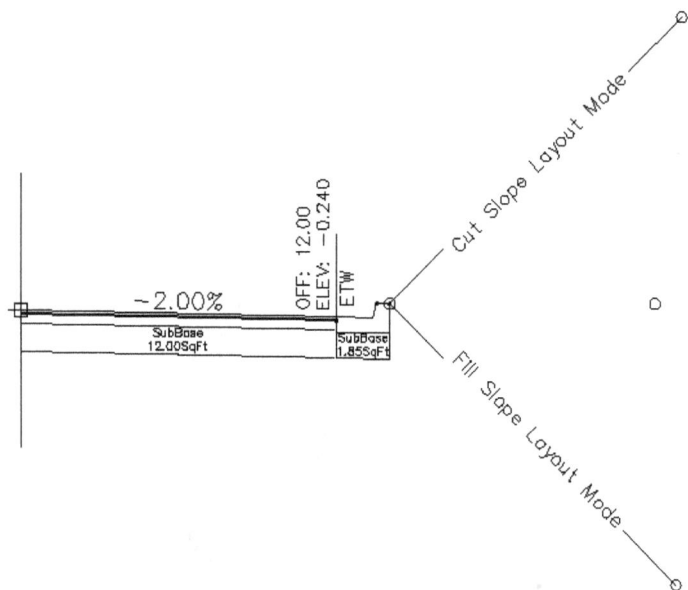

Figure 8–2

- Each subassembly attaches to the assembly connection point or to a point on an adjacent subassembly. You should assign each assembly a logical, unique name during creation. This is helpful later in the corridor creation process when you are working with very complex corridors that include intersections, transitions, and other components.

- Autodesk Civil 3D Help contains extensive documentation for each subassembly.

The Toolspace, *Prospector* tab lists each assembly with a further breakdown of each subassembly associated with it, in a tree structure, as shown in Figure 8–3.

Figure 8–3

To review their interconnections and parameters, select the assembly, right-click, and select **Assembly Properties**. The Assembly Properties dialog box opens as shown in Figure 8–4.

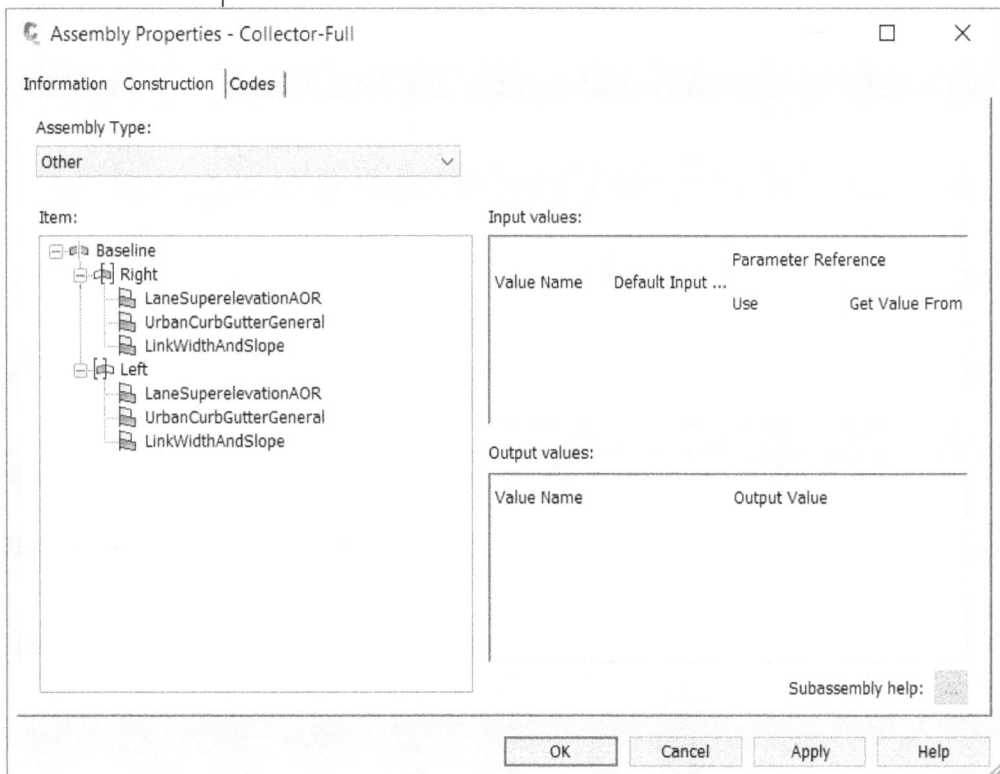

Figure 8–4

8.2 Modifying Assemblies

Attaching Subassemblies

The easiest way to add an Autodesk Civil 3D subassembly to an assembly is using the Tool Palettes. You can open the Tool

Palettes by clicking in the *Home* tab>Palettes panel, as shown in Figure 8–5, or in the *View* tab>Palettes panel. You can also use <Ctrl>+<3>.

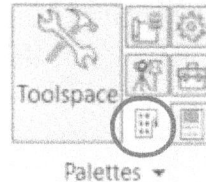

Figure 8–5

The Autodesk Civil 3D software provides a number of stock subassembly tool palettes, as shown in Figure 8–6. In addition, it is continually updating and adding new subassemblies with every release.

Figure 8–6

There are separate Tool Palettes for metric and imperial units. Ensure that you are using the correct palette. To select the correct palette, right-click on the Tool Palette band and select the required palette, as shown in Figure 8–7.

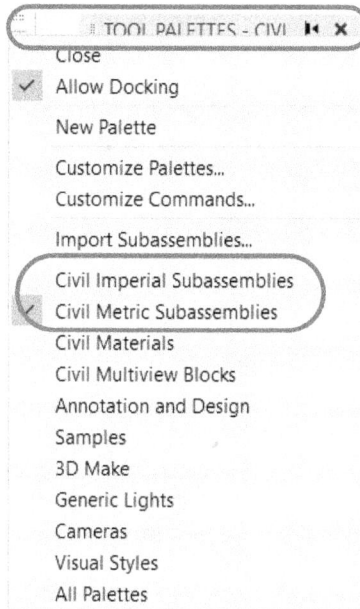

Figure 8–7

The Help file is an invaluable resource for an updated list, and information about the specific attributes and properties of each subassembly, as shown in Figure 8–8.

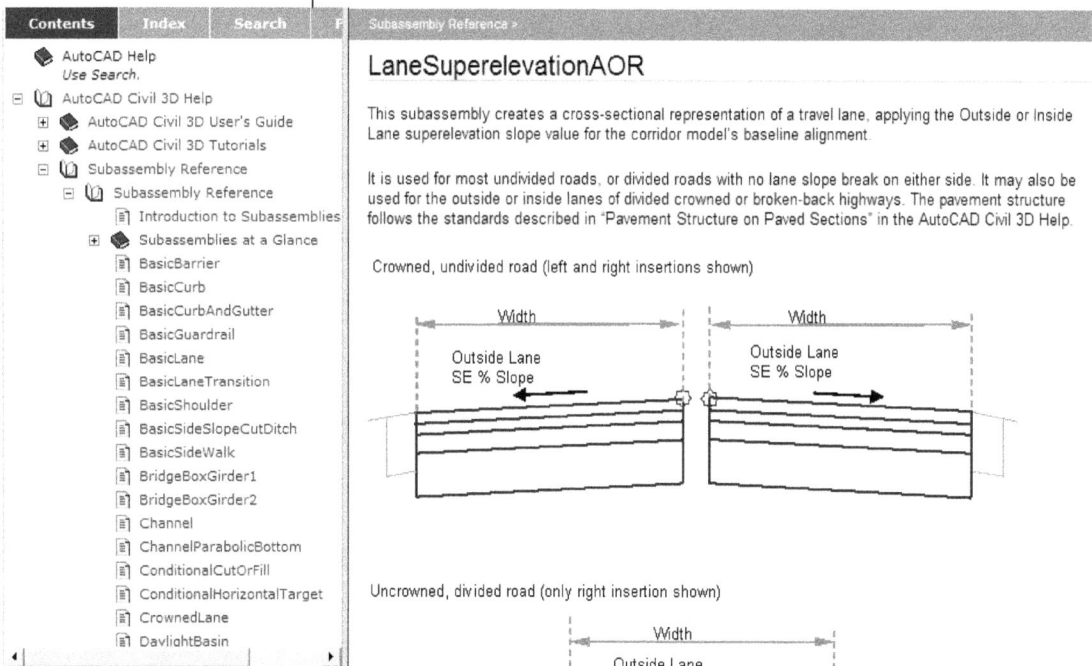

Figure 8–8

Additional subassemblies can be accessed using the Corridor Modeling catalogs. Open the catalog by selecting an assembly or subassembly from the drawing. In the *Assembly/Subassembly* tab>Launch Pad panel, click **Catalog**, as shown in Figure 8–9.

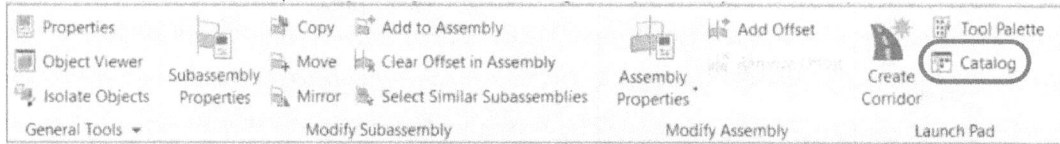

Figure 8–9

You can drag and drop the catalog onto a Tool Palette, if required. When working with the Tool Palettes and Properties palette, you might find it helpful to toggle off the **Allow Docking** option to prevent them from docking on the sides of the screen. Right-click on the palette's title bar to set the option, as shown in Figure 8–10.

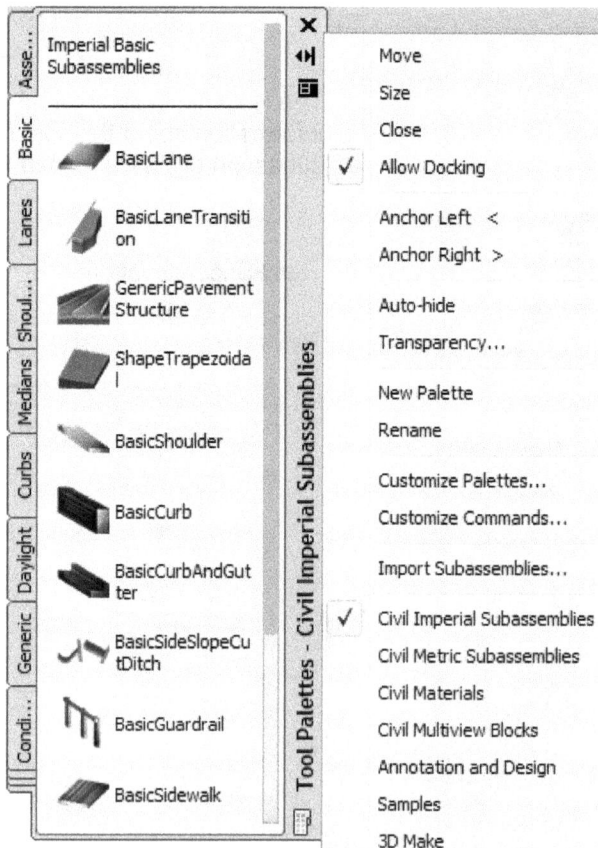

Figure 8–10

Detaching Subassemblies

Individual subassemblies can be deleted directly from an assembly with the AutoCAD® **Erase** command or using Assembly Properties. Assemblies can also be deleted with the **Erase** command.

Copying Assemblies

Assemblies can be copied with the AutoCAD **Copy** command. Copying an assembly creates an independent assembly without a relationship to the original. Select the assembly by selecting the **Assembly Baseline**.

Modifying Subassemblies

In the Autodesk Civil 3D software, subassemblies can be mirrored, copied, and moved across the assembly to which it is attached by selecting the subassemblies, right-clicking, and selecting **Mirror**, **Copy to**, or **Move to** or by clicking (Mirror), (Copy), or (Move), in the *Assembly* tab>Modify Subassembly panel. This enables you to create one side of the roadway and to create a mirrored image for the other side in one step.

> **Hint: AutoCAD Mirror, Move, or Copy Commands**
>
> The basic AutoCAD **Mirror**, **Move**, or **Copy** commands do not work for subassemblies. You need to use the special commands from the shortcut menu or in the Modify Subassembly panel.

Select Similar Subassemblies

It is often necessary to create multiple assemblies with the same subassemblies for various purposes. For example, a corridor that includes an intersection might need a full assembly that includes both sides of the road, an assembly that includes just the right side of the road, and another that includes just the left side of the road. It might also include two other assemblies that require the assembly marker to be placed at the edge of pavement rather than the crown, as shown in Figure 8–11.

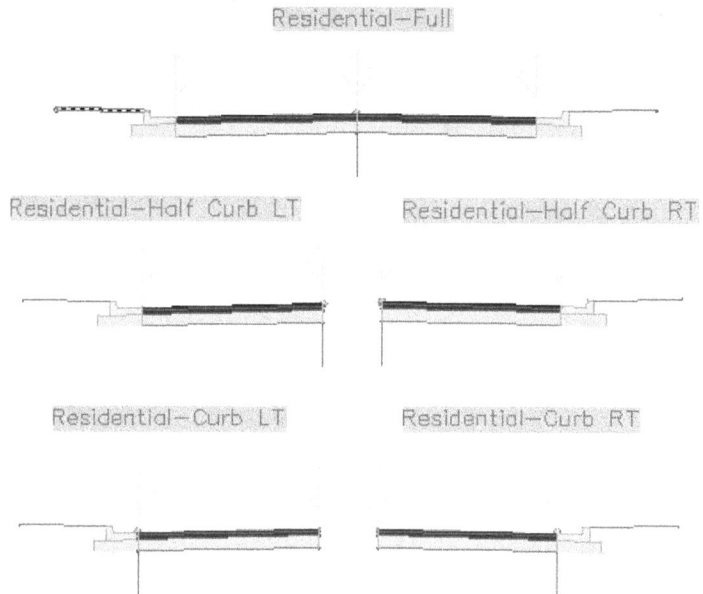

Figure 8–11

However, making changes to all of the assemblies when a design parameter changes can be time consuming. To ensure that all similar subassemblies are modified at the same time when a design change occurs you can select one subassembly,

click (Select Similar Subassemblies) in the *Assembly* tab> Modify Subassembly panel, and change the parameter in the AutoCAD properties palette.

Sharing Assemblies

Assemblies can be shared with the Autodesk Civil 3D software in three ways:

- Assemblies can be dragged from the drawing area to a Tool Palette. The Tool Palette can then be shared.

- The Content Browser can be used to add assemblies to a catalog.

- Assemblies can be placed in their own drawing files and shared by dragging the assembly drawing into the destination drawing file. If this method is used, the assembly drawing must only contain the assemblies that you want to share.

Getting More Information on Subassemblies

Many subassemblies have a large number of parameters. If you want to read the documentation on a subassembly, right-click on its tool icon in a Tool Palette and select **Help**. You can also find out more from Subassembly Properties and Assembly Properties using the **Subassembly help** icon, as shown in Figure 8–12.

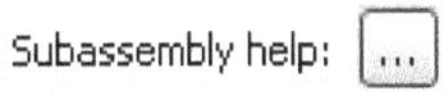

Subassembly help: [...]

Figure 8–12

Practice 8a | Creating Assemblies

Practice Objective

- Create and modify assemblies for use in a corridor model.

In this practice, you will create two assemblies: one for Jeffries Ranch Rd and the second for the Ascent Place. Create the Collector Road assembly.

Task 1 - Create the Collector Road assembly.

A typical cross-section of Jeffries Ranch Rd is shown in Figure 8–13. (See Appendix A for the design criteria.)

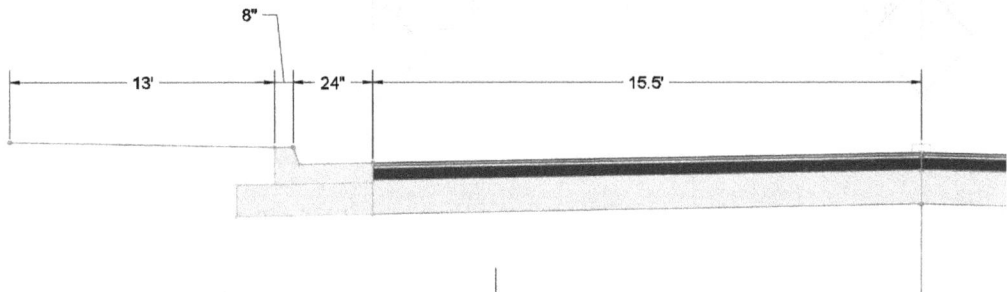

Figure 8–13

1. Open **COR1-A1-Corridor.dwg** from the *C:\Civil 3D Projects\ Working\Corridors* folder.

2. Hover the cursor over the Data Shortcuts and review the tooltip that displays, as shown in Figure 8–14. Ensure that your Data Shortcuts are set so the **Working Folder** is set to *C:\Civil 3D Projects\Data Shortcuts\Fundamentals* and the **Data Shortcuts Project Folder** to *Ascent-Development*. If required, right-click on Data Shortcuts to set the **Working Folder** and **Data Shortcuts Project Folder**.

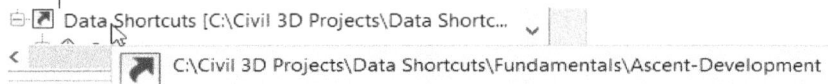

Figure 8–14

3. In the *Home* tab>Create Design panel, click (Create Assembly).

4. In the Create Assembly dialog box, name the new assembly **Collector-Full**. Set the *Assembly Type* to **Undivided Crown Road,** and leave the other settings at their defaults, as shown in Figure 8–15. Click **OK** to close the dialog box.

Figure 8–15

5. When prompted, locate the assembly baseline to the left of the profile view Jeffries Ranch Rd in the current drawing, as shown in Figure 8–16.

Once selected, the Autodesk Civil 3D software will change the view to zoom into the assembly baseline location.

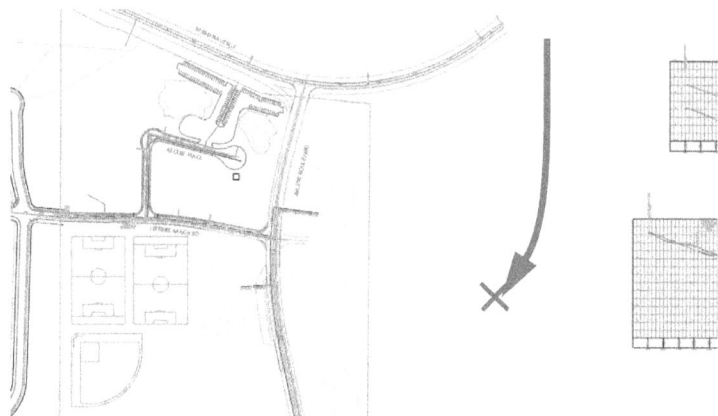

Figure 8–16

6. Open the Tool Palettes by clicking [icon] (Tool Palettes) in the *Home* tab>Palettes panel.

7. In the Lanes Tool Palette, select the **LaneSuperelevationAOR** subassembly to add it to your assembly. In the Properties palette, set the following, as shown in Figure 8–17:
   - *Side*: **Right**
   - *Width*: **15.5'**
   - *Slope*: **-2%**
   - Select the assembly baseline to attach the subassembly to the assembly.

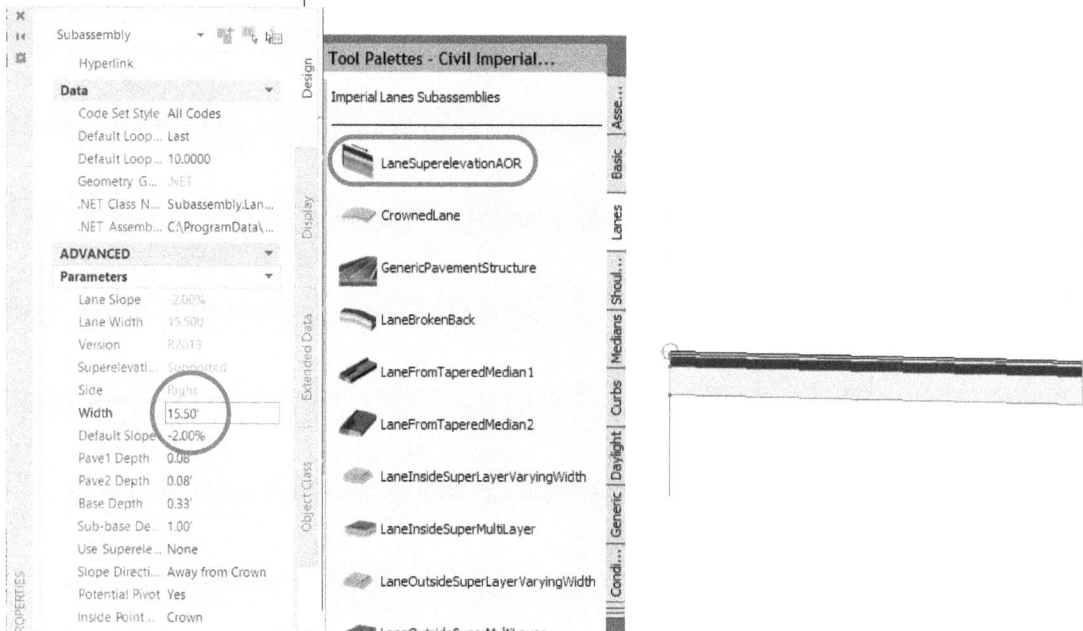

Figure 8–17

8. In the Subassemblies Tool Palette, select the *Curbs* tab and select the **UrbanCurbGutterGeneral** subassembly. In the Advanced Properties, set the following:
   - *Side*: **Right**
   - *Dimension B*: **24"**
   - Insert the subassembly by selecting the upper most circle at the end of the **LaneInsideSuper** subassembly, as shown in Figure 8–18. Do not Osnap to the endpoint, for this may not connect the two subassemblies properly. Press <Esc> to exit the subassembly command.

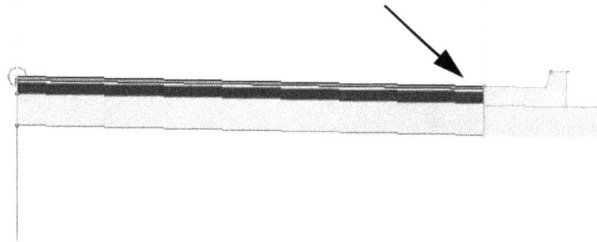

Figure 8–18

9. You will now create a subassembly that links the back of curb to property line. In the Subassemblies Tool Palette, select the *Generic* tab, and select the **LinkWidthAndSlope** subassembly. In the Advanced Properties, set the following:

   - *Side parameter:* **Right**
   - *Width*: **13'**
   - Insert the subassembly by selecting the circle at the end of the **UrbanCurbGutterGeneral** subassembly, as shown in Figure 8–19.
   - Press <Esc> to exit the subassembly command.

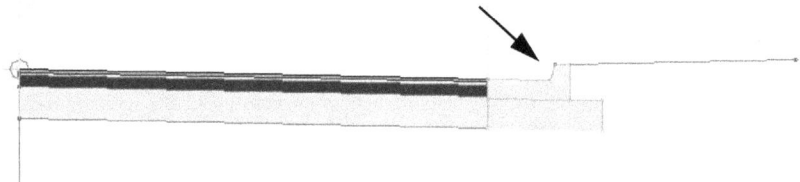

Figure 8–19

Do not select the assembly baseline, and do not use window crossing.

10. Select the three sub-assemblies that you just created on the right side, right-click, and select **Mirror**. At the *select marker point within assembly:* prompt, select the assembly baseline (the red vertical line), as shown in Figure 8–20, which represents the road center line.

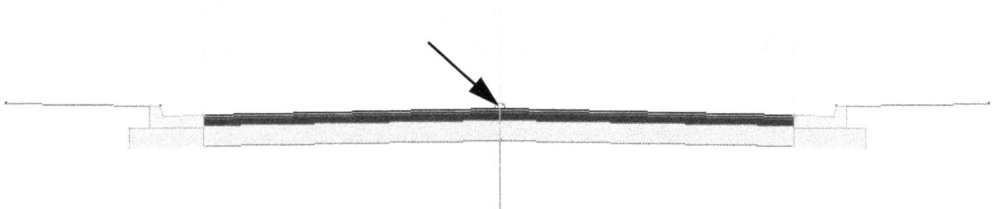

Figure 8–20

11. Save the drawing.

Task 2 - Create the Residential Road assembly.

Note that this task is similar to Task 1. You can use this Task as a test of your knowledge in creating a residential road assembly or you can skip this task and open the backup drawing in Task 3.

A typical cross-section of Ascent Pl is shown in Figure 8–21. (See Appendix A for design criteria.)

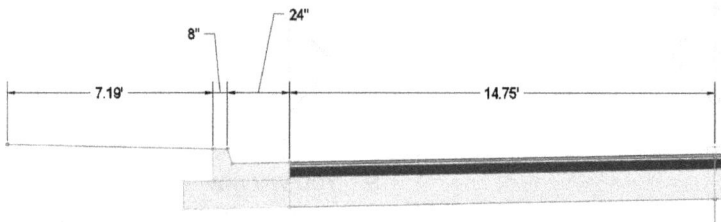

Figure 8–21

1. Continue working with the drawing from the previous task or open **COR1-A2-Corridor.dwg**.

2. In the *Home* tab>Create Design panel, click (Create Assembly).

3. In the Create Assembly dialog box, name the new assembly **Residential-Full**. Set the *Assembly Type* to **Undivided Crown Road,** and leave the other settings at their defaults and click **OK**. Click in the drawing to place the new assembly.

4. Follow the same steps in Task 1 to create the residential assembly. For this assembly:

   • Set the pavement LaneSuperelevationAOR *width* to **14.75'**.

   • **UrbanCurbGutterGeneral** subassembly *Dimension B* is set to **24"**.

   • LinkWidthAndSlope *width* to **27.193'**.

Task 3 - Copy and modify an assembly.

Copying an assembly can be helpful if you need another, similar assembly for other design purposes. In the following task, you will create assemblies that are required by the Intersection wizard for the intersection area of Jeffries Ranch Rd and Ascent Place. It would be helpful to understand the names and the configuration of the different assemblies.

You only need to select the red baseline, since all subassemblies are properly attached, they all will get copied with the baseline.

1. Start the AutoCAD **Copy** command. Copy the **Collector-Full** assembly to a location just below the original, as shown in Figure 8–22.

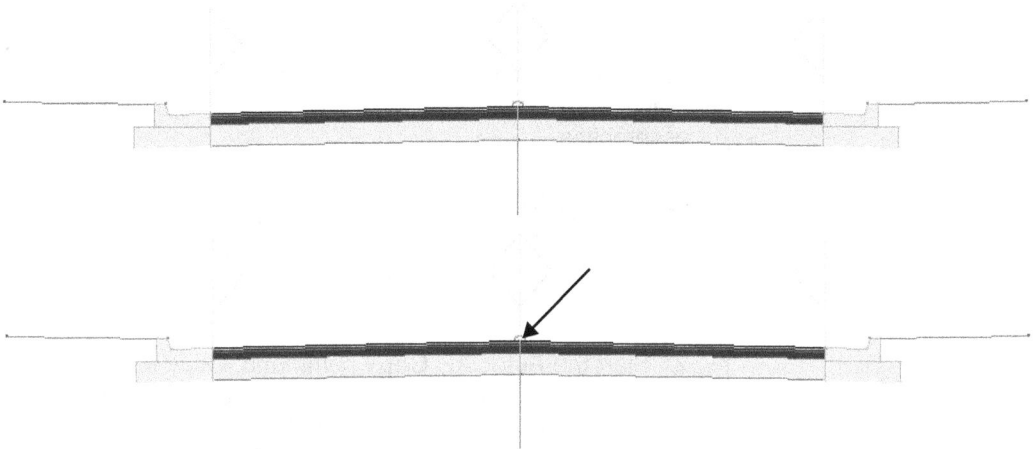

Figure 8–22

2. Select the bottom assembly baseline, right-click, and select **Assembly Properties**.

3. In the *Information* tab, change the *Name* to **Collector-Part Curb RT** and click **OK**.

4. Start the AutoCAD **Erase** command and erase the left **UrbanCurbGutterGeneral** and the left **LinkWidthAndSlope**, as shown in Figure 8–23.

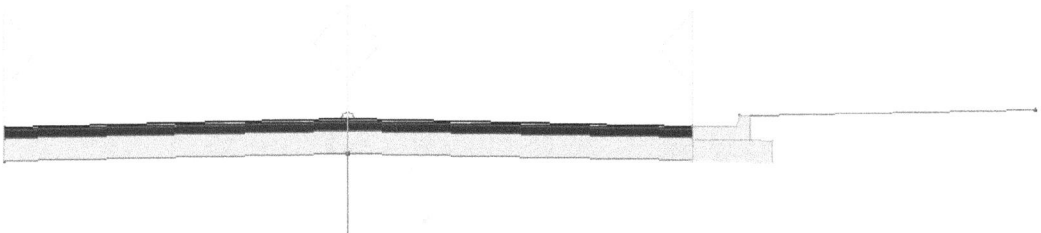

Figure 8–23

5. Save the drawing.

Practice 8b	# Creating Assemblies Additional Practice

Practice Objective

- Create and modify assemblies for use in an intersection model.

In the previous practice, you created all of the Jeffries Ranch Rd assemblies that were required for the intersection. In this practice, you will create all of the required Ascent Place assemblies.

Task 1 - Create the assemblies required for the intersection.

1. Open **COR1-B1-Corridor.dwg** from the *C:\Civil 3D Projects\ Working\Corridors* folder.

2. Start the AutoCAD **Copy** command. Copy the **Residential-Full** assembly to two locations below the original, as shown in Figure 8–24.

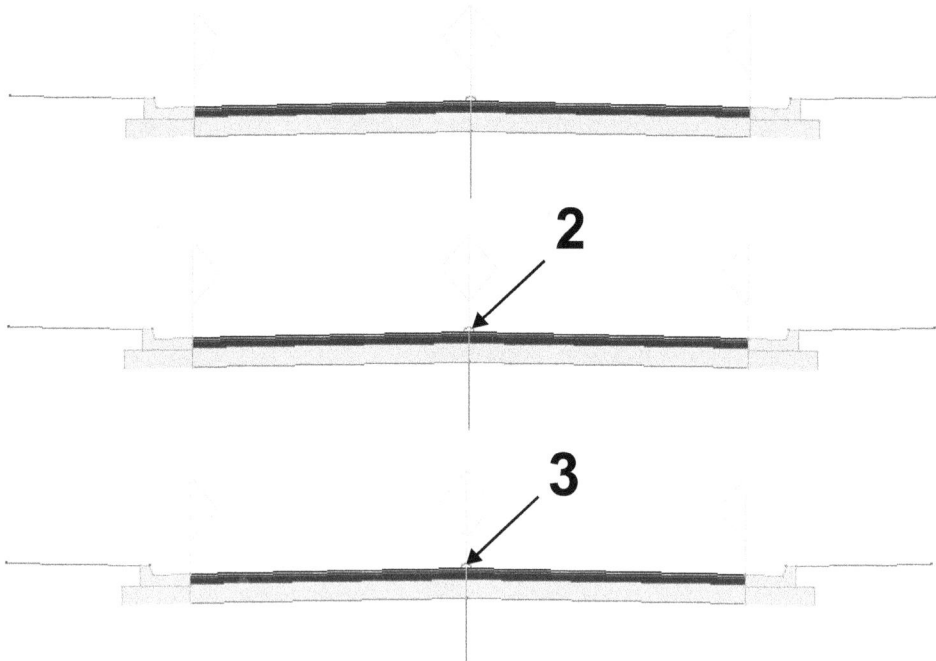

Figure 8–24

3. Select the second assembly baseline, right-click, and select **Assembly Properties**. In the *Information* tab, change the *Name* to **Residential-Half Curb LT** and click **OK**.

4. Start the AutoCAD **Erase** command and erase the right **LaneSuperelevationAOR**, the right **UrbanCurbGutterGeneral**, and the right **LinkWidthAndSlope**.

5. Select the third assembly baseline, right-click, and select **Assembly Properties**. In the *Information* tab, change the *Name* to **Residential-Half Curb RT** and click **OK**.

6. Start the AutoCAD **Erase** command and erase the left **LaneSuperelevationAOR**, the left **UrbanCurbGutterGeneral**, and the left **LinkWidthAndSlope**, as shown in Figure 8–25.

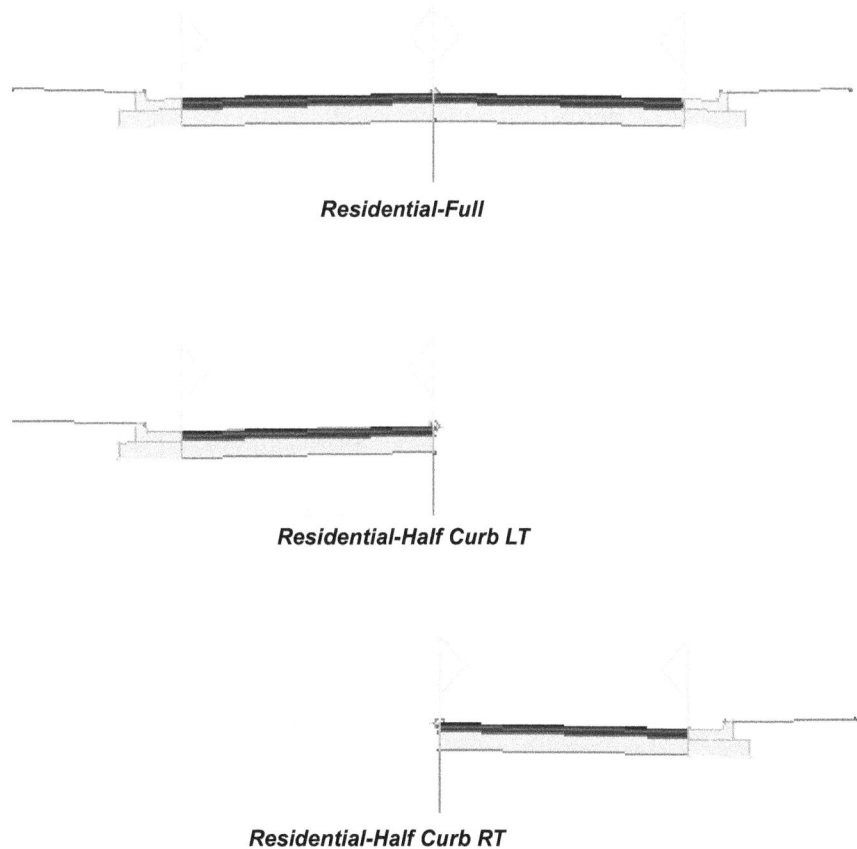

Residential-Full

Residential-Half Curb LT

Residential-Half Curb RT

Figure 8–25

Task 2 - Create a Curb Return assembly.

To include the intersection in the corridor model, you need another assembly to go around the curb returns. This assembly will have the assembly baseline at the edge of pavement or flange of the curb and gutter. It is important to create the assembly with the lane inserted first for the **Intersection** tool to be able to set the correct transitions at the centerline.

Open the Tool Palettes

by clicking 🖻 *in the View tab>Palettes panel, if it is not already open.*

1. In the *Home* tab>Create Design panel, expand **Assembly** and select **Create Assembly**.

2. In the Create Assembly dialog box, name the new assembly **Residential-Curb Return**. Leave the other settings at their defaults, and click **OK**. Click in the drawing to place the new assembly.

3. In the Lanes Tool Palette, select the **LaneSuperelevationAOR** subassembly to add it to your assembly. In the AutoCAD Properties Palette, confirm that the following are set:
   - *Side:* **Left**
   - *Width*: **14.75'**
   - *Slope*: **+2%**.

4. To add the Left lane subassembly, select the assembly baseline object.

5. In the Curbs tool palette, select the **UrbanCurbGutterGeneral** subassembly to add it to your assembly.

6. In the AutoCAD Properties Palette, confirm that the following are set:
   - *Side*: **Right**
   - *Dimensions B*: **24"**

7. Select the assembly baseline to add the curb and gutter, as shown in Figure 8–26.

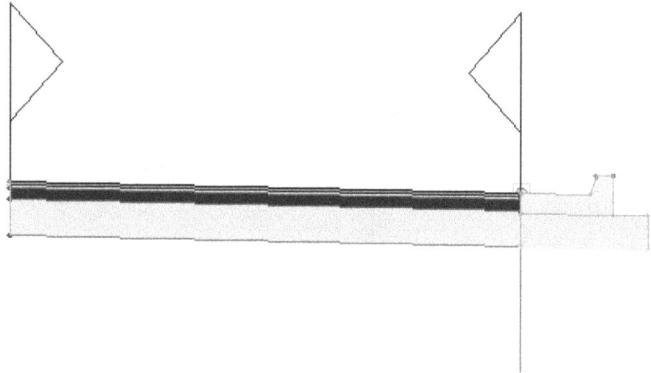

Figure 8–26

You will now create a subassembly that links the back of curb to the property line.

8. In the Subassemblies Tool Palette, select the *Generic* tab, and select the **LinkWidthAndSlope** subassembly.In the AutoCAD Properties Palette, in the Advanced Properties, set the following:

   • *Side*: **Right**
   • *Width*: **7.193'**

9. Insert the subassembly at the end of the **UrbanCurbGutterGeneral** subassembly, as shown in Figure 8–27.

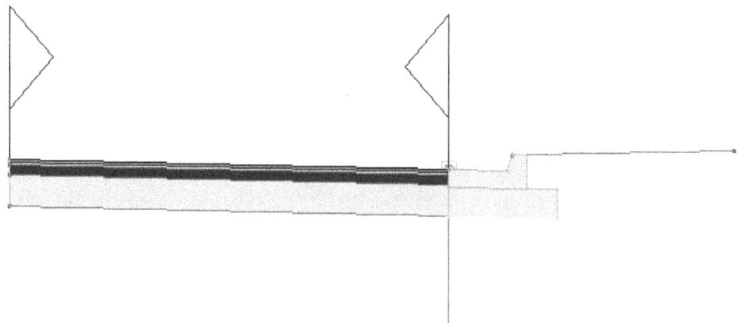

Figure 8–27

10. Press <Esc> to exit the subassembly command and save the drawing.

8.3 Corridor Properties

Once created, corridors are adjusted in the Corridor Properties dialog box.

Information Tab

The *Information* tab enables you to name the corridor (recommended) and add a description. The corridor style is not very pertinent since the **Code Set Styles** will control the appearance of the corridor.

Parameters Tab

The *Parameters* tab enables you to review and adjust corridor parameters, including which alignments, profiles, and assemblies are being used. Each unique road center line is listed as a *baseline*. In each baseline, there is at least one *region*. Each region is an area over which a specific assembly is applied. You can have multiple baselines and multiple regions in the same baseline as required. The *Parameters* tab is shown in Figure 8–28.

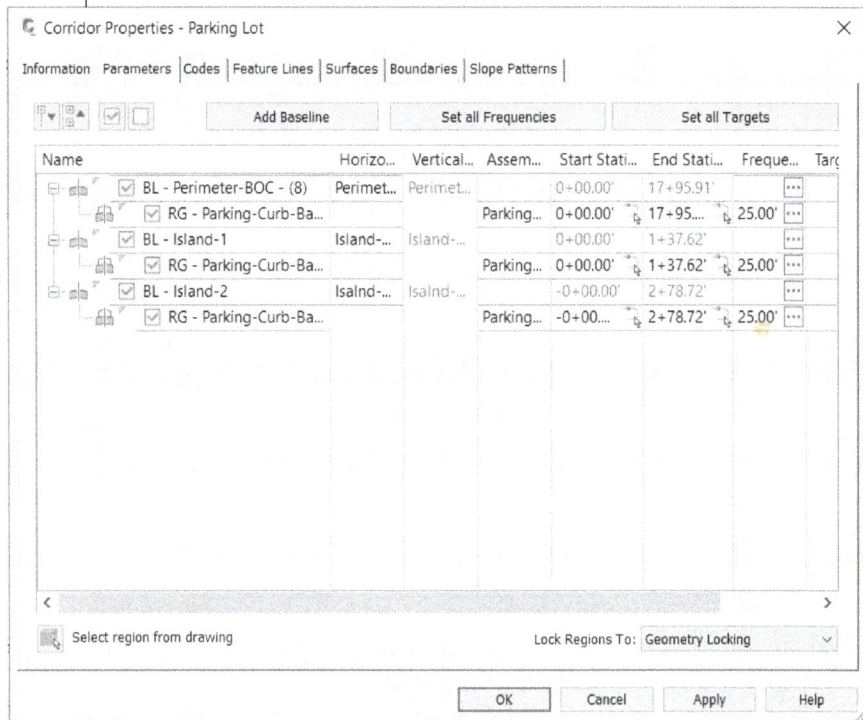

Figure 8–28

Each region has controls that enable you to review the Target Mapping, and the *Frequency* at which corridor sections should be created. If the corridor has had overrides applied using the Corridor Section Editor (select the corridor, *Corridor* tab> Modify panel), those can be reviewed here as well.

At the top of the dialog box are two important buttons: **Set all Frequencies** and **Set all Targets**. These can be used to assign frequencies and targets to all corridor regions. Otherwise, these properties can be adjusted for individual regions using ⊡ (Ellipsis), which is available in the *Frequency* and *Targets* columns.

Codes

*These can be preset through the Edit Command Settings dialog box for the various **CreateCorridor** commands.*

The *Codes* tab lists all of the codes that are available in the corridor based on the subassemblies in the assembly, as shown in Figure 8–29. These codes are combined into Code set styles.

They control the appearance of the corridor (and cross sections and assemblies) by applying styles to each of the subassemblies. Codes are also used to set section labels and for quantity take-off.

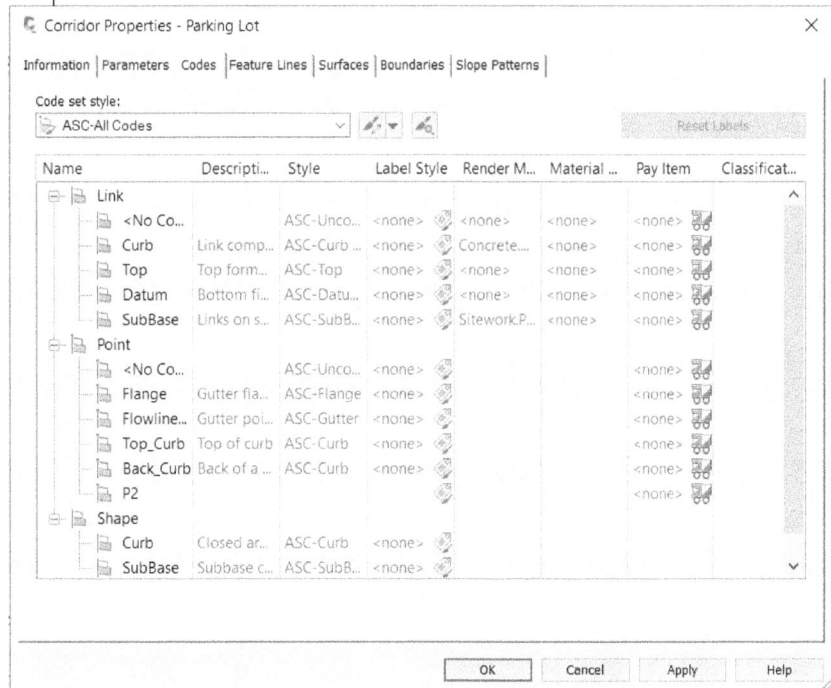

Figure 8–29

Feature Lines

Feature lines are named 3D linework that connect marker points (locations assigned point codes) in your assemblies, as shown in Figure 8–30. From any feature line listed in the *Feature Lines* tab, you can export a polyline or extract a linked or unlinked feature line (such as for grading purposes).

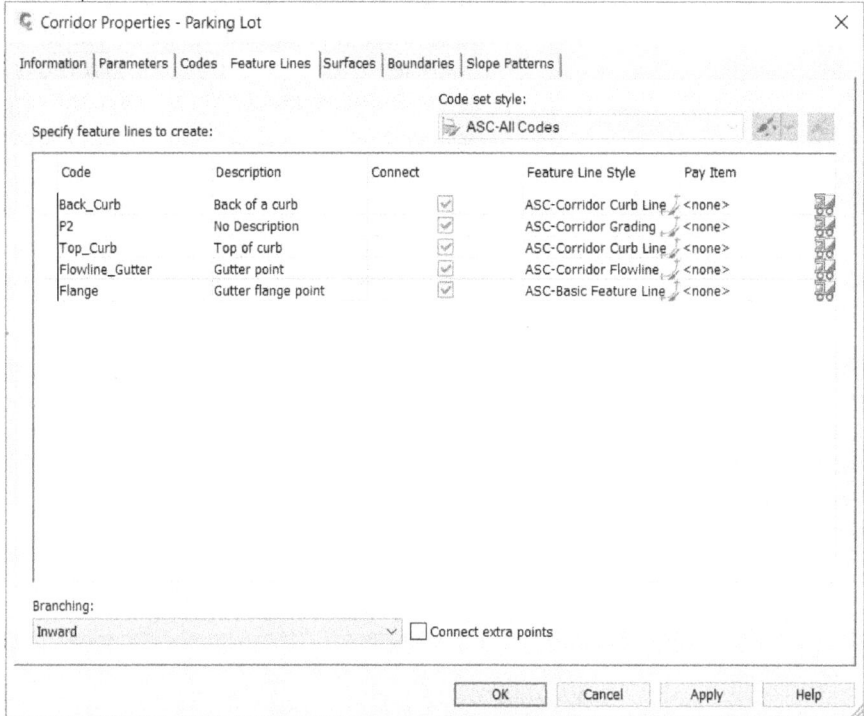

Figure 8–30

Slope Patterns

Slope patterns can be used to indicate whether an area of side slope is a cut or fill. The *Slope Patterns* tab is shown in Figure 8–31.

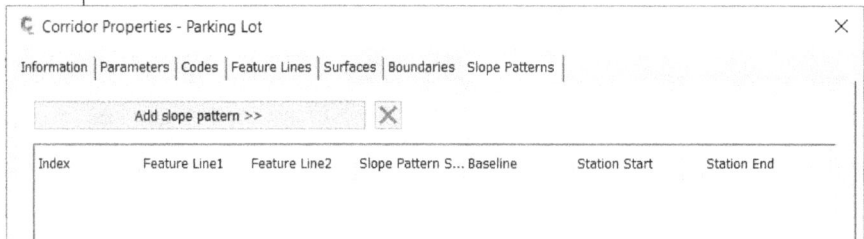

Figure 8–31

Corridor Contextual Ribbon

Most of the functions performed in the *Corridors Parameters* tab are also available in the ribbon in the *Corridor* contextual tab>Modify Region panel, as shown in Figure 8–32. For many users, this is the preferred option; they find it more intuitive because they can pick the regions of the corridor in the drawing and view the results.

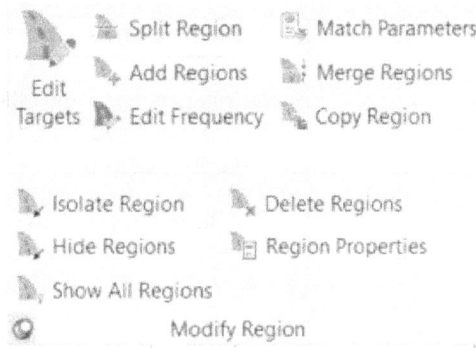

Figure 8–32

The Corridor Contextual Ribbon Modify Corridor panel also has **Corridor Surfaces**, **Code Sets**, **Feature Lines** and **Slope Patterns**, as shown in Figure 8–33.

Figure 8–33

Practice 8c

Create Corridors - Roads

Practice Objective

- Create a corridor model using previously created alignments, profiles, and assemblies.

Task 1 - Create a corridor with regions - Option #1.

In this practice, you will use the assemblies to create a corridor for both Jeffries Ranch Rd and Ascent Pl. You will also learn how to split a region.

1. Open **COR1-C1-A-Corridor.dwg** from the *C:\Civil 3D Projects\Working\Corridors* folder.

2. In the *Home* tab>Create Design panel, click 　 (Corridor). Enter the following (as shown in Figure 8–34):

    - Name it **Jeffries Ranch Rd**.
    - For the alignment, select **Jeffries Ranch Rd**.
    - For the profile, select **Jeffries Ranch Rd-DGN**.
    - For the subassembly, select **Collector-Full**.
    - Verify that the **Set baseline and region parameters** option is selected.

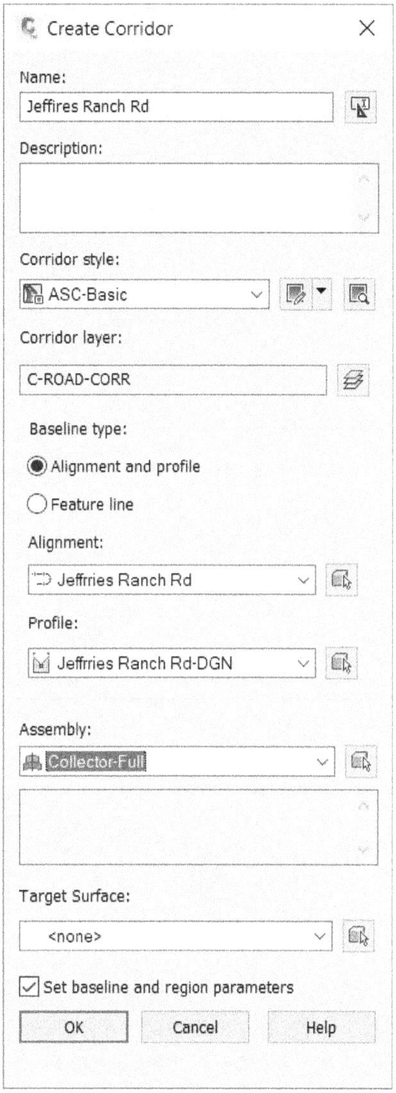

Figure 8–34

3. Click **OK**. The baseline and region parameters dialog box should open.

In this practice, you will create Jeffries Ranch Road and Ascent Place as two independent corridors. Note that this will also create two separate surfaces. As you will be creating an intersection in the Jeffries Ranch Rd, you need to create two regions: one before the intersection, and one after the intersection.

4. The dialog box identifies the Baseline (BL) as *BL-Jeffries Ranch Rd - (1)*. This baseline currently has one Region (RG). In the Baseline and Region Parameters dialog box, set the following options, as shown in Figure 8–35:

- Change the region name to **RG-Before Intersection**.
- Adjust the start station to **117.03'**.
- Right-click on RG-Before Intersection and select **Split Region**.

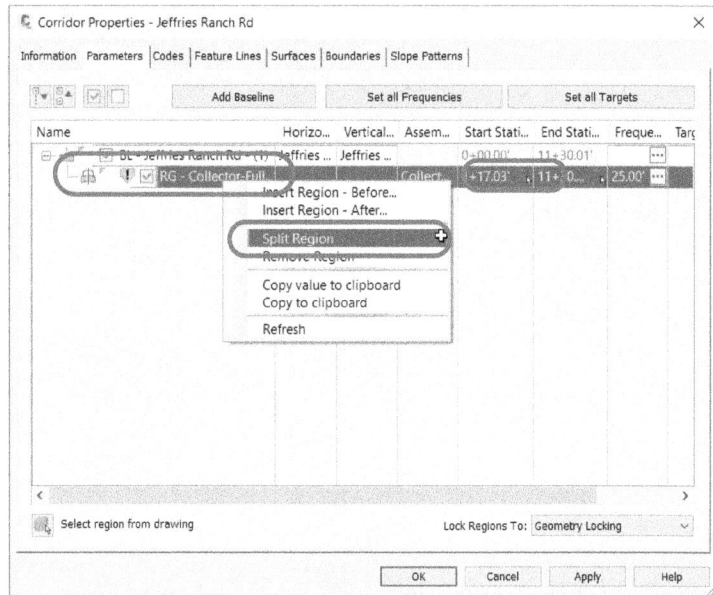

Figure 8–35

5. You now need to enter the start and end stations for the regions. You have already typed **117.03'** for the start station for the **RG-Before Intersection**. Enter the following values, as shown in Figure 8–36.
- RG-Before Intersection End station: **525.81'**
- RG-After Intersection Start station: **630.74'**
- RG-After Intersection End station: **1035.92'**
- Press <Enter> to return to the Baseline and Region dialog box.

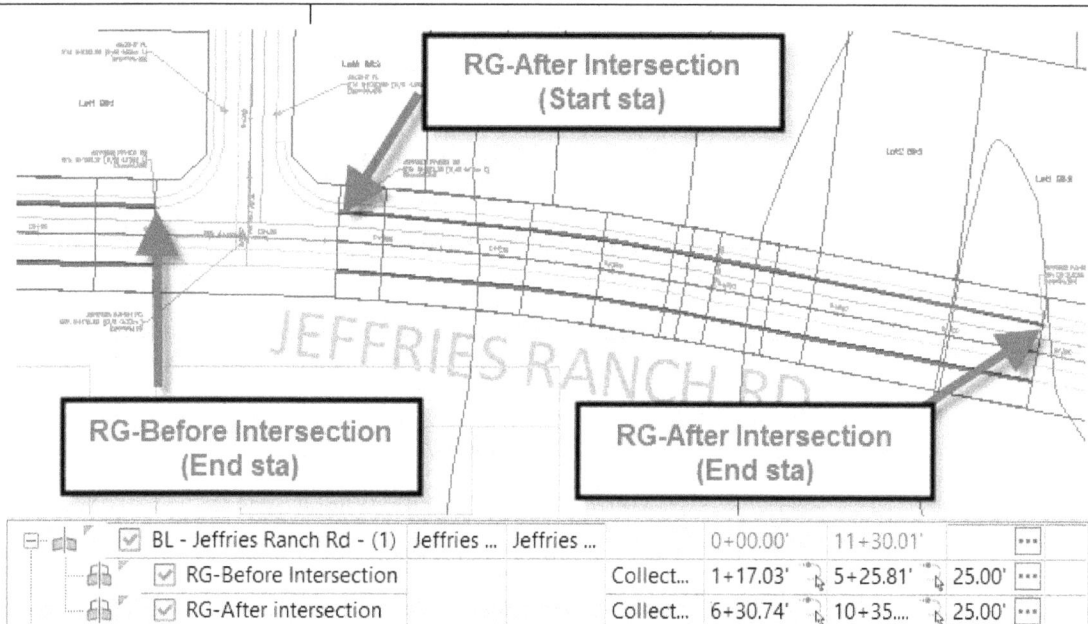

Figure 8–36

6. In the Baseline and Region Parameters dialog box, right-click on RG - Collector-Full - (1) and select **Remove Region**. Do the same for RG - Collector-Full - (3).

7. Click **OK** to apply the changes and close the dialog box. If prompted, rebuild the corridor.

8. Save the drawing.

Task 2 - Create a corridor with regions - Option #2.

In this task, you will create regions as in the previous task, but using the tools within the Corridor contextual ribbon and "eyeballing" the locations of the regions.

1. Open **COR1-C1-B-Corridor.dwg** from the *C:\Civil 3D Projects\Working\Corridors* folder.

2. As you did in Task 1, in the *Home* tab>Create Design panel,

   click ![icon] (Corridor). Enter the following:

   • Name it **Jeffries Ranch Rd**.
   • For the alignment, select **Jeffries Ranch Rd**.
   • For the profile, select **Jeffries Ranch Rd-DGN**.
   • For the subassembly, select **Collector-Full**.

3. **Do not** select the **Set baseline and region parameters** option. You will be using the corresponding tools within the contextual ribbon instead.

4. Click OK to close the *Create Corridor* dialog box.

5. The corridor is built with the default settings

6. Select the newly built corridor and in the *Corridor* contextual ribbon, Modify Region panel, select (![icon]) Split Region, as shown in Figure 8–37.

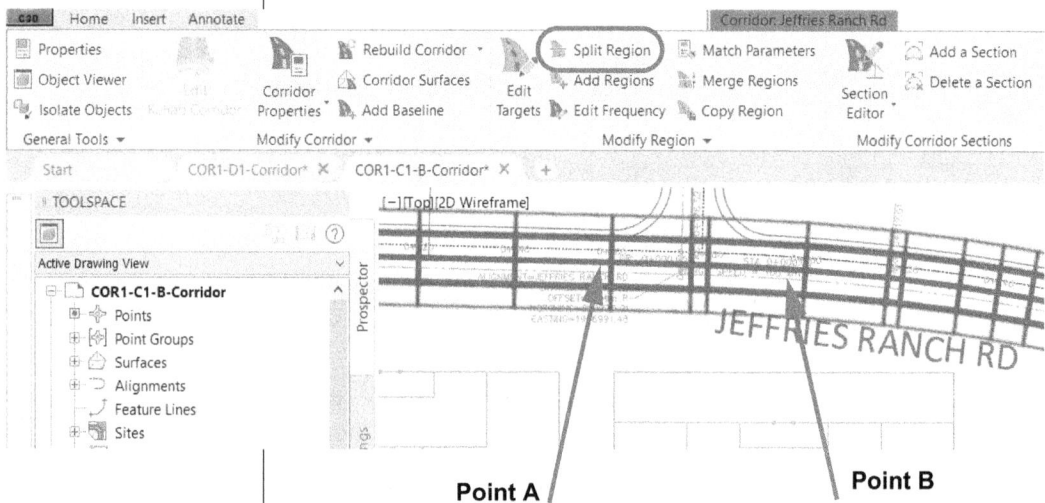

Point A   Point B

Figure 8–37

7. You are prompted to select the region to split. This is a newly created corridor, therefore it has only one region. Select anywhere within the corridor to select.

8. For the location to split the region, select somewhere near Point A. It doesn't need to be exact.

9. The Split Region command continues by asking for another region to split. Select the region to the East of the intersection.

10. For the location to split the region, select somewhere near Point B. It doesn't need to be exact.

11. Press <Enter> to finish the command.

12. There are now three regions, marked with triangular grips. Extend the Modify Region panel and select Delete Regions. Select the middle region, as shown in Figure 8–38.

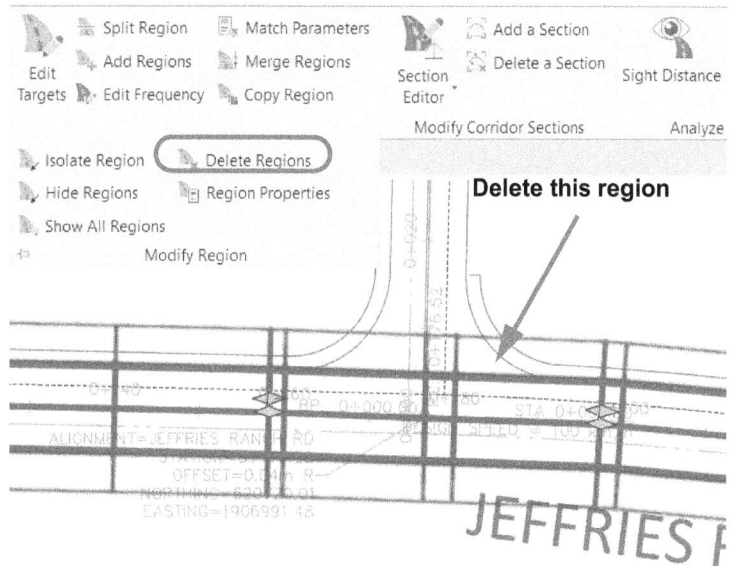

Figure 8–38

You didn't really need to create three regions. You could have split the corridor into two regions and simply dragged their edges to the intersection limits.

13. Now you can adjust the edges of the two remaining regions with the triangular grips.

14. Save the drawing.

Practice 8d

Create Corridors - Parking Lot

Practice Objectives

- Create a corridor model using previously created feature lines and assemblies.
- Add baselines and regions for the islands using Corridor Parameters.

Task 1 - Create a corridor representing the overall parking lot.

In this practice, you will use the perimeter feature line to create a corridor for the overall parking lot.

1. Open **PKCOR-B-Grading.dwg** from the *C:\Civil 3D Projects\Grading\Parking Corridor* folder.

2. In the *Home* tab>Create Design panel, click (Corridor). Do the following (as shown in Figure 8–39):

   - For the *Name*, type **Parking Lot**.
   - For the *Baseline type*, select **Feature line**.
   - For the *Site*, select **Multi-Family Site**.
   - For the *Feature line*, select **Perimeter-BOC**.
   - For the *Assembly*, select **Parking-Curb-Back**.
   - Verify that the **Set baseline and region parameters** option is *not* selected.

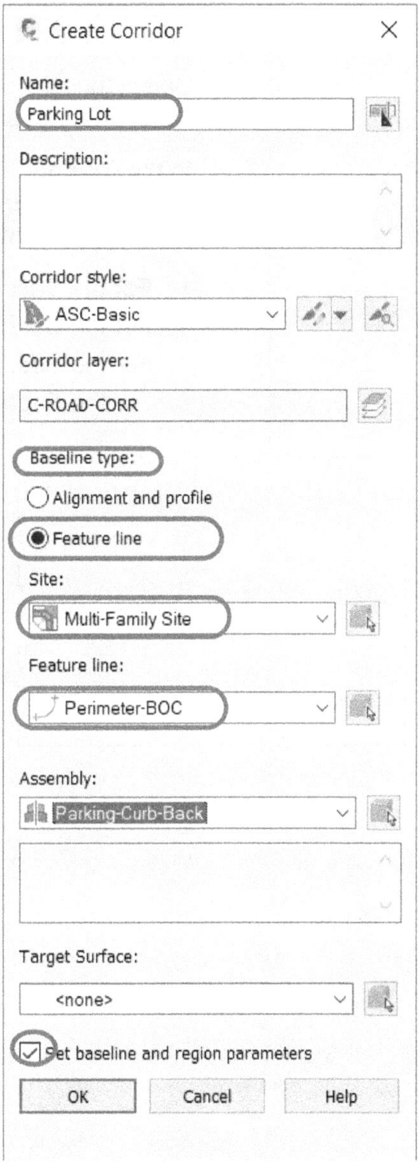

Figure 8–39

For now, ignore the inconsistencies within the corridor. They will be fixed later.

3. Click **OK**. The corridor is built.

4. Save the drawing.

Task 2 - Add islands to the corridor.

1. Select the corridor. Either through the right-click menu or the contextual ribbon, select **Corridor Properties**.

2. In the Corridor Properties dialog box, in the *Parameters* tab, click the **Add Baseline** button. Then, in the Create Corridor Baseline window, do the following (as shown in Figure 8–40):

   - For the *Baseline name*, enter **BL - Island-1**.
   - For the *Baseline type*, select **Feature line**.
   - For the *Site*, select **Multi-Family Site**.
   - For the *Feature line*, select **Island-1-BOC**.

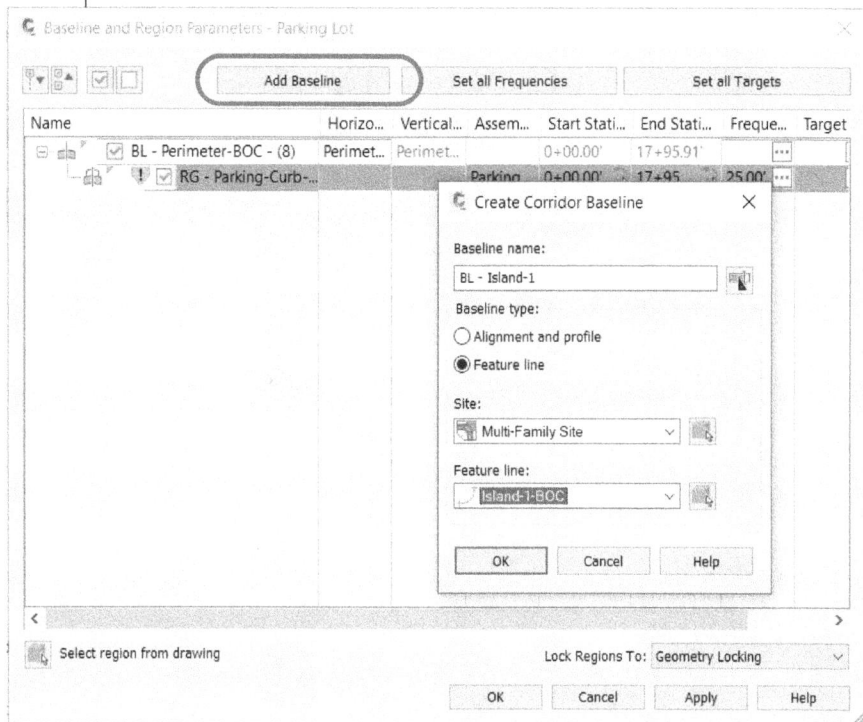

Figure 8–40

3. Click **OK** to close the Create Corridor Baseline window.

4. In the Corridor Properties dialog box, right-click on the newly created Baseline to add a region, then in the Create Corridor Region window, accept all the defaults as they are (as shown in Figure 8–41).

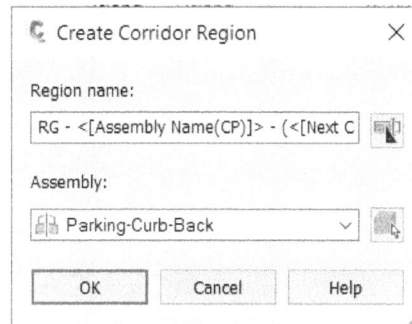

Figure 8–41

5. Click **OK** to close the Corridor Properties dialog box. When the warning box displays, select the **Rebuild the corridor** option, as shown in Figure 8–42.

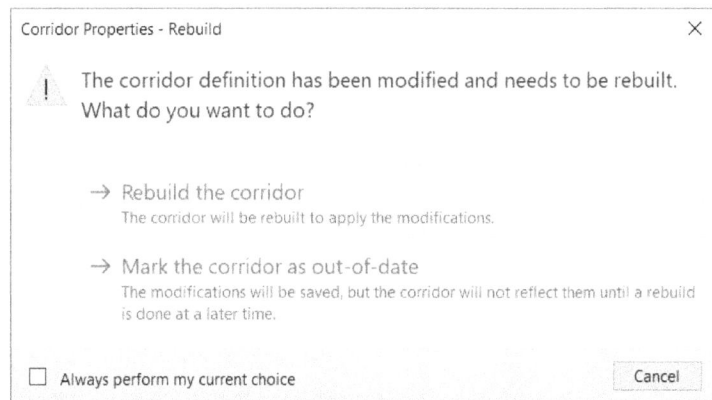

Figure 8–42

For now, ignore the inconsistencies within the corridor. They will be fixed later.

6. Save the drawing.

7. Repeat the same steps as before for the second island by selecting the corridor again. Through either the right-click menu or the contextual ribbon, select **Corridor Properties**.

8. In the Corridor Properties dialog box, click the **Add Baseline** button. Then, in the Create Corridor Baseline window, do the following (as shown in Figure 8–43):

   - For the *Baseline name*, type **BL - Island-2**.
   - For the *Baseline type*, select **Feature line**.
   - For the *Site*, leave this blank.
   - For the *Feature line*, click the green cube to select the feature line from the drawing.
   - Once the elongated feature line is picked in the drawing, the Site and Feature line names will be populated in the Create Corridor Baseline window.

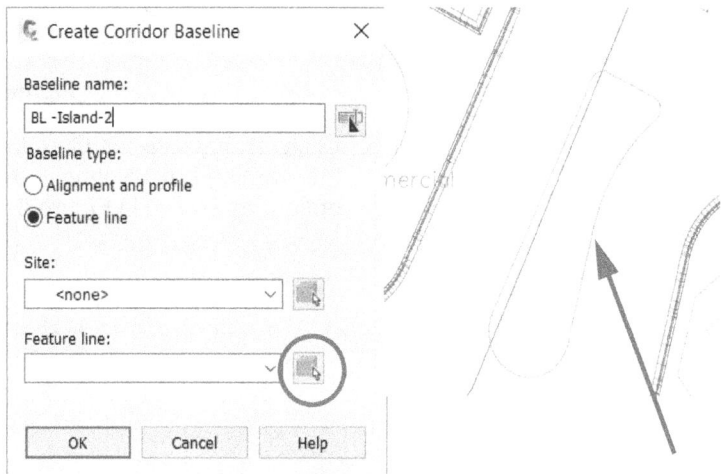

Figure 8–43

9. Click **OK** to close the Create Corridor Baseline window.

10. In the Corridor Properties dialog box, right-click on the newly created Baseline to add a region, then in the Create Corridor Baseline window, accept all the defaults as they are.

For now, ignore the inconsistencies within the corridor. They will be fixed later.

11. Click **OK** to close the Corridor Properties dialog box. When the warning box displays, select the **Rebuild the corridor** option.

12. Save the drawing.

8.4 Corridor Editing

In the typical Civil 3D workflow, you create the initial corridor, then edit and refine it. Corridors are perhaps the most complicated of all the Civil 3D (AEC) objects, with a multitude of settings and defaults. These settings are available in the different tabs of the Corridor Properties dialog box.

Corridor Bowties

In situations where there are tight curves or abrupt direction changes (such as corners) in the control line of the corridor, the corridor links can cross each other, resulting in links resembling bowties.

You can edit the feature settings of corridors to automatically clean bowties in corridors, as shown in Figure 8–44.

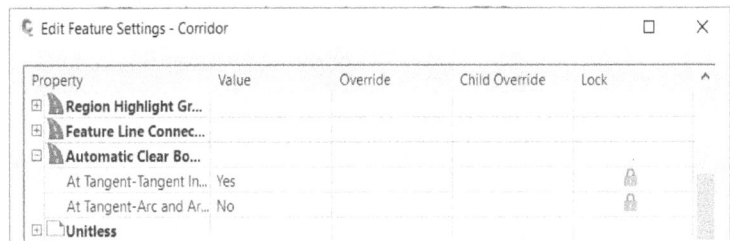

Figure 8–44

But bowties may still persist. In the *Corridor* contextual ribbon, there is a tool to fix such bowties, as shown in Figure 8–45.

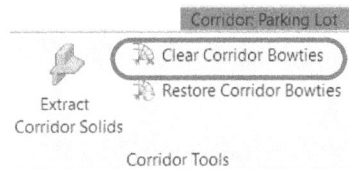

Figure 8–45

How To: Fix Bowties

1. In the *Corridor* contextual tab>Corridor Tools panel, click

   (Clear Corridor Bowties), as shown in Figure 8–45.
2. You are prompted to select the corridor baseline (either an alignment or a feature line). See **A** in Figure 8–46.
3. You are prompted for the starting subentity. Select the same baseline as you did previously, just *before* the bowtie. Take care that you understand the direction of the corridor and that the stationing of the starting subentity is lower than the ending subentity (next step). See **B** in Figure 8–46. The selected line segment highlights in red.
4. Specify the ending subentity, then select the baseline just *after* the bowtie. See **C** in Figure 8–46.
5. Next you determine where you want the resulting corridor feature lines to intersect. See **D** in Figure 8–46.
6. If there are more bowties to be cleared, you can move on to the next starting entity, or press <Enter> to rebuild the corridor and see the results.

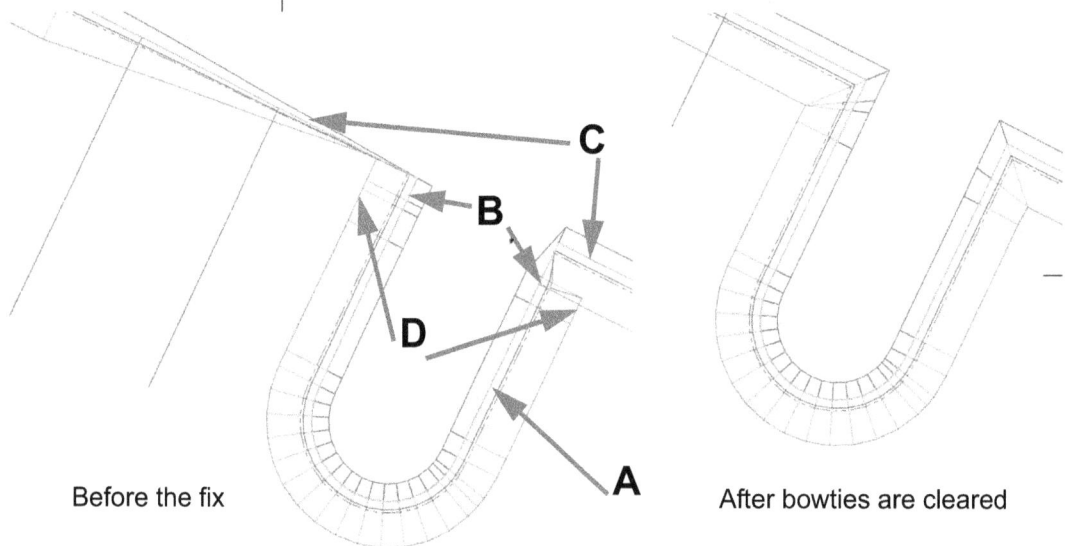

Before the fix   After bowties are cleared

Figure 8–46

Sometimes when the baselines change directions, the cleared bowties will remain and result in unsatisfactory conditions. For this reason, you can restore the original bowtie conditions.

How To: Restore Bowties

1. In the *Corridor* contextual tab>Corridor Tools panel, click
   (Restore Corridor Bowtie), as shown in Figure 8–47.

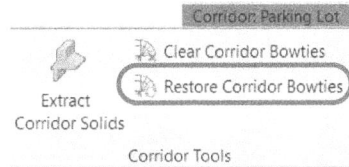

Figure 8–47

2. Since you invoked this command from the contextual corridor ribbon, Civil 3D already knows how many bowties have been cleared and highlights the first one. On the command line, it informs you how many bowties are cleared and the number of the current one.
3. You can choose to restore the current bowtie by simply pressing <Enter>, and it will move on to the next bowtie.
4. You can choose to ignore the bowtie by clicking **Skip** and it will move on to the next bowtie.
5. Once you are done selecting the bowties to be restored, select **Rebuild and restore** at the command line. The command terminates and the selected bowties are restored.
6. You can choose all bowties by clicking **All**. The command terminates and the bowties are restored.

Practice 8e | Corridor Editing

Practice Objectives

- Change the frequency of the corridor.
- Clean up the various bowties along the perimeter.
- Reverse the direction of the Island feature lines.

Task 1 - Changing corridor frequencies.

For the drawings in these exercises, the frequencies were preset through the Edit Command Settings dialog box for the various **CreateCorridor** commands for a satisfactory corridor. You will change them to see the results.

1. Open **PKCOR-C-Grading.dwg** from the *C:\Civil 3D Projects\Grading\Parking Corridor* folder.

2. Select the corridor. Either through the right-click menu or the contextual ribbon, select **Corridor Properties**. In the Corridor Properties dialog box, select the **Set all Frequencies** button. In the Frequency to Apply Assemblies window, change the Horizontal Baseline>Along curves to **Both** (using the drop-down list), as shown in Figure 8–48.

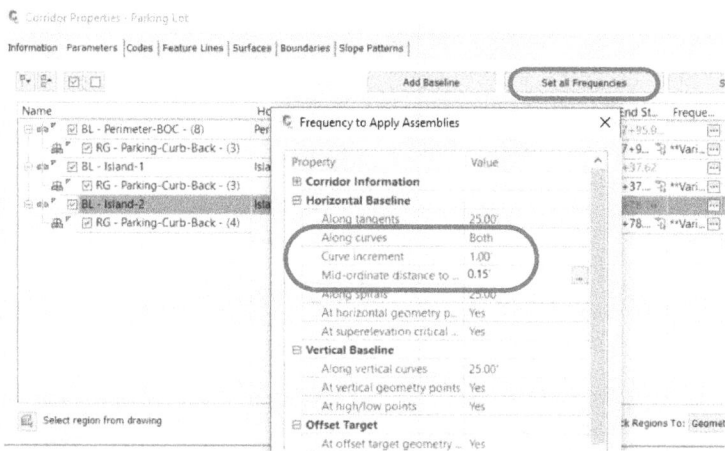

Figure 8–48

3. Change the Curve increment to **1.00'** and the Mid-ordinate distance to **0.15'**.

4. Click **OK** to close the Frequency to Apply Assemblies window.

Notice the increased placement along the curves, causing a smoother curve.

5. Click **OK** to close the Corridor Properties dialog box. When the warning box displays, select the **Rebuild the corridor** option.

6. Save the drawing.

Task 2 - Clearing bowties.

1. Select the corridor and through either the right-click menu or the *Corridor* contextual tab>General Tools expanded panel, send the corridor to the back. This will simplify picking the corridor baseline when clearing bowties.

2. In the *View* tab>Views panel, select **Problem Area** to view where some bowties might have occurred.

3. In the *Corridor* contextual tab>Corridor Tools panel, click
   (Clear Corridor Bowties), as shown in Figure 8–49.

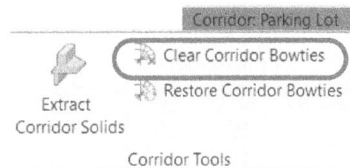

Figure 8–49

Your corridor and bowties may differ from the figure, depending on how the corridor is built.

4. Select the corridor baseline **A**, as shown in Figure 8–50.

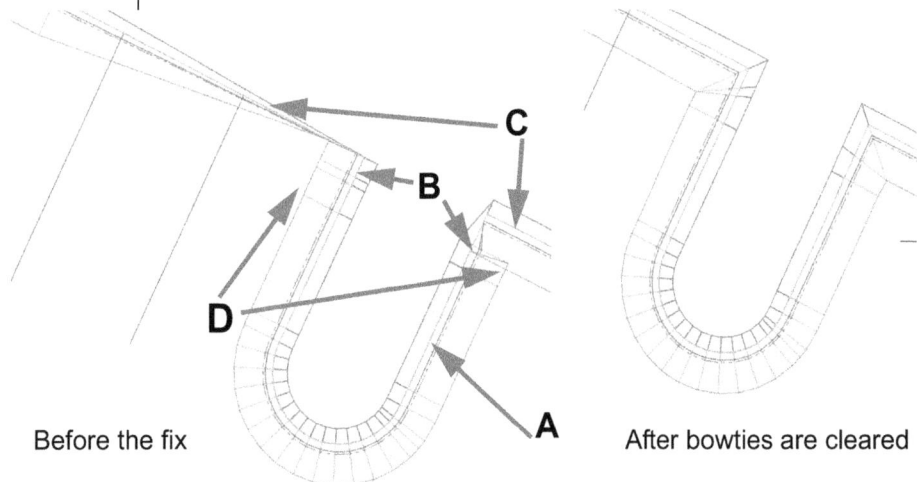

Before the fix

After bowties are cleared

Figure 8–50

5. When prompted to specify the starting subentity, select the same baseline as you did previously, just *before* the bowtie. See **B** in Figure 8–50. The selected line segment highlights in red.

6. When prompted to specify the ending subentity, select the baseline just *after* the bowtie. See **C** in Figure 8–50.

7. Next select the point where the resulting corridor feature lines are to intersect. See **D** in Figure 8–50.

8. At the command line, click **Specify another bowtie** to move on to the next corner. Repeat the same steps.

9. Press <Enter> to rebuild the corridor and study the results.

10. In the *View* tab>Views panel, select **Problem Area 2** to view where other bowties might have occurred.

11. Try to fix these as you did above. Chances are the left one will not clear properly. In the *Corridor* contextual tab>Corridor Tools panel, click (Restore Corridor Bowtie), as shown in Figure 8–51.

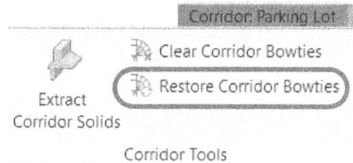

Figure 8–51

12. To move to the errant bowtie, keep selecting **Skip** (on the command line) until it is highlighted. You can pan and zoom to keep up with the bowties. Then select **Rebuild and restore** at the command line, as shown in Figure 8–52.

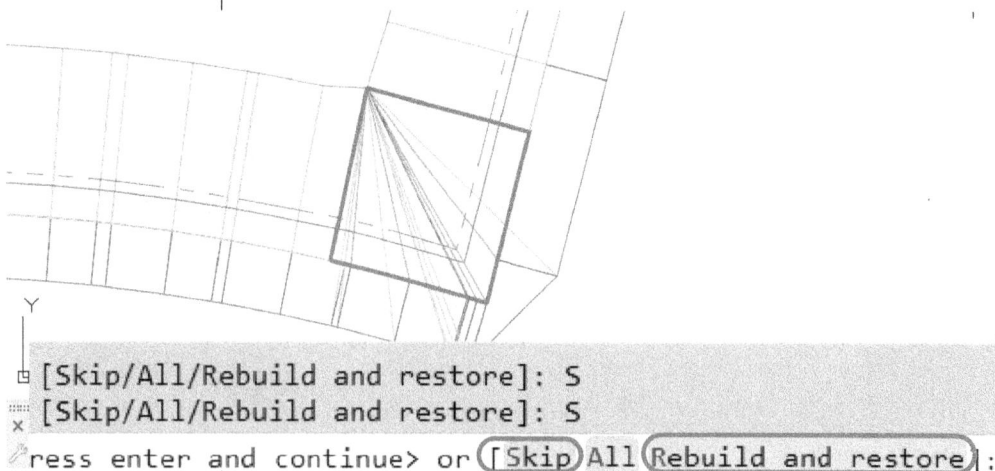

```
[Skip/All/Rebuild and restore]: S
[Skip/All/Rebuild and restore]: S
ress enter and continue> or [Skip] All Rebuild and restore]:
```

Figure 8–52

13. Select the feature line. The circular grips are *Elevation Points* of the feature line and reveal the problem of why the bowtie will not clear properly. As seen in Figure 8–53, the elevation point just after the intersection is too close to the intersection and needs to be eliminated.

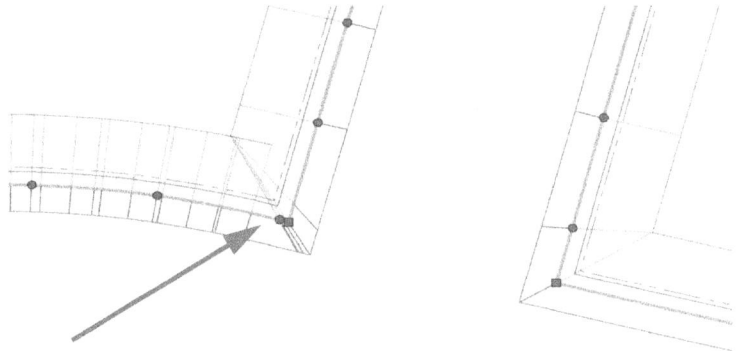

Figure 8–53

14. In the *Feature Line* contextual tab>Modify panel, click (Edit Geometry) to display the Edit Geometry panel.

15. In the Edit Geometry panel, click (Delete Elevation Point), as shown in Figure 8–54.

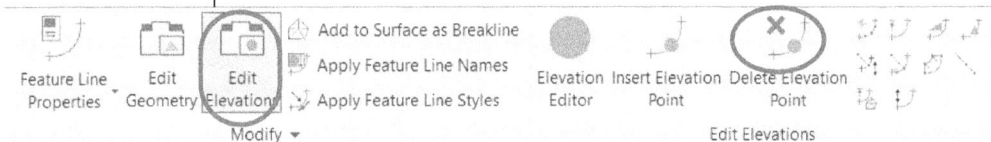

Figure 8–54

16. Select the errant elevation point and press <Enter> twice. You will notice that the circular grip has now been eliminated.

17. In the *Prospector* tab, note that the **Parking Lot** corridor is marked Out of Date (the yellow warning sign). Right-click on the name and select **Rebuild**, as shown in Figure 8–55.

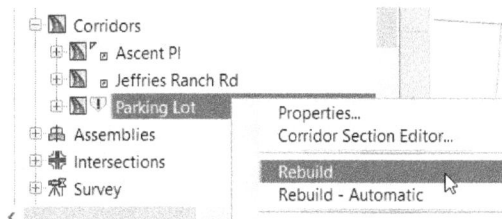

Figure 8–55

18. Click ☑ to close the Events Vista if it displays. Press <Esc> to end the command.

19. Now clear the bowtie as before.

20. In the *View* tab>Views panel, select **Parking Entrance** to view another troubling bowtie.

21. Clear the bowtie in the regular manner, but select the point on the outside where the resulting corridor feature lines are to intersect, as shown in Figure 8–56.

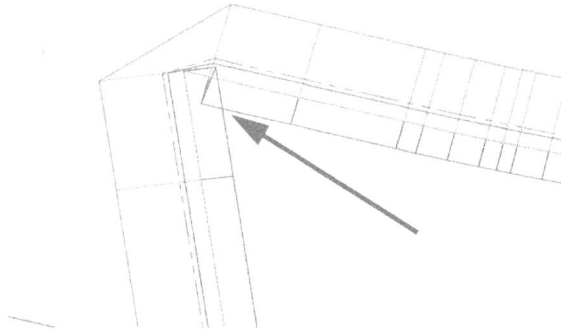

Figure 8–56

22. Continue clearing the rest of the bowties.

23. Save the drawing.

Task 3 - Reversing feature lines.

Careful inspection will reveal that the assemblies in the two island regions are attached to the wrong side (the curbs are facing inward). The feature lines need to be reversed and the corridor updated.

1. Note that the magenta links of the corridor representing the **LinkWidthAndSlope** subassembly, as shown in Figure 8–57, fall on the wrong side in the islands.

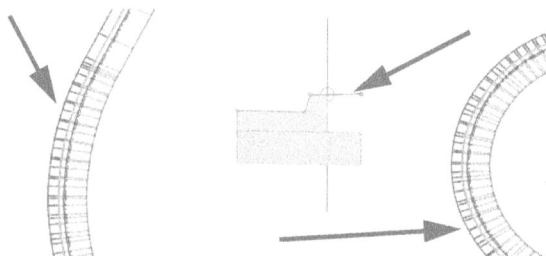

Figure 8–57

2. You need to reverse the island feature lines by selecting them one at a time.

3. In the *Feature Line* contextual tab>Modify panel, click
   (Edit Geometry). The Edit Geometry panel displays, as shown in Figure 8–58.

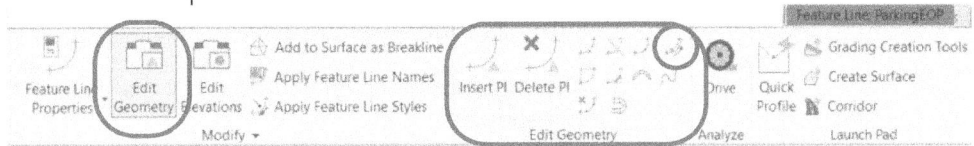

Figure 8–58

4. Click the (Reverse) command. The assemblies swap sides but are not yet connected (until the corridor is rebuilt).

5. Press <Esc> to clear the first feature line, then repeat the procedure for the other island feature line.

6. As before, rebuild the Parking Lot corridor.

7. Click to close the Events Vista if it displays. Press <Esc> to end the command.

8. Save the drawing.

8.5 Corridor Surfaces

The *Surfaces* tab in the Corridor Properties dialog box enables you to build the proposed surfaces based on corridor geometry. You can create these surfaces from corridor links or from feature lines based on marker points (point codes). As the corridor changes, its surfaces automatically update.

The two most common types of corridor surfaces are Top and Datum surfaces.

- **Top surfaces** follow the uppermost geometry of the corridor. These are useful for many purposes, such as in the display of finished ground contours or as a way of determining rim elevations of proposed utility structures.

- **Datum surfaces** generally follow the bottommost corridor geometry, where the corridor and the existing surface meet. These can be used in both Surface-to-Surface volume calculations and Section-based Earthworks calculations to determine site cut and fill totals (when compared to existing ground).

Other surfaces may be created and assigned materials for rendering purposes. Rendering can be done in Civil 3D; however, better results are achieved when using rendering-specific programs like Autodesk® 3DS Max®, Autodesk Navisworks®, etc.

Corridor surfaces: As with all Autodesk Civil 3D surfaces, these cannot contain vertical elements. Include slight offsets so that vertical curbing and similar geometry are not absolutely vertical.

Overhang Correction

In some configurations, Autodesk Civil 3D assemblies might have top or datum points or links in locations that might lead to incorrect surfaces, such as the datum surface represented by the heavy line in Figure 8–59.

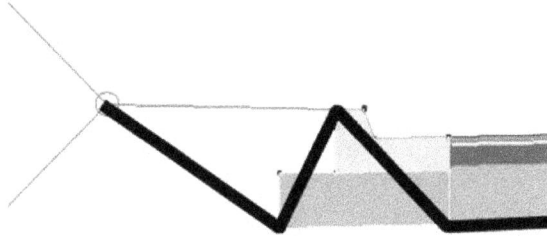

Figure 8–59

In these cases, the **Overhang Correction** option forces these surfaces to follow either the top or bottom of the corridor geometry, as shown in Figure 8–60. This setting is typically only required for Top and Datum surfaces.

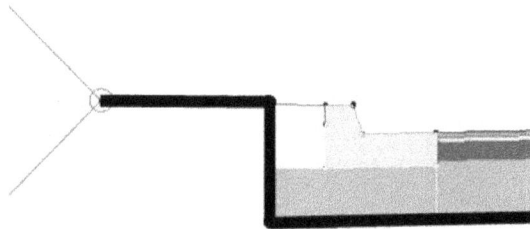

Figure 8–60

Surface Boundaries

Corridor surfaces, as with all Autodesk Civil 3D surfaces, often benefit from a boundary to remove unwanted interpolation between points. The *Boundaries* tab in the Corridor Surfaces dialog box enables you to add these boundaries in a couple of ways: by selecting a closed polyline or by interactively tracing the boundary using a jig.

The best option for Top and Datum surfaces is often to *automatically* add a boundary that follows the outermost edge on both sides. This can be done using the **Create Boundary from Corridor Extents** command.

For rendering specific surfaces (such as Asphalt, Concrete, etc.), you need to either trace the boundary or pick a polyline representing the boundary.

Practice 8f

Adding Surfaces and Boundaries

Practice Objectives

- Adding the top surface to the corridor.
- Extracting a feature line from the corridor.
- Add a boundary to the corridor surface.

Task 1 - Creating the top surface of the corridor.

1. Open **PKCOR-D-Grading.dwg** from the *C:\Civil 3D Projects\Grading\Parking Corridor* folder.

2. Select the corridor. Through either the right-click menu or the contextual ribbon, select **Corridor Properties**.

3. In the Corridor Properties dialog box, select the *Surfaces* tab.

4. Click ⬆ (Create a Corridor Surface) and do the following, as shown in Figure 8–61:

   - Name it **Parking Lot Surface - TOP**.
   - Set *Overhang Correction* to **Top Links**.
   - Change *Data type* to **Feature Lines**.
   - In the *Specify code* section, select **Back_Curb** and click

     ⊹ (Add Surface Item).
   - Repeat for the **Flange**, **Flowline_Gutter**, and **Top_Curb**, one by one.

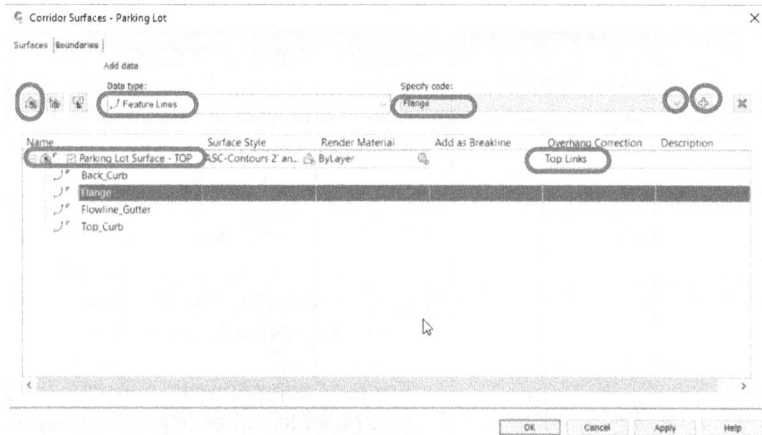

Figure 8–61

5. Click **OK** to close the Corridor Properties dialog box. When the warning box displays, select the **Rebuild the corridor** option.

6. The top surface is built, as shown in Figure 8–62.

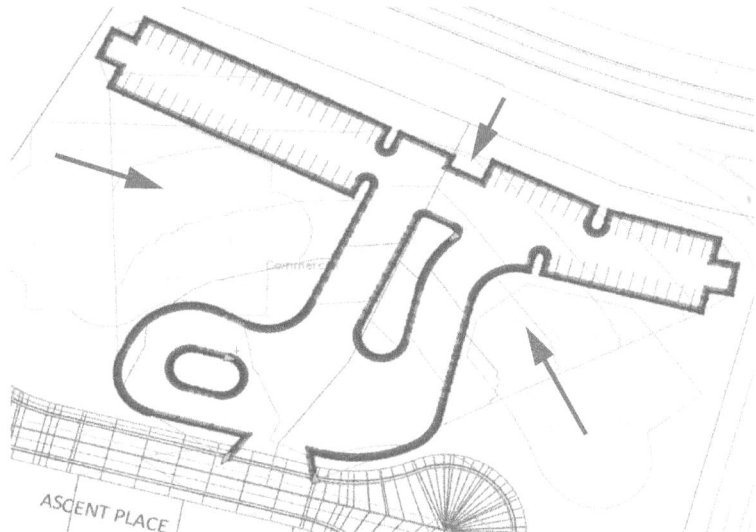

Figure 8–62

7. Save the drawing.

Task 2 - Extract corridor feature line.

The top surface expands beyond the parking lot and triangulates across the outer concave curves of the corridor. A boundary needs to be added to trim the surface back. In order to create the boundary, you will extract a feature line from the corridor and convert it to a closed polyline, which then can be chosen as the boundary of the surface.

1. Select the corridor. In the contextual ribbon, on the Launch

   Pad panel (far right), select   (Feature Lines from Corridor), as shown in Figure 8–63.

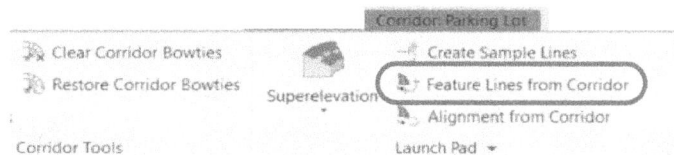

Figure 8–63

---

2. Hover over the outer edge of the corridor until you see the tooltip displaying **P2** and the outer edge highlights in red, as shown in Figure 8–64.

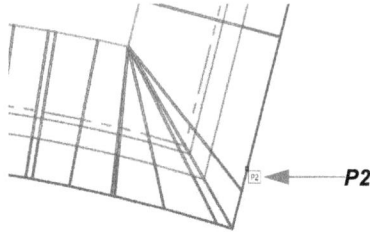

Figure 8–64

3. In the Extract Corridor Feature Lines window, press the **Settings...** button in the upper right corner.

4. In the Extract Corridor Feature Line Settings window, do the following, as shown in Figure 8–65:

   • Clear the *Dynamic link to corridor* checkbox.
   • Clear the *Apply Smoothing* checkbox.
   • Check the *Name* checkbox and name it **FL-Outer Limits**.
   • Click **OK** to exit the Extract Corridor Feature Line Settings window.

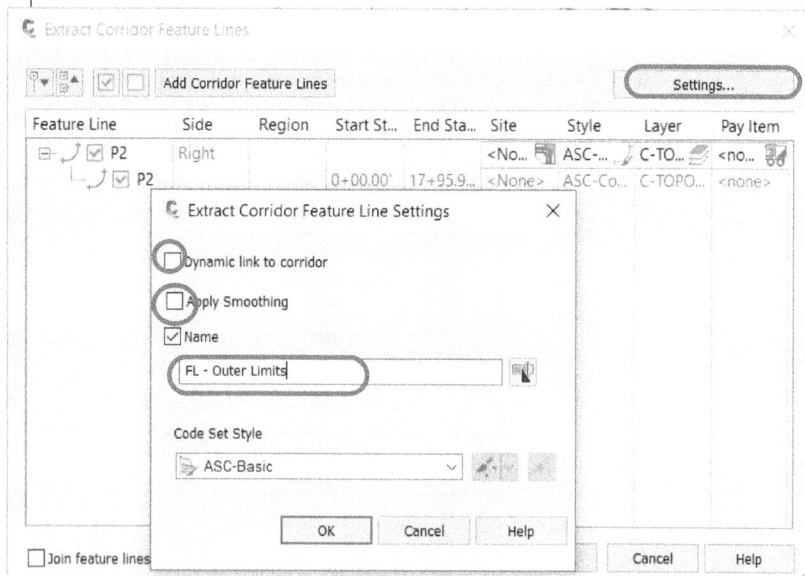

Figure 8–65

Since you are going to explode the feature line, there is no need to name it or change any of the settings.

5. In the Extract Corridor Feature Lines window, click **Extract**.

6. Invoke the AutoCAD Explode command (type **X** at the command line and press <Enter>) and select the extracted feature line. It becomes an AutoCAD 3D Polyline.

7. Select the 3D Polyline and, in the AutoCAD Properties panel, close the polyline (as shown in Figure 8–66).

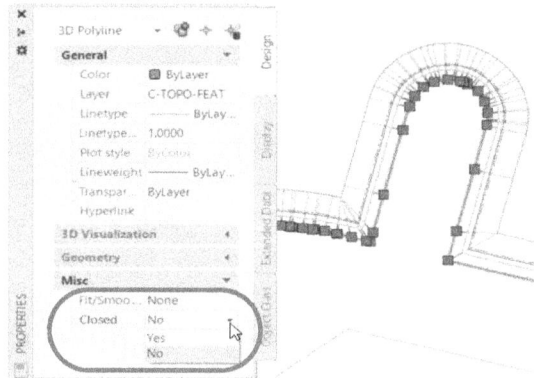

Figure 8–66

8. Save the drawing.

Task 3 - Create the corridor surface boundary.

1. Select the corridor. Through either the right-click menu or the contextual ribbon, select **Corridor Properties**.

2. In the Corridor Properties dialog box, select the *Boundaries* tab.

3. Right-click on the Parking Lot Surface - TOP and select **Add From Polygon...**, as shown in Figure 8–67.

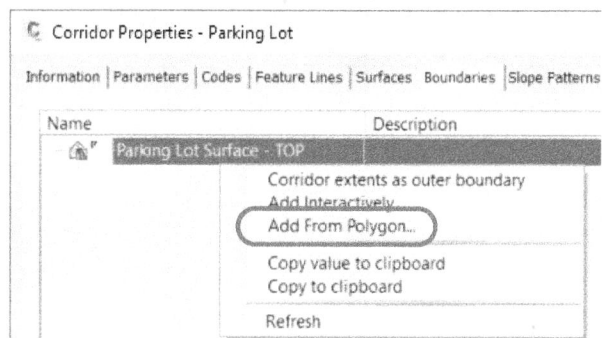

Figure 8–67

4. Select the 3D Polyline from the previous task.

5. Click **OK** to close the Corridor Properties dialog box. When the warning box displays, select the **Rebuild the corridor** option.

6. Save the drawing.

8.6 Sample Line Groups

Sample lines are objects that sample corridor elements for display in cross-sections and are used to form the basis of material lists that are used in corridor volumetric calculations. Sections are organized into groups for ease of selection and for managing common properties. A drawing can have any number of sample line groups for the same alignment.

Sample lines can be included in Data Shortcuts and referenced into your production drawings.

The **Sample Lines** command is located in the *Home* tab>Profile & Section Views panel, as shown in Figure 8–68.

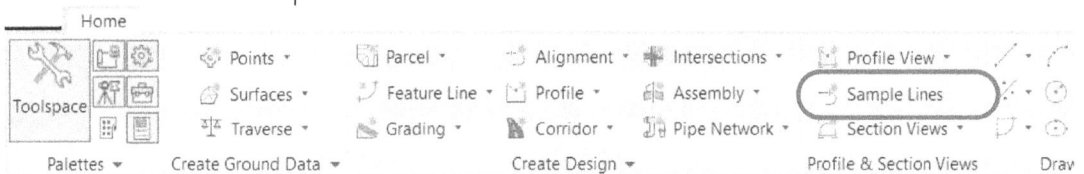

Figure 8–68

Selecting this command opens the Create Sample Line Group dialog box, as shown in Figure 8–69.

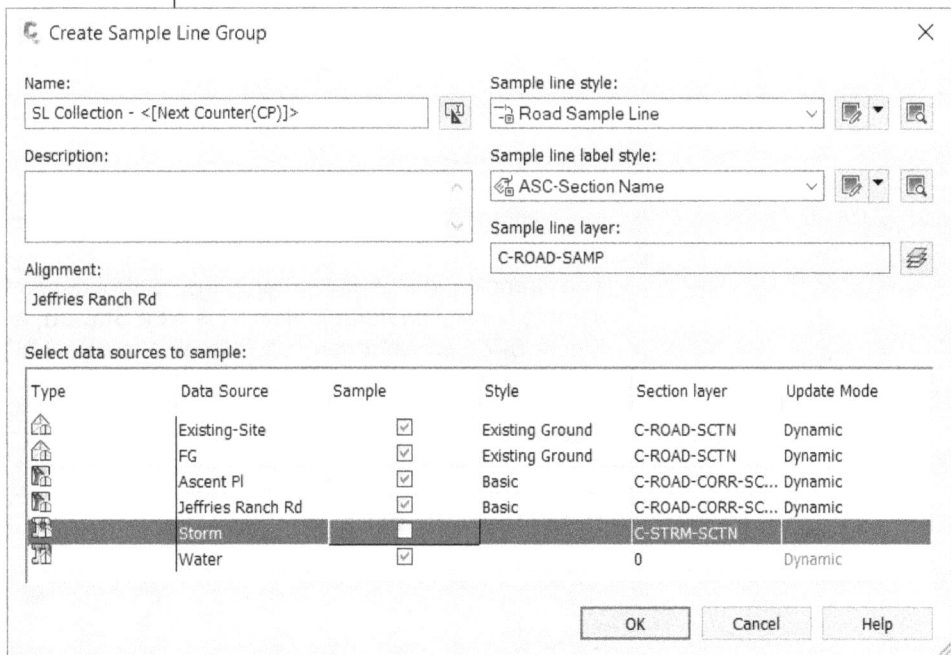

Figure 8–69

The Create Sample Line Group dialog box identifies all of the elements that might be included in the section:

- (corridor geometry)

- (terrain surfaces)

- (corridor surfaces)

- (pipe networks).

The *Select data sources to sample* area displays:

- The object type
- Where the object comes from
- Whether or not to sample the object
- The style to use for the sections
- The preferred layers
- The update mode for the section.

After adjusting the values for the Create Sample Line dialog box and clicking **OK**, the Sample Line Tools toolbar becomes active, as shown in Figure 8–70.

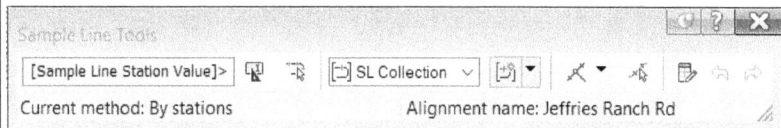

Figure 8–70

The Sample Line Tools toolbar is the control center for creating sample lines. The default method is **At a Station**, as shown in Figure 8–71, which means you are able to select a specific station at which to add a sample line.

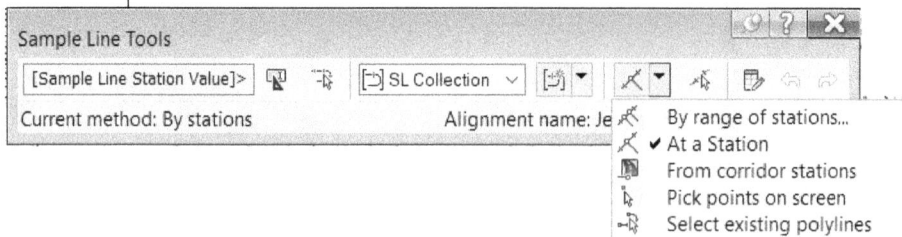

Figure 8–71

Other methods include:

- **By range of stations:** Enables you to specify a range of stations, sampling width, and other options where you want sample lines to be created. Sampling increments can be relative to an absolute station, or relative to a station range set.

- **From corridor stations:** Creates a sample line at all of the predefined corridor sections. This method also opens the Create Sample Line dialog box in which you can define the station range and swath widths for the sections.

- **Pick points on screen:** Enables you to select points in the drawing to define the path of the section. This type of section can have multiple vertices.

- **Select existing polylines:** Includes section lines based on existing polylines in the drawing. The polyline does not have to be perpendicular to the center line and can have multiple segments.

The dialog box that opens for the **By range of stations** option is shown in Figure 8–72.

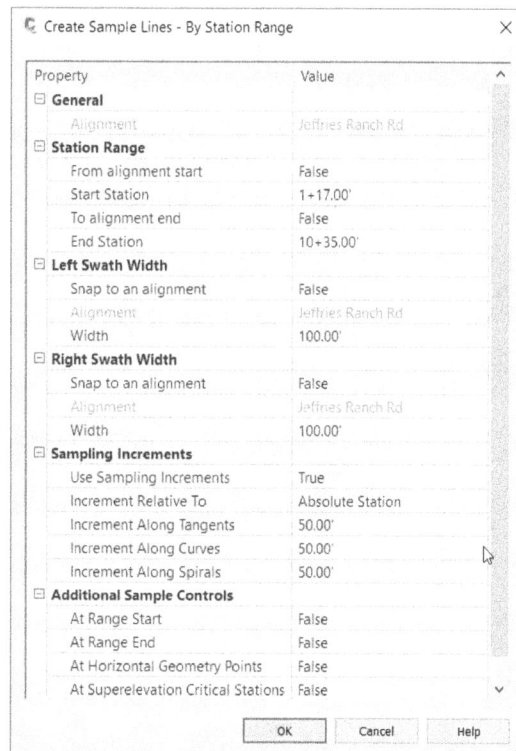

Property	Value
General	
Alignment	Jeffries Ranch Rd
Station Range	
From alignment start	False
Start Station	1+17.00'
To alignment end	False
End Station	10+35.00'
Left Swath Width	
Snap to an alignment	False
Alignment	Jeffries Ranch Rd
Width	100.00'
Right Swath Width	
Snap to an alignment	False
Alignment	Jeffries Ranch Rd
Width	100.00'
Sampling Increments	
Use Sampling Increments	True
Increment Relative To	Absolute Station
Increment Along Tangents	50.00'
Increment Along Curves	50.00'
Increment Along Spirals	50.00'
Additional Sample Controls	
At Range Start	False
At Range End	False
At Horizontal Geometry Points	False
At Superelevation Critical Stations	False

Create Sample Lines - By Station Range

Figure 8–72

After creating the sample line group, the Toolspace, *Prospector* tab lists the individual sample lines under the sample line group's name. Each entry in the list includes all of the sampled elements for a section, as shown in Figure 8–73.

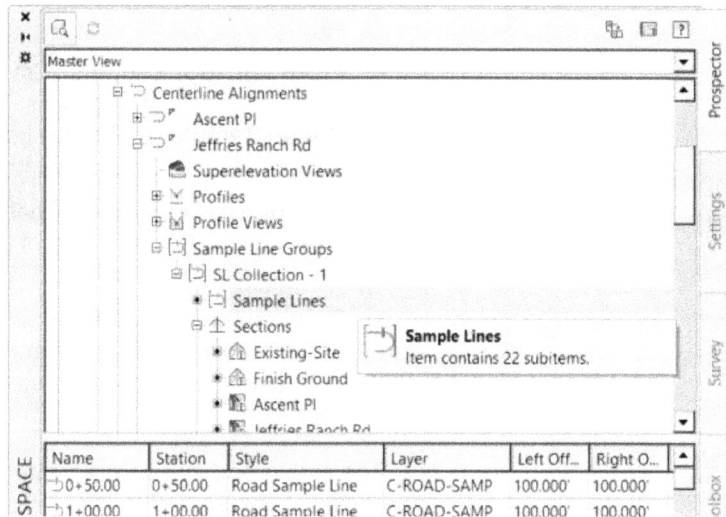

Figure 8–73

Modifying Sample Line Groups

New sample line groups can be added, existing groups can be deleted, swath widths (section sample width) can be adjusted, and new data sources can be added (such as newly created pipe networks) using the Modify drop-down list in the Sample Line Tools toolbar or the contextual *Sample Line* tab, as shown in Figure 8–74.

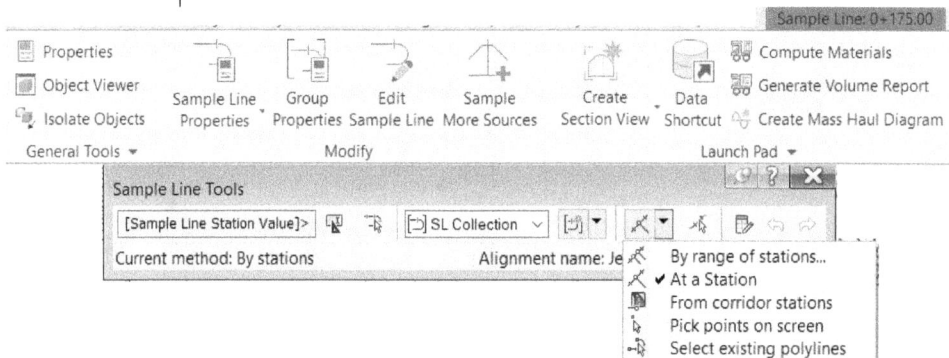

Figure 8–74

Sample line properties (such as display styles) can also be adjusted through the sample line group's properties, in the Toolspace, *Prospector* tab.

Practice 8g

Creating Sample Lines

Practice Objective

- Create sample lines and review sample line data in preparation for creating cross-section sheets.

Task 1 - Corridor Section Editor.

1. Open **COR1-F1-Corridor.dwg** from the *C:\Civil 3D Projects\ Working\Corridors* folder.

2. If not already set, change the *Annotation Scale* to **1"=30'** in the Status Bar, which is a scale more appropriate for displaying cross-sections.

3. Hover the cursor over the Data Shortcuts and review the tooltip which displays, shown in Figure 8–75. Ensure that your Data Shortcuts are set so the **Working Folder** is set to *C:\Civil 3D Projects\Data Shortcuts\Fundamentals* and the **Data Shortcuts Project Folder** to *Ascent-Development*. If required, right-click on Data Shortcuts to set the **Working Folder** and **Data Shortcuts Project Folder**.

⊟ 🗷 Data Shortcuts [C:\Civil 3D Projects\Data Shortc... ⌄

<   🗷   C:\Civil 3D Projects\Data Shortcuts\Fundamentals\Ascent-Development

Figure 8–75

4. Select the preset view **QTO-Corridors**.

5. In the *Home* tab>Profile and Section Views panel, click

   ⅃ (Sample Lines).

6. When prompted to select an alignment, press <Enter> and select **Jeffries Ranch Rd** from the list. Click **OK** to exit the dialog box.

The Create Sample Line Group dialog box opens, listing multiple data sources.

7. Verify that the *Sample* column is cleared of all but the **Existing-Site**, **FG**, **Jeffries Ranch Rd Datum**, **Jeffries Ranch Rd surface**, and **Water**, as shown in Figure 8–76. Leave the other settings at their defaults and click **OK**.

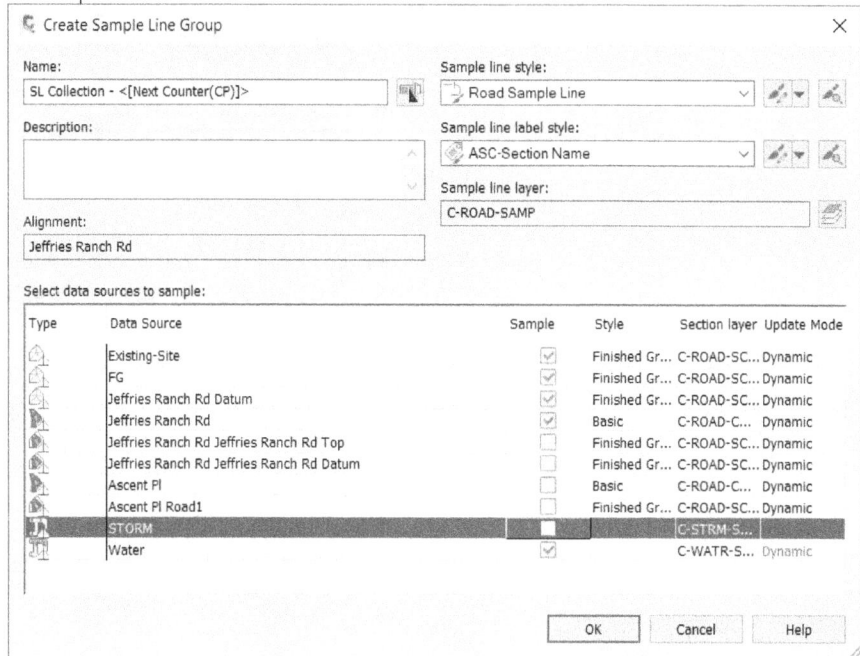

Figure 8–76

8. In the Sample Line Tools toolbar, select to create sample lines **By range of stations…**, as shown in Figure 8–77.

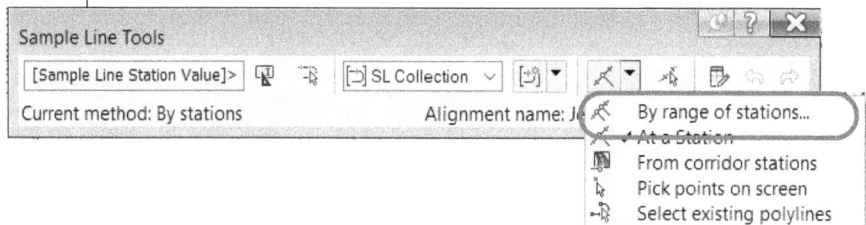

Figure 8–77

9. In the Create Sample Lines dialog box, review the settings, as shown in Figure 8–78.

   - Under *Station Range*, set *From alignment start* and *To alignment end* to **False**.

   - Set the *Start Station* to **117'** and the *End Station* to **1035'**.

   - Set both the Left and Right Swath Width[s] to **100'**.

   - Under *Sampling Increments*, set *Increment Along Tangents* and *Increments Along Curves* to **50'**.

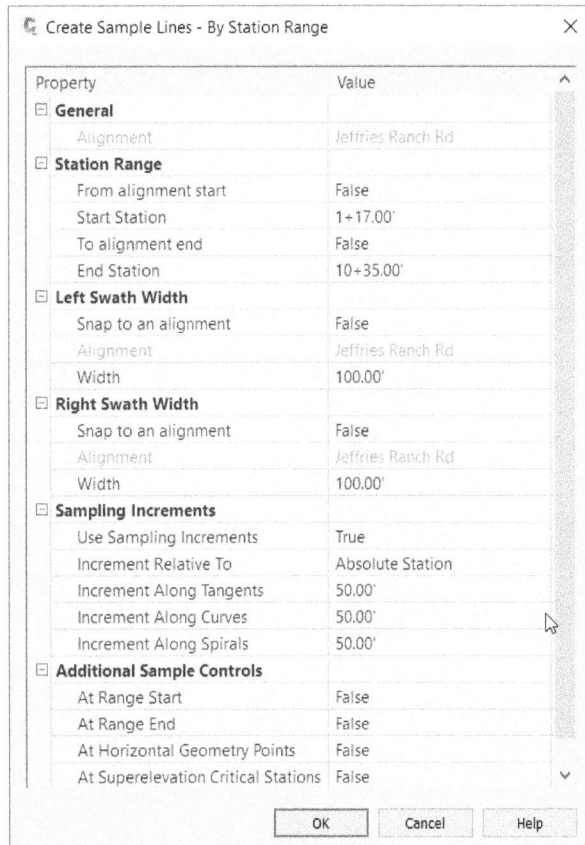

This is because the alignment extends beyond the design ground data.

Create Sample Lines - By Station Range		✕
Property	**Value**	
⊟ **General**		
Alignment	Jeffries Ranch Rd	
⊟ **Station Range**		
From alignment start	False	
Start Station	1+17.00'	
To alignment end	False	
End Station	10+35.00'	
⊟ **Left Swath Width**		
Snap to an alignment	False	
Alignment	Jeffries Ranch Rd	
Width	100.00'	
⊟ **Right Swath Width**		
Snap to an alignment	False	
Alignment	Jeffries Ranch Rd	
Width	100.00'	
⊟ **Sampling Increments**		
Use Sampling Increments	True	
Increment Relative To	Absolute Station	
Increment Along Tangents	50.00'	
Increment Along Curves	50.00'	
Increment Along Spirals	50.00'	
⊟ **Additional Sample Controls**		
At Range Start	False	
At Range End	False	
At Horizontal Geometry Points	False	
At Superelevation Critical Stations	False	

| OK | Cancel | Help |

Figure 8–78

10. Click **OK** when done.

11. In the Command Line, press <Enter> to close the dialog box.

12. Save the drawing.

Task 2 - Review Sample Line data.

1. In the Toolspace, *Prospector* tab, expand the *Alignment* collection, expand the *Centerline Alignments* collection, expand the *Jeffries Ranch Rd* collection, expand the *Sample Line Groups* collection, and select **SL Collection**, as shown in Figure 8–79.

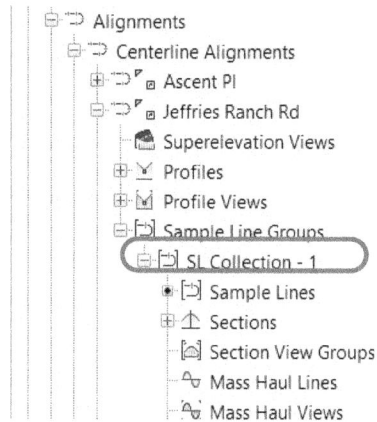

```
Alignments
  Centerline Alignments
    Ascent PI
    Jeffries Ranch Rd
      Superelevation Views
      Profiles
      Profile Views
      Sample Line Groups
        SL Collection - 1
          Sample Lines
          Sections
          Section View Groups
          Mass Haul Lines
          Mass Haul Views
```

Figure 8–79

2. Right-click and select **Properties**. In the Sample Line Group Properties dialog box, in the *Sections* tab, you can re-assign styles and layers, and add new data sources.

3. Click **Sample more sources...** in the top right corner.

Note that the Pressure Pipes do not display here.

4. Select **Storm** from the list on the left and click **Add**, as shown in Figure 8–80. Click **OK** to exit.

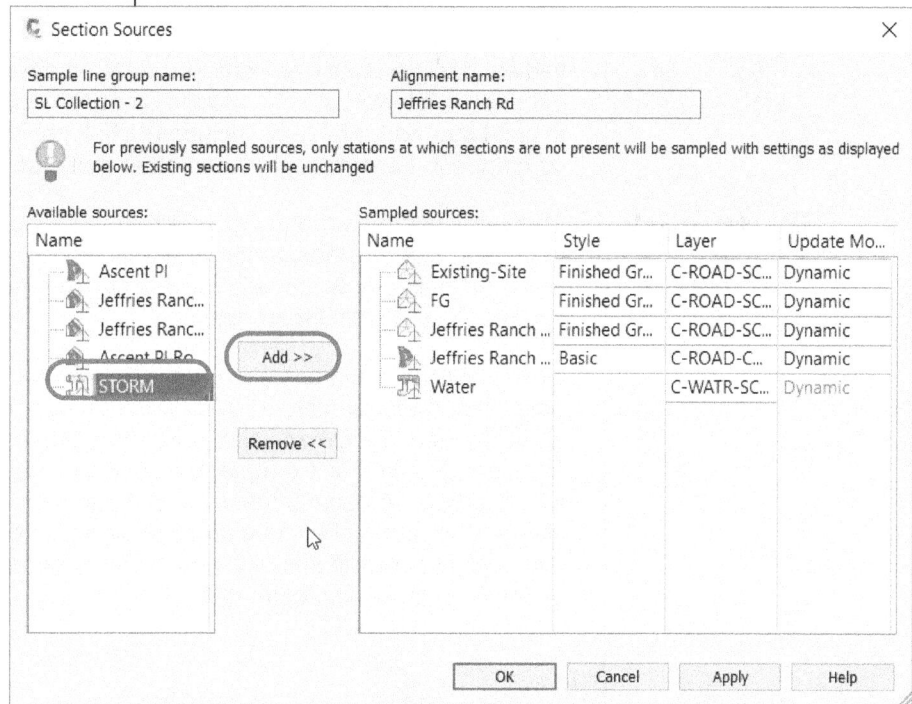

Figure 8–80

5. The *Sample Lines* tab enables you to change the swath widths of individual sections numerically. Click **OK** to exit.

6. Save the drawing.

8.7 Section Volume Calculations

Two types of quantity takeoffs can be calculated based on sections: earthwork volumes and material volumes. Earthwork volumes represent the amount of cut (existing material above the vertical design) or fill (the vertical design above the existing material). Material volumes are the amount of materials required to build the road. Materials include asphalt pavement, concrete curbing, sub-base materials, and other materials.

Earthwork Volumes

Earthwork volumes represent an amount of displaced surface materials. The displacement represents the excavation of high areas or filling of low areas in the existing ground surface, relative to the vertical road design.

One goal road designers strive for is to balance the amount of excavated material (called cut) and the amount of material to be added (called fill). On any site, not all of the excavated material (cut) is reusable. For example, the spoil materials could be from a bog, a type of material that does not compact well, or rock debris. The reuse of cut material can be a percentage of the overall cut value and affects the overall earthwork calculation. An example is shown in Figure 8–81.

Figure 8–81

Earthworks calculations are applied between the existing ground surface and the datum surface of an assembly. Note that the Datum Link is the last link of the assembly, and thus the corridor.

The datum surface represents the roadbed on which the sub-base gravel, asphalt, and concrete materials lie. Earthwork volumes affect the revisions that occur to a roadway design. For example, excessive cut material (i.e., material needing excavation) could lead to raising the vertical design or, if possible, moving the horizontal alignment to create less cut.

Mass Haul

A mass haul diagram can be generated and used as a visual representation of the cumulative cut and fill material volumes along a corridor. Contractors use mass haul diagrams as a primary tool in determining and balancing haulage costs when bidding on an earthwork job. Mass haul is the volume of excavated material multiplied by the distance it is required to be moved. When the mass haul line is above the balance line, it indicates how much cut there is going to be at that station. When the mass haul line is below the balance line, it indicates the volume to be filled. To generate a mass haul diagram, you need an alignment, a sample line group, and a materials list. The mass haul diagram calculates and displays the following:

- The distance over which cut and fill volumes balance.

- Free haul and overhaul volumes.

- Volumes offset by borrow pits and dump sites.

Construction costs can be reduced by enabling the designer to compare alternative designs, add dump sites, and borrow pits at key locations in the free haul distance, thus eliminating a portion of the overhaul volume. An example of a mass haul diagram is shown in Figure 8–82.

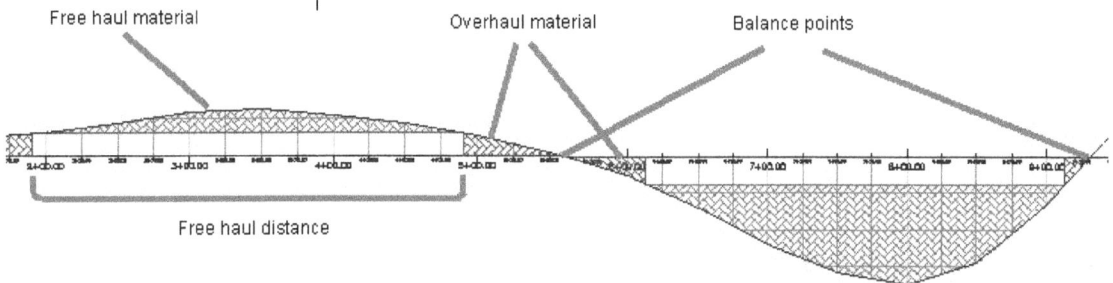

Figure 8–82

Material Volumes

Subassembly shapes represent the materials available for quantity takeoffs. These quantities come from the subassembly shapes (e.g., curb, pave, shoulder, sidewalk, etc.).

Quantity Takeoff Criteria

The Quantity Takeoff Criteria defines the surfaces and materials to be analyzed. Takeoff criteria can identify two surfaces for earthwork calculations and a list of shapes for material volumes.

The criteria style entries are generic because they are intended to be used on multiple corridors, which might contain different subassembly components. When computing section calculations, you are prompted to identify which entries correspond to the corridor shapes. The Quantity Takeoff Criteria dialog box is shown in Figure 8–83.

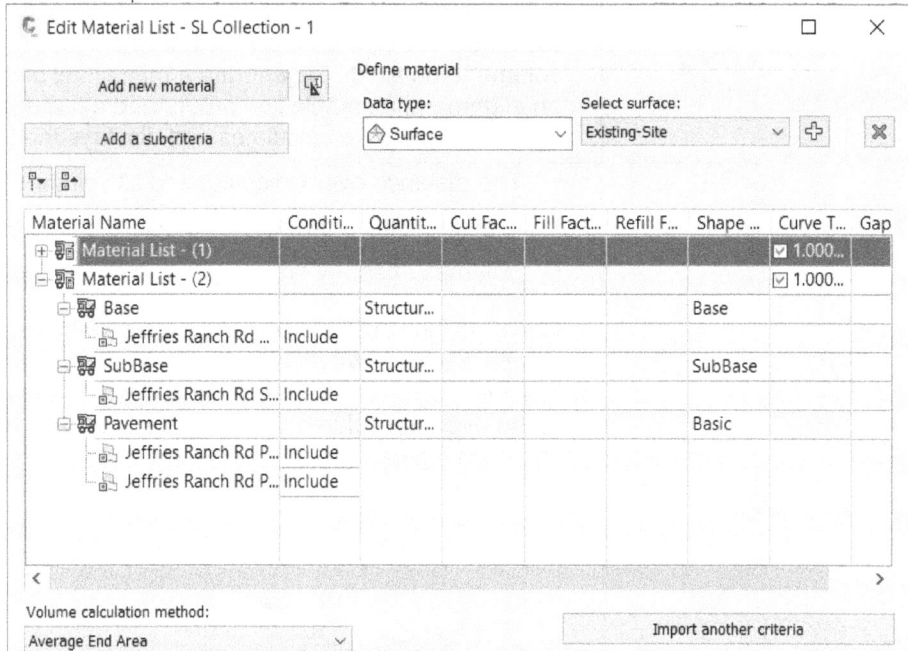

Figure 8–83

Define Materials

After defining the volume criteria, you create data from the criteria settings. In the *Analyze* tab>Volumes and Materials panel, click (Compute Materials) to set the alignment and a sample line group to use for data extraction. The command is shown in Figure 8–84.

Figure 8–84

When the Edit Material List dialog box opens, you can associate surfaces and/or structures (subassembly shapes) to the appropriate entries. Click **OK** to exit. The Autodesk Civil 3D software then calculates the required report data.

Practice 8h

Compute Materials

Practice Objective

- Calculate quantities of a corridor and display them.

Task 1 - Generate earthworks quantities.

In this task, you will compute the site cut and fill required to create the datum surface below the corridor. You will then calculate the construction materials that will be placed above the datum (asphalt, gravel, etc.).

1. Open **COR1-G1-Corridor.dwg** from the *C:\Civil 3D Projects\ Working\Corridors* folder.

2. In the *Analyze* tab>Volumes and Materials panel, click

    ![icon] (Compute Materials), as shown in Figure 8–85.

Figure 8–85

3. In the Select Sample Line Group dialog box, accept the default alignment **Jeffries Rand Rd** and sample line group **SL Collection - 1**, as shown in Figure 8–86. Click **OK**.

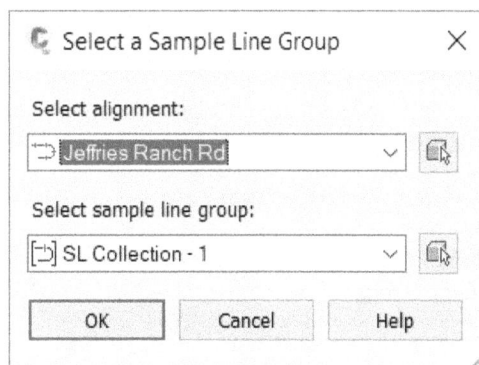

Figure 8–86

4. In the Compute Materials dialog box, select **Existing-Site** for the *EG* and **Jeffries Ranch Rd Datum** for the *DATUM*, as shown in Figure 8–87. Click **OK** when done.

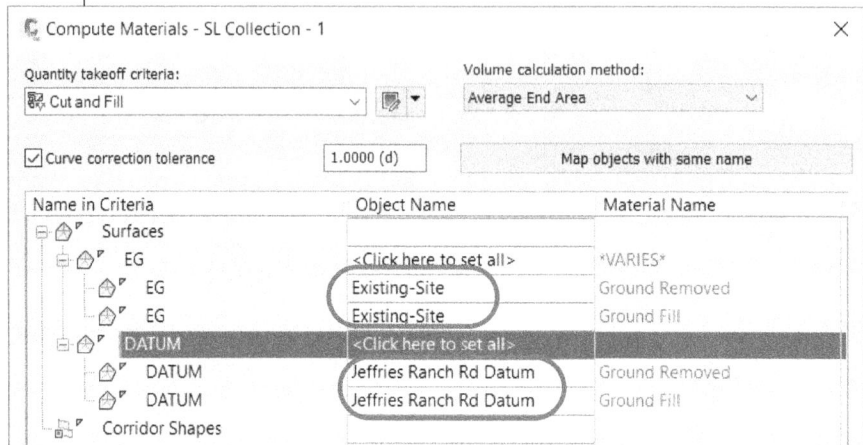

Figure 8–87

5. Generate a volume report. In the *Analyze* tab>Volumes and Materials panel, click ⊞ (Volume Report).

6. In the Report Quantities dialog box, ensure that you select the correct XSL file. Click 📂 next to the *Select a style sheet* field, as shown on the left in Figure 8–88. Browse to and select **earthwork.xsl**, as shown on the right, and open it. Click **OK** to close the Report Quantities dialog box.

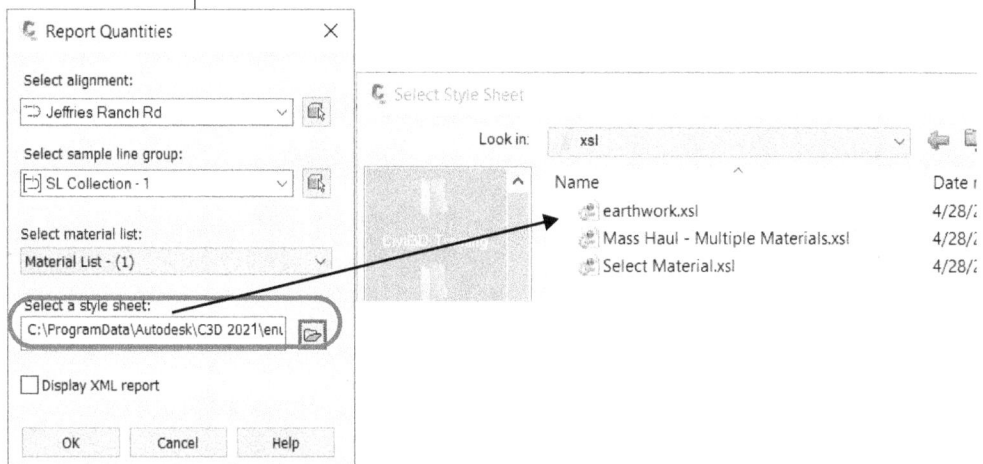

Figure 8–88

7. Internet Explorer will open when the HTML format report is created. Depending on your Internet Explorer security settings, you might be prompted to permit the script to run. Click **Yes** if this prompt displays. Your report displays similar to that shown in Figure 8–89.

Volume Report

Project: C:\Civil 3D Projects\References\DWG\Proposed\Corridor-Complete.dwg
Alignment: Jeffries Ranch Rd
Sample Line Group: SL Collection - 1
Start Sta: 1+50.000
End Sta: 10+00.000

Station	Cut Area (Sq.ft.)	Cut Volume (Cu.yd.)	Reusable Volume (Cu.yd.)	Fill Area (Sq.ft.)	Fill Volume (Cu.yd.)	Cum. Cut Vol. (Cu.yd.)	Cum. Reusable Vol. (Cu.yd.)	Cum. Fill Vol. (Cu.yd.)	Cum. Net Vol. (Cu.yd.)
1+50.000	89.56	0.00	0.00	31.28	0.00	0.00	0.00	0.00	0.00
2+00.000	145.03	217.21	217.21	16.14	43.90	217.21	217.21	43.90	173.31
2+50.000	1199.74	1160.83	1160.83	5.11	18.87	1378.05	1378.05	62.77	1315.27
3+00.000	1334.47	2346.50	2346.50	35.97	38.03	3724.54	3724.54	100.81	3623.74
3+50.000	1262.57	2404.67	2404.67	239.57	255.13	6129.21	6129.21	355.94	5773.27
4+00.000	704.95	1821.78	1821.78	564.45	744.47	7950.99	7950.99	1100.41	6850.58
4+50.000	0.37	653.07	653.07	1194.30	1628.47	8604.06	8604.06	2728.88	5875.18
5+00.000	0.00	0.35	0.35	1271.33	2282.99	8604.41	8604.41	5011.87	3592.54
5+50.000	0.00	0.00	0.00	1579.50	2639.65	8604.41	8604.41	7651.52	952.89

Figure 8–89

8. Close the HTML report.

9. Create an AutoCAD table listing earthwork volumes. In the *Analyze* tab>Volumes and Materials panel, select **Total Volume Table**, as shown in Figure 8–90.

Figure 8–90

10. Pick the *Cut and Fill with Net* Table Style, and accept the other defaults in the Create Table dialog box, as shown in Figure 8–91, and click **OK**. When prompted, click in empty space to create the table.

Figure 8–91

11. Select a point in Model Space to insert the table, as shown in Figure 8–92. Note that the top left of the table is the reference point.

				Total Volume Table			
Station	Fill Area	Cut Area	Fill Volume	Cut Volume	Cumulative Fill Vol	Cumulative Cut Vol	Net
1+50.00	31.28	89.56	0.00	0.00	0.00	0.00	0.00
2+00.00	16.14	145.03	43.90	217.21	43.90	217.21	173.31
2+50.00	5.11	1199.74	18.87	1160.83	62.77	1378.05	1315.27
3+00.00	35.97	1334.47	38.03	2346.50	100.81	3724.54	3623.74
3+50.00	239.57	1262.57	255.13	2404.67	355.94	6129.21	5773.27
4+00.00	564.45	704.95	744.47	1821.78	1100.41	7950.99	6850.58
4+50.00	1194.30	0.37	1628.47	653.07	2728.88	8604.06	5875.18
5+00.00	1271.33	0.00	2282.99	0.35	5011.87	8604.41	3592.54
5+50.00	1579.50	0.00	2838.65	0.00	7851.52	8604.41	952.89
6+00.00	1323.31	0.00	2687.79	0.00	10339.31	8604.41	-1734.90
6+50.00	947.48	0.00	2130.26	0.00	12469.57	8604.41	-3865.16
7+00.00	596.83	0.01	1447.90	0.01	13917.46	8604.41	-5313.05
7+50.00	88.79	15.37	642.39	14.93	14559.85	8619.34	-5940.51
8+00.00	0.00	494.19	82.19	479.25	14642.04	9098.59	-5543.45

Figure 8–92

12. Save the drawing.

Task 2 - Calculate material quantities.

Your assemblies include five defined shapes: Pave1 and Pave2 (the top two courses), Base, Sub-base, and Curb. The default Material List only includes one material for Pavement so you will need to adjust it. You will not calculate curb volume at this time.

1. In the *Analyze* tab>Volumes and Materials panel, click
   [icon] (Compute Materials).

2. In the Select Sample Line Group dialog box, accept the default alignment **Jeffries Ranch Rd** and sample line group **SL Collection - 1**, and click **OK**.

3. In the Edit Material List dialog box, click **Import another criteria**.

4. In the Select a Quantity Takeoff Criteria, select **Material List** and click **OK**.

5. In the Compute Materials dialog box, shown in Figure 8–93:
   - For *Pavement Material*, select **Jeffries Ranch Rd Pave1**.
   - For *Base Material*, select **Jeffries Ranch Rd Base**.
   - For *SubBase Material*, select **Jeffries Ranch Rd SubBase**.
   - Click **OK**.

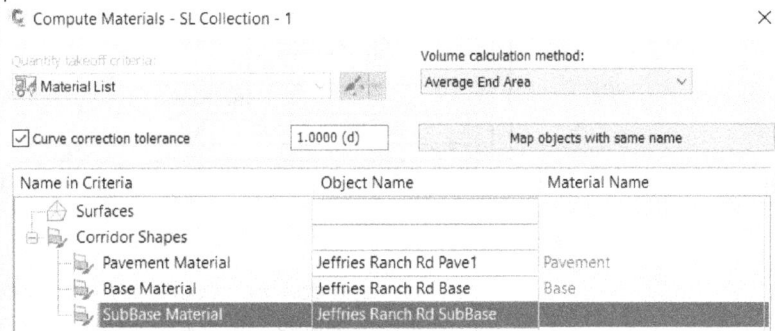

Compute Materials - SL Collection - 1

Name in Criteria	Object Name	Material Name
Surfaces		
Corridor Shapes		
Pavement Material	Jeffries Ranch Rd Pave1	Pavement
Base Material	Jeffries Ranch Rd Base	Base
SubBase Material	Jeffries Ranch Rd SubBase	

Figure 8–93

6. Click **OK** to close the dialog box and calculate the material.

7. Generate a volume report. In the *Analyze* tab>Volumes and Materials panel, select [icon] **Volume Report**.

8. In the Report Quantities dialog box, select **Material List - (2)** and ensure that you select the correct XSL file in the Select a style sheet drop-down list. Click ⬦ next to the drop-down list. Browse to and select **Select Material.xsl** and open it. Click **OK** to close the Report Quantities dialog box.

9. Internet Explorer will open as the Autodesk Civil 3D software creates an HTML format report. Depending on your Internet Explorer security settings, you might be prompted to permit the script to run. Click **Yes** if this prompt displays. The report will display with the volume of Pavement 1 from your corridor, as shown in Figure 8–94.

Material Report

Project: C:\Users\jmorris\AppData\Local\Temp\Corridor-Complete_1_29253_71bbc490.sv$
Alignment: Jeffries Ranch Rd
Sample Line Group: SL Collection - 1
Start Sta: 1+50.000
End Sta: 10+00.000

	Area Type	Area	Inc.Vol.	Cum.Vol.
		Sq.ft.	Cu.yd.	Cu.yd.
Station: 1+50.000				
	Pavement	2.57	0.00	0.00
	Base	10.32	0.00	0.00
	SubBase	37.79	0.00	0.00
Station: 2+00.000				
	Pavement	2.57	4.76	4.76
	Base	10.32	19.12	19.12
	SubBase	37.79	69.98	69.98
Station: 2+50.000				
	Pavement	2.57	4.76	9.53

Figure 8–94

10. Close the HTML report.

The road design, specifically the corridor assembly, has a second shape called Pave 2. This is also Pavement, but might be based on a different composition than Pave 1. You can quantify this value as a separate amount, but for demonstration purposes, you will create a total volume for Pavement.

11. In the *Analyze* tab>Volumes and Materials panel, click ▦ (Compute Materials).

12. In the Select Sample Line Group dialog box, accept the defaults and click **OK**.

13. In the Edit Material List dialog box, shown in Figure 8–95:

- In the *Name* column, select **Pavement**. Click ⊠ (Delete).
- Click **Add new material**.
- Click on the new material name and rename it **Pavement**.
- In the *Quantity Type* column, select **Structures**.
- In the Data type drop-down list, select **Corridor Shape**.
- In the Select corridor shape drop-down list, select **Jeffries Ranch Rd Pave 1**.
- Click ⊞ to add **Jeffries Ranch Rd Pave 1** to the *Pavement* collection.
- In the Select corridor shape drop-down list, select **Jeffries Ranch Rd Pave 2**.
- Click ⊞ to add **Jeffries Ranch Rd Pave 2** to the *Pavement* collection.
- Click **OK** to apply the changes and close the dialog box.

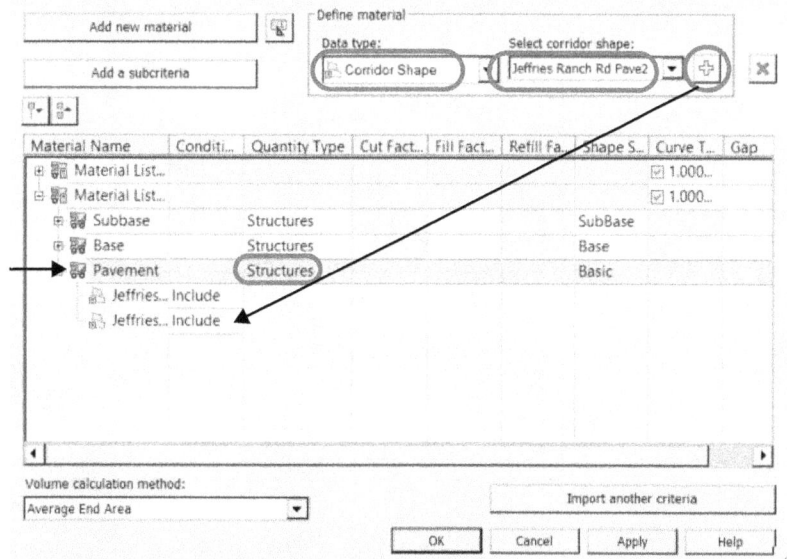

Figure 8–95

14. As in Steps 8 to 10, generate a volume report. In the *Analyze* tab>Volumes and Materials panel, select **Volume Report**.

- In the Report Quantities dialog box, ensure that you select the correct XSL file in the Select a style sheet drop-down list. Click ⌷ next to the drop-down list. Browse to and select **Select Material.xsl** and open it. Click **OK** to close the Report Quantities dialog box.

- Internet Explorer will open as the Autodesk Civil 3D software creates an HTML format report. Depending on your Internet Explorer security settings, you might be prompted to permit the script to run. Click **Yes** if this prompt displays. Your report will display, as shown in Figure 8–96.

Material Report

Project: C:\Users\jmorris\AppData\Local\Temp\Corridor-Complete_1_29253_71bbc490.sv$
Alignment: Jeffries Ranch Rd
Sample Line Group: SL Collection - 1
Start Sta: 1+50.000
End Sta: 10+00.000

	Area Type	Area	Inc.Vol.	Cum.Vol.
		Sq.ft.	Cu.yd.	Cu.yd.
Station: 1+50.000				
	Base	10.32	0.00	0.00
	SubBase	37.79	0.00	0.00
	Pavement	5.15	0.00	0.00
Station: 2+00.000				
	Base	10.32	19.12	19.12
	SubBase	37.79	69.98	69.98
	Pavement	5.15	9.53	9.53
Station: 2+50.000				

Figure 8–96

15. Create drawing tables displaying this information, using the **Material Volume Table** command in the Volumes and Materials panel, for each material, as shown in Figure 8–97.

Figure 8–97

16. Be sure you select **Material List - (2)** and then select which material you want to create the table for, as shown in Figure 8–98.

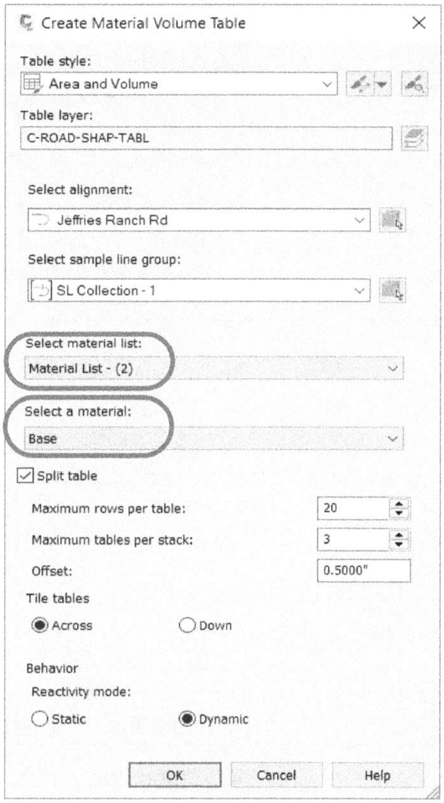

Figure 8–98

17. Repeat these steps to create a table for each of the three materials, as shown in Figure 8–99.

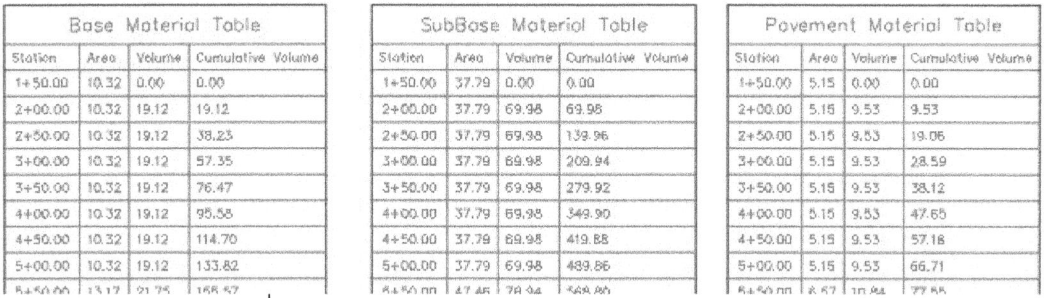

Base Material Table			
Station	Area	Volume	Cumulative Volume
1+50.00	10.32	0.00	0.00
2+00.00	10.32	19.12	19.12
2+50.00	10.32	19.12	38.23
3+00.00	10.32	19.12	57.35
3+50.00	10.32	19.12	76.47
4+00.00	10.32	19.12	95.58
4+50.00	10.32	19.12	114.70
5+00.00	10.32	19.12	133.82
5+50.00	13.17	21.75	155.57

SubBase Material Table			
Station	Area	Volume	Cumulative Volume
1+50.00	37.79	0.00	0.00
2+00.00	37.79	69.98	69.98
2+50.00	37.79	69.98	139.96
3+00.00	37.79	69.98	209.94
3+50.00	37.79	69.98	279.92
4+00.00	37.79	69.98	349.90
4+50.00	37.79	69.98	419.88
5+00.00	37.79	69.98	489.86
5+50.00	42.45	78.94	568.80

Pavement Material Table			
Station	Area	Volume	Cumulative Volume
1+50.00	5.15	0.00	0.00
2+00.00	5.15	9.53	9.53
2+50.00	5.15	9.53	19.06
3+00.00	5.15	9.53	28.59
3+50.00	5.15	9.53	38.12
4+00.00	5.15	9.53	47.65
4+50.00	5.15	9.53	57.18
5+00.00	5.15	9.53	66.71
5+50.00	8.57	10.84	77.55

Figure 8–99

Task 3 - Changing code set styles.

The corridors are now designed and ready to be shared with the rest of the design team. Before you share the corridors you need to make some changes to their display, so as not to show the assemblies. You can also change the display of the assemblies. This is done with the appropriate code set styles.

1. Select both corridors.

2. In the *Properties* Palette, under *Data*, click on the drop-down list for *Code Set Styles* and select **All Codes - No Display**, as shown in Figure 8–100.

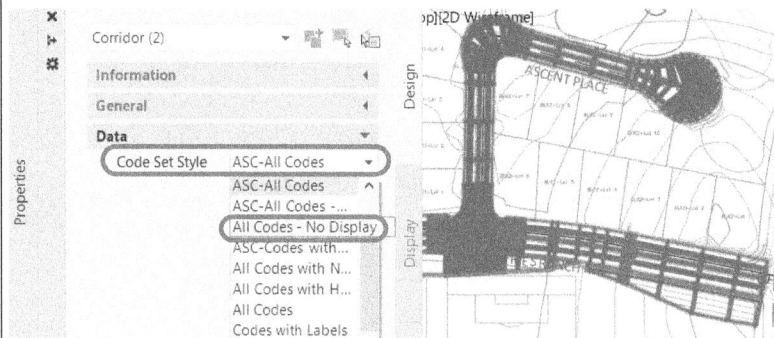

Figure 8–100

3. Note the changes in how the corridors are displayed.

4. Select the preset view **Assemblies**.

5. Change your drawing scale to **1"=40'**.

6. Select any one of the assemblies, and in the right-click menu, pick **Select Similar** (at the bottom of the list). This selects all assemblies in your drawing.

7. As you did above, change the *Code Set Styles* through the Properties palette. experiment with the different styles, and end up with **ASC-View-Edit**.

8. Save the drawing.

8.8 Section Views

A section view can display sampled surface sections, corridor assemblies, and pipes or structures where the Sample Lines have been placed. Similar to profiles, sections use a section view to annotate their elevations and center line offsets. Styles affect the look of a section view.

Section views can annotate an assembly's offsets, elevations, and grades. The *All Codes* style assigned to the assembly in the sample line group makes all of the points and links available for labeling. The Section Label styles do not interact with the assembly, only with the corridor surfaces.

- As with Profile views, Section views can be moved and retain the correct information.

- Section views can be created individually or in groups.

Section View Wizard

In the *Home* tab, the Profile & Section Views panel enables you to create a single section view, multiple sections organized into columns and rows, and project objects to a section view. The **Single** and **Multiple View** commands open the Section View wizard, which guides you through the process of creating Section views. There are six parts in the Section View wizard, as shown in Figure 8–101.

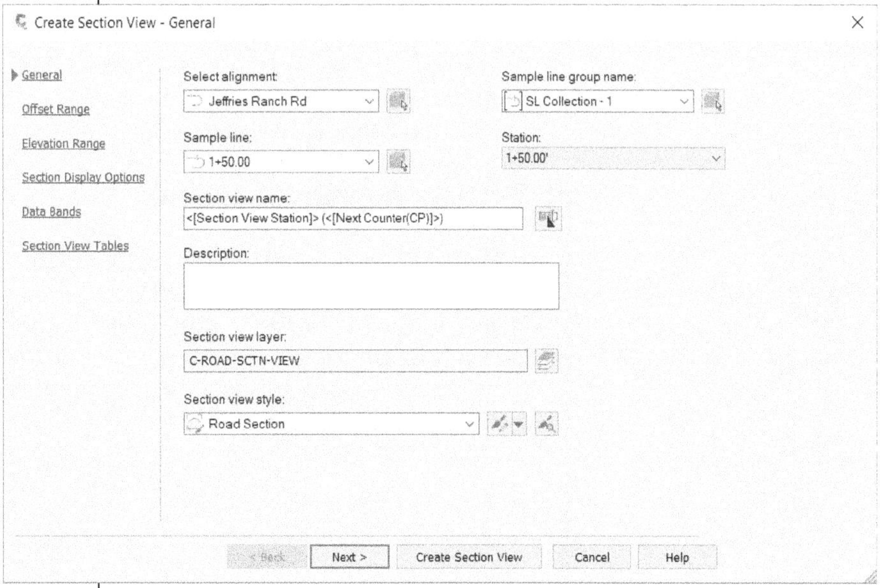

Figure 8–101

- **General:** Specifies basic information about the Section View, including which alignment to use, the sample group and line, and the view template. If creating multiple views, the Group Plot Style method specifies how to create multiple section views (**All** or **Page**). You can define page styles that define sheet sizes and plottable areas (sheet size minus margins and border).

- **Section Placement:** Only displays when you are creating multiple views. It enables you to set the Group Plot Style to use for setting the row and column settings for placing multiple section views.

- **Offset Range:** Enables you to set the width of the view.

- **Elevation Range:** Enables you to set the height of the view.

- **Section Display Options:** Enables you to select what gets drawn in the view and the section style.

- **Data Bands:** Enables you to specify one or more band set styles for the sections and their positions in the view.

- **Section View Tables:** Enables you to add and modify volume tables calculated using the Section view (a material list must be created from the sample line group for this option to be available).

Section View Styles

A Section View style defines the vertical and horizontal grid and its annotation. The horizontal lines represent the elevations and the vertical lines represent the center line offset.

Section View Band Styles

A band style defines the offset and elevation annotation at the bottom of a Section view. The style affects the annotation's format and the information that displays in the band. Using the band styles provided in the sample templates, set your existing ground surface as **Surface 1**, and the proposed surface (such as a Corridor Top surface) as **Surface 2**.

Section Styles and Section Label Styles

A section style assigns a layer and other layer properties to a surface section. The section label styles annotate grade breaks, slopes, and offsets.

Code Set Styles

In Multi-Purpose styles, **Code Set Styles** are collections of customized **Link, Point** and **Shape Styles**. The *All Codes* style assigns object and label styles for corridor assemblies. This is the default style for section labeling.

Code Set Styles define object styles for points, links, or shapes for corridors, assemblies, section and section views. It specifies which labels display in a Section view.

- All link styles annotate a grade or slope.

- All point styles annotate an offset and elevation.

Other Code Set Styles are available (or can be created or modified by the BIM Manager) for specific purposes, such as:

- Plotting with or without hatching

- Design development

- No Display

- Visualization

Page Styles

A page style defines the plottable area of a sheet size. The plottable area is what remains after removing the non-printing margins and border from the sheet size. The page style also defines a sheet grid. The Plot Group styles use the grid to space sections on a sheet.

Practice 8i

Plan Production Tools - Sections

Practice Objective

- Show what is happening with existing and proposed surface data at predefined intervals along an alignment using section views.

Task 1 - Create a Single Section view.

1. Open **PPR1-C1-PlanProduction.dwg** from the *C:\Civil 3D Projects\Plans* folder.

2. In the *Home* tab>Profile & Section Views panel, expand **Section Views** and click ⌂ (Create Section View), as shown in Figure 8–102. The Create Section View wizard opens.

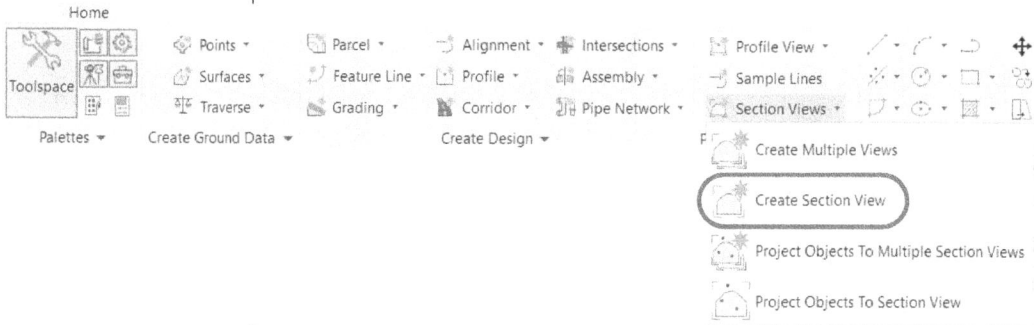

Figure 8–102

3. In the *General* page, in the *Sample Line* field, select **4+50.00** as shown in Figure 8–103. Set the *Section view style* to **Road Section** and click **Next>**.

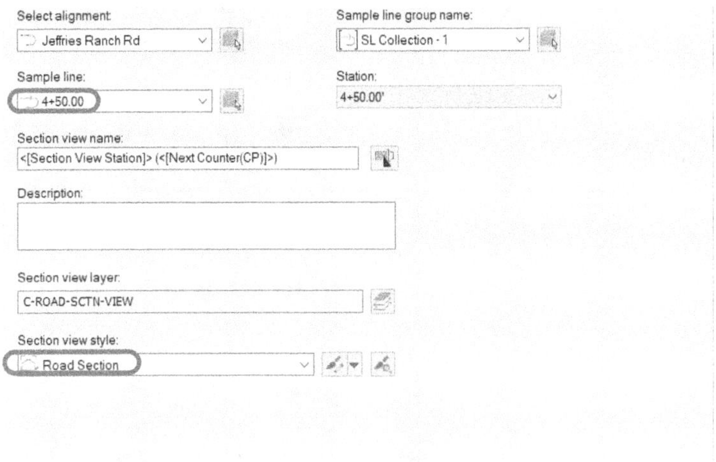

Figure 8–103

4. In the *Offset Range* and *Elevation Range* pages, accept the defaults and click **Next>**.

5. In the *Section Display Options* page, do the following:
   - Set the *Style* to **Existing Ground** for *Existing-Site*.
   - **ASC-View-Edit with Shading** for the *Jeffries Ranch Rd Corridor* section.
   - **Finished Ground** for the *FG* and *Jeffries Ranch Rd Datum*.
   - Assign the label options and styles to **_No Labels** for all, as shown in Figure 8–104 and click **Next>**.

Note that the quantity take offs only display if the material quantities are calculated before the section views are created.

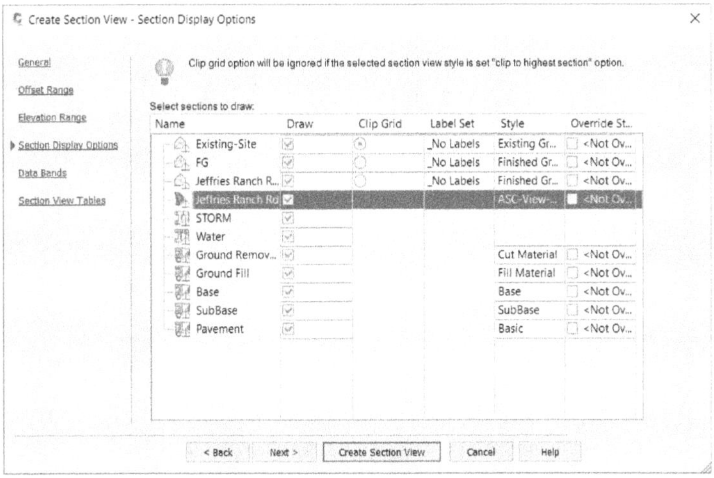

Figure 8–104

6. On the left, click **Section View Tables** or click **Next>** to skip setting the Data Bands because **No_Labels** was selected in Step 6.

7. In the *X Offset* field, type **0.25"** and click **Add>>** to add the Total Volume Table to the list. Then expand the Type drop-down list and select **Material**. Click **Add>>** again to include the material table in the section view, as shown in Figure 8–105. Select all of the materials in the **Select Materials** window.

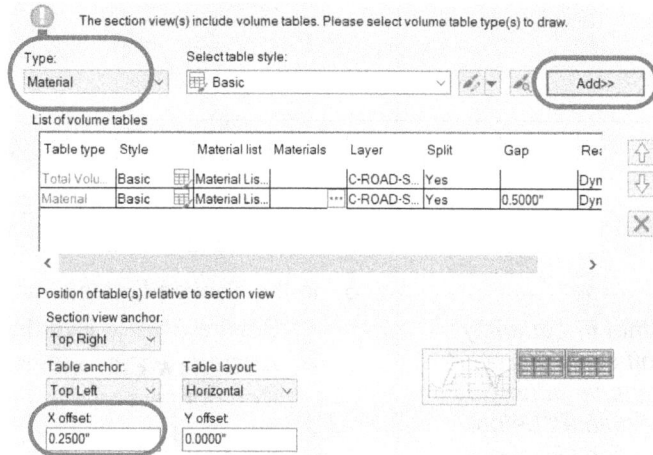

Figure 8–105

8. Click **Create Section View**. At the *Identify section view origin* prompt, click in empty space in Model Space, somewhere northeast of the surface.

9. Adjust the section by dragging or deleting unwanted labels. (Hold <Ctrl> when selecting.) The drawing is shown in Figure 8–106.

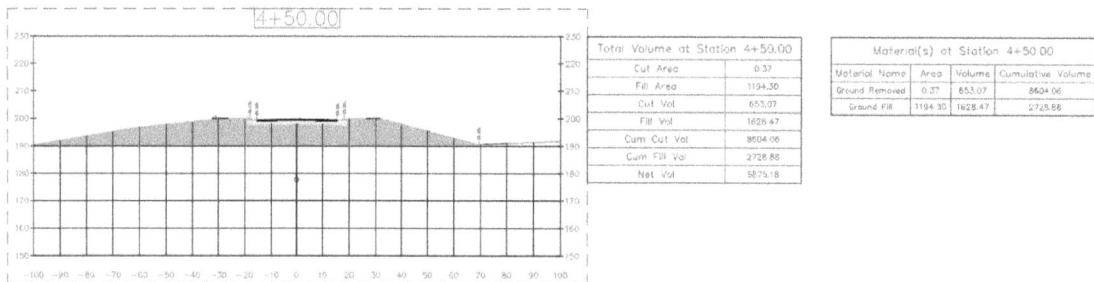

Figure 8–106

Task 2 - Create a Multiple Section view.

1. Open **PPR1-C2-PlanProduction.dwg** from the *C:\Civil 3D Projects\Plans* folder.

2. In the *Home* tab>Profile & Section Views panel, expand **Section Views** and click (Create Multiple Section Views).

3. In the Create Multiple Section Views - *General* dialog box, accept all the defaults and click **Next>**.

4. In the Create Multiple Section Views - *Section Placement,* for *Placement Options,* choose the **Production**, click on the Ellipsis (...) to open the *Select Layout as Sheet Template* window.

5. Select the Ellipsis(...) again to choose the proper template, browse to the *C:\Civil 3D Projects\Ascent-Config* folder and select **ASC-Training Section-I.dwt.** Click **OK**.

6. Select the **ARCH D Section 40 Scale** layout from the list, as shown in Figure 8–107.

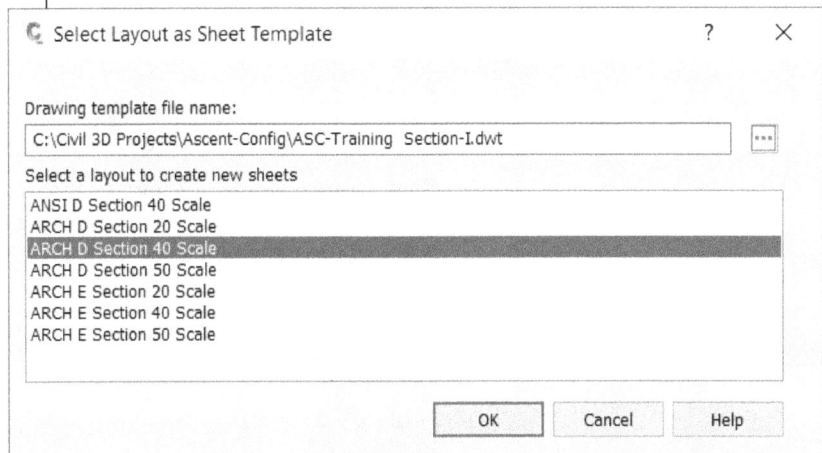

Figure 8–107

7. Accept the defaults for the next four windows by clicking **Next>,** until you come to the last window named Create Multiple Section Views - *Section View Tables.*

8. In the *X Offset* field, type **0.500"** and set *Table layout* to
    Vertical, then click **Add>>** to add the Total Volume Table to
    the list. Then expand the Type drop-down list and select
    Material. Click **Add>>** again to include the material table in
    the section view. Select all of the materials in the **Select
    Materials** window. Change the *Gap* for the Material table to
    0.250", as shown in Figure 8–108.

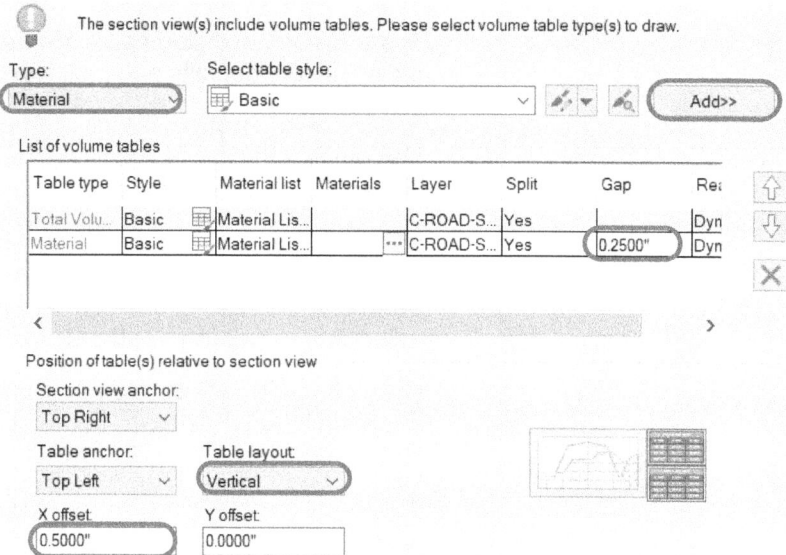

Figure 8–108

9. Click **Create Section View**. At the *Identify section view origin*
    prompt, click in empty space in Model Space, somewhere
    north of the previous section.

**Task 3 - Create section sheet files and add them to the
sheet set.**

---

1. Open **PPR1-C3-PlanProduction.dwg** from the *C:\Civil 3D
    Projects\Plans* folder.

2. In the *Output* tab>Plan Production panel, click (Create
    Section Sheets).

3. Fill in the following, as shown in Figure 8–109:

   - *Alignment*: **Jeffries Ranch Rd**
   - *Sample line group*: **SL Collection - 1**
   - *Section view group*: **Sample View Group**
   - *Layout name*: Select the name template icon and fill in **Section-<[Parent Alignment]>-<[Next Counter]>** in the New Template, as shown in figure Figure 8–109.

4. For *Sheet Set,* select *Add to existing sheet set* and use the ellipses (...) to browse to the *C:\Civil 3D Projects\Plans* folder and select **Ascent Phase1.dst.** If you did not complete the previous practice, select **Ascent Phase1A.dst** instead.

5. Click on **Create Sheets**.

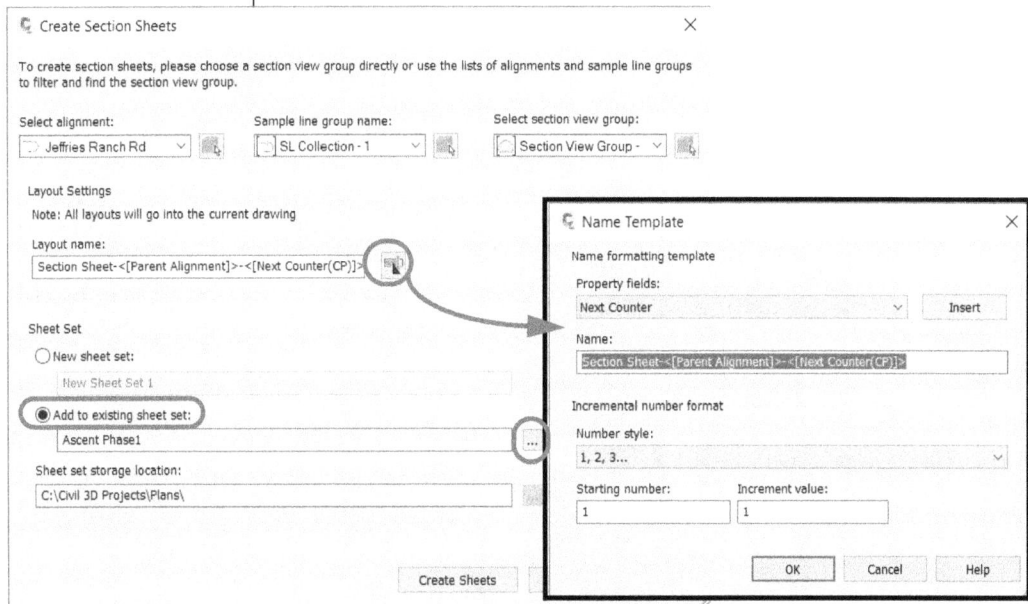

Figure 8–109

6. Click **OK** to dismiss the *Drawing will be saved* message.

7. Note the new layouts that have been created in the drawing.

8. Save the drawing.

SECTION
5

Pipe Networks

Pipe Networks

Exam Objectives Covered in This Chapter

5.1.a Describe the purpose of the part catalog and parts list

5.1.b Set the part catalog location

5.1.c Add and modify parts and part sizes in the parts list

5.1.d Identify the tools used to create and modify pipe networks

5.1.e Add parts, pipes and structures to a profile view

5.1.f Change the pipe network flow direction

5.1.g Annotate plan and profile pipe networks

5.2.a Create and edit the parts list

5.2.b Set the part catalog location

5.2.c Use the Pressure Network creation tools

5.2.d Add pipes, appurtenances, and fittings to a profile view

5.2.e Add plan and profile view labels

9.1 Pipes Configuration

The Toolspace, *Settings* tab contains values and styles affecting pipe networks. The *Parts Lists* and *Pipe Rules* are the most important settings. Parts Lists contain typical pipes, fittings, appurtenances, and structures for a utility. Pipe Rules trigger error messages if pipes/structures are not created in accordance with predefined constraints, such as the minimum or maximum pipe length or slope.

Edit Drawing Settings

The Edit Drawing Settings dialog box contains values affecting the pipe layout layers (e.g., pipe networks, fittings, profiles, and section views).

Pipe Network Feature Settings

The Pipe Network Edit Feature Settings dialog box contains values that assign styles, set the pipe network naming convention, set the default pipe and structure rules, and set the default location for pipe and structure labels. To open the Edit Feature Settings dialog box, right-click on Settings in the *Pipe Network* collection, and select **Edit Feature Settings**. The dialog box is shown in Figure 9–1.

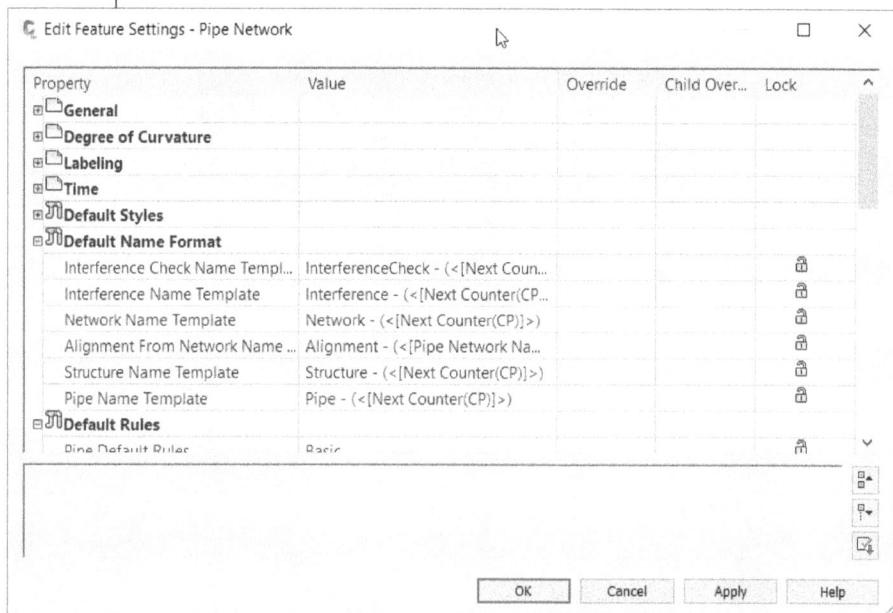

Figure 9–1

Pipe Catalog

The Autodesk Civil 3D software includes standard catalogs in both Imperial and Metric units. Catalog specifications define the size and shape of the underground structures and pipes for sanitary or storm gravity systems.

- The *Imperial Pipes* folder contains **Imperial Pipes.htm**, which displays the components of the Pipe catalog.
- The Pipe catalog includes circular, egg, elliptical, and rectangular shapes. For each pipe shape, the catalog includes inner and outer pipe diameters and wall thicknesses.

Pipe catalog components can be edited by selecting **Modify> Pipe network>Parts List>Part Builder**.

Structure Catalog

The Structure catalog includes specifications for inlets, junction structures (circular, rectangular, or eccentric) with or without frames, and simple junction shapes (rectangular or circular).

- The Structure catalog consists of tables and lists that define allowable sizes, thicknesses, and heights.

Pipe Network Parts Lists

While the catalogs are shared between multiple projects (and multiple users), each Autodesk Civil 3D drawing can contain any number of Part Lists that are specific to that drawing.

Part Lists are populated with pipes and structures from the catalog and are organized for a specific task (such as Sanitary Sewer and Drain).

- Parts Lists are in the Toolspace, *Settings* tab under the *Pipe Network* collection and *Pressure Network* collection, as shown in Figure 9–2.

- To display a parts list, right-click on its name and select **Edit**.

Figure 9–2

The Pipe Network parts list has typical pipe sizes in the *Pipes* tab and typical structures in the *Structure* tab, as shown in Figure 9–3. If required, you can change a pipe or structure size list, or add a new part type.

An important setting for each tab is *Rules*. Render Material affects how the pipes and structures display in 3D.

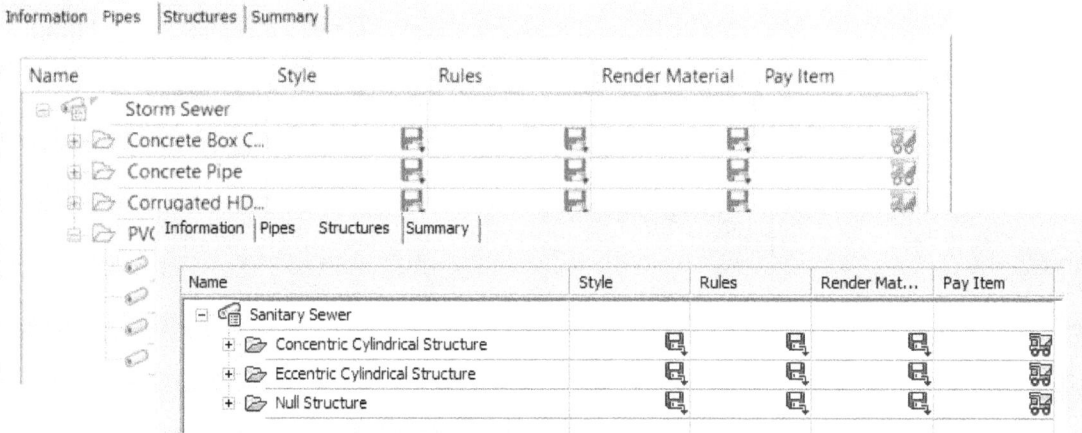

Figure 9–3

- To add a pipe size or structure size, select the part type heading, right-click, and select **Add a part size**. Then select a new part size from the size list, as shown in Figure 9–4.

Figure 9–4

- To add a new part family (e.g., concrete pipes for a sanitary system), select the name of the part list, right-click, and select **Add a part family**. Then select a new part family from the list of available parts in the catalog, as shown in Figure 9–5.

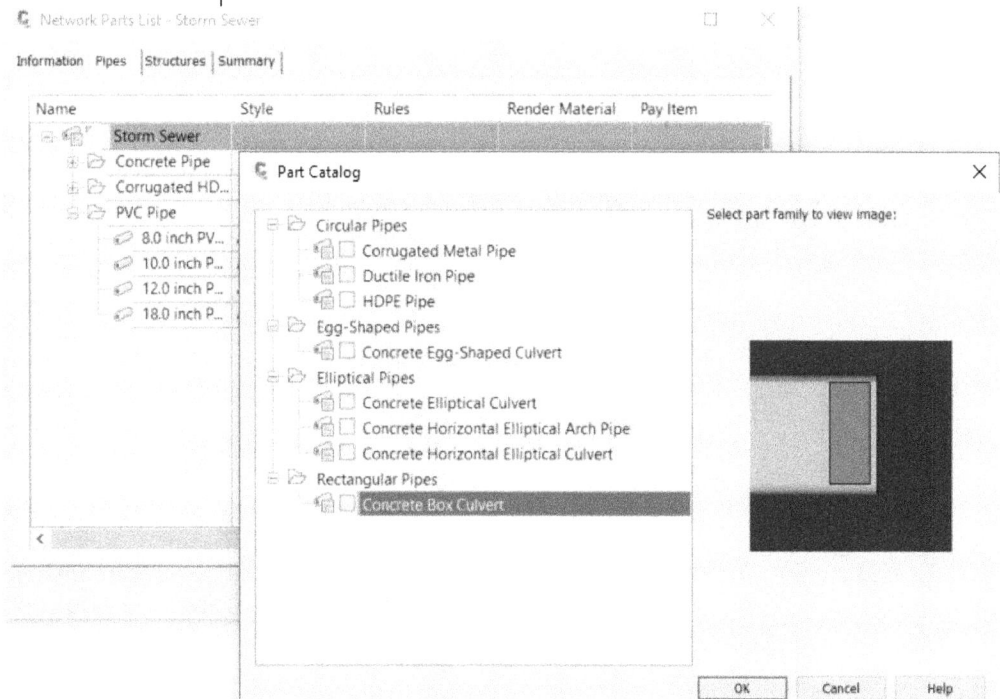

Figure 9–5

The *Pressure Network* parts list has typical pipe sizes in the *Pressure Pipes* tab, typical fitting sizes in the *Fittings* tab, and typical appurtenance sizes in the *Appurtenances* tab, as shown in Figure 9–6. If required, you can change any of the size lists, or add a new part type. *Render Material* affects how the various parts display in 3D.

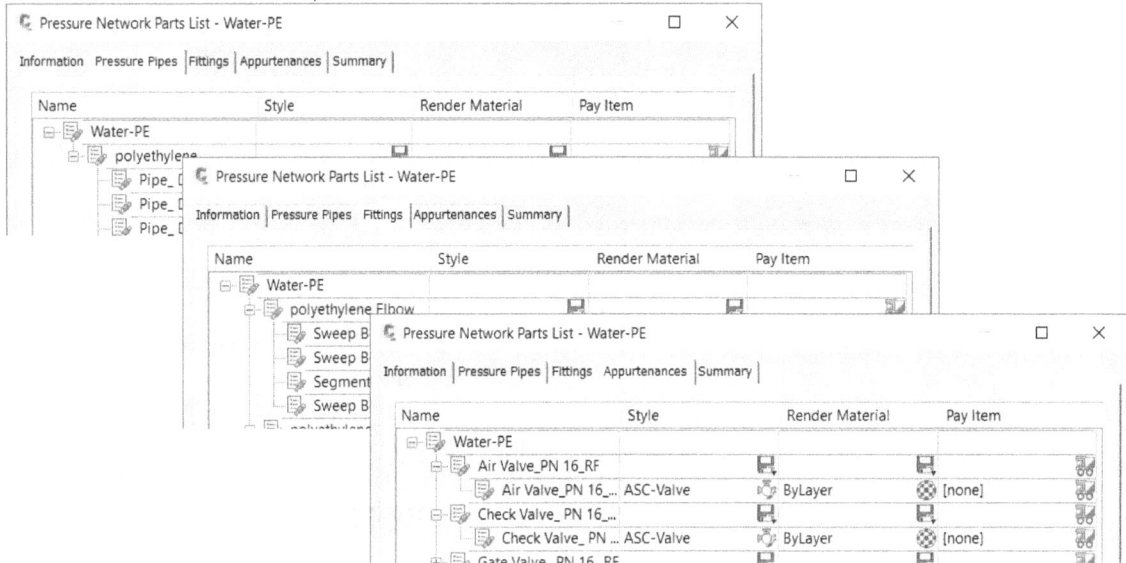

Figure 9–6

Pipe and Structure Styles

The pipe style defines how a pipe displays in plan, profile, and section views. The most used tab of a Pipe Style is the *Display* tab. By toggling on or off the Component display, a style affects how a network displays in the drawing window (e.g., as a single or double line), its layer name, and color.

A structure style defines how a structure displays in plan, profile and section views. The plan settings include the plan view symbol and how a structure displays in profile and section views (the outline of the 3D shape).

Pipe styles include the **Clean up Pipe to Pipe Intersections** option for networks, where one pipe connects to another (rather than to a structure). This enables the pipes to seem to join together. For this option to work, the pipes must be connected with a *null* structure.

Pipe and Structure Rules

Since pipes and structures often need more than one rule applied to them, individual rules are organized into collections called **rule sets**. Then the rules are prioritized from most important to least important by organizing the order in which they display in the list. You can have different sets for different types of pipe, sizes, and/or systems.

- Pipe rules define minimum/maximum slopes, cover, minimum/maximum pipe segment length, how pipes of different sizes align and how they are truncated when attached to a structure.

- Pipe rule sets are located in the Toolspace, *Settings* tab, in the *Pipe Rule Set* collection, as shown in Figure 9–7. To display or edit a rule set, right-click on it and select **Edit**.

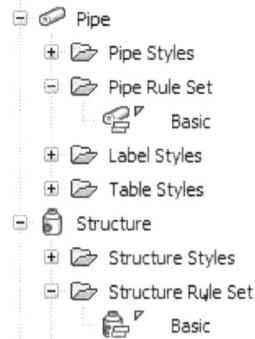

Figure 9–7

- Structure rules define the across structure drop's default value, maximum value, maximum pipe size and the sump depth.

- Structure rule sets are located in the Toolspace, *Settings* tab, under the *Structure Rule Set* collection.

Pressure Networks do not use rules.

Some pipe and structure rules directly control the layout of new pipes and structures, such as minimum and maximum slope. Some rules are checks that are made after creation, such as maximum pipe length. Rules, such as maximum pipe length, do not prevent you from creating a pipe that is over the maximum length. However, if a pipe is over the maximum length, you are prompted with a warning in the Toolspace, *Prospector* tab and in the Pipe Network Vistas, as shown in Figure 9–8.

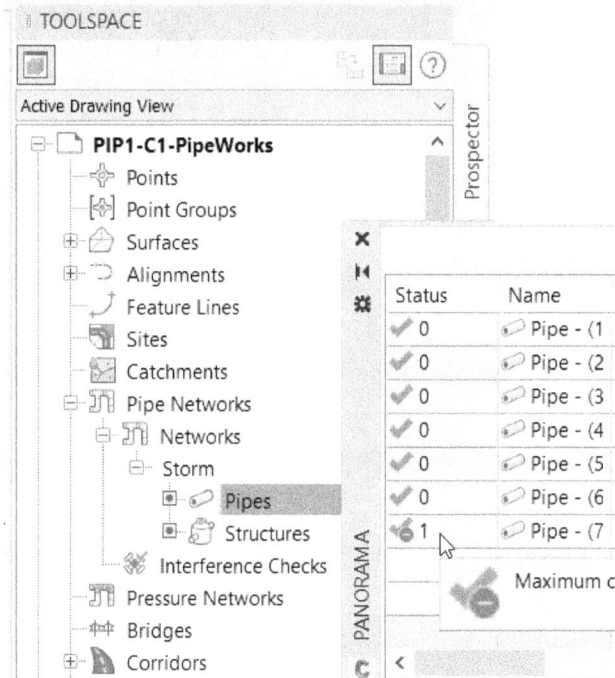

Figure 9–8

Reapplying Pipe Rules

Structure Invert Out elevations are automatically calculated based on the given rules when the structure is first created. Therefore, if new connecting pipes are added to a structure below the lowest invert, the outlet is not automatically lowered until you click 🖳 (Apply Rules) in the *Modify* tab>Pipe Network>Modify panel. An example is shown in Figure 9–9.

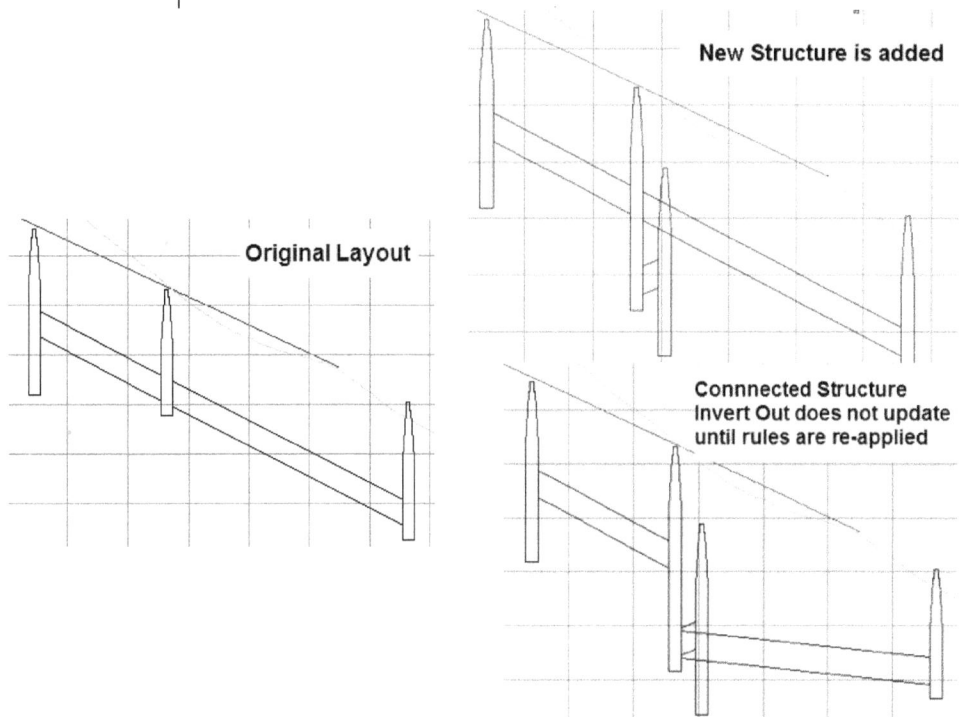

New Structure is added

Original Layout

Connnected Structure Invert Out does not update until rules are re-applied

Figure 9–9

Pipe Layers

Unlike most Autodesk Civil 3D objects, pipe network layers typically need to be manually reassigned when a pipe network is created. Layers need to be assigned for pipes and structures in plan, profile, and section views. For example, the default Autodesk Civil 3D templates automatically map to layers appropriate for storm drainage structures when using the Pipe Network Creation Tools and water structures when using the Pressure Pipe Creation Tools. The Pipe Network Layers dialog boxes are shown in Figure 9–10.

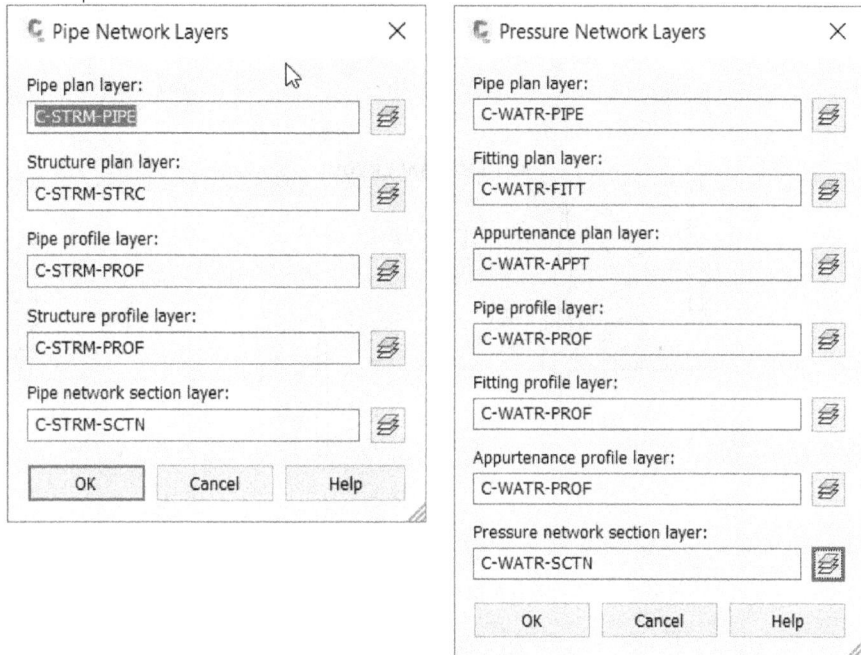

Figure 9–10

If creating a sanitary sewer line, each one needs to be remapped to layers specific to sanitary sewer utilities, such as the examples shown in Figure 9–11.

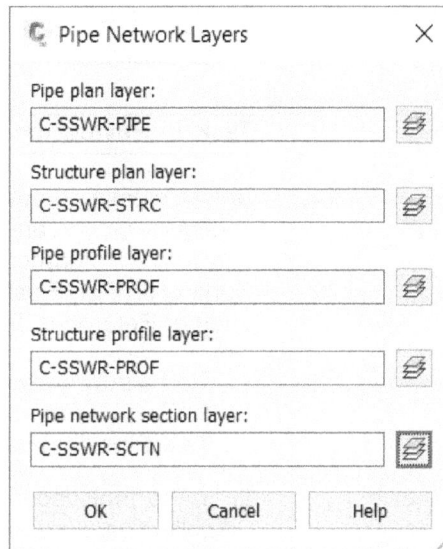

Figure 9–11

Practice 9a

Configuring Pipe Networks

Practice Objective

- Create a new Reference Template for Pipe Networks with settings for your organization.

Task 1 - Review the Storm Drain Parts List and Rules.

Before creating a network, you should become familiar with the configuration you are about to use. While you have already attached a Reference Template for the styles, now that you are working on Pipe Networks, you need to create and attach another Reference Template for Pipes.

1. Start a new drawing from **ASC-Base-Styles.dwt**. In the *C:\Civil 3D Projects\Ascent-Config* folder, save the file as **XXX-Pipe-Styles.DWG** (substitute your initials for XXX).

2. In the Toolspace, *Settings* tab, expand the *Pipe Network* collection, expand the *Parts Lists* collection, right-click on the *Storm Sewer* part list and select **Edit...**.

3. In the *Pipes* tab, the parts list currently contains a large number of concrete pipes. They are all assigned to use the Basic rule set and a pipe style that displays double lines in plan view, as shown in Figure 9–12.

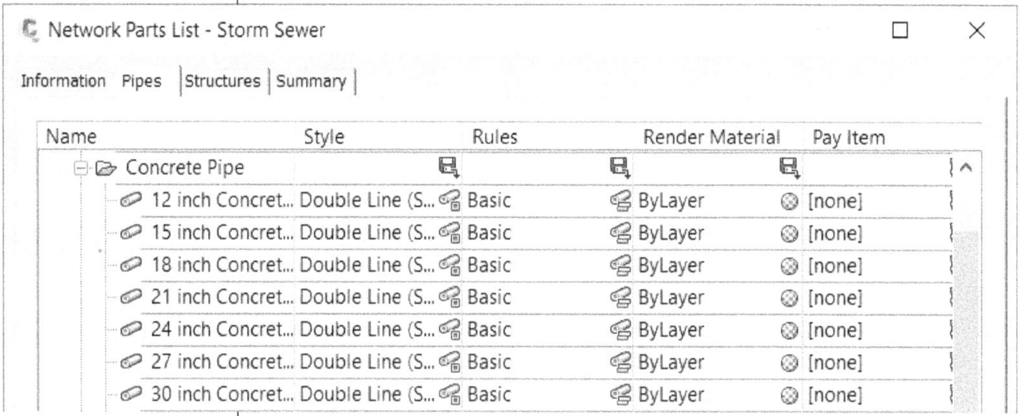

Name	Style	Rules	Render Material	Pay Item	
▷ Concrete Pipe					^
12 inch Concret...	Double Line (S...	Basic	ByLayer	[none]	
15 inch Concret...	Double Line (S...	Basic	ByLayer	[none]	
18 inch Concret...	Double Line (S...	Basic	ByLayer	[none]	
21 inch Concret...	Double Line (S...	Basic	ByLayer	[none]	
24 inch Concret...	Double Line (S...	Basic	ByLayer	[none]	
27 inch Concret...	Double Line (S...	Basic	ByLayer	[none]	
30 inch Concret...	Double Line (S...	Basic	ByLayer	[none]	

Network Parts List - Storm Sewer

Information Pipes Structures Summary

Figure 9–12

4. You don't need all these sizes. Click on the ones you want to remove, right-click and select **Delete**, as shown in Figure 9–13 (note that you can only do this one at a time). Ensure that you keep the 12", 15", 21", 30", and 60" parts.

Figure 9–13

5. Change the Styles of the smaller diameter pipes to be Single Lines. Select the pipes up to size 21" and select ⌕ (Pipe Style) and select *ASC-Single Line (Storm)* from the list, as shown in Figure 9–14. (You can only select one at a time.)

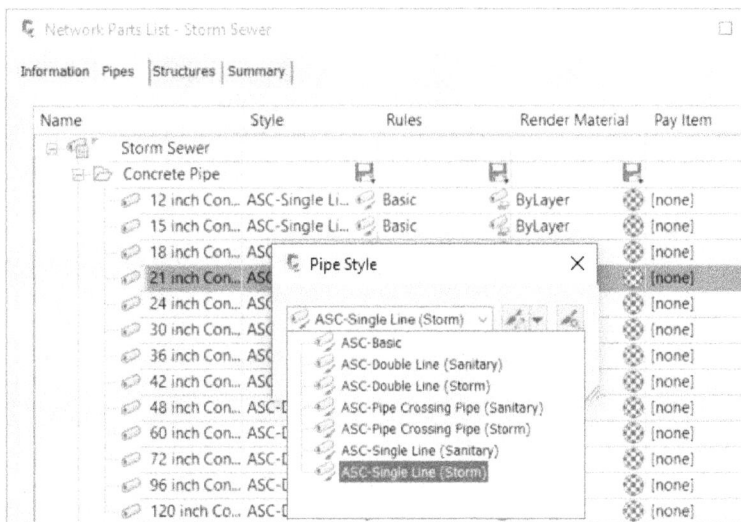

Figure 9–14

6. Delete the **Concrete Elliptical Culvert** type (if present) by right-clicking on it and selecting *Delete...*. Confirm that you want to delete this Pipe Type.

7. To add another Pipe type, under **Network Parts List - Storm Sewer**, right-click on **Storm Sewer** and select **Add part family...**, as shown in Figure 9–15.

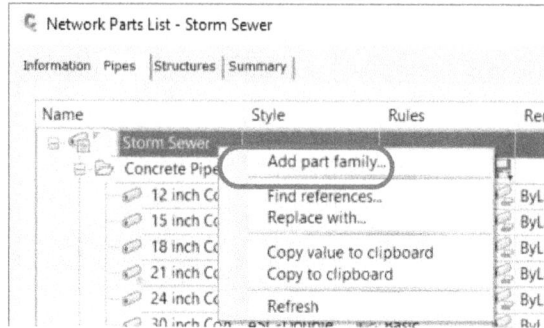

Figure 9–15

8. In the Parts catalog, select **PVC Pipe**, as shown in Figure 9–16. Click **OK** to close the dialog box. Note that the Pipe Parts already in your Parts List do not show in this list.

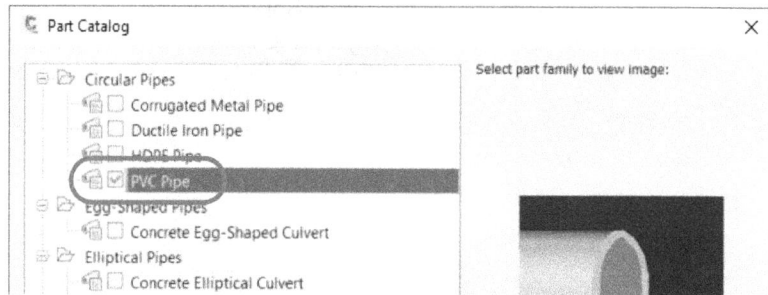

Figure 9–16

9. To add sizes to the part family, select **PVC Pipe**, right-click, and select **Add part size...**, as shown in Figure 9–17.

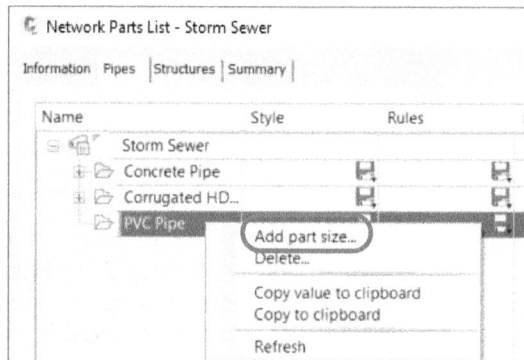

Figure 9–17

10. Select and add the pipe sizes: **8**, **10**, **12**, and **18**. Note that you cannot select all four of these sizes. You will need to add each one separately. To add part sizes, you can select individual sizes in the Value drop-down list (or select the checkbox in the *Add all sizes* column to add all of the available sizes), as shown in Figure 9–18. Ensure that the part Material is set to **PVC**. Click **OK** to add each one.

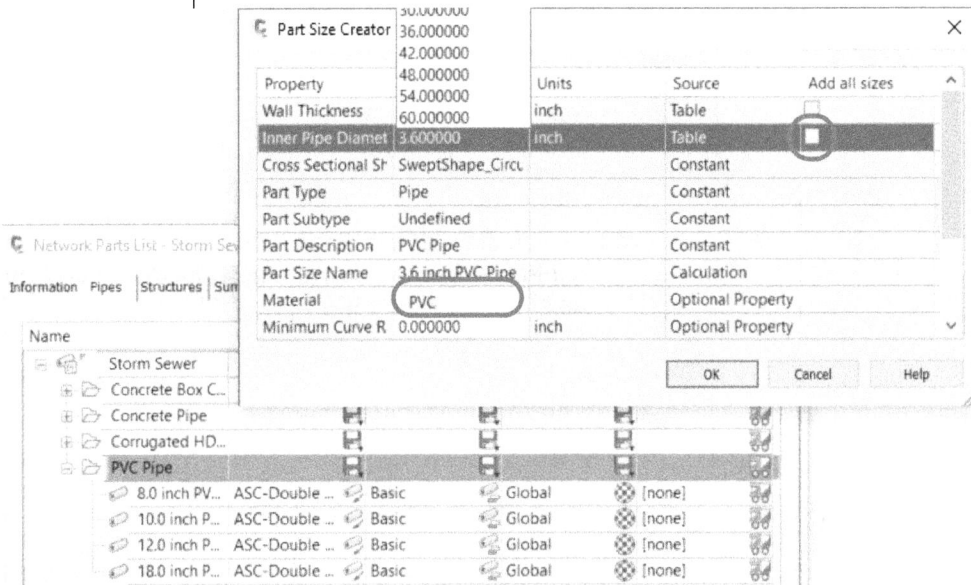

Figure 9–18

11. Change the Pipe Styles of the 8.0" and 10.0" PVC pipes to **ASC-Single Line (Storm)** as you had done previously.

12. When finished, the Network Parts List - Storm Sewer dialog box opens, as shown in Figure 9–19.

Figure 9–19

13. Select the *Structures* tab. The parts list includes a number of headwalls of different sizes, and catch basins and manholes. Each of these is assigned styles and rules specific to each type, as shown in Figure 9–20.

Name	Style	Rules	Render Material	Pay Item
⊟ Storm Sewer				
⊞ Concrete Rectang...				
⊞ Concentric Cylindr...				
⊞ Eccentric Cylindric...				
⊞ Null Structure				
⊞ Cylindrical Structu...				

Figure 9–20

14. As you did with the Pipes, add a Structure Part Family by right-clicking and selecting the Concrete Flared End Section, as shown in Figure 9–21.

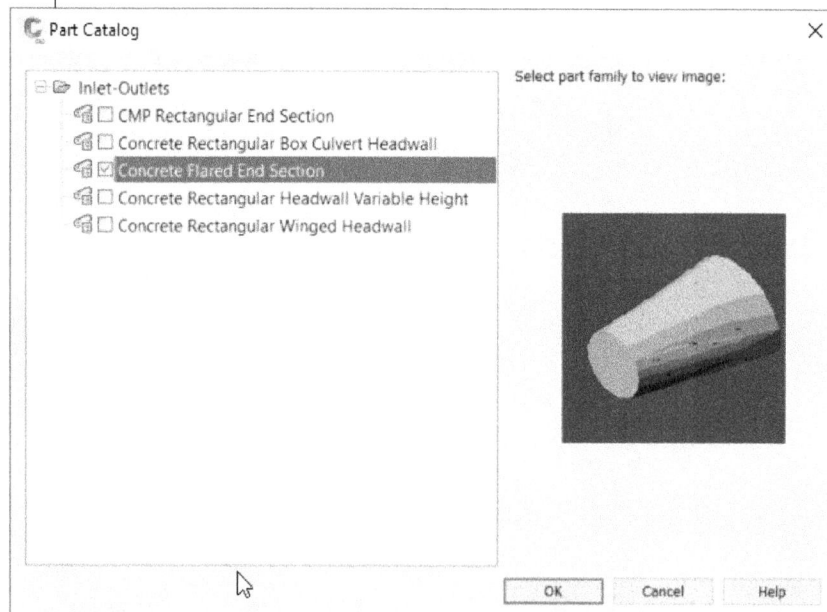

Figure 9–21

15. Add **12"** as the part size and click **OK** to exit the Part Catalog.

16. Click **OK** to exit.

17. In the Toolspace, *Settings* tab, expand the *Structure* collection, expand the *Structure Rule Set* collection, right-click on the **Basic** rule set and select **Edit...**, as shown in Figure 9–22.

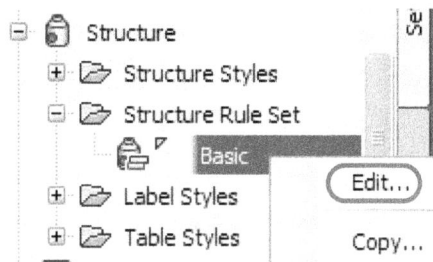

Figure 9–22

Using the arrows at the right side of the Rules tab enables you to prioritize the rules. The rules are processed sequentially from bottom to top. Therefore, place the most important rule at the top of the list.

For this Manhole, in the **Maximum pipe size check** rule you can use a maximum pipe diameter of **4'**. In the Pipe Drop Across Structure rule, you can have elevations based on **Inverts** and a drop across the manhole of **0.10'** with a **3'** maximum interior drop, as shown in Figure 9–23.

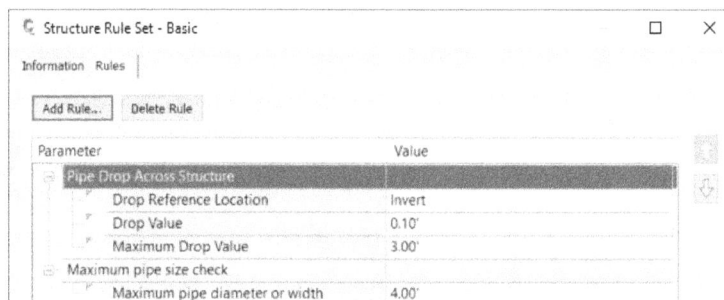

Parameter	Value
Pipe Drop Across Structure	
Drop Reference Location	Invert
Drop Value	0.10'
Maximum Drop Value	3.00'
Maximum pipe size check	
Maximum pipe diameter or width	4.00'

Figure 9–23

18. Review and click **Cancel** to exit without changes.

Task 2 - Review a pressure network parts list.

1. Open **C:\Civil 3D Projects\Ascent-Config\ ASC-Pipe-Styles-1.dwg**.

2. In the Toolspace, *Settings* tab, expand the *Pressure Network* collection, expand the *Parts Lists* collection, right-click on the **Water-Steel** part list and select **Edit...**, as shown in Figure 9–24.

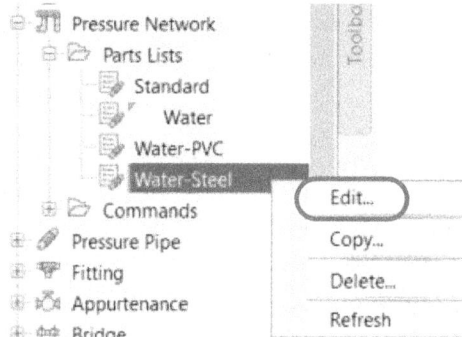

Figure 9–24

3. In the *Pressure Pipes* tab, review the available pipe sizes. To the right of the ductile iron family, select the disk to change all of the styles to **ASC-Double Line (Water)**, as shown in Figure 9–25.

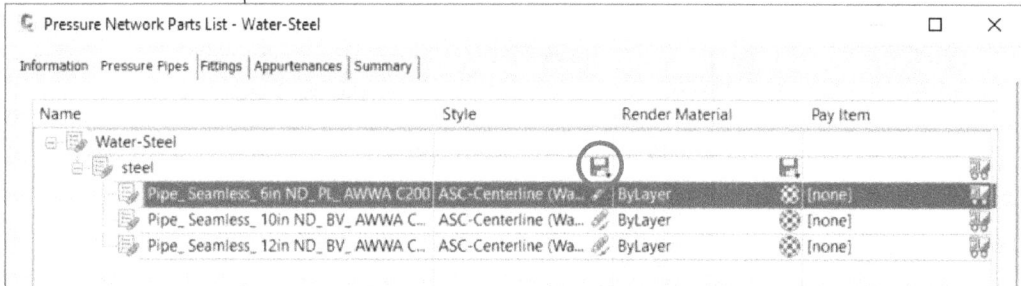

Figure 9–25

4. In the *Fittings* tab, review the available fittings. To the right of each family, select the disk to change all of the styles to **ASC-Fitting**, as shown in Figure 9–26.

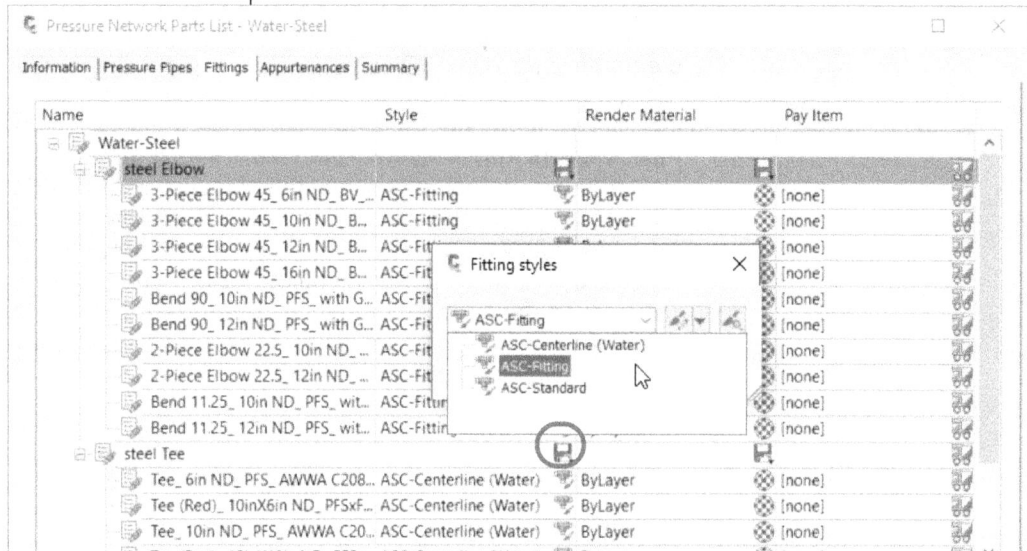

Figure 9–26

5. In the *Appurtenances* tab, review the available valves. To the right of each family, select the disk to set the style to **ASC-Valve**, as shown in Figure 9–27.

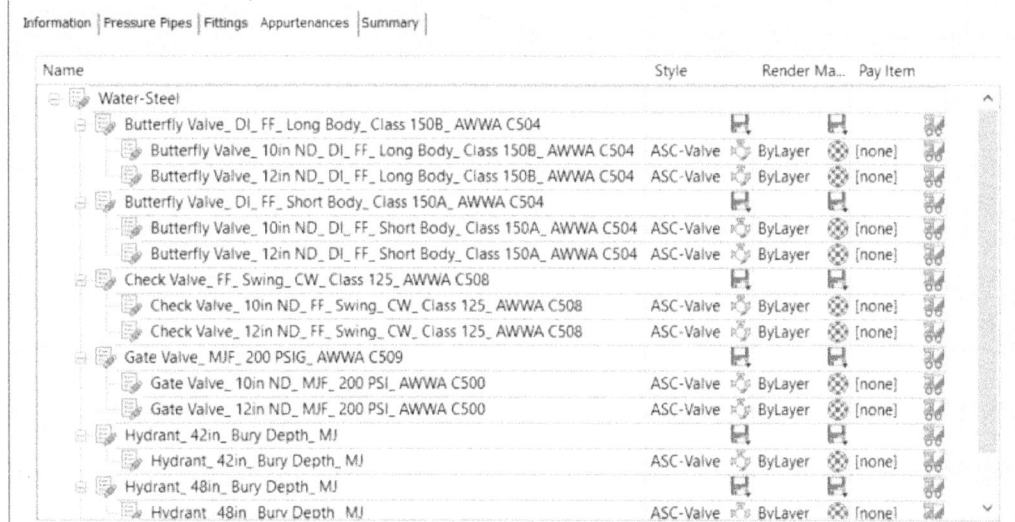

Figure 9–27

6. Click **OK** and save the drawing.

9.2 Creating Networks from Objects

In addition to creating networks by layout, a pipe network can be created from a 2D or 3D object, including a polyline or feature line. In the *Home* tab>Pipe Network panel, and click 🔧 (Create Pipe Network from Object) to start the creation of a pipe network. Next you are prompted to select the object or type **X** and press <Enter> to select objects from an external reference file. Once selected, a flow arrow displays along the pipe network. The flow is set to the direction in which you drew the original entity but you can reverse the direction by selecting **Reverse**. To leave the flow directions set as is, press <Enter> or select **OK**. A Create Pipe Network dialog box opens enabling you to:

- Name the network.

- Set the parts list.

- Select the default pipe and structure to use.

- Set the surface and alignment to reference.

- You can also clean up the drawing as you create the network, by selecting the **Erasing existing entity** option (if the entity is not part of an XREF), as shown in Figure 9–28.

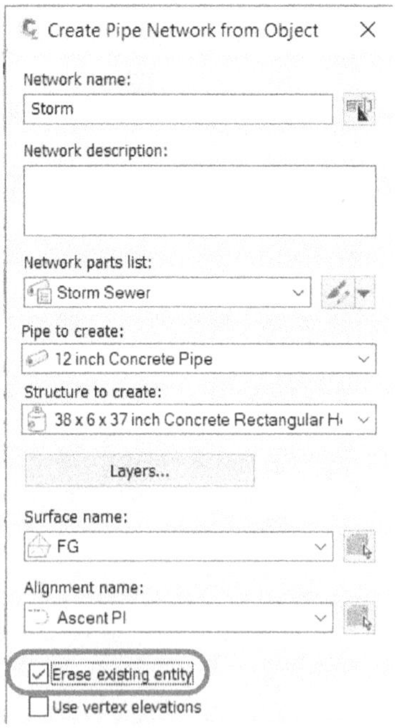

Figure 9–28

Practice 9b

Creating Pipe Networks by Layout

Practice Objective

- Create a gravity fed pipe network by layout.

Task 1 - Create a Pipe Network by Layout.

In this task, you will continue adding to the network using Autodesk Civil 3D's **Pipe Network** creation tool.

You will insert manholes based on Figure 9–29. The first structure, **pt1**, is located at station 11+00 of Jeffries Ranch Rd. The next structure, **pt2**, is located at the beginning of the curve, **pt3** is at the intersection of Jeffries Ranch Rd and Ascent Pl, and **pt4** is at a station of 0+098.87m along the Jeffries Ranch Rd alignment. Use the information shown in Figure 9–29 as a guide as you complete the following steps.

Figure 9–29

1. Open **PIP1-B1-PipeWorks.dwg** from the *C:\Civil 3D Projects\Working\PipeNetworks* folder.

2. Select the preset view **Pipe-Create**.

3. In Model Space, select a part in the STORM network. In the contextual tab>Modify panel, click 🔧 (Edit Pipe Network), as shown in Figure 9–30.

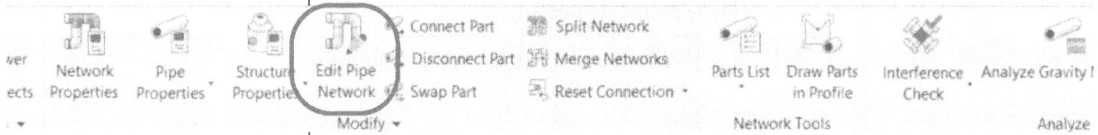

Figure 9–30

4. In the Network Layout Tools - STORM toolbar, shown in Figure 9–31:

- Click ⤵ (Alignment) and select **Jefferies Ranch Rd**.
- Select **68 x 6 x 57 inch Concrete Rectangular Headwall** for the manhole structure.
- Select **12.0 inch PVC Pipe** for the Pipe part.
- Toggle the slope to **Upslope**.
- Click 🗜 (Draw Pipe and Structure).

To find the PVC section, go to the bottom of the list, and then expand it to find the proper size.

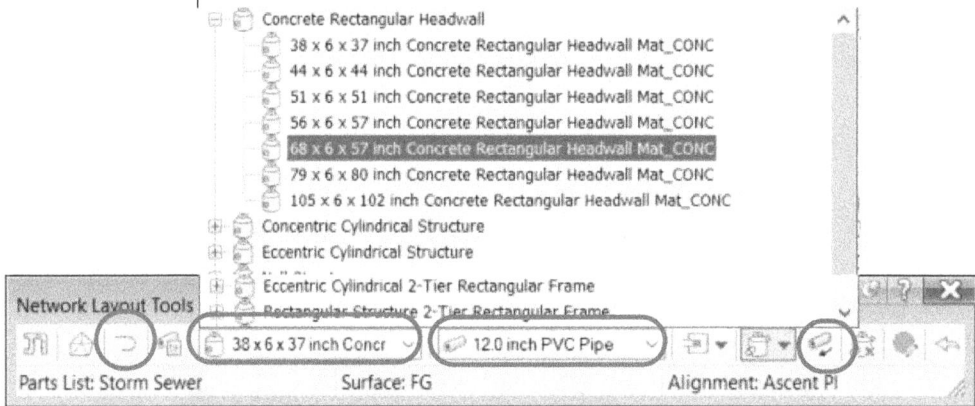

Figure 9–31

5. The Autodesk Civil 3D software prompts you for the locations of the structures. Select end point **pt1** and then select an approximate location near point **pt2** for the next structure location, as shown in Figure 9–32.

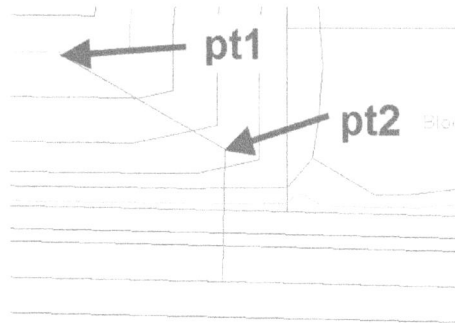

Figure 9–32

6. In the Network Layout Tools - STORM toolbar, select **Cylindrical Structure Slab Top Circular Frame>Slab Top Cylindrical Structure 15 dia 18 dia Frm 4 FrHt 4 Slab 3 Wall 4 Floor** for the manhole structure and toggle the slope to **Downslope**, as shown in Figure 9–33.

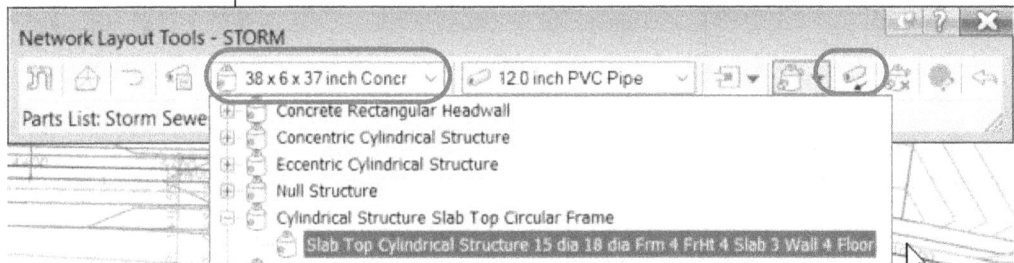

Figure 9–33

7. In the Command Line, you should be prompted for a structure insertion point. Select **Startpoint** for a new starting point.

8. The Autodesk Civil 3D software prompts you for the locations of the structures. Click (Station offset) in the *Transparent* Tab, as shown in Figure 9–34.

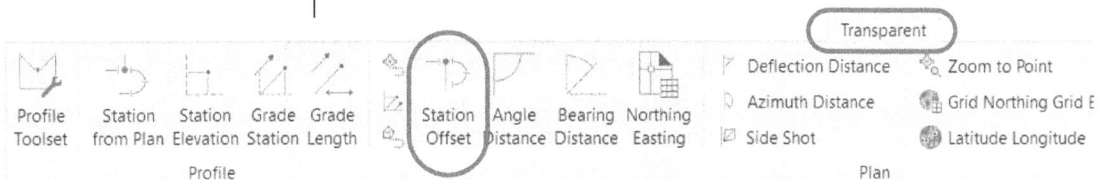

Figure 9–34

9. When prompted for an alignment, select the **Jeffries Ranch Rd** alignment (select an alignment label if it is difficult to select the alignment centerline). Type **1100'** for the station and type **0** for the offset. Press <Esc> to exit the **Transparent command** while remaining in the **Pipe Layout** command. Refer to Figure 9–29 at the start of this exercise.

10. Use the **end point** Osnap to select **pt2** for the next structure, as shown in Figure 9–29.

11. When prompted for the next structure, select **Curve** in the command options to draw a curved pipe. When prompted for the end of curve, select the manhole structure at the intersection of Jeffries Ranch Rd and Ascent Pl, as shown in Figure 9–35.

A symbol should display indicating that you are tying into a manhole. In Figure 9–35, the symbol is red; on your screen, it will be yellow.

Figure 9–35

You now want to use a different pipe size.

12. In the Network Layout Tools - STORM toolbar, expand the drop-down list and select **18.0 inch PVC Pipe**, as shown in Figure 9–36.

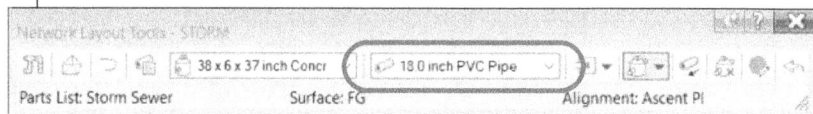

Figure 9–36

13. At the prompt for the end of curve, type **L** and press <Enter> to draw a line. When prompted to select the next structure location, click (Station offset). When prompted for an alignment, select the **Jeffries Ranch Rd** alignment (select an alignment label if it is difficult to select the alignment centerline). Type **324'** for the station, and type **0** for the offset. Press <Esc> to exit the command and press <Enter> to exit the prompt for the insertion point of a structure.

You have made a design change and decided to insert a manhole east of the original intended location, as shown in Figure 9–37. This requires you to make further adjustments to the network later in this chapter.

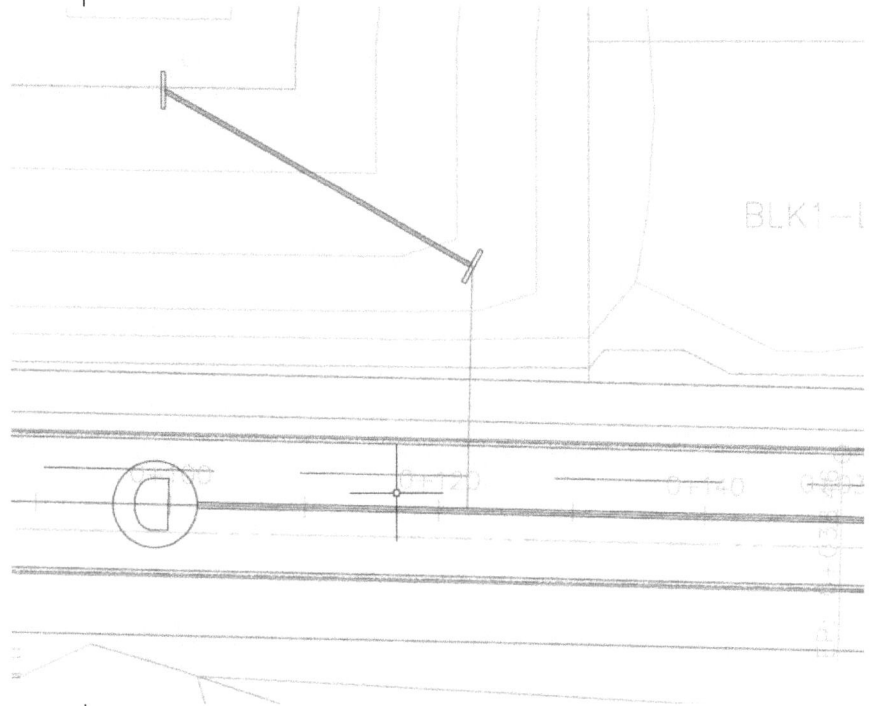

Figure 9–37

14. Close the Network Layout Tools toolbar by clicking the **X**.

15. Save the drawing.

Task 2 - View Pipe network in profile view.

1. Open **PIP1-B2-PipeWorks.dwg** from the *C:\Civil 3D Projects\Working\PipeNetworks* folder.

2. Draw a window from left to right around the pipes to select the last three pipes and four structures that you created in the last task, as shown in Figure 9–38. If the *Pipe Networks* contextual tab does not appear, then hit <Esc> to clear the selection set, then pick the three pipes and four structures individually.

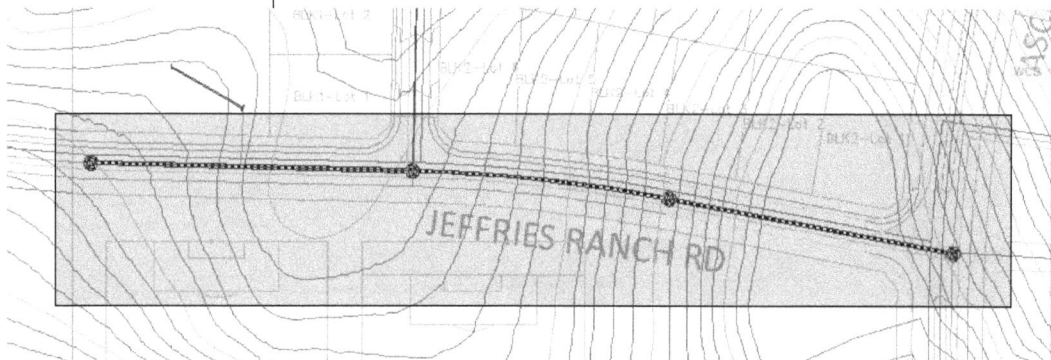

Figure 9–38

3. In the *Pipe Networks* contextual tab>Network Tools panel, click (Draw Parts in Profile).

4. When prompted to select the Profile view, select the Jeffries Ranch Road profile view to the right of the site plan. Press <Esc> to release the selected pipe network parts.

5. Because you only selected certain network parts to be added to the profile, you will now review the parts that are relevant to this profile view. Select the Profile view and in the contextual tab>Modify Views panel, click (Profile View Properties), as shown in Figure 9–39.

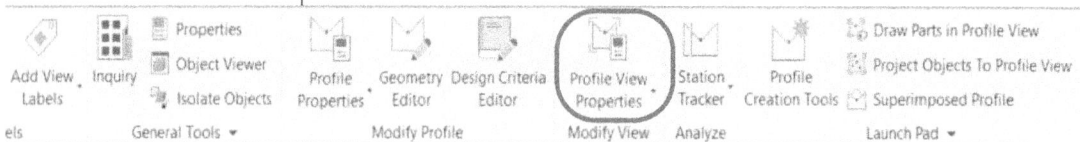

Figure 9–39

Note that your numbers might be slightly different. The key is that not all pipes and structures will be checked.

6. In the Profile View Properties - Jeffries Ranch Rd dialog box, in the *Pipe Networks* tab, ensure that only the following parts are enabled, as shown in Figure 9–40:
   - **Pipe - 5**, **6**, and **7**
   - **Structure - 4**, **7**, **8**, and **9**

Information | Stations | Elevations | Profiles | Bands | Hatch | Pipe Networks

Name	Draw		Description	Layer	Style	Style Override	
⊟ STORM							^
P-1	☐	No	12.0 inch PVC Pipe		Double Line (Stor...	☐ <Not Overridd...	
P-2	☐	No	12.0 inch PVC Pipe		Double Line (Stor...	☐ <Not Overridd...	
P-3	☐	No	12.0 inch PVC Pipe		Double Line (Stor...	☐ <Not Overridd...	
P-9	☐	No	24 inch Concrete P...		Double Line (Stor...	☐ <Not Overridd...	
P-6	☑	Yes	12.0 inch PVC Pipe	C-STRM-PROF	Double Line (Stor...	☐ <Not Overridd...	
P-7	☑	Yes	12.0 inch PVC Pipe	C-STRM-PROF	Double Line (Stor...	☐ <Not Overridd...	
P-8	☑	Yes	18.0 inch PVC Pipe	C-STRM-PROF	Double Line (Stor...	☐ <Not Overridd...	
St-9	☑	Yes	Slab Top Cylindric...	C-STRM-PROF	Storm Sewer Man...	☐ <Not Overridd...	
St-10	☑	Yes	Slab Top Cylindric...	C-STRM-PROF	Storm Sewer Man...	☐ <Not Overridd...	
St-8	☑	Yes	Slab Top Cylindric...	C-STRM-PROF	Storm Sewer Man...	☐ <Not Overridd...	
St-11	☑	Yes	48 x 48 Rect Two T...	C-STRM-PROF	Catch Basin	☐ <Not Overridd...	
St-1	☐	No	Slab Top Cylindric...		Storm Sewer Man...	☐ <Not Overridd...	
St-3	☐	No	Slab Top Cylindric...		Storm Sewer Man...	☐ <Not Overridd...	
St-2	☐	No	Slab Top Cylindric...		Storm Sewer Man...	☐ <Not Overridd...	∨

Figure 9–40

7. Click **OK** to close the dialog box and apply the changes.

8. Save the drawing.

9.3 Annotating Pipe Networks

As with other Autodesk Civil 3D labels, pipe network plan and profile labels are all style-based. A pipe label style can contain an extensive list of pipe network properties. The labels are scale- and rotation-sensitive and use the same interface for creating or modifying styles.

- The Autodesk Civil 3D software can label pipes and structures as you draft them or later as required.

- In the *Annotate* tab>Add Labels panel, expand **Pipe Network** and select **Add Pipe Network Labels...** or expand **Add Pressure Network** and select **Add Pressure Network Labels** to label individual objects or an entire network. The Add Labels dialog box is shown in Figure 9–41.

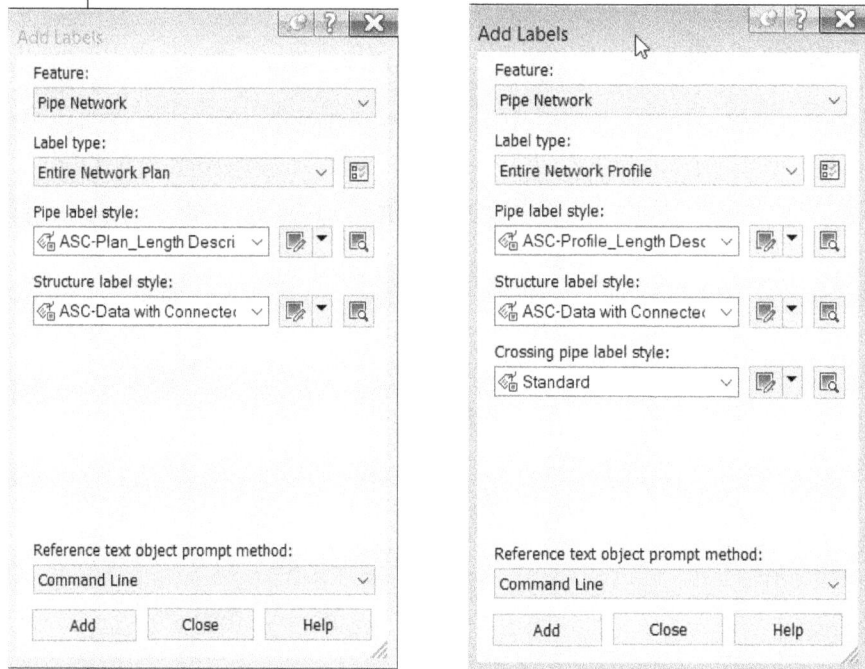

Figure 9–41

Most pipe labels annotate the length and slope of a specific pipe. If you have pipe bends and would rather not label each individual segment as a separate pipe, select the **Spanning** label type. It enables you to select multiple pipes that should be given a single label, which can include overall length, slope, and other properties.

Parts in a network can be renumbered quickly and easily by selecting **Modify>Pipe Network>Modify (panel)>Rename Parts**. Another method is to renumber each one manually using the Pipe Network Vistas view, which can be accessed in the Network Layout Tools toolbar, as shown in Figure 9–42. Labels automatically display the new part label.

Figure 9–42

Pipe Networks in Sections

To display pipe networks in sections, they need to be included as a data source for the sections' sample line group. If a sample line group has been created before a pipe network, they are not automatically included. To include them, open the sample line group's Properties dialog box, select the *Sections* tab, and click **Sample more sources...**, as shown in Figure 9–43.

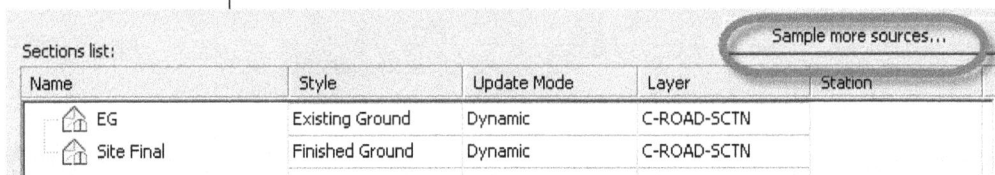

Figure 9–43

Pipe Network Reports and Tables

Pipe reports are available in the Toolspace, *Toolbox* tab (**Home>Palettes>Toolbox**), as shown in Figure 9–44.

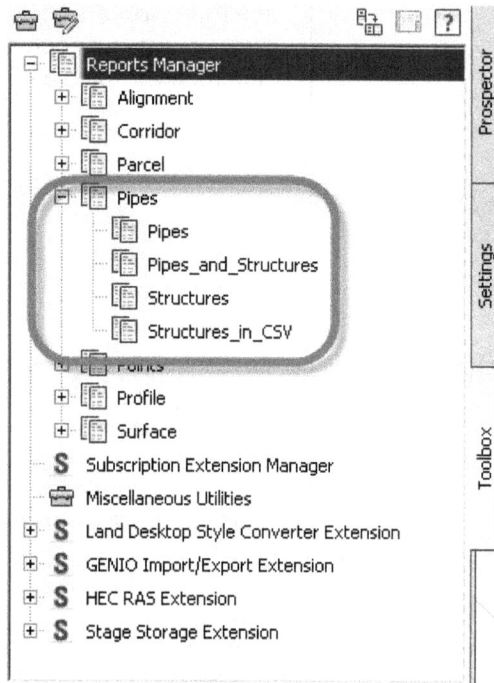

Figure 9–44

Pipe tables can be created inside drawing files using **Annotate> Add Tables>Pipe Network>Add Structure and Annotate> Add Tables>Pipe Network>Add Pipe**.

Practice 9c

Annotating Pipe Networks

Practice Objective

- Communicate important design information about pipe networks by adding labels to plan and profile views and creating reports.

Task 1 - Annotate pipe networks.

1. Open **PIP1-D1-PipeWorks.dwg** from the *C:\Civil 3D Projects\Working\PipeNetworks* folder.

2. Select the preset view **Pipe-Create**.

3. In the *Annotate* tab>Labels & Tables panel, select **Add Labels**, as shown in Figure 9–45.

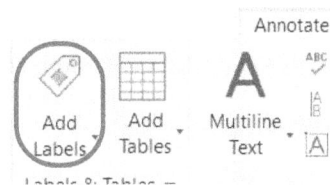

Figure 9–45

4. In the Add Labels dialog box, set the following parameters, as shown in Figure 9–46:

- *Feature:* **Pipe Network**
- *Label type:* **Entire Network Plan**
- *Pipe label style:* **ASC-Plan_Length Description and Slope**
- *Structure label style:* **ASC-Data with Connected Pipes (Storm)**

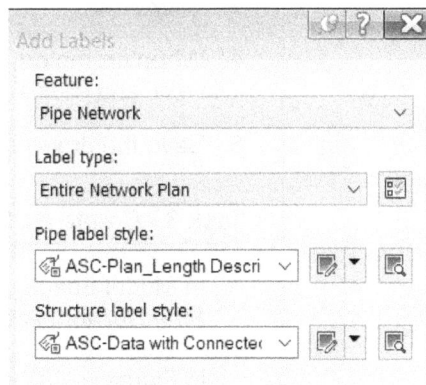

Figure 9–46

5. Click **Add**. When prompted, select any part in the **Storm network**.

6. Click **X** or click **Close** to close the Add labels dialog box.

7. Save the drawing.

Task 2 - Add labels to parts in the profile view.

1. In the *Annotate* tab>Labels & Tables panel, select **Add Labels**.

2. In the Add Labels dialog box, set the following parameters, as shown in Figure 9–47:

   - *Feature:* **Pipe Network**
   - *Label type:* **Entire Network Profile**
   - *Pipe label style:* **ASC-Profile_Length Description and Slope**
   - *Structure label style:* **ASC-Data with Connected Pipes (Storm)**

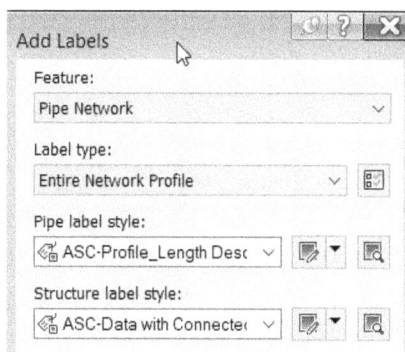

Figure 9–47

3. Click **Add**.

4. When prompted, select any of the network parts in the profile view, and click **X** to close the dialog box.

5. Save the drawing.

Task 3 - Create a Structure table.

1. In Model Space, select any Storm Pipe network part. In the *Pipe Networks* contextual tab>Labels & Tables panel (shown in Figure 9–48), expand ▦ (Add Tables) and select **Add Structure**.

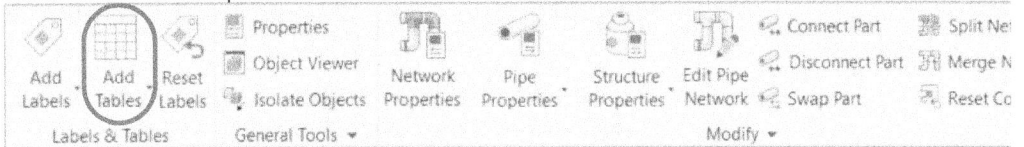

Figure 9–48

2. In the Structure Table Creation dialog box, for *Table style*, select **Structure with Pipes**. Select **Dynamic** and accept all of the other defaults. Click **OK** to close the dialog box, as shown in Figure 9–49.

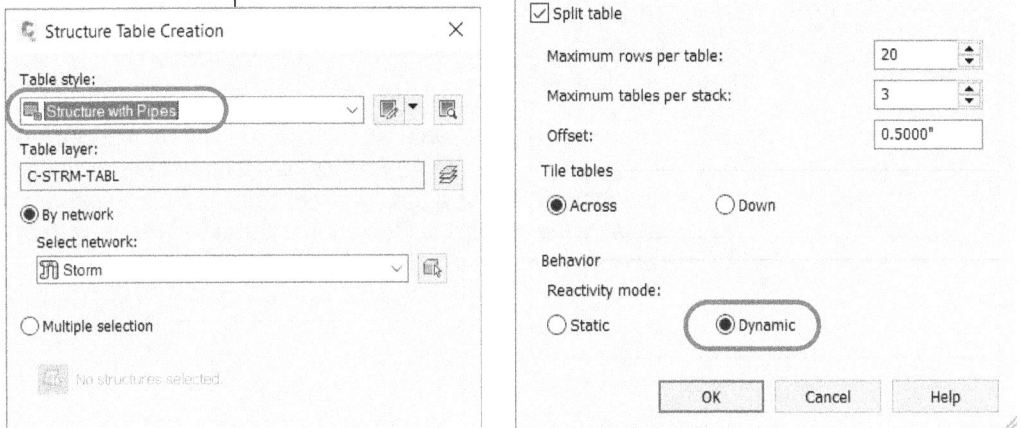

Figure 9–49

3. Zoom to an open space and insert the table, as shown in Figure 9–50.

Figure 9–50

4. Save the drawing.

9.4 Pressure Pipe Networks

Pressure Pipe Networks are used for designing and laying out pressurized systems, such as water networks. There are three types of pressure pipe network objects: Pipes, Fittings, and Appurtenances. You can create Pressure Pipes from existing objects (e.g., lines, arcs, 2D/3D polylines, splines, feature lines, alignments, survey figures, etc.), or by layout.

Pressure Pipes

To start the Pressure Pipe Layout command, in the *Home* tab> Create Design panel, expand **Pipe Networks** and click

(Pressure Network Creation Tools). This opens the Create Pressure Pipe Network dialog box, as shown in Figure 9–51. In it, you can type a name and description, set the parts list to use, and the surface and alignment to reference. You can also set label styles for pipes, fittings, and appurtenances so that they receive labels as you layout the pressure network.

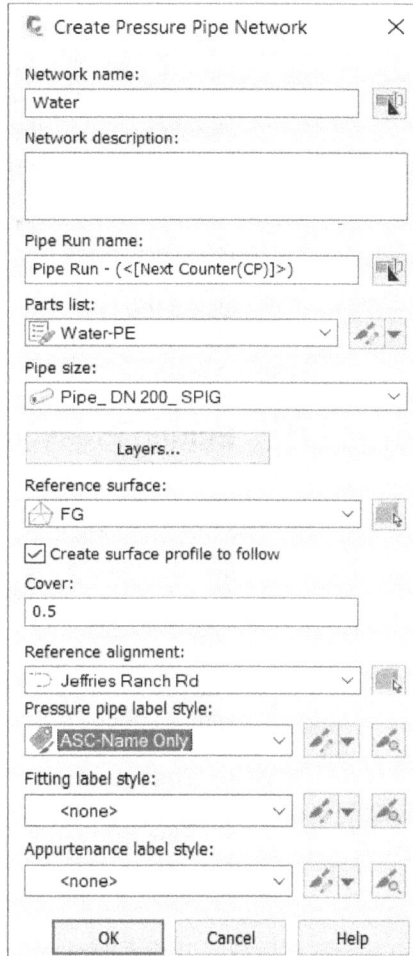

Figure 9–51

Once in the command, the *Pressure Network Plan Layout* contextual tab displays, as shown in Figure 9–52.

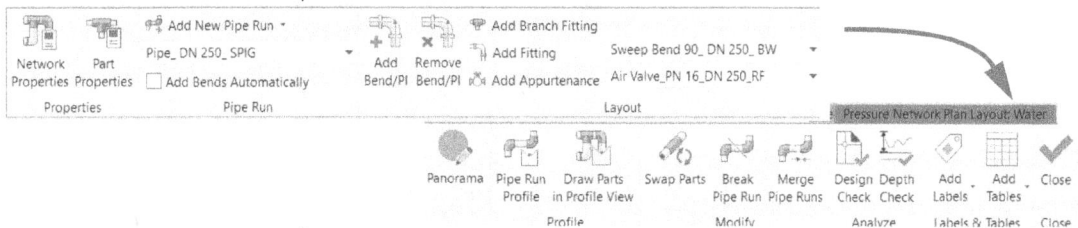

Figure 9–52

The reference surface and alignment that were set up during creation display in the Network Settings panel along with the current parts list. The Cover setting is also found in the Network settings panel and specifies the minimum depth the network should be below the selected surface. Ideally, you would select a finished ground surface. In the Layout panel, you can select the pipe material to use.

Pressure pipes can be laid out by themselves or with bends

Using the ☐ Add Bends Automatically (Add Bends Automatically) checkbox, in the *Layout* tab automatically places fittings that are included in the Pressure Networks parts lists.

Editing Pressure Networks

When selecting a part of a pressure pipe network *with a single click*, you select the underlying control alignment, which has the same name as the pipe run. The same the *Pressure Network Plan Layout* contextual tab displays (as shown previously in Figure 9–52).

The glyphs that appear are similar to the alignment glyphs, along with a special one as shown in Figure 9–53:

- Triangular Grip: Extending the pipe.

- Plus sign Grip: adding to the pipe run.

- Square Grip: move the pipe parallel to itself.

- Triangular Up Grip: move the PVI

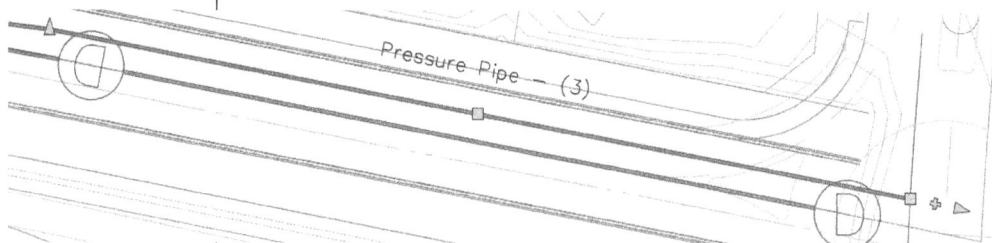

Figure 9–53

The first pick selects the alignment of the pipe run, the second click selects the pipe part.

Fittings

Fittings enable you to specify the T's and other bends to layout a pressurized utility network. Additional fittings can be added to the Autodesk Civil 3D software using the parts catalog. To add additional fittings to a network in the drawing click 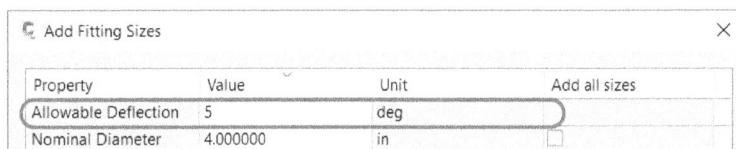 (Add Fitting) in the *Pressure Network Plan Layout* tab>Insert panel.

When configuring the fittings, you can specify the *allowable deflection* in degrees, as shown in Figure 9–54. This can be thought of as "wiggle room" within the fixture and is different for each material.

Property	Value		Unit	Add all sizes
Allowable Deflection	5		deg	
Nominal Diameter	4.000000		in	

Add Fitting Sizes

Figure 9–54

Included in the Pressure Pipes catalogs are the following fittings:

- Elbows (90, 60, 45, and 30 degrees)

- Tees

- Reducers

- Couplings

- Caps

The glyphs that appear when selecting the fitting (by clicking on it twice) are as follows, as shown in Figure 9–55:

- Arrow Grip: flip or mirror the fitting.

- Diamond Grip: move the fitting along the pipe.

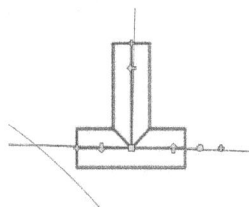

Figure 9–55

Branch Fittings

When pipes of different pipe runs intersect, there is a Branch Fitting tool (🖜) to connect them. If the appropriate fitting (such as a Tee fitting) is found within the parts list, it will connect the pipes appropriately. If there is no proper part in the parts list, Civil 3D will get as close as it can with the parts available.

Appurtenances

Appurtenances are valves, which can be added in the same manner as fittings. Click 🖜 (Add Appurtenance) in the *Pressure Network Plan Layout* tab>Insert panel.

Included in the Pressure Pipes catalogs are the following appurtenances:

- Gate Valves

- Butterfly Valves

- Air Valves

- Hydrants (above and below ground)

- Shut Off Valves

- Check Valves

- Globe Valves

Pressure Pipe Styles

In the fitting and appurtenance styles, you can choose to display the parts as boundaries, catalog-defined blocks, or user-defined blocks. For parts drawn in profile views, you can add masks to hide underlying geometry, you can add hatching to the parts, and you can crop the pipes at the extent of the profile view.

Pipe Runs

Pressure pipe networks are divided into Pipe Runs, which are branches to the overall network. Pipe runs can be added to profile views. Pipe runs are listed in the Prospector within the pressure pipe network.

You can create pipe runs using the following methods, as shown in Figure 9–56:

- By picking points designating the ends of the pipes.
- Selecting objects (lines, plines) to convert to a pipe run.
- Selecting existing pressure pipe parts.

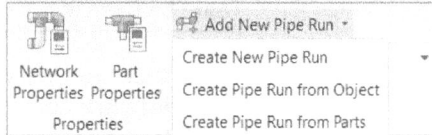

Figure 9–56

Swap Pressure Parts

Similar to gravity fed pipe networks, pressure pipe networks have the option to exchange one part for another, but in a different type, part family, or size. To start the command, select the part, right-click, and select **Swap Pressure Part.** The Swap Pressure Network Parts dialog box displays as shown in Figure 9–57.

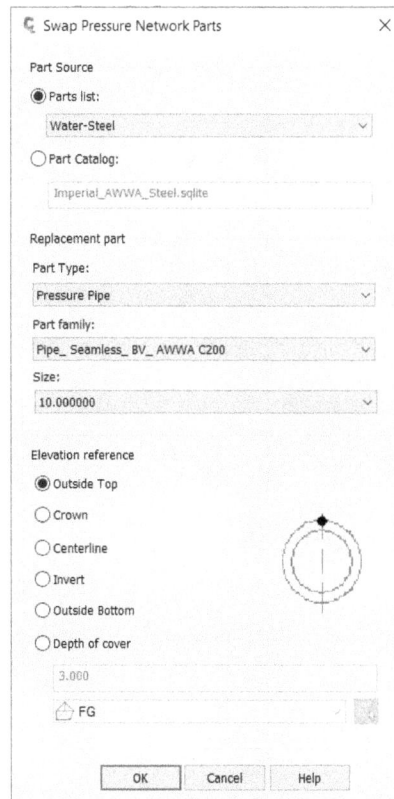

Figure 9–57

Practice 9d

Create a Pressure Pipe Network

Practice Objective

- Create and edit a pressure pipe network.

Task 1 - Create a pressure pipe network.

In this task, you will create a water network using the **Pressure Pipe Network** commands.

1. Open **PIP1-E1-PipeWorks.dwg** from the *C:\Civil 3D Projects\Working\PipeNetworks* folder.

2. Ensure that your Pressure Pipe Catalog is set correctly to **Imperial_AWWA_Steel.sqlite.** You do this by going to the Create Design panel drop down in the Home tab to set the Pressure Pipe Catalog, as shown in Figure 9–58.

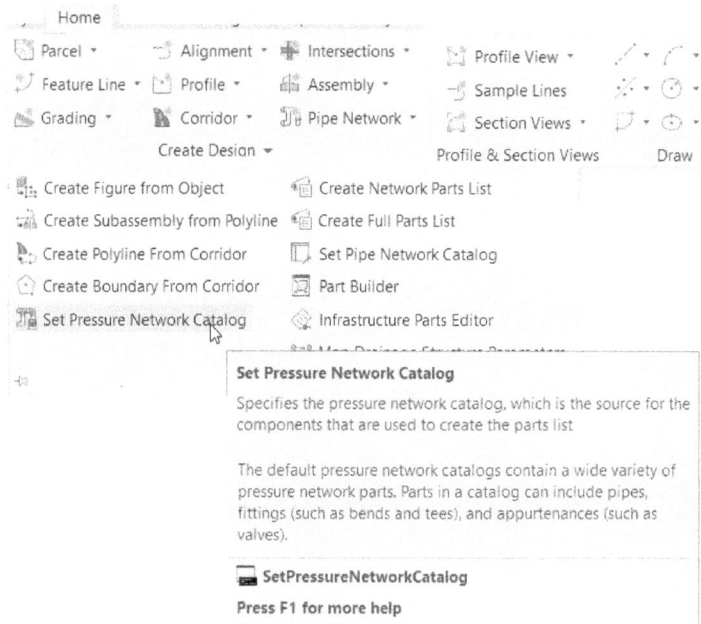

Figure 9–58

3. In the *Set Pressure Network Catalog* dialog box, select
   Imperial_AWWA_Steel.sqlite, as shown in Figure 9–59.

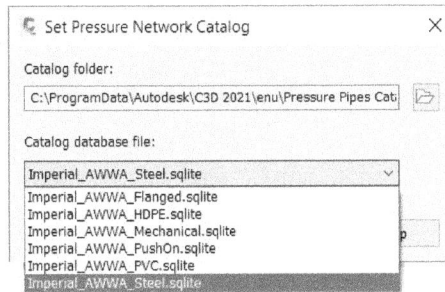

Figure 9–59

4. If **Imperial_AWWA_Steel.sqlite** does not appear in the list,
   change the path to *C:\ProgramData\Autodesk\C3D
   2021\enu\Pressure Pipes Catalog\Imperial* by clicking on the

   (Browse...) icon.

5. Select the preset view **Pipe-Create**.

6. In the *Home* tab>Layers panel, click (Layer Freeze).
   Select any Storm Sewer pipe network label (layer:
   C-STRM-TEXT) and any alignment label (layer:
   C-ROAD-TEXT), then press <Enter> to end the command.

7. The proposed water line has been sketched on the
   Base-Proposed-Engineering Xref drawing as a blue dashed
   line just north of the storm sewer along Jeffries Ranch Rd. A
   branch of proposed water line extend up Ascent Place, to the
   east of the road's center line.

8. In the *Home* tab>Create Design panel, expand **Pipe Network**

   and click (Pressure Network Creation Tools).

9. In the Create Pressure Pipe Network dialog box, set the following, as shown in Figure 9–60:

    *   *Network Name*: **Water**
    *   *Pipe Run Name*: **Jeffries Ranch Rd**
    *   *Parts List:* (use drop-down list) **Water-Steel**
    *   *Pipe Size*: Leave as is (you'll change it later)
    *   *Reference surface:* (use drop-down list) **FG**
    *   *Cover*: **3.00'**
    *   *Reference alignment:* (use drop-down list) **Jeffries Ranch Rd**
    *   *Pressure pipe label style*: (use drop-down list) **ASC-Name Only**

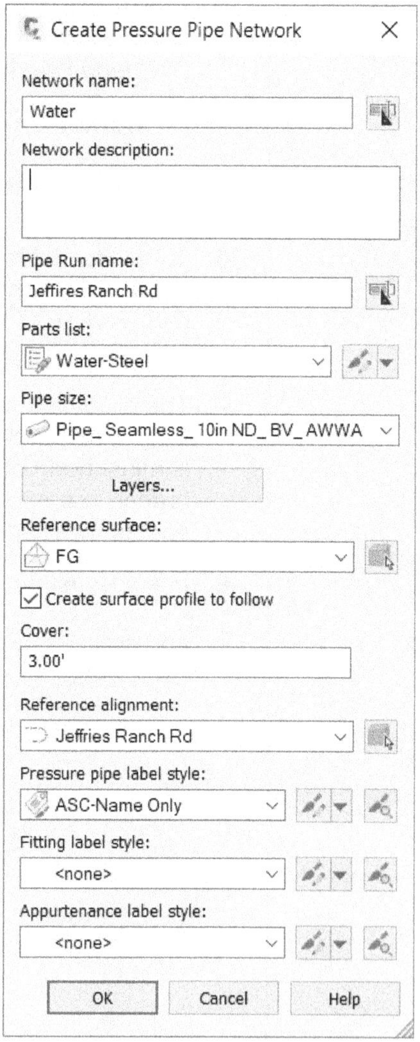

Figure 9–60

10. Click **OK** to accept the selection and close the dialog box.

11. In the *Pressure Network Plan Layout* contextual tab>Pipe Run panel, set the pipe size and material to **Pipe_Seamless_12in ND_BV_AWWA C200**, as shown in Figure 9–61.

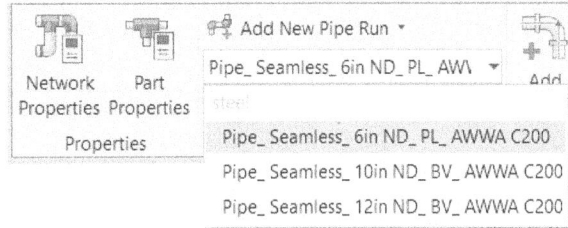

Figure 9–61

12. Ensure that **Add Bends Automatically** is checked in the *Pressure Network Plan Layout* contextual tab>Pipe Run panel

13. Using the **Endpoint** object snap to select the points along the dashed blue lines north of the storm sewer, as shown in Figure 9–62.

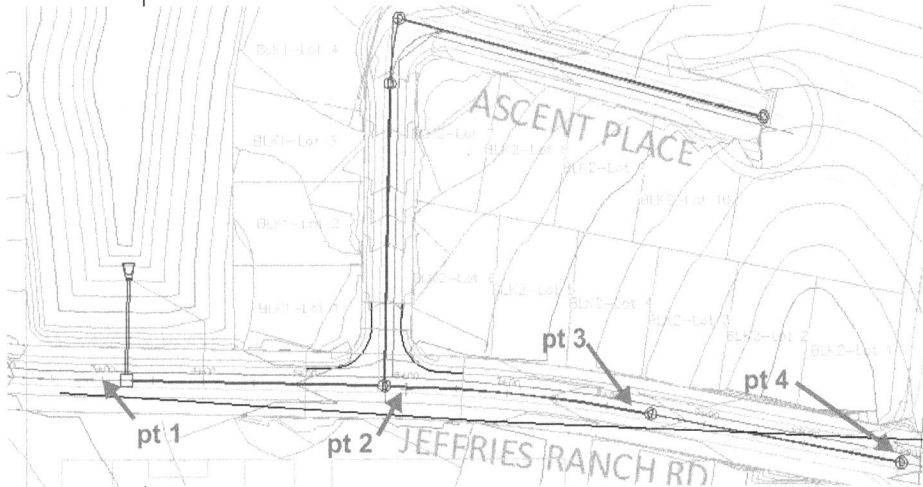

Figure 9–62

14. The second point is to the east of the Tee intersection of the blue reference lines.

15. The third point is above and slightly to the west of the storm sewer's second manhole.

16. The fourth point is at the intersection of Ascent Boulevard (not to be confused with Ascent Place!) and Jeffries Ranch Road.

17. Press <Enter> to end the command, click the green

    checkmark ( ) to close the Pressure Pipe Contextual ribbon, and save the drawing.

Task 2 - Place fittings and appurtenances and add a pipe run.

---

1. Open **PIP1-E2-PipeWorks.dwg** from the *C:\Civil 3D Projects\Working\PipeNetworks* folder.

2. Select one of the pressure pipes you created in the previous task. In the *Pressure Network Plan Layout:Water* contextual tab>Layout panel, expand the Fitting drop-down list and select **Tee (Red)_ 12inX10in ND_ PFSxFF_AWWA C208_ with Gasket SBR_ AWWA C111**, as shown in Figure 9–63.

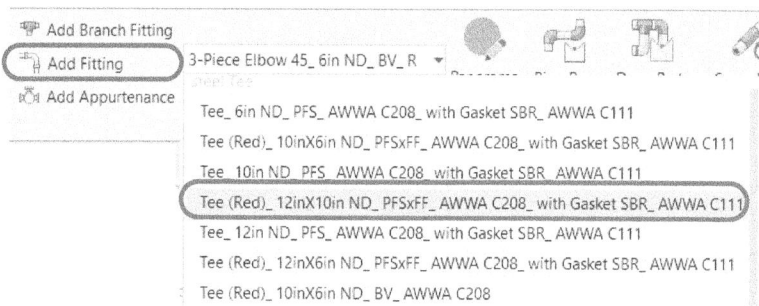

Figure 9–63

3. Click ⚙ (Add Fitting).

4. Select the point where the blue dotted lines intersect, as shown in Figure 9–64. Wait until you see the Broken Pipe glyph (⌐□ □⌐). Press <Esc> to end the command.

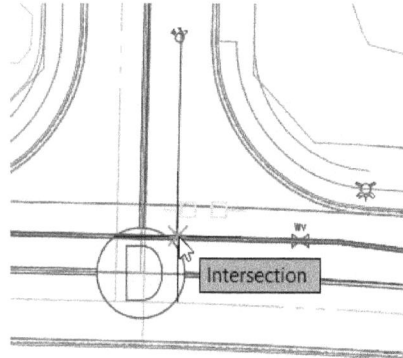

Figure 9–64

The first pick selects the alignment of the pipe run, the second click selects the pipe part.

5. If the fitting is set in the wrong rotation or location, select it by clicking it twice and pick the down arrow grip to flip the fixture.

6. After placing the fitting, note that you need to extend the pressure network along Ascent PI, as shown in Figure 9–65.

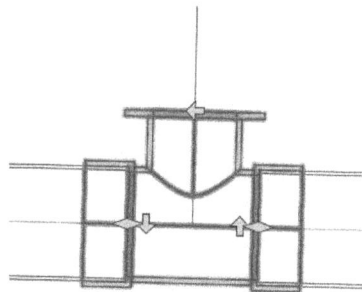

Figure 9–65

7. In the *Pressure Network Plan Layout:Water* contextual tab> Pipe Run panel, expand the Add New Pipe Run drop down and select **Create New Pipe Run** option, as shown in Figure 9–66.

Figure 9–66

8. In the Create Pipe Run dialog box, Enter **Ascent Place** for the *Pipe Run* name, ensure the *Cover* is set to **3.00'**, set the pipe size and material to **Pipe_ Seamless_ 10in ND_BV_ AWWA C200** and select **Ascent PI** as the *Reference alignment*, as shown in Figure 9–67.

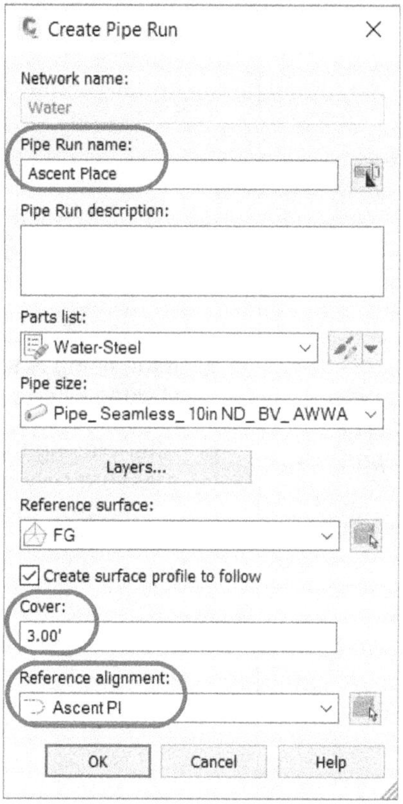

Figure 9–67

9. Select the ☐ Add Bends Automatically (Add Bends Automatically) checkbox.

10. Hover over the tee fitting that you placed until the fitting tooltip image and the Endpoint grip display, as shown in Figure 9–68. Click to accept the connection and start the new pipe.

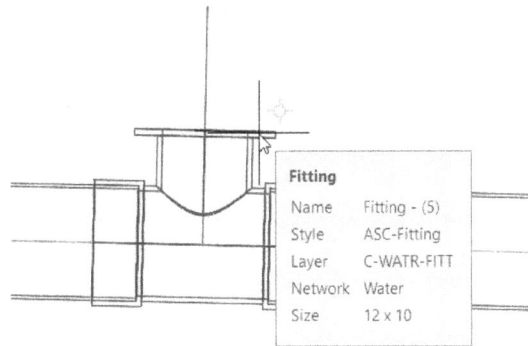

Figure 9–68

11. Use the **Endpoint** object snaps to help you select the next points, **pt2** through to **pt4**, as shown in Figure 9–69.

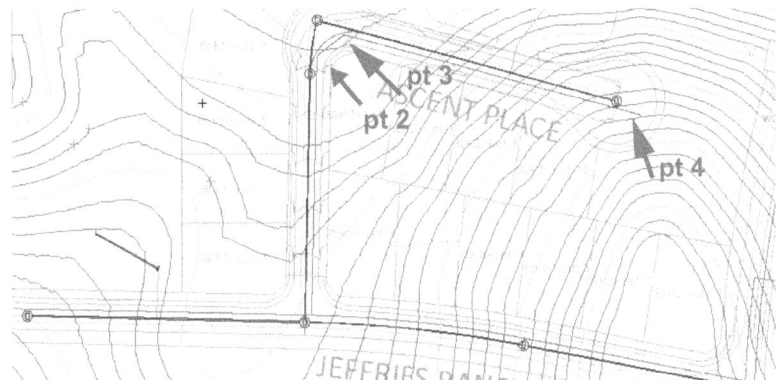

Figure 9–69

12. Select the preset view **Pipe-Intersection**.

13. In the *Pressure Network Plan Layout:Water* contextual tab> Pipe Run panel, expand the Add New Pipe Run drop down and select **Create Pipe Run from Object** option, as shown in Figure 9–70.

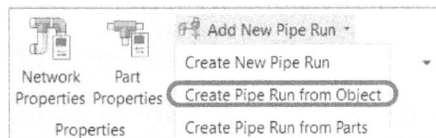

Figure 9–70

14. Type **X** to be able to pick the line that is part of the Xref.

15. Select the short blue line running between the hydrant symbol and the water main in the eastern portion of the intersection. Ensure that the direction arrow is pointing northward, if need be, type **R** to reverse the direction. See Figure 9–71.

16. In the Create Pipe Run from Objects dialog box, set the following, as shown in Figure 9–71, and then click **OK**:

Simply replace the text "Pipe Run" with "Hydrant".

- *Pipe Run name:* **Hydrant - (<[Next Counter(CP)]>)**
- *Pipe size:* **Pipe_ Seamless_ 6in ND_ BV_ AWWA C200**
- *Reference surface:* **FG**
- *Reference alignment:* **Jeffries Ranch Rd**
- *Horizontal offset distance:* **0.000**
- *Cover distance:* **3.00'**

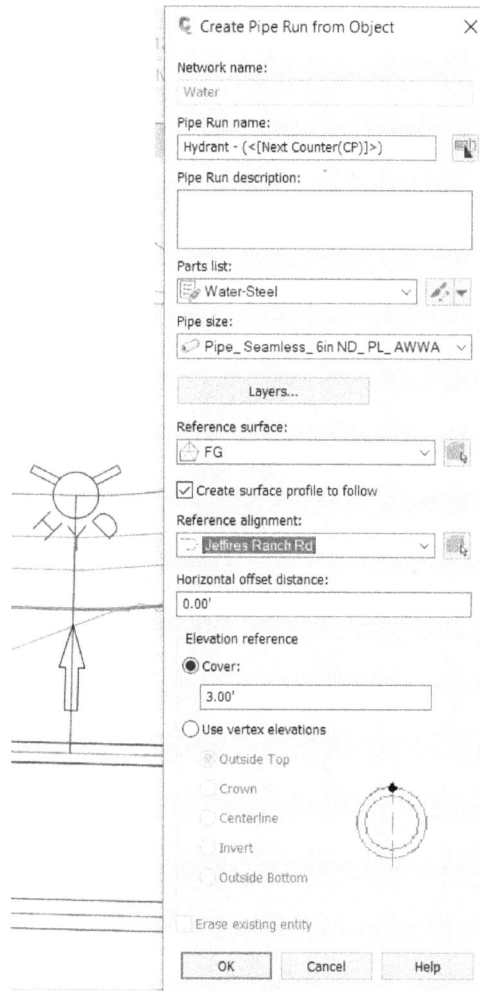

Figure 9–71

17. In the *Pressure Network Plan Layout:Water* contextual tab> Layout panel, select **Hydrant_ 42in_ Bury Depth_ MJ** from the Appurtenance drop-down list.

18. Click on 🔩 (Add Appurtenance), as shown in Figure 9–72.

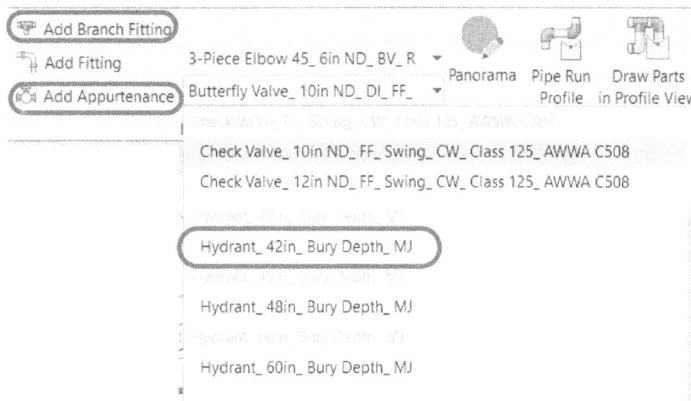

Figure 9–72

19. Select the endpoint of the water line you just created, make sure you get the special yellow glyph, and hit <Enter> to finish. Do not select the blue XREF line, but the end of the pipe.

20. In the *Pressure Network Plan Layout:Water* contextual tab> Layout panel, click on 🔧 (Add Branch Fitting).

21. For the *First pipe at intersection*, select the Jeffries Ranch Rd Waterline, for the second select the waterline running to the hydrant.

22. Save the drawing.

Task 3 - (Optional) Add more appurtenances.

---

1. (Optional) Repeat Steps 13 to 21 for the hydrant in the north-western portion of the intersection.

2. Place a gate valve near the WV (Water Valve) symbol along Jeffries Ranch Road and move as required.

3. Place a check valve near the WSO (Water Shutoff Valve) symbol along Ascent Place.

4. Turn off the **Base-Proposed Engineering|C-WATR** layer.

5. Save the drawing.

Task 4 - Draw pressure pipes in the profile view.

Continue working with the drawing from the previous task or open **PIP1-E3-PipeWorks.dwg**

1. Select the water line running along Jeffries Ranch Rd. *Pressure Network Plan Layout:Water* contextual tab>Profile panel, click (Pipe Run Profile).

2. In the Pipe Run Profile Settings dialog box, set the following, as shown in Figure 9–73:
   - *Offset to:* **Profile**
   - *Offset Distance:* **3.00'**
   - *Draw Profile in:* **Existing Profile View**

Figure 9–73

3. Click **OK**.

4. When prompted, select the **Jeffries Ranch Rd** profile view.

5. Repeat the same procedure for the Ascent Place pipe run.

6. Save the drawing.

Plan Production and Data Management

Styles

Exam Objectives Covered in This Chapter

6.1.a Use the text component editor

6.1.b Change the dragged state of a label

6.1.c Apply a label set to an object

10.1 Styles

Styles are preconfigured groups of settings (specific to an individual object type or label) that make the objects display and print the way you want them to. For example, in the list of surface styles shown in Figure 10–1, each surface style is configured differently to display different features, such as contours at different intervals and on the correct layers. The display of a terrain model could be changed by swapping one surface style for another. Styles enable an organization to standardize the look of their graphics by providing preconfigured groupings of display settings.

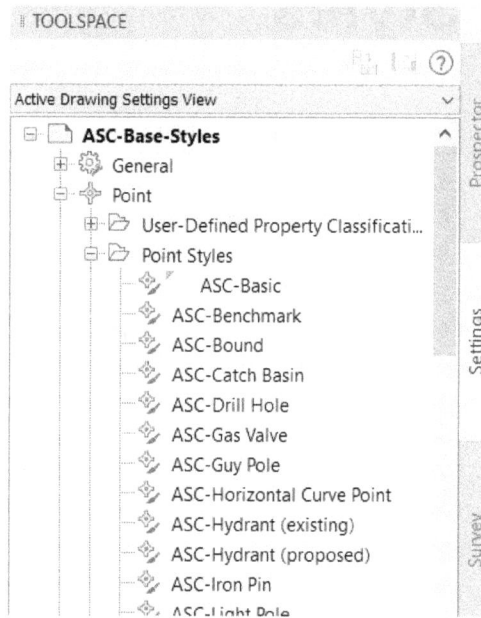

Figure 10–1

The two categories of styles you work with most often are Object Styles and Label Styles. Some objects have table styles as well. Object styles control how Autodesk Civil 3D objects (points, surfaces, alignments, etc.) display, what combination of components the object displays, which layers they display on, and many other settings. Label Styles are similar except that they control the text and other annotations associated with the objects.

For example, an alignment object style specifies many settings including the layers on which to draw tangents and curve segments (which might be different) and the symbols to add at certain points as required (such as a triangle at the PI point). Alignment label styles include major and minor station labels, the display of station equations, design speeds, and similar annotation. By separating object and label styles, you can mix and match the right combination for a specific object.

Styles are the lowest items in the Toolspace, *Settings* tree and are typically dependent on other settings above them. If a style is given a unique setting, different from feature settings or label style defaults (such as a different text height), then that style is considered to have an override.

Label Styles

Label styles produce annotation of values from existing conditions or a design solution. A label annotates a contour's elevations, a parcel's number and area, a horizontal geometry point's station on an alignment, etc.

A label style can have text, vectors, AutoCAD blocks, and reference text. The content of a label depends on the selected object's components or properties. For instance, a Line label can annotate bearing, distance, and coordinates, and use a direction arrow. A Parcel Area label can contain a parcel's area, perimeter, address, and other pertinent values. A surface label can include a spot elevation, reference for an alignment's station and offset, or other pertinent surface information.

- To access the values of a label style, in the Toolspace, *Settings* tab, select the style, right-click on its name, and select **Edit**.

- A style's initial values come from Edit Label Style Defaults and the style's definition.

- All labels use the same interface.

- The object properties available for each label vary by object type.

Each label style uses the same tabbed dialog box. The *Information* tab describes the style as well as who defined and last modified its contents. The values of the *General* tab affect all occurrences of the label in a drawing. For example, if Visibility is set to False, all labels of this style are hidden in the drawing. Other settings affect the label's text style, initial orientation, and reaction to a rotated view.

The *Layout* tab lists all of a label's components. A label component can be text, line, block, or tick. The Component name drop-down list (shown in Figure 10–2), contains all of the defined components for the style. When selecting a component name in the drop-down list, the panel displays information about the component's anchoring, justification, format, and border.

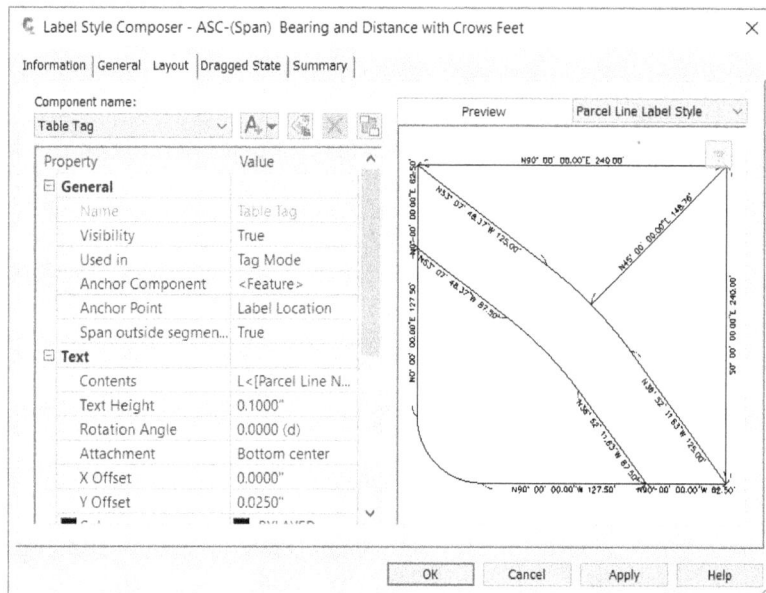

Figure 10–2

When defining a new text component, you assign it an object property by clicking ⋯ (Browse) for Contents. This opens the Text Component Editor dialog box, as shown in Figure 10–3. The Properties drop-down list displays the available object properties. The number and types of properties varies by object type. For example, a parcel area label has more and different properties than a line label does. Once a property has been selected, units, precision, and other settings can be set to display the property correctly in the label. Click ⇨ next to Properties to place the property in the label layout area to the right.

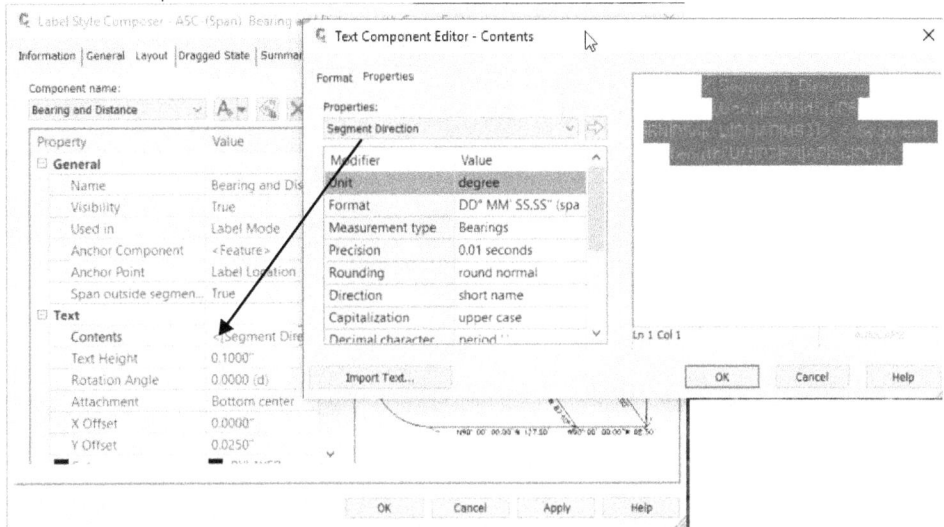

Figure 10–3

The values in the *Dragged State* tab define a label's behavior when it is dragged to a new location in the drawing.

The key to having the label display correctly when it is not in the dragged state, is to line up the Anchor Point of the component with the **Attachment** option for the text. Each has nine options from which to select. The options are shown in Figure 10–4.

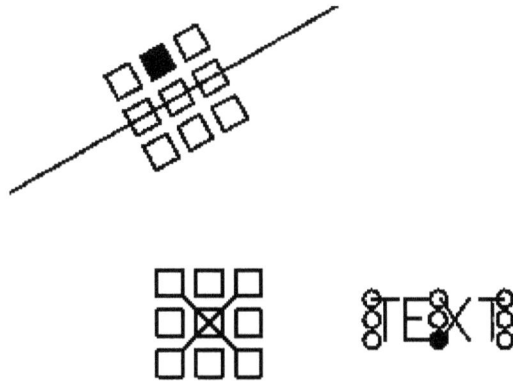

Figure 10–4

Lining up the square hatched Anchor Point with the circular hatched attachment option results in the text centered above the object similar to the bearing distance label shown in Figure 10–5.

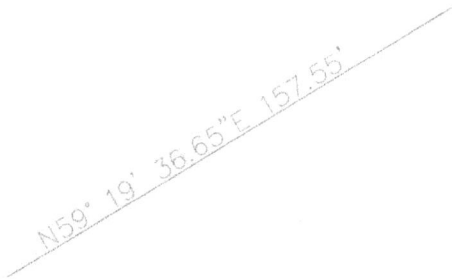

N59° 19' 36.65"E 157.55'

Figure 10–5

Practice 10a

Point Marker Styles

Practice Objective

- Create a point marker and label style to ensure that the correct symbol is assigned to specific points.

In this practice, you will create a new point style and apply it to an existing group of points.

Task 1 - Add a Block Symbol.

1. Open **SUV1-B1-Survey-.dwg** from the *C:\Civil 3D Projects\Working\Survey* folder.

2. To toggle off the aerial image, in the *Home* tab>Palettes panel, click ⬒ (Map Task Pane). When prompted, select **ON**.

The aerial image used in this chapter was attached using the AutoCAD® Map 3D FDO connection.

3. In the Task pane>*Display Manager* tab, clear the **Main Site Imperial** layer, as shown in Figure 10–6. Select *Map Base* again to clear the *Raster Layer* contextual tab. Close the map Task Pane.

Figure 10–6

4. In the Toolspace, *Settings* tab, expand the *Point* collection until *Point Styles* displays. Expand the *Point Styles* collection.

Review the Point Styles list and note that there is no light pole style.

5. In the *Point Styles* list, select the **ASC-Guy pole** style, right-click, and select **Copy…**.

6. In the *Information* tab, change the point style's name to **ASC-Light Pole.**

7. Select the *Marker* tab. Select the **Use AutoCAD BLOCK symbol for marker** option. In the block list, scroll across as required and select the AutoCAD block **ST-Light**, as shown in Figure 10–7.

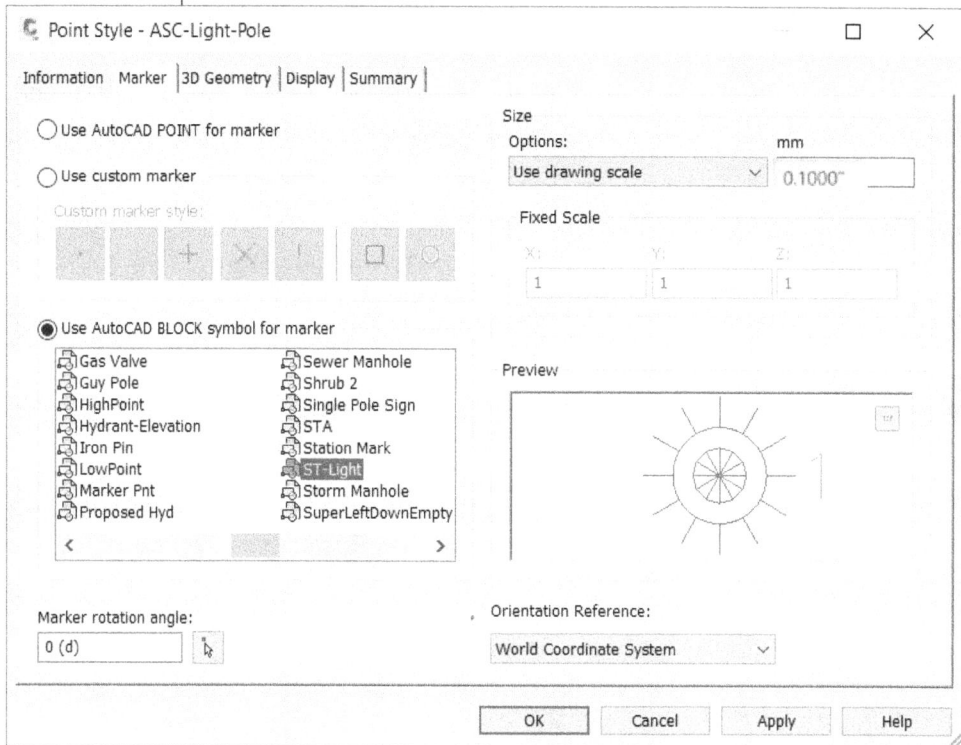

Figure 10–7

8. Select the *Display* tab and note that the layer settings are from the Guy Pole point style.

9. You can reassign the marker and/or label layer by selecting the layer name. Select the layer name to display the drawing layer list.

10. Click **New** in the top right corner of the Layer Selection dialog box. The Create Layer dialog box opens (as shown in Figure 10–8), enabling you to create new layers without having to use the Layer Manager.

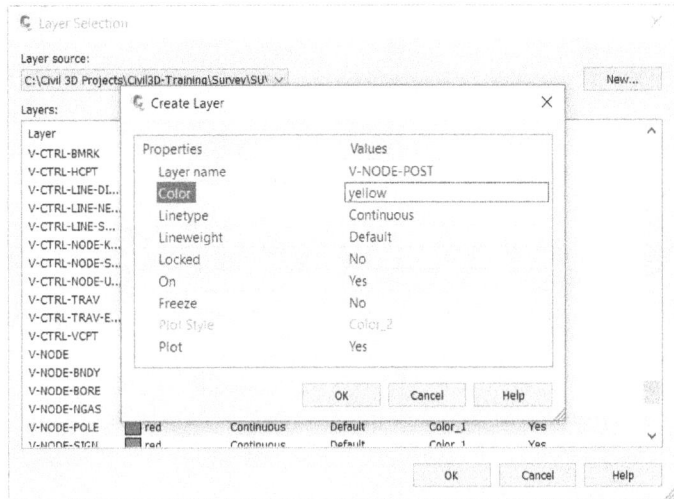

Figure 10–8

11. For the *Layer name*, type **V-NODE-POST**, and then set the *Color* to **yellow**, as shown in Figure 10–8. Click **OK** to exit the Create Layer dialog box. Click **OK** to exit the Layer Selection dialog box.

12. Click **OK** to create the point style.

13. Review the *Point Styles* list and note that **Light Pole** is now a point style, as shown in Figure 10–9.

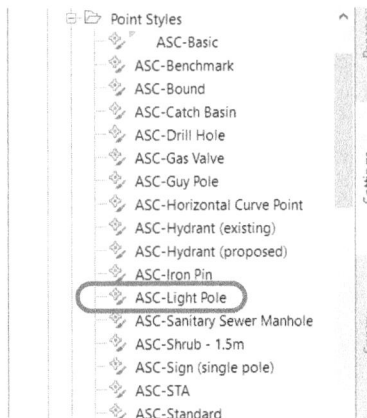

Figure 10–9

14. Save the drawing.

Task 2 - Create a Point Label Style's Components.

1. Open **SUV1-B2-Survey.dwg** from the *C:\Civil 3D Projects\ Working\Survey* folder.

2. In the Toolspace, *Settings* tab, expand the *Point* collection until the *Point Label Styles* list displays.

3. From the list of point label styles, select **ASC-Point#-Elevation-Description**, right-click, and select **Copy**.

4. In the *Information* tab, change the name to **ASC-Point#-Description-N-E**.

5. Select the *Layout* tab and do the following (shown in Figure 10–10):

   - Select **Point Number** in the *Component name* drop-down list.
   - Set the *Anchor Component* to **<Feature>**.
   - Set the *Anchor Point* to **Top Right**.
   - Set the *Attachment* to **Bottom left**.

These settings attach the bottom left of the label to the top right of the point object.

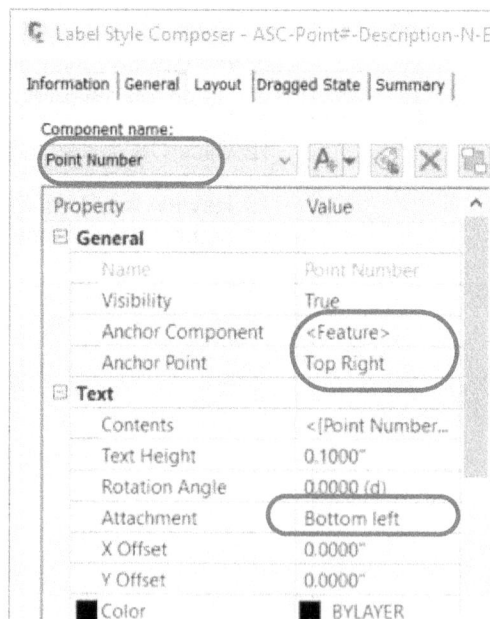

Figure 10–10

Since the elevation label is not required, you can delete it.

6. Select **Point Elev** in the Component name drop-down list and click ✕, as shown in Figure 10–11. At the *Do you want to delete it?* prompt, click **Yes**.

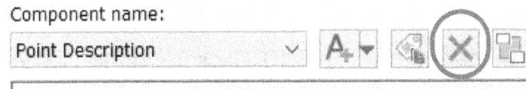

Component name:

Point Description

Figure 10–11

7. Select **Point Description** in the Component name drop-down list and do the following (shown in Figure 10–12):
   - Set the *Anchor Component* to **Point Number**.
   - Set the *Anchor Point* to **Bottom Left**.
   - Set the *Attachment* to **Top Left**.

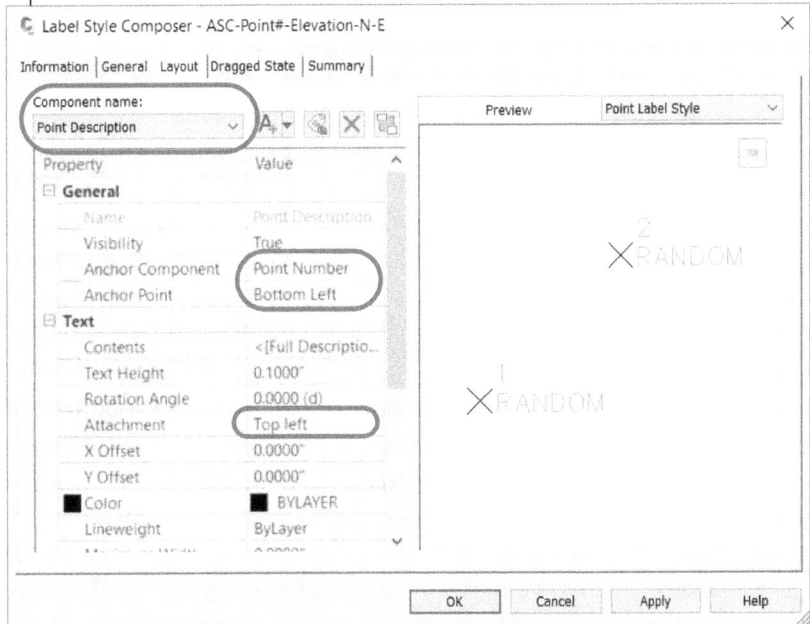

Label Style Composer - ASC-Point#-Elevation-N-E

Information | General | Layout | Dragged State | Summary

Component name:

Point Description

Preview   Point Label Style

Property	Value
General	
Name	Point Description
Visibility	True
Anchor Component	Point Number
Anchor Point	Bottom Left
Text	
Contents	<[Full Descriptio...
Text Height	0.1000"
Rotation Angle	0.0000 (d)
Attachment	Top left
X Offset	0.0000"
Y Offset	0.0000"
Color	BYLAYER
Lineweight	ByLayer

OK   Cancel   Apply   Help

Figure 10–12

You will now add a new text component to display the Northing and Easting.

8. Expand the **Create Text Component** flyout (shown in Figure 10–13) and select **Text** to create a text component.

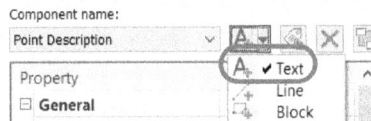

Component name:

Point Description

Property	
General	✔ Text
	Line
	Block

Figure 10–13

9. Change the default *Name* **text.1** to **Coordinates**, and then do the following:

    • Set the *Anchor Component* to **Point Description**.
    • Set the *Anchor Point* to **Bottom Left**.
    • Set the *Attachment* to **Top Left**.

You will now change the contents from the default label set by the Autodesk Civil 3D software to display the coordinates.

10. Click ⋯ in the *Contents* cell, next to *Label Text*, as shown in Figure 10–14.

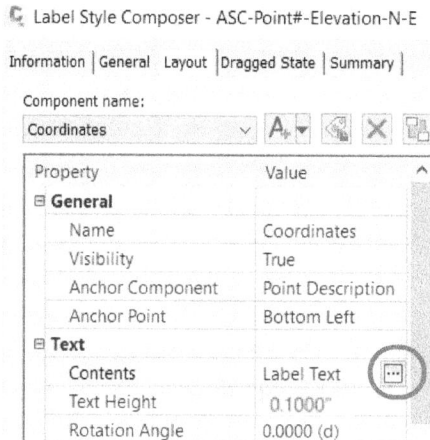

Figure 10–14

11. In the Text Component Editor dialog box, double-click on the text in the right side panel to highlight it and type **N:**.

12. Select **Northing** in the Properties drop-down list. Change the *Precision* to **0.001** and click ⇨, as shown in Figure 10–15, to add the code to display the northing.

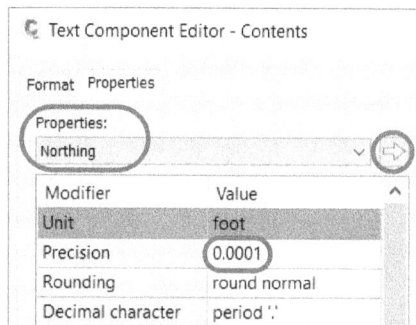

Figure 10–15

13. Click at the end of the code. Press **<Enter>** to insert a new line followed by the letter **E** and a colon. Then select **Easting** in the Properties drop-down list and add it to post the code in the right side panel. The following should be displayed:
    - N:<[Northing(Uft|P3|RN|AP|GC|UN|Sn|OF)]>
    - E:<[Easting(Uft|P4|RN|AP|GC|UN|Sn|OF)]>

In the easting, the value will be displayed to the 4th decimal, P4.
Change it so that it matches the northing.

14. Select all of the code for the easting. Change the *Precision* to **0.001** and click ⊡ to revise the easting code.

15. Select the *Format* tab and verify that *Justification* is set to **Left**. Click **OK** to accept the changes in the Text Component Editor dialog box, and click **OK** again to accept the changes in the Label Style Composer.

16. Save the drawing.

Task 3 - Apply Style Components.

---

1. Open **SUV1-B3-Survey.dwg** from the *C:\Civil 3D Projects\ Working\Survey* folder.

2. In the Toolspace, select the Toolspace, *Prospector* tab and expand the *Point Groups* collection until the *Street Light* point group displays. Select the **Street Light** group, right-click, and select **Properties**.

3. In the *Information* tab, expand the Point Style drop-down list and select **ASC-Light Pole**. Then expand the Point label style drop-down list and select **ASC-Point#-Description-N-E**, as shown in Figure 10–16.

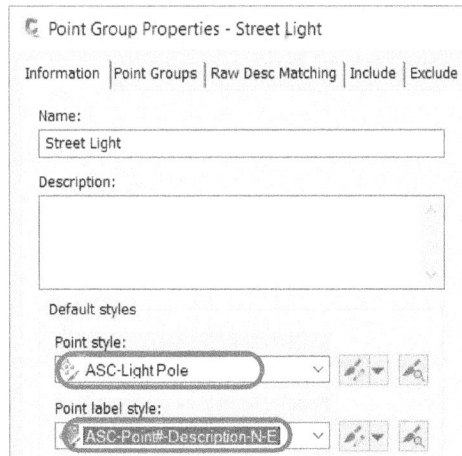

Figure 10–16

---

4. Click **OK** to accept the changes and close the dialog box.

*If the symbol and label do not change, in the Toolspace, Prospector tab, right-click on the Street Light point group and select **Update**.*

5. The symbols for the Light pole points have now been changed. Additionally, both the point symbols and point labels are annotative. In the Status Bar, expand the Annotation Scale drop-down list and change the scale of the drawing from *1"=80'* to **1"=40'**, as shown in Figure 10–17. The size of the labels and point symbols change.

Figure 10–17

6. Save the drawing.

Chapter 11

Plan Production

Exam Objectives Covered in This Chapter

6.2.a Create view frames

6.2.b Insert match lines on the view frames

6.2.c Create sheets from a view frame group

11.1 Plan Production Objects

The first step in using the Plan Production tools is to assemble all of the relevant data. This process is the same, whether you use the Autodesk Civil 3D Plan Production tools or not. Some of the steps you might use in assembling base plans and design models involve external referencing of pertinent data into your drawing to give the plan geographic reference (i.e., ROW lines, contours, survey data, aerial photographs, etc.). Autodesk Civil 3D design objects may also be data-referenced into these base plans and design models.

The Autodesk Civil 3D software provides a tool to help automate plan and production sheet creation: the Create View Frames wizard. It is the next step in plan production after the base plan has been created. Using this wizard, you can create View Frames, View Frame Groups, and Match Lines, all of which are plan production objects. The wizard is shown in Figure 11–1.

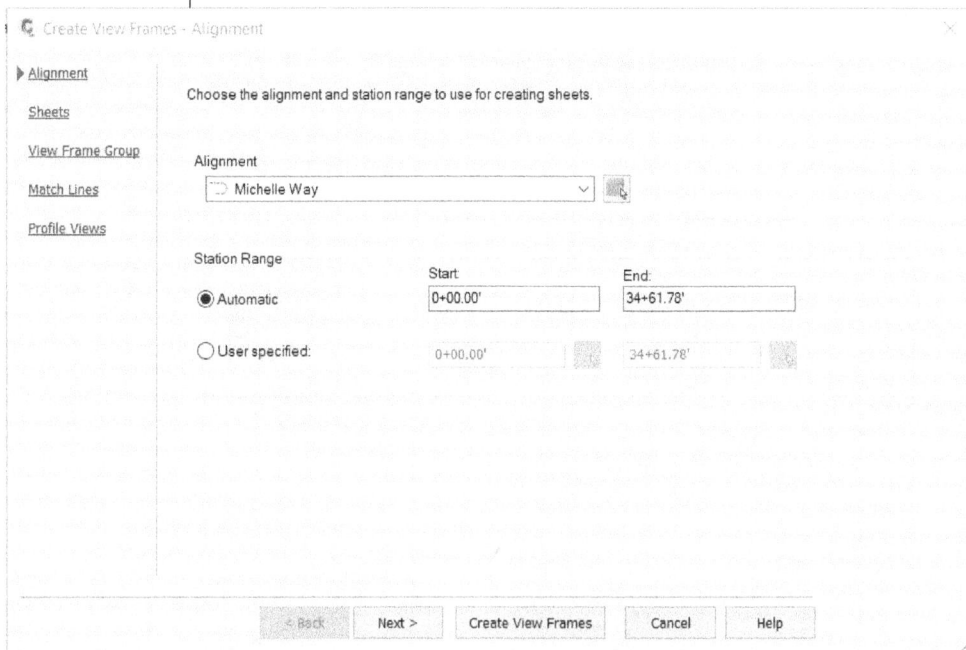

Figure 11–1

View Frames

View Frames are interactive, rectangular objects that are placed along a selected alignment. These rectangular shapes represent a view for each plan sheet that is created in the Autodesk Civil 3D software. View Frames divide the alignment into segments. These segments are based on the base drawing scale and the viewport proportion, size and settings on the Layout tab from the drawing template that is used to define the views.

View Frame Groups

View Frame Groups are collections of the View Frames along a single alignment. View Frame Groups enable you to manage a group of views, including properties, such as styles and labeling.

Match Lines

A Match Line is a line that designates a location along an alignment that is used as a common reference point for two adjacent plans. If you create plan and profile or profile only sheets, the **Insert Match Lines** option is automatically selected and you cannot edit it.

Match Lines, as with all other Autodesk Civil 3D objects, are style-driven.They include an option for hatching areas which are part of adjacent drawings.Typically, they have labels that can identify both adjacent plans, one plan, or no plans. You can also have these labels displayed at the top, bottom, or middle of the Match Line.

Practice 11a	# Plan Production Tools - View Frames

Practice Objective

- Create and edit view frames to divide the alignment into printable areas.

For this practice, two alignments from the project have been combined into one alignment and profile to better demonstrate the full power of the plan production tools in the Autodesk Civil 3D software when used with longer corridor projects. Combining alignments is not necessary or recommended for real projects.

Task 1 - Create View Frames.

1. Open **PPR1-A1-PlanProduction.dwg** from the *C:\Civil 3D Projects\Plans* folder.

This reference template has the profile view styles set to 1:5 exaggeration, whereas the Base-styles are set to 1:10.

2. Attach the **ASC-Profile-Styles.dwg** style reference template file from the *C:\Civil 3D Projects\Ascent-Config* folder as done earlier in this course. Ensure it is at the top of the list, as shown in Figure 11–2.

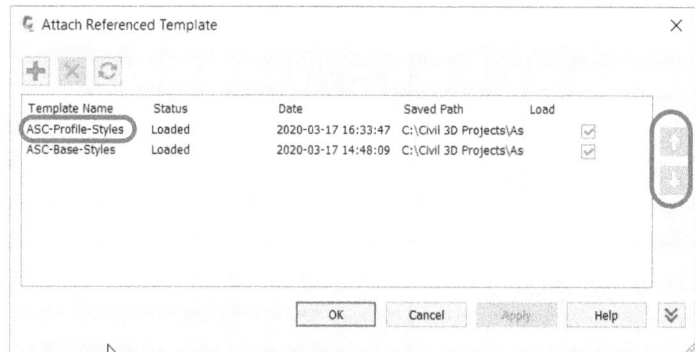

Figure 11–2

3. You will create the plan - profile sheets at a scale of 1"=20'. The sheets will be created more consistently if the Model Space scale matches the final output scale. If not already done, set the *Annotation Scale* to **1"=20'**, as shown in Figure 11–3.

Figure 11–3

4. In the *Output* tab>Plan Production panel, click (Create View Frames).

5. In the wizard, in the *Create View Frames - Alignment* page, do the following, as shown in Figure 11–4:

   - In the Alignment drop-down list, select **Michelle Way**.
   - In the *Station Range* area, select the **Automatic** option.
   - Click **Next>**.

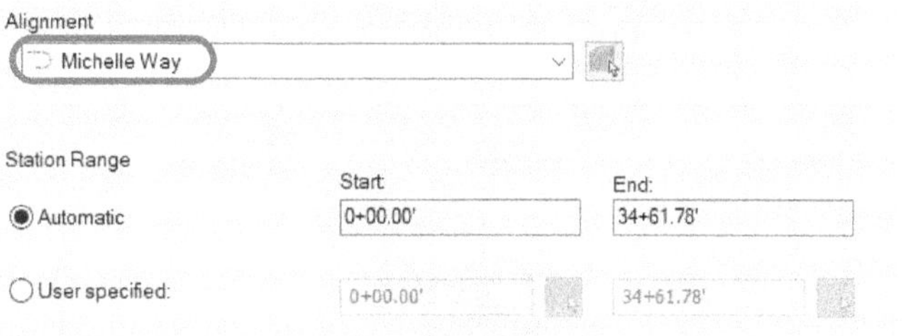

Figure 11–4

6. In the *Create View Frames - Sheets* page, do the following:
   - In the sheet settings, select the **Plan and Profile** option.
   - In the *Template for Plan and Profile sheet* area, click .
   - In the *Drawing template file name* field, click and browse to **ACS-Training Plan and Profile-l.dwt**. This file is located in *C:\Civil 3D Projects\Ascent-Config*.
   - In the *Select a layout to create new sheets* area, expand the drop-down list and select **Arch D Plan and Profile 20 Scale**, as shown in Figure 11–5.
   - Click **OK**.

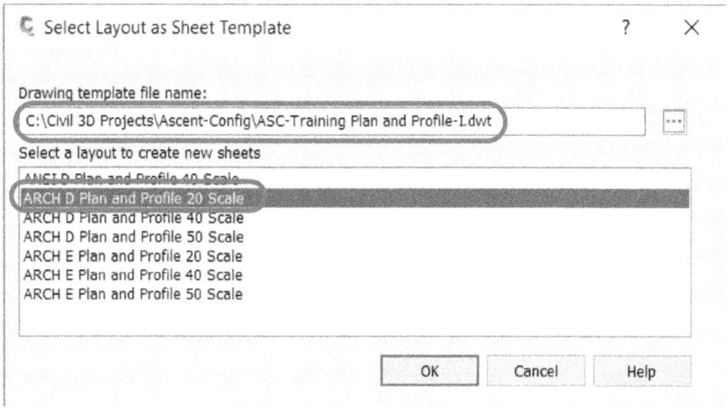

Figure 11–5

- For the *View Frame Placement*, select the **Along alignment** option, as shown in Figure 11–6.
- Click **Next>**.

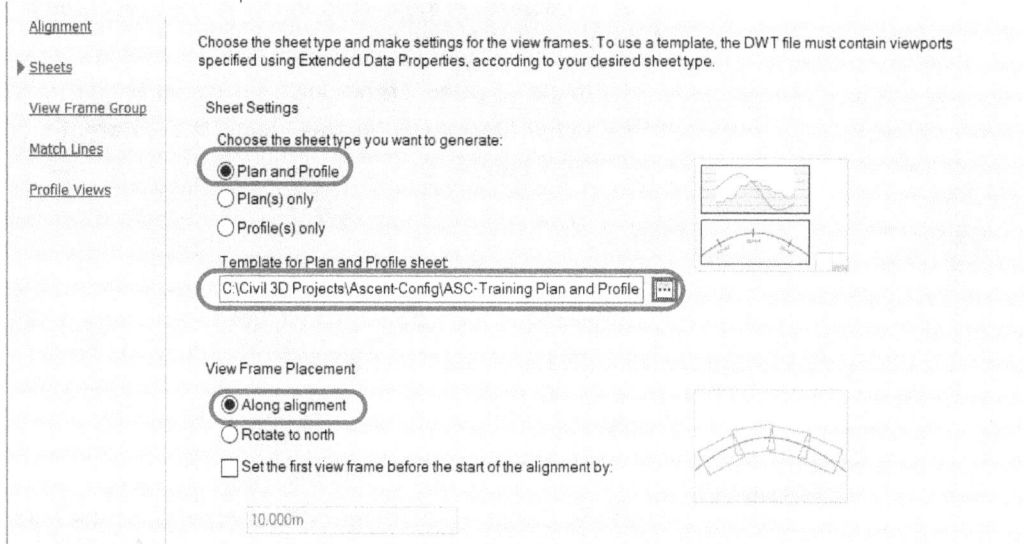

Alignment

▶ Sheets

View Frame Group

Match Lines

Profile Views

Choose the sheet type and make settings for the view frames. To use a template, the DWT file must contain viewports specified using Extended Data Properties, according to your desired sheet type.

Sheet Settings

Choose the sheet type you want to generate:

- ⦿ Plan and Profile
- ○ Plan(s) only
- ○ Profile(s) only

Template for Plan and Profile sheet:

C:\Civil 3D Projects\Ascent-Config\ASC-Training Plan and Profile [...]

View Frame Placement

- ⦿ Along alignment
- ○ Rotate to north

☐ Set the first view frame before the start of the alignment by:

10.000m

Figure 11–6

This will append the alignment name and a counter to the VFG.

7. In the *Create View Frames - View Frame Group* page, accept the default for the *Name*.

8. To name the View Frame with the starting station, click
   🔲 (Edit View Frame Name).

If these settings in the name template are standard, you can save them in the Setting tab in the master DWT file.

9. In the Name Template dialog box, shown in Figure 11–7:
   - In the *Name* field, type **VF - Sta**.
   - In the Property fields drop-down list, select **View Frame Start Raw Station**.
   - Click **Insert**.
   - Click **OK** to close the dialog box.

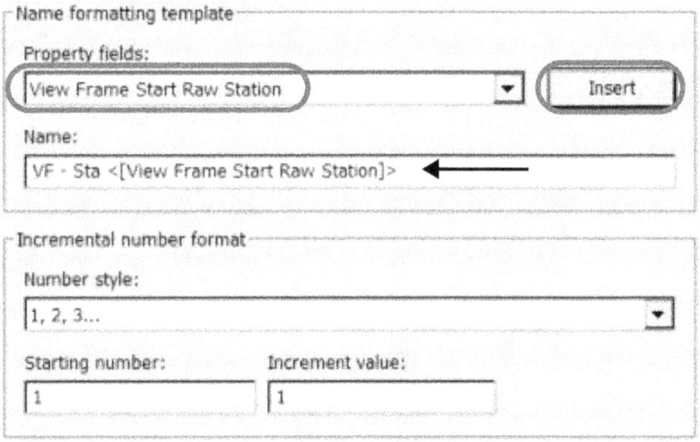

Figure 11–7

10. Accept the Label and Label style. Accept the Label location of **Top left** (as shown in Figure 11–8), and click **Next>**.

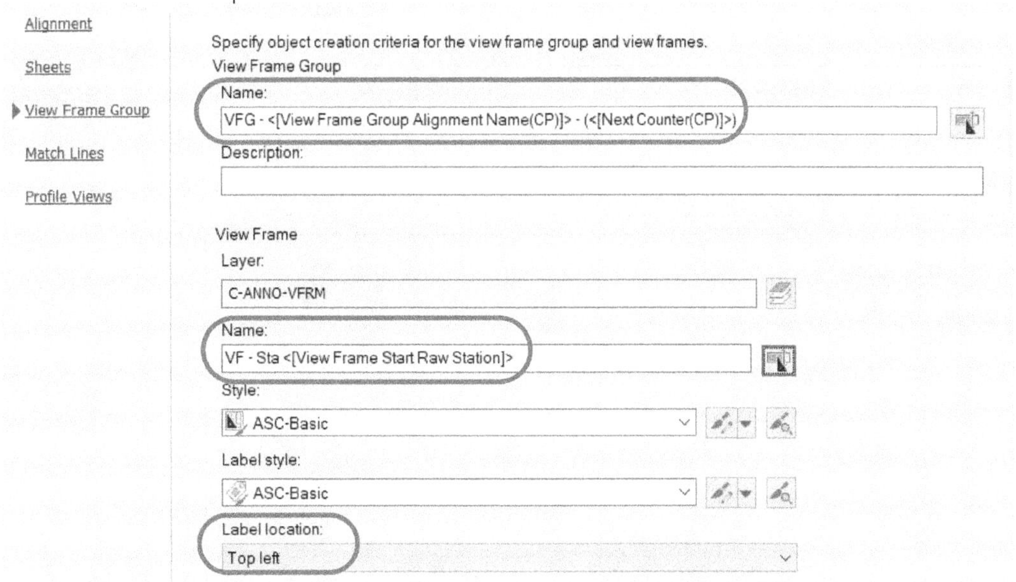

Figure 11–8

11. In the *Create View Frames - Match Lines* page, shown in Figure 11–9:

The procedure to do this is similar to Step 8.

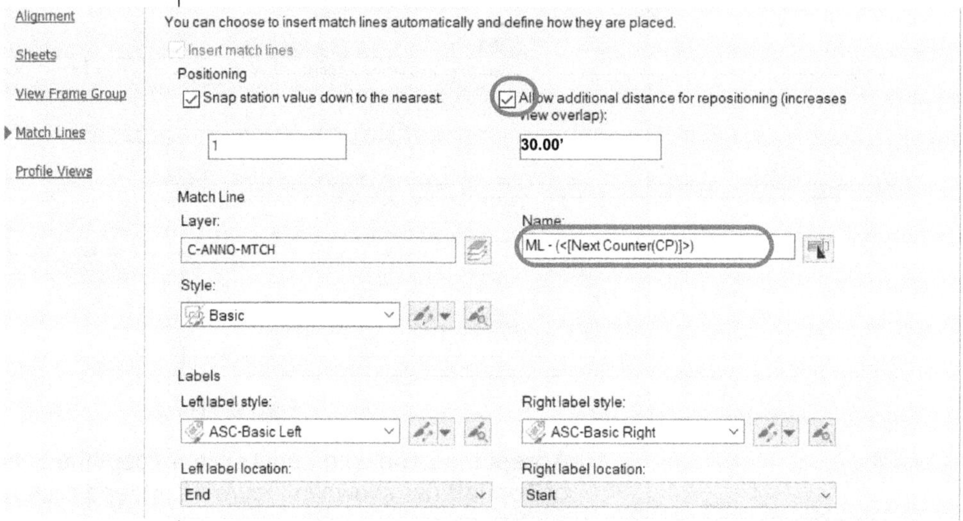

- Select **Allow additional distance for repositioning**.
- Change the *Match Line* name to **ML - <[Match Line Raw Station]>**.
- Accept all other defaults and click **Next>**.

Alignment

Sheets

View Frame Group

▶ Match Lines

Profile Views

You can choose to insert match lines automatically and define how they are placed.

☐ Insert match lines

Positioning

☑ Snap station value down to the nearest.   ☑ Allow additional distance for repositioning (increases view overlap):

[1]   [30.00']

Match Line

Layer: Name:

[C-ANNO-MTCH]   [ML - (<[Next Counter(CP)]>)]

Style:

[Basic]

Labels

Left label style: Right label style:

[ASC-Basic Left]   [ASC-Basic Right]

Left label location: Right label location:

[End]   [Start]

Figure 11–9

12. In the *Create View Frames - Profile Views* page, accept the default values for the *Profile View Style* and the *Band Set*. Click **Create View Frames**, as shown in Figure 11–10.

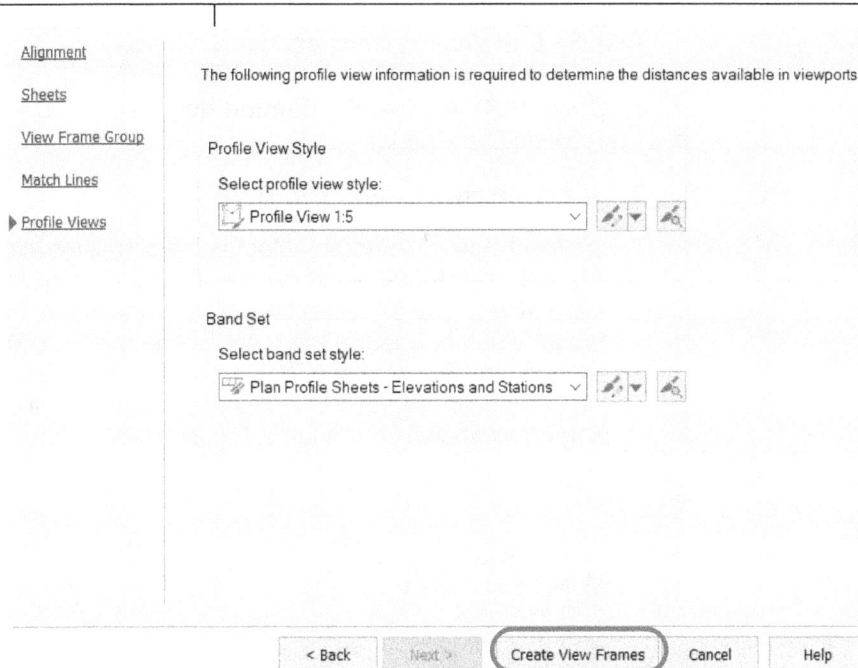

Alignment

Sheets

View Frame Group

Match Lines

▶ Profile Views

The following profile view information is required to determine the distances available in viewports.

Profile View Style

Select profile view style:

☐ Profile View 1:5   ∨

Band Set

Select band set style:

☐ Plan Profile Sheets - Elevations and Stations   ∨

< Back   Next >   (Create View Frames)   Cancel   Help

Figure 11–10

13. In the Toolspace, *Prospector* tab, expand the *View Frame Groups* collection, expand the *VFG - Michelle Way View Frame Group*, and then expand the *View Frames* collection and the *Match Lines* collection. Note that the Create View Frame wizard has created eleven Plan Production objects, six View Frames, and five Match Lines, as shown in Figure 11–11.

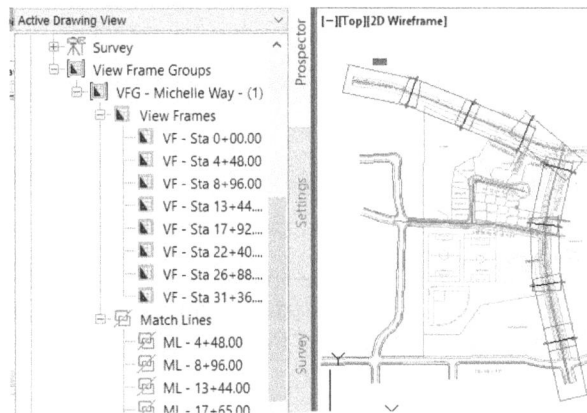

Figure 11–11

14. Save the drawing.

Task 2 - Edit View Frames and Match Lines.

1. Open **PPR1-A2-PlanProduction.dwg** from the *C:\Civil 3D Projects\Plans* folder.

2. Select the preset view PP-Edit VF.

3. In Model Space, select the Match Line object for Michelle Way **ML - 17+92.00**, as shown on the right in Figure 11–12. Alternatively, you can select the Match Line in the Toolspace, *Prospector* tab. Expand the *View Frame Groups* collection, expand the *VFG-Michelle Way* collection, expand the *Match Line* collection, select **ML - 17+92.00**, right-click, and select **Select**, as shown on the left in Figure 11–12.

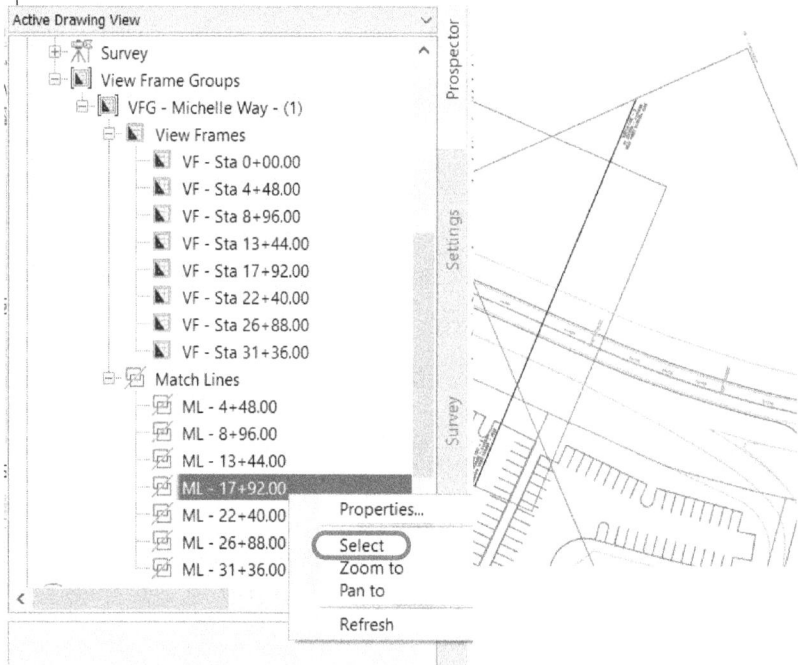

Figure 11–12

If Quick Properties does not display, in the Status bar, click ▣ (Quick Properties) to open it.

4. Select the move grip (the diamond grip), and type **1765**.

5. In the Quick Properties dialog box, also rename it as **ML - 17+65.00**, as shown in Figure 11–13. Press <Esc> to release the Match Line object.

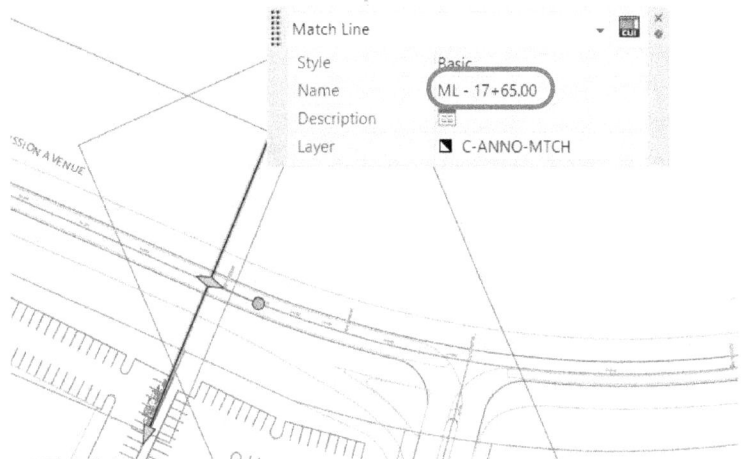

Figure 11–13

6. Now you can adjust the View Frame object corresponding to ML - 17+65.00. Select the View Frame object, select the rotation grip (the circular grip), and graphically rotate the View Frame object so that it is parallel to the Mission Avenue alignment, as shown in Figure 11–14.

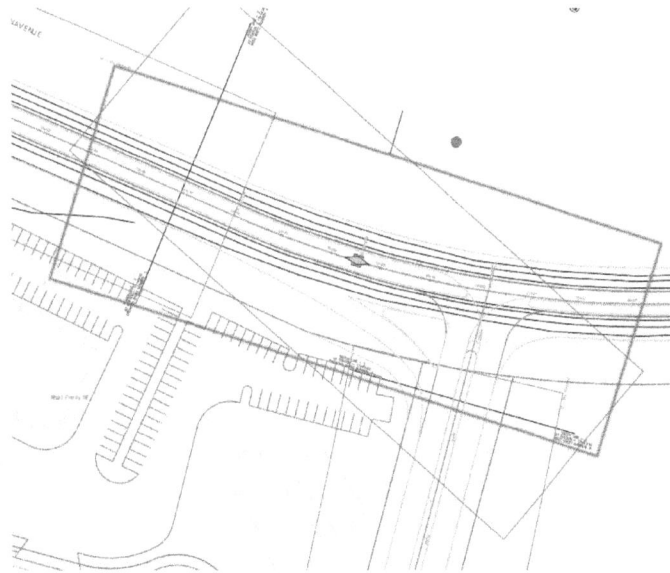

Figure 11–14

7. Press <Esc> to exit the View Frame object selection.

8. Save the drawing.

11.2 Creating Sheets

Once the Match Lines, View Frames, and associated View Frame Groups have been established, you can start the next phase of generating sheet sets.

The Autodesk Civil 3D software includes a wizard that helps you create sheets from the View Frames. The flexibility of this wizard, in addition to the selection of styles, enables you to create sheets that automatically conform to many of your organization's standards. The wizard is shown in Figure 11–15.

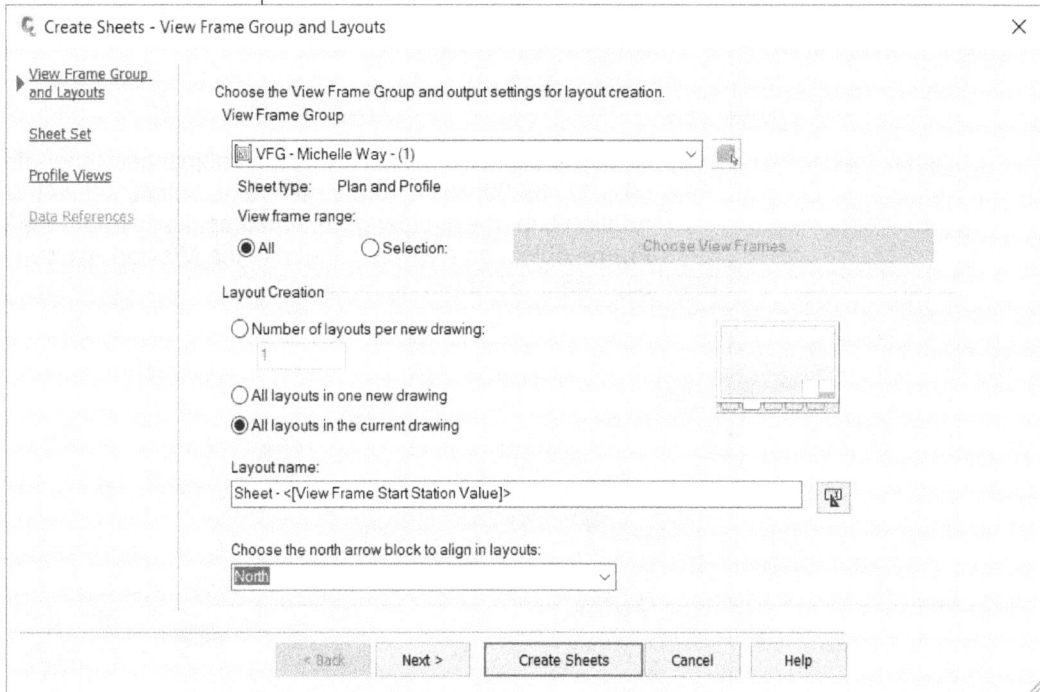

Figure 11–15

Since a dynamic link does not exist between the View Frames and the sheet, it is important that the required View Frames are established before creating the sheets. Changing or editing View Frames after the sheets are created has no effect on the sheets.

- In addition to using the wizard for creating sheets, this workflow also uses the AutoCAD Sheet Set Manager.

Practice 11b

Plan Production Tools - Sheet Generation

Practice Objective

- Create plan and profile sheets using the Plan Production tools and previously created View Frame objects.

1. Open **PPR1-B1-PlanProduction.dwg** from the *C:\Civil 3D Projects\Plans* folder.

2. In the *Output* tab>Plan Production panel, click 🖾 (Create Sheets).

3. In the wizard, in the *Create Sheet - View Frame Group and Layouts* page:
   - Ensure that the *View Frame Group* is **VFG - Michelle Way**.
   - Set the *View frame range* to **All**.
   - In the *Layout Creation* area, set the *Layout* creation to **All layouts in the current drawing**.
   - For the *Layout name*, click 🖾 (Edit Layout Name).

4. In the Name Template dialog box, shown in Figure 11–16:
   - In the *Name* field, delete the current name.
   - Type **Sheet-**.
   - In the Property fields drop-down list, select **View Frame Start Station Value**.
   - Click **Insert**.
   - Click **OK** to close this dialog box.

In a production environment, it is recommended NOT to have the layouts in your Design models, but to have them in a separate folder specifically for sheets.

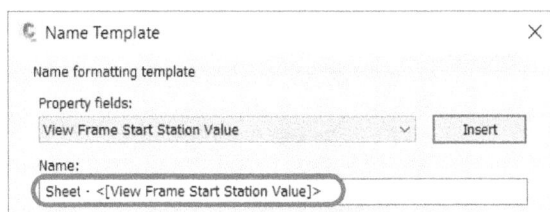

Figure 11–16

5. Expand the Choose the north arrow block to align in layouts drop-down list and select the **North** block, as shown in Figure 11–17. This North Arrow block is part of the *Template for Plan and Profile sheet* that you chose in the previous exercise. Once this is complete, click **Next>**.

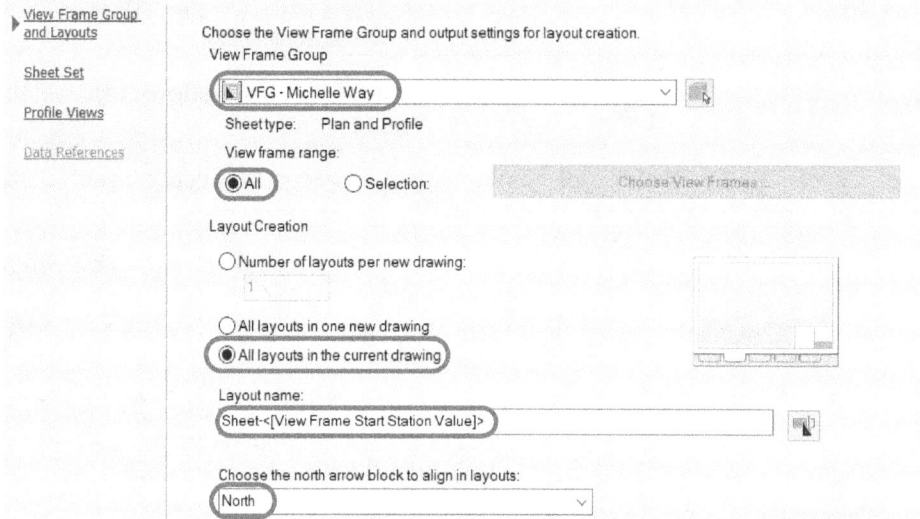

Figure 11–17

6. In the *Create Sheets - Sheet Set* page, set the following:
   - Select the **New sheet set** option and type **Ascent Phase1** in the *Sheet Set name* field. Leave the *Sheet set storage location* field set to the default (*C:\Civil 3D Projects\Plans*), as shown in Figure 11–18. Click **Next>**.

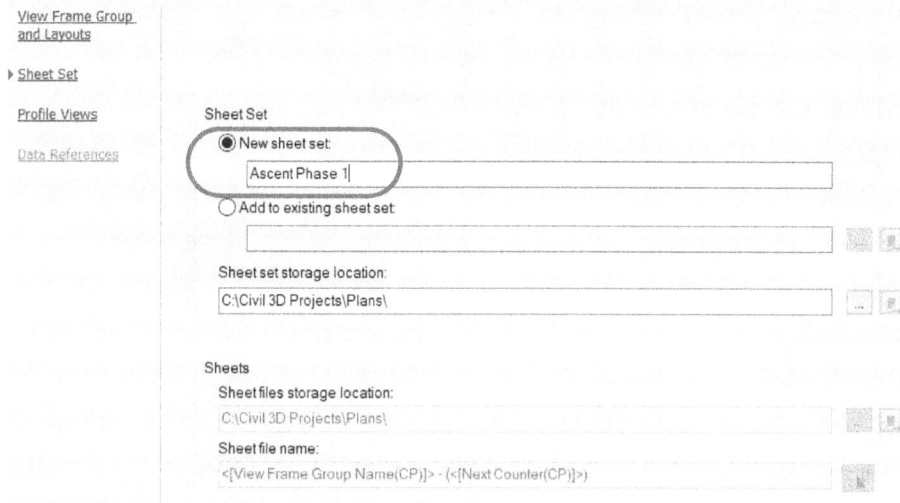

Figure 11–18

*These 1:5 profile views belong to the **ASC-Profile-Styles.dwg** style reference template you attached earlier.*

7. In the *Create Sheets - Profile Views* page, click on Choose settings for *Other profile views options*. In the Profile View wizard, ensure that the Split Profile views are as follows, as shown in Figure 11–19:

- *First View 1:5*
- *Intermediate View 1:5*
- *Last View 1:5*

8. Click **Finish** to dismiss the Profile View wizard, then accept the other defaults, and click **Create Sheets**.

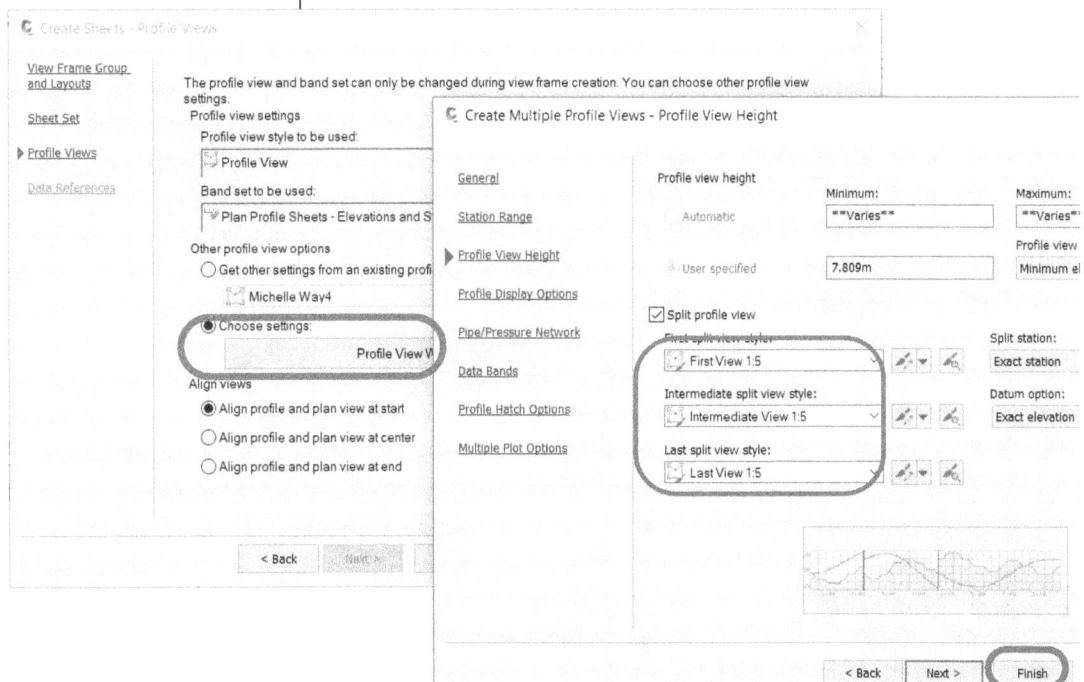

Figure 11–19

9. The wizard prompts you that the drawing will be saved before creating the new sheets. Click **OK** to accept this.

10. When prompted for the location of the profile, select a blank space in your drawing, as shown in Figure 11–20. The Autodesk Civil 3D software will use this location to insert a profile of your alignment. Since the point you pick will be the lower left corner of the Profile Views to be generated, assure there is nothing to the right and above that can overlap the new Profile Views.

[−][Top][2D Wireframe]

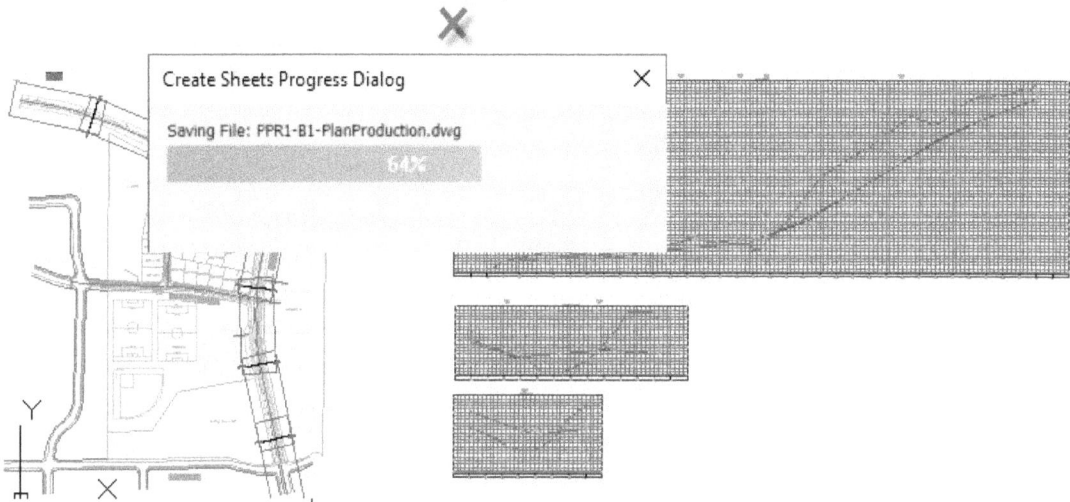

Figure 11–20

*You may have to regenerate (command **RE**) the drawing to update the newly created profile views.*

11. The Autodesk Civil 3D software creates the sheets and the Sheet Set Manager files. The Sheet Set Manager opens, as shown in Figure 11–21.

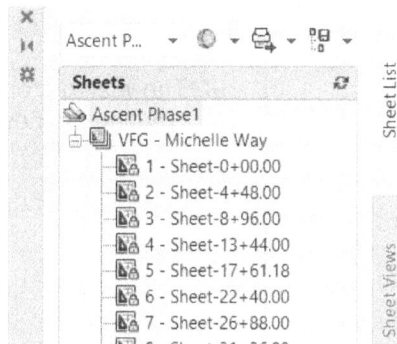

Figure 11–21

12. Hover the cursor over the filename in the Sheet Set Manager to display all of the properties of the sheet, including the name and location of the drawing file, as shown in Figure 11–22.

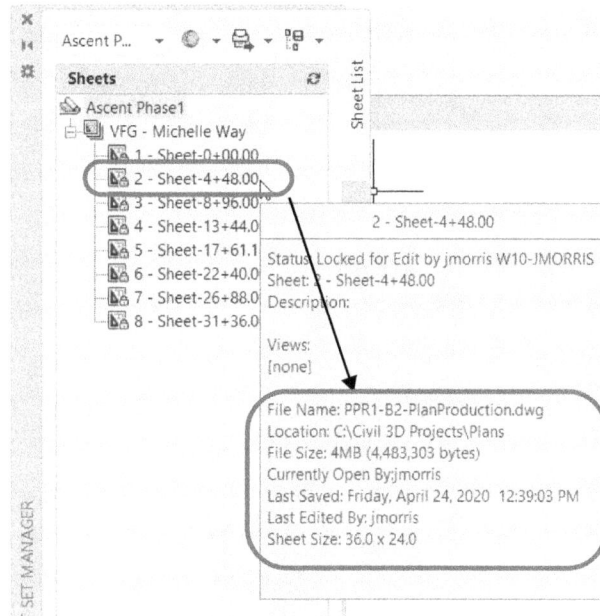

Figure 11–22

13. Save the drawing.

Chapter 12

Data Shortcuts

Exam Objectives Covered in This Chapter

6.3.a Differentiate between a data shortcut and external reference

6.3.b Explain the concepts and procedures for managing data shortcuts

6.4.a Create a reference to a Data Shortcut

12.1 Sharing Data

In the Autodesk Civil 3D workflow, you can use two methods of project collaboration to share Autodesk Civil 3D design data: Data Shortcuts (local based or through BIM 360) and Vault references.

Autodesk Vault and Data Shortcuts can be used to share design data between drawing files in the same project, such as alignment definitions, profiles, corridors, surfaces, pipe networks, pressure networks, sample line groups, and View Frame Groups. They do not permit the sharing of profile views, assemblies, or other Autodesk Civil 3D objects. Drawing sets using shortcuts typically use XREFs and reference other line work and annotations between drawings. Whether using Vault Shortcuts or Data Shortcuts, the process is similar.

The example in Figure 12–1 shows the sharing of data in a project collaboration environment. The data is divided into three distinctive levels. Using either Data Shortcuts or Autodesk Vault, these levels can be accessed and contributed to, on a local or remote server or across a WAN.

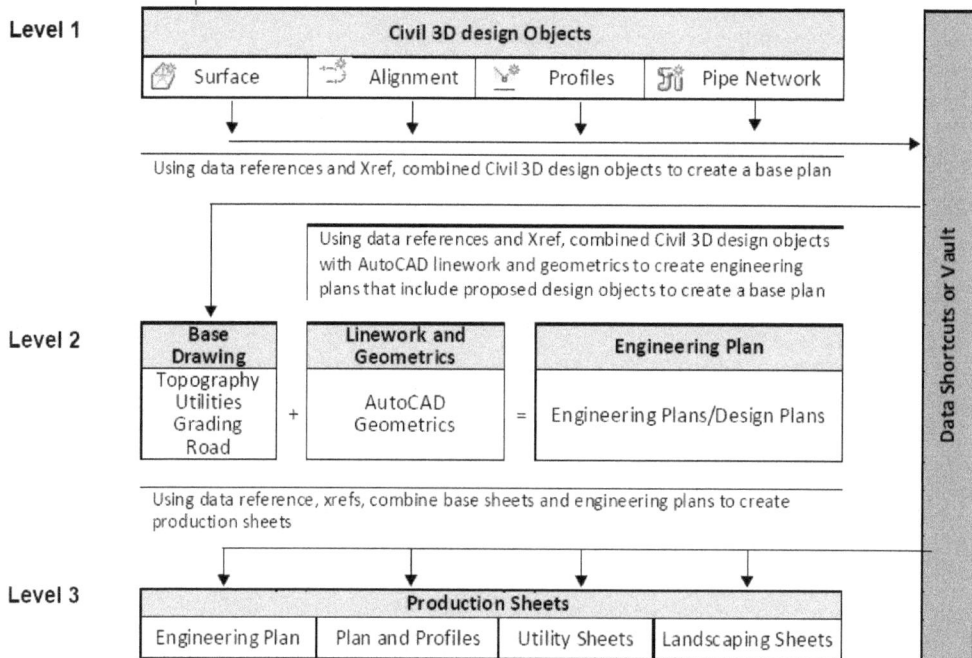

Figure 12–1

12.2 Using Data Shortcuts for Project Management

Data Shortcuts can be used to share design data between drawing files through the use of XML files. Using Data Shortcuts is similar to using the Autodesk Vault software, but does not provide the protection of your data or the tracking of versions the way the Autodesk Vault software does.

Data Shortcuts are managed using the Toolspace, *Prospector* tab, under the *Data Shortcuts* collection or in the *Manage* tab>Data Shortcuts panel, as shown in Figure 12–2. The shortcuts are stored in XML files in one or more working folders that you create. They can use the same folder structure as the Autodesk Vault software. This method simplifies the transition to using the Autodesk Vault software at a future time.

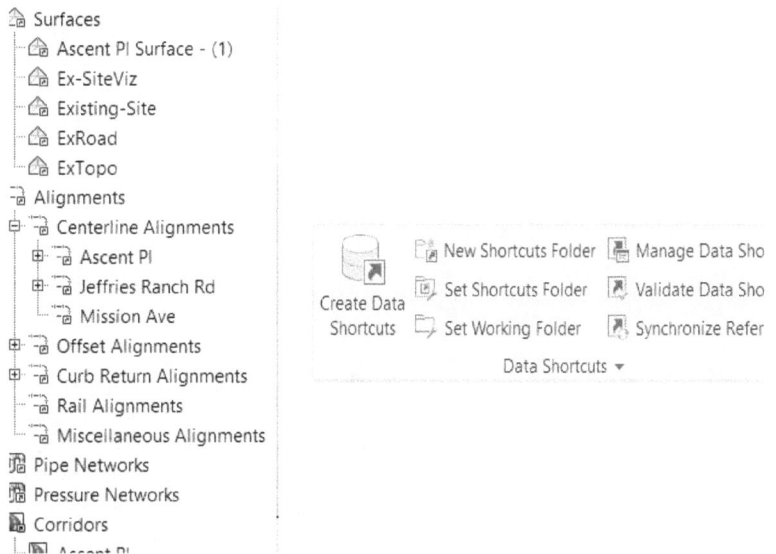

Figure 12–2

When the data shortcuts reside in a BIM 360 project in the cloud, it is designated as such in the Toolspace, *Prospector* tab with a small cloud symbol and a path pointing to the BIM 360 Project, as shown in Figure 12–3.

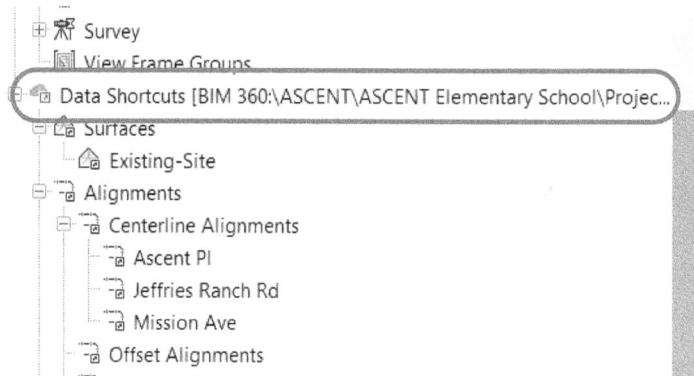

Figure 12–3

Similarly, when you are working in a drawing that resides in a BIM 360 project, in the Toolspace, *Prospector* tab, the drawing has a cloud symbol as a prefix, as shown in Figure 12–4.

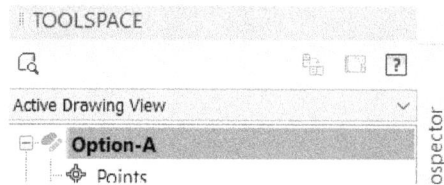

Figure 12–4

Whether using the Autodesk Vault software or Data Shortcuts (local based or through BIM 360), the intelligent Autodesk Civil 3D object design data can be consumed and used on different levels. However, this referenced data only can be edited in the drawing that contains the original object. As referenced data can be assigned a different style than those in the source drawing, you can separate the design phase (where drawing presentation is not critical) from the drafting phase (where drawing presentation is paramount). Therefore, after the styles have been applied at the drafting phase, any changes to the design have minimal visual impact on the completed drawings.

Changing the name of a drawing file that provides Data Shortcuts or the shortcut XML file itself invalidates the shortcut. In the *Manage* tab, there is a Data Shortcut Manager that is used to correct such issues. It is used to repair references broken through renamed drawings or re-pathing drawings containing the Civil 3D objects.

Update Notification

If the shortcut objects are modified and the source drawing is saved, any drawings that reference those objects are updated when opened. If the drawings consuming the data referenced in the shortcuts are open at the time of the edit, a message displays to warn you of the changes, as shown in Figure 12–5.

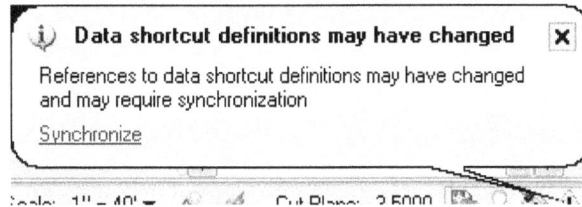

Figure 12–5

The following modifier icons help you to determine the state of many Autodesk Civil 3D objects.

▽	The object is referenced by another object. In the Toolspace, Settings tab this also indicates that a style is in use in the current drawing.
↱	The object is being referenced from another drawing file (such as through a shortcut or Autodesk Vault reference).
⚠	The object is out of date and needs to be rebuilt, or is violating specified design constraints.
◣	A Vault project object (such as a point or surface) has been modified since it was included in the current drawing.
◢	You have modified a Vault project object in your current drawing and those modifications have not yet been updated to the project.

Figure 12–6 shows how the modifier icons are used with an Autodesk Civil 3D object as it displays in the Toolspace, *Prospector* tab.

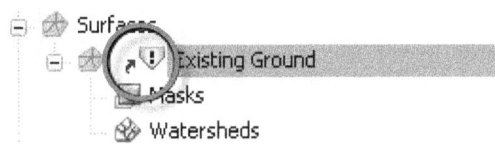

Figure 12–6

To update the shortcut data, select **Synchronize** in the balloon message or right-click on the object in the Toolspace, *Prospector* tab and select **Synchronize**.

BIM 360 Notification

In the debut release of BIM 360 Design Collaboration, there is no standard Civil 3D notification indicating that the Data Shortcuts have changed. For that, you need to go to the *Collaborate* tab and click ⟳ (Check Reference Status). It will examine if any of the referenced data items have changed and need updating.

Removing and Promoting Shortcuts

Shortcut data can be removed from the Shortcut tree in the Toolspace, *Prospector* tab by right-clicking on it and selecting **Remove**, but this does not remove the data from the drawing. To do so, right-click on the object in the Toolspace, *Prospector* tab and select **Delete**. This removes the shortcut data from the current list, so that the item is not included if a Data Shortcut XML file is exported from the current drawing.

You can also promote shortcuts, which converts the referenced shortcut into a local copy without any further connection to the original. You can promote objects by right-clicking on them in the Toolspace, *Prospector* tab and selecting **Promote**.

Data Shortcut Workflow

Whenever Civil is searching for folders, you can use the Autodesk Desktop Connector to browse to the local cache folders of files that reside in a BIM 360 project.

1. In the Toolspace, *Prospector* tab, right-click on Data Shortcuts and select **Set the Working Folder…**
2. In the Toolspace, *Prospector* tab, right-click on Data Shortcuts and select **New Data Shortcuts Folder…** to create a new project folder for all of your drawings.
3. Create or import the data that you want to share in the source drawing and save it in the current working folder under the correct project folder.
4. In the Toolspace, *Prospector* tab, right-click on Data Shortcuts and select **Associate Project to Current Drawing**.
5. In the Toolspace, *Prospector* tab, right-click on Data Shortcuts and select **Create Data Shortcuts**.
6. Select all of the items that you want to share, such as surfaces, alignments, profiles, etc., and click **OK**.
7. Save the source drawing (and close, as required).
8. Create and save a new drawing or open an existing drawing to receive the shortcut data. Expand the *Data Shortcuts* collection and the relevant object trees (*Surfaces, Alignments, Pipe Networks, View Frame Groups, etc.*).
9. Highlight an item to be referenced, right-click and select **Create Reference…**. Repeat, for all of the objects, as required. You are prompted for the styles and other settings that are required to display the object in the current drawing.

10. You might also want to add an XREF to the source drawing if there is additional AutoCAD® objects that you want to display in the downstream drawing.
11. The Autodesk Civil 3D tools for Data Shortcuts are located in the *Manage* tab (as shown in Figure 12–7), and in the Toolspace, *Prospector* tab.

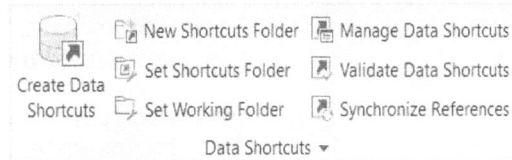

Figure 12–7

Workflow Details

- **Set Working Folder:** Sets a new working folder as the location in which to store the Data Shortcut project. The default working folder for Data Shortcut projects is *C:\Users\Public\Documents\Autodesk\Civil 3D Projects*.

- Obviously, in a shared working environment, the working folder needs to be accessible by all project team members. Often working folders are named by the year of the project, or perhaps the major clients for the project.

- For project team members who reside outside of your firewall, consider setting up a BIM 360 Project for design collaboration and file referencing.

- The default working folder is also used for Autodesk Vault projects and local (non-Vault) Survey projects. If you work with the Autodesk Vault software, local Survey, and Data Shortcut projects, you should have separate working folders for each project type for ease of management.

- **New Shortcuts Folder:** Creates a new folder for storing a set of related project drawings and Data Shortcuts.

- **Create Data Shortcuts:** Creates Data Shortcuts from the active drawing.

Data Shortcuts are stored in the *_Shortcuts* folder for the active project and used to create data references to source objects in other drawings. Each Data Shortcut is stored in a separate XML file.

Advantages of Data Shortcuts	• Data Shortcuts provide a simple mechanism for sharing object data, without the added system administration needs of the Autodesk Vault software.
	• Data Shortcuts offer access to an object's intelligent data while ensuring that this referenced data can only be changed in the source drawing.
	• Referenced objects can have styles and labels that differ from the source drawing.
	• When you open a drawing containing revised referenced data, the referenced objects are updated automatically.
	• During a drawing session, if the referenced data has been revised, you are notified in the Communication Center and in the Toolspace, *Prospector* tab.
	• When Data Shortcuts reside in a BIM 360 project, design collaboration and file referencing can be done beyond the firewall of your organization.
Limitations of Data Shortcuts	• Data Shortcuts cannot provide data versioning.
	• Data Shortcuts do not provide security or data integrity controls.
	• Unlike the Autodesk Vault software, Data Shortcuts do not provide a secure mechanism for sharing point data or survey data.
	• Maintaining links between references and their source objects requires fairly stable names. However, most broken references can easily be repaired using the tools in the Autodesk Civil 3D software.

Practice 12a

Starting a Project

Practice Objective

- Create a new data shortcut project with the correct working folder for the project being worked on.

In this practice, you will walk through the steps of creating project-based Data Shortcuts folders.

Task 1 - Set the working folder.

In this task, you will set up a new working folder as the location in which to store Data Shortcut projects. The default working folder for Data Shortcut projects is *C:\Users\Public\Documents\Autodesk\Civil 3D Projects*.

For this course, you will not be using a BIM 360 Project, as that requires access to BIM 360 Project and Project setup.

For information on practices for BIM 360 Collaboration with Civil 3D, see the Autodesk BIM 360: Fundamentals guide (published by ASCENT).

1. Open **DS-A1-Shortcuts.dwg** from the *C:\Civil 3D Projects\Data Shortcuts\Practice* folder.

2. Configure Civil 3D to reduce the fading of XREF files. Type *Options* on the command line. In the Options window, go to the *Display* tab and use the slider in the lower left corner to change the *Fade control* from the default value of 50% to 6% for the *Xref display*, as shown in Figure 12–8. Click **OK**.

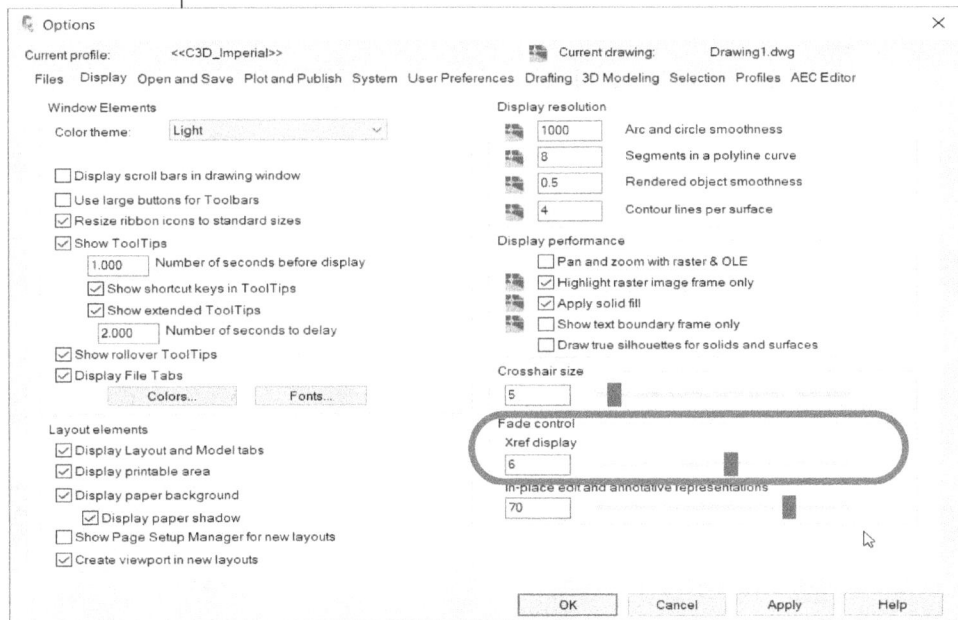

Figure 12–8

3. In the *Manage* tab>Data Shortcuts panel, click ☐ (Set Working Folder), as shown in Figure 12–9.

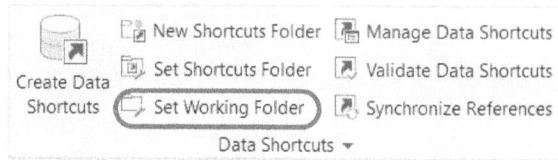

Figure 12–9

4. In the Browse For Folder dialog box, select the *Civil 3D Projects\Data Shortcuts* folder, right-click to create a new folder and name it Lesson. Click **Select Folder**.

Task 2 - Create new Shortcuts folders.

In this task, you will create a new folder for storing a set of related project drawings and Data Shortcuts. A second project folder is created to help you understand how to change the project in which you are working.

1. In the *Manage* tab>Data Shortcuts panel, click ☐ (New Shortcuts Folder), as shown in Figure 12–10.

Figure 12–10

2. In the New Data Shortcut Folder dialog box, type **Ascent Phase 1** for the name and select the **Use project template** option. Templates are found in the default folder *C:\Civil 3D Templates*; however, you will be using customized project templates. Pick on the ellipses, as shown in Figure 12–11, and browse to *C:\Civil 3D Projects\Ascent-Config\Ascent Project Templates*. From the Project templates available, select *Base Project*. The Autodesk Civil 3D software will replicate this template folder structure and all included forms and documents in the *Ascent Phase 1* project folder. Click **OK**.

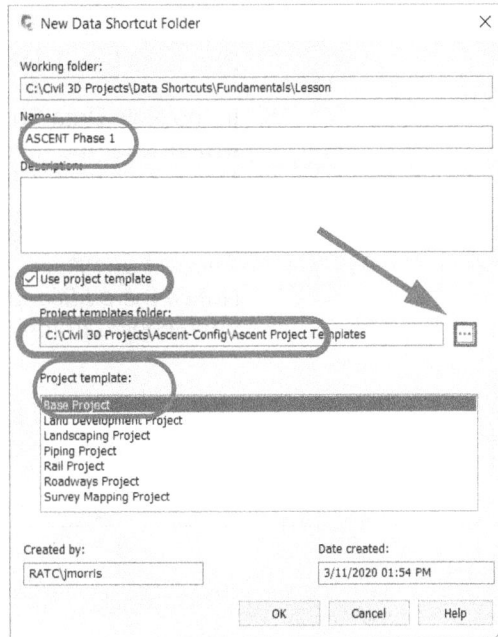

Figure 12–11

3. In the Toolspace, *Prospector* tab, a Data Shortcut folder is displayed in *C:\Civil 3D Projects\Data Shortcuts\ Lesson\Ascent Phase 1*. In Windows Explorer, verify that the *Civil 3D* folder structure is created for this project, as shown on the right in Figure 12–12.

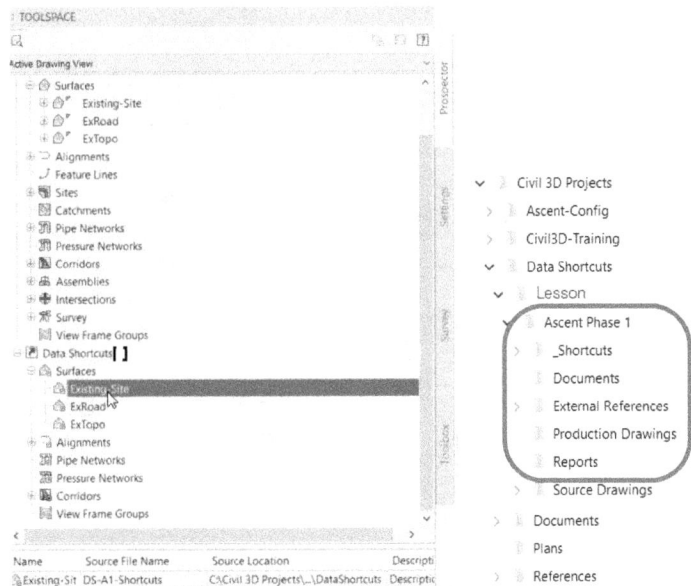

Figure 12–12

4. Create another new shortcuts folder. In the *Manage* tab>Data Shortcuts panel, click ⬚ (New Shortcuts Folder).

5. In the New Data Shortcut Folder dialog box, type **Ascent Phase 2** for the name and uncheck the **Use project template** option. Click **OK** to close the dialog box.

You now have two projects in the working folder: *Ascent Phase 1* and *Ascent Phase 2*, as shown in Figure 12–13. Notice the additional folders in *Ascent Phase 1*. These have been copied from the *Base Project* project template.

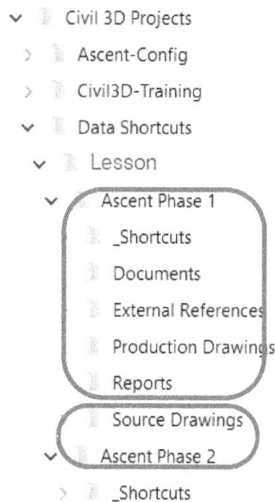

Figure 12–13

Task 3 - Set up the shortcuts folder.

Setting the shortcuts folder specifies the project path for Data Shortcuts. The path to the current *Data Shortcuts* folder (also known as the project folder) is specified in the Toolspace, *Prospector* tab, in the *Data Shortcuts* collection. The project folder typically contains both Data Shortcuts and source objects for data references.

1. In the *Manage* tab>Data Shortcuts panel, click ▦ (Set Shortcuts Folder).

2. The current *Data Shortcut* folder is indicated by a green circle with a checkmark. Select **Ascent Phase 1** to make it current and click **OK**, as shown in Figure 12–14.

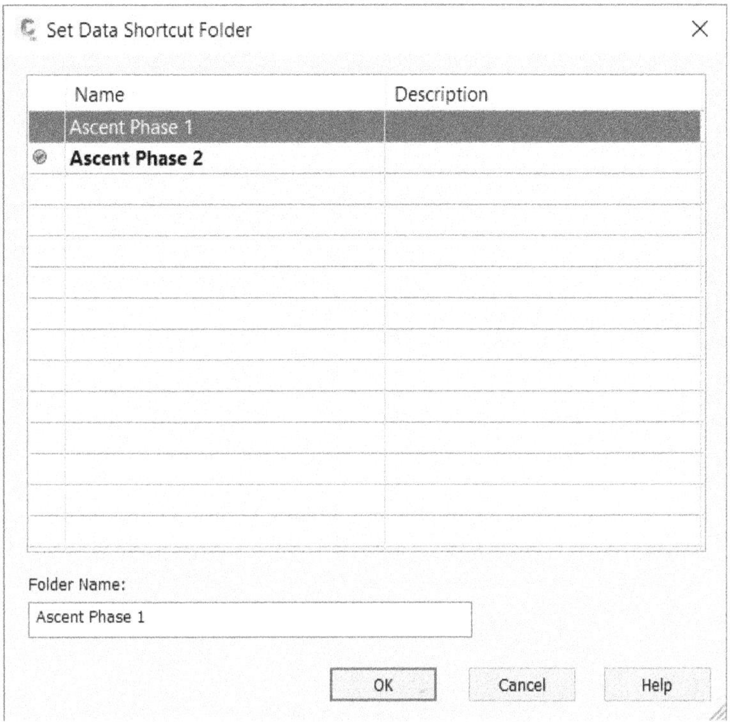

Figure 12–14

3. In the Toolspace, *Prospector* tab, right-click on Data Shortcuts and select **Associate Project to Current Drawing**, as shown in Figure 12–15.

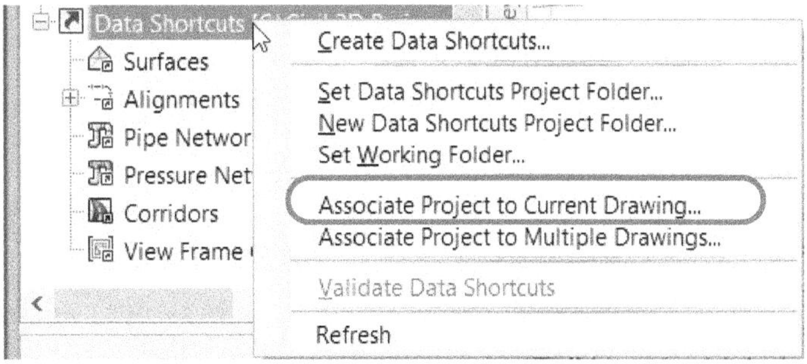

Figure 12–15

4. Verify that **Ascent Phase 1** is the selected project. Click **OK**.

Practice 12b	# Manage File Sizes with Data Shortcuts

Practice Objective

- Create Data Shortcuts from objects in a drawing to share with other team members.

In this practice, you will walk through the steps of creating project-based *Data Shortcuts* folders. It simulates a situation in which the existing conditions and/or design work has been done and you now need to share elements of the design with team members.

Task 1 - Create Data Shortcuts.

1. In the Toolspace, *Prospector* tab, verify that the Data Shortcuts points to the correct folder, as shown in Figure 12–16. By hovering over the Data Shortcuts heading, the full path gets revealed in the tooltip. If it is not set to *Ascent Phase 1*, then repeat the steps from the previous exercise.

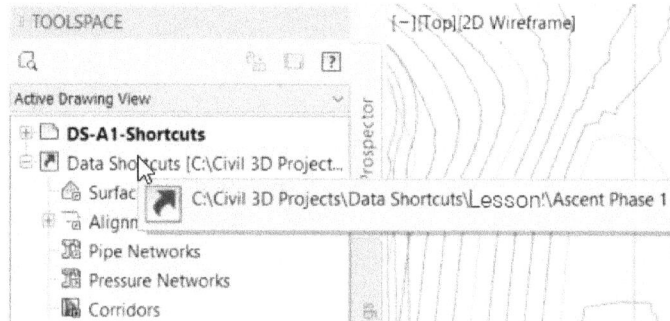

Figure 12–16

2. In the *Manage* tab>Data Shortcuts panel, click (Create Data Shortcuts).

3. If you receive a message that the drawing has not yet been saved, click **OK**. Save the drawing and start the **Create Data Shortcuts** command again.

4. In the Create Data Shortcuts dialog box, a list of all of the available objects for use in shortcuts displays. Select **Surfaces**, **Alignments**, and **Corridors** (as shown in Figure 12–17) and click **OK**.

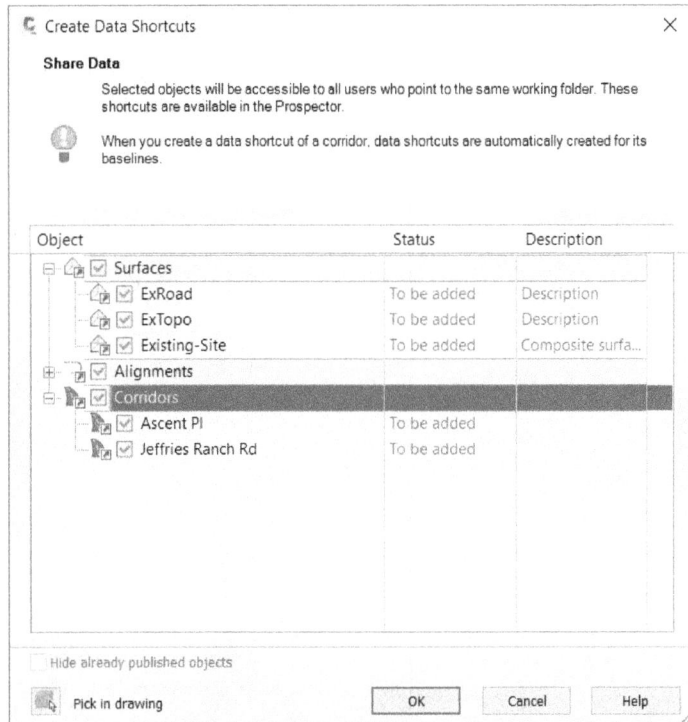

Figure 12–17

5. You have now created shortcuts for the surfaces, alignments, and corridors. This means that if the shortcuts and drawings are in a shared network folder, anyone on the network has access to these Autodesk Civil 3D objects.

Note that in the Toolspace, *Prospector* tab, under the *Data Shortcuts* and *Surfaces* collections, you can now access all of the surfaces. In the list view, the source filename and source path display, as shown in Figure 12–18.

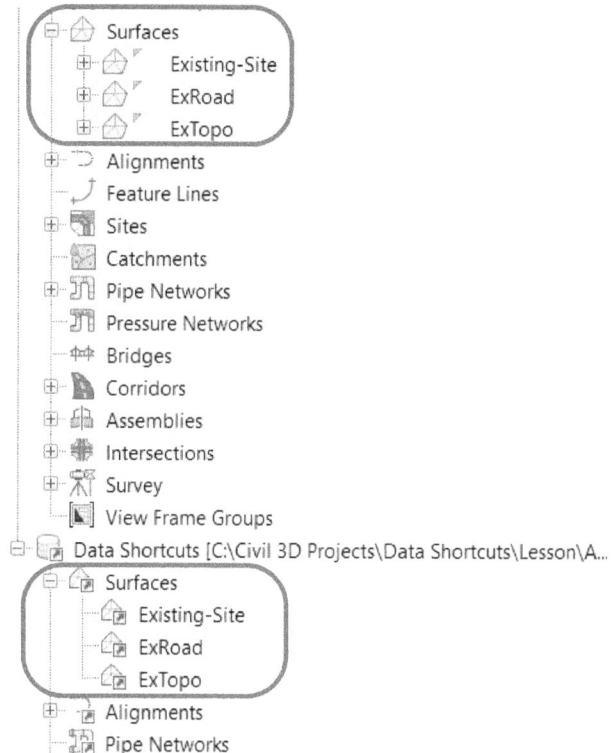

Figure 12–18

6. Save the drawing, but do not close it.

Task 2 - Data-reference Data Shortcuts.

---

1. Start a new drawing from the **ASC-C3D (CA83-VIF) NCS.dwt** file from the *C:\Civil 3D Projects\Ascent-Config* folder.

2. Save the file in *C:\Civil 3D Projects\Data Shortcuts\DWG* as **Reference File.dwg**.

3. In the Toolspace, *Prospector* tab, ensure that *Data Shortcuts* point to the *C:\Civil 3D Projects\Data Shortcuts\ Lesson\Ascent Phase 1* folder.

4. In the Toolspace, *Prospector* tab, right-click on **Data Shortcuts** and select **Associate Project to Current Drawing**, as shown in Figure 12–19.

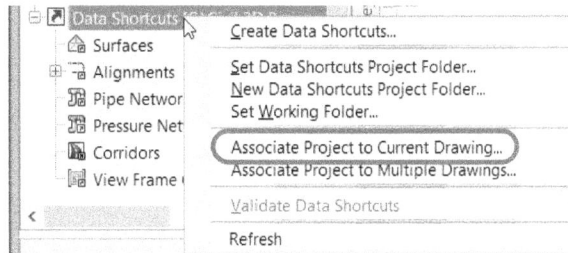

Figure 12–19

5. In the Toolspace, *Prospector* tab, under the *Data Shortcuts* collection, expand the *Surfaces* collection (if not already expanded) and expand the *Alignments>Centerline Alignments* collection, as shown in Figure 12–20.

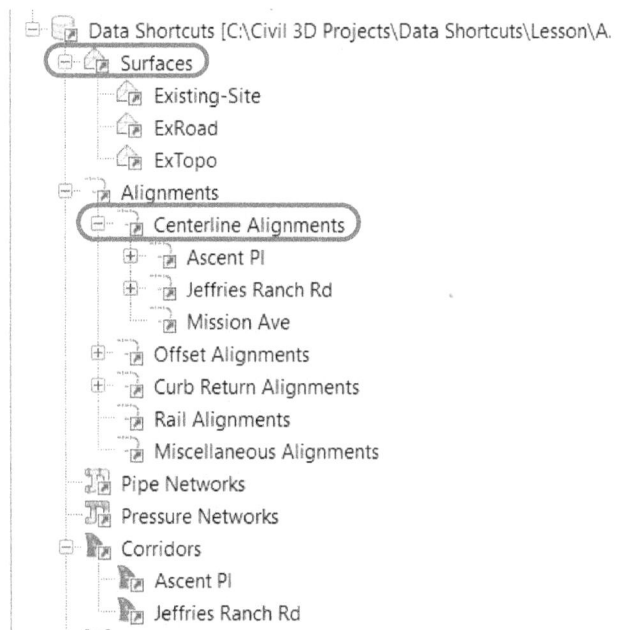

Figure 12–20

6. Under the *Surfaces* collection, select the surface **Existing-Site**, right-click, and select **Create Reference**, as shown in Figure 12–21.

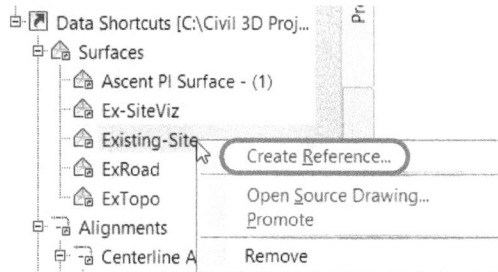

Figure 12–21

7. In the Create Surface Reference dialog box, do the following:
   - Type **ExSurface** for the *Name*.
   - Type **Data referenced surface** for the *Description*.
   - Select **Contours 2' and 10' (Background)** for the *Style*, as shown in Figure 12–22.
   - Click **OK** to close the dialog box.
   - Type **ZE** and press <Enter> to display the surface reference.

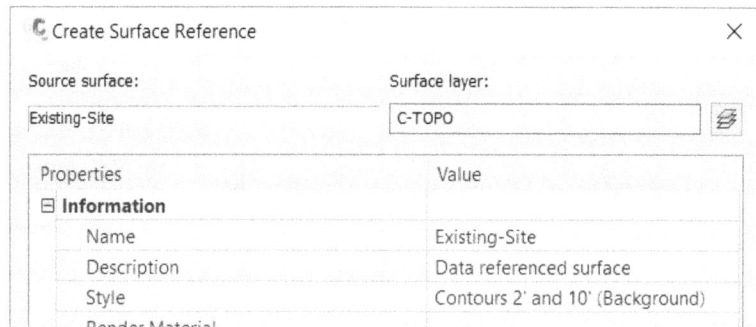

Figure 12–22

8. You will now create a data reference to the alignment. In the *Alignments* collection, right-click on **Ascent PI** and select **Create Reference**.

9. In the Create Alignment Reference dialog box, accept the default for the *Name*. Type **Data referenced alignment** for the *Description*. Set the *Alignment style* to **ASC-Layout** and set the *Alignment label set* to **ASC-Major and Minor only**. Click **OK** when done, as shown in Figure 12–23.

Figure 12–23

10. Zoom in to the end of the Ascent PI alignment, as shown in Figure 12–24.

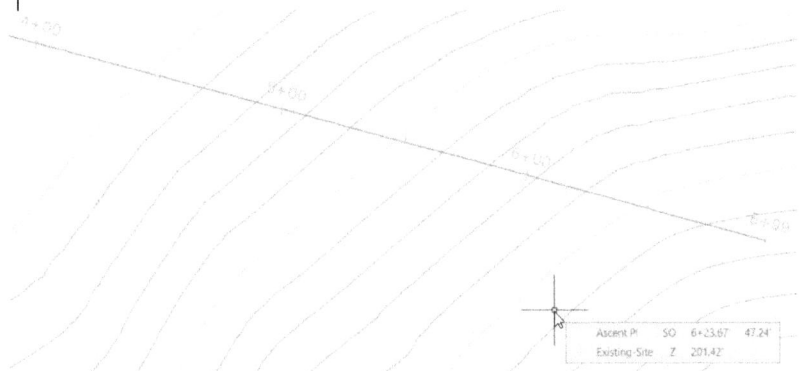

Figure 12–24

11. Create a data reference to the corridor: in the *Corridors* collection, right-click on **Ascent PI** and select **Create Reference**. Accept all of the defaults and then click **OK**.

12. In Model Space, select the **Ascent PI** referenced alignment.

Note that there are no grips and you cannot graphically redefine this alignment. However, you can add labels using the contextual tab.

13. In the contextual tab>Labels & Tables panel, expand Add Labels and select **Station/Offset - Fixed Point**, as shown in Figure 12–25.

Figure 12–25

14. When prompted to select a point, select the end point of Ascent PI, as shown on the left in Figure 12–26. Select the label and move its location so that it is easier to read, as shown on the right in Figure 12–26. Note that the station is **6+98.72**.

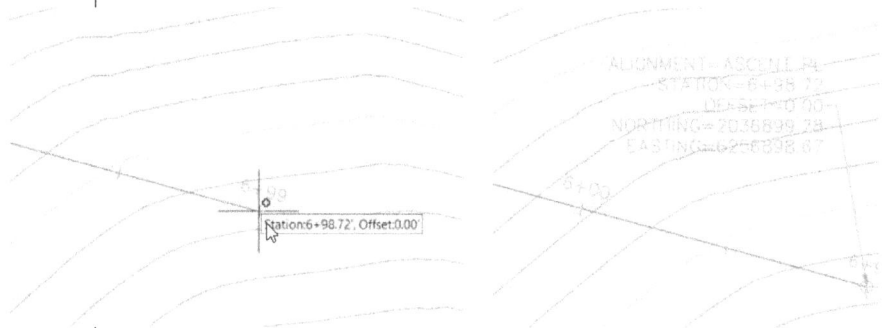

Figure 12–26

15. In the Toolspace, *Prospector* tab, expand the *Surfaces* and *ExSurface* collections, as shown on the left in Figure 12–27. Note that it does not contain the definition elements that might otherwise be displayed in a surface that is not data-referenced, as shown on the right in Figure 12–27. Therefore, you cannot edit or make design changes to a referenced surface.

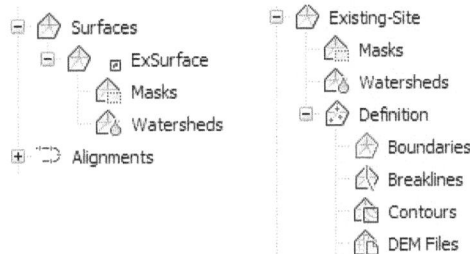

Figure 12–27

16. Save the drawing but do not close it.

Task 3 - Revise original referenced object.

---

1. In the Toolspace, *Prospector* tab, ensure that *Data Shortcuts* point to the *C:\Civil 3D Projects\Data Shortcuts\Lesson\ Ascent Phase 1* folder.

2. Ensure that the **Master View** is enabled in Toolspace so that all of the drawings that are loaded display. Select **DS-A1-Shortcuts**, right-click and select **Switch to**, as shown in Figure 12–28. **DS-A1-Shortcuts.dwg** is now the current drawing. However, if you had closed the drawing, you need to open **DS-A1-Shortcuts.dwg**.

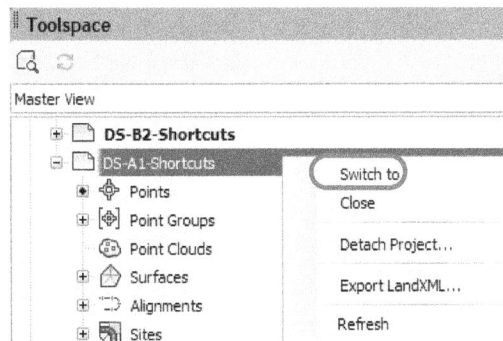

Figure 12–28

3. Zoom into the end of Ascent Pl to get a better view of the cul-de-sac.

---

4. You will now change the length of this alignment. In Model Space, select the alignment, select the grip that signifies the end of the alignment, and move it to the intersection where it crosses the cul-de-sac bulb, as shown in Figure 12–29.

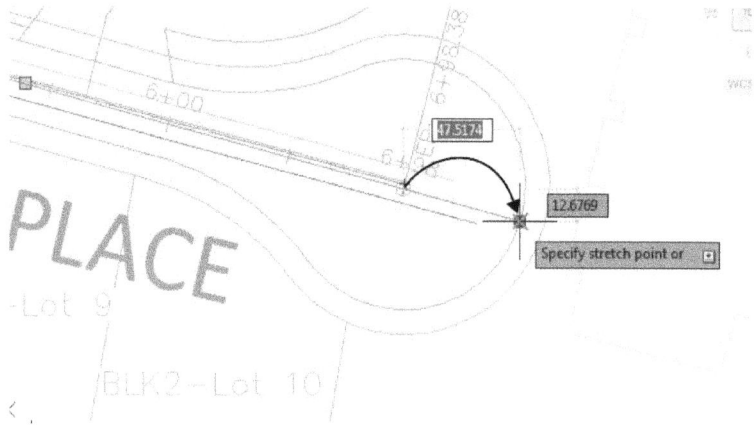

Figure 12–29

5. In the contextual tab>Modify panel, select **Alignment Properties**, as shown in Figure 12–30.

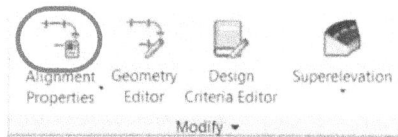

Figure 12–30

6. In the *Station Control* tab in the Alignment Properties - Ascent PI dialog box, set the reference point Station to **100**, as shown in Figure 12–31. A warning displays prompting you that changing the station will affect objects and data that have already been created. Click **OK** to dismiss the warning. Click **OK** to close the Alignment Properties dialog box.

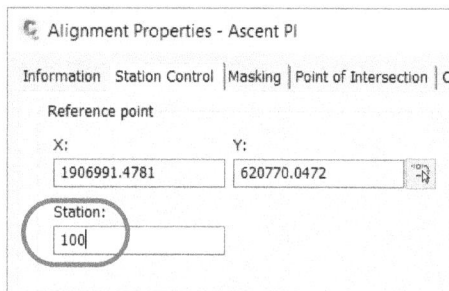

Figure 12–31

7. Save the drawing. This updates the Data Shortcut.

If you closed the drawing in Step 8, open the drawing Reference File.dwg.

8. If you are continuing with the drawing from the previous task, ensure that the Master view is enabled in the Toolspace so that you can see all of the drawings that are loaded. Select **Reference File**, right-click, and select **Switch to**. **Reference File.dwg** is now the current drawing.

9. In the Status Bar, you should see ⚓ (Data Shortcut Reference), as shown on the left in Figure 12–32. To synchronize your current drawing, right-click on see ⚓ (Data Shortcut Reference) and select **Synchronize**, as shown on the right in Figure 12–32.

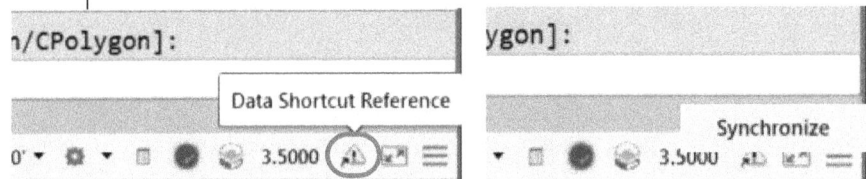

Figure 12–32

10. Alternatively, in the Toolspace, *Prospector* tab, select the alignment **Ascent PI** in the *Alignments* collection. Right-click and select **Synchronize**, as shown in Figure 12–33.

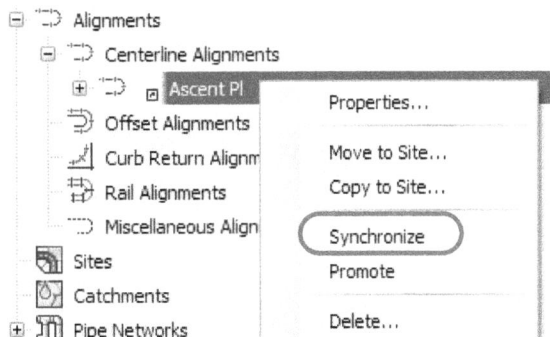

Figure 12–33

11. Note that the alignment has updated geographic information, as shown in Figure 12–34. The end of the alignment has been extended to intersect the cul-de-sac bulb, and the station label is updated to reflect the change to the original alignment design.

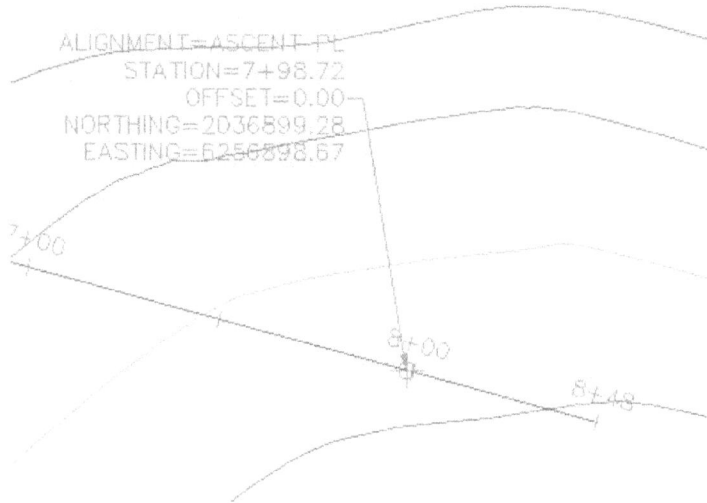

Figure 12–34

12. Save the drawing.

Index

www.ingramcontent.com/pod-product-compliance
Lightning Source LLC
Chambersburg PA
CBHW060950210326
41598CB00031B/4782

* 9 7 8 1 9 5 2 8 6 6 5 6 2 *